Lecture Notes in Computer Sc

T0237760

Commenced Publication in 1973
Founding and Former Series Editors:
Gerhard Goos, Juris Hartmanis, and Jan van Leeuwen

Koen Bertels   João M.P. Cardoso
Stamatis Vassiliadis (Eds.)

Reconfigurable Computing: Architectures and Applications

Second International Workshop, ARC 2006
Delft, The Netherlands, March 1-3, 2006
Revised Selected Papers

 Springer

Volume Editors

Koen Bertels
Stamatis Vassiliadis
Delft University of Technology
Computer Engineering Lab
Mekelweg 4, 2628 CD Delft, The Netherlands
E-mail: {k.l.m.bertels,s.vassiliadis}@ewi.tudelft.nl

João M.P. Cardoso
INESC-ID
Instituto Superior Técnico (IST)
Av. Alves Redol 9, 1000-029 Lisbon, Portugal
E-mail: jmpc@acm.org

Library of Congress Control Number: 2006929859

CR Subject Classification (1998): C, B, I.4

LNCS Sublibrary: SL 1 – Theoretical Computer Science and General Issues

ISSN   0302-9743
ISBN-10   3-540-36708-X Springer Berlin Heidelberg New York
ISBN-13   978-3-540-36708-6 Springer Berlin Heidelberg New York

Springer is a part of Springer Science+Business Media

springer.com

© Springer-Verlag Berlin Heidelberg 2006

Typesetting: Camera-ready by author, data conversion by Scientific Publishing Services, Chennai, India
Printed on acid-free paper   SPIN: 11802839   06/3142   5 4 3 2 1 0

Preface

The International Workshop on Reconfigurable Computing (ARC)[1] started in 2005 in Algarve, Portugal. The major motivation was to create an event where on-going research efforts as well as more elaborated, interesting and high-quality work on applied reconfigurable computing could be presented and discussed.

Over the last couple of years reconfigurable computing has become a well-known and established research area producing interesting as well as important results in both general and embedded computing systems. It is also getting more and more interest from industry which is attracted by the (design and development) flexibility as well as the performance improvements that can be expected from this technology. As reconfigurable computing has blurred the gap between software and hardware, some even speak of a radical new programming paradigm opening a new realm of unseen applications and opportunities.

The logo of the ARC workshop is the Nonius, a measurement instrument used in the Portuguese period of discoveries that was invented by Pedro Nunes, a Portuguese mathematician. As the logo suggests, the main motto of ARC is to help to navigate the world of reconfigurable computing. Driven by this motto, we hope ARC contributes to solid advances on reconfigurable computing.

The second edition of the International Workshop on Applied Reconfigurable Computing (ARC2006) was held at Delft University of Technology, Delft, The Netherlands, on March 1-3, 2006. More than 60 participants contributed to the success of this second edition. It is also a clear sign that the need exists for a high-level international forum to discuss and exchange ideas on reconfigurable computing.

Ninety-four papers were submitted to the workshop from 22 countries. After a careful review process, 22 papers were accepted as full papers (acceptance rate of 23.4%) and 35 as short papers (global acceptance rate of 60.64%). There were also keynote presentations by two invited, distinguished, international speakers. Besides the keynotes, the workshop also had a panel discussing hot issues related to reconfigurable computing. The workshop talks were organized around a number of themes, namely, applications, power, image processing, organization and architecture, networks and telecommunications and security.

Several persons contributed to the success of the workshop. We would like to acknowledge the support of the Program Committee members in reviewing papers and giving valuable suggestions for the workshop. Special thanks also to the auxiliary reviewers that contributed to the reviewing process, to all the authors that submitted papers to the workshop, and to all the workshop attendees.

---

[1] http://www.arc-workshop.org

For the second time, improved versions of the best papers of the workshop will be published in a special edition of the *Journal of Electronics,* a Taylor & Francis journal.

We consider the accepted papers to constitute a representative overview of ongoing research initiatives in this rapidly evolving field. We hope you have a pleasant reading, as we had.

Delft, The Netherlands   Koen Bertels
March 2006   João Cardoso
                                                          Stamatis Vassiliadis

Organization

ARC 2006 was organized by the Department of Electrical Engineering, Computer Science and Mathematics, Delft University of Technology, The Netherlands.

Organization Committee

General Chairs	Stamatis Vassiliades, Delft University of Technology, The Netherlands
	João M. P. Cardoso, University of Algarve, Portugal
Program Chair	Koen Bertels, Delft University of Technology, The Netherlands
Proceedings Chair	Arjan van Genderen, Delft University of Technology, The Netherlands
Organization Chair	Georgi Kuzmanov, Delft University of Technology, The Netherlands
Workshop Secretary	Lidwina Tromp, Delft University of Technology, The Netherlands

Program Committee

Andy Pimentel, University of Amsterdam, The Netherlands
António Ferrari, University of Aveiro, Portugal
Eduardo Marques, University of São Paulo, Brazil
George Constantinides, Imperial College, UK
Gordon Brebner, Xilinx, USA
Horácio Neto, INESC-ID/IST, Portugal
João M. P. Cardoso, University of Algarve, Portugal
José Nelson Amaral, University of Alberta, Canada
José Sousa, INESC-ID/IST, Portugal
Jürgen Becker, Universität Karlsruhe (TH), Germany
Koen Bertels, Delft University of Technology, The Netherlands
Marco Platzner, University of Paderborn, Germany
Markus Weinhardt, PACT Informationstechnologie AG, Germany
Mihai Budiu, Microsoft Research Silicon Valley, USA
Nader Bagherzadeh, University of California, Irvine, USA
Paul Chow, University of Toronto, Canada
Pedro Diniz, University of Southern California/ISI, USA
Pedro Trancoso, University of Cyprus, Cyprus
Peter Athanas, Virginia Tech., USA
Peter Cheung, Imperial College, UK

Ranga Vemuri, University of Cincinnati, USA
Reiner Hartenstein, University of Kaiserslautern, Germany
Roger Woods, The Queen's University of Belfast, UK
Roman Hermida, Universidad Complutense, Madrid, Spain
Russell Tessier, University of Massachusetts, USA
Stamatis Vassiliadis, Delft University of Technology, The Netherlands
Stephan Wong, Delft University of Technology, The Netherlands
Tim Callahan, Carnegie Mellon University, USA
Wayne Luk, Imperial College, UK

Additional Reviewers

Adeel Basit, Delft University of Technology, The Netherlands
Alastair Smith, Imperial College, UK
Alexander Thomas, Universität Karlsruhe (ITIV), Germany
Altaf Abdul Gaffar, Imperial College, UK
Balasubramanian Sethuraman, University of Cincinnati, USA
Behnaz Pourebrahimi, Delft University of Technology, The Netherlands
Ben Cope, Imperial College, UK
Carlo Galuzzi, Delft University of Technology, The Netherlands
Christian Schuck, Universität Karlsruhe (ITIV), Germany
Christopher Kachris, Delft University of Technology, The Netherlands
Christos Strydis, Delft University of Technology, The Netherlands
Cor Meenderinck, Delft University of Technology, The Netherlands
David Howland, University of Massachusetts, USA
Elena Moscu Panainte, Delft University of Technology, The Netherlands
Fethulah Smailbegovic, Delft University of Technology, The Netherlands
Filipa Duarte, Delft University of Technology, The Netherlands
Fredy Rivera, Complutense University, Madrid, Spain
Georgi Kuzmanov, Delft University of Technology, The Netherlands
Girish Venkataramani, Carnegie Mellon University, USA
Hassan Al-Atat, University of Cincinnati, USA
Ijeoma Sandra Irobi, Delft University of Technology, The Netherlands
Ioannis Sourdis, Delft University of Technology, The Netherlands
Jae Young Hur, Delft University of Technology, The Netherlands
Jianping Yan, University of Cincinnati, USA
Jonathan Allen, University of Massachusetts, USA
Jonathan Clarke, Imperial College, UK
Jorge Luiz e Silva, University of São Paulo, Brazil
José Canas Ferreira, Universidade do Porto, Portugal
José Carlos Alves, Universidade do Porto, Portugal
Jose Ignacio Hidalgo, Complutense University, Madrid, Spain
Jose Luis Imana, Complutense University, Madrid, Spain
Joseph Yeh, MIT Lincoln Laboratory, USA
Julio C. B. Mattos, Universidade Federal do Rio Grande do Sul, Brazil

Table of Contents

Applications

Power

Image Processing

Organization and Architecture

Networks and Communication

Security

Tools

Implementation of Realtime and Highspeed Phase Detector on FPGA

Andre Guntoro[1], Peter Zipf[1], Oliver Soffke[1],
Harald Klingbeil[2], Martin Kumm[2], and Manfred Glesner[1]

[1] Institute of Microelectronic Systems
Darmstadt University of Technology, Germany
guntoro@mes.tu-darmstadt.de
[2] Gesellschaft für Schwerionenforschung mbH
Darmstadt, Germany

Abstract. We describe the hardware implementation of a phase detector module which is used in a heavy ion accelerator for real-time digital data processing. As this high-speed real-time signal processing currently exceeds the performance of the available DSP processors, we are trying to move some functionality into dedicated hardware. We implemented the phase detection algorithm using a pipeline mechanism to process one data value in every clock cycle. We used a pipelined division operation and implemented an optimized table-based arctan as the main core to compute the phase information. As the result, we are able to process the two 400 MHz incoming data streams with low latency and minimal resource allocation.

1 Introduction

Control systems are now moved more into the digital domain since this provides better pre-processing, filtering, regulating, and post-processing compared to the analog domain [5,7]. Moreover, digital processing also provides a flexibility which is very hard to achieve in the analog domain, where hardware re-designs are necessary for each change.

Digital signal processors (DSP) are good candidates for those digital processing tasks for which results must be provided in (near) real-time [7]. One major problem in DSPs is that even though they provide special instruction sets which are dedicated for digital signal processing [2,8], they are not able to process data continuously like it is found in a specialized pipeline. Instead, junks of data have to be handled individually. In most of the cases, data processing which starts from pre-processing and ends at post-processing would not only bind a high share of the DSP's workload capacity, but possibly push the throughput below the required rate. One solution is to drop information by *subsampling* the incoming data so that it will not longer overload the DSP.

In certain applications, such as high-speed and real-time signal processing for which *resolution* and *accuracy* are the key points to produce a better system response and control results, subsampling can no longer be seen as a solution. One alternative approach to subsampling is the implementation of some dedicated hardware modules handling the critical tasks.

K. Bertels, J.M.P. Cardoso, and S. Vassiliadis (Eds.): ARC 2006, LNCS 3985, pp. 1–11, 2006.
© Springer-Verlag Berlin Heidelberg 2006

1.1 Background

One of the applications found in many signal control systems is the determination of the *phase difference* between two signals [4]. The calculated results will be used, for example, as a parameter to tune-up the oscillator of the second signal source to match to the first signal source.

Detection of the phase difference between two signals is actually a straight-forward task. But when looking at a specific application such as the *heavy ion acceleration control system*, phase detection needs to be performed in a *high frequency* domain and it must be done in *real-time*. A block diagram of such a system is shown in Fig. 1. Implemented on a commercial DSP board, a field-programmable gate array (FPGA) manages the interconnection between two DSPs, a host computer, analog-to-digital (ADC) and digital-to-analog converters (DAC). In our case, DSP A handles the communication with the host and also monitors the data, while DSP B processes the phase calculation.

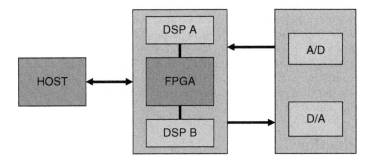

Fig. 1. The heavy ion acceleration control system

1.2 Problem Overview

Looking at both constraints, the high frequency data input and the need for real-time processing in our heavy ion accelerator control system, we have developed a dedicated hardware module on a FPGA to fulfill the performance requirements. This step was taken since the DSPs could not satisfy the given constraints.

One necessary key to calculate the phase difference is to resolve the phase information from the given discrete samples of each signal. The calculation of the phase involves first the usage of a *division operation* of the quadrature and in-phase components of the signal, and second the usage of the inverse trigonometry function *arctan* to compute the phase itself [3].

Two major problems can directly be seen from the above steps. One is concerning the division operation which obviously needs a lot of resources (both time and hardware allocation), and the other one is concerning the arctan computation, which is mainly implemented through iteration.

As our previous consideration is to follow the constraints but without neglecting the resource utilization of the FPGA, we have implemented a robust phase detector module which provides one result of the calculated phase from the continuous data stream in every clock cycle.

1.3   Paper Outline

The rest of this paper is organized as follows. Section 2 provides some background on how the computation of the phase detector is done. Section 3 discusses the hardware implementation of the phase detector. Section 4 describes the optimization which can be done in order to minimize the logic resources, and Section 5 discusses the result. Finally, Section 6 concludes the paper and points out our future plans for further developments of the system.

2   Theory of Phase Detector

The phase detection between two signals is actually done in two steps. At the first step, the phase information of every signal has to be resolved from the sampled input signal. This phase information is calculated by using the following formula:

$$\phi_X = f(x, y)$$
$$\tan(\phi_X) = \frac{y}{x} \tag{1}$$

where y and x represent the in-phase and quadrature components and they are defined as:

$$x = Q_1 - Q_2 \tag{2}$$

$$y = I_1 - I_2 \tag{3}$$

I_1, Q_1, I_2, and Q_2 themselves correspond to four subsequent samples of the input signal. Keep in mind that the calculation of the phase information has to be done for both input signals. Afterward, the output of the phase detector can be computed by calculating the difference between two resolved phase informations.

$$\phi_\Delta = \phi_1 - \phi_2 \tag{4}$$

3   Implementation

Due to the nature of the arctan function, the whole range of computation can be divided into several quadrants which will then restrict the range needed for calculation. This quadrant separation [6] can be formulated as:

$$\phi_X = \begin{cases} f(x, y) & |y| \le |x|, x \ge 0 \\ +\pi + f(x, y) & |y| \le |x|, x < 0, y \ge 0 \\ -\pi + f(x, y) & |y| \le |x|, x < 0, y < 0 \\ +\pi/2 - f(y, x) & |y| > |x|, y \ge 0 \\ -\pi/2 - f(y, x) & |y| > |x|, y < 0 \end{cases} \tag{5}$$

Fig. 2 illustrates the divided quadrants in in-phase and quadrature coordinate axes. It concludes that now it is only necessary to provide the range between $-\pi/4$ and $+\pi/4$ for the arctan computation.

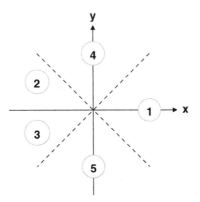

Fig. 2. Quadrant differentiation which is done in Equation 5

One of the important aspects of the phase detector application is that the detection is always used in a continuous input process. In order to provide maximum performance of the phase detector, we have taken a pipeline approach to implement this module. Thus, incoming subsequent samples can be processed in every clock cycle and the results are also available in every clock cycle with a minimal latency time, which is certainly needed in real-time data processing. The block diagram of the module is shown in Fig. 3. Here, the controller manages the data flow of every attached module. A FIFO (First In First Out) buffer is introduced to buffer the incoming data (organized as $32 \times [2 \times 16\text{-bits}]$ to incorporate the two input signals), whereas the phase calculation is realized in multiple pipeline stages. In the end the subtraction unit computes the difference between the two phases.

3.1   Stage 1 – Subtraction and Quadrant Determination

The first stage of the pipeline handles the preparation for the computation of the phase information. Here, two operations take place: One is the calculation for x and y, and the other is the determination of which quadrant should the result of arctan function belong to. The quadrant determination is computed according to the boundary condition given in Equation 5, where the input parameters are taken from the values of x and y.

Unlike x and y which are directly used in the next stage (division), the result of the quadrant determination will be used at the second and the last stages, whereas at the third stage the value will just be passed.

In our application the input data are received from an ADC which is configured to deliver 14-bits data width for each sample. As the register allocation, we have taken 16-bits data width to store the results.

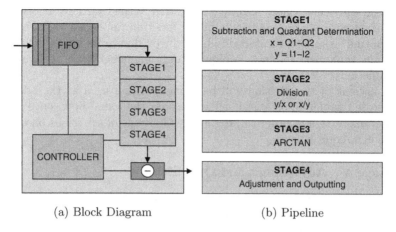

(a) Block Diagram   (b) Pipeline

Fig. 3. (a) represents the block diagram of the phase detector; (b) shows the detailed pipeline structure for calculating the phase information from the in-phase and quadrature components

3.2 Stage 2 – Division

Based on the result of the quadrant determination and the values of x and y, the second stage does the division. In case where the parameters are located in quadrants 4 or 5 (see Figure 2), the divisor and dividend have to be exchanged. Using this mechanism, we are restricting the range of the division result so that arctan will reside between $-\pi/4$ and $+\pi/4$. Furthermore, by using the absolute values of x and y as the inputs of this stage, the division result will confine in range of 0 to $\pi/4$. The reason of doing this at this early step is to deliver an easy optimization when designing the arctan function as hardware which will be discussed later on.

One main difficult task in this stage is the implementation of the division unit itself. Since a single cycle division algorithm would not allow us to operate the module at the high frequency, we have considered to use a pipeline version of the non-restoring division algorithm. Although it adds up to the latency, it will not lower the operating frequency. As the result, the second stage is again pipelined with an internal pipeline size which depends on the data width. Here, since we use 32-bits/16-bits division, it consumes 18 clock cycles (16+2) for the division stage itself.

3.3 Stage 3 – Arctan Calculation

At the third stage, the quotient of the division on the second stage is used as parameter to calculate the arctan function. Instead of using a CORDIC (COordinate Rotation DIgital Computer) algorithm [1] which requires several iteration steps in order to increase accuracy of the result, we have developed a table-based arctan function. The decision of taking this approach is that in our application we only need to compute the arctan function. At the first sight, it seems that table-based will occupy more resources compared to the CORDIC algorithm, but when it concerns only on one trigonometry function implementation, especially arctan, optimization can comfortably be deduced due to its behavior. Advantageously, the table-based approach requires only one clock cycle to compute the arctan function.

The quotient of the division will be truncated and used as the address for the generated table. The table itself represents the value between 0 and $\pi/4$ and is parameterized in order to provide a wide range of selections based on the application's requirement.

3.4   Stage 4 – Adjustment and Outputting

In the last stage, the result of the arctan computation is adjusted. Referring to Equation 5 and by using the already computed quadrant determination from the first stage, lookup table adjustment and addition take place here. The adjustment recovers the calculated angle from the previous stage to $-\pi/4$ and $+\pi/4$ and the addition extends the range to $-\pi$ and $+\pi$.

4   Arctan Optimization

At the beginning of the previous section, we have mentioned that we only need to compute arctan from $-\pi/4$ to $+\pi/4$. Since arctan is an asymmetric function, we can easily simplify the calculation by first taking the absolute value and afterwards do the conversion based on the trigonometry quadrant type. Thus the swing value will be limited from 0 up to $\pi/4$.

Since we have taken a table-based approach, two cases have to be taken into consideration in building this lookup table. One is concerning the bit width selection and the other is about the length of the table itself. For the first case, by taking 8-bits and 12-bits representations for these values, we are allowed to provide the resolution of $\pi/(4 \cdot 256) = 0.1758°$ and $\pi/(4 \cdot 4096) = 0.0109°$. For the last case, the determination of the table length can be adapted from the application's requirements. Three different table lengths for each table width have been simulated and the difference between the accurate value and the table is shown in Fig. 4. By increasing the table length, the data representation is more condensed. For example, with a table length of 256 we can only represent the data between 0 and 1 in 256 possibilities (resolution of 0.00391), whereas with a table length of 512 we have a resolution of 0.00195. In each case, the maximum error always leads to the same value since it depends on the table width and not on the table length. Table 1 summarizes the mean absolute and standard deviation of the error for each case.

5   Simulation and Synthesis

Inspecting the architecture presented in Section 3 and the lookup table optimization, two sources of error are introduced here. Despite the quotient of the

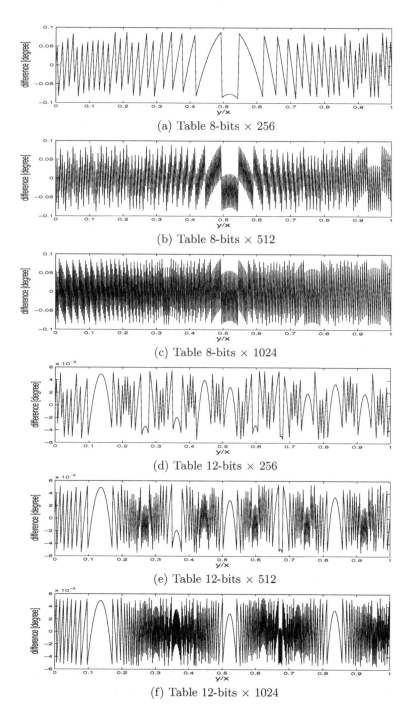

(a) Table 8-bits × 256

(b) Table 8-bits × 512

(c) Table 8-bits × 1024

(d) Table 12-bits × 256

(e) Table 12-bits × 512

(f) Table 12-bits × 1024

Fig. 4. Rounding errors due to the selection of 8-bits and 12-bits table width for different table lengths

Table 1. Mean absolute and standard deviation (all in degree unit) of the difference between accurate and table-based values for each table size

Table Size	$|\bar{x}|$	σ
8-bits × 256	0.04665	0.05365
8-bits × 512	0.04428	0.05157
8-bits × 1024	0.04411	0.05101
12-bits × 256	0.00277	0.00317
12-bits × 512	0.00277	0.00318
12-bits × 1024	0.00273	0.00314

division from Stage 2 delivers 16-bits resolution, we have taken only higher significant bits of the quotient as the input of the lookup table (depending on the preffered table length). This truncating error adds up with the error introduced by the 8-bits or 12-bits width arctan lookup table, leading to the total error shown in Fig. 5. In this figure, six different table dimensions are simulated to show the comparison of the overall performance for each different case. Table 2 summarizes the statistical results. As we can see, by increasing the length of the table we are able to improve the performance. Nevertheless, without modifying the table width we are not able to receive a significant improvement with respect to the consumption of hardware resources itself.

Table 2. Maximum error, mean absolute and standard deviation (all in degree unit) of the overall error from the division and table-base approach for every table width

Table Width	max	$|\bar{x}|$	σ
8-bits × 256	0.36247	0.18079	0.19835
8-bits × 512	0.31842	0.13461	0.15109
8-bits × 1024	0.27455	0.11336	0.13063
12-bits × 256	0.22200	0.09787	0.11271
12-bits × 512	0.11337	0.05178	0.05883
12-bits × 1024	0.05983	0.02861	0.03196

All six different table implementations have been synthesized to give us information about the resource allocation of the FPGA. As the target device in our design we have selected Xilinx Virtex2 XC2V2000. Table 3 describes the device utilization summaries for each table dimension. Depending on the application's requirements and available resources, we can optimize the generation of the arctan lookup table.

As in the prototyping the target device is clocked with 100 MHz, we are able to provide the calculation result with latency of 210 ns (with respect to the total

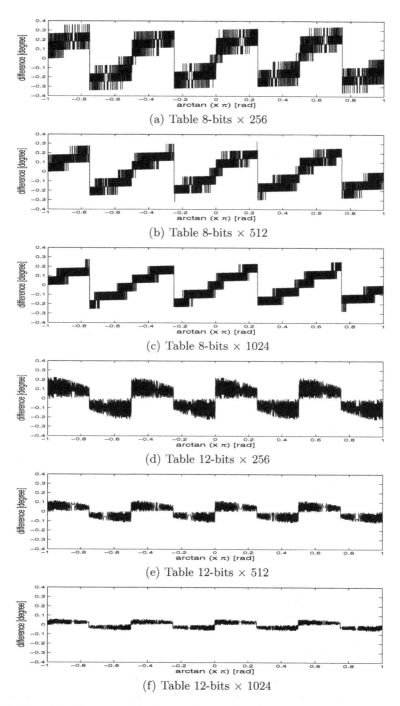

(a) Table 8-bits × 256

(b) Table 8-bits × 512

(c) Table 8-bits × 1024

(d) Table 12-bits × 256

(e) Table 12-bits × 512

(f) Table 12-bits × 1024

Fig. 5. Overall performance. Total error due to the usage of 8-bits width lookup arctan table and truncating effect of the quotient in division for different table lengths.

Table 3. Device utilization of the Virtex2 XC2V2000 for each different implementation of the phase detector

Table Size	Max Frequency	Slices	Flip Flops	4-input LUTs
Available		10752	21504	21504
8-bit × 256	173.989 MHz	500 (4.65%)	630 (2.93%)	547 (2.54%)
8-bit × 512	171.659 MHz	581 (5.40%)	718 (3.34%)	654 (3.04%)
8-bit × 1024	151.126 MHz	687 (6.39%)	811 (3.77%)	771 (3.59%)
12-bit × 256	169.190 MHz	569 (5.29%)	678 (3.15%)	626 (2.91%)
12-bit × 512	169.190 MHz	695 (6.46%)	797 (3.71%)	780 (3.63%)
12-bit × 1024	149.903 MHz	878 (8.16%)	910 (4.23%)	1026 (4.77%)

number of pipeline steps that is 21). Furthermore, as the phase detector processes four samples for each input signal and we implemented only one module for computing both input channels, the phase detector itself can process the data stream at the speed of 200 MHz. If higher frequency is demanded, by implementing two modules to resolve the phase information, we can make the phase detector to receive data as fast as 400 MHz. For comparison, the phase calculation was also programmed on the DSP (TMS320C6711; 100 MHz) and as the result the DSP can only process the data stream at 1.5 MHz.

6   Conclusions and Future Work

In this paper we have introduced the implementation of a phase detector on a XC2V2000 FPGA. The objective is to make the real-time signal data processing required by our application possible. Our solution to the problem is to implement the critical task as a specialized hardware pipeline. Optimization and resource allocation can be selected depending on the granularity of the application's requirements without consuming too many logic resources. We also have shown that our dedicated hardware phase detector is capable to fulfill the constraint of the high-speed signal processing by working on two 400 MHz incoming data streams, which is 266× faster than the DSP solution. The output has a latency of only 210 ns which is excellent for the digital control system to provide a stable control behavior and a quick system response time.

Thanks to the FPGA we are now able to deliver flexibility to the design. By implementing a processor core inside the FPGA, we have the possibility to extend the phase detector module so that it will be integrated within the processor itself. Thus, additional pre- and post-processing can be done and control system algorithms can easily be programmed. Furthermore, moving some more functionalities from the software algorithm to hardware helps to optimize the whole system response, thus making this real-time signal processing a less critical task.

References

1. R. Andraka. A survey of CORDIC algorithms for FPGA based computers. *FPGA 98 Monterey CA USA*, 1998.
2. Introduction to DSP, 2004. http://www.bores.com/courses/intro/chips/.
3. A. Dhodapkar and J. Smith. Comparing Program Phase Detection Techniques. In *Proceedings of the 36th International Symposium on Microarchitecture*, 2003.
4. M. Hind, V. Rajan, and P. Sweeney. Phase shift detection: a problem classification. In *IBM Research Report*, 2003.
5. J. Iverson. Digital Control Technology Enhances Power System Reliability and Performance. In *Technical Information from Cummins Power Generation*. Cummins Power Generation, 2004.
6. H. Klingbeil. A Fast DSP-based Phase-detector for Closed-loop RF Control in Synchrotrons. *IEEE Transaction on Instrumentation and Measurement*, 2004.
7. W. Steven. *The Scientist and Engineering's Guide to Digital Signal Processing*. California Technical Publishing, 1997.
8. DSP Tutorial, 2001. http://www.wave-report.com/tutorials/DSP.htm.

Case Study: Implementation of a Virtual Instrument on a Dynamically Reconfigurable Platform

Gerd Van den Branden[1,2], Geert Braeckman[1], Abdellah Touhafi[1,2], and Erik Dirkx[2]

[1] Erasmushogeschool Brussel, Departement IWT, Nijverheidskaai 170,
1070 Brussel, Belgium
gerd.van.den.branden@ehb.be,
geert.braeckman@ehb.be, abdellah.touhafi@docent.ehb.be
[2] Vrije Universiteit Brussel (VUB), Pleinlaan 2, 1050 Brussel, Belgium
efdirkx@info.vub.ac.be

Abstract. This paper discusses our experiences in porting a virtual instrumentation machine, which is a tool to create virtual instruments for the measurement of sound and vibrations to a dynamically reconfigurable platform. Hereby we follow a generic approach and we focus on maximizing reusability of elements that are available in the software based environment. Furthermore we analyze the final result and discuss the benefits and drawbacks of the reconfigurable platform with associated CAD tools we chose to use.

1 Introduction

Today there is a lot of interest in dynamic reconfiguration. However, there still isn't much rumor of applications that really make use of this so called feature. Because dynamic reconfiguration is in fact a new design paradigm, we believe that there exists a great design productivity gap. In an effort to fill this gap we experimented with partial and dynamic reconfiguration in order to deduce a consistent design flow.

This paper gives a clean overview on how an existing application, designed to run on a general purpose desktop PC environment, can be ported to a dynamically reconfigurable platform. The objective is that this will result in a considerable decrease in execution time and even in a decrease in power consumption, without losing much flexibility or introducing much complexity. To achieve this goal we developed a framework which we will use to come to the final, generic, implementation.

The rest of this paper is constructed as follows. In Section 2 we explain what is meant by a virtual instrumentation machine and how it can be used to create a custom measurement infrastructure, which we call a virtual instrument. We present a software-environment where this can be done in an accurate and cost effective way. Finally, the benefits and drawbacks of this environment are discussed for a virtual instrument running on a Pentium IV desktop PC. In Section 3 we will outline the details of porting the virtual instrumentation machine towards a dynamically reconfigurable platform. Then in Section 4 we discuss the implementation on an xc2vp30 FPGA and an ML310 development board, both from Xilinx Inc. [1]. We outline some difficulties we encountered and propose possible solutions, if any.

K. Bertels, J.M.P. Cardoso, and S. Vassiliadis (Eds.): ARC 2006, LNCS 3985, pp. 12–17, 2006.
© Springer-Verlag Berlin Heidelberg 2006

2 A Virtual Instrumentation Machine

A virtual instrumentation machine must be seen as a design environment that enables the creation of a custom measurement system. In this context, an example virtual instrument is depicted in Figure 1. It shows a tool that captures audio data and displays the energy spectrum. This is a simple straight forward example, but more complex constructions with split- and merge- points, are off course also possible.

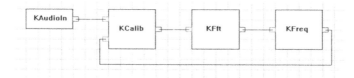

Fig. 1. A virtual instrument to display the frequency spectrum of audio data

For the rapid implementation of virtual instruments we developed an automation tool. This software-environment allows one to define a virtual instrument by means of interconnectable multi-port operations (which we will call *objects* from here on), whereby the sources are data-acquisition elements and the sinks are storage elements. Furthermore it is possible to assign a number of parameters to each object.

Once the user has completely defined the virtual instrument, an evaluation is executed on it. First a numbered graph representation is created using an ASAP (as soon as possible) numbering strategy. Next a consistency checking is executed on the instrument. This includes a type checking, a port checking and a check to ensure that no infinite loops were created. When no errors are detected, a serialized file is generated that implements the virtual instrument. With this representation of the virtual instrument, we can move on to the simulator. For more documentation about the details of this software environment and how to use it, we refer the interested reader to the publications and documentation that can be found on our web-site [2, 3].

The purpose of the virtual instrumentation machine was to provide a cheap alternative for measuring and analyzing sound and vibrations without the need of buying each time a specific and expensive measurement apparatus, and without loosing much accuracy compared with those state-of-the-art analyzers [4].

However, there are some serious shortcomings when real-time measurements need to be done. For example, on a Pentium IV desktop environment (1.4 GHz), we are capable of analyzing one channel in real-time. But, when we define a multi-channel system (e.g. in a multi-sensor environment), we miss the real-time deadlines. It is clear that the equipment lacks the necessary computing power to provide correct results in such an environment. The reason is that every object is executed serially on a single general purpose Von-Neumann like processor, which offers greater flexibility and programmability at the cost of lower performance.

3   Migrating to Dynamic Reconfiguration: A Natural Evolution

Migrating towards dynamic reconfiguration for this application is a natural choice because the objects that compose the virtual instrument lend themselves well to be executed in reconfigurable hardware. Partitioning is easy because the objects correspond nicely to isolated operations. In addition, the scheduling problem can be recycled from the numbered graph representation. Figure 2 shows the flow of how this is done.

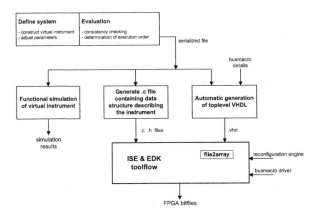

Fig. 2. General flow for the virtual instrumentation machine

3.1   Composing the Virtual Instrument

For the composing phase, we can reuse almost the entire front-end and GUI of the software environment we have available. When no errors are generated after the evaluation phase, all information is written to a serialized file. Unto this point, there is no difference with the flow outlined in section 2, and we can rigorously take advantage of what has been done in the past. However, before we write the serialized file, we include some additional information to it compared with the original software based implementation. This extra information simply represents quantification information about the number of reconfigurable modules that will be used in the final system and information about which off-chip peripherals interface with the platform we use (e.g. if the system will use external DDR SDRAM memory). This number is entered manually by the end-user of the tool.

The simulation process is essential to ensure that the composed instrument behaves as supposed to. The simulator takes the serialized file which describes the virtual instrument, and uses this information to build a data structure preserving the circuit graph. For simulation purposes, each object has been mapped to a software simulation with the expected behavior. Simulation results are written to files on a module base, so we have one file for each instantiated object.

On the FPGA, in a later phase, each object will eventually occupy a reconfigurable area.

3.2 The Reconfiguration Engine

The Reconfiguration Engine is implemented as a software program that will run on a microprocessor on the target platform. It is designed in a generic and scalable manner such that it can drive a number of modules varying from only one to as many as the FPGA can contain. In Section 4 we discuss this limit, and provide a general way to deduce it for an arbitrary system.

When a reconfigurable area comes available, the engine reads and stores the data from that module and saves the state of the internal registers of the module. Thereafter it loads a new configuration and restores the state of the internal registers according to the new configuration. The computation data is then written to the module's memory and finally the module is activated.

3.3 Generating the Hardware

The reconfigurable system is composed of communicating modules with a unified interface. There are two types of modules: fixed and reconfigurable. The reconfigurable module makes sure that it produces the correct results before it alerts the fixed module that the results are available.

Every object that corresponded to a computational operation in our original software implementation will now be implemented by a reconfigurable module. The fixed module will run the reconfiguration engine, the global communication control between the implemented reconfigurable modules, the sources and the sinks, and the communication with "off chip" devices.

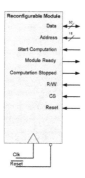

Fig. 3. Black box representation of a generic reconfigurable module

Figure 3 shows the interface of a reconfigurable module. The reconfigurable modules are available as VHDL descriptions in a library. They are described according to the principles of genericity and modularity as explained before. Automatic Generation of Toplevel VHDL.

According to the information contained in the serialized, we are able to automatically generate a VHDL description of the toplevel file for the dynamically reconfigurable system. The toplevel VHDL file of the system instantiates all reconfigurable modules and at least the interface with the fixed module.

3.4 Creating the Dynamically Reconfigurable System

Now all elements are available to assemble the complete system and finalize the design phase. We do this according to the framework depicted in Figure 4. We developed and validated this framework to create partially and dynamically reconfigurable systems. We refer to [5] and to our website [2] for more detailed information about how to read and use the framework.

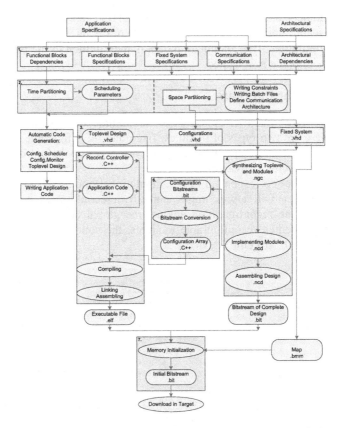

Fig. 4. The implementation phase of the final system is done according to this framework

4 Results

We implemented our virtual instrumentation machine on a Xilinx ML310 board. This board contains a Xilinx XC2VP30 Virtex-II Pro FPGA, 256 MB of external SDRAM and a RS232 connector. The SDRAM is reserved to store the different partial bitfiles and the source code that is executed on the on-chip PowerPC405 processor. The source code contains the reconfiguration engine, drivers for the customized communication structure, and the drivers for the ICAP primitive.

We experimented with dynamically reconfigurable systems that implement one fixed and one reconfigurable module and with systems with one fixed and two reconfigurable modules. In our setup we had to deal with uncompressed partial bitfiles of about 100 kB. If we clock the ICAP at a rate of 50 MHz, reconfiguring a module takes about 2ms [1]. If we process data that comes at a rate of 48 kHz, a buffer with a depth of about 150 32-bit words is needed to ensure safe real time operation. For simplicity reasons we implemented buffers of 512 words.

In this configuration, with a maximum of 64 communication lines (two 32-bit gpio_modules), the maximum number of reconfigurable modules is limited to six, because in our implementation there is a separate CS and comp_stop signal line for each individual module, while the other lines are shared among all modules (see Figure 3). Our experience however, is to minimize the number of reconfigurable modules, and to maximize the area of the fixed module. The latter is useful to maximize the available BRAM memory in the fixed module that serves as a cache memory to pre-load reconfiguration streams. The former is useful to master overall complexity and speed.

Due to conflicting architectural constraints of the board and the device, the external storage capacity was not accessible. Therefore we were limited to creating dynamically reconfigurable systems with one reconfigurable module, where the partial bitstreams and a limited part of the source code are both contained in the internal BRAM memory of the fixed system. Tests with multiple reconfigurable modules are executed, but without the use of dynamic reconfiguration. As a consequence, the entire reconfiguration engine is only simulated. However, we emphasize that we succeeded in dynamically reconfiguring the platform, initializing the module, starting its computation, collecting the results, and reading out and saving its state.

We end this paper by stressing the importance of the completeness and accuracy of the architectural specifications of the dynamically reconfigurable component, as well as the target board. The relevance is illustrated clearly in the fact that those specifications serve as an input for the framework we proposed in Figure 4. Great up-front care is required in order to avoid obstructions at the final assembling phase of the design, and to master the engineering cost of the application. This paper contributes in this matter by providing a validated framework to fixate the flow, by reciting problems that can occur, and by relating design guidelines to them.

References

1. Xilinx User Guide 012, Virtex-II PRO Platform FPGA Handbook, San José (2002)
2. http://elektronica.ehb.be/reco/
3. http://akoestiek.ehb.be/
4. Touhafi, A., Braeckman, G., Raadschelders, M.: Implementation of an Integrated Virtual Instruments Environment for Acoustic Measurements, International Conference on Noise and Vibration Measurement (ISMA), ISBN 90-73802-79-2, Leuven (2002)
5. Van den Branden, G., Touhafi, A., Dirkx, E.: A Design Methodology to Generate Dynamically Self-Reconfigurable SoCs for Virtex-II Pro FPGAs. FPT05, NUS Singapore (2005)
6. Thorvinger, J., Lenart, T.: Dynamic Partial Reconfiguration of an FPGA for Computational Hardware Support, Masters Thesis, Lund Institute of Technology (2004)
7. Xilinx Application Note 290: Two Flows for Partial Reconfiguration: Module Based or Difference Based, http://www.xilinx.com/bvdocs/appnotes/xapp290.pdf, San José (2004)

Configurable Embedded Core for Controlling Electro-Mechanical Systems

Rodrigo Piedade and Leonel Sousa

Electrical and Computer Engineering Dept., IST/INESC-ID
Lisboa, Portugal
rmpi@sips.inesc-id.pt

Abstract. This paper proposes a configurable embedded core for controlling electro-mechanical systems for continuous periodical movements. These are sub-systems that must operate and be controlled simultaneously with data or signal processing. The core integrates, for example, the control loop of two practical systems for typical light deflection purposes. An application is presented where the core is also applied for developing a complete image projection system. Experimental results show that an FPGA with modest resources, namely the *SPARTAN-IIs300e*, is able to fulfill the basic requirements of these applications.

1   Introduction

The purpose of this paper relies on controlling mechanical systems which have a continuous behavior, in a sense that its dynamic must not change, with the use of configurable controllers. These systems can be generally actuated by DC motors rotating at known angular speeds. Systems have to be modeled for being included in feedback control loops, for example by identifying its frequency response characteristics.

Electro-Mechanical systems usually integrate several mechanical devices which have to be controlled in a conjugated way. These are complex systems which also require real-time data and information processing performed in the digital domain. A unified architecture for simultaneously processing and controlling may require configurable logic structures in order to fulfil specifications, namely time restrictions, programmability and power consumption.

This paper proposes a configurable control core to be embedded in general electro-mechanical systems. The core implements the feedback control linear approach in Field Programmable Gate Arrays (FPGA). It can accommodate nested loops as well as independent parallel control structures and it can be attached to different processing units for specific applications. An example is provided for implementing a specific video projection system, by combining the specific core with a video processing unit.

K. Bertels, J.M.P. Cardoso, and S. Vassiliadis (Eds.): ARC 2006, LNCS 3985, pp. 18–23, 2006.

2   Characteristics of Mechanical System and Control Loop

By looking at a DC motor as a frequency oscillator, which generates a periodic signal in its speed sensor with frequency proportional to its input, it can be directly integrated in a Phase-Locked Loop (PLL) for speed control purpose [1].

The PLL scheme, presented in figure 1(a), is a non-linear loop that results from multiplying the reference and the output signals, to obtain the phase error of the two signals. The mean value of the error signal is the input of the Voltage Controlled Oscillator (VCO), which is directly implemented by the motor itself.

In an incremental operating linear approach, (figure 1(b)) for the lock range, the Phase Detector (PD) turns into a sum for phase error, so the behavior can be specified with linear analysis, with the poles of the system defining the jitter and the noise rejection. The DC motors frequency response can be approximated to a first-order low-pass filter. The static gain becomes the ratio of rotation over DC input and the pole the cutoff frequency of the overall mechanical system.

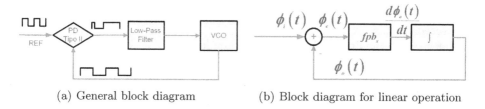

(a) General block diagram   (b) Block diagram for linear operation

Fig. 1. Block diagram of a PLL

Let us consider, for example, two mechanical systems for light deflection purposes, composed by mirrors with a continuous movement.

The first example is from a LASER printer (figure2(a)). Its a three-phase Motor with rotation proportional to the voltage input. Its frequency response was obtained by analyzing the sensor frequency signal to a voltage step input. This signal, captured by the magnetic field effect of a magnet over a coil, was registered by a sound card. The frequency response of the Motor integrated in a PLL was analyzed with a Spectrum Analyzer is presented in figure 2(b). The peak lobe represents the synchronism frequency and the side lobes the jitter.

The second mechanical system (see figure 2(c)) consists of a DC Motor with a crank-shaft mechanic elevating a rectangular plate mirror. In this case, the sensor signal frequency is very low, dozen of Hertz, due to the fact that one revolution corresponds to one pulse of the magnetic sensor installed on the motor's flywheel. Thus, knowing the static gain of the system, a coarse grain approach in order to estimate the frequency response is to simulate and adjust the system behavior as a first-order low-pass filter with the same input. This system is actuated by a Pulse Width Modulation (PWM) generator over the power supply of the DC Motor for an operating frequency of 2.5kHz. A low-pass filter smoothly actuates

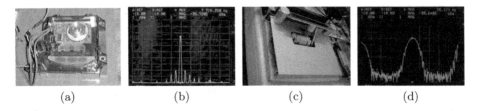

(a)   (b)   (c)   (d)

Fig. 2. a) and c) Mechanical systems of 1st and 2nd example respectively. b) and d) sensor signals spectrums of 1st and 2nd example respectively.

the PWM output, adjusting the gain-pole of the loop [5], reaching synchronism, as depicted in figure 2(d).

3   Embedded Control Core

The Control core was described in VHDL and was implemented in a *Spartan-II300e* FPGA [2]. PLL units for controlling the motors are accomplished in this configurable core, being the sensors signals sampled and the references signals generated on it.

Referring to the first of the previous examples, the blocks needed are the reference generator and the tri-state PD, while for the second example a PWM generator and a low-pass filter are also required. The use of configurable technology allows to have both loops operating at the same time. The maximum operating frequency of the logic devices is high enough for this kind of control, since it is known that the system's bandwidth is limited by mechanical factors that result in a low cutoff frequency. So there is room for plenty of signal processing during a time sampling.

3.1   Main Components of the Core

The reference generator is composed of two cascade counters: an inner counter defines the time base while the outer one specifies half period of the square reference cycle. The implemented PDs operate like the 4046 phase detector circuit [3]. The state machine can be implemented with two flip-flops and a reset unit (see figure 3(a)). The flip-flops are set in the positive edge transitions of the sensor signal or reference. The reset module operates in parallel with the flip-flops, resetting them whenever simultaneously the '1'-state occurs. Reset signal has the shape of a pulse to allow in the next sample the set-state of the flip-flops. The implemented filter has a Infinite Impulse Response (IIR) (see figure 3(b)). Processing is implemented in 32 bit fixed-point arithmetic, but using the Q16 format (16 bits for the fractional part). The decision unit is used to implement the three-state imposed by the phase detector. In high impedance situation, the filter is turned off and the output remains with the value of the previous sample.

The PWM generator is implemented with a 11-bit counter. A constant is used to define the number of clock cycles for the '1'-state output, leaving

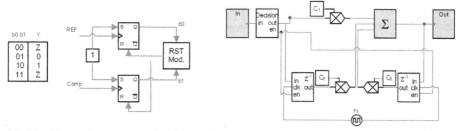

(a) The phase detector truth table and implementation

(b) Discrete Low-pass filter (fs = 1kHz)

Fig. 3. Diagram of the PD and the filter

'0'-state output when the count values are higher than the constant. This resolution generates 2047 different pulse width signals.

3.2   Experimental Results

The control core, with all presented blocks, is described in VHDL and synthesized for the *Spartan-IIs300e* by using the ISE 6.3. It can be observed in table 1 that only about 14% of the total number of slices and 7% of the total number of Flip-Flops (FFs) are required to implement the core realizing two nested control loops. Moreover, it can be concluded that most of the hardware resources provided by the FPGA is still available for data processing or other control loops.

4   Application of the Core to Implement a LASER Image Projector System

A mechanical light deflection system, for two dimensional scanning of a Light Amplification by Stimulated Emissions of Radiation (LASER) beam, was developed based on the proposed control core. The purpose of this system is the projection of images and video sequences [6], [7]. It uses the first mechanical system, referred to in section 2, as the line scanning system, the other as the vertical

(a) LASER image projector   (b) Some image projection results

Fig. 4. Developed prototype and results

Table 1. Projection system synthesis report: Control units, processing unit for buffering the image data and a camera interface for a maximum operating frequency of 40MHz [4]

Resources	Available	Ref. Gen.	PD	LP Filter	PWM Gen.	Image	Camera
Slices	3072	79 (3%)	9 (1%)	269 (9%)	24 (1%)	139(5%)	200(7%)
Slice	6144	70 (2%)	11 (1%)	132 (3%)	12 (1%)	214(2%)	266(5%)
LUTs:	6144	96 (2%)	16 (1%)	427 (7%)	44 (1%)	119(2%)	270(5%)
IOBs:	146	2 (2%)	3 (1%)	33 (23%)	33 (23%)	16(11%)	64(5%)
BRAMs:	16					5(31%)	1(7%)

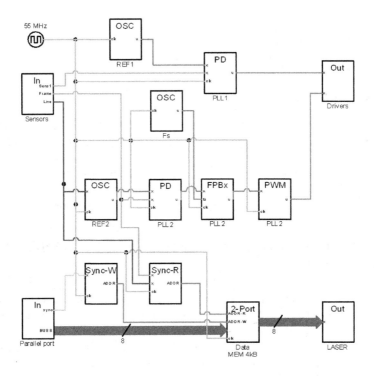

Fig. 5. Projection system block diagram

scanning system and a solid-state LASER diode with a 655nm light emission wavelength and 50mW of optical power. The prototype of the developed system (see figure 4(a)) uses the *Spartan-II300e* FPGA, not only for control but also to process and store images (see figure 5). The proposed control core is embedded with an additional control module for modeling the LASER beam intensity and a processing unit. The processing unit is an aggregation of sub-units, corresponding to the writing and reading memory process and the dual-port memory buffer. The writing process performs the storage of a frame fed by an external image supplier, which can be a Personal Computer (PC) for static images or a digital video camera (OV9650 with a maximum XVGA resolution) [4], into a Block RAMs (BRAMs). The reading process reads the image pixel information at a specified constant rate, according to the line pulse signal generated by the horizontal scanning sub-system. This process generates the vertical scanning system reference after reaching the counting of the image bottom's lines. The final result of the projection system is present in figure 3.2. These images have 20×100 pixel resolution with a 8-bit of resolution per pixel, being originally from gray-scaled bitmaps. This resolution was chosen only for prototyping and it does not arise from any limit imposed by the hardware. Experimental results are shown in table 1.

5   Conclusions

This paper proposes a configurable embedded core for controlling electro - mechanical systems. The core implements a configurable set of control loops based on the digital PLL architecture. As it has been shown, the implementation only requires a few hardware resources of a low cost FPGA and can be easily applied for controlling simultaneous multiple mechanical devices control. The successful implementation of a prototype for video projection shows the practical usefulness of this core. This embedded core will be deployed in the future for developing electro-mechanical applications.

References

1. R. Best. *Phase-Locked Loops : Design, Simulation, and Applications*. McGraw-Hill Professional, fifth edition, 2003.
2. Coreworks. *Basic Board FPGA Development and Evaluation Board User Manual*, 2004.
3. Fairchild. Cd-4046bc, micropower phase-locked loop, October 1987.
4. J. Germano, R. Baptista, and L. Sousa. Configurable platform for real time video processing and vision systems. In *In XX Conference on Design of Circuits and Integrated Systems (DCIS'05)*, November 2005.
5. K. Ogata. *Modern Control Engineering*. Prentice-Hall, fourth edition, 2001.
6. R. Piedade. Image projector based on mechanical laser beam deflection, (written in portuguese). Technical report, Instituto Superior Técnico, 2005.
7. R. Piedade and L. Sousa. Laser image projector using reconfigurable logic control. In *Submitted to Jornadas Sobre Sistema Reconfigurveis (REC'06)*, November 2005.

Evaluation of a Locomotion Algorithm
for Worm-Like Robots on FPGA-Embedded
Processors

J. Gonzalez-Gomez, I. Gonzalez, F. Gomez-Arribas, and E. Boemo

Computer Engineering School, Universidad Autonoma de Madrid, Spain
{Juan.Gonzalez, Ivan.Gonzalez, Francisco.Gomez, Eduardo.Boemo}@uam.es

Abstract. In this paper, a locomotion algorithm designed for an eight modules worm-like robot has been successfully tested on three different FPGA-embedded processors: MicroBlaze, PowerPC and LEON2. The locomotion of worm-like robots, composed of a chain of equal linked modules, is achieved by means of wave propagation that traverse the body of the worm. The time the robot needs to generate a new motion wave, also known as the gait recalculation time, is the key to achieve an autonomous robot with real-time reactions. Algorithm execution time for four different architectures, as a function of the total number of articulations of the robot, are presented. The results show that a huge improvement of the gait recalculation time can be achieved by using a float point unit. The performance achieved using the LEON2 with FPU is 40 times better than LEON2 without FPU, using only 6% of additional resources.

1 Introduction

Modular self-reconfigurable robots offer the promise of more versatility, robustness and low cost[1]. They are composed of modules, capable of attach and detach one to each other, changing the shape of the robot. In this context, the word "reconfigurable" means the ability of the robot to change its form, not a hardware reconfigurable system. In the last years, the number of robot following this approach has growth substantially[2].

One of the most advanced systems is Polybot[1][3], designed at Palo Alto Research Center (PARC). This robot has the capability to achieve different reconfigurations, such as moving as a wheel, using a rolling gait, then transforming itself into a snake and finally becoming a spider. Currently, the third generation of modules (G3) is being developed[4]. Each module has its own embedded PowerPC 555 processor with a traditional processor architecture.

An additional step on versatility is the use of Field Programming Gate Array (FPGA) technology instead of a conventional microprocessor chip. It gives the designer the possibility of implementing new architectures, faster control algorithms, or dynamically modify the hardware to adapt it to a new situation. In summary, modular reconfigurable robot controlled by a FPGA are not just able to change their shapes, but also their hardware and therefore, complete versatility can be achieved.

K. Bertels, J.M.P. Cardoso, and S. Vassiliadis (Eds.): ARC 2006, LNCS 3985, pp. 24–29, 2006.

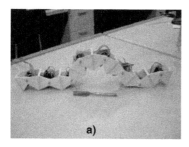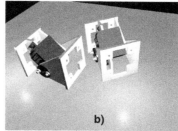

Fig. 1. a) "Cube revolutions" worm-like robot, composed of eight similar linked modules, connected in phase. **b)** A CAD rendering of two unconnected Y1 modules.

As previous work, an implementation of a FPGA-based worm-like robot locomotion was successfully carried out[5]. The Xilinx MicroBlaze[6] soft-processor was used for the algorithm execution and custom cores were added for servo positioning.

In this paper the locomotion algorithm for an eight modules worm-like robot (figure 1a) is evaluated in different FPGA embedded processors: MicroBlaze, PowerPC[7] and LEON2[8]. The time this algorithm takes to complete the movement generation is calculated as a function of the number of nodes of the robot, giving information about the scalability. This experimental results will be used in future work to select the architectures that fit best a particular application.

2   Locomotion Algorithm for Worm-Like Robots

The prototype of the worm-like robot, called "Cube Revolutions", is shown in figure 1a. It is composed of 8 similar linked modules, connected in phase. Therefore it can only move in a straight line, forward and backward. The first generation of the modules created, named Y1 (1b), were made of PVC and contains only one degree of freedom, actuated by a servo. Technical details and aditional information can be found in [5].

The locomotion of the robot is achieved by means of precalculated data matrix, that store the position of all the articulations at different time slots. This control data arrangement is denominated gait control table[1]) (GCT).

Each row of the table contains the position of the articulations at instant t_i, that is, the shape of the robot at t_i. The whole matrix determines the evolution of the shape of the robot in time.The robot will move correctly if the GCT is well calculated. In order to achieve locomotion, the controller reads the table, row by row, producing the pulse width modulations (PWM) signals that actuate the servos.

The proposed locomotion algorithm generates well-constructed gait control tables that allow the robot to move forward and backward. A wave propagation model is used for its calculation, building the tables from the parameters of the wave: amplitude, waveform, wavelength and frequency.

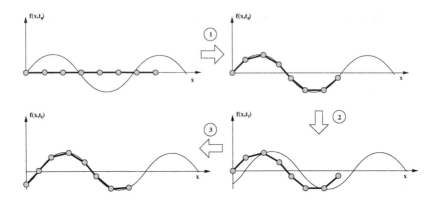

Fig. 2. An example of the algorithm used to generate the control tables. The first two rows of the gait control table are calculated.

Figure 2 shows an example of how the algorithm calculates the first and second rows of the gait control table. It consist of two stages. First, the angles of the articulations are calculated by "fitting the worm to the wave". Then, the wave is shifted (that is, the time is incremented) and the robot is fitted to the wave again. These steps are repeated until the wave has move a distance equal to the wavelength.

The algorithm has a geometric approach and is based on rotations of 2D points, therefore, sine, cosine and arctan function are widely used.

3   Implementation on Embedded FPGA Processors

3.1   Algorithm Operation Analysis

The whole algorithm has been implemented in C language, using double precision floating point. The profiling analysis of the algorithm shows that the 71.4% of the execution time is spent in float point operations. The 21.23% is used for integers operations and the final 7.37% for remainder operations, including trigonometric ones. The profile suggests the use of a float point unit (FPU) for improving the execution time.

3.2   Target Architectures

Table 1 shows the four architectures used for the evaluation of the algorithm. Three FPGA-embedded processor has been tested: LEON2, Xilinx MicroBlaze and a PowerPC core embedded in the Xilinx Virtex II Pro FPGA. The PowerPC is the processor employed in PolyBot G3, the most advanced modular reconfigurable robots designed at PARC.

The soft core processors (SCP) have been implemented using similar architectural features: without hardware multiplier/divisor units and with similar data

Table 1. Architectures used for the evaluation of the algorithm

Target architectures	1	2	3	4a	4b
Processor	LEON	LEON+ Meiko FPU	MicroBlaze	PowerPC	
Frequency	25 Mhz		50MHz	50Mhz	100Mhz
FPGA	Virtex XC2000E			Virtex II Pro	

and instruction caches. Architectures 1 comprises only one LEON2 SCP. Architecture 2 adds the Meiko FPU[8]. The third architecture is a Xilinx MicroBlaze SCP. The final architecture consists of an embedded PowerPC core.

Architectures 1 to 3 have been evaluated in hardware on the RC1000 development board from Celoxica that includes a Xilinx Virtex E FPGA. The architecture 4 has been implemented on a Alpha Data ADM-XPL board in a Virtex II Pro.

4 Results

Xilinx XST is used for the synthesis of MicroBlaze. Symplify Pro is used for the synthesis of the LEON2 processor. The reason why Simplify Pro is not used for the synthesis of the MicroBlaze processor is the fact that MicroBlaze processor is distributed as a parametrizable netlist, i.e. it is already synthesized. PowerPC implementation have been developed using the Xilinx Embedded Development Kit.

4.1 Synthesis Results

The results are shown in table 2. Since MicroBlaze processor is highly optimized for Xilinx FPGA circuit the resources used are lower than for the LEON2 processor. LEON2 is written not only for FPGA circuit so it is very difficult for a synthesis tool to synthesize LEON2 with the same low FPGA resource optimization as MicroBlaze. Also, as can be seen in table 1 the maximum clock frequency achieved for MicroBlaze is 50Mhz, whereas LEON2 runs at 25Mhz in the selected FPGA device.

The improved architecture LEON2 with FPU unit only suppose a 6% of additional resources.

Table 2. Implementation results for architectures 1,2 and 3

Processor	Slices	BRAM
MicroBlaze	1321 (6%)	74 (46%)
LEON2	4883 (25%)	43 (26%)
LEON2+Meiko FPU	6064 (31%)	40 (25%)

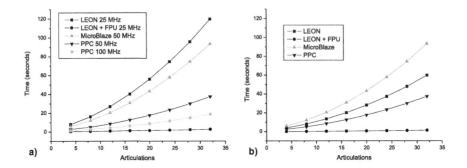

Fig. 3. a) GRT comparison for the four architectures evaluated, as a function of the number of articulations. **b)** Normalized results supposing a 50MHz system clock frequency for all architectures.

4.2   Algorithm Execution Time

The algorithm has been compiled for the different architectures and it is loaded from external memory and executed. The execution of the algorithm determines the time the robot needs to generate a new kind of movement. This time is called gait recalculation time (GRT). If a worm-like robot capable of having a fast reaction is needed for a particular applications, a low GRT is required.

Figure 3a shows the GRT for the four architectures, as a function of the numbers of articulations. Figure 3b compares the different architectures working at 50MHz. Due to the limitations of the chosen architecture FPGA device, the 50Mhz data for the LEON2 processor has been estimated supposing a half cycle time.

As it was expected, the GRT increases with the number of articulation of the robot. Also, the PowerPC reaches a significantly better result than the other two processors, because it is a hard core with specific hardware functional units.

The most outstanding result is obtained with architecture 2 (LEON + FPU). For an 8 articulations worm-like robot, the performance achieved using the LEON2 with FPU is 40 times better than LEON2 without FPU, using a 6% additional resources. This performance is 6.5 times better than the obtained with the 100Mhz PowerPC implementation.

5   Conclusion and Further Work

The worm like-robot locomotion can be realized by means of the propagation of waves through the body of the robot. The algorithm generates the gait control tables from the wave applied. The gait recalculation time is the key parameter in order to achieve an autonomous robot with real-time reactions.

The algorithm has been successfully implemented and executed on three different embedded processors in FPGA: LEON2, MicroBlaze and PowerPC. The

GRT has been measured in four architectures, as a function of n, the number of total articulations. Results show that GRT can be drastically improved by means of the use of an FPU unit. A 25MHz LEON2 with an Meiko FPU is almost one order of magnitude faster than an PowerPC working at 100Mhz. This makes evident one of the advantages of the use of a FPGA instead of a traditional processor: designers and researchers can improve the robot by introduction architectural changes and adding custom hardware cores.

The LEON2 with an FPU is a very good option when a low GRT is required. In not critical applications the use of the MicroBlaze saves about the 75% of the area, leaving this percentage free for the implementation of new hardware cores.

The current worm like-robot prototype, "Cube Revolutions", can only move on a straight line. The movement on a plane will be studied in further works. The same locomotion algorithm will be used, but calculating two gait control tables from two different waves: one for the articulations in the plane parallel to the ground and the other in the perpendicular plane. The final locomotion will be generated as a composition of the two waves.

References

1. Mark Yim, Ying Zhang & David Duff, Xerox Palo Alto Research Center (PARC), "Modular Robots". IEEE Spectrum Magazine. Febrero 2002.
2. Mark Yim, David G. Duff, Kimon D. Roufas, "Polybot: a Modular Reconfigurable Robot", IEEE intl. Conf. on Robotics and Automation (ICRA), San Francisco, CA, April 2000.
3. D. Duff, M. Yim, K. Roufas,"Evolution of PolyBot: A Modular Reconfigurable Robot", Proc. of the Harmonic Drive Intl. Symposium, Nagano, Japan, Nov. 2001, and Proc. of COE/Super-Mechano-Systems Workshop, Tokyo, Japan, Nov. 2001.
4. M. Yim, Y. Zhang, K. Roufas, D. Duff, C. Eldershaw, "Connecting and disconnecting for chain self-reconfiguration with PolyBot", IEEE/ASME Transactions on mechatronics, special issue on Information Technology in Mechatronics, 2003.
5. González-Gómez J., Aguayo E., Boemo E.,"Locomotion of a Modular Worm-like Robot using a FPGA-based embedded MicroBlaze Soft-processor".Proc. of 7th International Conference on Climbing and Walking Robots, Madrid, Spain, Sep. 2004.
6. Xilinx Inc. "MicroBlaze Processor Reference Guide, Embedded Development Kit. Version 6.2"
7. Xilinx Inc. "PowerPC Processor Reference Guide, Embedded Development Kit. Version 6.2"
8. Gaisler Research, "http://www.gaisler.com". (March, 2005)

Dynamic Partial Reconfigurable FIR Filter Design

Yeong-Jae Oh, Hanho Lee, and Chong-Ho Lee

School of Information and Communication Engineering
Inha University, Incheon, Korea
rokmcno6@gmail.com,
{hhlee, chlee}@inha.ac.kr

Abstract. This paper presents a novel partially reconfigurable FIR filter design that employs dynamic partial reconfiguration. Our scope is to implement a low-power, area-efficient autonomously reconfigurable digital signal processing architecture that is tailored for the realization of arbitrary response FIR filters using Xilinx FPGAs. The implementation of design addresses area efficiency and flexibility allowing dynamically inserting and/or removing the partial modules to implement the partial reconfigurable FIR filters with various taps. This FIR filter design method shows the configuration time improvement, good area efficiency and flexibility by using the dynamic partial reconfiguration method.

1 Introduction

FIR filters are employed in the majority digital signal processing (DSP) based electronic systems. The emergence of demanding applications (image, audio/ video processing and coding, sensor filtering, etc.) in terms of power, speed, performance, system compatibility and reusability make it imperative to design the reconfigurable architectures. This paper presents a partially reconfigurable FIR filter design that targets to meet all the objectives(low-power consumption, autonomous adaptability/reconfigurability, fault-tolerance, etc.) on the FPGA. FPGAs are programmable logic devices that permit the implementation of digital systems. They provide an array of logic cells that can be configured to perform a given functionality by means of a configuration bitstream. Many of FPGA systems can only be statically configured. Static reconfiguration means to completely configure the device before system execution. If a new reconfiguration is required, it is necessary to stop system execution and reconfigure the device it over again. Some FPGAs allow performing partial reconfiguration, where a reduced bitstream reconfigures only a given subset of internal components. Dynamic Partial Reconfiguration (DPR) allows the part of FPGA device be modified while the rest of the device (or system) continues to operate and unaffected by the reprogramming [1]. Module-based partial reconfiguration was proposed by Xilinx [3][4]. And now many researchers have been proposed many partial reconfiguration methods (JBits, PARBIT, etc) [1][2]. The modular design flow allows the designer to split the whole system into modules.

K. Bertels, J.M.P. Cardoso, and S. Vassiliadis (Eds.): ARC 2006, LNCS 3985, pp. 30–35, 2006.
© Springer-Verlag Berlin Heidelberg 2006

2   Reconfigurable FIR Filter Design

The FIR filter computes an output from a set of input samples. The set of input samples is multiplied by a set of coefficients and then added together to produce the output as shown in Fig. 1. Implementation of FIR filters can be undertaken in either hardware or software [5]. A software implementation will require sequential execution of the filter functions. Hardware implementation of FIR filters allows the filter functions to be executed in a parallel manner, which makes improved filter processing speed possible but is less flexible for changes. Thus, reconfigurable FIR filter offers both the flexibility of computer software,

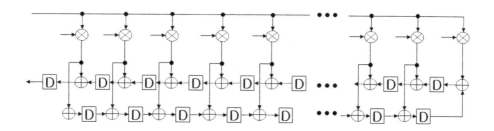

Fig. 1. n-tap transposed FIR filter

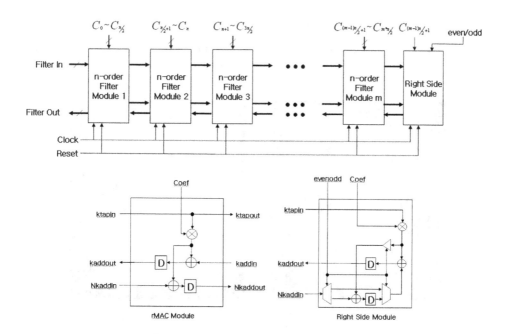

Fig. 2. Block diagram of (a) partial reconfigurable m n order FIR filter, (b) reconfigurable multiply-accummulate (rMAC) modules

and the ability to construct custom high performance computing circuits. Fig. 2 shows the partial reconfigurable m n order FIR filter, which consists of m n order filter modules and right side module. These FIR filter is consisted of m filter modules, which connected by bus macros on FPGA. And each filter module consists of $n/2$ reconfigurable multiply-accumulate (rMAC) unit, which includes the serial-to-parallel register to get coefficient inputs in serial.

3   Implementation

This section describes the implementation method of 20-tap FIR filter, which is reconfigured partially from 12-tap FIR filter. The whole system is implemented on a Xilinx Virtex2p30 FPGA device.

3.1   HDL Coding and Synthesis

This step is composed to following two phase:

Top Module Design: In this phase, designer must consider each sub-module interconnection, area assignment and bus macro assignment.

Reconfigurable Sub-module Design: This phase is same to traditional HDL design method. But designer must consider input and output assign rule for partial reconfiguration.

3.2   Module-Based Design

Modular Design Implementation step comprises following three phase: 1) Initial budget phase, 2) Active module implementation, 3) Final assembly.

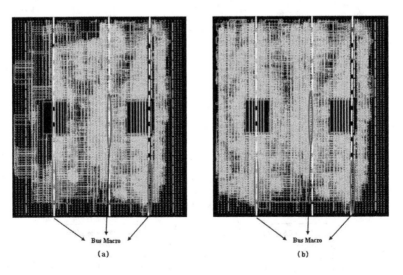

Fig. 3. PAR map of (a) 12-tap and (b) 20-tap FIR filter using DPR

Initial Budget: In this phase, the team leader assigns top-level constraints to the top-level design. Top-level constraint needs to area constraint and bus-macro assignment. This step is as sequence of top module design. In this step, designer must do bus macro manual setting, sub module area constraint by using floorplanner and top module IOB assignment. Bus macro is limited by target size. Through equation (1), designer can estimate maximum usable bus macro.

Active Module Implementation: In this phase, the team members implement the reconfigurable modules. That is, partially reconfigurable sub-modules are generated by top module and .ucf file. Each sub-module generates a partial bitstream during this step. Fig. 3 shows a post-PAR (placement and routing) diagram. Through n-order filter module1 is reconfigured to bypass module and module2 is reconfigured to 4-tap module on 12-tap FIR filter while other module is processing, 20-tap FIR filter is composed by partial reconfiguration of module1 showing Fig. 3(b).

Final Module Assmble: In the phase, designer assembles on system from partially generated modules. All partial modules generated in active module implementation step are combined to the top-level module.

4   Experiment and Result

The partial reconfiguration of reconfigurable symmetric transposed FIR filters was implemented on Xilinx Virtex2pro FPGA device using test environment shown in Fig. 4[6]. XUPV2P FPGA test board and Agilent logic analyzer were used for board level verification. And configuration bitstream download is operated by Xilinx Platform Cable USB and IMPACT. For dynamic partial reconfiguration experiment, the partial reconfigurable module1 and module2 were reconfigured bypass module and 4-tap module respectively while other areas of modules remain operational. For verification, we have performed following two methods. First, 12-tap and 20-tap FIR filters before/after partial reconfiguration have been simulated to verify the output results on FPGA test board using Xilinx ChipScope Pro Analyzer. Second, each module has been assigned by identification number such as bypass=00, 2-tap=01, 4-tap=10, 6-tap=11, and then during the partial reconfiguration process the waveform of logic analyzer shows the change of identification number to verify the partial reconfiguration of FIR filter. Because most of modules are operating except reconfigured module, module identification number is changed continuously. After completing DPR, the waveform shows the output change from 3D(111101) to 31 (110001). This result shows that module2 is reconfigured partially from 6-tap module to bypass module. And measured reconfiguration time shows about 112.5 ms. Otherwise, the full reconfiguration is processed after FPGA reset. Measure reconfiguration time is about 3.05 s. Thus the reconfiguration time of DPR FIR filter is reduced about 1/30 compared to full reconfiguration of FIR filter. For performance comparison, we have implemented FIR filter using variable multipliers, multiplexer

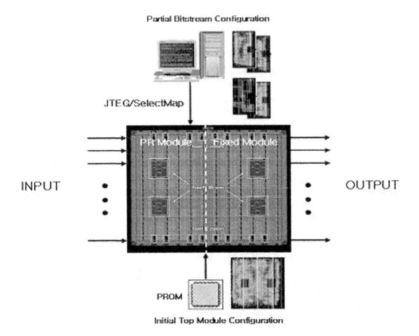

Fig. 4. Test Environment

Table 1. FPGA device utilization for several FIR filters (GF: General symmetric FIR filter, MBF: Multiplexer-based reconfigurable FIR filter, DPR: Reconfigurable FIR fiter using DPR)

	GF	MBF	DPR
Slice	3,058	5,349	4,733
LUT	5,980	9,669	8,427
Equivalent Gate	N/A	76,024	68,063

based reconfigurable FIR filter and reconfigurable symmetric transposed FIR filter. Table 1 shows the utilization of slice, LUT and equivalent gate count after technology mapping. The reconfigurable symmetric transposed FIR filter using DPR can save about 11.5% slice compared to the multiplexer based reconfigurable FIR filter. Compared to the general symmetric FIR filter, the number of slice increased about 54% because of adding bus macro, serial-to-parallel register and a little controller. But if we want to change one tap in general symmetric FIR filter, we must do the full reconfiguration, which requires the slow configuration time. However, reconfigurable symmetric transposed FIR filter using DPR method requires the partial reconfiguration of about 1,499 slices for one coefficient tap that adds flexibility allowing dynamically inserting and/or removing the coefficient taps.

5 Conclusion

In this paper, we present a reconfigurable FIR filter design using dynamic partial reconfiguration, which has area efficiency, flexibility and configuration time advantage allowing dynamically inserting and/or removing the partial modules. The proposed method produces a reduction in hardware cost and allows performing partial reconfiguration, where a reduced bitstream reconfigures only a given subset of internal components. In the future, self-reconfigurable hardware platform using microcontroller unit and configuration memory will be promising solution for automatic partial reconfiguration of digital circuit in the run-time environment.

Acknowledgement

This research was supported by the MIC (Ministry of Information and Communication), Korea, under the ITRC (Information Technology Research Center) support program and supported by Inha University research grant.

References

1. Mesquita, D., Moraes, F., Palma, J., Moller, L., Calazanas, N.: Remote and Partial Reconfiguration of FPGAs: tools and trends. International Parallel and Distributed Processing Symposium,(2003).
2. Raghavan, A. K., Shutton, P.: JPG-A partial bitstream generation tool to support partial reconfiguration in Virtex FPGAs. Proc. Of the International Parallel and Distributed Processing Symposium, (2002)
3. Xilinx Inc.: XAPP 290: Two flows for Partial Reconfiguration: Module Based or Difference Based. www.xilinx.com, Sept. (2004)
4. Xilinx Inc.: Development System Reference Guide. www.xilinx.com.
5. Meyer-Baese, U.: Digital Signal Processing with Field Programmable Gate Arrays. Springer, (2001).
6. Xilinx: Managing Partial Dynamic Reconfiguration in Virtex-II Pro FPGAs. Xcell Journal, Xilinx, Fall (2004)

Event-Driven Simulation Engine for Spiking Neural Networks on a Chip

Rodrigo Agis, Javier Díaz, Eduardo Ros, Richard Carrillo,
and Eva. M. Ortigosa

Dpto. Architecture and computers technology of the University of Granada, Spain
{ragis, jdiaz, eros, rcarrillo, eva}@atc.ugr.es
http://atc.ugr.es

Abstract. The efficient simulation of spiking neural networks (SNN) remains as an open challenge. Current SNN computing engines are still far away of being able to efficiently simulate systems of millions of neurons. This contribution describes a computing scheme that takes full advantage of the massive parallel processing resources available at FPGA devices. The computing engine adopts an event-driven simulation scheme and an efficient *next-event-to-go* searching method to achieve high performance. We have designed a pipelined datapath in order to compute several events in parallel avoiding idle computing resources. The system is able to compute approximately 2.5 million spikes per second. The whole computing machine is composed only by an FPGA device and five external memory SRAM chips. Therefore the presented approach is of high interest for simulation experiments that require embedded simulation engines (for instance in robotic experiments with autonomous agents).

1 Introduction

The simulation of biologically plausible neural networks is a challenging task. Several properties of the biological nervous systems must be taken into consideration in order to build up an efficient computing scheme:

Biological neural networks are composed by massive parallel computing resources organized in very densely connected topologies.

Most of the information exchanged between the different computing elements (neurons) is encoded in spikes.

The firing rate of biological neurons is low (with maximum rates of approximately 100 Hz). Therefore, the global activity depends on the network size and average neuron firing rate.

On the other hand the current technology has very different characteristics that can be exploited adopting proper computing schemes:

In general, digital circuits are able to work at very high clock rates (MHz or even GHz).

K. Bertels, J.M.P. Cardoso, and S. Vassiliadis (Eds.): ARC 2006, LNCS 3985, pp. 36–45, 2006.

The physical circuit connectivity is limited to 2-D patterns that consume large device resources. Therefore densely connected topologies are impossible to implement directly on VLSI technology.

Although there are hardware approaches that implement in FPGA efficient time-driven simulation schemes [1, 2, 3, 4], the features enumerated above have motivated the development of event-driven processing schemes. This computing scheme is usually implemented in software [5, 6, 7, 8 and 10], but has been also adopted in hardware approaches [11, 12]. In event-driven simulation schemes, the neuron state variables are updated when it fires or receives a spike. Therefore, the simulation engine is able to jump from one spike to the next one. In this way all the activity (spikes) of a network is queued in a chronological order and processed sequentially. This scheme is very appropriate for sequential computing platforms (such as conventional computers). On the other hand, since all the events need to be processed in a chronological order this scheme is hardly parallelizable.

In this work we present a specific purpose computing architecture to efficiently simulate spiking neural networks adopting an event-driven scheme. The common approach is based on a queue of events ordered chronologically. In this case, the goal is to reduce the number of accesses required for the correct insertion of a new spike in its correct position. Contrary to this approach, we use a disordered event list, the processing scheme searches for the *next-event-to-go* before each computing loop. For this purpose we implement a parallel searching strategy that takes full advantage of the parallel processing resources available in FPGA devices. We also implement a pipelined processing structure to further accelerate the simulator but this requires the consideration of inter-spike dependency risks. In this work we focus on processing speed as the main performance indicator, therefore the goal is to design a system able to process the maximum number of spikes per second.

2   Description of the Computing Scheme

The computing scheme is illustrated in Fig. 1. The event list is stored on embedded memory resources in order to facilitate the insertion and searching processes. On the other hand the neural state variables and the network topology are stored on external memory SRAM.

2.1   Scalable Next-Event Selection: Pick-Up Strategy

In order to facilitate the insertion processes we use a disordered event list. In this case each time we need to extract an event we search for the one with a minimum *time label*. We implement a parallel searching strategy taking full advantage of the parallel computing resources of the FPGA devices. Each event is characterized by four fields: time label, synapse identifier, source neuron and

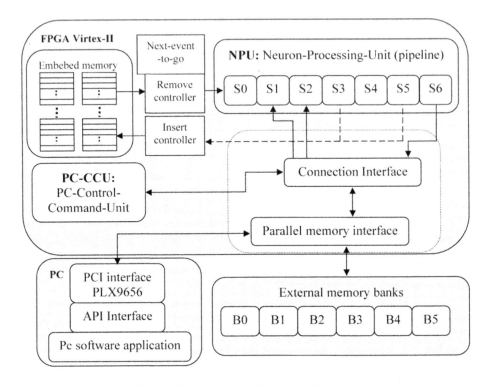

Fig. 1. Computing architecture schematic

target neuron. We distribute the storage of the time labels in different dual port embedded memory blocks (EMBs) of 512x32 bits to allow parallel access to a high number of elements. We implement parallel comparator circuits of 4 and 8 elements each. And we use distributed memory buffers to segment the searching process in several comparator stages in a micro-pipelined structure (as shown in Fig. 2).

The reconfigurability of the FPGA makes easy to change the amount of memory resources allocated for specific tasks. Therefore, depending of the global network activity it may be convenient to use more or less embedded memory blocks for the time labels of the spikes. We have implemented a pipelined searching structure to efficiently handle event list of up to 2^{14} spikes. The events are distributed in 128 dual port EMBs in order to allow reading 256 elements in parallel to fill a buffer implemented in distributed memory. This allows these 256 elements to access to 32 comparator circuits of 8 elements each producing 32 candidates that are stored in the second buffer (on distributed memory). These 32 elements access to 4 comparator circuits of 8 elements each producing 4 candidates that are stored in the third buffer. Finally, a single comparator of 4 elements provides the access to out of these primary 256 elements. After this is done, this winning event is stored as the one with the minimum time label. This scheme is further expanded sequentially in the following manner; the next event that goes out of

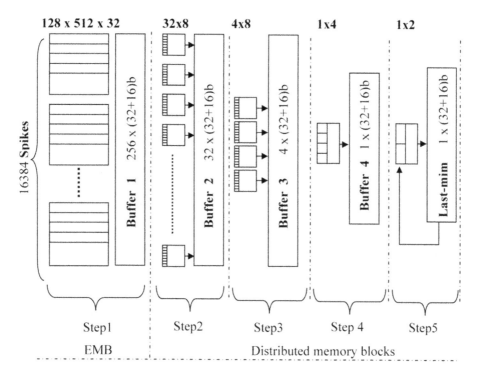

Fig. 2. Parallel searching tree

this pipelined searching structure is compared with the one stored previously *Last-mim*. In this way, with this last sequential comparator cycle we are able to manage event lists of up to 2^{14} elements consuming up to 69 clock cycles. Note that in order to pipeline this processing datapath we need to store in buffers (distributed memory) not only the time labels but also an index to identify the original spike (in embedded memory block that is being processed). In fact, this scheme can be further scaled up using external memory banks to manage larger event list at the cost of reducing the searching speed significantly when all the input memory resources are saturated. This is amply discussed in [13].

$$N_{clk\_cycles\_searching} = 4 + \left\lceil \frac{T_{EMB}}{256} \right\rceil \qquad (1)$$

The number of clock cycles required in this searching structure ($N_{clk\_cycles\_search}$) is illustrated follows expression (1). The expression (1) is the ceiling function where T_{EMB} denotes the number of spikes stored in all the EMBs used by the searching module and $\lceil \rceil$ denotes the function that produces the first entire above the considered real number. The offset of 4 is given by the number of cycles consumed filling the pipeline structure.

Note that after the *next-event-to-go* is found all the data fields of this event need to be retrieved which also consumers another 5 cycles.

2.2   Pipelined Event-Processing Datapath

The computing strategy is outlined in the block diagram of Fig. 3. The different stages are the following: S0) the *next-event-to-go* is searched (this is done through a parallel searching tree as described in the previous section), S1) access to memory to retrieve the source neuron state variables and the connection characteristics, S2) load the target neuron state, S3) the next spike (if the remain spike of the output connection tree to be processed) of this source neuron connection tree is inserted in the event list, S4) the target neuron state is updated (including learning), S5) the axon-hillock is processed (spike firing decision) and S6) store the target neuron state and connection weight (updated in the learning module).

When a neuron fires it produces multiple spikes that will reach different target neurons according to the network topology. Each connection is characterized by a weight and a synaptic delay. In order to restrict the number of spike insertions, in each computation cycle we consult the output connection tree (ordered according to the synaptic delays) of a neuron that has fired and we insert only the next-event according to the synaptic delay. This keeps the event list at a manageable size.

We have implemented a pipelined event-processing datapath consisting in the 7 stages outlined in Fig. 3. Note that for event list up to 2048 the next-event searching structure consumes less than 13 clock cycles, therefore not degrading the global processing performance. All the processing stages are quite balanced being the limiting one the spike insertion process that requires 13 clock cycles. This leads to a performance of more than 2.5 million of spikes per second with

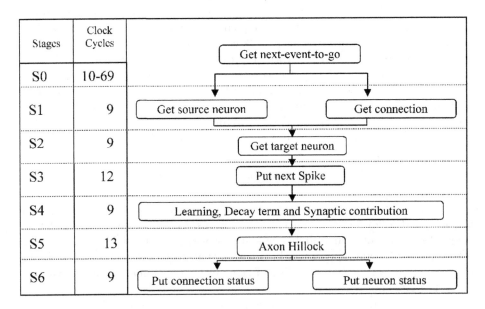

Fig. 3. Pipeline datapath. Seven stages in the datapath.

a system clock rate of 33 MHz and provided that the event list size is smaller than 2048 elements.

The clock cycles consumption of each of the stages of the pipelined datapath is included in Fig. 3. The stage S0 consumes between 10 and 69 cycles because the number of the clock cycles depends of the size of the event list. But even with the optimized stage, without a global coarse pipeline we obtain a data throughput between 464000 and 272000 spikes per second. This has motivated the pipelined processing structure that allows performances between 2.5 and 0.478 million spikes per second. We need to take into account that depending on the network topology we will have up to 10% of performance degradation due to inter-spike risks. This occurs, when S5 (Axon Hillock) puts a new event in the event list with a time label which is bellow the one of the last spike that entered the pipeline structure. In this case is necessary to reset the whole datapath to keep the chronological processing order. The performance values on Fig. 5 have been obtained with a circuit running at 33 Mhz.

2.3   Neural Model

The described general architecture is valid for multiple neuron models. In fact, the neural state computation is a single processing stage that can be seen as a black box.

The only restriction is that the neural model allows the neural state variables to be updated discontinuously. Currently we are using the proposed platform to test bio-inspired robotic control experiments [14] with the neural model illustrated in the Table 1.

Fig. 4 illustrates the neural model described in Table 1. Fig. 4.a represents the spike time dependent plasticity (STDP) expressed in the first equation of table 1. Fig. 4.b represents the passive decay term, it plots the time dependent

Table 1. Neural model characteristics. V_x denotes the membrane potential and W the connection weight. The weigth is uploaded according to the first expresion. The conection betwen cells K and J is made stronger on weaker depending on the inter-spike time betwen the events produced by the two neurons.

Stage	Feature	Clock cycles	Expression
S4	Learning of synapse (i)	3	$\Delta W_i^{t_k} = 27 .(t_k^i - t_j^i). e^{\frac{(t_j^i - t_k^i)}{10}}$
	Passive decay	4	$V_x = V_x - \left[\frac{V_{max}}{\tau} . (t_k - t_j) \right]$
	Synaptic contribution	2	$V_x = V_x + W_i$
S5	Axon Hillock (spike insertion)	13	$Out = \begin{cases} 1 & if \ V_x \geq V_{threshold} \\ 0 & if \ V_x < V_{threshold} \end{cases}$

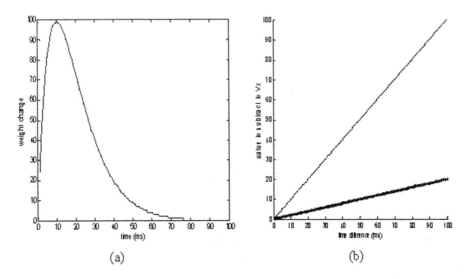

Fig. 4. Neural model. (a) Spike-time dependent plasticity and (b) Membrane potential passive decay term.

term that needs to be subtracted to the membrane potential according to the second equation of table 1. We particularize different neural models with specific values of τ (Purkinje cell model with a stronger passive decay term represented in the upper trace and Granular cell model with weaker passive decay term in the lower trace).

3   Simulation Performance and Hardware Resources

The complete processing datapath consumes 74 clock cycles (provided that the event list has less than 1024 elements). But using a pipeline processing strategy we process one spike each 13 clock cycles (provided that the interspike risks do not affect significantly the system performance). Therefore, with a system clock frequency of 33 MHz, the achieved performance is approximately 2.5 million spikes per second. Comparing the performance with other approaches is difficult since each of them use different neural models. Currently one of most efficient event-driven software versions [5] is able to compute up to 0.8 Mspikes/second using an AMD processor at 2.8 GHz. It is significant to note that through the design of a specific purpose datapath working at a clock rate about 2 orders of magnitude lower than conventional computers we are able to outperform in more than a factor of 2 the processing performance. Other simpler spiking neurons simulator we able to process higher rates [6, 7] but only including simplified neural models network topologies. It is also remarkable that the exploration of other neural models (even of higher complexity) would not significantly degrade the system performance if the computation can be done in less than 13 independent steps or split in several pipelined processing stages. The data throughput

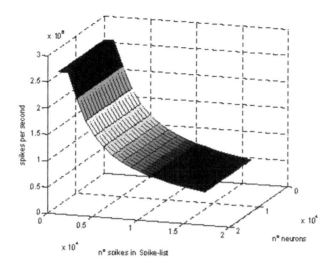

Fig. 5. Performance vs global network activity and network size

Table 2. Hardware resources consumption. Design compiled on a Virtex II 6000 [15].

Pipeline state	#System Gates	EMBs	# Clock cycles
S0	4.823.495	64	10-69
S1	2450	-	9
S2	919	-	9
S3	1172	-	12
S4	1955	-	9
S5	1182	-	13
S6	1451	-	9

(D_t) follows expression (2) which is independent on the network size and includes a degradation term (A_{risks}) dependent on the inter-spike risks. This factor will not be significant in realistic networks in which spikes of output connection trees will be almost consecutively processed.

$$D_t = \frac{f_{clk}}{A_{risks} + \max\left[13, \ N_{clk\_cycles\_search}\right]} \qquad (2)$$

The performance follows rigorously the characterization expression outlined above. The surface Fig.5 has been done using a network topology (all-to-all connectivity with short synaptic delays). In this case the inter-spike risks do not affect significantly the system performance. As it can be seen the performance does no depend of the network size, only of the global activity achieving a maximum performance of 2.5 millions spikes per second. The hardware resources consumption is summarized in the table 2.

4   Discussion

The main innovation of the presented approach is the efficient use of the parallel computing resources of FPGA devices for an event-driven processing scheme. We have adopted a strategy that handles efficiently disordered event list which is a completely novel approach. We have used extensively parallel computing in the *next-event-to-go* searching structure that has been implemented with a finely pipelined searching tree.

The whole computing scheme is also implemented in a coarse pipelined datapath of 7 stages. Here is required to handle inter-spike risks, but they are not significant in realistic networks in which spikes of specific output connection trees will be processed almost consecutively. But, depending on the network topology more pipelined stages may not be handled efficiently, since the effect of inter-spike risks may become larger.

Although comparisons between different event driven approaches are difficult, since different authors adopt different neural models and computing strategies, the presented approach exhibits very promising performance results. It outperform in more than a factor of two a similar approach implemented in software [5]. This is very important also taking into account that the presented computing scheme can embed more complex neural models without significantly degrading the system performance. In this sense, we call this approach *scalable in the neural model complexity*.

Another important point is that since the described computing platform is very general and can be easily adapted for different neural models, it is interesting to explore different neural features in the framework of massive simulations or real-time experiments requiring very short time responses.

Acknowledgements. This work has been supported by the Spanish national grant DEPROVI (DPI-2004-07032) and the EU projects SENSOPAC and DRIVSCO.

References

1. E.L. Graas, E.A. Brown and R.H. Lee, "An FPGA-based approach to high-speed simulation of conductance-based neuron models", Neuroinformatics, vol. 2., pp. 417-435, 2004.
2. Ros, E., Ortigosa, E. M., Agis, R., Carrillo, R., Prieto, A., Arnold, M., "Spiking neurons computing platform", Lecture Notes in Computer Science, Vol. 3512, pp. 471-478, 2005.
3. Ros, E., Ortigosa, E. M., Agis, R., Carrillo, R., Arnold, M., "Real-time computing platform for spiking neurons (RT-Spike)", Submitted to IEEE Transactions on Neural Networks, 2005.

4. Glackin B., McGinnity T.M., Maguire L.P., Wu Q.X., Belatreche A., "A Novel Approach for the Implementation of Large Scale Spiking Neural Networks on FPGA Hardware", Lecture Notes in Computer Science, pp. 552-563, 2005.
5. Ros, E., Carrillo, R., Ortigosa, E. M., Barbour, B., Agís, R., 2005. Event-driven Simulation Scheme for Spiking Neural Models based on Characterization Look-up Tables. Submitted to Neural Computation.
6. Delorme, A., Gautrais, J. van Rullen, R., Thorpe, S. (1999). SpikeNET: A simulator for modelling large networks of integrate and fire neurons. In J. M. Bower (Ed.), Computational Neuroscience: Trends in research 1999, Neurocomputing, Vols. 26-27, 989-996.
7. Delorme, A., Thorpe, S. (2003). SpikeNET: An event-driven simulation package for modelling large networks of spiking neurons. Network: Computation in Neural Systems, Vol. 14, 613-627.
8. Mattia, M., & Del Guidice, P. (2000). Efficient event-driven simulation of large networks of spiking neurons and dynamical synapses. Neural Computation, 12(10), 2305-2329.
9. Reutimann, J., Guigliano, M., Fusi, S. (2003). Event-driven simulation of spiking neurons with stochastic dynamics.Neural Computation, 15, 811-830.
10. Makino, T., 2003: A Discrete-Event Neural Network Simulator for General Neuron Models. Neural Comput & Applic, 11. 210-223.
11. T. Schoenauer, S. Atasoy, N. Mehrtash, H. Klar, "NeuroPipe-Chip: A Digital Neuro-Processor for Spiking Neural Networks," IEEE Trans. Neural Networks, vol. 13(1), pp. 205-213, 2002.
12. N. Mehrtash, D. Jung, H.H. Hellmich, T. Schoenauer, V.T. Lu, H. Klar, "Synaptic Plasticity in Spiking Neural Networks (SP^{2}INN): A System Approach, " IEEE Transactions on Neural Networks , vol. 14(5), 2003.
13. R. Agís, E. Ros, J. Díaz, R. Carrillo, R. Rodriguez, "Memory Management in FPGA based platforms for event driven processing systems", Submitted to ARC'06.
14. 14 C. Boucheny, R. Carrillo, E. Ros, O. J-M D. Coenen, "Real-Time spiking neural network : an adaptive cerebellar model," Lecture Notes in Computer Science, vol. 3512, pp. 136-144, 2005.
15. Xilinx, 1994-2003. [Online]. Available: http://www.xilinx.com

Towards an Optimal Implementation of MLP in FPGA

E.M. Ortigosa[1], A. Cañas[1], R. Rodríguez[1], J. Díaz[1], and S. Mota[2]

[1] Dept. of Computer Architecture and Technology, University of Granada,
E-18071 Granada, Spain
{eva, acanas, rrodriguez, jdiaz}@atc.ugr.es
[2] Dept. of Informatics and Numerical Analysis, University of Córdoba,
E-14071 Córdoba, Spain
smota@uco.es

Abstract. We present the hardware implementation of partially connected neural network that is defined as an extended of the Multi-Layer Perceptron (MLP) model. We demonstrate that partially connected neural networks lead to a higher performance in terms of computing speed (requiring less memory and computing resources). This work addresses a complete study that compares the hardware implementation of MLP and a partially connected version (XMLP) in terms of computing speed, hardware resources and performance cost. Furthermore, we study also different memory management strategies for the connectivity patterns.

1 Introduction

The implementation of Artificial Neural Networks (ANNs) as embedded systems using FPGA devices has become an interesting research field in the last years [1,2,3,4,5]. The work presented here studies the implementation viability and efficiency of ANNs into reconfigurable hardware (FPGA) for embedded systems, such as portable real-time ASR (Automatic Speech Recognition) devices for consumer applications, vehicle equipment (GPS navigator interface), toys, aids for disabled persons, etc. The application chose has been the ASR and among the different ANN models available used for ASR, we have focused on the Multi-Layer Perceptron (MLP).

The hardware implementation of ANNs usually focuses on the conventional software model and tries to parallelize the whole processing scheme. Nevertheless, the optimization of the traditional ANN model towards a less densely connected network leads to a significant improvement in the system computing speed (requiring less memory and computing resources). In this way, the main innovation of this contribution is the description of a modified version of the MLP called eXtended Multi-Layer Perceptron (XMLP) [6] towards a less densely connected network.

The paper is organized as follows. Section 2 briefly describes the MLP and XMLP models. Then we describe and evaluated the detailed hardware implementation strategies of the MLP and XMLP and we presents the discussion of the results (Section 3). Finally, Section 4 summarizes the conclusions.

K. Bertels, J.M.P. Cardoso, and S. Vassiliadis (Eds.): ARC 2006, LNCS 3985, pp. 46–51, 2006.

2   MLP / XMLP

2.1   Multi-Layer Perceptron (MLP)

The MLP is an ANN with processing elements or neurons organized in a regular structure with several layers: an input layer (that is simply an input vector), some hidden layers and an output layer. For classification problems, only one winning node of the output layer is active for each input pattern.

Each layer is fully connected with its adjacent layers. There are no connections between non-adjacent layers and there are no recurrent connections. Each of these connections is defined by an associated weight. Each neuron calculates the weighted sum of its inputs and applies an activation function that forces the neuron output to be high or low.

In this way, propagating the output of each layer, the MLP generates an output vector from each input pattern. The synaptic weights are adjusted through a supervised training algorithm called backpropagation [7].

The most frequently activation function used is the sigmoid, although there are other choices such as a ramp function, a hyperbolic tangent, etc.

2.2   Extended Multi-Layer Perceptron (XMLP)

The XMLP is a feed-forward neural network with an input layer (without neurons), a number of hidden layers selectable from zero to two, and an output layer. In addition to the usual MLP connectivity, any layer can be two-dimensional and partially connected to adjacent layers. As illustrated in Fig. 1, connections come out from each layer in overlapped rectangular groups. The size of a layer l and its partial connectivity pattern are defined by six parameters in the following form: $x(g_x, s_x) \times y(g_y, s_y)$, where x and y are the sizes of the axes, and g and s specify the size of a group of neurons and the step between two consecutive groups, both in abscissas (g_x, s_x) and ordinates (g_y, s_y). A neuron i in the X-axis at layer $l+1$ (the upper one in Fig. 1) is fed from all the neurons belonging to

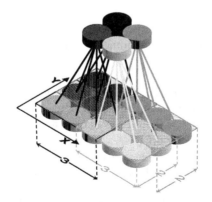

Fig. 1. Structure of an XMLP layer and its connections to the next layer

the i-the group in the Xaxis at layer l (the lower one). The same connectivity definition is used in the Y-axis. When g and s are not specified for a particular dimension, the connectivity assumed for that dimension is $g_x = x$ and $s_x = 0$, or $g_y = y$ and $s_y = 0$. Thus, MLP is a particular case of XMLP where $g_x = x$, $s_x = 0$, $g_y = y$ and $s_y = 0$ for all layers.

3   Hardware Implementation: XMLP vs MLP

In order to illustrate the hardware implementation of the MLP and XMLP systems, and address a complete comparative study of these ANNs, we have chosen a specific speaker-independent isolated word recognition application [8]. Nevertheless, many other applications require embedded systems in portable devices (low cost, low power and reduced physical size).

For our test bed application, we need an MLP / XMLP with 220 scalar data in the input layer and 10 output nodes in the output layer. The network input consists of 10 vectors of 22 components (10 cepstrum, 10 Δcepstrum, energy, Δenergy) obtained after preprocessing the speech signal. The output nodes correspond to 10 recognizable words extracted from a multi-speaker database [9]. After testing different architectures [6], the best classification results (96.83% of correct classification rate in a speaker-independent scheme) have been obtained using 24 nodes in a single hidden layer, with the connectivity of the XMLP defined by 10(4,2)×22 in the input layer and 4×6 in the hidden layer.

For the MLP / XMLP implementations, we have chosen fix point computations with two's complement representation and different bit depths for the stored data (inputs, weights, activation function, outputs, etc). It is necessary to limit the range of different variables: inputs to the MLP / XMLP and output of the activation function (8 bits), weights (8 bits) and inputs to the activation function, which is defined by a Look-Up-Table (LUT) that stores the useful values. After taking all these discretization simplifications the model achieves similar classification results. The results of the hardware system differ in less than 1% from the software full resolution results.

The systems have been designed and translated to EDIF files using DK Design Suite tool from Celoxica [10]. Then, the designs have been placed and routed in a Virtex-E 2000 FPGA using the development environment ISE Foundation 3.5i from Xilinx [11].

We have evaluated the serial and parallel approaches. The serial version emulates the software implementation, using only one processing unit that is multiplexed to compute all the neurons of the ANN. On the other hand, the parallel version makes use of one processing unit per neuron at the hidden layer. In addition, we have implemented three different versions of approaches using different memory resources: (A) using only distributed memory resources, (B) using distributed memory resources and embedded memory blocks and (C) using only embedded memory blocks.

Tables 1 and 2 summarize the hardware implementation characteristics of the MLP and XMLP respectively.

Table 1. Implementation characteristics of the MLP designs. (A) Only distributed RAM (B) Both EMBs RAM and distributed RAM. (C) Only EMBs RAM.

MLP design	# slices	# EMBs RAM	# sys. gates (S_g)	Max.Freq. (MHz)	# cycles	D_t (data/s)	S_g / D_t
		$\mathbf{H}_r$		**Perf.**			$\mathbf{P}_c$
A: Serial	2582	0	245268	19.7	5588	3535	69.38
A: Parallel	6321	0	333828	17.2	282	60968	5.48
B: Serial	710	11	218712	16.1	5588	2671	81.86
B: Parallel	4411	24	518928	16.7	282	59326	8.75
C: Serial	547	14	248996	15.3	5588	2733	91.07
C: Parallel	4270	36	695380	15.4	282	54692	12.71

Table 2. Implementation characteristics of the XMLP designs. (A) Only distributed RAM (B) Both EMBs RAM and distributed RAM. (C) Only EMBs RAM.

XMLP design	# slices	# EMBs RAM	# sys. gates (S_g)	Max.Freq. (MHz)	# cycles	D_t (data/s)	S_g / D_t
		$\mathbf{H}_r$		**Perf.**			$\mathbf{P}_c$
A: Serial	2389	0	181858	22.3	2595	8592	21.17
A: Parallel	5754	0	258808	20.8	167	124844	2.07
B: Serial	1700	5	154806	14.0	2595	5384	28.75
B: Parallel	5032	96	1722376	15.6	167	93170	18.49
C: Serial	1608	10	202022	13.0	2595	4990	40.48
C: Parallel	4923	147	2526915	15.4	167	92365	27.36

The tables include the consumption of hardware resources of each approach in terms of slices and embedded memory blocks (EMB). We also calculate a global hardware resource indicator as the total number of equivalent system gates (S_g) consumed by each implemented version. The gate counting used on Virtex-E devices is consistent with the system gate counting used on the original Virtex devices [11].

In order to evaluate the computing speed we include the maximum clock frequency allowed by each implementation (this is given by the ISE Foundation after the synthesization stage) and the number of clock cycles consumed to evaluate a single input vector. We have also calculated a global performance indicator as the data throughput (D_t) of the system, i.e. the number of input vectors processed per second (note that each vector consist of 220 components).

Finally, to better illustrate the trade off between these two characteristics, which can be adopted as a convenient design objective during the architecture definition process, we have evaluated the performance cost (P_c) achieved by each implementation as the ratio $P_c = S_g$ / D_t. This feature indicates the hardware resources required to achieve a data throughput of one. Therefore, we can compare directly the hardware resources of the different approaches to achieve the same performance. The comparative results are summarized in Fig 2.

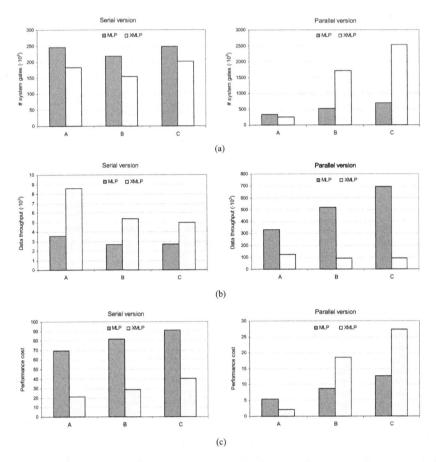

Fig. 2. XMLP vs. MLP in the serial (left) and parallel (right) approaches: a) Number of equivalent system gates, S_g. b) Data throughput, D_t. c) Performance cost, P_c.

We can see that the XMLP significantly improves all the indicators—hardware resources consumption (S_g), performance as data throughput (D_t) and performance cost (P_c)—compared to MLP. In both, the serial and parallel version, XMLP improves all the indicators by a factor of two approximately.

Among the three versions evaluated regarding the data storage strategy (A, B and C), we see that the best approach is the one that only makes use of distributed memory resources (A). This is so, because the network memory requirements per neuron is small (220 input weights for each hidden neuron) compared to the size of the embedded memory blocks (512 elements). Therefore, the embedded memory resources are being used inefficiently (although this factor depends on the network topology, mainly on the hidden neuron fan-in). This is more dramatic in the XMLP where the number of inter-neuron connections is greatly reduced. In this case, the use of only distributed memory is mandatory since the embedded memory blocks are very inefficiently used given the reduced number of weights that are stored in each of them, provided that the parallel version needs to access in parallel to the weights of different hidden neurons.

4   Conclusions

The main innovative idea of this contribution regarding hardware implementation of neural networks is that the final approach, can be highly improved if the previous software simulations include the possibility of simplifying the network topology (reducing the number of interneuron connections). Along this line we have defined an extended multilayer perceptron that allows the definition of networks of different interlayer topologies. This aspect has a great impact on the neural network implementation on specific hardware as has been shown in Section 3. Choosing between different topologies can be done in preliminary software simulations applying for instance genetic algorithms to obtain the best configuration before the hardware implementation is addressed.

Acknowledgement

This work has been supported by TIN2004-01419 and SENSOPAC proyects.

References

1. Zhu, J., Sutton, P.: FPGA Implementations of Neural Networks – a Survey of a Decade of Progress, LNCS, 2778 (2003), 1062–1066
2. Zhu, J., Milne, G., Gunther, B.: Towards an FPGA Based Reconf. Comp. Environment for N. N. Impl., in Proc. 9th Intl.Conf. on ANN, 2 (1999), 661–667
3. Gonçalves, R. A., Moraes, P.A.,...: ARCHITECT-R: A System for Reconfig. Robots Design, in ACM Symp. on Appl. Comp., ACM Press (2003), 679–683
4. Hammerstrom, D.: Digital VLSI for Neural Networks, The Handbook of Brain Theory and Neural Networks, Second Edit., Ed. Michael Arbib, MIT Press (2003)
5. Gao, C., Hammerstrom, D., Zhu, S., Butts, M.: FPGA implementation of very large associative memories, in: FPGA Implementations of Neural Networks, Omondi, A.R.; Rajapakse, J.C. (Eds.), Springer Berlin H., New York (2005)
6. Cañas, A., Ortigosa, E.M., Díaz, A., Ortega, J.: XMLP: A Feed-Forward Neural Network with two-dimensional Layers and Partial Connectivity, LNCS, 2687 (2003), 89–96
7. Widrow, B., Lehr, M.: 30 years of adaptive neural networks: Perceptron, Madaline and Backpropagation, Proc. of the IEEE, 78 (9) (1990), 1415–1442
8. Ortigosa, E.M., Cañas, A., Ros, E., Carrillo, R.R.: FPGA implementation of a perceptron-like N. N. for embedded applications, LNCS, 2687 (2003), 1–8
9. Waibel, A., Hanazawa, T., Hinton, G., Shikano, K., Lang, K.: Phoneme Recognition Using T-D N.N. IEEE T. on Ac., Sp. and Sig. Proc., 37 (3)(1989)
10. Celoxica: Technical Library, http://www.celoxica.com/techlib/
11. Xilinx, http://www.xilinx.com/

Energy Consumption for Transport of Control Information on a Segmented Software-Controlled Communication Architecture

Kris Heyrman[1], Antonis Papanikolaou[2], Francky Catthoor[3], Peter Veelaert[4], Koen Debosschere[5], and Wilfried Philips[6]

[1] Hogeschool Gent, Schoonmeersstraat 52, B-9000 Gent, Belgium, and IMEC, Kapeldreef 75, B-3001 Leuven, Belgium
kris.heyrman@hogent.be
[2] IMEC
papaniko@imec.be
[3] IMEC, and Katholieke Universiteit Leuven, Kasteelpark Arenberg 10, B-3001 Heverlee, Belgium
francky.catthoor@imec.be
[4] Hogeschool Gent
peter.veelaert@hogent.be
[5] ELIS, Ghent University, St-Pietersnieuwstraat 41, B-9000 Gent, Belgium
koen.debosschere@ugent.be
[6] TELIN, Ghent University
wilfried.philips@ugent.be

Abstract. The segmented bus is a power-efficient architecture for intra-tile SoC communication, where energy is saved by switching off unused bus segments cycle-by-cycle. We determine the pattern of switch control bits and calculate the cost of transporting them. A test case indicates that the cost is much lower than the gain obtained from the segmentation, and that the prospects of segmented buses remain promising.

1 Trends in Communication Architecture: Software Control, Heterogeneity and Parallelism

In embedded systems, minimal energy dissipation and fast performance are challenging targets, while flexibility is necessary for quick time-to-market.

Software control over the architecture is a definite trend in processor and memory architecture design, addressing the need to reduce energy consumption. It makes sense that the communication network is also controlled by software. The drawback is the extra functionality required from the compiler and possibly increased design complexity. Once the necessary design tools are developed these drawbacks will be overcome.

A second trend in embedded system design is a move towards *heterogeneous* architectures. Heterogeneity is a step towards power efficiency, since it allows circuit activity to be confined to portions of an hierarchy, while non-utilized portions of the hierarchy do not consume power. Also, to optimize energy consumption, memory organizations are becoming multi-layered, with each layer

K. Bertels, J.M.P. Cardoso, and S. Vassiliadis (Eds.): ARC 2006, LNCS 3985, pp. 52–58, 2006.

consisting of memories of different size and type, like in the TI C5510 [13] or those designed according to the DTSE methodology described in [2].

Finally, hardware *parallelism* enables designers to either decrease an application's execution time or trade off execution time for lower energy consumption, e.g. by decreasing the supply voltage. In both cases, the amount of data to be transferred per cycle is high, since a number of parallel resources need to be kept busy in order to achieve the expected volume. This implies that the communication network should provide large enough bandwidth. This should be achieved by parallelism in communication, not by overclocking the network.

2   The Segmented Bus Architecture

In this paper we advocate the use of heavily segmented buses, which make a very energy-efficient software-controlled architecture. Because of the scaling down of technology, power lost to drive the capacitance of long lines will ultimately outweigh the power lost in active circuits. Isolating those segments of a bus that are not in use, cycle-by-cycle, can deliver important savings in the power budget. This architecture is shown in Figure 1. To see the type of environment where segmented buses become useful, Figure 2 shows a 14-bus system in the context of a VLIW processor cluster. The energy gains achieved by segmenting long bus interconnect wires have been reported in [3,11], but the energy needed for steering the buses was neglected.

The control bits bits required are 4 per bus and per individual segmentation switch. The control bit format has been chosen for energy saving (frequent changes require only one bit to change) but could still be improved upon if the energy to transport the bits would turn out to be excessive.

We will call E_{seg} the total energy consumed on a segmented bus system. E_{unseg} is the energy consumed on an equivalent bus which has no segmentation switches. SG, the segmentation gain, consists of the energy consumed by all segments that do not need to be driven, integrated over the duration of the application. At first sight, it looks like $SG = E_{unseg} - E_{seg}$ There is, however also

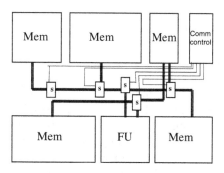

Fig. 1. The architecture of the segmented buses communication network includes parallel buses, segmentation switches, control wires and a communication controller

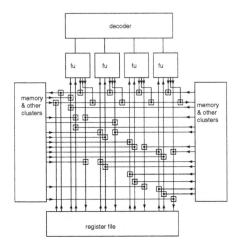

Fig. 2. VLIW processor cluster with a multiple segmented bus

a segmentation loss SL, which has two components: $SL = SL_{transport} + SL_{gen}$ SL consists of the cost incurred to transport control bits from the source of control to the switches, since this would not have to be done if the bus was non-segmented, and the cost to generate the bits from memory addresses or from the instruction flow. The cost of decoding the control bits is considered here as negligible, as it is certainly in the limit when technology scales down: we only need a small number of minimum-size gates, and in the limit their consumption is much smaller than E_{seg}.

$SL_{transport}$ does not depend on the method of generating the bits. The controller can be implemented either as an address-based path decoder using a memory-mapped look-up table or as a instruction-driven component which is part of the program flow generated by the compiler: the required control bits for the switches are inserted in the application code as separate network configuration instructions. In either case, scheduling is done at compile time and can be seen to be under software control.

With the first solution (path decoder), the routing need not be fully determined at compile-time, although the scheduling must have been done. The solution is compatible with common register indirect addressing modes, where the addresses at runtime are not necessarily known to the compiler at compile time. The second solution (fully compiled control) requires a cost that the first does not have: not only the schedule but also the actual path information must be fetched from instruction memory. It offers more possibilities for power efficiency: hierarchical activity clustering [7] is possible and distributed loop buffers can be employed that bring instruction decoding costs down in data-intensive applications of the sort that we contemplate on SoCs.

We will not consider SL_{gen} further in this paper. It is in fact the subject of further work. We suspect that there is a scalability issue at work here. For simple networks an address-based path decoder is probably optimal but it may well be that for complex networks instruction-driven switching is better. Suffice it to say that at least for small networks SL_{gen} scales well with technology, and that for scalability with network complexity, $SL_{transport}$ does not depend on it.

3 Method: Segmented Bus Analysis

When developing a method for segmented bus analysis, we perform tasks that are part of design-time analysis or need to be done compile-time by the control-bit emitting compiler. Since we have as yet no such compiler, we designed a program that undertakes some of the extra tasks on a profiled run of the application.

We use an optimization toolset (Atomium/MA [1]) to allocate and assign the memories for the application, i.e. to design the memory hierarchy for a given application (or set of applications). The functional units are assigned from the C code, in our experiments. Ultimately, this is of course also a task for the compiler. Storage bandwidth optimization is again done by the optimization toolset. The methodology presented in [14] is used to define the number of parallel communication resources needed to satisfy the application bandwidth requirements. Based on high-level application mapping, the peak bandwidth is extracted and a sufficient number of parallel buses is allocated. The bus connections are defined based on the synthesis of the memory organization. The layouts are made according to the practice of activity-aware floorplanning [7]. All segment lengths, including control bit segments, are extracted from a commercial routing tool [10].

From the data obtained from the optimization tool, which includes profiling together with floorplanning information, we recover the execution schedule for each basic block, recover the memory assignment, reconstruct the access tree, and collapse it into a per-cycle node tree of concurrent accesses. Then, for each path through the bus geometry, we decide what the switch positions must be. Walking in time sequence through the tree of cycles that the application consists of, we resolve each transfer to a set of control bits to be emitted, and from the dynamic behavior of the control bits calculate the energy required to transport the information, taking into account the physical lengths involved.

In essence, then, our power figures are derived from the characteristic capacitances and resistances of the technology node employed ($130nm$ CMOS in our case), the activity of the segments as derived from the access schedule, and the wire lengths from the floorplan. Achieving the figures is not automatic, but comes from the fact that a physical design methodology optimized for low power is followed throughout.

4 Application: Digital Audio Broadcast (DAB) Receiver

In order to estimate control power, we have made 4 different floorplans for a DAB receiver. Each represents a different trade-off between power efficiency and circuit area, resulting in a different on-chip memory count and complexity of the bus structure. The DAB receiver has three functional units: a FFT subsystem, a Viterbi decoder, and a deinterleaver.

After data storage and bandwidth exploration (DTSE) analysis [2] of the problem, 4 different sets of optimizations are chosen to set 4 alternative tasks for the design process. The solutions all feature 3 parallel buses and an unequal number of memories: 4, 8, 10 and 12. They all have an 8-bit bus, which in some solutions is extended to include some 16-bit segments, and two 32-bit buses.

5   Observations

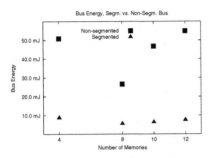

Fig. 3. Comparison of E_{seg} vs. E_{unseg} for 4 design choices

When analyzing typical activity patterns from this design, observing local switch activity would encourage us to seek for clusters of switches, that can be efficiently driven from loop buffers. We find that if some two switches change data direction, all switches in-between also change data direction and show activity. This would in general be bad for the locality of switching activity. The effect is counteracted by the fact that because of power-aware floorplanning, active connections will be short and the number of switches in between them will be few.

Using the switch control patterns and the segment and control bit line lengths, we can calculate the energies. In Figure 3, E_{seg} is compared with E_{unseg}, for all 4 design choices. The comparison confirms the advantage of a segmented bus from the standpoint of power efficiency. We see that E_{seg} and E_{unseg} both reach a minimum which is not radically different between the 4 solutions. This would indicate that segmentation does not impose different optimization targets for physical layout than a non-segmented solution.

In Figure 4, we compare $SL_{transport}$ with E_{seg}. It is of a lower order of mag-

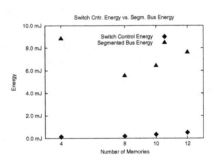

Fig. 4. Comparison of $SL_{transport}$ vs. E_{seg} for 4 design choices

nitude. Intuitively, this can be attributed to a good choice of the switch codes, reducing the number of active control wires. Moreover, there are many more active data and address lines than control bit lines. Also there is only limited activity on some buses in some branches of the program, thanks to activity-aware placement. We can observe from the test-case of the DAB receiver that:

E_{seg} is 17-21% of E_{unseg}.

$SL_{transport}$ is much smaller than SG. It is in the range of 1.5-6% of E_{seg}. So a further reduction of the $SL_{transport}$ is not required[1].

Clustering the switches may make sense both locally and per bus. Often the switches do not change state because the bus is not in use. At other times, there are frequent patterns on a section of a bus because only short sections are being used.

For long periods, switching often occurs on every cycle. This follows from what the storage bandwidth optimization considers to be a cycle: a period through which accesses to external memory are scheduled. Consecutive cycles during which only internal registers are accessed, are not counted. Only if the access schedule would be completely the same for two cycles, w.r.t. sources and sinks as well as data direction, would there not be any switching activity. (Or else when the bus is simply not used.)

6   Related Work

Segmented buses are not novel as such, having been developed in the context of super-computing, to speed up parallel computations in the mid 90's; cfr, for instance, Li [9]. Chen et al [3] have illustrated their potential for energy optimization. They did not show how to program or control such an architecture.

Most research on communication architectures has been focused on inter-tile communication. The architecture discussed in this paper is intended for intra-tile communication and uses finer-grain segmentation and simpler control. In this area, the literature is limited. Current industrial SoC implementations rely on textbook [4] solutions such as point-to-point connections [5], shared buses [12] and crossbars [8]. These are general purpose architectures, that do not provide the energy-efficiency and scalability required for massively parallel processing [6].

The term "segmented bus" is at times used to refer to multiple inter-tile buses interconnected by bridges. Our "segmented bus" is different, taking segmentation to its logical consequence: not only are intra-tile and inter-tile buses decoupled, but every segment of the intra-tile bus can be decoupled to save power.

7   Conclusions

We have discussed a software-controlled energy-efficient segmented bus communication architecture for SoC designs, and compared the energy required to distribute the switch control bits with the energy consumed by the segmented bus itself, and also with the energy that would be consumed by the bus, were it not segmented. From a test case design we found that the energy costs of driving the switches are appreciably lower than the gain obtained. If we take the viewpoint of control energy, the case for the segmented bus still stands. We

---

[1] This is due to our judicious choice for software control. The picture would have been quite different if we would have used a full hardware-based NoC routing solution.

should not go for optimization of the transport component, but instead look for the ways to optimize the energy cost of fetching the control information.

References

1. "The ATOMIUM tool suite", http://www.imec.be/design/atomium/
2. F. Catthoor et al., "Custom memory management methodology exploration of memory organization for embedded multimedia system design", Kluwer, June 1998,
3. J.Y. Chen et al., "Segmented bus design for low-power systems", IEEE VLSI, Mar 1999.
4. J. Duato et al., "Interconnection networks, an engineering approach", IEEE Computer Society, Jun 1997.
5. S. Dutta et al., "Viper: a multiprocessor SoC for advanced set-top box and digital TV systems", IEEE Design & Test, Sep 2001.
6. A. Gangwar et al., "Evaluation of bus based interconnect mechanisms in clustered VLIW architectures", DATE, 2005.
7. J. Guo et al., "Physical design implementation of segmented buses to reduce communication energy", ASP-DAC, 2006.
8. B. Khailany et al., "Imagine: media processing with streams", IEEE Micro, Mar 2001.
9. Y. Li et al, "Prefix computation using a segmented bus", Southeastern Symposium on System Theory, Apr 1996.
10. "Blast Chip 4.0 User Guide *Magma Design Automation*, Cupertino, CA 95014, pp.271-351", http://www.magma-da.com
11. A.Papanikolaou et al., "Architectural and physical design optimizations for efficient intra-tile communication", Proc. Intnl SoC Symp., Finland, Nov 2005.
12. "TMS320VC5471 fixed-point digital signal processor data manual", http://focus.ti.com/docs/prod/folders/print/tms320vc5471.html
13. "TMS320VC5510/5510A Fixed-Point Digital Signal Processors", http://focus.ti.com/docs/prod/folders/print/tms320vc5510.html
14. T. Van Meeuwen et al., "System-level interconnect architecture exploration for custom memory organisations", ISSS, 2001.

Quality Driven Dynamic Low Power Reconfiguration of Handhelds

Hiren Joshi[1], S.S. Verma[2], and G.K. Sharma[3]

[1] M.L.V. Textile and Engineering College, Bhilwara, India
hiren@mlvti.ac.in
[2] Flextronics Software Systems, Gurgaon, India
verma.shyam@flextronicssoftwaresystems.com
[3] ABV-Indian Institute of Information Technology and Management, Gwalior, India
gksharma@iiitm.ac.in

Abstract. Run time reconfiguration of mobile devices to optimize power according to user experience is a significant research challenge. The paper investigates a novel technique of generating power-optimized bitstream to be used for on-the-fly remote-reconfiguration of mobile devices. The approach dynamically minimizes the bitwidths of variables of applications residing in mobile and allows the user to tradeoff between power and quality. Experimental results for MPEG2 decoder show that the approach is able to reduce power consumption dynamically by 33.58% for 25% PSNR degradation.

1 Introduction

To fulfill the user Requested QoS (RQoS), designers reserve extra resources that lead to an inefficient design in terms of power. This penalty of power for getting better quality starts creating problem when the user is out of power. Therefore, the system needs to have real time properties and must adapt itself with respect to changes in user requirement of QoS. When user feels that a device is running out-of-power, he can save power by requesting low quality of service. The proposed well-structured framework presents a practical approach for run-time optimization for power in mobile devices. This framework is experimented on bitwidth optimization for MPEG-2 and results agreed with the practical importance of runtime and remote optimization of bitwidth for power saving.

For optimization of multimedia algorithms during high-level synthesis, *lossless bitwidth optimization* is exposed greatly [1,2,3]. But *lossy bitwidth optimization* has not been exposed very well. The root cause behind this is that the lossy approach depends upon application. But the overall saving can be increased if *Quality driven lossy approach* is adapted according to run-time requirements. In *lossy approach* we reduce the bit width of different variables of algorithms beyond the permissible limit and achieve significant power saving. Although the application of lossy approaches results in a moderately degraded quality but with this acceptance one can save significant amount of power.

K. Bertels, J.M.P. Cardoso, and S. Vassiliadis (Eds.): ARC 2006, LNCS 3985, pp. 59–64, 2006.
© Springer-Verlag Berlin Heidelberg 2006

2 Framework

The framework presents a practical approach for run-time high-level optimization of power with user-desired compromise in quality. Framework supports series of static and dynamic optimizations like loop unrolling, dynamic voltage scaling etc. and generates bitstream for partial reconfiguration of mobile architecture. As quality requirement changes dynamically, quality related optimizations must be done dynamically while quality independent optimization must be applied statically. In this paper we focused on "Quality Independent Bitwidth Optimization" (QIBO) and "Quality Dependent Bitwidth Optimization" (QDBO) and results are verified for the practical importance of runtime and remote bitwidth optimization for power saving.

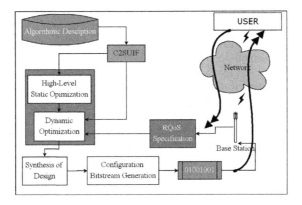

Fig. 1. Processing at Remote Server

The framework as shown in fig. 1 explains the overall approach.Whenever user(client) feels that the device is running out-of-power, and if one wishes to save power, initiates the process by selecting the required level of QoS and send it to remote server. Server calculates the new optimized design and extracts the reconfiguration bit-stream, which when sent to the client, reconfigures the device for reduced power consumption and compromised quality.

3 Bitwidth Analysis

The quality observable at the mobile device is a function of the accuracy and therefore depends upon bitwidths used in representation of all intermediate variables in the algorithm.We have proposed a two fold scheme of saving in the bitwidths of variables. First we find the bits in each variable, which are not affecting the output quality. This normally includes the blank MSB bits (e.g. in an integer variable which is assigned a value 4, the 29 MSB bits out of total reserved 32 bits are blank) and some LSB bits.

Input: Min_Err
Output: msb_saving, lsb_saving

1: **vector** msb_saving (1 to n) $\leftarrow$ 0
2: **vector** lsb_saving (1 to n) $\leftarrow$ 0
3: **vector** $variables$(1 to n)
4: **constant** $assigned\_bit\_width \leftarrow$ 32
5: **for all** i such that $0 \leq i \leq n$ **do**
6:   **for** $k = 0$ to $assigned\_bit\_width$ **do**
7:     lsb_saving(i) $\leftarrow$ lsb_saving(i) + 1
8:     Calculate MSE with lsb_saving in bitwidth
9:     **if** $(MSE \leq Min\_Err)$ **then**
10:       **continue**
11:     **else**
12:       lsb_saving(i) $\leftarrow$ lsb_saving(i) - 1
13:       **break**
14:     **end if**
15:   **end for**
16:   **for** $k = 0$ to $assigned\_bit\_width$ **do**
17:     msb_saving(i) $\leftarrow$ msb_saving(i) + 1
18:     Calculate MSE with msb_saving in bitwidth
19:     **if** $(MSE \leq Min\_Err)$ **then**
20:       **continue**
21:     **else**
22:       msb_saving(i) $\leftarrow$ msb_saving(i) - 1
23:       **break**
24:     **end if**
25:   **end for**
26: **end for**

Fig. 2. Algorithm of QIBO

Input : Req_PSNR, lsb_saving
Output : lsb_saving, $Error$

1: $Req\_MSE \leftarrow$ $255 * 255/(10^{Req\_PSNR/10})$
2: **vector** $variables$ [1 to n]
3: $var\_sel \leftarrow$ 0
4: **while** $var\_sel = -1$ **do**
5:   $Error \leftarrow Req\_MSE$
6:   **for all** i such that $0 \leq i \leq n$ **do**
7:     lsb_saving(i) $\leftarrow$ lsb_saving(i) + 1
8:     Calculate MSE with lsb_saving in bitwidth
9:     **if** $(MSE \leq Error)$ **then**
10:       $Error \leftarrow MSE$
11:       $var\_sel \leftarrow i$
12:     **end if**
13:     lsb_saving(var_sel) $\leftarrow$ lsb_saving(var_sel) - 1
14:   **end for**
15:   Increment lsb_saving(var_sel) by 1
16:   $Error$ = Calculate MSE with new bitwidths specified by lsb_saving
17: **end while**

Fig. 3. Algorithm of QDBO: No. of variable in function is n. lsb_saving are saving in variable from LSB side. $PSNR$ is Peak Signal to Noise Ratio. MSE is New MSE each time bitwidth changes.

This analysis can be done once, statically for an algorithm and is named as Quality Independent Bitwidth Optimization (QIBO). The QIBO is lossless i.e. bitwidth saving in this phase does not introduce error and thus does not affect the output quality. Secondly bitwidths of all variables are gradually decreased from LSB side till the degradation in quality up to acceptable level. For getting maximum saving with fewer penalties on quality we have proposed a greedy approach. This phase is named as Quality Dependent Bitwidth Optimization (QDBO).

3.1   Quality Independent Bitwidth Optimization (QIBO)

For static analysis we have used a pseudo-simulation method, bitwidths are varied from MSB as well from LSB side till the MSE remains less than threshold

(MIN_Err). MSE is calculated by adding difference i.e. error between all pixels of original and new image as follows.

$$MSE = \frac{1}{n^2} \sum_{i=0}^{n-1} \sum_{j=0}^{n-1} \{f^{'}(i,j) - f(i,j)\}^2 \qquad (1)$$

The QIBO phase generates two vectors lsb_saving and msb_saving. The vectors are n-bit long. The ith bit, in msb_saving vector represents the bit saving from MSB side in the ith variable. Similarly i^{th} bit in the lsb_saving vector represents the bit saving from LSB side in the ith variable. The QIBO is done only once for any algorithm and results are made available for the QDBO at remote server.

3.2   Quality Dependent Bitwidth Optimization (QDBO)

The key idea over here is that once the user selects the required quality at which he is comfortable the tolerable error is calculated for this quality-level. Precision of all the variables are again fine-tuned and the narrowest bitwidth of each variable is determined that retains the requested quality level.

The QDBO phase initiated at server every time after receiving the required PSNR from the user and then acceptable MSE for the desired PSNR is calculated. The QDBO uses lsb_saving vector as starting point and further increase the bit saving at each position in the vector by one. The corresponding error is each case is calculated and finally bit saving in the bit of lsb_saving vector which introduces minimum error, is only considered. The lsb_saving vector is modified by making increment in the corresponding bit, all other bits remain unchanged. At the same time the bitwidth of the variable under consideration is reduced by one from LSB side, see fig. 4. The process is repeated till the error introduced remain lower then the MSE. The final bit saving in each variable is reflected by the two vectors msb_saving and lsb_saving.

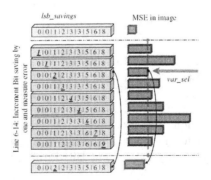

Fig. 4. Selection of Target Variable During QDBO

4   Experiments and Result

For the validation of proposed methodology, the experiments were solely based upon functionality of *MPEG2decoder*. What follows is the experiment on *idctrow* and *idctcol*, the compute-intensive functions of *MPEG2decoder*.The functions contain 9 integer variables (x0 to x8) with a total bitwidth $32 * 9 = 288$ bits. We refine bitwidth of each of 9 variables firstly by applying QIBO and then QDBO. Thus each variable is fine-tuned to contribute maximum in power saving. We calculated these bitwidths for 40 dB to 26 dB PSNR which was calculated with reference to the image obtained using standard implementation of MPEG decoder. The framework supports every positive PSNR but our experiments showed that the quality of image less than 26dB is degraded beyond the acceptable range, thus presenting only the saving between 40dB to 26dB PSNR (Table 1).

Table 1. Power consumption and bitwidth saving with PSNR: Here bit saving due to dynamic analysis is shown. Power is reducing with decreasing PSNR. Average power saving for *idctrow* and *idctcol* is 28.77% and 23.26%.

PSNR	idctrow		idctcol	
	Dynamic Bit-Saving	Power Consumption	Dynamic Bit Saving	Power Consumption
40	16	20.62	23	19.84
38	27	19.33	36	18.66
36	43	17.46	46	17.77
34	51	16.53	57	16.78
32	58	15.71	64	16.16
30	79	13.26	64	16.16
28	80	13.14	82	14.55
26	87	12.32	83	14.46

The power saving results were extracted using the tool Xpower of Xilinx Inc. The code of *idctrow* and *idctcol* was firstly converted into equivalent VHDL code and then synthesized using Xilinx synthesis tools for Virtex-II series FPGA. The synthesized design was used to estimate power consumption in the above functions using Xpower. The process was repeated for each PSNR ranging between 40dB to 26dB with the optimum bitwidth suggested by the present framework (fig. 5(a),fig. 5(b)).

5   Conclusion

The methods presented here show the great potential of incorporating user experience of quality in power optimization in an inherent dynamic environment of mobile systems. The framework explores the power saving capability of run-time bitwidth optimization with acceptable compromise in quality of multimedia.

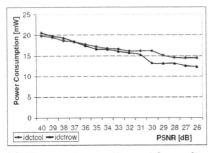

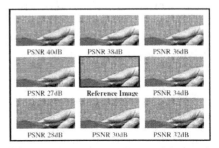

(a) Power consumption with quality specification

(b) Visual Image quality results with decreasing PSNR

Fig. 5. Experimental Results Obtained for Mobile Device

Other high level optimization mixing with QoS may provide better and wider ranging quality/energy tradeoffs, and are subject of our future work.

References

1. M.Stephenson, J.Babb and S.Amarasinghe. "Bit Width Analysis with Application to Silicon Compilation", in Proc. of *Conference on Prog. Language Design and Implementation*, 108-120, 2000.
2. M. Budiu, S.C. Goldstein. "Bit-value Inference: Detecting and Exploiting Narrow Bitwidth Computations", in Proc. of 6th *International Euro-Par Conference*, August 2000.
3. S. Mahlke, R. Ravindran, M. Schlansker, R. Schreiber, T. Sherwood. "Bitwidth Sensitive Code Generation in A Custom Embedded Accelerator Design System", *Technical Report*, HP Labs, Palo Alto, CA.
4. S Mohapatra, R Cornea, N Dutt, A Nicolau, N Venkatasubramanian "Integrated Power Management for Video Streaming to Mobile Handheld Devices", in Proc. of 11th *ACM International Conference on Multimedia*, 582-591, 2003.

An Efficient Estimation Method of Dynamic Power Dissipation on VLSI Interconnects

Joong-ho Park[1], Bang-Hyun Sung[1], and Seok-Yoon Kim[2]

[1] Department of Computer, Soongsil University,
1-1 Sang-Do 5 Dong, Dong-Jak Gu,
Seoul, Korea
{joongs, bhsung}@ic.ssu.ac.kr
[2] Department of Computer, Soongsil University,
1-1 Sang-Do 5 Dong, Dong-Jak Gu,
Seoul, Korea
ksy@comp.ssu.ac.kr

Abstract. Up to the present, there have been many works to analyze interconnects on timing aspects, while less works have been done on power aspects. As resistance of interconnects and rise time of signals decrease, power dissipation associated with interconnects is ever-increasing. Hence, an efficient method to compute power dissipation on interconnects is necessary and in this paper we propose a simple yet accurate method to estimate dynamic power dissipation on interconnects. We propose a new reduced-order model to estimate power dissipation on large interconnects. Through the proposed model which is directly derived from total capacitance and resistance of interconnects, we show that the dynamic power dissipation on whole interconnects can be approximated, and propose an analytic method to compute the power dissipation. The results of the proposed method applied to various RC networks show that maximum relative error is within 7% in comparison with HSPICE results.

1 Introduction

Owing to the process technology advances, the number of transistors that can be accumulated in a single chip amounts to tens of millions, which allows the realization of SoC (System-on-a-Chip) technology. Electric power dissipation is one of the most important issues that limit the performance of circuits, and it shows an increasing trend as the chip density increases. Hence the estimation of power dissipation during design process and design of circuits that can reduce power are very important. Until now, the analysis on dynamic power dissipation has been focused on gates since the portion of gate power dissipation has been the most in chip. However, as the effect of interconnects may not be neglected, it is evident now that the power dissipation on interconnects should be accounted [1]-[3]. Especially, the increase in interconnect resistance through UDSM (ultra deep submicron) process technology manifests the necessity. The

K. Bertels, J.M.P. Cardoso, and S. Vassiliadis (Eds.): ARC 2006, LNCS 3985, pp. 65–74, 2006.

increase in resistance means that more energy is dissipated on interconnect and it is reported that about 30% of whole chip power is dissipated on interconnect in some cases [1]-[3] . If the width of interconnect decreases due to the process technology advances, which results in resistance increase, then this proportion would grow. Also, the trend [4] that signal rise time shortens add to the increase in interconnect power dissipation. As the signal rise time decreases, the power dissipation of interconnect shows an increasing pattern.

So far, $(1/2)CV^2$ expression has been widely used in interconnect power analysis [5] , assuming interconnect as a single capacitor model. Since the resistance of interconnects can not be neglected, this model lacks in accuracy. Several methods to improve the accuracy of $(1/2)CV^2$ have been introduced [6], [7] , and the method to analyze the power distribution on interconnects using poles and residues has been proposed in [1] . It is shown in [1] that the power distribution analysis on interconnects is feasible in frequency domain using poles and residues. However, high complexity is inevitable when calculating the power dissipation of the whole interconnects since poles and residues of the current flowing through each resistance have to be calculated. Therefore, this paper proposes an algebraic method of estimating the power dissipation on the whole interconnects based on a reduced model. This paper is composed as follows. Following this introduction, reduced-order model for power dissipation analysis is proposed in Section 2 and a simple algebraic expression to calculate power dissipation on interconnects is derived in Section 3. Simulation results are given in Section 4 to show that the power dissipation of whole interconnects can be estimated through the proposed algebraic model. Finally, Section 5 gives a conclusion

2   Modeling of Interconnect for Power Dissipation Analysis

In case of large (detailed) models, accuracy can be met while paying enormous analysis time and time requirement can be met with a small (rough) model while giving up some accuracy. Therefore, the purpose of this section is to propose a model that can provide the convenience of analysis while preserving the accuracy worthy of trusting. The proposed model has the advantage of being constructed directly from the extracted variables without special reduction process, and still yields fairly accurate results.

2.1   Reduced – Order Model for Power Dissipation Analysis

Considering both the operating speed of chips and necessity for a simple model, a reduced-order model for power dissipation analysis of interconnects is proposed in this section. Considering the trend of circuit designs, it is observed that the operating frequency goes higher and resistance of interconnects increases, which makes it feasible that total resistance of interconnects can not be ignored compared to driver's output resistance. That is, most of capacitance load is shielded by interconnect resistance as seen from the driver side. Especially, the increase in interconnect resistance is important from the viewpoint of estimating power dissipation on interconnects since more energy is now dissipated on interconnects. To analyze the power dissipation on interconnects correctly, hence, we need as many number of resistors as possible for the model. However, although the accuracy of analysis improves if the order of the reduction model goes higher, the efficiency of analysis decreases. Hence, we propose a second-order RC model that can keep reasonable accuracy.

2.2   Modeling Method of the Proposed Second-Order RC Model

Various reduction techniques to analyze large circuits are introduced and applied appropriately in many fields in [12] - [15]. A modeling method proposed in this section can be composed directly by extracted resistance and capacitance values. The admittance of interconnects from the driving point is given by (1), where, Rt and Ct are the total resistance and capacitance of interconnect, respectively[8]

$$Y(s) = \sqrt{\frac{sC_t}{R_t}} tanh(\sqrt{sC_tR_t}) \tag{1}$$

Also, the driving point admittance of the circuit is represented in (2),

$$Y(s) = \frac{b_0 s + b_1 s^2}{1 + a_0 s + a_1 s^2} \tag{2}$$

where $a_0 = R_1C_1 + R_1C_2 + R_2C_2, a_1 = R_1R_2C_1C_2, b_0 = C_1 + C_2, b_1 = R_2C_1C_2$.
    In the meantime, applying MacLaurin series to $tanh(\sqrt{sC_tR_t})$ in (1) and arranging it yields(3),

$$Y(s) = \sqrt{\frac{sC_t}{R_t}} tanh(\sqrt{sC_tR_t})$$
$$= m_1 s + m_2 s^2 + m_3 s^3 + m_4 s^4 + ... \tag{3}$$

where $m_1 = C_t, m_2 = -\frac{1}{3}R_tC_t^2, m_3 = \frac{2}{15}R_t^2C_t^3, m_4 = -\frac{17}{315}R_t^3C_t^4$. Applying moment matching between (2) and (3), a_0, a_1, b_0 and b_1 can be represented as (4).

$$a_0 = \frac{m_3m_4 - m_2m_3}{m_2^2 - m_1m_3}$$
$$a_1 = \frac{m_3^2 - m_2m_4}{m_2^2 - m_1m_3} \tag{4}$$
$$b_0 = m_1$$
$$b_1 = m_2 + m_1a_0$$

Using (4), R and C values in the second-order reduced model can be obtained from R_t and C_t values as shown in Fig.1.

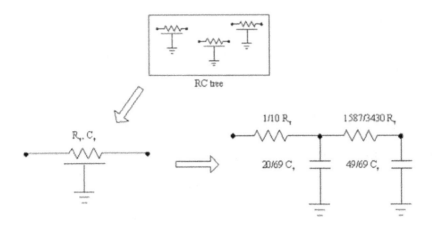

Fig. 1. Reduction of RC trees

3   Estimation of Dynamic Power Dissipation for Saturated Ramp Input

Inputs to gates and interconnects in actual circuits are usually saturated ramp signals that are characterized with finite rise times. Power dissipation on interconnects tends to increase as the signal rise time shortens. However, previous analysis methods presented so far have addressed only step input case due to the complexity reason, which corresponds to the maximum power dissipation [1], [15]. Hence, an analysis method for ramp input case with finite signal rise time is required in order to analyze power dissipation on interconnects accurately. In this section we define ramp input in frequency domain and propose the estimation method for power dissipation on interconnects using this definition.

3.1   Definition of Saturated Ramp Signal

A saturated ramp signal with a finite rise time can be represented as the addition of two functions given by (5) in time domain [16]. tr and V_{dd} represents signal rise time and input voltage,respectively, and U(t) denotes unit step.

$$V_{ramp}(t) = \frac{V_{dd}}{t_r}[tU(t) - (t - t_r)U(t - t_r)](t \geq 0) \tag{5}$$

Using Laplace transform, (5) can be transformed to (6) in frequency domain

$$V_{ramp}(t) = \frac{V_{dd}}{t_r}\frac{1}{s^2}(1 - e^{-st_r}) \tag{6}$$

Expanding $(1-e^{-st_r})$ in (6) using MacLaurin series and arranging it yields (7).

$$V_{ramp}(s) = \frac{V_{dd}}{t_r}\frac{1}{s^2}(1 - e^{-st_r}) \tag{7}$$

$$= \frac{V_{dd}}{s}(1 - \frac{st_r}{2} + \frac{s^2t_r^2}{6} - \frac{s^3t_r^3}{24} + ...)$$

3.2 Estimation Method for Dynamic Power Dissipation

When an RC circuit is given, power dissipation happens only in resistance part of the circuit, and power dissipation on interconnects can be estimated by summing up all the contribution of power dissipated at each resistor of interconnect model. That is, once RC tree model is composed for interconnect consisting of several URC segments, then the RC tree model can be reduced using current moment at the driving point as shown in Fig. 2. Sum of power dissipations in R_1 and R_2 can be assumed as an approximation of sum of power dissipation in each resistor of the RC tree circuit. During the transition period of input signal, the power dissipation in a resistor can be given by (8), where I(t) denotes the current flowing into resistor R_i

$$E = R_i \int_0^\infty I^2(t)dt \tag{8}$$

As shown in (8), we can calculate power dissipation in a resistor if the current flowing into the resistor is known. Then, power dissipation for the reduced model in Fig. 2 can be expressed as (9).

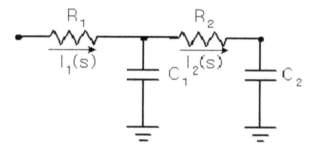

Fig. 2. Interconnect model for power dissipation analysis (I(s): current flowing into resistor)

$$E = R_1 \int_0^\infty I_1^2(t)dt + R_2 \int_0^\infty I_2^2(t)dt \tag{9}$$

$$
\begin{aligned}
I_1(s) &= \frac{R_2C_1C_2s + (C_1 + C_2)}{R_1R_2C_1C_2s^2 + (R_1C_1 + R_1C_2 + R_2C_2)s + 1}V_{dd}(1 - \frac{st_r}{2}) \\
&= \frac{K_{1_{I_1}}}{s + P_1} + \frac{K_{2_{I_1}}}{s + P_2} + d
\end{aligned} \tag{10}
$$

$$
\begin{aligned}
I_2(s) &= \frac{C_2}{R_1R_2C_1C_2s^2 + (R_1C_1 + R_1C_2 + R_2C_2)s + 1}V_{dd}(1 - \frac{st_r}{2}) \\
&= \frac{K_{1_{I_1}}}{s + P_1} + \frac{K_{2_{I_1}}}{s + P_2}
\end{aligned} \tag{11}
$$

$$P_1 = \frac{-(R_1C_1 + R_1C_2 + R_2C_2) + \sqrt{(R_1C_1 + R_1C_2 + R_2C_2)^2 - 4(R_1R_2C_1C_2)}}{2R_1R_2C_1C_2} \quad (12)$$

$$P_2 = \frac{-(R_1C_1 + R_1C_2 + R_2C_2) - \sqrt{(R_1C_1 + R_1C_2 + R_2C_2)^2 - 4(R_1R_2C_1C_2)}}{2R_1R_2C_1C_2} \quad (13)$$

Assuming that input signal is a saturated ramp given by (7), $I_1(s)$ and $I_2(s)$ can be expressed in (10) and (11), where P_1 and P_2 denote the poles of $I_1(s)$ and $I_2(s)$ and $K_{i_{I_j}}$ denotes the residue of currents for each pole. Note that all the terms after the second term in (7) are truncated and poles of $I_1(s)$ and $I_2(s)$ are same as shown in (10) and (11), where $d = -\frac{V_{dd}t_r}{2R_1}$

$$K_{1_{I_1}} = \frac{V_{dd}P_1^2P_2(2R_2C_1C_2 + (R_2C_1C_2P_1 + R_2C_1C_2P_2 - C_1 - C_2)t_r)}{2(P_1 - P_2)}$$
$$- \frac{(C_1 + C_2)V_{dd}P_1P_2 + dP_1P_2}{(P_1 - P_2)}$$

$$K_{2_{I_1}} = \frac{V_{dd}P_1^2P_2(2R_2C_1C_2 + (R_2C_1C_2P_1 + R_2C_1C_2P_2 - C_1 - C_2)t_r)}{2} - K_{1_{I_1}}$$

$$K_{1_{I_2}} = \frac{-V_{dd}C_2P_1P_2(t_rP_1 + 2)}{2(P_1 - P_2)}$$

$$K_{2_{I_2}} = \frac{-V_{dd}C_2P_1P_2t_r}{2} - K_{1_{I_2}} \quad (14)$$

$$\int_0^\infty I^2(t)dt = \sum_{i=0}^q K_iI(-P_i) \quad (15)$$

As explained in Section 2, values of R_1, R_2, C_1, and C_2 can calculated directly from R_t and C_t and poles can be calculated by (12) and (13). Also, residues of currents for each pole are given by (14). And, $\int_0^\infty I^2(t)dt$ in (9) can be represented as (15) using poles and residues [1], where P_i denotes poles and K_i denotes the current residue associated with P_i. Applying (12), (13), (14) and (15) to (9) yields (16), which estimates the dynamic energy dissipation on interconnects. As shown in the above, poles and residues of the second-order reduced model are first calculated using R_1, R_2, C_1, and C_2 values of the reduced model, and then the power dissipation on interconnects can be estimated by plugging these poles and residues into the algebraic expression given in (16).

$$E = R_1 \int_0^\infty I^2(t)dt + R_2 \int_0^\infty I_2^2(t)dt$$

$$= R_1(K_{1_{I_1}}(\frac{K_{1_{I_1}}}{-P_1 - P_1} + \frac{K_{2_{I_1}}}{-P_1 - P_2})$$

$$+ K_{2_{I_1}}(\frac{K_{1_{I_1}}}{-P_2 - P_1} + \frac{K_{2_{I_1}}}{-P_2 - P_2}))$$

$$+ R_2(K_{1_{I_2}}(\frac{K_{1_{I_2}}}{-P_1 - P_1} + \frac{K_{2_{I_2}}}{-P_1 - P_2})$$

$$+ K_{2_{I_2}}(\frac{K_{1_{I_2}}}{-P_2 - P_1} + \frac{K_{2_{I_2}}}{-P_2 - P_2})) \tag{16}$$

4   Simulation Results

Simulation results for general tree structures of interconnects are presented in this section to verify the validity of the proposed method. We assume a 2.5V saturated ramp input is applied to interconnect circuits. Power estimation results using the proposed method in this paper are compared with those of HSPICE as the rise times of input signal varies

4.1   RC Tree Examples

We have simulated the tree-shaped interconnect consisting of several URC segments, shown in Fig. 3. The numbers in Fig. 3 denote the total resistance (Ω) and capacitance (pF), respectively, for each URC segment. These URC segments have been modeled using ladder circuits composed of RC cells, in which the number of cells, N, can be chosen from (17).

$$f_{max} \leq | \frac{2N^2}{R_t C_t}(1 - cos\frac{(2N-1)\pi}{2N}) | \tag{17}$$

where f_{max} is the maximum frequency of interest [11]. Table 1 shows the comparison of power dissipation estimated by the proposed method and HSPICE, as the signal rise time varies. It is shown in Table 1 that the errors of the proposed method are within a 2% range when compared with HSPICE results.

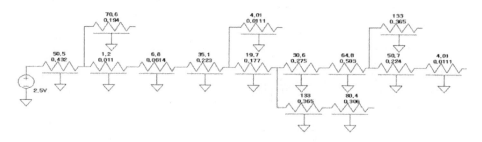

Fig. 3. An RC tree example

Table 1. Power dissipation (unit : J) and relative error of the proposed method compared to HSPICE

Rising Time	Proposed Method	HSPICE	Relative Errors
1.00E-11	3.9355E-11	3.8761E-11	+1.53%
1.00E-12	4.0161E-11	4.0152E-11	+0.02%
1.00E-13	4.0248E-11	4.0447E-11	-0.49%
1.00E-14	4.0257E-11	4.0477E-11	-0.54%
1.00E-15	4.0257E-11	4.0480E-11	-0.55%
1.00E-16	4.0257E-11	4.0480E-11	-0.55%
0(STEP)	4.0258E-11	4.0480E-11	-0.55%

4.2   General RC Network Example

Circuit that use in simulation includes all of RC network that it is no branch and branch, and the size also is various. We have simulated various circuit examples of many different sizes which include the both cases with and without branches. Relative errors of the proposed method are tabularized in Table 2 against the HSPICE results when signal rise time and number of nodes vary. It is noticed in Table 2 that the accuracy of the proposed method is not compromised much.

Table 3 shows power dissipation comparison and relative errors when signal rise time varies for two circuit examples. Although it is observed that the relative errors grow bigger as signal rise time becomes slow, the proposed method will still be a good estimator for power dissipation, considering that signal rise time ever increases as the circuit technology advances.

Table 2. Relative errors of power dissipation [J] versus signal rise time in various circuits

	0p(Step)			1p		
# of nodes	HSPICE	Our Method	Error	HSPICE	Our Method	Error
100	8.9250E-11	3.9375E-11	+0.1399%	8.9141E-11	8.9315E-11	+0.1951%
200	9.8125E-11	9.8137E-11	-0.0119%	9.8097E-11	9.8027E-11	+0.0712%
300	1.0594E-10	1.0606E-10	-0.1094%	1.0591E-10	1.0595E-10	-0.0347%
400	1.1406E-10	1.1399E-10	+0.0652%	1.1403E-10	1.1388E-10	+0.1348%
500	1.2219E-10	1.2202E-10	+0.1423%	1.2216E-10	1.2191E-10	+0.2074%
Maximum	0.1423%			0.2074%		
	10p			100p		
# of nodes	HSPICE	Our Method	Error	HSPICE	Our Method	Error
100	8.8456E-11	8.8785E-11	+0.3715%	8.5608E-11	8.4164E-11	-1.6872%
200	9.7845E-11	9.7343E-11	+0.5160%	9.5468E-11	9.4495E-11	+1.0296%
300	1.0566E-10	1.0526E-10	+0.3777%	1.0329E-10	1.0241E-10	+0.8554%
400	1.1379E-10	1.1319E-10	+0.5285%	1.1142E-10	1.1034E-10	+0.9752%
500	1.2191E-10	1.2122E-10	+0.5671%	1.1956E-10	1.1837E-10	+1.0017%
Error	0.5671%			1.0017%		

Table 3. Power dissipation comparison and relative errors for various signal rise time

	Circuit 1			Circuit 2		
	HSPICE	Our Method	Error	HSPICE	Our Method	Error
1p	4.9589E-10	5.1243E-10	+3.3355%	2.5742E-10	2.5739E-10	-0.0109%
50p	4.9365E-10	5.0893E-10	+3.0961%	2.5432E-10	2.5205E-10	-0.8923%
100p	4.9166E-10	5.0553E-10	+2.8218%	2.5194E-10	2.4717E-10	-1.8939%
150p	4.8984E-10	5.0223E-10	+2.5298%	2.4995E-10	2.4276E-10	-2.8764%
200p	4.8816E-10	4.9901E-10	+2.2220%	2.4820E-10	2.3880E-10	-3.7881%
250p	4.8661E-10	4.9589E-10	+1.9069%	2.4663E-10	2.3532E-10	-4.5858%
300p	4.8516E-10	4.9287E-10	+1.5899%	2.4519E-10	2.3229E-10	-5.2606%
350p	4.8377E-10	4.8994E-10	+1.2747%	2.4385E-10	2.2972E-10	-5.7936%
400p	4.8246E-10	4.8710E-10	+0.9616%	2.4259E-10	2.2762E-10	-6.1725%
450p	4.8121E-10	4.8435E-10	+0.6535%	2.4141E-10	2.2598E-10	-6.3902%

5 Conclusion

The proposed method works on a reduced-order model to take the simple estimation by reducing the original interconnect into a second-order RC model. This reduction process is directly achieved using total resistance and capacitance values of interconnect segments. We have simulated various circuit examples of many different sizes in which each node may or may not have branches. Simulation results for various RC networks show that the maximum relative error is within 7% in comparison with HSPICE results. The estimation method proposed in this paper may provide an important measure in placement & routing(P&R) phase of design process, for example, in a form of power dissipation-aware P&R.

Acknowledgements

This work was supported by grant No. R01-2005-000-11215-0(2005) from the Basic Research Program of the Korea Science & Engineering Foundation and by the Soongsil University Research Fund.

References

1. Y. Shin, T. Sakurai: Power Distribution Analysis of VLSI Interconnects Using Model Order Reduction. IEEE Tran. Computer-Aided Design, vol 21, pp. 739-745, June 2002
2. D. Lur, C. Sevensson: Power dissipation Estimation in CMOS VLSI Chips. IEEE Journal of Solid-State Circuits, vol. 29, pp.663-670, June 1994
3. Micheal K. Gowan, Larry L. Biro, Daniel B. Jackson: Power Considerations in the Design of the Alpha 21264 Microprocessor. in Proc. IEEE DAC, June 1998
4. M. Celik, L. T. Pileggi, A. Odabasioglu: IC Interconnect Analysis, Kluwer Academic Publishers, 2002
5. J. M. Rabaey: Digital Integrated Circuits, A Design Perspective, Prentice Hall, Inc., New Jersey, 2003

6. T. Uchino, J. Cong: An Interconnect Energy Model Considering Coupling Effects. in Proc. IEEE DAC, June 2001
7. P. Heydari, M. Pedram: Interconnect Energy Dissipation in High-Speed ULSI Circuit. in Proc. IEEE Int. Conf. VLSID, 2002
8. P. R. O'Brien, T. L. Savarino: Modeling the Driving-Point Characteristic of Resistive Interconnect Accurate Delay Estimation. in Proc. IEEE ICCAD, 1989
9. S. Y. Kim, Modeling and Analysis of VLSI Interconnects, Sigma Press, 1999
10. H. B. Bakoglu, Circuit, Interconnections, and Packaging for VLSI, Addison Wesley, 1990.
11. N. Gopal: Fast Evaluation of VLSI Interconnect Structures Using Moment-Matching Methods. Ph.D. Thesis, Univ of Texas at Austin, Dec. 1992
12. L. T. Pileggi, R. A. Rohrer: Asymptotic Waveform Evaluation for Timing Analysis. IEEE Trans. Computer Aided Design, vol. 9, 1990
13. A. Odabasioglu, M. Celik, L. T. Pileggi: PRIMA: Passive Reduced Order Interconnect Macromodeling Algorithm. IEEE Tran. Computer Aided Design, vol. 18, no 8, pp. 645-654, Aug. 1998
14. E. Acar, A. Odabasioglu, M. Celik, L. T. Pileggi: S2P: A Stable 2-pole RC Delay and Coupling Noise Metric. in Proc. Great Laked Symposium VLSI, 1999
15. W. K. Kal, S. Y. Kim: An Analytical Calculation Method for Delay Time of RC-class Interconnect. in Proc. IEEE ASP-DAC, 2000
16. A. B. Khang, Muddu: An Analytical Delay Model for VLSI Interconnects under Ramp Input. in UCLA CS Dept. TR-960015, 1996

Highly Paralellized Architecture for Image Motion Estimation

Javier Díaz[1], Eduardo Ros[1], Sonia Mota[2], and Rafael Rodriguez-Gomez[1]

[1] Dep. Arquitectura y Tecnología de Computadores, Universidad de Granada, Spain
[2] Dep.Informática y Análisis Numérico, Universidad de Córdoba, Spain
{eros, jdiaz, rrodriguez}@atc.ugr.es
smota@uco.es

Abstract. Optical flow computation is a well-known topic with a large number of contributions describing different models and their accuracies but real-time implementation of high frame-rate sequences remains as an open issue. The presented approach implements a novel superpipelined and fully parallelized architecture for optical flow processing with more than 70 pipelined stages that achieve a data throughput of one pixel per clock cycle. This customized DSP architecture is capable of processing up to 45 Mpixels/s arranged for example as 148 frames per second at VGA resolution (640x480 pixels). This is of extreme interest in order to use high frame-rate cameras for reliable motion processing. We justify the optical flow model chosen for the implementation, analyze the presented architecture and measure the system resource requirements. Finally, we evaluate the system comparing its performance with other previous approaches. To the best of our knowledge, the obtained performance is more than one range of magnitude higher than any previous real-time approach described in the literature.

1 Introduction

Optical flow is a well known research field used to recover 2-D motion from image sequences. There are different approaches based on image block-matching, gradient constraints, phase conservation or energy models [1]. Until now, most of the comparative studies focused on the different estimation approaches and their accuracies [1], [2]. Nevertheless some of them also covered the implementation feasibility [3]. They show that best accuracy is achieved using phase-based and differential methods but, though these models work fine for low motion velocities, they fail when trying to estimate fast motion (their accuracies are significantly degraded due to the temporal aliasing) [4], [5]. The temporal aliasing problem is a complex topic where we can not isolate the temporal sampling rate and the image structure. The spatial frequency has significant importance to calculate the maximum speed which can be recovered from an image sequence according to the Nyquist-Shannon theorem [4], [5].

Our approach focuses on the utilization of digital cameras of high frame-rate acquisition as a valid alternative to reduce temporal aliasing. Advances in imaging sensor technology make possible to acquire more than 1000 frames per second (fps) (see products from the web sites: http://www.coreco.com, http://www.hitachi-service.net/, http://www.ims-chips.com/index.php3) prompting us to develop

K. Bertels, J.M.P. Cardoso, and S. Vassiliadis (Eds.): ARC 2006, LNCS 3985, pp. 75 86, 2006.
© Springer-Verlag Berlin Heidelberg 2006

processing architectures running at higher frame-rates than standard video at 30 fps. Though the 1000 fps is still far away from our processing capabilities, an over-sampled factor of 4 or 5 dramatically reduces the motion aliasing presented in most common scenarios. The utilization of a high frame-rate cameras reduces the motion range presented at the video sequence, allowing gradient models to achieve an outstanding accuracy.

In previous works, Lucas & Kanade (L&K) gradient based method [1], [6] is highlighted as a good candidate to be implemented on hardware with affordable hardware resources consumption [2], [3], [7], [8]. The comparison of L&K with other differential approaches [9], [10], (also of feasible hardware implementation as indicated in [11]), concludes that the L&K least-squares fitting approach achieves the best accuracy.

In this work we present a novel superpipelined processing architecture capable of computing one pixel per clock cycle. This architecture significantly improves our previous works [7], [8] thanks to the new fine-grain pipeline, a nobel memory management unit which enable the utilization of FIR temporal filters and improved image differentiation technique. It allows real-time processing of oversampled frame-rates, which opens the door to utilize the advanced image sensors to achieve high accuracy of optical flow. In the next sections we illustrate the superpipelined architecture, evaluate their performance, system resources consumption and we compare our results with other previous approaches.

2   Gradient Model Parameters

On the previous discussion we have presented the L&K model as a good candidate for real-time optical flow computation. The L&K algorithm belongs to gradient-based techniques which mean that the estimation of pixel velocities is based on image derivatives and the assumption of constant luminance over a temporal window is required. The velocities are computed as convolution with separable kernels which operate as discrete derivatives. L&K method constructs a flow estimation based on the first-order derivatives of the image. Using least-square fitting, the model extracts an estimation of pixel motion based on the hypothesis of velocity similarity on their neighbourhood For details, please see [1], [6].

Most of the literature works utilize the derivative kernels and model parameters presented in [1] but, as J. Brandt described in [12], they are suitable of significant improvement. We encourage the reading of that work for the correct understanding of such modifications. To summarize, the processing stages developed in our system are the following:

1. Pre-filtering with a separable kernel of 3x3x3, *P=[1, 2, 1]/4* The utilization of this small smoothing kernel allow high optical flow estimation density because it does not reject the high frequency terms and at the same time also contributes as anti-aliasing filter.
2. Complementary derivative kernels (2-D smoothing and 1-D derivation for each axe derivative) such as designed by Simoncelli [13]. These kernels increase the architecture complexity compared with previous approaches [7], [8], but significantly improve the accuracy of the system [12]. In terms of performance,

they represent a computation load increment of a factor of 3 but this is not a problem when designing customized hardware because it can be implemented in the pipeline structure without throughput degradation.

3. The image derivatives I_x, I_y and I_t (subscript stands for axe direction derivative) are cross-multiplied to get the five products $I_x \cdot I_x$, $I_y \cdot I_y$, $I_x \cdot I_y$, $I_x \cdot I_t$, and $I_y \cdot I_t$ and then are locally weighted on a neighbourhood area Ω. The weighing operation is implemented as separable convolution operations over the derivatives products using the 2-D spatial central-weighting separable kernel *[0.0625, 0.25, 0.375, 0.25, 0.0625]*.

4. Finally, the weighted image derivatives products are combined to get the pixel velocities estimation [1].

The overall support of the system is 11x11x7 pixels using the parameters described above, thus just 7 images storage is required which is feasible on systems embedded on a single chip. In a previous implementation of the L&K model [7], [8], we used the Fleet et al. [14] IIR temporal filter which requires just 3 images storage. The drawback of such approach is that IIR filters produce lower accuracy in the estimated optical flow and need higher fixed-point bit-width to compute filter values.

3 Hardware Architecture

Nowadays, standard PC processors have significant computing performance thanks to the high system clock frequency and to the MMX and SSE instruction extensions which give them DSP capabilities. Nevertheless, although there are some optical flow approaches running on software in near real-time [15], the intensive computation required to process optical flow makes non viable to process oversampled sequences in real-time. DSP and multimedia processors are specifically suitable for embedded large processing [16] but their computing performances are still far from allowing real-time computing of optical flow at more than 30 fps. Therefore we consider reconfigurable hardware the best target technology.

We use a pipelined architecture (Fig. 1). The basic computational stages represent the different steps of L&K algorithm briefly described on section 2. The system has been designed as an embedded processing platform which can be used on mobile applications and thus, user interface, hardware controller for memory, VGA visualization and input camera interface have been embedded on the same FPGA device. This strategy enables the utilization of the system combined with a high frame-rate camera as a *smart sensor* on diverse potential applications. The different elements that form the system are represented on Fig. 1. Note that the thin dotted line marks the optical flow processing core whose stages can be summarized as follows:

a) S_0. Gaussian-filter smoothing stage.
b) S_1. The FIR temporal filter computes the temporal derivative and space-time smoothed images.
c) S_2. Spatial derivatives and complementary Gaussian filtering operations.
d) S_3. Construction of least-square matrices for integration of neighborhood velocities estimations.

e) S_4. Custom floating-point unit. Final velocity estimation requires the computation of a matrix inversion, which includes a division operation. At this stage the resolution of the incoming data bits is significant and expensive arithmetic operations are required. Thus fixed-point arithmetic becomes unaffordable, prompting us to design a customized floating-point unit.

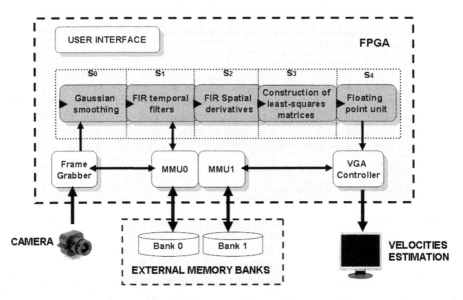

Fig. 1. Optical flow system structure. Thin dotted line marks the processing core. Light-colour blocks indicate hardware controllers inside the FPGA and external memories. The user interface consists on a LCD display plus mode-selection buttons. All the computation has been done inside the FPGA device.

3.1 Superpipelined Architecture

We have described the coarse pipelined system of 5 stages. Now we outline the number of parallel units used at each stage and the number of fine-grain pipeline stages per unit. In fact previous approaches used a coarse pipeline processing architecture able to process up to 41 *Kpps (Kpps ≡ kilo pixels per second)* [7], [8]. The previous scheme, with a pipelined structure divided on 5 basic stages, would lead to high performance but still far from high frame-rate processing requirements. The main reason is that the coarse architecture in Fig. 1 utilizes a structure similar to DSP processor. There is a trade-off between pipeline length and system performance based on the dependence problems (in DSPs branch conditions often stop the pipeline which represents a significant time loss). Therefore, long pipelines are not presented on standard DSPs and microprocessors. On the other hand, we describe here a specific purpose processing architecture that highly benefits of a fine grain pipeline datapath.

According to [17], the best architecture should be a superscalar and superpipelined structure. This design strategy has been adopted in our approach and is one of our novel contributions compared with [7], [8]. Furthermore, this processing strategy leads to an outstanding processing performance. In Fig. 1 we present the global scheme. Each coarse stage has been finely pipelined leading to a processing datapath of more than 70 stages just for the optical flow computing core. The number of scalar units grows at stages in which L&K model requires to maintain the system throughput. This parallelism expansion represents:

1. Stage S_0 uses one scalar unit for spatial smoothing with 12 pipeline stages.
2. Stage S_1 uses two scalar units, one for temporal smoothing and another one for temporal differentiation. Each one requires 9 pipeline stages.
3. Stage S_2 uses 3 parallel scalars units of 12 pipeline stages; corresponding to the 3 dimensions (I_x, I_y, and I_t) in which are computed the image derivatives.
4. Provided that 5 cross-product ($I_x \cdot I_x$, $I_y \cdot I_y$, $I_x \cdot I_y$, $I_x \cdot I_t$, and $I_y \cdot I_t$) are computed at stage S_3, the systems uses 5 parallel units of 12 pipeline stages to comply this requeriment. These scalar units compute the weighted sum of these cross-products needed at the least-squares fitting.
5. Finally, stage S_4 uses one scalar unit of 25 pipeline stages to compute the final motion for each pixel but internally several parallel pathways drive the data process.

Stage S_4 is critical in terms of system frequency, resources and accuracy. The incoming data use fixed point representation of 18 bits and this stage requires the operations of multiplication, addition/subtraction and division without loosing accuracy. From our previous analysis [7], [8], we decide using floating point data which allows obtaining the required precision with reasonable resources consumption (as is shown on table 1). Fig. 2 presents the architecture of this stage, based again on a high pipelined and parallel datapaths to achieve a high system throughput. The whole stage requires 25 cycles. Data conversion, multiplication, addition and subtraction are computed in just one cycle but division requires 15 cycles. This is the stage limiting the system clock frequency and it could be even further pipelined to increase the clock frequency if necessary.

Special consideration must be taken about the temporal filtering stages (smooth and derivation filters). The limited number of memory banks accessible on board constraints the available system parallelism (which translates in performance degradation) and increments the design complexity. Therefore an efficient *memory management unit (MMU)* becomes of great interest to abstract the sequential access inherent to this kind of devices. For this purpose we create *Virtual memory ports (VMP)* whose behavior emulates parallel independent real memory ports. High abstraction HDL makes feasible to describe systems at a high abstraction level but finally, low level hardware imposes strong constraints to the feasibility of the system. We have designed a shell to expand the parallelism of this sequential elements in such a way that the design process of the system can be done without taking care about this low level considerations. According to this strategy, algorithmic implementations as the one proposed here can be designed at a higher abstraction level. The main idea for this implementation is to combine the following concepts/properties:

a. Nowadays, long memory words (36 bits) make feasible to store up to four 9-bit-width data at each memory address with more than 512Kaddress [18] (up to 5 images of 720x576 pixels per memory chip).

b. A throughput of one pixel per cycle is possible using pipelined packing and unpacking circuits, which requires memory access only each 4 clock cycles.

We have designed a MMU which benefits from the previous architectural descriptions. Depending on the number of VMPs required and packing/unpacking possibilities (provided by the memory word bit-width), a state machine is used to feed the VMP registers sequentially, achieving a final performance of one data per cycle. Furthermore, this architecture is scalable because an increment of N in the number of VMPs available on one memory only modifies the required access cycles on a factor of N. This can be further optimized by incrementing the MMU clock frequency by this factor with respect to the global system clock frequency. There is only one limitation, due to the packing and unpacking circuits, random access is limited to a multiple of 4 and for efficient data management they should be stored on memory in a consecutive packed way.

The MMU architecture is illustrated on Fig. 3 for a four VMP case. Note that a VMP is composed by 4 addresses register (read or write type) plus a data-write register with packing circuits or by a data-read register with unpacking circuitry.

The new high level abstraction provided by the MMU makes feasible the implementation of FIR temporal filters using a high abstraction level description. Previous implementation of L&K used IIR filters to reduce the memory access but the drawback was the accuracy degradation [7], [8], [14]. The presented architecture allows the easy management of a large number of read-write processes necessary for FIR temporal filters with a minimum FPGA logic which clearly justifies the design of the presented MMU architecture.

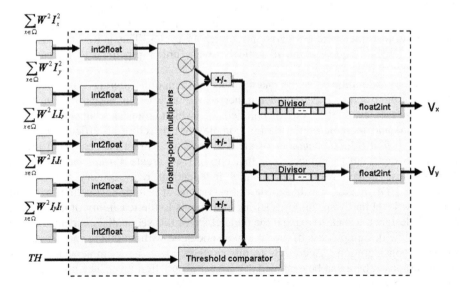

Fig. 2. Architecture schematic of the floating-point unit. Pipeline stage S_4.

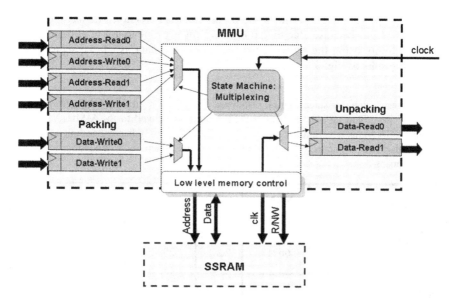

Fig. 3. MMU schematics for a 4 VMPs expansion-case. VMPs are represented by one address register (type Read or Write) and a Data-Write or Data-Read register. Low level memory control manages the data and address signals as well as the SSRAM clock, read-no-write signal (R/NW), etc. The state machine feeds four VMPs sequentially and manages the low level memory access. Packing/unpacking circuits achieve a total throughput of one pixel per clock cycle. This architecture allows us to multiply by 4 the equivalent memory parallel access.

4   System Resources and Performance

The whole system has been successfully implemented and tested on a stand-alone board for image processing applications [19]. This board is provided with a Virtex II XC2V6000-4 Xilinx FPGA as processing element including also video input/output circuits and user interfaces/communication buses. Table 1 summarizes the estimation of the system resources consumption for each pipeline stage to determine the critical circuits in terms of frequency and resources cost.

The computations use fixed point arithmetic on stages S_0 to S_3 and floating point on stage S_4. We include the values of the requirements for pipeline stage S_4 with different approaches. Rows number 5, 6 and 7 include an approach using a customized floating point representation. It uses one bit for the sign and customized bits for the mantissa and the exponent as indicated on Table 1. The final rows present an implementation using fixed point arithmetic. Because the input data to this stage uses 18 bits data, their implementation with fixed point arithmetic needs at least 36 bits to avoid loss of accuracy. It is clear that floating point representation fits better this stage provided that the dynamic range is larger, which is very important to represent small numbers after the division operation without requiring bits extension. Several bits configurations of the implementation floating point data have been implemented. The number of bits dedicated to the mantissa allows us to define the accuracy vs. performance of the system. In the final version we have utilized a mantissa of 11 bits because, due to that optical flow is prone to noise, good results can be achieved only using the most significant bits of the data as can be seen from the illustrative results of Fig. 4.

Table 1. Basic pipeline stages gates resources consumption (results taken from the DK synthesizer [19]). Non motion core indicates the logic associated to the MMU, Video input controller, VGA signal generation, user interface, etc. Last rows indicate the implementation of stage S_4 with different parameters and data representation, where *man* stands for mantissa and *exp* for exponent.

Pipelined stages	NAND gates	FFs	Memory bits	Max clock frequency (MHz)
S_0 Gaussian smoothing + Non motion core modules	66213	2081	20208	45
S_1 FIR temporal filters	156266	529	73728	67
S_2 FIR spatial derivatives	454087	639	221184	60
S_3 Construction of Least squares matrices	478034	1873	221184	51
S_4 Floating point unit (11 man + 7 exp)	57167	3488	0	45
S_4 Floating point unit (17 man + 7 exp)	131193	4938	0	36
S_4 Floating point unit (23 man + 7 exp)	207428	7698	0	34
S_4 Fixed point unit (36 bits)	345981	1080	0	31

Fig. 4.a corresponds to a diverging tree sequence produced by the simulated approaching of the camera to the tree. All the spurious deviations of the flow from a central expansion are artefacts produced in areas with low image structure. Fig. 4.b corresponds to a simulated flight over the Yosemite Valley. In this figure we have areas with fast motion components (clouds on the top, and closer rock on the bottom left of the image). The optical flows obtained in these regions are noisier due to the model restrictions. In these areas oversampled sequences would lead to more reliable flow estimations. Nevertheless, the overall motion patterns are quite regular and accurate. We have tested the global accuracy of the flow using the configurations of S_4 indicated in table 1 and they lead to similar results (using the benchmarking sequences of [1]).

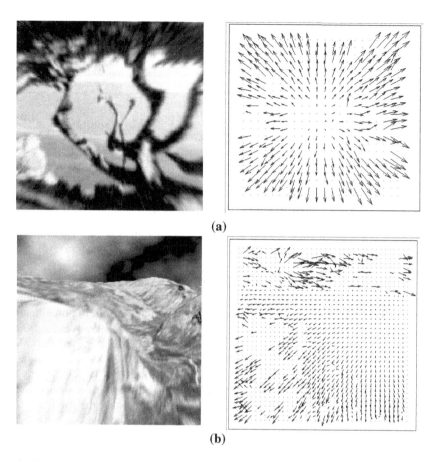

(a)

(b)

Fig. 4. Optical flow processing results (11 bits for the mantissa in S_4) for a coupled of sequences used in [1] and available at: ftp://ftp.vislist.com/SHAREWARE/CODE/OPTICAL-FLOW/. (a) Diverging tree sequence. (b) Yosemite Fly-Through sequence. The flow is represented as vectors with module proportional to the motion speed.

Finally, Table 2 shows the hardware costs of the whole designed system (processing motion core, MMUs, frame-grabber, VGA output and user-interface) and its performance. The image resolution can be selected according to image input camera standard or processing capabilities. This architecture is scalable being possible to reduce the system parallelism (and performance) to fit on a smaller device. Furthermore, the processing core can be replicated (more than 75% of system resources of a Virtex II XC2V6000 are available) and the frame-grabber can be easily modified (thanks to the MMU architecture) to split the image and send it to several processing units. This high level scalability allows multiplying the processing performance on this board but since the architecture already fulfils the requirements to compute in real-time sequences at a high frame-rate we have not addressed this issue.

Table 2. System resources required on a Virtex II XC2V6000-4. The system includes the optical flow processing unit, memory management unit, camera Frame-grabber, VGA signal output generation and user configuration interface. (*Mpps: mega-pixels per second* at the maximum system processing clock frequency, *EMBS*: embedded memory blocks).

Slices / (%)	EMBS / (%)	Embedded multipliers / (%)	Mpps	Image Resolution	Fps
8250 (24%)	29 (20%)	12 (8%)	45.49	640x480 1280x960	148 37

4.1 Performance Comparison with Other Approaches

The implementation of the optical-flow algorithm with FPGAs has only been addressed by some authors in very recent years. In our previous work [7], [8], a basic implementation of L&K model was proposed and we presented a detailed study about the performance vs. system resources trade-off. These papers also cover the topic of system degradation related with the different stages bit-width. Although the performance was quite high (2857 Kpps), neither the image resolution or frame-rates perform the high frame-rate requirements addressed here. The iterative algorithm of Horn & Schunk (H&S) [20] has also been implemented by different authors. Martin et. al. [21] presented a system implementation that fits quite well the specification of a standard frame-rate optical flow system capable to process up to 3932 Kpps. The main disadvantage of that approach is that the model itself obtains poor accuracy as shown by Barron et al. [1]. Using the block-matching approach, the implementation described by Niitsuma & Maruyama [22] achieves 30 fps of image size 640x480 but with high hardware cost (90% slices of a XC2V6000 FPGA) and without sub-pixel accuracy. Finally, the model described here, running in software on an Intel Pentium 4 HT, 3200 MHz, can compute 47.6 fps of 160x120 pixels (914 Kpps) and this can be further optimized using MMX and SSE instructions. The problem is that it consumes all the computing resources of the machine.

Our system has been experimentally tested running up to 45 MHz and due to the fine-grain pipelined architecture; we have computed 45 Mpps which is more than one order of magnitude higher than previous approaches. Since the referenced works are very recent (some of then using the same evaluation devices), the outstanding performance of our approach is not provided by technology improvements but rather by a very efficient processing architecture that extensively uses the parallel resources of the FPGA device.

5 Conclusions

The presented system outperforms in more than one order of magnitude any previous approach, validating the proposed architecture. The necessity of a system for high frame-rate optical flow processing has been clearly motivated because of two main reasons: it decreases temporal aliasing and it better fits to the first order gradient constraint assumption. Current image sensors make possible very fast image acquisition and simple gradient based optical flow approaches seem to be one of the most suitable alternatives for real-time processing system onto customized hardware.

According to this we have implemented an improved version of the L&K model [12] which complements the capabilities of high frame-rate cameras providing real-time image motion analysis.

We have presented a novel architecture that addresses the real-time optical flow computation of high frame-rate and high resolution sequences using a FPGA device as processing element. We have described the architecture and illustrated how parallelism and superpipelined structures can be defined for image processing applications. We finally have evaluated the system resource consumption and performance of an implementation on a stand-alone platform which fulfils the high frame-rate optical flow requirements. The comparison with previous works clearly shows the outstanding performance of the system and opens the door to a wide range of application fields.

Future works will cover the utilization of such systems on real-world applications using moving robotics platforms, such as robot navigation, tracking, as well as structure extraction from motion analysis.

Acknowledgments

This work has been supported by the Spanish project National Project DEPROVI (DPI2004-07032) and by the EU grant DRIVSCO (IST-016276-2).

References

[1] Barron, J.L., Fleet, D.J., Beauchemin, S.: Performance of optical-flow techniques. *International Journal of Computer Vision*, vol. 12, n°1, (1994) pp. 43-77.

[2] McCane, B., Novins, K., Crannitch D. and Galvin B.: On Benchmarking Optical Flow. *Computer Vision and Image Understanding*, vol. 84, (2001) pp. 126–143.

[3] Liu, H.C., Hong, T.S., Herman, M., Camus, T., and Chellappa, R.: Accuracy *vs.* Efficiency Trade-offs in Optical Flow Algorithms. *Computer Vision and Image Understanding*, vol.72, 3, (1998) pp. 271-286.

[4] Weber, J. and Malik, J.: Robust computation of optical flow in a multi-scale differential framework. *International Journal of Computer Vision*, vol. 14, (1995) pp. 67-81.

[5] Lim, S., Apostolopoulos, J.G., Gamal, A.E.: Optical flow estimation using temporally oversampled video. *IEEE Transactions on Image Processing*, vol. 14, 8, (2005) pp. 1074-1087.

[6] Lucas, B.D. and Kanade T.: An Iterative Image Registration Technique with an Application to Stereo Vision. *Proc. of the DARPA Image Understanding Workshop*, (1984), pp. 121-130.

[7] Díaz, J., Ros, E., Mota, S., Carrillo, R., Agís, R.: Real time optical flow processing system. *Lecture Notes in Computer Science*, vol. 3203, (2004) pp.617-626.

[8] Díaz, J., Ros, E., Ortigosa, E. M. and Mota, S.:FPGA based real-time optical-flow system. *IEEE Transactions on Circuits and Systems for Video Technology*, Accepted for publication.

[9] Bainbridge-Smith, A. and Lane, R.G.: Determining Optical Flow Using a Differential Method. *Image and Vision Computing,* vol. 1, (1997) pp. 11-22.

[10] Bainbridge-Smith, A. and Lane, R.G.: Measuring Confidence in Optical Flow Estimation. *IEE Electronic Letters,* vol. 10, (1996) pp. 882-884.

[11] Maya-Rueda, S., Arias-Estrada, M.: FPGA Processor for Real-Time Optical Flow Computation. *Lecture Notes in Computer Science,* vol. 2778, (2003), pp. 1103-1016.

[12] Brandt, J.W.: Improved Accuracy in Gradient Based Optical Flow Estimation. *Int. Journal of Computer Vision,* vol. 25, 1, (1997), pp. 5-22.

[13] Simoncelli, E. P.: Design of multi-dimensional derivatives filters. Proc. *IEEE International Conf. on Image Processing,* Austin Tx, (1994), pp. 790-794.

[14] Fleet, D.J. and Langley, K.: Recursive filters for optical flow. *IEEE Transactions on Pattern Analysis and Machine Intelligence,* vol. 17, 1, (1995) pp. 61-67.

[15] Bruhn, A., Weickert, J., Feddern, C., Kohlberger, T., Schnorr, C.: Variational optical flow computation in real time. *IEEE Transactions on Image Processing,* vol. 14, 5, (2005) pp. 608-615.

[16] Dumontier, C., Luthon, F., Charras, J.P.: Real-time DSP implementation for MRF-based video motion detection. *IEEE Transactions on Image Processing,* vol. 8, 10, (1999) pp. 1341-1347.

[17] Forsell, M. J.: Architectural differences of efficient sequential and parallel computers. *Journal of Systems Architecture: the EUROMICRO Journal,* vol. 47, 13, (2002) pp. 1017-1041.

[18] SRAM ZBT memories, part number: 71T75602. Datasheet available at: www.idt.com.

[19] Celoxica company. Web site and products information available at: www.celoxica.com.

[20] Horn, B.K.P. and Schunck, B.G.: Determining optical flow. *Artificial Intelligent* vol. 17, (1981) pp 185-204.

[21] Martín, J.L., Zuloaga, A., Cuadrado, C., Lázaro, J., Bidarte, U.: Hardware implementation of optical flow constraint equation using FPGAs. *Computer Vision and Image Understanding* No. 3, (2005) pp. 462-490.

[22] Niitsuma, H. and Maruyama, T.: Real-Time Detection of Moving Objects. *Lecture Notes in Computer Science, FPL 2004,* vol. 3203, (2004) pp. 1153-1157.

Design Exploration of a Video Pre-processor for an FPGA Based SoC

Niklas Lepistö, Benny Thörnberg, and Mattias O'Nils

Department of Information Technology and Media
Mid Sweden University
Holmgatan 10, Sundsvall, Sweden
{niklas.lepisto, benny.thornberg, mattias.onils}@miun.se

Abstract. FPGA based implementation of embedded systems has many attractive characteristics such as: flexibility, low cost, high integration, embedded distributed memories and extensive parallelism. One application where there is a significant possible potential for FPGA is for the implementation of real-time video processing. In this paper we present an analysis of a video pre-processor and how this affects the FPGA and RAM resource usage and performance. From these results we indicate the best space-time mapping of operations under different design constraints. These results can be used as a decision base when implementing an FPGA based video enabled display unit.

1 Introduction

The necessity for real-time video processing capabilities in embedded systems is generally increasing with time. Many systems which have previously only provided a simple graphical user interface are now required to support real-time video processing. Real-time video processing is a very data intensive task when compared to many of the normal tasks performed by embedded systems. Even in simple real-time video operations where the algorithmic complexity of the processing is very low, the mere transfer of image data may consume significant system resources [1].

FPGAs provide an efficient alternative for implementing video processing applications. Modern FPGAs include resources such as embedded memories and hardware multipliers which make them suitable for real time video applications. Due to the possibility of parallelizing computationally intensive tasks, FPGAs offer significantly higher performances than general purpose processors (GPP) and digital signal processors (DSP)[2]. The increased performance provided by an FPGA makes it possible to integrate the tasks performed by multiple GPPs or DPSs in a single chip[3]. An FPGA based system also provides an advantage regarding customizability allowing the designer to move computationally intensive tasks to hardware.

The increased integration possibilities offered by FPGAs in turn leads to added design challenges when attempting to achieve the maximum level of integration. The main challenge is often the sharing of the system's memory resources between the different components implemented in the FPGA [4,5]. The

K. Bertels, J.M.P. Cardoso, and S. Vassiliadis (Eds.): ARC 2006, LNCS 3985, pp. 87–92, 2006.

goal of this design exploration is to identify the best space-time mapping for an
FPGA based video pre-processor regarding memory requirements and memory
bandwidth.

The presentation of this work is organized as follows. Next section presents
an overview of a video pre-processor and a description of the design exploration,
followed by a formal description and analysis of the video pre-processor. Finnally
the results from the analysis is discussed and concluded.

2   Video Pre-processor Analysis

The purpose of the video pre-processor is to provide an effective co-processor
for the display of multiple video channels in an FPGA based system. The pre-
processor should, in real-time, perform horizontal *mirroring*, *zoom* in and *zoom
out* and *cropping* of the frame before displaying it, as depicted in Figure 1.

To extract the correct storage requirements and memory access rate we present
a formal description of all video processing operations shown in Figure 1. We
have chosen not to fully define the operations at frame borders in order for the
complexity of the formulae to be maintained at a reasonable level. A linear estimation of the neighborhood pixels located outside the frame is the standard
method used.

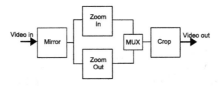

Fig. 1. Data flow for the video pre-processor functionality

The design exploration is done by altering the space-time mapping of the
operators used in the system. Space-time mapping is the process of placing the
order and schedule of the processes and operators, such that one or several
design constraints are fulfilled. Three different space time mapping alternatives
are evaluated for each operator: (1) Keep execution order and use registers and
external memory only, (2) Keep execution order and use registers and internal
memory, (3) Reorder execution order and use registers and internal memory.

Five different design metrics are analyzed in this section: (1) internal memory
usage, (2) external memory usage, (3) mean access rate, (4) peak access rate
and (5) the number of used DMA channels.

The required buffer size for each operator is analyzed such that the minimum
buffer size for each mapping of operations is derived. In the same way the memory
access rate is analyzed.

The bit width to an external memory is set at a constant of 32 bits. Only
relative memory activities are analyzed in this paper, thus access rates generated
by the display update and memory accesses from the processor are ignored in

this analysis. The design exploration has been done using 18 bit color and a frame resolution of 760×580.

The crop operation will not be included in the design exploration since the crop operation does not require any buffers and thus will not generate any memory traffic for any type of configuration.

Let $P_{frc}^{RGB} \in R^4$ be a RGB color coded pixel at the spatio-temporal position $(f, r, c) \in Z^3$. A color frame F_f^{RGB} at the temporal position f is denoted as,

$$F_f^{RGB} = \left\{ \begin{array}{l} P_{frc}^{RGB} | 1 \leq r \leq R \wedge 1 \leq c \leq C \wedge \\ 0 \leq P_{frc}^{RGB} \leq 2^{n_c} - 1 \end{array} \right\}, \tag{1}$$

where R and C are the number of rows and columns defined as $R \in Z$ and $C \in Z$. n_c is the number of bits which represents each color component of RGB.

A color video stream is denoted as $F^{RGB} = \{F_f^{RGB} | f \in Z\}$ and the sub frame of F_f^{RGB} is defined as:

$$F_\varphi^{RGB} = \left\{ \begin{array}{l} P_{\varphi rc}^{RGB} | 1 \leq \rho \leq P \wedge 1 \leq \gamma \leq \Gamma \wedge \\ 0 \leq P_{\varphi rc}^{RGB} \leq 2^{n_c} - 1 \end{array} \right\}, \tag{2}$$

where P and Γ are the number of rows and columns defined as $P \in Z$ and $\Gamma \in Z$.

Definition 1. *The operation* Crop *performs both a horizontal and vertical crop of each frame in the video stream and is the mapping* $M_\varphi^{CROP}(A_f^{RGB})$ *from the input color frame* A_f^{RGB} *to the output color frame* B_φ^{RGB} *and is defined as,*

$$M_\varphi^{CROP}(A_f^{RGB}) = \left\{ \begin{array}{l} A_f^{RGB} \rightarrow B_\varphi^{RGB} | B_{\varphi\rho\gamma}^{RGB} = A_{f(\rho+x)(\gamma+y)}^{RGB} \\ s.t.\ A_{frc}^{RGB} \in A_f^{RGB} \wedge B_{\varphi\rho\gamma}^{RGB} \in B_f^{RGB} \wedge \\ 1 \leq \rho \leq P \wedge 1 \leq \gamma \leq \Gamma \end{array} \right\}, \tag{3}$$

where x and y are the start coordinates of the new frame within the old frame. P and Γ represents the number of rows and columns.

Definition 2. *The operation* Mirror *performs a horizontal mirroring of each video frame and is the mapping* $M_f^{MIRROR}(A_f^{RGB})$ *from one input color frame* A_f^{RGB} *to the output color frame* B_f^{RGB} *and is defined as,*

$$M_f^{MIR}(A_f^{RGB}) = \left\{ \begin{array}{l} A_f^{RGB} \rightarrow B_f^{RGB} | B_{frc}^{RGB} = A_{fr(C-c+1)}^{RGB} \\ s.t.\ A_{frc}^{RGB} \in A_f^{RGB} \wedge B_{frc}^{RGB} \in B_f^{RGB} \end{array} \right\}. \tag{4}$$

For ordered execution, i.e., pixels produced in the same order as they are consumed, the minimum buffer size for the mirror operation is derived from Equation 4 as $\Psi_{order}^{MIR} = n_c(C+1)$. If the pixel production is allowed to be reordered, the required buffer size is reduced to $\Psi^{MIR} = 0$. When the memory access rate for the operator is derived for the configuration when the buffer is placed outside the FPGA, this involves all pixels being read and written to the external memory through a DMA channel, as $\Omega_{mean,peak}^{MIR} = 2CRBn_c/n_m$. In this equation, B

is the number of frames per second and n_m is the external memory bit width. Since reordering does not use any buffers, it will not add any memory accesses. The access rate is expressed as additional memory accesses, which involves those generated when video information is written to the video buffer and is added into the design exploration phase. Using the resolutions and configurations defined in the previous section the design metrics for the mirror operation are shown in Table 1.

Definition 3. *The operation* Zoom In *enlarges a selected are in a video stream and is the mapping $M_f^{IN}(A_f^{RGB})$ from one input color frame A_f^{RGB} to the output color frame B_f^{RGB} and is denoted as,*

$$
M_f^{IN}(A_f^{RGB}) = \left\{
\begin{array}{l}
A_f^{RGB} \to B_f^{RGB} | B_{frc}^{RGB} = A_{f(r/W+x)(c/W+y)}^{RGB} \\
s.t.\ A_{frc}^{RGB} \in A_f^{RGB} \wedge B_{frc}^{RGB} \in B_f^{RGB} \wedge \\
1 \leq x \leq R/W \wedge 1 \leq y \leq R/W
\end{array}
\right\},
\tag{5}
$$

where W is the degree of magnification, $W \in Z$.

For ordered execution the minimum buffer size for zoom in is calculated as $\Psi_{order}^{IN} = N_c RC(W-1)/W^2$ where W is the degree of magnification, $W \in [1,2,3]$. For the reordered implementation of the operator, the memory requirement will be reduced to $\Psi_{reorder}^{IN} = n_c$. The memory access rate using an external buffer and ordered execution is derived as $\Omega_{mean,peak}^{IN} = (W+1)CRBn_c/N_m$. For reordered execution the peak access rate can be derived as $\Omega_{peak}^{IN} = CRBW^2 n_c/n_m$ for a buffer of size n_c and $\Omega_{peak}^{IN} = CRBWn_c/n_m$ for a buffer of size $n_c C/W$. The design metrics for the zoom in operator are labeled Zi in table 1. This is an attempt to fully explore the effects that different internal buffer sizes have on the system; this includes the two cases described above and are indicated as a and b for case 3.

Definition 4. *The operation* Zoom Out *scales down each frame in a video stream and is the mapping $M_f^{OUT}(A_f^{RGB})$ from one input color frame A_f^{RGB} to an output color frame B_f^{RGB} and is denoted as,*

$$
M_f^{OUT}(A_f^{RGB}) = \left\{
\begin{array}{l}
A_f^{RGB} \to B_\varphi^{RGB} | B_{\varphi\rho\gamma}^{RGB} = 2^{-W} \sum_{x=0}^{W-1}\sum_{y=0}^{W-1} A_{f(W\rho-x)(W\gamma-y)}^{RGB} \\
s.t.\ A_{kfrc}^{RGB} \in A_f^{RGB} \wedge B_{\varphi rc}^{RGB} \in B_\varphi^{RGB} \wedge \\
1 \leq \rho \leq P \wedge 1 \leq \gamma \leq \Gamma \wedge k \in D^{RGB}
\end{array}
\right\},
\tag{6}
$$

where $P = R/W, \Gamma = C/W$ and W is the degree of magnification, $W \in Z$.

The minimum buffer requirement for the zoom out operator, both ordered and reordered execution, is derived as $\Psi_{order,reorder}^{OUT} = n_c C/W$. Since both execution styles will have the same memory access rate, it will be derived as $\Omega_{order,reorder}^{OUT} = CRBn_c/n_m$ for the external buffer configuration and as $\Omega_{mean,peak}^{OUT} = 0$ for the internal.

Table 1. Cost figures of the *Mirror, Zoom In* and *Zoom Out* operators

	Allocated Memory		Accesses/s		DMA channels
Case:Operator	Internal	External	Mean	Peak	
1:Mi	0	13 698	14 877 000	14 877 000	1
2:Mi	13 698	0	0	0	0
3:Mi	0	0	0	0	0
1:Zi	18	1 735 650	22 315 500	22 315 500	1
2:Zi	1 983 600	0	0	0	0
3a:Zi	18	0	0	119 016 000	0
3b:Zi	6 840	0	0	29 754 000	0
1:Zo	18	6 840	14 877 000	14 877 000	1
2-3:Zo	6 840	0	0	0	0

3 Discussion

From the results presented in the previous section, it is difficult to obtain an overview regarding the best solution. It is necessary to firstly identify which of the costs actually determine the final system's cost.

For the external memory the maximum value is less than one Mbyte, which is quite small and will only have a marginal effect on the cost of the final system. The mean access rate is an indication of the average energy consumption rather than a required speed when selecting RAM memory and FPGA. However, peak access rate will determine the minimum speed required when selecting RAM memory for the system. Internal RAM will affect the size of the selected FPGA and the number of DMA channels will affect the scalability, since too many DMA channels will cause difficulties with the bus scheduling.

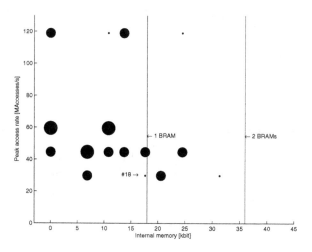

Fig. 2. Design parameter consideration where peak access rate is plotted vs. internal memory and the number of DMA channels

Thus, these three costs must be considered when selecting the implementation style for the system. In Figure 2, all solutions are plotted as the peak memory access rate vs. the required internal memory. Additionally, the size of the dot indicating a solution is proportional to the number of DMA channels required for the solution. Although this plot gives no information concerning the index it does offer a good visualization of the design space. The internal memory size is also indicated as the number of Xilinx Spartan 3 block RAMs. From this plot, solution #18, as indicated in Figure 2, will offer the best implementation configuration. Solution #18 will implement the zoom out using ordered execution and the remainder using reordered execution. All buffers will be implemented on the FPGA.

4   Conclusion

This paper analyzes the implementation costs of a pre-processor for the display of video information in a FPGA based System on Chip. The analysis focuses on the memory part of the system since this determines the real cost of the system. We have found that the pre-processor can be implemented on a FPGA using only one block RAM (18 kbits), with no extra external memory and only one DMA channel. This solution has a reasonable peak memory access rate of 30 Maccesses/s. Hence, the low implementation cost and the reasonable memory access rate makes the identified solution scalable. Thus it is possible for several pre-processors to be placed in parallel in order to handle multiple video channels.

References

1. Craig Sanderson, Dave Shand, "FPGAs Supplant Processors and ASICs In Advanced Imaging Applications", FPGA and Structured ASIC Journal, www.fpgajournal.com.
2. Fan Yang, Michel Paindavoine, "Implementation of an RBF Neural Network on Embedded Systems: Real-Time Face Tracking and Identity Verification", IEEE Transaction on Neural Networks, Sept. 2003, pp. 1162-1175.
3. K. Morris "Beyond Processors" FPGA and Structured ASIC journal, www.fpgajournal.com, Oct 2003.
4. F. Catthoor, S. Wuytack, E. De Greef, F. Balasa, L. Nachtergaele, A. Vandecappelle, "Custom Memory Management Methodology - Exploration of Memory Organisation for Embedded Multimedia Systems Design", Kluwer Academic Publishers, 1998.
5. Domingo Benitez, "Performance of Remote FPGA-based Coprocessor for Image-Processing Applications", Proceedings of Euromicro Symposium on Digital System Design 2002.

QUKU: A Fast Run Time Reconfigurable Platform for Image Edge Detection

Sunil Shukla[1,2], Neil W. Bergmann[1], and Jürgen Becker[2]

[1] ITEE, University of Queensland, Brisbane,
QLD 4072, Australia
{sunil, n.bergmann}@itee.uq.edu.au
http://www.itee.uq.edu.au/
[2] ITIV, Universität Karlsruhe,
76131 Karlsruhe, Germany
{shukla, becker}@itiv.uni-karlsruhe.de

Abstract. To fill the gap between increasing demand for reconfigurability and performance efficiency, CGRAs are seen to be an emerging platform. In this paper, a new architecture, QUKU, is described which uses a coarse-grained reconfigurable PE array (CGRA) overlaid on an FPGA. The low-speed reconfigurability of the FPGA is used to optimize the CGRA for different applications, whilst the high-speed CGRA reconfiguration is used within an application for operator re-use. We will demonstrate the dynamic reconfigurability of QUKU by porting Sobel and Laplacian kernel for edge detection in an image frame.

1 Introduction

With the rapid emergence of multi-protocol standards, the need for a platform which is able to reconfigure itself rapidly and on the fly has grown tremendously. This situation demands a high level of flexibility, as seen in GPP (General Purpose Processor), performance and power efficiency. GPP has failed to show its mark in terms of processing efficiency. To fill the gap between flexibility and efficiency, several architectures have been proposed.

Generally, ASICs are seen as the only low-power solution which can meet this demand for fast computational efficiency and high I/O bandwidth. However, the NRE cost of ASICs are a strong motivation for some sort of general purpose computing chip with better power efficiency than microprocessors. Recently, coarse grained reconfigurable architectures (CGRA) have been developed to bridge the gap between power-hungry microprocessors and single-purpose ASICs. Coarse-grained arrays have the advantages of power-efficiency for their intended application domain, and also they are designed with efficient implementation of dynamic reconfiguration supported in hardware and in design software. Furthermore, this dynamic reconfiguration can be very fast, since configuration codes are very short. But their use remains in question due to the lack of a well defined design flow and commercial availability. Traditionally, FPGAs have been thought of as a prototyping device for small scale digital systems. However current generation mega-gate FPGA chips have changed this perception. FPGAs can be reconfigured for an unlimited number of times to

K. Bertels, J.M.P. Cardoso, and S. Vassiliadis (Eds.): ARC 2006, LNCS 3985, pp. 93–98, 2006.

implement any circuit. FPGAs have proved their usability in control intensive as well as computational intensive tasks. An attractive feature of FPGAs is the ability to partially and dynamically reconfigure the FPGA function.

The next section gives a short overview of FPGA based reconfigurable architectures. Section 3 describes the QUKU architecture. Section 4 describes the run time reconfigurability of QUKU. Section 5 discusses the implementation results followed by conclusion.

2   Related Work

Some other systems consisting of MPU and FPGAs have been proposed in past [3, 4, 5, 6, 7, 8]. Guccione [9] provides a detailed list of FPGA based reconfigurable architectures. YARDS [5] is a hybrid system of MPU connected with an array of FPGA and has been targeted for telecommunication applications. Spyder [7] consists of a processor with 3 reconfigurable execution units working in parallel. The configuration of the execution units is determined from the set of applications. DISC [6] is an FPGA based processor which loads application specific instruction from a library of image processing elements. It takes advantage of the partial reconfiguration feature of FPGA and implements a system analogous to memory paging in software. PRISM [8] is a reconfigurable architecture built using hardware-software co-design concepts. For each application, new instructions are compiled, synthesized and loaded. GARP [4] combines a MIPS processor with a reconfigurable array to achieve accelerated performance in certain applications.

3   QUKU Architecture

QUKU [1, 2] is a merger of two technologies: CGRAs and FPGAs. Fig 1 shows the system level description of QUKU. It consists of a dynamically reconfigurable PE array, configuration controller and address controller for data and result memory along with a Microblaze based soft processor. QUKU is a coarse-grained PE matrix overlaid on a conventional FPGA. The aim is to develop a system which is based on commercially available and affordable technologies, but at the same time provides active support for fast and efficient dynamic reconfiguration. Our system is unique in that it provides two levels of application-specific reconfigurability. The operation of each PE, and the interconnections between PEs can be reconfigured on a cycle-by-cycle basis, giving maximum reuse of arithmetic and logical operators without long reconfiguration delays. However, the CGRA does not suffer from the normal CGRA problem of trying to identify the optimal mix of operators for all present and future applications to be used on that array. Rather, the structure of the CGRA can be periodically re-optimized for each new application at a cost of several milliseconds of FPGA reconfiguration time.

A commonly perceived obstacle to provide algorithm speedup is the difficulty of designing custom hardware for each new algorithm. The QUKU architecture moves the design problem from a complex hardware design problem to a simpler problem of programming a PE array. QUKU compiles these PEs to a heterogeneous array, with each PE optimized for just the range of operations it requires to implement for one application set. It is our conjecture that such a PE array has the potential to provide area and power efficiencies not normally associated with FPGAs, and this paper outlines some of our initial investigations into this potential.

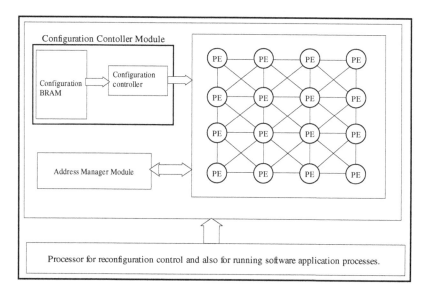

Fig. 1. System level diagram of QUKU

4 Run Time Reconfiguration

In [2] we have described the design process and shown that QUKU performance is much better than a FPGA based soft processor implementation. In this section, we will describe the configuration memory organization to support run time reconfiguration of whole or partial PE array.

As shown in fig. 1, the configuration controller is responsible for the loading of different modules on the PE array. The configuration BRAM contains configuration codes for up to four modules. Fig 2 shows the address space of modules and the configuration word structure. The first location of a module configuration space is reserved for specifying the address of PEs involved in the module mapping. Address of PE is written in decoded form say, if a module is to be loaded on PE 0, 1, 2, 4, 7, 8 and 10 then it is written in the address location as "0000010110010111". This ensures that the corresponding PEs can be reset before they are loaded with the new configuration. Actual PE configuration word starts after the PE reset information. A PE array consists of 16 PEs. Each PE may have three configuration layers: start, middle and end layer. Each configuration layer is programmed to run for a certain number of iterations as a 10 bit value in iteration counter. The iteration counter value is written with the configuration bits in odd numbered locations. The even numbered locations contain the address of PEs for which the configuration is valid.

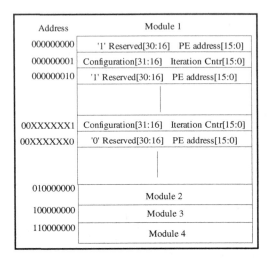

Fig. 2. Configuration BRAM memory structure

Depth of the address space is decided by the worst case in which no two PEs share the same configuration. For this worst case, each PE requires 3 configuration word (start, middle and end layer) and each configuration word along with address occupies two locations leading to a total of 96 (16X3X2) locations, plus one location for the reset information. Hence a total of 97 locations are required. To keep the memory map simple, this depth is extended to the nearest power of 2, making it 128. To mark the end of configuration, we have reserved bit 31 of the even numbered location. The last configuration word is indicated by a '0' at bit 31 in the even numbered location.

4.1   Run Time Reconfiguration for Image Processing Kernel

In this section, we will be concentrating on edge detection algorithms that find widespread application in image processing [10,11]. There are a lot of methods for edge detection. But most of them can be grouped into either gradient or Laplacian. Gradient method looks for finding out minima or maxima in the first derivative while Laplacian method looks for zero crossings in the second derivative.

We have mapped Sobel and Laplace edge detection algorithms on QUKU. The Sobel and Laplacian masks are shown in Fig. 3. Sobel edge detector uses a pair of 3X3 convolution masks, one estimating the gradient in X direction and the other in Y direction. The approximate gradient magnitude is then obtained by adding the X and Y gradients The Laplacian technique uses a 5X5 convoluted mask to approximate the second derivative in both X and Y directions. The idea of generating gradient from image frame, utilizes the concept of sliding window over the image frame. The mask is slid over an area of the input image. The new value is calculated for the middle pixel, then the mask is slid one pixel to the right. This continues from left to right and top to bottom.

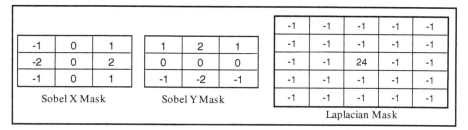

Fig. 3. Sobel & Laplacian filter mask for edge detection in image frame

5   Result Analysis

For edge detection purpose, we have chosen an image with 336 rows and 341 columns (fig. 4(a)) of pixels. Fig. 4(b) and 4(c) represents the image obtained after applying Laplacian and Sobel edge detection algorithms respectively. Initially, Laplacian kernel was mapped followed by Sobel kernel.

Table 1. Result comparison for Laplacian and Sobel kernel implementation on QUKU

Application	Execution time/frame	Configuration time
Laplacian Kernel	33.5 ms	105 ns
Sobel kernel	54.4 ms	105 ns

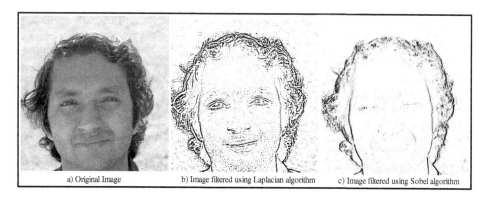

a) Original Image   b) Image filtered using Laplacian algorithm   c) Image filtered using Sobel algorithm

Fig. 4. Original image and image after processing with Laplacian and Sobel filter

6   Conclusion

In this paper we showed how QUKU can be dynamically reconfigured at the application level within a few clock cycles. The configuration time was found to be a very small fraction (10^{-7}) of the execution time. The preliminary results support the fact that QUKU can be used in real time image processing applications and can be dynamically reconfigured at a very fast speed to switch between different kernels

Development of QUKU is still in progress. This first set of experiments is mostly to confirm the APEX design flow, and to establish performance and reconfigurability features. We are yet to develop a Microblaze based soft processor interface to QUKU for system and software control.

Acknowledgement

This project is proudly supported by the International Science Linkages programme established under the Australian Government's innovation statement, Backing Australia's Ability.

References

1. Sunil Shukla, Neil Bergmann, Jürgen Becker, "APEX – A Coarse Grained Reconfigurable Overlay for FPGA", Proceedings of the IFIP VLSI SoC 2005, pp 581-585
2. Sunil Shukla, Neil Bergmann, Jürgen Becker, "QUKU: A Two-Level Reconfigurable Architecture", accepted for presentation in ISVLSI 2006
3. Alexandro M. S. Adário, E. L. Roehe and S. Bampi, "Dynamically Reconfigurable Architecture for Image Processor Applications", DAC 99, New Orleans, Louisiana
4. Hauser, J. R.; Wawrzyneck J., "GARP: A MIPS Processor with a Reconfigurable Coprocessor" Proceedings of FCCM (1997), pp 24-33
5. A. Tsutsui, T. Miyazaki, "YARDS: FPGA/MPU Hybrid Architecture for Telecommunication Data Processing". Proceedings of FPGA 1997, pp. 93-99
6. M. J. Wirthlin, B. L. Hutchings, "DISC: The dynamic instruction set compiler", in FPGAs for Fast Board Development and Reconfigurable Computing, Proc. SPIE 2607, pp. 92-103 (1995)
7. C. Iseli, E. Sanchez, "Spyder: A Reconfigurable VLIW processor using FPGAs" in proceedings of FCCM, 1993, pp. 17 – 24
8. P. Athanas, H. F. Silverman, "Processor Reconfiguration through Instruction Set Metamorphosis", IEEE Computer, March 1993, pp. 11-18
9. S. Guccione, "List of FPGA based Computing Machine", online at http://www.io.com/~guccione/HW_list.html
10. L. S. Davis, "A survey of edge detection techniques", Computer Graphics and Image Processing, vol. 4, no. 3, pp. 248-270, September 1975
11. V. S. Nalwa and T. O. Binford, "On detecting edges", IEEE Transactions on Pattern Analysis and Machine Intelligence, vol. PAMI-8, no. 6, pp. 699-714, November 1986

Applications of Small-Scale Reconfigurability to Graphics Processors

Kevin Dale[1], Jeremy W. Sheaffer[1], Vinu Vijay Kumar[2], David P. Luebke[1],
Greg Humphreys[1], and Kevin Skadron[1]

[1] Department of Computer Science
[2] Department of Electrical and Computer Engineering
University of Virginia*

Abstract. We explore the application of *Small-Scale Reconfigurability*
(SSR) to graphics hardware. SSR is an architectural technique wherein
functionality common to multiple subunits is reused rather than replicated, yielding high-performance reconfigurable hardware with reduced
area requirements. We show that SSR can be used effectively in programmable graphics architectures to allow double-precision computation
without affecting the performance of single-precision calculations and to
increase fragment shader performance with a minimal impact on chip
area.

1 Introduction

Every hardware system makes a tradeoff between performance and flexibility. At
one end of the spectrum, general purpose processors provide maximum flexibility
at the expense of performance, area, power consumption, and price. Custom
ASICs are the other extreme, providing maximum performance at a minimum
cost, albeit for only a very narrow set of applications.

Modern graphics hardware requires both high performance and flexibility,
placing it somewhere between these two extremes. Traditional intermediate hardware solutions like FPGAs are inappropriate for graphics processors because of
their large size and low performance relative to their fixed-logic counterparts [1].
Small-scale reconfigurability (SSR) provides an attractive compromise; systems
that use SSR components can approach the high speed and small size of ASICs
while providing some specialized configurability. In this paper, we explore the
applicability of SSR to programmable graphics hardware.

The simplest example of a reconfigurable component is two fully functional
components connected with a multiplexer (see Fig. 1). Although these two components are disjoint, in typical usage they will contain substantially similar redundant substructures, which is precisely the situation in which SSR performs
best. Rather than replicate all of the redundant structure, one can instead reuse
common substructure within a single component.

A common SSR unit is the morphable multiplier. These multiplier-adders can
be reconfigured into a multiplier or an adder in a single cycle. When used to

---

* {kdale, jws9c, vv6v, luebke, humper, skadron}@virginia.edu

K. Bertels, J.M.P. Cardoso, and S. Vassiliadis (Eds.): ARC 2006, LNCS 3985, pp. 99–108, 2006.

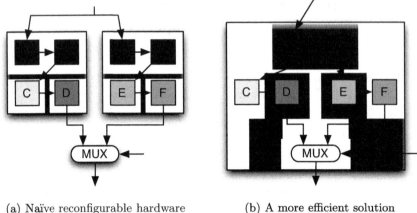

(a) Naïve reconfigurable hardware   (b) A more efficient solution

Fig. 1. A naïve implementation of reconfigurable hardware can be built by simply multiplexing between two distinct, unmodified units (a), but a more efficient design would reuse common substructure to avoid replication (b)

create single-precision floating point units, morphable multipliers yield a nearly 17% reduction in total area when compared to the sum of the sizes of their constituent parts [2].

Graphics processors, like specialized multimedia processors and DSPs, are a particularly suitable target for SSR due to their vector-processor like operations. When the same operation is performed repeatedly in SIMD fashion, reconfiguration and its associated overhead is infrequently needed, and any cost can be amortized over many instructions. Furthermore, SSR-based components typically have lower static power requirements because less hardware goes unused.

2   Related Work

Dynamically reconfigurable hardware has been a popular topic in recent computer architecture literature, especially in the FPGA and reconfigurable computing communities. The configurability of these systems serves myriad design goals, among them improved performance, power, area, and fault tolerance characteristics.

Even et al. describe a dual mode IEEE multiplier—a pipelined unit capable of producing one double-precision or two single-precision multiplications every clock cycle with a three cycle latency [3]. The authors argue that the reuse of substructure yields a cheap device that performs well for both precisions. They further claim that the single precision mode is particularly useful for SIMD applications, like graphics, because it is conducive to systems on which the same operation is regularly repeated on large numbers of data points.

Guerra et al. explore *built-in-self-repair* (BISR) and its application to fault tolerance, manufacturability, and application-specific programmable processor design [4]. Previous work in the area of dynamic repair had made use of specialized redundant units to replace damaged units; their paper describes the synthesis of more general units that can replace any of several units on a chip when damage is detected. The authors coin the term HBISR (*heterogeneous BISR*) for the technique.

A *morphable multiplier* is a device capable of performing either a floating point multiply or add using the same hardware structure [2]. Morphable multipliers require less area than the sum of the area needed for a separate multiplier and adder (in fact, they require only slightly more than a multiplier alone), while imposing negligible performance penalties.

Metrics like area, performance, and power are easily quantified, but it is less obvious how to measure the increasingly important metric of hardware flexibility. Compton and Hauck have defined a testing method and quantification metric for flexibility of reconfigurable hardware [5]. Other examples of relevant research in reconfigurable hardware include Kim et al. [6] and Chiou et al. [7].

The work in this paper makes use of Brook [8], a stream-based programming language which allows the programmer to write general-purpose applications for a GPU without worrying about the sometimes byzantine details of GPU programming. Our experiments all use Chromium [9] to intercept and analyze streams of graphics commands made by real applications. The primary advantage of using Chromium is that we ensure that our workloads are not contrived. Although we use Brook and Chromium without modification, we have enhanced the Qsilver graphics architectural simulator [10, 11] to model the necessary aspects of the fragment pipeline. A detailed description of our modifications to QSilver and our experimental setup are presented in Sect. 3 and Sect. 4.

3   Simulation Setup

Qsilver is a simulation framework for graphics architectures that can simulate low-level GPU activity for any existing OpenGL application [10]. Qsilver uses Chromium [9] to intercept and transform an OpenGL application's API calls and create an annotated trace that encapsulates geometry, timing, and state information. This trace serves as input to the Qsilver simulator core, which performs an accurate timing simulation of the graphics hardware and produces detailed statistics.

Qsilver is configured at runtime with a description of its pipeline. In these experiments we simulate an NV4x-like architecture, with a pipeline configuration similar to that of NVIDIA's 6800 GT, so we configure Qsilver to model a system with 6 vertex pipelines and 16 fragment pipelines. The fragments are tiled in blocks of 2 × 2, so we effectively have 4 tile pipelines, each of which can process 4 fragments simultaneously. NV4x GPUs use a similar tiled configuration in the fragment engine [12].

To account for modifications to the fragment pipeline, we enhanced Qsilver to track fragment shader activity. Our modified Qsilver simulator stores a per-triangle identifier which uniquely specifies which, if any, fragment shader was bound when that triangle was being rendered. We also store the text of the fragment shaders so that they can be analyzed by the Qsilver simulator core.

Both of the following experiments hold fixed the graphics pipeline described above and focus on the programmable path of the fragment engine. While the NV4x vertex engine follows a MIMD architecture, its fragment engine is truly SIMD in nature. Additionally, in many modern games the majority of fragments are shaded by fragment programs (see Fig. 5), so we focus our efforts on the programmable path in the fragment engine.

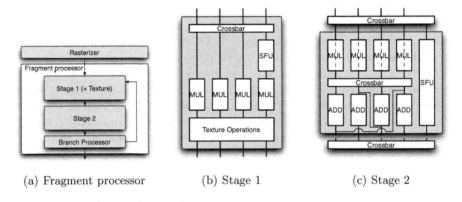

(a) Fragment processor   (b) Stage 1   (c) Stage 2

Fig. 2. Baseline fragment units used for comparison. Stage 2 can take up to three 4-channel operands, one of which directly feeds the ADD units and whose data path is represented here by dashed lines. Note the additional data paths that cascade the ADD units; these allow for a single-pass dot product [13].

Our baseline fragment pipeline, depicted in Fig. 2, is similar to that found in NV4x GPUs[1]. A single fragment unit contains two stages; four-channel fragments (RGBA) reach stage 1 from either the rasterizer or fragment pipeline loopback. Stage 2 can execute instructions in parallel with stage 1 in *dual-issue* mode as well sequentially, taking its operands from the output of stage 1. Crossbars route operands to the appropriate functional units, and *Special Function Units* (SFUs) are used to perform special scalar operations like reciprocal square root. The fragment units can also operate in *co-issue* mode, whereby a single 4-channel data path functions as two distinct data paths, with independent instructions executing in parallel, on the same unit, across these two data paths—e.g., a 3-vector and a scalar, or two 2-vectors [12].

---

[1] Based on those details that have been made available to the public or indirectly obtained via patents and extensive benchmark tests. For additional details, see [12] and [13].

4 Experiments and Results

In this section, we describe two experiments we performed to validate our hypothesis that using SSR components in a modern GPU architecture can benefit certain applications. We show improved performance in the recent game Doom III with only a minimal impact on GPU die area and also demonstrate that double-precision floating point capabilities can be added to the fragment pipeline without affecting the performance of single-precision applications.

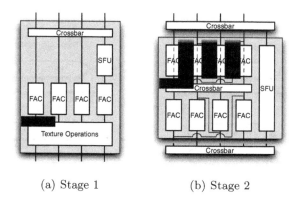

(a) Stage 1   (b) Stage 2

Fig. 3. Proposed SSR fragment units for the first experiment. FAC modules are Flexible Arithmetic Units, and they replace each of the ADD and MUL units in our baseline architecture.

4.1 Increased Throughput

We first compared the simulated performance of the NV4x-like fragment pipeline to that of an SSR fragment pipeline architecture, whose fragment units are depicted in Fig. 3. The fragment units in our target SSR architecture are similar to those in the baseline architecture; however, we replace both the multipliers and adders in stages 1 and 2 with single-precision Flexible Arithmetic Units (FACs). An FAC can be very quickly reconfigured to perform either a multiplication or an addition and uses only slightly more gates than a multiplier. With current technology, these FACs can produce a result every cycle and can be reconfigured between cycles, assuming a 400 MHz clock and a two-stage pipeline [2]. Finally, in the first set of FACs in our SSR architecture, we duplicate the accumulate data paths from the baseline architecture's ADD units. These data paths require a trivial amount of additional area overhead.

In addition to supporting all the existing functionality of our baseline units, the modified SSR units provide new scheduling opportunities beyond those of the baseline. First, the baseline fragment pipe is only capable of performing a single full-precision 4-vector addition per pass in stage 2 [13], while the SSR pipeline is capable of performing three in one pass—one in stage 1 and two chained additions in stage 2 (see Fig. 4a). Moreover, there is more freedom to schedule dot product and multiply-accumulate operations, both of which are extremely common in fragment programs. For example, the SSR pipeline can execute a 32-bit 3-channel dot product (DP3) and dependent scalar-vector multiplication—e.g., the expression $(A \cdot B)C$—in a single pass by computing the per-channel multiply of A and B in stage 1, accumulating the channel products to obtain $A \cdot B$ in the first set of FACs in stage 2, and performing a scalar-vector multiply in its second set of FACs (Fig. 4b). Extending this scheduling approach to co-issue configurations is straightforward.

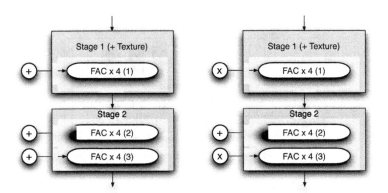

(a) Single-pass configuration for multiple 4-vector additions.

(b) Single-pass configuration to compute $(A \cdot B)C$.

Fig. 4. Two example configurations that provide additional scheduling opportunities for the SSR fragment pipeline

Given these additional scheduling opportunities and the known scheduling constraints of NV4x GPUs, we hand-scheduled fragment programs intercepted from a 50-frame Doom III demo (see Fig. 5), which was then simulated under Qsilver. We used *NVShaderPerf*[2]—a utility that displays shader scheduling information for NVIDIA hardware—to schedule programs for our baseline architecture simulation. While NV4x GPUs have dedicated hardware for performing common half-precision operations in parallel with full-precision operations, none of the fragment programs tested included any half-precision operations. However, to be sure of a legitimate comparison of performance along the full-precision path, we forced *NVShaderPerf* to schedule programs for our NV4x-like architecture using the full-precision path only. We limited program schedules for the SSR architecture to the full-precision path as well.

From the simulation of this data stream, we obtained a 4.27% speedup over the entire graphics pipeline for the SSR architecture. Equally as important, based on conservative inverter-equivalent gate count estimates[3], each FAC requires 12,338

---

[2] Unified compiler version 77.80.

[3] All area estimates are given in terms of inverter-equivalent gate area unless otherwise specified.

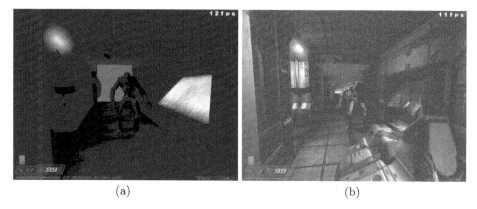

(a)   (b)

Fig. 5. Screen captures from Doom III. On the left, the color of each pixel is modulated to indicate which fragment program generated it. The right image is the unmodified rendering from the game. Notice that the majority of pixels are generated by programmable fragment shaders.

gates, only 710 more than a single-precision multiplier (11,628 gates). Replacing the adders (7,782 gates) requires 4,556 additional gates. This additionally requires the small overhead of a multiplexer to configure the FACs. Given these gate estimates, with 16 fragment pipelines, the cost of our proposed use of SSR is 382,464 gates, which is less than 0.2% of the total area of NVIDIA's 6800 GT (an estimated 222 million transistors[14]).

4.2   Dual-Mode IEEE Adders and Multipliers

The GPGPU and scientific computing communities would like to have the ability to perform double-precision calculations on the GPU. Unfortunately for them, the gaming industry drives the graphics hardware industry, and games do not currently require double-precision. We present a method here that can satisfy the demands of the scientific community without compromising the performance of the single-precision path so crucial to video game performance.

A dual-mode floating point unit is a small-scale reconfigurable unit capable of performing two simultaneous single-precision operations or one double-precision operation. Dual-mode units can be fully pipelined to produce results every cycle. Like other SSR units, dual-mode multipliers and adders require internal multiplexers for path selection. Additionally, they require a rounding unit capable of flexible rounding modes. The total additional structure for this modification is insignificant [3].

We simulate a pipeline in Qsilver that uses dual-mode multipliers and adders in the fragment engine, where we replace pairs of single-precision FPUs in the baseline architecture with a single corresponding dual-mode FPU. This effectively gives us an 8-wide double-precision fragment engine with approximately half the throughput of the single-precision configuration. Double-precision configuration also requires that we retask pairs of 32-bit registers as single 64-bit registers. With half as many fragment pipelines, each double-precision pipe has the same number of available 64-bit registers as each single-precision pipe has 32-bit registers (four 32-bit registers per fragment in the case of NV4x GPUs [12]). By a similar argument, the bandwidth requirements for the memory and register bus systems in 8-wide double-precision mode should not exceed those of the original 16-wide single-precision configuration.

We have conservative area estimates for a double-precision adder and multiplier of 13,456 gates and 37,056 gates, respectively. The real overhead here comes from replacing each pair of single-precision FPUs with one dual-mode FPU, at an approximate cost of 815,744 gates over the entire fragment engine, or 0.4% of the 6800 GT's total area. Note that we have modified only the multiplication and addition units, so additional precision is not available for specialized operations such as logarithms or square roots. Although many scientific applications would benefit greatly from high precision addition and multiplication alone, a full double-precision arithmetic engine would be ideal. Dual-mode reciprocal, square-root, logarithm, and other specialized units are a topic for future exploration.

To validate our SSR-based graphics architecture capable of both single- and double-precision, we traced four Brook demo programs through Qsilver:

1. **bitonic_sort**, a parallel sorting network
2. **image_proc(25,25)**, an image convolution shader
3. **particle_cloth(5,10,15)**, a cloth simulation
4. **volume_division(100)**, a volume isosurface extractor.

The results are summarized in Table 1. This table lists the cycle counts for each application in both single- and double-precision modes. Note that the double-precision calculations never require more than twice as long as the corresponding single-precision calculation. Because the timing results are identical for dual-mode units configured in single-precision mode and dedicated single-precision units, we have shown that by using SSR we can add double-precision addition and multiplication to the graphics pipeline with only a modest increase in gate count and without affecting the performance of the commonly-used single-precision path.

5   Conclusions

We have extended Qsilver to record information on fragment program state in its annotated trace. Our modified Qsilver core then uses this new information, along with fragment program listings and timing information, to model the programmable fragment engine of an NV4x-like architecture. With this framework in place, we have demonstrated the applicability of Small-Scale Reconfigurability to graphics architectures. We have shown that it is possible to increase the throughput of the fragment engine with only a small increase in die area. In addition, we have demonstrated that dual-mode multipliers and adders can provide double-precision in the fragment engine to support scientific computing in the

Table 1. Single- and double-precision GPGPU computations using SSR. Each application comes with the Brook distribution. The *32-bit cycles* row shows the GPU cycle count for our NV4x-like architecture. Note that these timings are identical whether we are using a dual-mode unit configured in single-precision mode or a dedicated single-precision unit. The *64-bit cycles* row shows the cycles required for double-precision after reconfiguration. As expected, none of the programs takes more than twice as long with double-precision than with single-precision.

Demo	bitonic_sort	image_proc	particle_cloth	volume_division
32-bit cycles	468	1,292	19,504	254,923,418
64-bit cycles	877	2,525	38,959	509,846,783
32-bit→64-bit speedup	.534	.512	.501	.500

GPGPU community with no detriment to the gamers who drive the market. The vector-like operations performed on GPUs make them a particularly good target for such techniques, since need for reconfiguration is rare in SIMD environments, and since the cost of reconfiguration is amortized over many operations.

6   Future Work

The fragment engine is one of many elements of the graphics pipeline. Applications of SSR will likely yield similar performance improvements in other units as well. Another area of exploration that is likely to be fruitful for SSR is power consumption. Whenever portions of a chip are unused, they use no dynamic power, but they leak static power. By their very nature, SSR components are rarely idle, and should therefore leak a minimum of static power. Power leakage is currently a major issue with GPUs, and reducing leakage becomes crucial as continuing improvements in chip manufacturing technology exacerbate this problem [10].

Acknowledgments

We would like to thank John Lach for his input on SSR and Peter Djeu for his collaboration on Chromium extensions. This work was funded by NSF grants CCF-0429765, CCR-0306404, and CCF-0205324.

References

[1] Vijay Kumar, V., Lach, J.: Designing, scheduling, and allocating flexible arithmetic components. In: Proceedings of the International Conference on Field Programmable Logic and Applications. (2003)
[2] Chiricescu, S., Schuette, M., Glinton, R., Schmit, H.: Morphable multipliers. In: Proceedings of the International Conference on Field Programmable Logic and Applications. (2002)

108   K. Dale et al.

[3] Even, G., Mueller, S.M., Seidel, P.M.: A dual mode IEEE multiplier. In: Proceedings of the International Conference on Innovative Systems in Silicon. (1997)

[4] Guerra, L.M., Potkonjak, M., Rabaey, J.M.: Behavioral-level synthesis of heterogeneous bisr reconfigurable asic's. IEEE Transactions on VLSI (1998)

[5] Compton, K., Hauck, S.: Flexibility measurement of domain-specific reconfigurable hardware. In: Proceedings of the ACM/SIGDA Symposium on Field-programmable Gate Arrays. (2004)

[6] Kim, K., Karri, R., Potkonjak, M.: Synthesis of application specific programmable processors. In: Proceedings of Design Automation. (1997)

[7] Chiou, L.Y., Bhunia, S., Roy, K.: Synthesis of application-specific highly efficient multi-mode cores for embedded systems. ACM Transactions on Embedded Computing Systems (2005)

[8] Buck, I., Foley, T., Horn, D., Sugerman, J., Fatahalian, K., Houston, M., , Hanrahan, P.: Brook for GPUs: Stream computing on graphics hardware. ACM Transactions on Graphics (2004)

[9] Humphreys, G., Houston, M., Ng, R., Ahern, S., Frank, R., Kirchner, P., Klosowski, J.T.: Chromium: A stream processing framework for interactive graphics on clusters of workstations. ACM Transactions on Graphics **21**(3) (2002) 693–702

[10] Sheaffer, J.W., Luebke, D.P., Skadron, K.: A flexible simulation framework for graphics architectures. In: Proceedings of SIGGRAPH/Eurographics Workshop on Graphics Hardware. (2004)

[11] Sheaffer, J.W., Skadron, K., Luebke, D.P.: Studying thermal management for graphics-processor architectures. In: Proceedings of 2005 IEEE International Symposium on Performance Analysis of Systems and Software. (2005)

[12] Kilgariff, E., Fernando, R. In: The GeForce 6 Series GPU Architecture. Addison-Wesley Pub Co (2005) 471–491

[13] Seifert, A.: NV40 technology explained (2004) `http://3dcenter.org/artikel/nv40_pipeline/index3_e.php`.

[14] Medvedev, A., Budankov, K.: NVIDIA GeForce 6800 Ultra (NV40) (2004) `http://www.digit-life.com/articles2/gffx/nv40-part1-a.html`.

An Embedded Multi-camera System for Simultaneous Localization and Mapping

Vanderlei Bonato, José A. de Holanda, and Eduardo Marques

Institute of Mathematics and Computing Sciences,
University of São Paulo, São Paulo, Brazil

Abstract. This paper presents an embedded multi-camera system for Simultaneous Localization and Mapping (SLAM) for mobile robots. The multi-camera system has been designed and implemented as a SoC (System-on-a-Chip), using reconfigurable computing technology. In this system the images are captured in real-time by means of four CMOS digital cameras. After some pre-processing steps, those images are sent to an embedded softcore processor by a direct memory access (DMA) channel. In this system, images are captured, pre-processed and sent to the embedded processor at 30 frames per second in color mode and 60 frames per second in gray-scale mode. This paper also shows the main advantages of using multi-cameras to implement SLAM based on the Extended Kalman Filter.

1 Introduction

Robots have been used in industries since they were invented. Nowadays they are still expanding and a new generation of service robots for personal use is appearing. This category of robots is produced for a mass market and is used mainly in the domestic environment (household). Besides the price represents only a fraction of robots' prices used for industrial purposes. Nowadays, there is in a great quantity of robots to vacuum dust, to cut grass and to entertain on the market. Other models of robots for surveillance, the elderly and child care are also being introduced.

Recent technological advances in VLSI are making possible an entire range of new applications embedded on chips. Mobile robots is an area of increasing interest, either in the research community, or commercial ventures. However, such robots require powerful underlying computing systems, often in the form of dedicated hardware. Reconfigurable computing technology, specially FPGAs (Field-Programmable Gate Arrays), are creating new opportunities for the implementation of mobile robots [9]. For instance, its application in aerospace science is a reality [13]: Xilinx's FPGAs were used by robots recently sent to Mars by NASA (National Aeronautics and Space Administration).

The use of FPGAs is a flexible alternative to implement complex models, as the hardware functionality can be changed according to the task to be executed [5]. It can also be argued that FPGAs are able to execute image processing

K. Bertels, J.M.P. Cardoso, and S. Vassiliadis (Eds.): ARC 2006, LNCS 3985, pp. 109–114, 2006.

algorithms with speed comparable to graphics processing custom chips [14]. Relying on this technology, we present the implementation of a *multi-camera* for SLAM (Simultaneous Localization and Mapping) algorithm [10] using four smart cameras distributed along the robot perimeter. In general terms, a smart camera system can be seen as a camera, which captures not only images, but also high-level descriptions of a scene [12]. By doing so, other applications besides SLAM could be enhanced by our system, such as surveillance, motion analysis, pattern identification, virtual reality systems, and man-machine communication.

The multi-camera system described in this paper aims to improve the robustness of the SLAM algorithms based only on vision. In addition, it also aims to reduce the computational complexity of the SLAM implemented with Extended Kalman Filter (EKF). This strategy of using multi-cameras for SLAM has been discussed in [7], where two independent cameras are used to increase the EKF convergency speed to reduce the computational complexity of this filter.

The remaining of this paper is organized as follows. Sect. 2 presents the multi-camera system components. Sect. 3 explains the advantages of using this system, followed by experimental results in Sect. 4. Finally, Sect. 5 concludes the article.

2 The Multi-camera System

The multi-camera system was designed to work as an accurate vision sensor for SLAM algorithms based on EKF. The system is composed of four CMOS cameras connect to the Nios-Stratix Development board [2]. This kind of reconfigurable technology provides resources enough to implement complex system as a SoPC (System-on-a-Programmable-Chip) [6].

2.1 Hardware Implementation

Most of SLAM systems are implemented in general purpose architecture, being more specific, in personal computers, such as Desktops or Notebooks. The implementation in this kind of architecture is easier than that on-a-chip, since the system designers do not need to configure hardware implementation details, such as the hardware/software codesign [11]. However, when the SLAM processing architecture must be customized to an embedded system, for instance personal robots, a general purpose architecture will probably not be suitable for it, since this kind of system normally requires low power, small size, and low cost.

In Fig. 1 is presented the hardware integration of the smart cameras with the Nios II softcore processor [1], which will run the SLAM algorithms. To connect these components, the Avalon Switch Fabric bus with a direct memory access (DMA) is being used to speed up the communication. The DMA reads data from the smart cameras and send them to the SLAM processor memory.

2.2 Smart Camera

The functional structure of the smart camera system is shown in the block diagram in Fig. 2. The structure consists of a pipeline of blocks for image

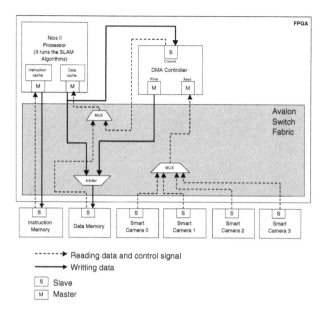

Fig. 1. Hardware system integration

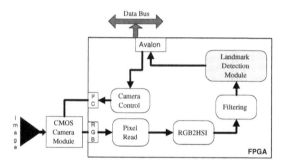

Fig. 2. Vision system blocks diagram

pre-processing operations, which are implemented in hardware and executed in parallel, and of a module for detecting natural landmarks, which is being implemented in software. These landmarks are references used in the map generated by the EKF SLAM algorithm [4]. Each of those blocks is responsible for a specific image processing step, such as image capturing, RGB to HSI color conversion and image filtering. These image pre-processing steps are described in [3].

3   Multi-cameras and EKF

The multi-camera system needs a lot of hardware resources to be implemented. However, this amount of resource usage can be compensated, since the accuracy and convergency speed of the EKF increase with the quantity of sensors, as can be seen in Fig. 3. In this demonstration, the signal accuracy is given by an unidimensional gaussian density function. The EKF integrates the four sensor information and generates the μ. With this result, we can notice that the μ data is the most precise. The EKF equations used in this graphical demonstration can be found in [8].

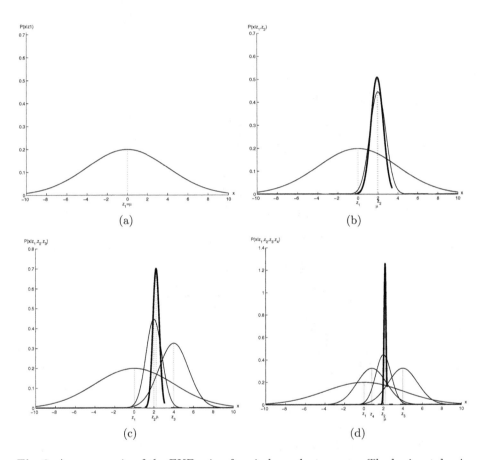

Fig. 3. Accuracy gain of the EKF using four independent sensors. The horizontal axis shows the data from four sensors (cameras) (z_1, z_2, z_3, z_4) and the vertical axis shows the probability of this data to be correct.

4   Experimental Results

This section presents some experimental results related to the multi-camera system described in this paper, in particular its performance, and hardware and software resources employed. The development of a prototype system has been done mainly using two Altera tools: Quartus II V4.2, and SOPC Builder. The hardware platform is composed of a Nios-Stratix development board, featuring an EP1S10F780C6 FPGA. This reconfigurable device contains 10.570 logical elements, and 920 Kbits of RAM memory. The processor used to implement the detection of natural landmark is the Nios II softcore, which is synthesized as a component into the FPGA board. The development board with the four smart cameras will be embedded in a pioneer 3DX robot base, as shown in Fig. 4.

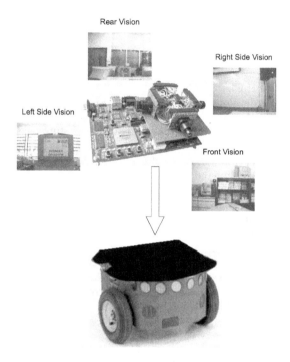

Fig. 4. Multi-camera system embedded in the Pioneer 3DX robot base

The communication channel among the cameras and the Nios II processor, where the SLAM algorithm will be implemented (see Fig. 1), achieved at least 30 frames per second in color mode and 60 frames per second in gray-scale mode. The image resolution in both modes is 320x240 pixels. This integration was done by the Avalon Switch Fabric bus provided by SOPC Builder tool, where an DMA channel reads data from the smart-cameras and sends them to the memory data of the Nios II processor. The resource usage to implement this multi-camera system is 5,699 logic elements and 603KBits of memory from the P1S10F780C6 FPGA.

5   Conclusion

In this paper we have shown a multi-camera system for mobile robots, which provides data to a SLAM algorithm based on EKF. This system is implemented as a SoPC using FPGA technology. The evaluation of a prototype implementation showed that the multi-camera system achieved a real-time performance. At a resolution of 320x240 pixels, the system was able to process 30 frames per second in color mode and 60 frames per second in gray-scale mode. It means that the whole system can capture images from the image sensors, run the pre-processing steps, and finally send the data to the SLAM processor in real-time. In addition, as only 53% of the FPGA capacity is used, it should be possible to add new image processing functions, if required by other applications.

References

1. Altera Corp. Nios II CPU. 2004.
2. Altera Corp. Nios development kit, stratix edition. 2005.
3. Vanderlei Bonato, Adriano K. Sanches, M.M. Fernandes, João M. P. Cardoso, E. D. V. Simoes, and Eduardo Marques. A real time gesture recognition system for mobile robots. In *International Conference on Informatics in Control, Automation and Robotics (ICINCO-2004)*, pages 207–214, Setúbal, Portugal, 2004.
4. Johann Borenstein, Commander H. R. Everett, and Liqiang Feng. Where am i? sensors and methods for mobile robot positioning. 1996.
5. Stephen Brown and Zvonko Vranesic. *Fundamentals of digital logic with VHDL design.* Mc Graw Hill, Toronto, 2 edition, 2005.
6. Ali Habibi and Sofiène Tahar. A survey on system-on-a-chip design languages. In *The 3rd IEEE International Workshop on System-on-Chip for Real-Time Applications*, pages 212–215, Calgary, Alberta, Canada, 2003.
7. Gab-Hoe Kim, Jong-Sung Kim, and Ki-Sang Hong. Vision-based simultaneous localization and mapping with two cameras. In *IEEE International Conference on Intelligent Robots and Systems*, pages 3401–3406, 2005.
8. Peter S. Maybeck. *Stochastic models, estimation, and control*, volume 1. Academic Press, London, 1979.
9. Lara Simsie. Using programmable logic for embedded systems. Technical report, Altera Corporation, December 2003.
10. Randall Smith, Matthew Self, and Peter Cheeseman. Estimating uncertain spatial relationships in robotics. pages 167–193, 1990.
11. Bräunl Thomas. *Embedded Robotics: Mobile Robot Design and Applications with Embedded Systems.* Springer-Verlag, Berlin and Heidelberg, 2003.
12. Wayne Wolf, Burak Ozer, and Tiehan Lv. Smart cameras as embedded systems. *IEEE Computer Society*, pages 48–53, 2002.
13. Xilinx Inc. Aerospace & defense. 2004.
14. Pavel Zemcik. Hardware acceleration of graphics and imaging algorithms using fpgas. pages 25–32, 2002.

Performance/Cost Trade-Off Evaluation for the DCT Implementation on the Dynamically Reconfigurable Processor

Vu Manh Tuan, Yohei Hasegawa, Naohiro Katsura, and Hideharu Amano

Graduate School of Science and Technology, Keio University
3-14-1 Hiyoshi, Kohoku-ku, Yokohama, Kanagawa 223-8522, Japan
drp@am.ics.keio.ac.jp

Abstract. The Dynamically Reconfigurable Processor (DRP) developed by NEC Electronics is a coarse grain reconfigurable processor with the capability of changing its hardware functionality within a clock cycle. While implementing an application on the DRP, designers face the task of selecting how to efficiently use resources in order to achieve particular goals such as to improve the performance, to reduce the power dissipation, or to minimize the resource use. To analyze the impact of trade-off selections on these aspects, the Discrete Cosine Transform (DCT) algorithm has been implemented exploiting various design policies. The evaluation result shows that the performance, cost and consuming power are influenced by the implementation method. For example, the execution time can reduce 17% in case of using the distributed memory against the register files; or up to 40% whether the embedded multipliers are used.

1 Introduction

Dynamically reconfigurable devices have the potential to provide high processing performance, flexibility and power efficiency especially for a wide range of stream and network processing applications. Recently, the development of dynamically reconfigurable processors such as DRP [1], DAPDNA-2[2], XPP[3] and D-Fabrix[4] have been received much attention for their remarkable achievements. Such devices incorporate following characteristics:

1. A dynamically reconfigurable processor consists of an array of coarse-grained processing elements (PEs), distributed memory modules and finite-state-machine-based sequencers. Execution circuits can be freely configured by programming the instruction set of the PEs and wiring between PEs. The chip achieves high performance using customized data path configurations comprised of arrays of PEs.
2. An application can be implemented either as multi-task or time-division execution. A multi-context mechanism, which stores a number of configuration data for the same PE array, allows the capability of changing the hardware functionality of the on-chip circuit, often in one clock cycle.
3. High-level design languages, automatic synthesis techniques and place-and-route tools are often applied to ease the development process.

K. Bertels, J.M.P. Cardoso, and S. Vassiliadis (Eds.): ARC 2006, LNCS 3985, pp. 115–121, 2006.
© Springer-Verlag Berlin Heidelberg 2006

While developing a certain application, there is often a trade-off to be made between improving the performance and reducing the cost. In order to quantitatively analyze the impact of resource usage on the performance and the power dissipation of a dynamically reconfigurable processor, a typical task DCT used in JPEG codes is chosen to implement on the target device DRP-1 using different design policies.

The rest of this paper is organized as follows. Section 2 describes the DRP architecture, which is the target device of this study. The evaluation results and analysis are illustrated in the Section 3. Finally, the conclusion of this research is mentioned in Section 4.

2 DRP Overview

DRP is a coarse-grain dynamically reconfigurable processor that was released by NEC Electronics in 2002 [1]. DRP-1 is the prototype chip fabricated with 0.18-um 8-metal layer CMOS processes. It consists of 8-tile DRP Core, eight 32-bit multipliers, an external SRAM controller, a PCI interface, and 256-bit I/Os. The structure of DRP-1 is shown on the Fig.1.

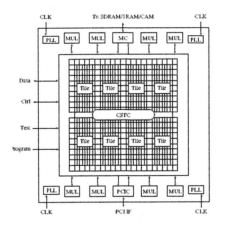

Fig. 1. DRP-1 architecture   **Fig. 2.** DRP tile architecture

The primitive unit of DRP Core is called a `Tile', and the number of Tiles can be expandable, horizontally and vertically. The primitive modules of the Tile are processing elements (PEs), State Transition Controller (STC), 2-ported memories (VMEMs: Vertical MEMories), VMEM Controller (VMCtrl) and 1-ported memories (HMEMs: Horizontal MEMories). The structure of a Tile is shown in Fig. 2. Each has an 8-bit ALU, an 8-bit DMU, and an 8-bit x 16-word register file. These units are connected by programmable wires specified by instruction data. PE has 16-depth instruction memories and supports multiple context operation which can be changed with a clock cycle by an instruction pointer delivered from STC.

An integrated design environment, called Musketeer, is available for DRP-1. It includes a high level synthesis tool, a design mapper for DRP, simulators, and a layout viewer tool. Applications can be written in a C-like high level hardware description language called BDL, synthesized, and mapped directly onto the DRP-1.

3 Trade-Off of the Design Policies

This section presents quantitative evaluation results of different DCT implementations with following evaluation metrics.

- **Performance:** The performance of an implementation can be expressed by its execution time for a given set of data. The execution time is computed as the product of the delay or the critical path and the number of execution clock cycles.
- **Power and energy consumption:** The power consumption for an application can be estimated from the power profile based on the simulation. Here, the energy consumption, which is defined as the product of the power consumption and the execution time, can be used as a general measure for evaluation. The energy consumption is also the total energy necessary for executing a target application. Small energy consumption means the high degree of efficiency in the computation.
- **Required resource:** The required resource of each implementation is the total number of PEs used for each context. It shows not only the PE usability, but also the parallel processing capability of the application.

Following design policies are chosen and compared with each other in order to clarify the performance/cost trade-off.

- Memory array vs. register array
- Multiplier use vs. no-multiplier use
- Optimum context sizes

3.1 Memory Array vs. Register Array

In BDL, an array variable can be assigned either to registers or to memory modules. The difference is that while a memory access requires a clock latency, data read out from a register file can be processed in the same clock.

Table 1. DCT implementation using different types of array

	VMEM	HMEM	Register
Delay or critical path (ns)	72.512	75.264	104.112
Execution time (μs)	8.05	8.35	9.68
Power consumption (mW)	368.97	356.56	315.53
Energy consumption (μsW)	2.97	2.98	3.05
Clock cycles	111	111	93

Table 1 shows the results of the DCT implementation when the input data block is stored in VMEMs, HMEMs and registers respectively. The DCT version using the VMEM has the best result in terms of the critical path, while the execution time of the case of using register is the worst because of the large delay time by reading registers in the same clock cycle. However, the register-based design achieves the best result in terms of the number of clock cycles; and it also consumes small power consumption. Execution with low clock frequency but small number of steps can reduce power. In terms of the execution time and the energy consumption, the VMEM use policy out-performs the register use policy by about 17% and 3% respectively. Although the power of register based design is small, the total energy consumption is increased be-cause of its long execution time.

Fig. 3 illustrates the required resources where "*PEs*" denotes the number of required PEs in each context. From Fig. 3, it is easy to point out that al-though the number of contexts is different the required number of PEs is well distributed into each context, while the PE usability in VMEM and HMEM cases is quite imbalanced. Since the total cost is depending on the

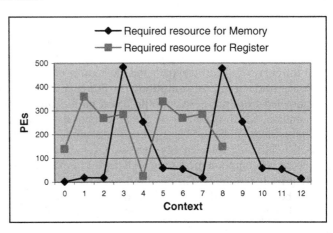

Fig. 3. Required resource for Memory and Register-use policy

maximum number of required PEs in all contexts, the register based design is advan-tageous from the viewpoint of the cost.

3.2 Multiplier Use vs. No-Multiplier Use

The DRP supports two types of multiplication. If the multiplier factor is a constant, the multiplication is automatically transformed into shifts and additions by the DRP com-piler. On the other hand, since the DRP has eight 32-bit multipliers distributed on the top and the bottom of the chip (Fig. 1), multiplications can be performed using these embedded multipliers. Using the multipliers has two limitations: their numbers are limited, and there is a delay of two clock cycles from the input of data until the result is available although pipelined operation is allowed.

Table 2. DCT implementation using different strategies of multiplication

	Memory		Register	
	Multiplier	No-multiplier	Multiplier	No-multiplier
Delay or critical path (ns)	30.611	72.512	53.913	104.112
Execution time (μs)	4.87	8.05	6.74	9.68
Energy consumption (μsW)	3.74	2.97	3.37	3.05

Table 2 shows the results of the DCT implementation in case multipliers are used or not for the memory-based design and the register-based design respectively. The results prove that although multipliers are located far from PEs and have certain limitations; their use could lead to satisfactory outcomes. Using the multipliers achieves the shortest critical path as well as the highest throughput. However, in terms of the power consumption and the number of clocks, using the multipliers does not outperform the case without them; especially, the design using multipliers dissipate almost double power as that without multipliers, although the power of multipliers itself is not counted in the value because of the problem of the profiler. The large power consumption, in this case, mainly comes from its high clock frequency.

The energy consumption proves that, in general, the no-multiplier policy is more efficient than the multiplier-use policy as illustrated on the above table. In terms of the execution time, the multiplier-use with memory policy outperforms the no-multiplier policy by about 40%. Nonetheless, the no-multiplier with memory design consumes power about 53% less than the multiplier-use design; more importantly, the no-multiplier design proves to be more effective about 10% in term of the energy consumption.

Fig.4 presents the resource required in the DCT implementation using the multipliers for the memory-based design and the register-based design. The necessary resources when the multipliers are not used are shown in Fig.3. As expected, the use of multiplier reduces the resources dramatically.

In general, the best version of the DCT implementation is the case when using the multipliers coupled with VMEM based design in terms of both the performance and the resource usage. On the contrary, in terms of the

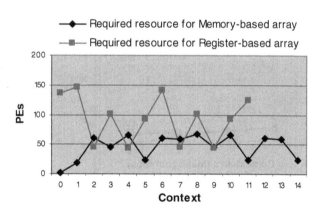

Fig. 4. Required resource when using multipliers

power efficiency, the case when the multipliers are not used and data are stored in the registers is the best, although it is the worst from the viewpoint of the performance and the resource usage.

3.3 Optimum Context Sizes

Fig. 5 presents different parameters of the DCT implementation on the DRP against the context size. Evaluation results of performance show that execution time can be reduced with a large context size because of the parallel processing. On the other hand, the critical path tends to increase when the context size becomes large with some exceptions. Therefore, the performance improvement by increasing the context size faces a certain limitation.

In contrast with the performance, the power consumption seems to increase with the larger context size. The reason is that the larger context size means the more number of PEs used to form computation circuits, which requires more power. Besides, as the context size becomes larger, additional wires are necessary to connect more PEs together, so the power dissipation tends to increase. Nevertheless, the energy consumption reduces when the context size becomes large, since the execution time is reduced. As a result, it is likely that the larger context size provides the better performance/cost ratio for solving DCT.

From Fig. 5, it is quite clear that there exists an optimum context size, where both the performance and the power dissipation are well balanced. In case of the DCT application, when the context size is 6, the execution time, the power dissipation and the energy consumption are not much different from that of the maximum context size. More importantly, the energy consumption shows that the 6-tile case is the best case in terms of performance and the cost.

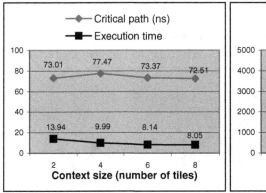 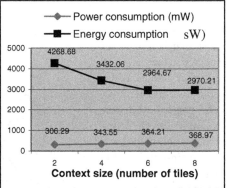

Fig. 5. Critical path, Execution time, Power and Energy consumption vs. context size

4 Conclusion

This paper presents the performance/cost trade-off when designing applications on a dynamically reconfigurable processor based on implementations of the DCT algorithm. Results show that implementation policies on the array data allocation and usage of multipliers influence the performance, cost and power consumption. The optimal context size also should be chosen. Based on the analysis, a tool for rapidly developing a prototype or a model of target applications to help the designers' decision is required.

References

[1] M.Motomura, "A Dynamically Reconfigurable Processor Architecture", In Microprocessor Forum, Oct. 2002.

[2] IPFlex. http://www.ipflex.com/.

[3] PACT. http://www.pactcorp.com/.

[4] Elixent. http://www.elixent.com/.

[5] M. Suzuki, Y. Hasegawa, Y. Yamada, N. Kaneko, K. Deguchi, H. Amano, K. Anjo, M. Motomura, K. Wakabayashi, T. Toi, and T. Awashima, "Stream Applications on the Dynamically Reconfigurable Processor", In Proceedings of International Conference on Field Programmable Technology (FPT2004), pages 137-144, Dec. 2004.

Trigonometric Computing Embedded in a Dynamically Reconfigurable CORDIC System-on-Chip

Francisco Fons[1], Mariano Fons[1], Enrique Cantó[1], and Mariano López[2]

[1] Departament d'Enginyeria Electrònica, Elèctrica i Automàtica
Universitat Rovira i Virgili, ETSE, Tarragona, Spain
[2] Departament d'Enginyeria Electrònica
Universitat Politècnica de Catalunya, EPSEVG, Vilanova i la Geltrú, Spain

Abstract. This work presents the custom-made design of a 32-bit fixed-point trigonometric computer based on the CORDIC (Coordinate Rotation Digital Computer) algorithm and embedded in an AT94K40 system-on-chip device. This platform –composed of a 8-bit MCU that handles the program flow and a dynamically reconfigurable FPGA that synthesizes an evolvable slave coprocessor to speed up the calculus– provides a balanced control-computing architecture to efficiently process functions as $\sin(z)$, $\cos(z)$, $\mathrm{atan}(y/x)$ and $\mathrm{sqrt}(x^2+y^2)$. This approach reaches significant area-time optimizations over other traditional software-oriented solutions inspired on powerful stand-alone microprocessors.

1 Introduction

Nowadays trigonometric computing is present in a broad field of engineering applications: navigation systems that calculate trajectories in real-time (robotics) or image processing (fingerprint minutiae-oriented matching in biometrics) are some examples. An efficient technique for this computing is the CORDIC method. The development of FPGA-based systems emerged as a viable means of offsetting software-oriented alternatives in such kinds of compute-intensive applications. Also, CORDIC designs exhibit potential characteristics to exploit by flexible hardware: reconfigurable computing technologies permit to improve the CORDIC implementation mainly by taking advantage of the high similarity between the different CORDIC operation modes.

Next, section 2 summarizes the CORDIC concept. Section 3 covers the technical criteria followed to embed the trigonometric coprocessor in the AT94K40 device. Finally, experimental results and conclusions are presented in sections 4 and 5.

2 CORDIC Algorithm

The CORDIC concept allows the computing of elementary operations such as products, divisions and trigonometric/hyperbolic functions. It consists in performing a linear, circular or hyperbolic rotation of a 2-D vector a desired angle *6* decomposing this into a sum of micro-rotations of predefined elementary angles θ_i expressed as values that depend on the *i*-th power of 2, thus left in a good place to be efficiently computed by hardware through simple shift-add operations, and where the result is

K. Bertels, J.M.P. Cardoso, and S. Vassiliadis (Eds.): ARC 2006, LNCS 3985, pp. 122 127, 2006.
© Springer-Verlag Berlin Heidelberg 2006

more and more accurate as the number of iterations n increases since the vector orientation is successively closer to its target. When adapted to a circular rotation, CORDIC computes the functions sine-cosine and the magnitude-phase of the vector.

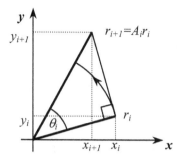

Fig. 1. Circular CORDIC rotation of a vector in a 2-D coordinate system

The CORDIC algorithm for trigonometric computing [1] is defined by the equations:

$$x_{i+1} = x_i - s_i y_i 2^{-i}, \quad y_{i+1} = y_i + s_i x_i 2^{-i}, \quad z_{i+1} = z_i - s_i atan2^{-i}, \tag{1}$$

where x and y are the coordinates of the vector, z is the angle accumulator that stores the effective rotation and s is the sign of rotation. Moreover, as depicted in Fig. 1, a CORDIC micro-rotation is not a pure rotation but a rotation with an intrinsic increase of the magnitude r of the vector quantified by the scale factor A:

$$A_n = \prod_{i=0}^{n-1} \sqrt{1 + tan^2 \theta_i} = \prod_{i=0}^{n-1} \sqrt{1 + 2^{-2i}}. \tag{2}$$

The CORDIC algorithm can operate in two different modes:

- In rotation mode, the initial coordinate components (x_0, y_0) of the vector and the desired rotation angle $z_0 = \theta$ are given in order to compute the new components after the rotation. For this, in each rotation step i, fixed angles $\theta_i = atan2^{-i}$ are subtracted or added from/to the angle accumulator z so that this variable approaches to zero. This iterative decision rule relating to the direction of rotation is described next:

$$s_i = \begin{cases} -1, & z_i < 0 \\ +1, & z_i \geq 0 \end{cases} \quad \begin{matrix} i = 0, \ 1,... \ n-1 \\ n \to \infty \end{matrix} \qquad \begin{cases} x_n = A_n (x_0 cos z_0 - y_0 sin z_0) \\ y_n = A_n (y_0 cos z_0 + x_0 sin z_0) \\ z_n \to 0 \end{cases} \tag{3}$$

The functions $cos\theta$ (x data-path) and $sin\theta$ (y data-path) are obtained if z_0 is initialized to θ and the initial vector is of magnitude $1/A_n$ and aligned with the abscissa.

- In vectoring mode, given the components (x_0, y_0) of the vector, its magnitude and phase (cartesian-to-polar coordinates conversion) are computed by rotating the input vector until it is aligned with the X axis. If z_0 is started to zero, after n iterations it will contain the effective rotated angle $\theta = atan(y_0/x_0)$. Apart, simultaneously, another result stored in x is the magnitude of the original vector scaled by A_n:

$$s_i = \begin{cases} +1, & y_i < 0 \\ -1, & y_i \geq 0 \end{cases} \qquad \begin{array}{l} i = 0, \ 1, \dots \ n-1 \\ n \to \infty \end{array} \qquad \left| \begin{array}{l} x_n = A_n \sqrt{x_0^2 + y_0^2} \\ z_n = z_0 + atan(y_0/x_0) \\ \quad y_n \to 0 \end{array} \right. \qquad (4)$$

3 Hw/Sw Co-design and Dynamic Partial Reconfiguration

The Hw/Sw co-design of CORDIC systems inspired on FPGA outperforms other software-only approaches based on DSP, CISC or RISC processors basically thanks to the customization of both shift-add mechanism –key aspect of this algorithm– and operands data width –which together with the number of iterations n constitute the two factors (data truncation error and angular error respectively) that determine the results accuracy [2]–. In addition, an outstanding feature emerges from section 2: the only difference between the calculus of sine/cosine and arctangent/magnitude is found in the sign criterion s_i since the CORDIC equations (1) remain invariable in both rotation and vectoring modes. This fact lets inspire the implementation on flexible hardware; our approach splits the computer into a static hardware skeleton and a re-configurable part that evolves at run-time depending on the trigonometric function to compute. Like this, our CORDIC computer is embedded in a system-on-chip with dynamic partial reconfiguration performances. The chosen platform is the Atmel AT94K40 device especially thanks to its fine-grained architecture: the system is all integrated in a chip composed of an 8-bit AVR MCU and an AT40K40 FPGA where the entire device or select portions can be reconfigured at run-time through an internal configuration controller, while the remaining logic keeps active [3]. With regard to Hw/Sw partitioning, the presence of a FPGA makes possible to use a CPU of lower power; under a master-slave topology, the MCU handles the data while the FPGA computes elementary functions such as $sin(z_0)$, $cos(z_0)$, $atan(y_0/x_0)$ and $magn(y_0,x_0)$.

```
long sin(char);          long atan(char, char);
long cos(char);          long magn(char, char);
```

Code 1. Prototypes of the trigonometric functions

When the user application calls a function supported in hardware, as Code 1, the MCU reconfigures specific FPGA cores and the FPGA performs the calculus. For this, software is organized in a model of two layers: a low-level or hardware abstraction layer composed of the library of drivers that define the platform-dependant routines and a high-level or application layer that constitutes the code fully portable and transparent to any platform. Concerning hardware, many research efforts have been focused on CORDIC-based architectures for computing [4]. Our design makes use of an iterative bit-parallel CORDIC architecture, as depicted in Fig. 2. The system consists of a CPU responsible for executing the program, an I/O interface to exchange the function arguments and results between MCU-FPGA, a CORDIC core that carries out the computing and, finally, three reconfigurable blocks that allow to optimize some distributed parts of this multipurpose computer to make it so much generic as possible. After reset, the bitstream composed of the basic CORDIC circuitry is automatically loaded into the FPGA. From now on, only partial reconfigurations are required

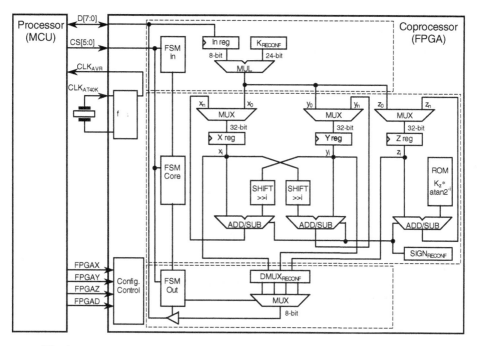

Fig. 2. Block diagram of the AT94K40-based trigonometric CORDIC coprocessor

to customize the coprocessor to the concrete function on demand or in progress. Like this, the MCU downloads the partial bitstream through the configuration controller interface of four 8-bit buses, FPGAX, FPGAY, FPGAZ and FPGAD.

4 Performance Evaluation

The coprocessor, described in C and VHDL, handles 8-bit integers as inputs and gives 32-bit data in fixed-point representation of 6 decimal digits as result. The trigonometric calculus is carried out in 32 iterations. The hardware design comprises 1423 logic cells (61.8% of FPGA resources). Our interest is focused on the reconfigurable 4x1 or 3x2 look-up table (LUT) present in each logic cell of the FPGA. The behavior of the system is made conditional on the three reconfigurable blocks:

- K_{RECONF}. The CORDIC results are affected by the gain factor A_n defined in Eqn. (2). Its inverse, $K_n = 1/A_n$, in our design is a pre-calculated constant multiplied to the initial values x_0 and y_0 to compensate this amplifier effect. Furthermore, another constant is applied to the 8-bit integer z_0 to scale the angle in degrees but in 6-digit fixed-point. Thus, two 24-bit constants K are assigned depending on the variable (X-Y or Z) to transfer from the MCU to the FPGA: instead of using a *mux2x24* with its select lines controlled by a FSM, this multiplexing is achieved by reconfiguring an only logic cell of the FPGA. In fact, the MCU can reconfigure the LUT of a logic cell to negate or not its input and generate thus two outputs that are applied to the bits that differ from a constant to another, as depicted in Fig. 3. The input is permanently tied to '0' and

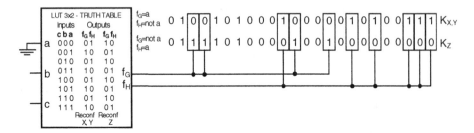

Fig. 3. Multiplexing of K_{RECONF} by dynamic partial reconfiguration

the output switching takes place by reconfiguring the logic function. In this way, the routing of the design is fixed and only some logic resources change.

- SIGN$_{RECONF}$. In rotation mode, z_i takes charge of the addition/subtraction decision shown in Eqn. (3) whereas in vectoring mode y_i is the selection key in accordance with Eqn. (4). In this way, the sign controller can be implemented in an only logic cell through a LUT of 2 inputs, the signs of y_i and z_i. By solely reconfiguring the 8-bit truth table of that logic cell, one of both sign criteria is applied to the three adder/subtract modules synthesized in the coprocessor of Fig. 2.

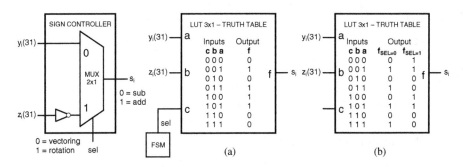

Fig. 4. Sign controller. Static version (a) versus dynamic version (b).

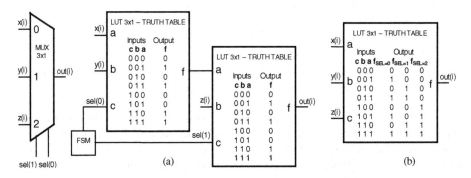

Fig. 5. Static 3x1-multiplexer (a) versus dynamic 3x1-multiplexer (b)

- $DMUX_{RECONF}$. The result of 32-bit wide is located in one of the registers x_i, y_i or z_i depending on the processed function and it is sequentially transferred to the MCU through an 8-bit data bus. A static *mux4x8* selects each of the four bytes that compound the 32-bit data whereas the choice of x, y or z is done by a dynamic multiplexer composed of 32 *mux3x1*, each of them performed in a reconfigurable LUT.

Table 1. Comparison of different Hw/Sw implementations of the CORDIC algorithm

Platform (Operating System)	Time (ns)	Development Tools
Pentium 4 @ 2.66GHz (MS-WinXP)	5050	MS Visual C++ 6.0 (Win32)
AMD K6-2 @ 450MHz (MS-DOS)	13200	Borland C++ 3.1 (MS-DOS)
AT94K40 Coprocessor @ 12.5MHz	* 5840/17040	Atmel System Designer/IAR

* best/worst case depending on the number of hardware modules reconfigured

The performance of our coprocessor has been compared with a software-based implementation on different PC platforms. Taking in mind the working frequency, our prototype carries out the calculus in much less clock cycles than any software approach. In addition, reconfiguration allows to simplify the hardware design, improve the routing, reduce the critical path and merge both operation modes of the algorithm.

Table 2. Experimental results of the reconfigurable coprocessor

Hw Resources	Data	Execution Time (ns)	Data	Compute Error	Data
Flip-Flops	125	Data-Control I/O	3920	Sine	$\leq 10^{-6}$
Gates	1177	Reconf. Kmul	960	Cosine	$\leq 10^{-6}$
IO cells	33	Reconf. Sign	640	Arctangent	$\leq 10^{-6}$
Total logic cells	1423	Reconf. Dmux	10560	Magnitude	$< 2 \cdot 10^{-6}$

5 Conclusions

This work discusses the development of a CORDIC trigonometric computer based on dynamic partial reconfiguration and mapped on an AT94K40 device. The design pursues to optimize the routing and multiplexing of physical signals through a multiplexing strategy performed on-the-fly by reconfiguration techniques. The result is an area-saved embedded system that only just running at low frequencies computes sine, cosine, arctangent or square root operations at rates comparable to PC platforms.

References

1. Vladimirova T., Tiggeler, H.: FPGA Implementation of Sine and Cosine Generators Using the CORDIC Algorithm. MAPLD'99 (1999)
2. Ligon, W. B. et al.: Implementation and Analysis of Numerical Components for Reconfigurable Computing. Proceedings IEEE Aerospace Conference, Vol. 2 (1999)
3. Atmel Corporation: AT94K Series Cache Logic® (Mode 4) Configuration. (2001)
4. Andraka, R.: A Survey of CORDIC Algorithms for FPGA Based Computers. Proceedings 6th International Symposium on FPGAs, Monterey, USA (1998) 191-200

Handel-C Design Enhancement for FPGA-Based DV Decoder

Sławomir Cichoń, Marek Gorgoń, and Mirosław Pac

AGH University of Science and Technology
Biocybernetic Laboratory, Department of Automatics
Al.Mickiewicza 30, 30-059 Kraków, Poland
blizniak_s@tlen.pl, mago@agh.edu.pl, pacm@poczta.onet.pl

Abstract. In the paper the authors present an implementation of the algorithm of DV Decoder conformant to IEC-61834-2 standard in re-programmable resources . A software implementation has been realized and then transferred to the Handel-C language. By parallelization of the algorithm and using language mechanisms in Handel-C the processing efficiency has been increased 10 times with respect to the initial hardware implementation. The implementation has been verified in hardware-software environment with real data transmitted on-line from a DV camcorder.

Keywords: Parallel algorithm, high level languages, video decompression, field programmable gate array.

1 Introduction

Application of the latest production technologies for semiconductors stimulates a great development dynamics in the field of reprogrammble devices and reconfigurable systems. Although the general philosophy of reprogrammable devices remains the same for years, the style and techniques of the design, the method for algorithm allocation in the resources is continuously being developed. A very interesting direction is the development of all manner of methods allowing the designs of reprogrammable devices based on the widely known methods for algorithm design. The required features of such tools include a user-friendly graphical interface, possibly highest level of independence between the algorithm description tools and the implementation tools and generally high standards of software quality. These criteria are met, among others, by the high level languages (HLL).

In the presented implementation the primary evaluation criterion for the application will be the possibility of executing the requested operations in real time. The starting point was a floating point version of the algorithm, realized in "ANSI C"language. The goal of the study was the algorithm's representation in a fixed-point version, adapted to the capability of a reprogrammable system, and then the construction of a parallelized implementation, working in real time in the FPGA device. The whole algorithm has been split into a series of processing stages and then each individual task has been optimized and highly parallel

K. Bertels, J.M.P. Cardoso, and S. Vassiliadis (Eds.): ARC 2006, LNCS 3985, pp. 128–133, 2006.

execution mode has been proposed. Effective execution of the algorithm written in Handel-C language requires a proper approach and deep knowledge of the mechanism offered by the language. In the paper the techniques applied in the Handel-C implementations are described.

1.1 DV Decoding Algorithm

Figure 1 presents a schematic version of the algorithm implemented in the DV decoder. Proper implementation of the Inverse Discrete Cosine Transform (IDCT) and Inverse Variable Length Coding is of fundamental importance for the quality and efficiency of the decompression system.

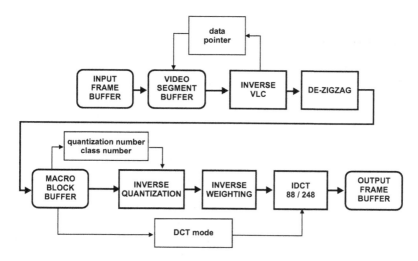

Fig. 1. Image decompression scheme In the DV standard

The problem of implementation of video compression/decompression algorithms in FPGA devices is a widely explored subject, because of the search for solutions featuring both high effectiveness and low cost. The application of FPGA devices in the acceleration process is an alternative to software implementations, consuming considerable part of the processor's resources. Vast segment of the low-end digital camcorder market is represented by devices employing the DV compression, described in the [1] standard. The physical interface is provided by the IEEE-1394 connection, conformant to the [2] standard, realizing the data transfer from the camcorder in real time. The possibility of application of DV standard in FPGA devices has been described in [3], however the realizations of commercial DV decoders so far has been based on the ASIC decoders, sometimes supported by reconfigurable devices [4], [5].

The DCT transform is a topic thoroughly discussed in literature [6]. Since intra-frame based compression is used, there are two DCT modes in DV to cope with the amount of picture movement in a frame. The 8-8-DCT mode and the 2-4-8-DCT mode.

For calculation of 1D-8-IDCT an algorithm proposed by Loeffler [7] has been applied, in the version slightly modified by Eijndhoven and Sijstermans [8]. The algorithm enables the evaluation of 8-point IDCT be merely 14 multiplication operations.

The second important operation is the inverse coding VLC. This stage, in various modifications and with various forms of the coding words table, is present in almost all standards of the video signal compression. An example of architecture of VLC decoders can be found in [9]. As the implementation in the FPGA device is considered, the VLC decoding process is the most complicated operation, which also demands the highest amount of logical resources.

2   Handel-C Implementation

2.1   Initial Implementation

The video signal is transmitted sequentially, therefore it has been decided to apply the medium grane pipeline, in which the processing elements are attributed to the individual decompression stages. In each pipeline cycle a compressed video block is requested from the external memory, which is subject to the decoding process.

A well functioning pipeline should be decomposable into a set of operations, which exhibit comparable execution times. It is a way to avoid bottlenecks in the system. In the initial implementation (ver.1) the pipeline has not been properly balanced.

In order to balance the pipeline in the first stage the decomposition of compressed data transfer and inverse VLC operation has been redesigned (ver.2) and to some extent the division and modulo operators have been eliminated. In ver.1,2 in a single IDCT processing element the ICDT-p1 and ICDT-p2 operations have been executed in sequence. In ver.3 these two operations have been separated and in the main pipeline two elements, working in parallel, have been inserted. The next improvement was the introduction of an additional CLR operation for clearing the table of decoded coefficients of DCT block (ver.4). One more step was the replacing of multiplication operations by the multipierless multiplication (ver.5) [10]. The next iteration comprised the implementation of two identical pipeline architectures for parallel processing of two video blocks (ver.6). At the same time for improvement of efficiency and maximum clock frequency the optimal constructions of software loops and other Handel-C mechanisms have been also applied (ver.7).

2.2   IDCT Code Performance Improvement

Two-dimensional IDCT transform has been replaced by an equivalent two-stage sequence of 1D IDCTs. For the 8-8 IDCT case two passes of one-dimensional 8-point IDCT (1D-8-IDCT) are carried out. For 2-4-8 IDCT in the first pass 1D 4-point IDCT (1D-2-4-IDCT) is calculated twice for the sums and differences of sample values respectively, and then the result is treated by a 1D-8-IDCT.

In the initial version of IDCT *(ver.1,2)* the first and second pass of 1D-IDCT are executed in sequence. The number of Handel-C clock cycles required for calculation of 2D-IDCT is therefore the sum of cycles required for execution of two 1D-IDCT passages. In version 2 the access to the Block-RAM memory has been partially done in parallel with arithmetic operations, what has resulted in execution of 1D-8-IDCT and 1D-4-8-IDCT in considerably lower number of cycles. An essential efficiency improvement has been achieved in version 3 due to parallelization of the first and second passage of 1D-IDCT. In such a way two elements: IDCT-p1 and IDCT-p2 has been placed in the pipeline. In addition in version 6 the time of 1D-IDCT calculation has been decreased by grouping of arithmetic operations and Block-RAM memory access operations.

2.3   Final Implementation

The operation of processing elements has been organized in a pipelining scheme. In the pipeline at the single block level the following processing elements are employed: CLR, IVLC, IQNO, IWGHT, IDCT-p1, IDCT-p2. The pipeline at the single block level is doubled, i.e. in the pipeline work period two video blocks are always decompressed at the same time using two identical sets of processing elements *(ver 6,7)*.

Table 1. Number of Handel-C clock cycles for the implemented hardware modules

Operation	Transfer from SRAM	CLR	IVLC	IQNQ	IWGHT (8-8DCT)	IDCT-p1 (2-4-8DCT)	IDCT -p1	IDCT -p2	Transfer to SRAM
Number	24	65	typic. 90-100	67	66	80	88	80	106

Realization times of individual operations for the final implementation are presented in Table 1. The memory clearing operation CLR has been separated. For the inverse multiplication in the IWGHT operation it can be noticed that the number of clock cycles required for executing the operation for an individual block has been reduced to 66.

Figure 2 presents the values of average decompression rate for consecutive implementation versions. The initial implementations, although working with high frequency, exhibited very low efficiency, about 2-5 fps, because of far from optimal algorithm decomposition to the pipeline form. Although consecutive implementations did not result in increasing the clock frequency, still the number of frames processed per second was systematically growing, because of the reduction of the number of clock cycles for the critical stage in the pipeline. The processing frequency was systematically, reaching the required number of 25fps, and even exceeding it up to 30fps.

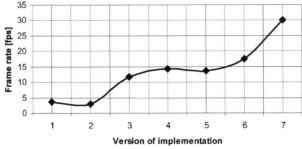

Average decompression rate

Fig. 2. Average decompression rate changes during consecutive phases of the implementation

Table 2. Number of Handel-C clock cycles for the implemented hardware modules

Maximum clock frequency of FPGA	52 MHz
Frame rate for FPGA implementation	Not less the 25 fps Max: 30.13 fps
Frame rate for PC implementation 2 GHz	10-15 fps
PSNR[dB] Software/Hardware (Quality of HW implementation)	48- 52 (average 49)
PSNR[dB] DirectShow DV Video Decoder/Hardware (Quality of implemented algorithm)	42 - 52 (average 47)

In Table 2 the final FPGA implementation and the PSNR quality factor are compared for the software implementation and the final version of hardware implementation.

3   Conclusions

The DV decoder described in the previous sections has been fully implemented for the VirtexE, using Handel-C descriptions of modules and their synchronization. The application of high-level allowed for realization of a properly functioning implementation of a complex system with relatively low amount of effort and time. Using the methods described here approximately tenfold decoder efficiency increase has been achieved in relation to its initial hardware version, what has resulted in its real time operation. The work on improvement of the system functioning were of twofold nature. On one hand by parallelization the number of clock cycles required for execution of individual operations has been reduced. On the other hand it was necessary to keep relatively high values of the system clock frequency. The optimization of the arithmetic logic, consisting of splitting the algorithm into eliminatory operations, and reduction of the depth of asynchronous logic at the expense of increasing the number of synchronous logic layers is a typical algorithm decomposition task for hardware implementations.

As can be seen from the present study the simultaneous analysis of both parameters is necessary: i.e. the number of clock cycles for the critical element of the pipeline and the maximum clock frequency of the FPGA device. Improvement of both aspects seems to be a way to reaching a solution close to optimal with respect to time.

References

1. IEC 61834-2 (1998-08) Recording - Helical-scan digital video cassette recording system using 6.3 mm magnetic tape for consumer use (525-60, 62550, 1125-60 and 1250-50 systems). IEC (1998)
2. IEEE Std 1394-1995 IEEE Standard for a High Performance Serial Bus. IEEE (1995)
3. Dhir A.: IEEE 1394 and HAVi Are the Leading Technologies for Wired Home Networking. Xcell Journal, No. **43** (2002) 48–51
4. Divio and Xilinx Collaborate to deliver next-generation DV codec and decoder reference design. On-line:
   `http://www.xilinx.com/prs_rls/design_win/01130divio.htm`
5. Merlin 2003 DV and MPEG-2 recorder and Dual Stream Decoder, Users Manual. On-line: `http://www.skymicro.com/filesm2k3/MerlinUser.pdf`. Skymicro Inc. (2003)
6. Richardson I.E.G.: Video Codec Design. 1-st edn. John Wiley&Sons, Chichester (2002)
7. Loeffler Ch., Ligtenberg A., Moschytz, G.S.: Practical Fast 1-DCT Algorithms with 11 Multiplications. Proc. of the International Conference on Acoustics, Speech, and Signal Processing. IEEE (1989) 988–991
8. van Eijndhoven, J. Sijstermans F.: Data Processing Device and method of Computing the Cosine Transform of a Matrix. PCT Patent No, WO 9948025 (1999)
9. Nikara J., Vassiliadis S., Takala J., Sima M., Liuha P.: Parallel Multiple-Symbol Variable-Length Decoding. Proceedings of ICCD - VLSI in Computers and Processors. IEEE (2002) 126–131
10. Wiatr K., Jamro E.: Implementation of Multipliers in FPGA Structures. Proc. of IEEE International Symposium on Quality Electronic Design. IEEE Computer Society, Los Alamitos, USA (2001) 415–420

Run-Time Resources Management on Coarse Grained, Packet-Switching Reconfigurable Architecture: A Case Study Through the APACHES' Platform

Alex Ngouanga[1], Gilles Sassatelli[1], Lionel Torres[1], Thierry Gil[1],
André Borin Suarez[2], and Altamiro Amadeu Susin[2]

[1] LIRMM - UMR 5506, 161 rue Ada,
34392 Montpellier, France
{ngouanga, sassatelli, torres, gil}@lirmm.fr
http://www.lirmm.fr
[2] Instituto de Informaica – UFRGS, Av. Bento Gonçalves 9500,
Porto Alegre, 91501-970, Brasil
{borin, susin}@inf.ufrgs.br
http://www.inf.ufrgs.br

Abstract. The increasing number of cores used on a single die in response to the power-computing applications tends to orient SoCs more and more toward communication-centric concept. Networks-on-chip (NoC) are good candidates providing both parallelism and flexibility. Nevertheless they imply to consider the notion of locality when distributing the computation among a set of cores. Defining an optimal placement at compile-time is difficult since other applications may temporarily make use of some of the processing resources. This paper explores the opportunity of dynamically mapping task graphs through using different placement algorithms, experiments and comparisons are conducted on a homogeneous coarse-grain reconfigurable architecture running JPEG applications. Results show that run-time task mapping is possible and brings interesting benefits over a random or static placement, especially when contention effects stemming from the communication medium are taken into account.

1 Introduction

The explosion of standards in 3G and more generally wireless systems goes along with a widening spectrum of applications that portable devices have to support. Designing a chip for every single device tends to become less feasible (SoC complexity, lifecycle of multimedia product, increasing NRE costs for deep-submicron).

A considered way to overcome these problems relies on flexibility, i.e. reusing a same chip for a range of products or even several generations of the same product. This approach allows sharing the NRE costs, and the design phase comes down to a software customization phase. Reconfigurable architectures provide this flexibility at the price of a silicon area overhead highly dependent on the level of flexibility. Dynamic reconfiguration allows decreasing this cost trough making better use of reconfigurable resources at run-time. FPGAs allow emulating any digital functionality

K. Bertels, J.M.P. Cardoso, and S. Vassiliadis (Eds.): ARC 2006, LNCS 3985, pp. 134 145, 2006.
© Springer-Verlag Berlin Heidelberg 2006

but also present some flaws when targeting a multi-applications system: since several applications have to be executed concurrently according to hardly predictable scenarios (e.g. set of algorithms executed concurrently at a given time) place and route phase (P&R) has to be executed at run-time. A means exist for overcoming that, which is grounded on a predefined floor-planning of the FPGA [4-8]. This approach whilst effective, does suffer from huge reconfiguration times, each core being made of several thousand gates.

Coarse grained reconfigurable architecture is generally based on a array of processing elements (PEs) [10][11] operating at word-level.   Usually these architectures better support run-time reconfiguration and therefore for run-time placement manipulations. One serious limitation of these architectures for performing run-time placement lies in the often systolic organization of the PEs. This usually prevents from placing different tasks at a distance greater than one (fragmentation of the computation) which is often unavoidable if the task graphs are complex. This work aims at exploring scalable alternative principles enabling to dynamically map applications made of task graphs onto a homogeneous array of processing elements.

This paper is organized as follows:

Section 2 presents the APACHES architecture, the hardware testbed used for our experiments as well as the underlying principles of task mapping. Section 3 presents the targeted design flow for evaluating the task mapping on APACHES as well as the used algorithms. Section 4 presents the implementation results including detailed information regarding communication cost when deploying the computation among different PEs. Section 5 concludes on the performed experiments and draws some perspectives of this work and its applicability on different architectures.

The main goal herein is not to target high computing performances, but just to show that run time tasks placement on multiple PE array is possible and allow to improve initial performances.

1.1 Related Work and Context Approach

Most platform implementations found in the literature [6][14][12] make use of heterogeneous elements. This type of solutions is often more efficient in terms of performance and power consumption (dedicated or typed cores likes DSPs). Nevertheless, this also limits the solution space for the task mapping concept because of the lack of support from certain PEs for some operations. SCORE [13] performs dynamic task mapping on a paged FPGA though virtualization of reconfigurable hardware. The cost of swapping pages is important, therefore top-level DFG (Data Flow Graph) are packed into clusters for limiting the reconfiguration cost. In [4-8] authors propose an interesting approach enabling to dynamically move tasks from software to reconfigurable hardware and the other way around under operating system control. The hardware partition relies on a run-time reconfigurable FPGA with a predefined floor planning (tiles); communications are handled by a packet-switching NoC. Among other possibilities, this allows to move some tiles for limiting physical link sharing and therefore improve performance. This approach whilst effective, does not allow adopting a new placement for each core each time a new task is mapped, because of the relatively huge FPGA reconfiguration times. To the best of our knowledge, no investigation has yet been conducted in order to determine the opportunity of performing task mapping at run-time on homogeneous processing arrays but on coarse grained architectures where tasks are limited to simple operations. The work presented throughout this paper is considering a reconfigurable architecture made of tiny processing elements (microcontroller-like architecture) connected through a packet-switching Network-on-Chip (NoC). The experiments conducted aim at determining whether performing defragmentation (i.e. run-time task-mapping in our context) brings benefits when several applications are concurrently running on the same large array of processing elements.

2 The Workbench: APACHES

APACHES is an acronym of a Parallel Architecture Composed of Homogeneous Elements' Set.

2.1 Platform Description

Our platform is composed of tiny homogeneous processing elements (PEs) communicating together through a packet-switching network on chip (NoC). The choice of the communication infrastructure has been done according to the considerations mentioned above; employing a 2D Mesh NoC allows to abstract communications and therefore eliminates the need to take care of routing at the application level. In our architecture data to be transmitted from a core to another one are split into packets. A packet is made of the destination address and a payload. Packet routing is fully handled by the NoC routers. The router architecture is depicted in figure 1; 2 ports (North and South) are represented for the sake of clarity. More generally, routers are composed of five incoming queue, one for each port (North, South, East, West and Local), an arbiter which handles the request from the buffers and a routing logic implementing the routing algorithm.

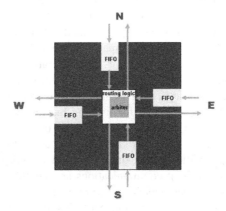

Fig. 1. Schematic representation of the Hermes switch

The number of nodes in the platform is fully parameterizable. The version used in this article features 16 elements, grouped in cluster of configurable size (4 PEs in fig 2). The topology of the NoC utilized is a mesh and the chosen processing element is a very compact MIPS-like processor (Fig 2) with 16 Kbytes of local memory. The interfacing between a router and the attached PE is done using the OCP protocol [15].

Two different classes of processing elements are used in APACHES:

-Processing nodes
A processing node handles the computation of tasks and behaves as a slave receiving orders from master nodes.

-Master nodes, or network controllers (NCs)
Master nodes act as I/O controllers and also decide the placement of each task onto the processing array.

Depending on the chosen array size, one or several masters are used; each one being responsible of the processing of a PEs cluster. They also handle the task placement algorithm according to the task graph to map onto the architecture, send tasks instruction code to each selected nodes and finally inject or collect the data of the platform.

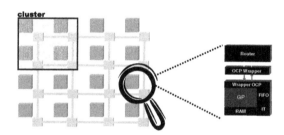

Fig. 2. Schematic representation of the platform APACHES

The chosen NoC supports several routing algorithms, however only the simpler XY routing (data routed towards destination according to the X-axis, then Y-axis) technique is used (deadlock free)[3].

Task Placement
In Figure 3 a global description of APACHES functioning is depicted. To ease the explanation a 3x3 platform has been selected. The node (0,4) and (2,0) (fig 3) are the network controllers, the remaining ones are processing elements. In figure 3.a, an application is running on the platform. When a new application has to be mapped on the grid the system performs sequentially the following tasks:

1. A new placement is computed by the master node and that for all tasks of all applications.
2. If the new placement implies to relocate some tasks of the already running applications, the master first moves those tasks to their new locations. This is done through issuing a 'send code' request to each concerned PE which specifies the new location of the task (fig 3.b).

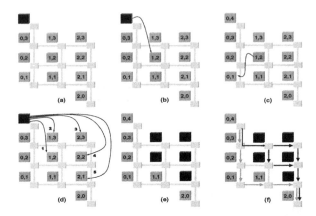

Fig. 3. Task placement and data routing

3. The task codes of the new application are sent to the PEs they have been assigned to (fig 3.c & fig 3.d).
4. The system resumes execution of stalled tasks and starts processing of the newly assigned application (fig 3.e).

Data routing

In figure 3.f the two applications are now running on the platform according to the new placement given by the task mapping algorithm executed on the master (0,4) (fig 3.a). Data are streamed from the master to the first PEs of the 2 applications' task graphs, and communications between the different tasks are automatically established through the NoC. A routing table storing the addresses of all other tasks of the application is kept up-to-date in the network controller. This update is done when a new task placement is triggered during execution for ensuring that data keep being sent to the right PEs (new tasks placement).

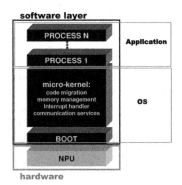

Fig. 4. Hardware and Software layer of APACHES' platform PE

Software layer

Each PE runs a small footprint multitasking kernel enabling the capabilities detailed above. Figure 4 shows the memory layout for each PE. The multitasking support is implemented in a preemptive fashion; a programmable interrupt controller periodically generates interrupts for distributing PE time among running processes: on each interrupt, the kernel scheduler resumes execution of a previously stalled process. No hardware memory management unit (MMU) is present and therefore all task codes are compiled in PIC (Placement Independent Code) mode. Upon reception of a new task, the memory manager allocates a memory block of sufficient size and the task is put in the scheduler task list. The entire kernel occupies less than 2kbytes.

2.2 Mapping Task on APACHES at Run-Time

Applications are described as task graphs. A single task can be handled by each PE. No placement information is provided *a priori;* placement is mainly performed according to locality matters: physical links sharing is prevented for limiting as much as possible communication overheads.

Task mapping concept

Whenever a new application needs to be mapped onto the array a new placement is computed by one network controller thanks to the task mapping it executes. Depending on the used algorithm and current scenario (number, position and complexity of task graphs) the time required for computing a new placement varies. This time should ideally be negligible compared to the processing time of the task which has triggered a new mapping. The main advantage of re-performing a global placement each time a new application has to be mapped is to lower contentions within the array, and therefore increase performance.

Task mapping algorithm

The task mapping problem is to succeed to split an application in a given number of tasks in order to limit communications, synchronizations and well-balance computation load.

In general, finding optimal solutions for mapping problems and the scheduling of inter-machine communications in Parallel Computing environments is NP-complete requiring the development of near-optimal heuristic techniques.

Two placement algorithms were tested to perform dynamic task mapping: simulated annealing and force directed. The first one is based on the simulation of a physical phenomenon, which changes randomly the tasks position on the network, estimates the cost and accepts or rejects changes according to a "temperature" criterion. The second one calculates the tasks positioning taking into account the "resulting force" produced by the attraction between communicating tasks. This attraction force is proportional to the communication volume between the linked tasks.

Force directed algorithm: This algorithm relies on a physically inspired phenomenon where system equilibrium is reached when the distance between weights (the tasks) connected together by strings (graph edges) is minimum. The string stiffness is here proportional to communication volume (link throughput) therefore providing an increased priority to highly communicating tasks.

1. Place randomly the tasks in the network
2. Choose one task
3. Calculate the new placement using the equations:

$$px_j = \frac{\sum\limits_{i=1}^{N} V_{ij} Cx_i}{\sum\limits_{i=1}^{N} V_{ij}} \qquad py_j = \frac{\sum\limits_{i=1}^{N} V_{ij} Cy_i}{\sum\limits_{i=1}^{N} V_{ij}}$$

Where Cx_i is the coordinate x of the node i, Cy_i is the coordinate y of the node i and V_{ij} is the communication volume between node i and node j.

4. If the position is not empty, search the nearest empty position.

The procedure is repeated for each node until the tasks position in the network becomes stable.

The advantage of this method is that an optimized solution is quickly obtained. The drawback is that the solution may, in some cases, fall in a local minimum.

Simulated annealing: This well-known algorithm is a search technique where a single solution is randomly modified. An energy is defined which represents how good the solution is. The goal is to improve this solution by minimizing its energy. Changes which lead to a lower energy are always accepted; some of those which lead to an energy increase are accepted, this is determined by the probability law $e^{\Delta E/kT}$. Where ΔE is the change in energy, k is a constant and T is the Temperature

1. Place randomly the tasks in the network and initialize the temperature value according to the temperature curve (normalized).
2. Evaluate the cost of the placement.
3. Randomly change the position of two tasks in the network.
4. Evaluate the new cost of the placement.
5. If the new cost is lower than the previous one, accept changes; if the cost is higher than the previous one, then the probability of acceptance of the new value is given by the temperature curve.
6. Update the temperature value.

Repeat steps 2 to 6 until the temperature reaches a certain value.

For each state of the system (i.e. the different positions of tasks set) the placement cost results from the weighting of path length between different cores by their communication volume. The cost function is summarized by the following equation:

$$\text{cost} = \sum_{i=1}^{N} \sum_{j=1}^{M} V_{ij} L_{ij}$$

Where V_{ij} is the volume of communication between node i and node j and Lij is the path length on the network between node i and node j.

3   Results

3.1   Experimental Protocol

To test **APACHES** and the task mapping concept, a JPEG encoder and two others synthetic scenarios have been used.

The implementation of the JPEG encoding uses two network controllers. The first one performs tasks mapping, instruction code dispatch and data injection. The other one simply acts as a sink. The application has been broken into 4 main functions and its tasks graph is represented in Fig 5.

In this implementation, data are injected into the macro pipeline by one network controller (NC) and collected by the other one.

Fig. 5. Example of a simple application graph: the JPEG encoder macro pipeline

Two synthetic scenarios are created to test the execution time of the tasks mapping algorithm. The graph of the first synthetic application is composed of four macro pipelines of three tasks. The data are injected and collected by the same network controller element in each pipeline. The graph of the second synthetic application is also composed of 4 macro pipelines which unlike the first one count a different number of nodes. This kind of graphs used to appear in many streaming applications, which tend to be very regular and with a sequence of processing steps being applied over a data stream.

3.2   Performance Results

Table 1 presents the execution time of the tasks mapping algorithms considering different NoC sizes and graph sizes. The number of graph tasks has a greater influence than the NoC size on the time needed to execute the force directed algorithm. It's the opposite for the simulated annealing algorithm. Therefore the first algorithm is then more scalable than the second one. Thus if a huge APACHES is used, a 10x10 for example, the process time for a given task graph will remain the same for the directed algorithm whereas it will dramatically increase for the simulated annealing.

Table 1. Execution time for different algorithm (cycles)

Algorithms, graph size and NoC Size	Simulated Annealing	Force Directed
JPEG (8 nodes) APACHES4x4	3771030	270741
Synthetic 1 (12 nodes) APACHES4x4	6840670	470341
Synthetic 2 (16 nodes) APACHES6x6	5716176	499721
JPEG (8 nodes) APACHES4x4	3771030	270741
Synthetic 1 (12 nodes) APACHES4x4	6840670	470341

Table 2 presents the total length of the communication path (expressed in number of NoC links) between the tasks for all three approaches. Figure 6 depicts the placement yielded by respectively the simulated annealing and the force directed algorithms when running four JPEG dataflow. Both placements are optimal; link sharing is limited as much as possible and only affects network controllers (NCs) due to the used topology: a single physical link exists between each NC and the rest of the PE array.

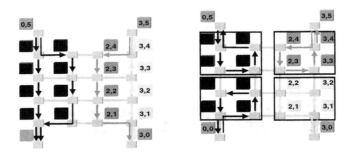

Fig. 6. Force directed and simulated annealing task placement results for 4xJPEG(16 nodes)

Table 2. Total length of the communication path between tasks in APACHES (hops)

Algorithm, graph size and NoC Size	Simulated Annealing	Force Directed
JPEG (8 nodes) APACHES4x4	6	6
Synthetic 1 (12 nodes) APACHES4x4	21	23
Synthetic 2 (16 nodes) APACHES6x6	19	18
JPEG (8 nodes) - 4x4	6	6
Synthetic 1 (12 nodes) APACHES4x4	21	23

Table 3 shows the improvements achieved for the different scenarios (multiple JPEG streams and multiple synthetic scenarios). The second and the third columns refer respectively to a random and a force directed placement; the last to the speedup obtained. For the second and the third JPEG implementation presented in table 2 each stream uses respectively one and two NCs (fig 6). In this table only the time to process one block is considered (i.e. no macro-pipeline).

Table 3. Random mapping versus run-time mapping considering a synchronized NoC (cycles)

Algorithm, graph size and NoC Size	Initial execution time	Optimized execution time	speedup
2 x JPEG (8 nodes) 4x4APACHES	40172	36512	9.1%
4xJPEG 16nodes+1NC APACHES4x4	43633	36536	16.2%
4xJPEG 16nodes+2NC APACHES4x4	42785	35851	16.2%
Synthetic 1 (12 nodes) APACHES4x4	13186	7745	41%
Synthetic 2 (16 nodes) APACHES6x6	17775	12491	29.7%

Table 4 presents different JPEG implementations on APACHES; one compact (1 PE) and two pipelined (2 PEs and 4 PEs). The process time, given in cycle, of each task of the JPEG algorithm is: RGB2YUV (5500), DCT (5397), Quantification (6509) and VLC (16281). As expected the pipelined implementations exhibit better performance than the single-PE one. The speedup achieved is around two. However there's no significant difference between the two pipelined versions. This is essentially due to the VLC (critical path of the pipeline 16281 cycles) which slows down the whole pipeline and creates a major bottleneck. Duplicate this task is one explored way to speedup the stream (software level). Another one is to enhance the PE of the APACHES platform by adding to each of them a reconfigurable function unit [1] which will help them to process more efficiently data at a bit level.

Table 4. Comparison between different jpeg implementations on APACHES

Feq=50MHz	1 PE	2 PEs pipelined	4 PEs pipelined
1000 blocs processing (cycles)	34.505e6	18.096e6	16.973e6
Throughput (kBytes/s)	5.796	11.052	11.783
speedup	1	1.9	2.1

Table 5 presents detailed performance results when the communication architecture and the PE are using the same clock (50 MHz). Values between brackets are the execution time in cycles for the considered placement algorithm. The speedup achieved for the JPEG algorithm is around 2 for both placement algorithms.

Table 5. Random mapping versus run-time mapping considering a synchronized NoC

Feq=50Mhz	Random placement 4xJPEG 16 nodes	Simulated annealing placement 4xJPEG 16 nodes	Force directed placement 4xJPEG 16 nodes
First bloc latency (cycles)	15363(0)	9132(6816413)	9299(508894)
Throughput (kbytes/s)	25	48.6	45
speedup	1	1.944	1.8

Table 6 presents the same set of results when the communication architecture uses a much slower clock (5MHz). As expected, this tends to increase contentions in the network and therefore increase the benefits of using an optimized placement for decreasing physical link sharing. In this case also, simulated annealing proves to yield a better result, achieving a speedup of 5.6x.

Table 6. Random mapping versus run-time mapping considering a desynchronized NoC

feq$_{processing}$ =50Mhz feq$_{communication}$=5Mhz	Random placement 4xJPEG 16 nodes	Simulated annealing placement 4xJPEG 16 nodes
First bloc latency (cycles)	77834	15529(6816413)
Throughput (kbytes/s)	8	44.862
Speedup	1	5.60775

4 Conclusion and Future Works

A flexible homogeneous processing array supporting dynamic placement has been presented. First results show that relocating tasks at run time is feasible without a huge performance overhead. The achieved application speedup is highly dependent on the performance of the communication architecture. However, the time required for the placement algorithms to converge is quite high and using that approach is relevant only for applications which are running over a long period.

Current work aims at implementing and validating that approach on several applications concurrently running on the architecture; but also to estimate the power consumption gain obtained using a desynchronized NoC. We're also considering a decentralized version of the force directed algorithm, each PE running an OS service. Evaluating the force applied by each other tasks. When the resulting force exceeds a given threshold, task migration to the new location is triggered.

Future work consists of exploring the opportunity of dynamically and automatically duplicating some tasks of the graph depending on system state (for instance battery level in embedded system) and requirements (performance). But also to add to each PE of the APACHES platform a reconfigurable unit in order to speedup the process time of channel coding and cryptographic algorithms.

References

[1] Lodi, et al., "A VLIW Processor With Reconfigurable Instruction Set for Embedded Application" IEEE Journal of Solid State Circuit, Vol. 38, no. 11, Novembre 2003

[2] W. J. Dally, B. Towles, "Route Packets, Not Wires: On-Chip Interconnection Networks", Proceedings of the Design Automation Conference, pp. 684-689, Las Vegas, NV, June 2001

[3] Moraes, F. G.; Mello, A. V. de; Möller, L. H.; Ost, L.; Calazans, N. L. V.. "A Low Area Overhead Packet-switched Network on Chip: Architecture and Prototyping.", IFIP VLSI SOC 2003, International Conference on Very Large Scale Integration. 2003, Darmstadt

[4] Marescaux T., Mignolet J-Y., Bartic A., Moffat W., Verkest D., Vernalde S., Lauwereins R. "Networks on Chip as Hardware Component of an OS for reconfigurable Systems" FPL 2003

[5] Nollet V., Coene P., Verkest D., Vernalde S., Lauwereins R., "Designing an Operating System for Heterogeneous Reconfigurable SoC" 10th Reconfigurable Architectures Workshop (RAW), Nice, France, 2003

[6] Mignonet J-Y., Nollet V., Coene P., Verkest D., Vernalde S., Lauwereins R., "Infrastructure for design and management of relocatable tasks in a heterogeneous reconfigurable system-on-chip" Proceedings of the DATE'03 conference, pages 986-991, Munich, March 2003, ISBN 0-7695-1870-2

[7] Nollet V., Avasare P., Mignolet J-Y., Verkest D., "Low cost Task Migration Initiation in a Heterogenous MP-SoC" Proceedings of the DATE'05 conference

[8] Nollet V., Marescaux T., Verkest D., "Operating System Controlled Network on Chip" DAC'03

[9] Steiger C., Walder H., Platzner M., "Operating Systems for Reconfigurable Embedded Platform: Online scheduling of Real-Time Tasks", IEEE Transactions on Computers, vol 53, no 11, november 2004

[10] Sassatelli G., Torres L., Benoit P., Gil T., Diou C., Cambon G., Galy J., "Highly Scalable Dynamically Reconfigurable SystolicRing-Architecture for DSP applications", IEEE DATE'02 , France, 2002

[11] Baumgarte V., May F., Nückel A., Vorbach M., Weinhardt M., "PACT-XPP A Self-Reconfigurable Data Processing Architecture", The Journal of supercomputing, vol 26, pp 167-184 septembre 2003

[12] OMAP2420 www.ti.com

[13] Caspi E., Chu M., Huang R., Weaver N., Yeh J., Wawrzynek J., and A. DeHon, "Stream Computations Organized for Reconfigurable Execution (SCORE)", FPL'2000, LNCS 1896, pp. 605-614, 2000.

[14] Heysters P., Smit G., "A Flexible and Energy-Efficient Coarse-Grained Reconfigurable Architecture for Mobile Systems", The Journal of supercomputing, vol 26, pp 283-308 novembre 2003

[15] OCPIP specification version 2.0, Available at www.ocpip.org

A New VLSI Architecture of Lifting-Based DWT

Young-Ho Seo[1] and Dong-Wook Kim[2]

[1] Department of Information and Communication Engineering, Hansung University
389, Samsung-dong 3ga, Sungbuk-gu, Seoul, 136-792, Korea
yhseo@hansung.ac.kr
http://www.hansung.ac.kr/~design
[2] Department of Electronic Materials Engineering, Kwangwoon University
447-1, Wolgye-Dong, Nowon-Gu, Seoul, 139-701, South Korea
dwkim@kw.ac.kr

Abstract. In this paper, we proposed a new architecture of lifting process for JPEG2000 and implemented it as an ASIC. It includes a new cell-structure that executes a unit lifting calculation to satisfy the property of lifting process of a repetitive arithmetic with a unit process. After the operational sequence of lifting arithmetic was analyzed in detail and the causality was imposed to implement in H/W, the unit cell was optimized. A new simple lifting kernel was organized possible by repeatedly arranging the unit cells and a lifting processor was realized with the kernel for Motion JPEG2000. From the comparison with previous works, we could conclude that the proposed architecture shows excellent properties in considering both the cost and the performance.

1 Introduction

As JPEG2000 [1] extends its application areas, research on 2DDWT (2Dimensional DWT) has increased. Recent research on DWT has focused on a form of lifting which shows excellent performance compared to the conventional convolution method. A lifting method has advantages of lower memory requirement and lower number of memory-accesses. Also it has the same arithmetic structure in forward and inverse transforms [2,3,4]. A block-based processing [2] and its structure to interleave the data with a (5,3) filters [3] have been studied. Also, a lifting structure for EZW (Embedded Zero tree Wavelet) algorithm [4] and a structure to expand the unit operation of prediction-and-update to the whole data [5] were proposed. For them to be applicable, the calculation unit and related lifting structure must be designed to follow the various principles of JPEG2000 [6]. In H/W, if the data-pass part doesn't have a perfect pipeline architecture, the critical path may show a large delay. If one tries to retain the simplicity in the structure by direct mapping into a H/W, it may not perform the continuous input of the data properly and may induce an unclear relation between the lifting operation and internal memory [5,6]. A lifting operation with an entire pipeline architecture and expandable H/W structure was introduced to solve these problems [7]. Although it showed high-speed operation, it has defects that it requires a lot of pipelining registers and cannot clearly show the line-based lifting characteristics because of its direct mapping of lifting arithmetic to H/W.

K. Bertels, J.M.P. Cardoso, and S. Vassiliadis (Eds.): ARC 2006, LNCS 3985, pp. 146–151, 2006.
© Springer-Verlag Berlin Heidelberg 2006

2   Proposed Lifting Architecture

In this chapter, we re-schedule the lifting arithmetic for H/W implementation and propose a cell structure for the unit operation of lifting. With this cell in H/W, we propose a lifting kernel to execute the horizontal and vertical lifting operation.

2.1   Architecture of Line-Based Filtering Cell

The procedure of the lifting operation is expressed graphically as Figure 1. Lifting consists of the same four steps of multiplication-and-addition with only different coefficients.

Since lifting has the same horizontal operating structure, it can be replaced by one line as the right-bottom of Figure 1. Even in a line, since the same operating process is repeated, it can be constructed with one unit arithmetic as the left-bottom one. This cell must satisfy the basic demand that the continuous data inputting sequence must be processed without overlapping.

The timing sequence of lifting operation satisfying the requirement is depicted in Figire 2, where $\otimes$ and $\oplus$ mean multiplication and addition, respectively. Each operation is configured with one multiplier and one adder since the unit arithmetic cannot execute both multiplication and addition simultaneously. The operation method and the retained data in the required register and the data saved in the register are shown in Figure 2 according to the order of clock sequencing.

We propose a VLSI architecture of a unit cell (Lifting-Based Filtering Cell, LBFC) which can accept the input data continuously and accommodate both (5,3) and (9,7) filters at the same time, which is in Figure 3(a). The architectures are transformed by the re-scheduled operation code. The proposed H/W can have five pipeline stages.

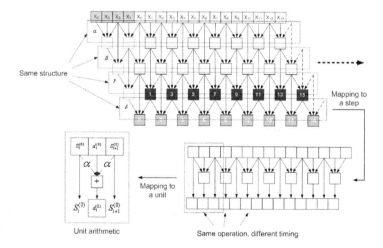

Fig. 1. Unit arithmetic of 1D lifting by structure mapping

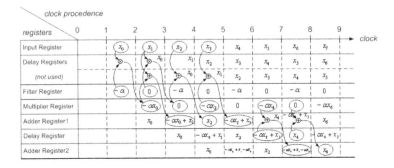

Fig. 2. Time rescheduling of lifting

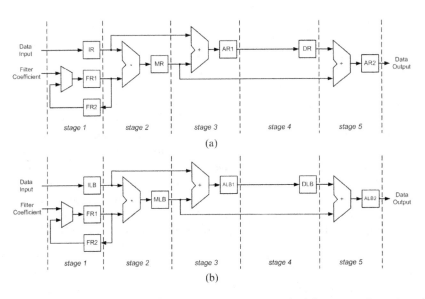

Fig. 3. Architecture of LBFC. (a) horizontal (LBFC_hor). (b) vertical (LBFC_ver).

To use the line-based filtering for vertical DWT, each register in Figure 3(a) should be substituted with a line buffer, the result of which is shown in Figure 3(b). Vertical LBFC has the same architecture as the horizontal one and the coefficients in the four subbands in a level are sequentially processed ($LL_{x,y} \rightarrow LH_{x,y} \rightarrow HL_{x,y} \rightarrow HH_{x,y}$).

2.2   Proposed Architecture of Lifting Processor

LBFC performs the unit arithmetic of lifting, which is the fundamental for a VLSI architecture. Horizontal or vertical LBFCs organize the corresponding LFDWT (Lifting Filter for DWT), which performs the entire lifting. The VLSI architecture of it is depicted in Figure 4. The (9,7) filter needs four LBFCs and twenty clocks of delay time since an LBFC has five steps of pipelining. While only two LBFCs are needed for the (5,3) filter. Thus the throughput of a (5,3) filter is twice of a (9,7) filter. As shown in Figure 4, the two LBFCs before the MUX operate in parallel. The results are MUXed into the next two LBFCs that operate in parallel, too. The lifting-based filtering is performed level by level. Data from the previous level (LL data only) is inputted according to the clock (frequency is f) and the four calculated coefficients are outputted in series with the same speed to the clock, which means input and output of this architecture have the same data rate. IS and FS perform the inverse and forward scaling, respectively.

Our architecture of the implemented lifting processor is shown in Figure 5. It consists of A/D Interface to interface with an external A/D converter, SDRAM

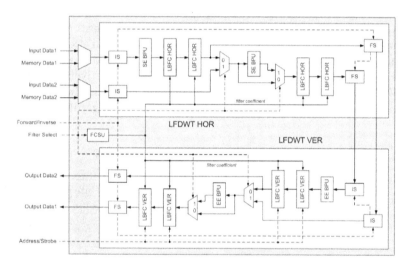

Fig. 4. Architecture of Lifting Kernel with LFDWT

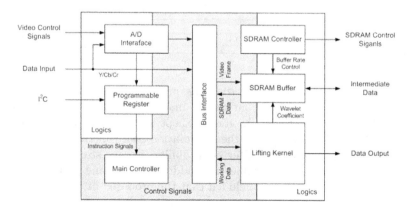

Fig. 5. Architecture of lifting processor

Controller and SDRAM buffer for data access with external SDRAM, Lifting Kernel to perform lifting operation, Programming Register for storing instructions, and Main controller to control overall operation. It accepts input data directly through the "Data Input" port, from A/D converter, or through "Intermediate Data" from SDRAM by SDRAM Controller and SDRAM buffer. The overall operation sequence depends on the configuration of Programming Register which is accessed and programmed by "I^2C" port and is performed by Main Controller.

3   Implementation and Experimental Results

After synthesis by Synopsys, the total gate count for Lifting Processor was 89,239, among which Lifting Kernel and SDRAM Controller occupies 83,798 and 5,439 gates respectively. Line Buffer in Lifting Kernel uses registers instead of memory because it is configured with large number of 4×4 storage cells. which needs relative smaller amount of H/W. If memory is used, SRAM or DRAM supported by memory compiler of vendor needs relatively larger amount of H/W. Using the registers for storage element of small size in Lifting Kernel has an additional advantage of easiness in transplanting regardless of the ASIC library.

Table 1. Resource usage of proposed H/W

Arch.	Filter	Tile Size	×	+	Storage Size	Output Rate	Operation Frequency	Gate Count	Control Complexity
Ferretti [5]	(9,7) (5,3)	256×256	36 36	36 36	18.5Kbit 17.5Kbit	f f	- -	- -	Simple Simple
Andra [6]	(5,3)	129×129	4	8	18.5Kbit	f	200MHz	15,000 (0.18μm)	Simple
Dillen [7]	(9,7)/ (5,3)	256×256	8	16	57.6Kbit	$f/2$	110Mhz (FPGA)	2,363SL (+3,449Reg)	Complex
Ours	(9,7)/ (5,3)	512×512	16	8	256Kbit	f	150Mhz	32,262 (0.35μm)	simple

As explained above, Lifting Kernel was implemented into both ASIC and FPGA. Specific results and comparison results with the previous researches are shown in Table 1, respectively. All items except the first row are related to the lifting algorithm. As well known, the convolution-based method occupies large H/W resource. By considering filter adaptability, storage size according to the image size, the number of multiplier and adder for the same performance, and the complexity of control, we concluded that the proposed lifting kernel has the best characteristics.

4 Conclusion

In this paper, we proposed a new architecture of the lifting method for JPEG2000 and developed an efficient hardware based on a unit arithmetic cell. Depending on the time-sequenced input data, we re-adjusted the arithmetic order of the lifting and implemented the cell-based architecture for DWT using the lifting scheme. We also proposed an architecture that accommodates both the filters of (5,3) and (9,7) for loss and lossless transform of JPEG2000 standard. We simplified and optimized the architecture and its control for its operation and implementation in H/W. Since the proposed hardware is based on the unit cell of LFBC and LFDWT, and has the uniform architecture, the output ratio is linearly increased as the number of operating cells. The proposed architecture is implemented into both the ASIC and FPGA. After examining the results, we concluded from comparing with the previous researches that the proposed architecture has very excellent characteristics by considering the operational speed, required H/W resources, control complexity, etc.

Acknowledgement

This work is financially supported by the Ministry of Education and Human Resources Development (MOE), the Ministry of Commerce, Industry and Energy (MOCIE) and the Ministry of Labor (MOLAB) through the fostering project of the Lab of Excellency.

References

1. M. Boliek, C. Christopoulos, and Eric Majani : JPEG2000 part-I final draft international standard: ISO/IEC JTC1/SC29 WG1 (2000)
2. K. K. Parhi and T. Nishitani: VLSI architectures for discrete wavelet transforms: IEEE Trans. VLSI Syst., vol. 1 (1993) 191-202
3. A. Grzeszczak, M. K. Mandal, S. Panchanathan, and T. Yeap: VLSI implementation of discrete wavelet transform: IEEE Trans. VLSI Syst., vol. 4 (1996) 421-433
4. G. Lafruit, L. Nachtergaele, J. Bormans, M. Engels, and I. Bolsens: Optimal memory organization for scalable texture codecs in MPEG-4: IEEE Trans. Circuits Syst. Video Technol., vol. 9 (1999) 218-243
5. M. Ferretti and D. Rizzo: A parallel architecture for the 2-D discrete wavelet transform with integer lifting scheme: J. VLSI Signal Processing, vol. 28 (2001) 165-185
6. K. Andra, C. Chakrabarti, and T. Acharya: A VLSI architecture for lifting-based forward and inverse wavelet transform: IEEE Trans. on Signal Processing, vol. 50, no. 4 (2002)
7. G. Dillen, B. Georis, J. D. Legat, and O. Cantineau: Combined Line-Based Architecture for the 5-3 and 9-7 Wavelet Tansform of JPEG2000: IEEE Transactions on Circuit Syst. Video Technol, vol. 13, no. 9 (2003)

Architecture Based on FPGA's for Real-Time Image Processing

Ignacio Bravo, Pedro Jiménez, Manuel Mazo, José Luis Lázaro, and Ernesto Martín

Electronics Department. University of Alcalá.
Alcalá de Henares (Madrid), Spain
{ibravo, pjimenez, mazo, lazaro, ernesto}@depeca.uah.es
http://www.depeca.uah.es

Abstract. In this paper an architecture based on FPGA's for real time image processing is described. The system is composed of a high resolution (1280×1024) CMOS sensor connected to a FPGA that will be in charge of acquiring images from the sensor and controlling it too. A PC sends certain orders and parameters, configured by the user, to the FPGA. The connexion between the PC and the FPGA is made through the parallel port. On the other hand, the resolution of the captured image, as well as the selection of a window of interest inside the image, are configured by the user in the PC. Finally, a system to make the convolution between the captured image and a nxn-mask is shown.

1 Introduction

One of the most important goals in vision-applications is the description of a certain scene in an automatic way. Description is understood as the localization and identification of the objects in the scene, depending on their features [1]. The main handicap in vision applications is the high computational cost that the algorithms that extract those features of the scene it implies. Nowadays, the large size images makes the number of operations needed increase considerably. Moreover, if real time performing is desired, execution-time of algothim must be as low as possible.

Usually, the platforms used to implement these algorithms are systems based on sequential programs. These are not, however, the most suitable elements for this kind of applications from the performance point of view, so, the search for new image processing systems is justified. In this sense, most of the vision systems can be divided in three levels, attending to the computational features: low level (such as filtered or convolutions), medium level (such as image segmentation) and high level (such as matching algorithms) [2].

It is, thus, important to select the necessary hardware platform depending on the complexity of the processing tasks. Since a conventional PC cannot carry out a bit operations concurrently, the system performance on a PC for image processing would be very poor. However, an ad-hock hardware design platform may overcome this problem. On the contrary, the kinds of operations to be done

K. Bertels, J.M.P. Cardoso, and S. Vassiliadis (Eds.): ARC 2006, LNCS 3985, pp. 152–157, 2006.

keeping high performance are relatively simple (filtering, image decompression, etc.). If it is desired to implement more complex algorithms, they must be re-formulated in order to exploit the characteristics of the platform where they are implemented.

In this work a platform based on a FPGA and intended for vision applications is presented. It will be in charge of: capturing images provided by a high resolution sensor, applying a convolution with a mask over that image and further transmission of that preprocessed image to a PC by USB bus. The whole architecture is depicted in the figure 1.a).

The sensor chosen is the MT9M413, by Micron [3]. This monochrome sensor has as best feature the high speed that it can reach: 500fps with a 1280x1024 pixel-resolution. Its internal architecture permits connection with an external controller, allowing other operations to be carried out, as exposition-time configuration or choosing the desired window, by means of a set of control-signals.

The rest of the chapter is organized as follows: chapters 2 and 3 describe general remarks and a block diagram of the proposed design. Finally, a results section where time-relations and consumed resources inside the FPGA are shown.

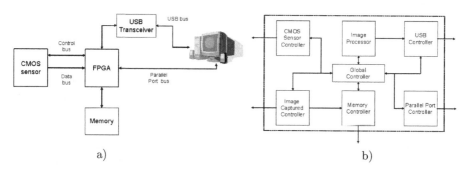

a)   b)

Fig. 1. a) Block-diagram of the developed real-time image-processing system. b) Block-diagram of the implemented system.

2   System Description

As it has been already said, one of the goals of this work has been the design of a specific architecture for image processing. The whole system is controlled by a FPGA of the Virtex II-Pro family, by Xilinx (XC2VP7) - aVirtex II Pro device has been chosen because of its versatility. This FPGA is mainly in charge of:

PC-parallel port of communication: It is only used to configure some parameters of the CMOS sensor (exposition time, window selection, status, etc). It is used used for this purpose due to its high speed and simplicity. Hence, an interface or parallel-port controller has been implemented in the FPGA which manages properly the data lines and the control lines of the parallel port. A PC will communicate with the FPGA through the parallel port using a set of registers implemented in the FPGA. The global controller of the FPGA (see Fig.1.b) will be in charge of handle the information from/to each register.

Memory controller: The system includes 8 Mbytes of external SDRAM memory where captured images, and further processed ones, are stored. The main feature of this kind of memories is the need of continuous refresh. Other features of these memories are: data-bus width: 32 bits, maximum clock frequency: 125MHz, memory internal configuration: 4 banks x 512K x 32bits (8MB), manual refresh control and different access modes dependin g on the data-burst size to be read and written. The memories have $\overline{CAS}$, $\overline{RAS}$ and $\overline{WE}$ control signals to manage the writing, reading and refreshing processes. The memory controller has also been designed using VHDL.

USB controller: This other communication channel is used to transmit processed images. The FPGA has been connected to an external USB-transceiver, the GT3200 by SMSC, in order to send images at high speed. This solution provides a simple communication channel between the FPGA and the PC. The transceiver implements the USB 2.0 protocol so, the maximum data transfer speed rate could reach 480Mbps (60MBps). The interface designed in the FPGA has been developed from the one shown in www.opencores.org [4]. The maximum speed supported by this bus permits transfering images without any problems. For all these reasons, the use of this channel to send processed images from the FPGA to the PC is suitable.

Image processing: In this case, a convolution with a squared nxn-elements mask is made. The mask size is configurable in compilation time but its values are assigned by the user at execution time. This block can be replicated or made more complex as long as the process algorithms require or the FPGA resources allow.

Image-capture and CMOS sensor controller: The sensor used has some control signals that must be enabled from the FPGA. Besides, apart from the image processing block, and depending on the desired image size, an average or decimating of the captured image is made. Two solutions have been designed for our proposal in case that the size of the desired window is smaller than the maximum size:

a) The first one has been making a decimate (D) of value 8, 4, 2 or 1. This option is the simplest one to realize as the system keeps only one row and one pixel out of D rows and D pixels respectively. In this way, the final size of the image is reduced by a DxD factor. However, this choice presents the serious drawback of excessive aliasing.

b) The second option consists in implementing a module (binning block) that averages the samples that are desired to be decimated. If this choice is taken an average of all the decimated samples will be done so that a result affected by less aliasing is obtained, in respect with the previous case.

Both choices are selectable by the user. Its internal structure can be seen in figure 2.a).

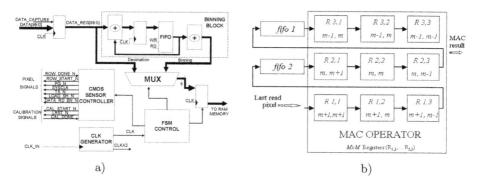

Fig. 2. a) Internal structure of the CMOS sensor controller and the image capturing system of the developed system. b) Convolution process between an image and a 3x3 mask.

3   Image Processor

Once the image has been captured, and a decimate or an average has been carried out, the image is processed. In this work, a system able to make a convolution a mask formed by the coeffients of $n \times n$ elements has been developed. These coefficients may be changed by the user through the parallel port. The maximum convolution-mask size depends on the resources of the FPGA and it must be specified during design time.

The new approach proposed is a block based on the use of some FIFO memories, which allows generating an output pixel at each clock cycle once the inicial latency has passed (see Fig. 2.b). The block stores every complete row of the image in a FIFO, so each pixel is ready to use when the calculation of the convolution for each row takes place [5].

This way the latency of the system is minimized and at the same time the use of the memory is optimized as data do not need to be stored to computed the convolution. As it is shown in Fig. 2.b, once the last pixel of the image has arrived multiplication by the last coefficient of the mask ($C_{m,m}$) is done, as well as the sum (first term in the sum in (1)) with the accumulated rest from the whole previous convolution operation (1).

$$R_{i,j} = P_{m,m} \cdot C_{m,m} \sum_{k=1}^{M} \sum_{l=1}^{m-1} C_{k,l} \cdot P_{i+k-m,j+l-m} \tag{1}$$

Where the second term in (1) is what it has been called accumulated result of the MAC-operation. The lapse of time since the the camera delivers the last pixel of the image, until the last convolution is performed generating the last result, is call *latency* (L_i), and is calculated as:

$$L_i = (X \cdot m + m + 1) \times T_{CLK} + W \cdot T_{CLK} \tag{2}$$

The first term corresponds to the time needed to process all the remaining points after the last pixel has been captured, and W is the processing-system depth. Here, the pixel capture-time, the multiplication and the sum are included. Finally, T_{CLK} is the period of the system clock-signal.

4   Results and Conclusions

In this section, an example of a captured and further processed image is shown, as well as an analysis of the resources and the time consumed by the system.

A 1024x1024 size image has been taken and a 4x4 binning has been carried out so that the final size becomes 256x256 pixels (see Fig. 3.a). Further, a convolution with an edge-detection specific mask is applied to the image (see Fig. 3.b). Thanks to the binning operation the image size can be efficiently reduced without loosing too much resolution. In this case the mask C is the 3x3 Laplacian operator, normalized to integer values. This mask is specially useful for image edge-detection.

In table 2 the results form the point of view of the resources consumed for a Virtex Pro (XC2VP7) with 4928 Slices are shown.

The maximum frequency allowed is over 100 MHz but, however, the global clock of the system runs at 100 MHz, so the system has been tested for this frequency. For this value the memory has 2 cycles latency.

Table 1. Consumed-resources summary of the binning-based design for a XC2VP7

Consumed slices 1084 slices (21 %)	
Capture:	130 Slices
Binning:	344 Slices
Convolution:	444 Slices
Max. freq:	166,66 M:z
RAM blocks:	6 (3 FIFO's)
Multipliers:	9 hardware multiplier

$$T = T_{capture} + L_{total} \quad , \text{ where } T_{capture} = 132 \times 1024 \times T_{CLKCAMARA} \quad (3)$$

$$L_{total} = L_{capture} + L_{binning} + L_{conv} = 10T_{CLK} + 4T_{CLK} + (\frac{n}{B}^2 + 4) \times T_{CLK} \quad (4)$$

Where L_{TOTAL} is the total latency time, being $T_{CLKCAMERA}$ the camera clock-period, n, the maximum square-matrix size (1024) T_{CLK} the FPGA clock period and B the binning factor. Hence, for $B = 4$ (256×256 size of the output image), $T_{CLK} = 100$ MHz and $T_{CLKCAMERA} = 10$ MHz, the system spends about 3.5 ms, what implies a total processing speed of 74 frames/s.

As conclusions, we may note that the architecture presented in this work has been designed to be used as base-platform for different artificial vision applications. The use of a high resolution and high frequency sensor, together with a FPGA, allows this platform to be used for many different algorithms. Also, a very fast image-convolution system has been shown in this work. Finally, the PCA (Principal Component Analysis) algorithm is currently being developed based on this platform.

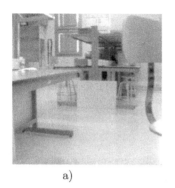
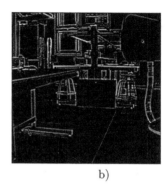

a)   b)

Fig. 3. a) Image-size reduction by means of a 4×4 binning. b) Application of a 3×3 mask to the image on left side.

Acknowledgements

This work has been possible thanks to the project *SILPAR* project of Ministerio de Ciencia y Tecnología (ref: DPI2003-05067) and "Cátedra de control electrónico en transportes" founded by *LOGYTEL* and *RENFE*.

References

1. Ratha N.K., Jain A.K.. Computer Vision Algorithms on Reconfigurable Logic Arrays. IEEE Transactions on Parallel and Distributed Systems. Vol. 10, No. 1. (1999) 29-43.
2. Hamid G. An FPGA-Bases Coprocessor for Image Processing. IEE Colloquium on Integrated Imaging Sensors and Processing, 1994, pp: 6/1 - 6/4.
3. Datasheets 1.3 Megapixel CMOS Active pixel digital image sensor: MT9M413.
4. Usselmann, R. USB Function IP Core Rev 1.5. www.opencores.org. 2002
5. Bravo, I.; Hernandez, A.; Gardel, A.; Mateos, R.; Lazaro, J.L.; Diaz, V.; Different proposals to the multiplication of 3/spl times/3 vision mask in VHDL for FPGA's Proceedings of IEEE Conference on Emerging Technologies and Factory Automation, 2003. ETFA '03. Vol 2, pp:208-211. 2003

Real Time Image Processing on a Portable Aid Device for Low Vision Patients

E. Ros[1], J. Díaz[1], S. Mota[2], F. Vargas-Martín[3], and M.D. Peláez-Coca[3]

[1] Dep. Arquitectura y Tecnología de Computadores, Universidad de Granada, Spain
[2] Dep.Informática y Análisis Numérico, Universidad de Córdoba, Spain
[3] Departamento de Física, Universidad de Murcia, Spain
{eros, jdiaz}@atc.ugr.es, smota@uco.es,
{vargas, mdpelaez}@um.es

Abstract. Low vision patients are subjects with very restricted visual fields or low contrast. There are different pathologies affecting this kind of patients. From a functional point of view the residual vision can be classified in three categories: low contrast vision, tunnel vision and peripheral vision. This contribution describes simple real-time image processing schemes that can help this kind of patients. The presented approaches have been implemented in specific hardware (FPGA device) to achieve real-time processing with low cost portable systems. This represents a very valid alternative to optical aids that are widely used in this field.

1 Introduction

There are several kinds of low vision patients suffering pathologies that reduce their visual fields. The pathologies can be classified in two types:

- Degenerative: in this case the visual capability gets degraded progressively.
- Post-traumatic: the visual field restriction has been produced by an accident, and the damage is permanent but stable.

The residual vision can have different characteristics. There are patients that loose their peripheral vision (they suffer from tunnel vision). These patients are able to read and watch TV, because both tasks require a very small visual field (fovea vision). However, their capability to walk and navigate in an urban environment is very limited. Other patients loose their fovea vision (due to macular degeneration for instance); they suffer from peripheral vision. In this case, the subject loses his central visual field; they can walk easily and avoid objects but they can hardly read and watch TV. Finally, there are other pathologies (such as retinitis pigmentosa) that produce low resolution vision. The prevalence of these different kinds of anomalies is very low (about 17 per thousand). Normally these patients use lenses based devices [1], [2] to partially compensate this restricted vision, although different research groups explore the possible use of electronic technology for real-time image processing in this field [3], [4], [5]. There are also commercial products [6] but they are video magnifiers, with low portability and only providing zooming capabilities.

K. Bertels, J.M.P. Cardoso, and S. Vassiliadis (Eds.): ARC 2006, LNCS 3985, pp. 158–163, 2006.
© Springer-Verlag Berlin Heidelberg 2006

The motivation of using reconfigurable hardware (FPGAs) in this application can be summarized in the following points:

1. The population suffering these pathologies is reduced and very diverse. Each patient has his own requirements: tunnel vision, peripheral vision, low contrast, etc; furthermore each patient may suffer from a kind of limited vision in different degrees. Therefore, instead of developing a different platform for each of these visual restrictions, a single hardware platform can be customized for different image processing tasks.
2. Temporal disease evolution. The systems need to be adapted to the pathology evolution in the degenerative cases.
3. Portability. The image processing device needs to be carried by the patient in order to be used for walking and similar tasks.
4. Low cost: these devices represent only aids, in the absence of a definitive solution to their limited vision. Each patient has different requirements, which make the system difficult to be used by different subjects without reconfiguring it.

The complete system for low vision aids is shown in Fig. 1. It is composed of a camera (image acquisition), a FPGA device (for real-time image processing) and a portable display (HMD: Head Mounted Display) NOMAD ND2000 16 ° HF.

Fig. 1. Low vision aid composed of a camera, a FPGA prototyping board and a HMD

In this work we describe the design and hardware resources cost of a real-time image processing device for this kind of application. We use a low cost FPGA prototyping platform (RC100 of Celoxica [7] shown in Fig. 1) that includes video input and VGA output.

2   Real Time Image Processing

We have focused on the implementation of three simple image processing algorithms that are useful for the described pathologies. In this way, a single board could be fabricated for the different pathologies. The medical specialist only needs to program the configuration EPROM with the proper file to adapt the device to a specific pathology and a restriction degree.

The three developed applications are: Contrast enhancement. For patients with low contrast vision, edges multiplexing with the original image in the central visual field (useful for patients with tunnel vision) and digital zoom of the image for patients with peripheral vision.

2.1 Contrast Enhancement

The contrast enhancement that we have implemented consists in extracting the edges and superimpose them with the original image at the same position with a polarity that depends on the context (this requires a not transparent HMD). That means that we redraw a black trace on a light background and a white trace on a dark background, as it can be seen in the marked area in Fig. 2.a. After testing different contrast enhancement algorithms we have chosen this approach due to its high quality and low computational requirements. The patient can control the relative intensity of the re-drawn edges with two buttons.

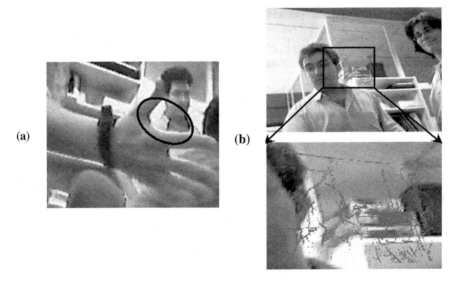

(a)   **(b)**

Fig. 2. (a) Contrast enhancement. (b) Global scene structure multiplexing (edges multiplexed in the central visual field). The bottom figure shows a detail of the patient's visual field.

2.2 Global Scene Structure Multiplexing

The patients with tunnel vision have a very restricted central visual field but of high resolution. For these patients it is useful to have information of a wider visual field to be able to walk easily. For this purpose, as an alternative to wide angle lenses [8] other authors have proposed the possibility of drawing the edges of a wider visual field on the central visual area. In this case, the patient can focus his attention on the edges to walk and neglect them or even switch them off for other tasks. This kind of image processing is shown in Fig. 2.b. This application requires a see-through HMD as shown in Fig. 1. It is important to give the patient the possibility of controlling easily (with two buttons) the edges threshold. In this way, he controls the amount of information that is displayed on the top of the central visual field.

2.3 Digital Zoom

The patients with peripheral vision have a wide visual field but with low resolution. Currently, telescopic devices (based on lenses) are being used as aids [9] to read. For this kind of pathology we have implemented a digital zoom, in this way the patient can control easily (with two buttons) the zoom used in each moment.

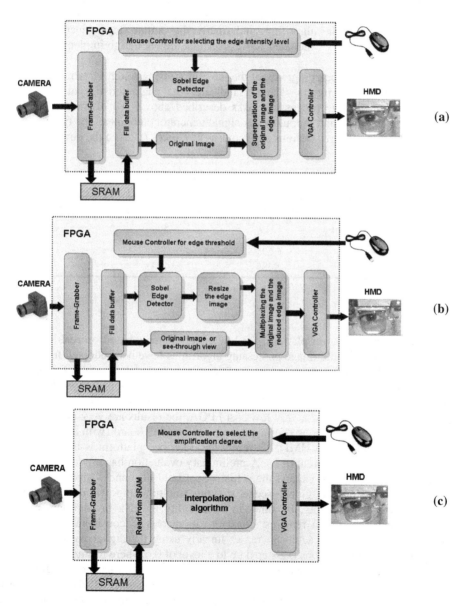

Fig. 3. Block diagrams of the different systems. (a) Contrast enhancement. (b) Global scene structure multiplexing. (c) Digital zoom.

3   Image Processing Implemented in Specific Hardware

The three designs have been included in an EPROM memory on the RC100 prototyping board shown in Fig. 1. In this way, the platform can be configured for each particular task For the three algorithms, the FPGA (Spartan-E 200K) of Xilinx [10] included in the board is configured with an embedded frame-grabber as front end, that receives the images from the camera. After this stage the image processing module depends on the algorithm, and finally the output stage generates a VGA format image. The FPGA includes 200K gates that are enough to implement the three described applications.

Fig. 3 shows the block diagrams of the three processing schemes, which have been implemented in the circuits. Table 1 indicates the characteristics of the circuits designed for the image processing tasks described above. All of them include the input (frame grabber) and output (VGA signal generator) modules. The frame grabber has been used in the three designs and requires 757 slices (32% of the device).

Table 1. Hardware resources cost using a FPGA Spartan-E 200K of Xilinx

	Number of Slices	Device use (%)	Frames/sec
Contrast enhancement	1319	56	25
Edges multiplexing	2350	99	25
Digital Zoom	948	40	25

4   Discussion

We have described an aid platform for low vision patients based on real-time image processing. Three simple image processing algorithms have been adopted for the three described pathologies: tunnel vision, peripheral vision and low contrast vision. The circuits implemented for these processing tasks have been described, and the implementation costs (in terms of the device usage) have been evaluated. Taking into account that we have used a very low cost FPGA, the results are very promising. The complete platform is composed of a camera, a processing board (with a FPGA device as processing chip) and a HMD. Currently the described platform is being evaluated with real patients in different tasks. A preliminary evaluation has produced promising results: a) we are able to expand the actual visual field of tunnel vision patients by a factor of 4.5 using the global scene structure multiplexing without significantly degrading the visual acuity, b) although their ability to walk in environments with obstacles experimentally remains constant, it increases considerably the users confidence, c) the visual acuity increases linearly using the digital zoom application with different augmentations (x2 steps) up to a level of 0.6 where it saturates towards a value of one [11], and d) the contrast enhancement application has been evaluated by [12]. We also have tested the system autonomy. The nomad HMD uses its own batteries with about 8 hours of autonomy. We measured the current consumption of the FPGA platform which is 410 mA (80 mA coming from the camera). We use a standard Ni-Mh battery of 2400 mA, providing a total system autonomy of five and half hours.

The main contribution of the presented work is the implementation of specific hardware for simple real-time processing tasks for specific visual pathologies. Other simple image processing tasks (image polarization inversion, contrast inversion) have already been implemented and are also being evaluated for different diseases. The great variability in the pathology affection levels and also the gradual evolution of the pathology makes reconfigurable hardware a very appropriate technology for this kind of applications.

Acknowledgments

Supported by grants DPI200407032, FIS-PI021829, and FUNDALUCE. All authors but M.D. Peláez-Coca have a patent applications pending regarding some of the technologies, and have interests in the devices discussed herein.

References

1. Peli, E.: Field Expansion for Homonymous Hemianopia using Prism and Peripheral Diplopia. Technical Digest on Vision Science and it Applications, Vol. 1. Optical Society of America, Washington, DC (1999), pp. 74-77
2. Kozlowski, J.M., Mainster, M.A., Avila, M.P.: Negative-lens field expander for patients with concentric field constriction. Arch. Ophthalmol, Vol. 102, (1984), pp. 1182-4.
3. Vargas-Martin, F., Peli, E.: Augmented view for restricted visual field: multiple device implementations. Optometry and Vision Science, Vol. 79, 11, (2002) pp 715-723.
4. Toledo, F. J., Martínez, J. J., Garrigós, F. J., Ferrández, J. M.: An Augmented Reality Visual Prothesis for People Affected by Tunneling Vision. LNCS, Vol. 3561, (2005) pp. 319-326.
5. Venkatachalam, R., Strong, J.G., Wong, W., Hornsey, R.: Digital Zoom for Low Vision Enhancement Systems. IS&T/SPIE Sym. on Elec. Im., San Jose, USA (2004), pp. 18-22.
6. Clarity company web site: http://www.clarityusa.com/products.htm
7. Celoxica company web site: http://www.celoxica.com.
8. Peli, E.: Vision multiplexing: an engineering approach to vision rehabilitation device development. Optom Vis Sci 78, 5, (2001) pp. 304-315.
9. Cohen, J.M.: An overview of enhancement techniques for peripheral field loss. J Am Optom Assoc, Vol. 64, (1993) pp. 60-70.
10. Xilinx company web site: http://www.xilinx.com.
11. Vargas-Martín, F., Peláez-Coca, M. D., Ros, E., Diaz, J., Mota, S.:A generic real-time video processing unit for low vision. ICS, Vol. 1282, (2005), pp. 1075-1079.
12. Peli, E., Kim, J., Yitzhaky, Y., Goldstein, RB., Woods RL.: Wide-band enhancement of television images for people with visual-impairments. J Opt Soc Am A, 21, 6, (2004) pp. 937-950.

General Purpose Real-Time Image Segmentation System

S. Mota[1], E. Ros[2], J. Díaz[2], and F. de Toro[3]

[1] Dep. Informática y Análisis Numérico,
Universidad de Córdoba, Spain
[2] Dep. Arquitectura y Tecnología de Computadores,
Universidad de Granada, Spain
[3] Dep. Teoría de la Señal, Telemática y Comun.,
Universidad de Granada, Spain
smota@uco.es, eros@atc.ugr.es, jdiaz@atc.ugr.es, ftoro@ugr.es

Abstract. This paper describes a general purpose system based on elementary motion and rigid-body detection that is able to efficiently segment moving objects using a sparse map of features from the visual field. FPGA implementation allows real-time image processing on an embedded system. The modular design allows to add other modules and to use the system in very diverse applications.

1 Introduction

It is known that the detection and analysis of motion are achieved by neural operations in biological systems, starting with registration of local motion signals, at low level processing stages, within restricted regions of the visual field, and continuing with the integration of those local motion features into global descriptions of the direction, speed and object motion, in higher level processing stages. This bottom-up strategy is adopted in the proposed system and is implemented in an FPGA device.

The system described uses the motion information to solve the segmentation problem. In other words, firstly the system extracts the structure of the scene that is mainly embodied in highly contrasted features (edges), as biological systems do when using specific cells (local contrast on-centre-off-surround and vice versa) [1, 2, 3], the next point is to detect moving objects through a multiplicative correlation detectors (Elementary Motion Detectors – EMD) described by Reichardt [4], that emulate the dynamics of early visual stages in insects. Both processes take place at low level processing stage.

In mid-level neural layer, that follows a competitive scheme, the system filters the moving features; in other words, segment the moving objects using velocity channels which define the motion of a rigid body [5].

The next sub-sections describe the low-level (Sobel based edge extraction [6] and Reichardt based motion detection) to mid-level (integration of local signals) neural processing scheme that adopts the presented hardware system, and the evaluation results.

K. Bertels, J.M.P. Cardoso, and S. Vassiliadis (Eds.): ARC 2006, LNCS 3985, pp. 164–169, 2006.

2   Hardware Implementation

A conventional monochrome CCD camera provides 30 frames per second of
640x480 pixels and 256 gray levels. These input frames are processed using a
Virtex-II FPGA (XC2V1000 device) [7] and 2 banks of ZBT SRAM.

The algorithm allows us to build a modular architecture that takes full advantage of the parallelism and pipeline resources inherent to the FPGA platforms.
Each functional module adopts a micro-pipelined processing scheme that computes one pixel per clock cycle, and the whole system follows the macro-pipelined
structure (both, macro- and micro- pipeline are shown in Fig. 1). The system
is structured in the following processing units: Frame-Grabber (S1); Memory
management modules; Edges extraction (S2); Direction selective pixel wise correlation with different velocities (S3); Velocity estimation stage that follows a
Winner-takes-all structure to compute the maximum. (S4); Selection of dominant moving features (S5).

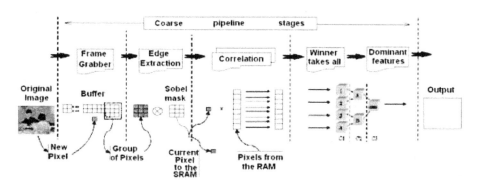

Fig. 1. Pipelined structure of the system

Now we briefly summarize the main micro-pipeline characteristics of each
processing stage in the implemented design. The input image is received by the
frame-grabber (S1) that stores the data into a FIFO buffer, implemented on an
embedded memory block. This FIFO structure allows us to extract the spatial
edges (S2) of the image by convolution with a Sobel 3x3 mask. The edge pixels
are stored in the external SRAM bank 1. During correlation stage, each EMD
correlates the outputs from its two detector cells, which have a characteristic
temporal separation (Δt).

This behavior is emulated by hardware doing a correlation of the current
pixel with pixels from a different frame, and placed at different spatial positions.
This choice characterizes the set of different velocities of the collection of EMDs.
Hence, it is necessary to store, at least, the edges of one previous image, to
correlate them with the pixels from the current image. The system has one frame
of latency due to the correlation module requirements that do not represent a
problem for processing. This is a usual 'limitation' of systems that require a
temporal processing.

The micro-pipeline structure in stage S3 works in the way that the edge extraction module provides a pixel from the current image, this current pixel is provided to the correlation stage and is also stored in the external memory bank. The current pixel is correlated, in parallel, with different pixels of a previous image that we have recovered from the memory bank.

During the S1 and S2 stages the pipeline structure is composed by a single data path, but at the correlation stage the pipeline structure is composed by different parallel data paths, one for each correlation, taking again advantage of the parallelism of the FPGA device.

The current velocity of the processed pixel will be the maximum among the correlation values. In order to compute the maximum as fast as possible (velocity estimation stage) we have used the micro-pipelined winner-takes-all scheme (S4) shown in Fig. 1. Each cube at C1 stage in Fig. 1 represents a correlation value. All the correlations values are obtained in parallel at the same clock cycle. Then we compare the correlation values by pairs in the same clock cycle to obtain local maximums (C2). Finally, the velocity estimation (C3) is the maximum between A and B. The micro-pipelined winner-takes-all scheme (S4) illustrated in Fig. 1 allows the global computation of one pixel per clock cycle, with a latency that depends on the number of primary correlation values, i.e. the number of velocities that we can compute. The advantage of this strategy is that we can compute as many velocities as necessary if we have enough equivalent gates to implement the parallel comparator-based structure. The output of the winner-takes-all-stage (S4) is stored in the external memory bank to be filtered with the results of the dominant features stage (S5).

The next stage (S5) segments the moving objects using more global motion information. A first stage defines velocity channels in overlapping regions of the image. Each velocity channel integrates the pixels that share the same velocity at the window. Next, the pipeline follows a similar scheme as the velocity estimation stage described above, i.e., the velocity channels compete among them, and the winner (this that integrates the maximum number of features sharing the same velocity) is the one that defines a moving object (we have define a rigid body moving along the scene) in this window. The necessity of storing data in the external SRAM banks forces us to design a module that allows the writing and reading to/from the SRAM banks as many times as necessary. This process of storing data consumes 2 cycles per pixel.

The pipeline structure of Fig. 1 consumes one cycle per stage due to the parallelism used; therefore, the limitation of the system is in the external memory banks access. In spite of this, the system is able to process images of 640x480 pixels at the speed of 512 frames per second, when the global clock is running at 31.5 MHz. Table 1 summarizes the main performance and hardware cost of the different parts of the system implemented and the whole system. The Virtex-II FPGA has one million system gates, distributed in 5120 slices, and 40 embedded memory blocks of a total of 720 Kbits. The ISE environment provides us the results in Table 1, which are rough estimations extracted from sub-designs compilations. When the system is compiled as a whole many resources are shared.

Note that the percentage of device occupation is 66%. This enables the possibility of using other devices with less equivalent gates (i.e. lower cost), computing higher resolution images with parallel processing units or adding other processing blocks towards specific application tasks. The spare equivalent gates can be employed in other processing stages, for example in a tracking process that alerts the driver when an overtaking car is detected (an example of this scenario is given in the next section). The circuit characterized in table 1 only includes lateral motion detection based on vertical edges. This approach is well suited for the goal real world application.

Table 1. Hardware cost of the different stages of the described system (estimated by the ISE environment). The global clock of the design is running at 31.5 MHz, and the image size is 640x480 pixels.

Pipeline stage	Number of Slices	% device occupation	% on-chip memory
Frame-Grabber	904	17	3
Edges extraction	185	3	2
Correlation process	2,296	44	0
Dominant features	1,033	20	0
Total system	3,415	66	5

3 Evaluation

The presented evaluation uses two real sequences. The first sequence was taken from the movie "Modern times" by C. Chaplin. The sequence shows two people moving sideways (Chaplin is moving leftwards while the waitress is moving rightwards) in front of a static camera. The system task is to segment both people. The other sequence shows a real overtaking sequence. The camera is onto the driver-mirror in a moving car. The scene shows an overtaking vehicle approaching to the vehicle in which the camera is mounting on. This example is a complex scenario, due to the ego-motion of the camera all the points are moving through the scene, and the system task is to segment the overtaking vehicle.

It is a difficult task to evaluate the segmentation quality of the algorithm using real images since pixels are not labeled according to the object they belong to. Therefore, we manually labeled the moving objects in the image, i.e. we carefully mark the goal objects labeling each pixel belonging to them, and then, we will compare the results of the automatic motion-driven segmentation with the marked labels.

We define the segmentation rate as the ratio between the well classified features in an object and the total number of moving features segmented that belong to this object. Figure 2 shows the results of segmentation rate. They are always above 85% when rigid body motion filtering is applied, these results improve the segmentation without filtering stage, which are below 80% when a static camera is used and below 70% when the camera has ego-motion.

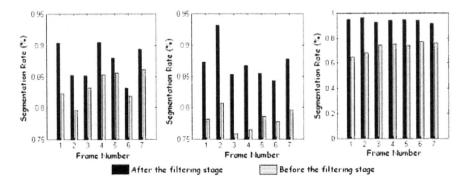

Fig. 2. Segmentation rate through different images of the: **(a)** Moving person to the right on the Chaplin's sequence; **(b)** Moving person to the left on the Chaplin's sequence; **(c)** Overtaking vehicle on the car sequence

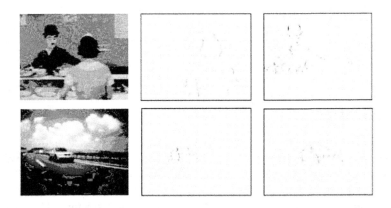

Fig. 3. Original images and motion-driven segmented objects

Fig. 3 shows the experimental results on real sequences. Rigid body motion detection allows us to minimize the noisy patterns and to segment the two people in Chaplin's sequence (the waitress and Chaplin are segmented) and the overtaking car in the overtaking sequence.

4   Conclusions

This contribution describes a general purpose segmentation system based on motion detection. The front-end of the system are Reichardt motion detectors (EMDs). We define filters based on motion patterns of the image that seem to correspond to moving objects. These filters effectively clean noisy patterns (due to the temporal aliasing) and help to segment the moving object (if present). This filtering technique is a robust scheme because it is only based on a rigid body motion rule. It detects areas with a population of features moving coherently (with the same speed and direction), being good candidates for a moving rigid body. In this way, the moving features are processed in a competitive manner, only patterns that activate a whole population of detectors with a similar velocity pass through this dynamic filter stage.

The results with real sequences have been evaluated. The hardware cost of the proposed system is low and allows the use of cheaper devices than other vision based algorithms. The described real-time computing scheme in embedded FPGA systems (portable) together with the very promising results obtained in the general context posed, opens good application perspectives in diverse fields (robot vision, automobile industry, surveillance, etc).

The system architecture based on independent processing units (modular architecture), each of them working at one pixel per clock cycle, allows us to add other units to the whole system. The new units could be connected to the whole system to pre- or post- process the sequences to address different applications or could constitute a parallel processing with a final information fusion. Some of these schemes will be part of our future work.

The presented scheme is based on a sparse map of pixels (less of 15% of the pixels in each frame have information different from 0). If we exploit this characteristic adopting an event-driven computing scheme we can increment the computing power of the system, the frame-rate of the camera, etc.

Acknowledgements. This work has been supported by the National Project DE-PROVI (DPI2004-07032) and the European Project DRIVSCO.

References

1. Hubel, D., Wiesel, T.: Receptive fields, binocular interaction and functional architecture in the cat's visual cortex. J.Physiol., 160 (1962) 106-154.
2. Petkov, N., Kruizinga, P.: Computational models of visual neurons specialized in the detection of periodic and a periodic oriented visual stimuli: bar and grating cells. Biolog. Cyber. 76(2), (1997) 83-96.
3. Dresp, B., Grossberg, S.: Contour integration across polarities and spatial gaps: from local contrast to global grouping. Vision Research 37 (1997) 913-924.
4. Reichardt, W. Autocorrelation, a principle for the evaluation of sensory information by the central nervous system. Sensory Communication. MIT Press (1961) 303-317.
5. Mota, S., Ros, E., Ortigosa, E.M., Pelayo, F. J.: Bio-Inspired motion detection for blind spot overtaking monitor. I. Journ. Robot. Autom. 19(4), (2004) 190-196.
6. Gonzalez, R. and Woods, R.: Digital image processing. Addison Wesley (1992)
7. http://www.xilinx.com/xlnx/xil_prodcat_landingpage.jsp?title=Platform+FPGAs

Implementation of LPM Address Generators on FPGAs

Hui Qin[1], Tsutomu Sasao[1], and Jon T. Butler[2]

[1] Department of Computer Science and Electronics, Kyushu Institute of Technology
680–4, Kawazu, Iizuka, Fukuoka, 820–8502, Japan
[2] Department of Electrical and Computer Engineering, Naval Postgraduate School
Code EC/Bu, Monterey, CA 93943-5121

Abstract. We propose the *multiple LUT cascade* as a means to configure an n input *LPM (Longest Prefix Match) address generator* commonly used in routers to determine the output port given an address. The LPM address generator accepts n-bit addresses which it matches against k stored prefixes. We implement our design on a Xilinx Spartan-3 FPGA for $n = 32$ and $k = 504 \sim 511$. Also, we compare our design to a Xilinx proprietary TCAM (ternary content-addressable memory) design and to another design we propose as a likely solution to this problem. Our best multiple LUT cascade implementation has 5.20 times more throughput, 31.71 times more throughput/area and is 2.89 times more efficient in terms of *area-delay* product than Xilinx's proprietary design. Furthermore, its area is only 19% of Xilinx's design.

1 Introduction

The need for higher internet speeds is likely to be the subject of intense interest for many years to come. A network's speed is directly related to the speed with which a node can switch a packet from an input port to an output port. This, in turn, depends on how fast a packet's address can be accessed in memory. The **longest prefix match** (**LPM**) problem is one of determining the output port address from a list of **prefix vectors** stored in memory. For example, if the prefix vector 01001**** is stored in memory, then the packet address 010011111 matches this entry. That is, each bit in the packet address matches exactly the corresponding digit in the prefix vector or there is a * or *don't care* in that digit. If other stored prefixes match the packet address, then the prefix with the least *don't care* values determines the output port address. That is, the memory entry corresponding to the longest prefix match determines the output port.

An ideal device for this application is a **ternary content-addressable memory** (TCAM). The descriptor "ternary" refers to the three values stored, 0, 1, and *. Unfortunately, TCAM dissipates much more power than standard RAM [1].

Several authors have proposed the use of standard RAM in LPM design. Gupta, Lin, and McKeown showed a mechanism to perform LPM every memory access [2]. Dharmapurikar, Krishnamurthy, and Taylor propose the use of Bloom filters to solve the LPM problem [3]. Sasao and Butler have shown that a fast, power-efficient TCAM realization using a look-up table (LUT) cascade [4].

In this paper, we propose an extension to the LUT cascade realization: a *multiple LUT cascade* realization that consists of multiple LUT cascades connected to a special

K. Bertels, J.M.P. Cardoso, and S. Vassiliadis (Eds.): ARC 2006, LNCS 3985, pp. 170–181, 2006.
© Springer-Verlag Berlin Heidelberg 2006

encoder. This offers even more efficient realizations in an architecture that is more easily reconfigured when additional prefix vectors are placed in the prefix table.

We have implemented six types of LPM address generators on the Xilinx Spartan-3 FPGA (XC3S4000-5): Four different realizations using multiple LUT cascades, one using Xilinx's TCAM realization based on the Xilinx IP core, and one using registers and gates. In addition, we compare the six types of LPM address generators on the basis of delay, *delay-area* product, throughput, throughput/area, and FPGA resources used.

The rest of the paper is organized as follows: Section 2 describes the multiple LUT cascade. Section 3 shows other realizations for the LPM address generators. Section 4 presents the implementations of the LPM address generator using an FPGA. Section 5 shows the experimental results. Section 6 concludes the paper.

2   Multiple LUT Cascades

2.1   LPM Address Generators

A content-addressable memory (CAM) [5] stores 0's and 1's and produces the address of the given data. A TCAM, unlike a CAM, stores 0's, 1's, and *'s, where * is a *don't care* value that matches both 0 and 1.

TCAMs are extensively used in routing tables for the internet. A routing table specifies an interface identifier corresponding to the longest prefix that matches an incoming packet, in a process called **Longest Prefix Match (LPM)**. In the PLM table, the ternary vectors have restricted patterns: the prefix consists of only 0's and 1's, and postfix consist of only *'s (*don't cares*). In this paper, this type of vector is called a **prefix vector**.

Definition 2.1. *An n-input m-output k-entry* **LPM table** *stores k n-element prefix vectors of the form* $VEC_1 \cdot VEC_2$, *where* VEC_1 *is a string of 0's and 1's, and* VEC_2 *is a string of *'s. To assure that the longest prefix address is produced, TCAM entries are stored in descending prefix length, and the first match determines the LPM table's output. An address is an m-element binary vector for* $m = \lceil \log_2(k+1) \rceil$, *where* $\lceil a \rceil$ *denotes the smallest integer greater than or equal to a. The corresponding* **LPM function** *is a logic function* $f : B^n \rightarrow B^m$, *where* $f(\overrightarrow{x})$ *is the smallest address of an entry that is identical to* $\overrightarrow{x}$ *except possibly for don't care values. If no such entry exists,* $f(\overrightarrow{x}) = 0^m$. *The* **LPM address generator** *is a circuit that realizes the LPM function.*

Example 2.1. *Table 1 shows an LPM table with 5 4-element prefix vectors. Table 2 shows the corresponding LPM function. It has 16 entries, one for each 4-bit input. The output address is stored for each input corresponding to the address of the longest prefix vector that matches it.*   *(End of Example)*

2.2   An LUT Cascade Realization of LPM Address Generators

An LPM function can be realized by a single memory. However, this often requires prohibitively large memory size. We propose functional decomposition [6,7] to realize the LPM function with lower storage requirements. For a given LPM function $f(\overrightarrow{x})$, let $\overrightarrow{x}$ be partitioned as $(\overrightarrow{x}_A, \overrightarrow{x}_B)$. The decomposition chart of f is a table with 2^{n_A}

Table 1. LPM table

Address	Prefix Vector
1	1000
2	010*
3	01**
4	1***
5	0***

Table 2. LPM function

Input	Output Address	Input	Output Address
0000	5	1000	1
0001	5	1001	4
0010	5	1010	4
0011	5	1011	4
0100	2	1100	4
0101	2	1101	4
0110	3	1110	4
0111	3	1111	4

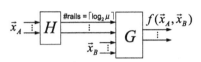

Fig. 1. Decomposition for the LPM function f

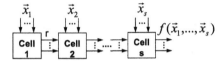

Fig. 2. LUT cascade

columns and 2^{n_B} rows, where n_A and n_B are the number of variables in $\vec{x}_A$ and $\vec{x}_B$, respectively. Each column and row is labeled by a binary number, and the corresponding element in the table denotes the value of f. The column multiplicity, μ, is the number of different column patterns of the decomposition chart. Then, using functional decomposition, the function f can be decomposed as $f(\vec{x}_A, \vec{x}_B) = G(H(\vec{x}_A), \vec{x}_B)$, as shown in Fig. 1, where the number of rails (signal lines between two blocks H and G) is $\lceil \log_2 \mu \rceil$. By iterative functional decomposition, the given function can be realized by an LUT cascade, as shown in Fig. 2 [8,9].

Theorem 2.1. *[4] An n-input LPM address generator with k prefix vectors can be realized by an LUT cascade, where each cell realizes a p-input, r-output combinational logic function. Let s be the necessary number of levels or cells. Then,*

$$s \le \lceil \frac{n-r}{p-r} \rceil, \tag{1}$$

where $p > r$ and $r = \lceil \log_2(k+1) \rceil$.

2.3   LPM Address Generators Using the Multiple LUT Cascade

A single LUT cascade realization of an LPM function often requires many levels. Since the delay is proportional to the number of levels in a cascade, we wish to reduce the number of levels. According to (1), if we increase p, the number of inputs to each cell, then the number of levels s is reduced. For each increase by 1 of p, the memory needed to realize the cell is doubled. However, as shown in Fig. 3, we can use the multiple LUT cascade to reduce the number of levels s while keeping p fixed. For an n-input LPM function with k prefix vectors, let the number of rails of each LUT cascade be r. First, partition the set of prefix vectors into g groups of $2^r - 1$ vectors each, except the last

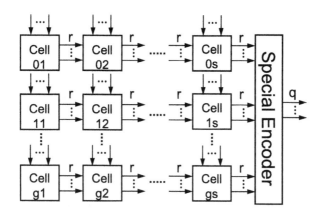

Fig. 3. Architecture of the multiple LUT cascade

group, which has $2^r - 1$ or fewer vectors, where $g = \lceil \frac{k}{2^r - 1} \rceil$. For each group of prefix vectors, form an independent LPM function. Next, partition the set of n inputs into s groups. Then, realize each LPM function by an LUT cascade. Thus, we need a total of g LUT cascades, and each LUT cascade consists of s cells. Finally, use a **special encoder** to produce the LPM address. Let v_i $(i = 1, 2, ..., g)$ be the i-th input of the special encoder, and let v_{out} be the output value of the special encoder. That is, v_i is the output value of the i-th LUT cascade, where its binary output values are viewed as a standard binary number. Similarly, v_{out} is the output of the special encoder, where its binary output values are viewed as a standard binary number. Then, we have the relation:

$$v_{out} = \begin{cases} v_i + (i - 1)(2^r - 1) & \text{if } v_i = 0 \text{ and } v_j = 0 \text{ for all } 1 \le j \le i - 1 \\ 0 & \text{if } v_i = 0 \text{ for all } 1 \le i \le g. \end{cases}$$

Note that v_{out} is the position of a prefix vector v in the complete LPM table, while i is the index to the LUT cascade storing v. $(i - 1)(2^r - 1)$ is the position in the LPM table of the last entry of the previous $(i - 1)$-th LUT cascade or is 0 in the case of the first LUT cascade. Adding v_i to this yields the position of v in the complete LPM table.

Example 2.2. *Consider an n-input LPM function with k prefix vectors. When $k = 1000$ and $n = 32$, by Theorem 2.1, we have $r = 10$. Let $p = r + 1 = 11$. When we use a single LUT cascade to realize the function, by Theorem 2.1, we need $\lceil \frac{n-r}{p-r} \rceil = 22$ cells, and the number of levels of the LUT cascade is also 22. Since each cell has 11 address lines and 10 outputs, the total amount of memory needed to realize the cascade is $2^{11} \times 10 \times 22 = 450,560$ bits. Note that the memory size of each cell, $2^{11} \times 10 = 20,480$ bits, is too large to be realized by a single block RAM (BRAM) of our FPGA, which stores $18,432$ bits.*

However, if we use a multiple LUT cascade to realize the function, we can reduce the number of levels and the total amount of memory. Also, the cells will fit into the BRAMs in the FPGAs. Partition the set of vectors into two groups, and realize each group independently; then, we need two LUT cascades. For each LUT cascade, the *number of vectors is 500, so we have $r = 9$. Also, let $p = r + 2 = 11$. Then, we need $\lceil \frac{n-r}{p-r} \rceil = 12$ cells in each cascade. Note that the number of levels of the LUT cascades is 12, which is smaller than the 22 needed in the single LUT cascade realization. Since each cell consists of a memory with 9 outputs and at most 11 address lines, the total amount of memory is at most $2^{11} \times 9 \times 12 \times 2 = 442,368$ bits. Also, note that the size of the memory for a single cell is $2^{11} \times 9 = 18,432$ bits. This fits exactly in the BRAMs of the FPGAs.*

Thus, the multiple LUT cascade not only reduces the number of levels and the total amount of memory, but also adjusts the size of cells to fit into the available memory in the FPGAs. *(End of Example)*

Fig. 3 shows the architecture of the multiple LUT cascade. The realization with this architecture is the **multiple LUT cascade realization**. It consists of a group of LUT cascades and a special encoder. The inputs of each LUT cascade are common with other LUT cascades, while the outputs of each LUT cascade are connected to the special encoder. Each LUT cascade realizes an LPM function, while the special encoder generates the LPM address from the outputs of cascades.

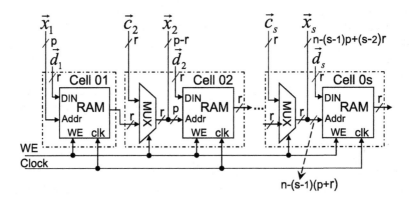

Fig. 4. Detailed design of the LUT cascade

For an n-input LPM function with k prefix vectors, the detailed design of the LUT cascade is shown in Fig. 4, where $\vec{x}_i$ $(i = 1, 2, ..., s)$ denotes the primary inputs to the i-th cell, $\vec{d}_i$ $(i = 1, 2, ..., s)$ denotes the data inputs to the i-th cell and provides the data value to be written in the RAM of the i-th cell, r denotes the number of rails, where $r \leq \lceil \log_2(k+1) \rceil$, $\vec{c}_j$ $(j = 2, 3, ..., s)$ denotes the additional inputs to the j-th cell and is used to select the RAM location along with $\vec{x}_j$ for write access. Note that $\vec{c}_j$ and $\vec{d}_i$ are represented by r bits. All RAMs except perhaps the last one have p address lines; the last RAM has at most p address lines. When *WE* is high, the $\vec{c}_j$ is connected to the RAM to write the data into the RAMs. When *WE* is low, the outputs of the RAMs are connected to the inputs of the succeeding RAMs, and the circuit works as a cascade to realize the LPM function. Note that the RAMs are synchronous RAMs. Therefore, the LUT cascade resembles a shift register.

Example 2.3. *Table 3 shows a 6-input 3-output 6-entry LPM table, and the corresponding LPM function is shown in Table 4. Note that the entries in the two tables are similar. Table 4 is a compact truth table, showing only non-zero outputs. Its input combinations are disjoint. Thus, the two tables are the same except for three entries.*

Single Memory Realization: *The number of address lines is 6, and the number of outputs is 3. Thus, the total amount of memory is $2^6 \times 3 = 192$ bits.*

Single LUT Cascade Realization: *Since there are $k = 6$ prefix vectors of the function, by Theorem 2.1, the number of rails is $r = \lceil \log_2 (6+1) \rceil = 3$. Let the number of address lines for the memory in a cell be $p = 4$. By partitioning the inputs into three disjoint sets $\{x_1, x_2, x_3, x_4\}$, $\{x_5\}$, and $\{x_6\}$, we have the cascade in Fig. 5 (a), where only the signal lines for cascade realization are shown, and other lines such as for storing data are omitted for simplicity.*

The total amount of memory is $2^4 \times 3 \times 3 = 144$ bits, and the number of levels is $s = 3$. Note that the single LUT cascade requires 75% of the memory needed in the single memory realization.

Multiple LUT cascade Realization: *Partition Table 3 into two parts, each with three prefix vectors. The number of rails in the LUT cascades associated with each separate LPM table is $\lceil \log_2 (3+1) \rceil = 2$. Let the number of address lines for the memory in a cell be $p = 4$. By partitioning the inputs into two disjoint sets $\{x_1, x_2, x_3, x_4\}$ and*

Table 3. 6-entry LPM table

Address	Prefix Vector
1	100000
2	10010*
3	1010**
4	101***
5	10****
6	1*****

Table 4. Truth table for the corresponding LPM function

Input						Output			LUT
x_1	x_2	x_3	x_4	x_5	x_6	out_2	out_1	out_0	Cascade
1	0	0	0	0	0	0	0	1	Upper
1	0	0	1	0	*	0	1	0	Cells 1
1	0	1	0	*	*	0	1	1	and 2
1	0	1	1	*	*	1	0	0	Lower
1	0	0	*	*	*	1	0	1	Cells 3
1	1	*	*	*	*	1	1	0	and 4

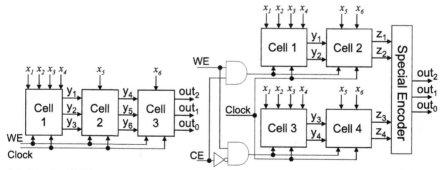

(a) Single LUT cascade realization   (b) Multiple LUT cascade realization

Fig. 5. Single LUT cascade realization and the multiple LUT cascade realization

Table 5. Truth tables for the cells in the multiple LUT cascade realization

Cell 1 and Cell 2 (upper LUT cascade)												Cell 3 and Cell 4 (lower LUT cascade)											
x_1	x_2	x_3	x_4	y_1	y_2	x_5	x_6	z_1	z_2	v_1	v_{out}	x_1	x_2	x_3	x_4	y_3	y_4	x_5	x_6	z_3	z_4	v_2	v_{out}
1	0	0	0	0	0	0	0	0	1	1	001	1	0	1	1	0	0	*	*	0	1	1	100
1	0	0	1	0	1	0	*	1	0	2	010	1	0	0	*	0	1	*	*	1	0	2	101
1	0	1	0	1	0	*	*	1	1	3	011	1	1	*	*	1	0	*	*	1	1	3	110
Other values				1	1	*	*	0	0	0	†	Other values				1	1	*	*	0	0	0	†
					Other values			0	0	0	†						Other values			0	0	0	†

† depends on values from the other LUT cascade

$\{x_5, x_6\}$, *we obtain the realization in Fig. 5 (b). The upper LUT cascade realizes the upper part of the Table 4, while the lower LUT cascade realizes the lower part of the Table 4. The contents of each cell is shown in Table 5.*

Let v_1 be the output value of the upper LUT cascade, let v_2 be the output value of the lower LUT cascade, and let v_{out} be the output value of the special encoder. Then, in Table 5, (z_1, z_2) viewed as a standard binary number, has value v_1, while (z_3, z_4) viewed as a standard binary number, has value v_2. The special encoder generates the LPM address from the pair of outputs, (z_1, z_2) and (z_3, z_4) :

$$out_2 = \bar{z}_1 \bar{z}_2 (z_3 \vee z_4),$$
$$out_1 = z_1 \vee \bar{z}_2 z_3 z_4,$$
$$out_0 = z_2 \vee \bar{z}_1 z_3 \bar{z}_4.$$

Note that (out_2, out_1, out_0) viewed as a standard binary number, has value v_{out} corresponding to the address in Table 3. The total amount of memory is $2^4 \times 2 \times 4 = 128$ bits, and the number of levels is 2. Note that the multiple LUT cascade realization requires 89% of the memory and one fewer levels than the single LUT cascade realization.

(End of Example)

3 Other Realizations

3.1 Xilinx's TCAM

Xilinx [10] provides a proprietary realization of a TCAM that is produced by the Xilinx CORE Generator tool [11]. Since a TCAM can directly realize an LPM address generator, we compare our proposed multiple LUT cascade realization with Xilinx's TCAM. In the Xilinx CORE Generator 7.1i, we used the following parameters to produce TCAMs.

- *SRL16 implementation.*
  Standard Ternary Mode: Generate a standard ternary CAM.
- *Depth-* Number of words (vectors) stored in the TCAM: k.
  Data width- Width of the data word (vector) stored in the TCAM: n.
- *Match Address Type-* Three options: Binary Encoded, Single-match Unencoded, and Multi-match Unencoded. We used the Binary Encoded option.
- *Address Resolution-* Lowest or Highest. We used the Lowest option.

3.2   Registers and Gates

We also compare our proposed multiple LUT cascade realization with a direct realization using registers and gates, as shown in Fig 6. We use a register pair (Reg. 1 and Reg. 0) to store each digit of a ternary vector. For example, if the digit is * (*don't care*), the register pair stores (1,1). Thus, for n bit data, we need a $2n$-bit register. The comparison circuit consists of an n-input AND gate and n 1-bit comparison circuits, each of which produces a 1 if and only if the input bit matches the stored bit or the stored bit is *don't care* (* or 11).

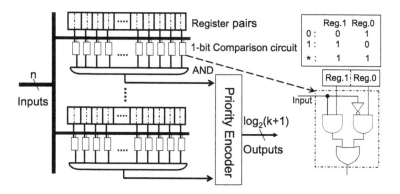

Fig. 6. Realize the address generator with registers and gates

For each prefix vector of an n-input LPM address generator, we need a $2n$-bit register, n copies of 1-bit comparison circuits, and an n-input AND gate. For an n-input address generator with k registered prefix vectors, we need k copies of $2n$-bit registers, nk copies of 1-bit comparison circuits, and k copies of n-input AND gates. In addition, we need a priority encoder with k inputs and $\lceil \log_2 (k + 1) \rceil$ outputs to generate the LPM address. If the n-input AND gate is realized as a cascade of 2-input AND gates, this circuit can be considered as a special case of the multiple LUT cascade architecture, where $r = 1$, $p = 2$, and $g = k$. Note that the output encoder circuit is a standard priority encoder.

4   FPGA Implementations

We implemented the LPM address generators for 32 inputs and 504~511 registered prefix vectors on Xilinx Spartan-3 FPGAs (XC3S4000-5) [12] by using the multiple LUT cascade, Xilinx CORE Generator 7.1i, and registers & gates. The FPGA device XC3S4000-5 has 96 BRAMs and 27648 slices. Each BRAM contains 18K bits, and each slice consists of two 4-input LUTs, two D-type flip-flops, and multiplexers. For each implementation, we described the circuit by Verilog HDL, and then used Xilinx ISE 7.1i to synthesize and to perform place and route.

First, we used the multiple LUT cascade to realize the LPM address generators. To use the BRAMs in the FPGA efficiently, the memory size of a cell in the LUT cascade should not exceed the BRAM size. Let p be number of address lines of the memory in the cell. Since each BRAM contains $2^{11} \times 9$ bits, we have the relation: $2^p \cdot r \le 2^{11} \times 9$, where r is the number of rails. Thus, we have $p = \lfloor \log_2 (9/r) \rfloor + 11$, where $\lfloor a \rfloor$ denotes the largest integer less than or equal to a.

We designed four kinds of LPM address generators $r6p11$, $r7p11$, $r8p11$, and $r9p11$, as shown in Table 6, where the column **Number of prefix vectors** denotes the number of registered prefix vectors, the column r denotes the number of rails, the column p denotes the number of address lines of the RAM in a cell, the column **Group** denotes the number of LUT cascades, and the column **Level** denotes the number of levels or cells in the LUT cascade.

To explain Table 6, consider $r8p11$ which is shown in Fig 7. For $r8p11$, since the number of rails is $r = 8$, the number of groups is $\lceil \frac{510}{2^8 - 1} \rceil = 2$. Thus, we need two LUT cascades. Since each LUT cascade consists of 8 cells, the number of levels of $r8p11$ is 8. To efficiently use BRAMs in the FPGA, the number of address lines of the RAM in the cell is set to $p = \lfloor \log_2 (9/8) \rfloor + 11 = 11$. Let v_1 be the values of the outputs of the upper LUT cascade, let v_2 be the values of the outputs of the lower LUT cascade, and let v_{out} be the values of the outputs of the special encoder. Then, we have the relation:

$$v_{out} = \begin{cases} v_2 + 255 & \text{if } v_1 = 0 \text{ and } v_2 = 0, \\ v_1 & \text{otherwise.} \end{cases}$$

This expression requires 11 slices to implement on the FPGA. After synthesizing and mapping, $r8p11$ required 16 BRAMs and 69 slices. From this table, we can see that decreasing r, increases the number of groups, but decreases the number of levels.

Table 6. Four Multiple LUT Cascade Realizations

Design	Number of prefix vectors	r	p	Group	Level
$r6p11$	504	6	11	8	6
$r7p11$	508	7	11	4	7
$r8p11$	510	8	11	2	8
$r9p11$	511	9	11	1	12

r: Number of rails
p: Number of address lines of the RAM in a cell
Group: Number of LUT cascades

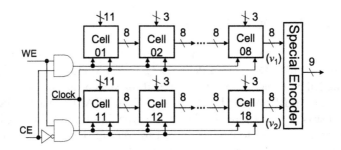

Fig. 7. Architecture of $r8p11$

Next, we used the Xilinx CORE Generator 7.1i tool to produce Xilinx's TCAM. Since the Xilinx CORE Generator 7.1i does not support TCAMs with 32 inputs and 505~511 registered prefix vectors, we designed a TCAM with 32 inputs and 504 registered prefix vectors. After synthesizing and mapping, the resulting TCAM required 8,590 slices. Note that Xilinx's TCAM requires one clock cycle to find a match.

Finally, we designed the LPM address generator with $n = 32$ inputs and $k = 511$ registered prefix vectors using registers and gates, as shown in Fig 6. This design is denoted **Reg-Gates**. Note that the number of inputs is 32 and the number of outputs is 9. After synthesizing and mapping, this design required 27,646 slices.

5   Performance and Comparisons

In Table 7, we show the performance of multiple LUT cascade realizations (i.e., $r6p11$, $r7p11$, $r8p11$, and $r9p11$), and compare them with Xilinx's TCAM and Reg-Gates. In Table 7, the column **Level** denotes the number of levels or cells in the LUT cascade, the column **Slice** denotes the number of occupied slices, the column **Memory** denotes the amount of memory required, and the column **F_clk** denotes the maximum clock frequency. The column **tco** denotes maximum clock-to-output propagation delay. (It is the maximum time required to obtain a valid output at output pin that is fed by a register after a clock signal transition on an input pin that clocks the register). The column **tpd** denotes the maximum propagation time from the inputs to the outputs. The column **Th.** denotes the maximum throughput. Since the LPM address generator has 9 outputs, it is calculated by:

$$\text{Th.} = 9 \cdot \text{F\_clk}.$$

For Reg-Gates, **Delay** denotes the maximum delay from the input to the output and is equal to **tpd**. For multiple LUT cascade realizations and Xilinx's TCAM, **Delay** denotes the total delay, and is calculated by:

$$\text{Delay} = \frac{1000 \cdot \text{Level}}{\text{F\_clk}} + tco,$$

where 1000 is a unit conversion factor.

Consider the area occupied by the various realizations. From the Spartan-3 family architecture [12], we can see that the area of one BRAM is at least the area of 16 slices (a slice consists of two "4-input LUTs", two flip-flops, and miscellaneous multiplexers).

An alternative estimate shows that the area of one BRAM is equivalent to that of 96 slices, as follows. In the Xilinx Virtex-II FPGA, one "4-input LUT" occupies approximately the same area as 96 bits of BRAM (also containing 18K bits) [13]. Note that both "4-input LUTs" and BRAMs of the Virtex-II FPGA are similar to those of the Spartan-3 FPGA. Thus, we can deduce that one BRAM of the Spartan-3 FPGA occupies about the same area as $192 \ (= 18 \times 1024/96)$ "4-input LUTs". If we view one "4-input LUT" as approximately one-half a slice according to our discussion in the previous paragraph, we conclude that one BRAM has about the same area as $96 \ (= 192/2)$ slices. Thus, estimates of the area for one BRAM vary between the area for 16 to 96 slices. For this analysis a worst case of 96 slices/BRAM was used.

Table 7. Comparisons of FPGA implementations of the LPM address generator

Design	Level	Slice	Memory (BRAM)	F_clk (MHz)	tco/tpd (ns)	Th. (Mbps)	Area (slice)	Th./Area ($\frac{Mbps}{slice}$)	Delay (ns)	Area-Delay (slice-ns)
r6p11	6	178	48	103.89	24.89 (tco)	935	4786	0.195	82.64	395.53
r7p11	7	116	28	113.77	23.46 (tco)	1024	2804	0.365	84.99	238.31
r8p11	8	69	16	139.93	20.91 (tco)	**1259** (*best*)	1605	0.785	79.57	127.71
r9p11	12	99	12	139.08	13.72 (tco)	1252	**1251** (*best*)	**1.001** (*best*)	100.00	**125.10** (*best*)
Xilinx's TCAM	1	8590			22.52	13.48 (tco)	203	8590	0.024	**57.88** (*best*)	497.23
Reg-Gates		27646				58.67 (tpd)		27646		58.67	1621.99

Area: We assume that the area for one BRAM is equivalent to the area for 96 slices

In Table 7, the column **Area** denotes the equivalent utilized area, where the area for one BRAM is equivalent to the area for 96 slices. The column **Th./Area** denotes the efficiency of throughput per area for one slice. The column **Area-Delay** denotes the *area-delay* product. The value denoted by *best* shows the best result.

Xilinx's TCAM has the smallest delay, but requires many slices. Reg-Gates has almost the same delay as Xilinx's TCAM, but requires about three times as many slices as Xilinx's TCAM. Note that Reg-Gates requires no clock pulses in the LPM address generation operation, while the others are sequential circuits that require clock pulses. Since the delay of Reg-Gates is 58.67 ns, the equivalent throughput is $(1000/58.67) \times 9 = 153$ (Mbps), which is lower than all others.

All multiple LUT cascade realizations have higher throughput, smaller area, higher throughput/area, and are more efficient in terms of *area-delay* than Xilinx's TCAM. r9p11 has the smallest area, the highest throughput/area, the most efficient in terms of *area-delay*, but has the largest delay. r8p11 has the highest throughput, and has the smallest delay among all multiple LUT cascade realizations. Furthermore, in terms of *area-delay*, r8p11 has almost the same performance as r9p11. Thus, r8p11 is the best multiple LUT cascade realization that has 5.20 times more throughput, 31.71 times more throughput/area, and is 2.89 times more efficient in terms of *area-delay* product than Xilinx's TCAM, while the area is only 19% of Xilinx's TCAM.

6   Conclusions

In this paper, we presented the multiple LUT cascade to realize LPM address generators. Although we illustrated the design method for $n = 32$ and $k = 504 \sim 511$, it can be extended to any value of n and k.

We implemented four kinds of LPM address generators (i.e. r6p11, r7p11, r8p11, and r9p11) on the Xilinx Spartan-3 FPGA (XC3S4000-5) by using the multiple LUT cascade. For comparison, we also implemented Xilinx's proprietary TCAM, and

Reg-Gates by using registers and gates on the same type of FPGA. Xilinx's TCAM has the smallest delay, but requires many slices. Reg-Gates has almost the same delay as Xilinx's TCAM, but requires the largest area and requires about three times as many slices as Xilinx's TCAM. All multiple LUT cascade realizations have higher through-put, smaller area, higher throughput/area and more efficient in terms of *area-delay* product than Xilinx's TCAM.

Acknowledgments

This research is partly supported by a Grant-in-Aid for Scientific Research from JSPS, MEXT, a grant from Kitakyushu Area Innovative Cluster Project, and by NSA Contract RM A-54.

References

1. Micron Technology Inc.: Harmony TCAM 1Mb and 2Mb, Datasheet, January 2003
2. Gupta, P., Lin, S., McKeown, N.: Routing lookups in hardware at memory access speeds, Proc. IEEE INFOCOM (1998) 1241-1247
3. Dharmapurikar, S., Krishnamurthy, P., Taylor, D.: Longest prefix matching using Bloom filters, Proc. ACM SIGCOMM (2003) 201-212
4. Sasao, T., Butler, J. T.: Implementation of multiple-valued CAM functions by LUT cascades, Proc. IEEE International Symposium on Multiple-Valued Logic (May 2006) (accepted for publication)
5. Shafai, F., Schultz, K.J., Gibson, G.F.R., Bluschke, A.G., Somppi, D.E.: Fully parallel 30-MHz, 2.5-Mb CAM, IEEE Journal of Solid-State Circuits, Vol. 33, No. 11 (1998) 1690-1696
6. Ashenhurst, R. L.: The decomposition of switching functions, Proc. International Symposium on the Theory of Switching (1957) 74-116
7. Sasao, T.: Switching Theory for Logic Synthesis, Kluwer Academic Publishers (1999)
8. Sasao, T., Matsuura, M., Iguchi, Y.: A cascade realization of multiple-output function for reconfigurable hardware, Proc. International Workshop on Logic and Synthesis (2001) 225-230
9. Sasao, T., Matsuura, M.: A method to decompose multiple-output logic functions, Proc. 41st Design Automation Conference (2004) 428-433
10. http://www.xilinx.com
11. http://www.xilinx.com/products/design_resources/design_tool/grouping/design_entry.htm
12. Xilinx, Inc.: Spartan-3 FPGA family: Complete data sheet, DS099, Aug. 19, 2005
13. Sproull, T., Brebner, G., Neely, C.: Mutable codesign for embedded protocol processing, Proc. IEEE 15th International Conference on Field Programmable Logic and Applications (2005) 51-56

Self Reconfiguring EPIC Soft Core Processors

Rainer Scholz and Klaus Buchenrieder

Universität der Bundeswehr München, Germany
rainer.scholz@unibw.de,
klaus.buchenrieder@unibw.de

Abstract. In this paper, we present a new kind of reconfigurable soft core processor based on the concept of Explicitly Parallel Instruction Computing (EPIC). The implementation targets a dynamic System-on-a-Chip utilizing Field Programmable Gate Arrays. In contrast to established EPIC cores, the number of functional units is adjusted at runtime and depends only on the available resources of the FPGA. Thus, our EPIC core dynamically trades space versus processing performance. Since we employ only standard functional units, we can use off-the-shelf EPIC compilers for efficient code generation.

1 Introduction

The capacity of Field Programmable Gate Arrays (FPGA) is constantly growing and thus, Systems-on-a-Programmable-Chip (SoPC) are becoming increasingly popular. Soft core processors, i.e. processors implemented with a Hardware Description Language (HDL) and subsequently configured on a FPGA fabric, are widespread in SoPCs, because of the advantages discussed in [14]. Major benefits are, that a higher level of design reuse, a reduced obsolescence risk, a simplified design update or change and increased design implementation options through design modularization can be achieved easily.

Challenging designs, however, require a lot of resources on the FPGA. With the use of partial run-time reconfiguration (pRTR) it is becoming harder to predict the exact chip area that is utilized by the SoPC. This complicates the task of choosing the right soft core, matching the requirements of the specific system. A high-performance core uses a lot of chip space, while a small core might not always reach the computing power required by the application.

2 Background

Several soft core processors are readily available. Beside commercial intellectual property cores like Altera's Nios [4], Xilinx' Microblaze [5] and Actel's ARM7-based CoreMP7 [9] open source cores, such as [8] emerged in recent years. Most of these computing engines offer an interface for core extensions with user defined instructions. This mechanism enables users to design and synthesize custom instructions for the processor core to take advantage of hardware parallelism.

K. Bertels, J.M.P. Cardoso, and S. Vassiliadis (Eds.): ARC 2006, LNCS 3985, pp. 182–186, 2006.

Clearly, loops, recurring groups of instructions, and other time consuming operations can be sped up significantly. Beside all these advantages, existing cores predominantly execute instructions serially, not exploiting instruction level parallelism.

Explicitly Parallel Instruction Computing (EPIC) can resolve these issues. EPIC is a computing paradigm fostering the exploitation of instruction level parallelism (ILP)[3]. Parallel executable instructions are hereby grouped in a flexible manner. In contrast to very long instruction word (VLIW) architectures, grouped instructions are independent of the number of functional units (FU) in the processor. In the EPIC approach, one can distinguish three types of FUs: integer, floating point and branch units. Additional features encompass static scheduling by the compiler as well as control- and data speculation. The most prominent EPIC processors are the processors in Intel's Itanium family [12], based on Intel's and HP's IA64 architecture [13].

As a baseline for this research, two approaches, the Adaptive EPIC (AEPIC) [1] and the customisable EPIC [2], require attention.

The AEPIC combines the EPIC paradigm with reconfigurable logic. Here the source code is partitioned into pieces executed on the EPIC core and entities, that are synthesized to so-called configurable functional units (CFU). These CFUs are then reconfigured during run-time. CFU loading and execution is initiated by special EPIC-style instructions, thus complex and highly specialized compilers are required.

Another approach dealing with EPIC and configurable logic are the customisable EPIC processors . Here, the number of functional units, the instructions and the number of registers is determined at compile time. The execution parameters depend on the program to be run. Like this an optimized EPIC core for a special application is generated. As the AEPIC does, the customisable EPIC also requires specialized compilers. In contrast to the Adaptive EPIC concept, this approach is not only limited to configurable logic.

3   Self Reconfiguring EPIC Soft Core Processors

Based on the EPIC paradigm explained above, we develop a novel EPIC Core, that benefits from run-time reconfigurable hardware and operates with machine code generated by existing EPIC compilers. One of our main objectives is to ease the use of our processor core by providing well-engineered development software. For this reason, the adopted compiler will most likely be based on the Trimaran framework [11], a complete framework for building EPIC compilers, that offers the ability to exploit ILP.

3.1   Functional Units

Since the EPIC machine code is designed independently from the number of functional units and targets instruction level parallelism, it is possible to utilize the number of available functional units. Based on this, the main aspect of our EPIC Soft Core will be the ability to change the number and nature (i.e. integer, floating point or branch unit) of its functional units at run-time. The number of configured FUs depends only on the usable space on the FPGA while their characteristic depends on the operations to be executed. A scheduling unit distributes the instructions.

3.2   Registers

Another advantage of the Self Reconfiguring EPIC Soft Core is the ability to adapt its number of registers during run-time. Using this mechanism, context switching can be accelerated if there is enough space on the FPGA. If possible, another preconfigured set of registers is used instead of pushing all registers onto the stack. Only the connecting wires to the registers are parametrized to access an other register set. As a result, performance and chip space is dynamically traded-off.

3.3   Example for an Operating EPIC Soft Core

The EPIC Soft Core , as depicted in Fig. 1, consists of an instruction-queue, an unit for dispatching and scheduling of instructions and a varying number of floating point or integer units and registers. In the initial state, the core operates with a floating point and an integer unit. When a large number of integer operations needs to be computed, an initial reconfiguration step is performed. In this step, an integer unit is added to speed up integer calculations. If no floating point operations are foreseeable but numerous integer operations waiting, the floating point unit is replaced by another integer unit as shown in step 2. In step 3, a call to a subroutines is realized by adding another register set.

3.4   Prototype

Our current EPIC Soft Core implementation is realized on an RC200 [15] development platform from Celoxica. The prototyper hosts a Xilinx Virtex II FPGA [6]. For the programming and configuration of the self reconfiguring EPIC we exclusively use the Xilinx ISE [7] tool suite. For building the first prototype we have chosen the Oregano 8051 IP core [16] as a baseline, because of its clear structure and good documentation. In our work, we modified the core's control unit such that either one or two integer FUs can be chosen. For additional flexibility, the FUs are dynamically reconfigurable.

In the initial research, several experiments have successfully been conducted. In our first implementation, the principle of operation was validated by manual initiation of the reconfiguration via a JTAG interface during run-time.

Current work targets to reconfigure the FUs via Xilinx' ICAP Port [10], triggered automatically by an on-chip decision unit. Here, the control unit will be expanded to deal with a larger number of ALUs. In our upcoming version, the instruction set will be enlarged to execute code produced by off-the-shelf compilers.

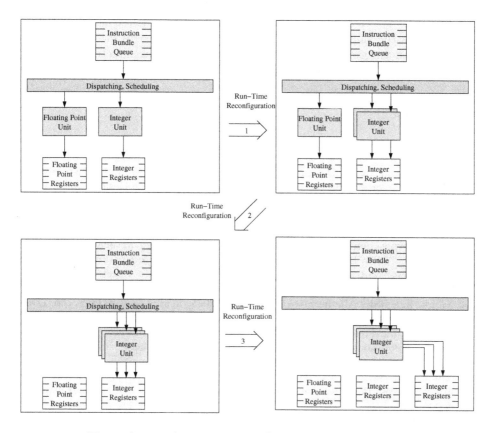

Fig. 1. A typical reconfiguration flow of the EPIC Soft Core

4   Summary and Conclusions

In this short contribution, we introduce a new type of a soft core processor. By its way of exploiting parallelism, the self reconfiguring EPIC soft core is able to trade off dynamically between chip area and computing performance. Due to its support of standard compilers, the opportunities of this kind of core are obvious.

In future work, we will improve the prototype based on the given concepts and provide benchmark results. These results will lead to further improvements in the architecture. Additional benefits are expected from:

reducing the instruction set of the FUs,
scheduling reconfiguration by the compiler,
enforcing more parallel source code by augmenting the used high level language with explicit parallel instructions,
allowing custom instructions, which compute more complex functions in hardware.

First experiments have shown, that our core may run on much lower clock rates compared to traditional soft cores when sufficient reprogrammable resources are available. We believe this results in much lower power consumption but still provides the same computing performance compared to other soft cores. Depending on the comparison we will discover, if our architecture enables a trade-off between chip space and power consumption as well.

References

1. Surendranath Talla: Adaptive explicitly parallel instruction computing. PhD thesis, New York University, 2000.
2. W. W. S. Chu, R. G. Dimond, S. Perrott, S. P. Seng and W. Luk: Customisable EPIC Processor: Architecture and Tools. Proc. Conference on Design, Automation and Test in Europe - Volume 3, 2004.
3. Michael S. Schlansker, B. Ramakrishna Rau: EPIC: An Architecture for Instruction-Level Parallel Processors. HP Laboratories Palo Alto, February 2000.
4. Altera Corporation: Nios Embedded Processor System. www.altera.com/nios.
5. Xilinx, Inc.: MicroBlaze Soft Processor Core. www.xilinx.com/microblaze.
6. Xilinx, Inc.: Virtex-II Platform FPGAs: Complete Data Sheet. March 2005, http://direct.xilinx.com/bvdocs/publications/ds031.pdf.
7. Xilinx, Inc.: ISE, All the Speed You Need. 2005, http://www.xilinx.com/ise/devsys_overview.pdf.
8. opencores.org: Free Open Source IP Cores and Chip Design. www.opencores.org.
9. Actel Corporation: CoreMP7 - Bringing ARM7 to the Masses. www.actel.com/arm7
10. Xilinx, Inc.: Virtex-II Platform FPGA User Guide, pages 297f., Internal Configuration Access Port (ICAP). March 2005, www.xilinx.com/bvdocs/userguides/ug002.pdf.
11. The Trimaran Consortium: An Infrastructure for Research in Instruction-Level Parallelism. www.trimaran.org.
12. Intel Corporation: Intel Itanium 2 Processor. www.intel.com/itanium.
13. Jerry Huck, Dale Morris, Jonathan Ross, Allan Knies, Hans Mulder and Rumi Zahir: Introducing the IA-64 architecture. IEEE Micro, 20(5):1223, 2000.
14. RC Cofer and Ben Harding: FPGA Soft Processor Design Considerations. Programmable Logic DesignLine, October 2005, www.pldesignline.com/showArticle.jhtml?articleID=172300690.
15. Celoxica Limited: Platform Developers Kit, RC200/203 hardware and PSL Reference Manual. 2004, http://www.celoxica.com/techlib/files/CEL-W04091016TC-135.pdf.
16. Oregano Systems Design & Consulting GesmbH: MC8051 IP Core, Oregano Systems 8-bit Microcontroller IP-Core. Version 1.2, June 2002, http://www.oregano.at/ip/8051.htm

Constant Complexity Management of 2D HW Multitasking in Run-Time Reconfigurable FPGAs*

S. Román, J. Septién, H. Mecha, and D.Mozos

Departamento de Arquitectura de Computadores y Automática,
Universidad Complutense, 28040 Madrid, Spain

Abstract. This paper presents a constant complexity and fast algorithm for the management of run-time reconfigurable resources by an operating system with extended hardware multitasking functionality. Our algorithm manages a two dimensional reconfigurable device by dividing the resource area into four partitions with different sizes. Each partition has an associated queue where the hardware manager places each arriving task depending on its size, shape, deadline requirements and the state of queues. It is possible to merge partitions for tasks not fitting any partition. The sizes of the partitions may be adapted to different circumstances.

1 Introduction

The size and density of present FPGA devices together with features such as partial run-time reconfiguration make them very suitable for a variety of applications with an inherent parallelism [1,2]. Reconfigurable HW can be viewed as a large two-dimensional processing area which holds a set of tasks previously compiled to a relocatable HW bitmap, loaded for execution at a free section of the FPGA. Each HW task can enter or leave the FPGA without affecting the other executing tasks. This HW multitasking should be managed by the same Operating System (OS) that manages SW resources[3]. This new functionality poses several problems such as deciding which parts of the application should be executed in the HW device or where to locate tasks in it.

There are several works about this topic: [4,5] deal with the problems derived of dynamically managing 2D Run Time Reconfigurable (RTR) resources. All of them propose complex algorithms to keep the information of the available FPGA area. However, [6] simplifies the algorithm by dividing the FPGA area in four partitions of equal area. Excessive area is wasted when the tasks are too small for the partitions, and bigger tasks have to be discarded. [7] have presented an algorithm in which they split the FPGA in several blocks with different sizes, but they have applied this only to 1D FPGAs.

* This research was supported by Spanish Ministerio de Ciencia y Tecnología, through the research grant TEC2005-04752/MIC.

K. Bertels, J.M.P. Cardoso, and S. Vassiliadis (Eds.): ARC 2006, LNCS 3985, pp. 187–192, 2006.
© Springer-Verlag Berlin Heidelberg 2006

Our O(1) algorithm makes fast decisions about allocation and scheduling for incoming tasks, does not need complex data structures and the different sizes of the partitions provide enough flexibility to achieve a good use of the FPGA area. Other features allow taking run-time decisions to solve punctual overloading problems and the possibility of adapting partitions' sizes to different distributions of workloads. Although we present a version of our algorithm for 2D FPGAs, the algorithm is easily translated to 1D management for an existing reconfigurable device such as Virtex II.

2   System Architecture

Our system model is shown in fig.1(left). Tasks may be initially executed in SW or HW, depending on the task time constraints, and the available SW and HW resources. Traditional OS functionality has been extended with the RTR HW manager, that decides where and when to place each arriving task. Fast decision making is decisive in this type of environment.

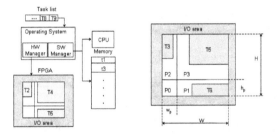

Fig. 1. System model

FPGA and task models are shown in fig.1(right). The FPGA is a 2D grid of identical cells. We reserve a peripheral bus that guarantees tasks' I/O access around a rectangular core of W x H cells used for task execution. The core is divided into four partitions with different sizes that execute one task at a time. Core partitions are defined by two dividing lines: $x = w_p$ and $y = hp$. We then have P0, P1, P2 and P3. The exact values of wp and hp (and thus the relative size of the partitions) may be changed during run-time according to the profile of the task set being processed. Tasks are rectangles which include all the necessary processing and internal routing resources. Each task comes as a tuple: $T_i = \{w_i, h_i, tarr_i, tex_i, tmax_i\}$, where w_i is the task width, h_i its height, $tarr_i$ the clock cycle in which it arrives, tex_i the execution time for the task and $tmax_i$ the time constraint for the task. They are always placed at the selected partition at the outer corner, in order to guarantee access to the bus. Tasks may be rotated.

The main features of the management algorithm are shown in fig.2. Each partition Pi has an associated queue Qi that keeps pending tasks allocated to it.

Each of the queues has a waiting time, wt_i, which is the sum of the execution times of the tasks in it plus the remaining time for the task in the partition to finish execution. As each new task arrives, the Scheduling-Allocating Unit (SAU) examines its size and time constraints, and writes the task into the queue where it fits better, determining the location and time for the task execution on the FPGA. The Execution Unit works in parallel with the SAU. It reads tasks from the queues and sends them to the FPGA every time one or more tasks finish execution. The Dynamic Adjustment Unit (DAU) examines the performance of the algorithm and decides what changes are needed and when to apply them. If the algorithm performance decreases, it may change some of the decision taking parameters or the configuration of the partitions.

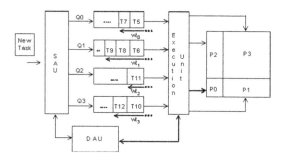

Fig. 2. HW manager structure

We have carried out several tests in order to prove that our $O(1)$ complexity algorithm may compete in performance with other common algorithms such as First Fit (FF), of $O(n^4)$ for the 2D allocation problem (n is the dimension of a square FPGA). They have been published in [8].

3   Partition Merging

There may be some tasks that do not fit any partition. In this case two (or the four) free partitions may be used jointly in order to allocate them. This partition merging is a temporary solution for such tasks. The possible combinations of partitions are: P0+P1, P0+P2, P1+P3, P2+P3 or P0+P1+P2+P3. The SAU examines which is the best possible combination of partitions to allocate the task. It first looks for the two smallest possible partitions that may be merged. Then it examines if waiting for both partitions to be free at the same time complies with the time restrictions of the task. If it does not, it continues looking for other combinations of partitions until it finds one that does.

The merging process leads to the appearance of gaps in the scheduling of tasks due to the necessity of waiting for the partitions to become free at the same time. Once there is a gap in any of the queues, the SAU will always try to fill them with as many as possible tasks. The gaps are marks placed at the queues' parameters and need not be written into a separate "gap queue" thus not increasing our algorithm's complexity (with the cost of having only one gap per queue).

4 Dynamic Adjusting to Task Profile Variations

Our algorithm works well enough when the tasks are of different and varied sizes, which we call a heterogeneous task set. For such task profile, the statistical distribution of sizes is in accordance with the FPGA distribution of area into partitions. Natural queue balance of workload is attained by writing each arriving task into the queue where it best fits in terms of less area wasted (approximate 25% of tasks are written into each queue). If the tasks arriving are very similar in size and shape, the queue balance is disturbed and one of the queues appears much more loaded than the rest, resulting in a low use of FPGA area and excessive execution delay for the tasks arriving.

We have tested several types of reactions of our algorithm to different changes in task profiles. We have seen that different types of actions are needed depending on the situation:

1. Peak: a high number of tasks of the same size arrive in a short lapse of time. This causes a temporary overloading of one of the queues. The solution consists in forcing queue balance by relocating one task from the overloaded queue.
2. Long peak: a peak that exceeds a certain threshold. The solution is to make a change in the queue selection criterium.
3. Profile change: the number of tasks of similar size arriving may be considered a permanent change in the task profile. In this case we can choose between two policies: clustering tasks into the same partition or re-arranging the size of the partitions. We now analyse the suitable strategies for different task profiles.

Small task profile: the size of the partitions needs to be changed so that many tasks currently being classified as small may be classified as medium (sent to Q1 and Q2 instead of Q0) and therefore some tasks going to Q1 and Q2 will go to Q3. This is achieved by reducing hp and/or wp so that the size of P0 decreases. The mean area used increases significantly when the size of the partitions is well adjusted to the task profile features, but is still too low for a satisfactory performance. In this case, the only possible solution is to execute more than four tasks on the FPGA at the same time by means of task clustering.

Medium task profile: if the majority of tasks are being sent to Q1 and Q2, the way to better adjust partitions size to task profile is to increase the size of P0 and therefore to reduce P3.

Large task profile: this is one of the toughest problems to solve by any algorithm, as having a majority of large tasks (we are calling large any task that is over 25% of FPGA size) in a very saturated environment may mean that the device has become insufficient. Here we need to distinguish between two cases:

1. Tasks are too big for P0, P1 or P2 but of a size around 25% of FPGA size, so we may execute four of them simultaneously. They are not requiring partition merging. The solution is to set FPGA partitions to very similar sizes, to decrease P3 and to increase P1, P2 and P0.

2. Tasks are of such large size, more than 25% of FPGA size, that only one of them may be executed in the FPGA at a time. They are requiring partition merging frequently, and the solution is to increase P3 to a size large enough to avoid frequent merging.

```
If queue unbalance triggers the alarm:
        force queue balance by moving one task from queue
        set timer T1 and calculate % area used
        if T1 expires without another alarm:
                do nothing /* this was a peak */
        else /* this is a long peak */
                change queue selection to force queue balance
                set timer T2 and calculate % area used
                when T2 expires:
                        reset queue selection to minimum area waste
                        if % area used during T2 > % area used during T1:
                                do nothing
                        else /* this is a profile change */
                                change the size and/or symmetry of partitions
```

Fig. 3. HW manager structure

Before a new task is written into the queues, the DAU examines how it affects queue balance and is responsible for triggering an alarm when the workload in the queues is going in a too unbalanced direction. The criterium we are using to detect queue unbalance (QUB) is to compare the difference between the maximum waiting time of any of the queues with the minimum waiting time of the queues relative to the mean execution time of tasks. The DAU triggers the alarm when QUB exceeds a certain threshold. The algorithm that the DAU uses for the alarm management at run-time is shown in fig.3.

5   Experimental Results

We have simulated the possible situations the DAU may encounter during execution by means of task sets consisting of 200 tasks each. The baseline is a completely heterogeneous task set in which the three different types of situations have been reproduced. We have simulated the three different reactions of our algorithm and the performance results. We are using the mean percentage of FPGA area and the number of time units used for the execution of the whole task set as performance metrics and we are comparing the algorithm performance when the alarm system is disabled and enabled. We have also simulated a long peak of medium tasks and a change in the task profile. Results in table 1 show how the performance of the algorithm is improved when the DAU is active and solves the problems caused by variations in task profile.

Table 1. Performance comparison results obtained

Event	Simulation	Time units	% area used
Small peak	Alarm disabled	275	61.5
Small peak	Alarm enabled	266	63.6
Long peak	Alarm disabled	277	61.2
Long peak	Alarm enabled	266	63.7
Profile change	Alarm disabled	229	50.0
Profile change	Alarm enabled	187	61.2

6   Conclusions

Our $O(1)$ algorithm is fast in scheduling and allocating incoming tasks in a heavily loaded environment and may compete in performance with other high complexity algorithms such as First Fit. The performance of the algorithm is optimum for heterogeneous task sets and good enough in situations where the workload is unbalanced in relation to partitions, as we have seen it is capable of absorbing peaks of homogeneous workloads. It also guarantees execution of tasks not fitting any partition and may adapt the partitions' sizes to the features of the task set.

References

1. Compton, K., Hauck, S.: Reconfigurable Computing: A Survey of Systems and Software. ACM Computing Surveys (2002) pp 171–210
2. Budiu, M.: Application-Specific Hardware: Computing Without CPUs. Fourth CMU Symposium on Computer Systems (2001) pp 1–10
3. Diessel, O.: Opportunities for Operating Systems Research in Reconfigurable Computing. Technical report ACRC-99-018 (1999)
4. O.Diessel: On Dynamic Task Scheduling for FPGA-based Systems. International Journal of Foundations of Computer Science, IJFCS'01 (2001) pp 645–669
5. Handa, M., Vemuri, R.: An efficient algorithm for finding empty space for online FPGA placement. DAC (2004) pp 960–965
6. Merino, P., López, J., Jerome, M.: A hardware operating system for dynamically reconfiguration of FPGAs. FPL'98 (1998) pp 431–435
7. Walder, H., Platzner, M.: Online scheduling for block-partitioned reconfigurable devices. DATE'03 (2003) pp 10290–10295
8. Román, S., Septién, J., Mecha, H., Mozos, D., Tabero, J.: Partition-based algorithm for efficient 2D HW multitasking. EUROMICRO WIP (2003) pp 26–27

Area/Performance Improvement of NoC Architectures

Mário P. Véstias[1] and Horácio C. Neto[2]

[1] ISEL/INESC-ID, Portugal
mvestias@deetc.isel.ipl.pt
[2] INESC-ID, Portugal
hcn@inesc-id.pt

Abstract. The design of electronic systems in a System-on-Chip (SoC) depends on the reliable and efficient interconnection of many different components. The Network-on-Chip (NoC) has emerged as a scalable communication infrastructure with high bandwidth able to tackle the communication needs of future SoC. In this paper, we present a generic NoC architecture that can be customized to the specific communication needs of an application in order to reduce the area with minimal degradation of the latency of the system.

1 Introduction

The constant increase of gate capacity and performance of single chips made it possible to implement complex systems in a single chip (System-on-Chip - SoC) able to tackle the demanding requirements of many embedded systems. An approach to the design of such systems in a single hardware chip is to reuse hardware/software IP cores, resulting in a considerable number of autonomous interconnected cores.

Traditional interconnection architectures, such as a single shared bus or a hierarchy of buses, are no longer a solution to support the increasing interconnection complexity and bandwidth demands of such hardware/software platforms due to their poor scalability and shared bandwidth. It is expected that in the future the aggregate communication bandwidth between cores will scale up to values much larger than the Gbytes/s range for many video applications [1].

To overcome these problems, the Network-on-Chip (NoC) has been introduced as a new interconnection paradigm able to integrate a number of IP cores while keeping a high communication bandwidth between them [2][3]. A NoC is made of a set of similar components designated routers interconnected to each other to forward data through the interconnection structure.

Routers introduce a relative area overhead and increase the average communication latency. Therefore, in the design process it is important to consider mechanisms to reduce the area and the average latency of the NoC infrastructure. Some approaches have already been proposed to minimize the average communication delay and the area overhead of NoC. In [4], Murali and DeMicheli

K. Bertels, J.M.P. Cardoso, and S. Vassiliadis (Eds.): ARC 2006, LNCS 3985, pp. 193–198, 2006.
© Springer-Verlag Berlin Heidelberg 2006

presented a mapping algorithm aiming to minimize the average communication delay. Lei et al. [5] use a two step genetic algorithm to map tasks looking to maximize timing performances. In [6], Kreutz et al. proposed three different routers with different performance, energy and area occupation and an algorithm to find the best combination of routers. All these approaches are mainly concerned with average latency reduction, except the work of Kreutz, which also considers area.

In this paper, we propose a generic NoC architecture that can be customized to the specific communication needs of an application in order to reduce the area with minimal degradation of the latency of the system. We have developed a generic router that can have from 1 to 4 local connections to IP cores allowing neighbor routers to communicate through a single router, which will potentially reduce the average latency communication. Our generic router has been characterized and a set of NoC instances have been implemented to demonstrate the area improvement that can be attained with our generic architectures.

2   Network-on-Chip Architecture

A NoC consists of a set of routers interconnected according to a certain topology. A router is used to route messages along the topology. In a typical NoC, a router is connected to at most four neighbor routers and to a local core. Among the many interconnection topologies, the most used is a mesh topology because a 2D network fits naturally in a 2-dimensional chip. Each core connects to the communication infrastructure through only one router, and links between routers have the same bandwidth (see example in figure 1).

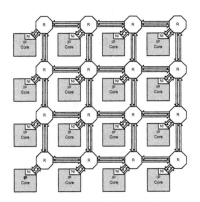

Fig. 1. Typical NoC Architecture

Homogeneous interconnection architectures are easily scaled up and facilitate modular design, but are not tailored to the application characteristics. They are probably the best choice for general-purpose computing. However, systems developed for a particular class of applications can benefit from a more heterogeneous communication infrastructure that provides high bandwidth in a localized fashion where it is needed to eliminate bottlenecks [7]. The traditional NoC structure does not take advantage of this property in spite of the physical proximity of the cores. To obtain NoC solutions with lower area overhead and average communication latency, we propose the design of a NoC based on the generic architecture of figure 2.

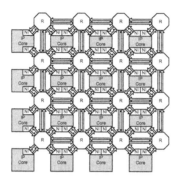

Fig. 2. Generic NoC Architecture

In the generic NoC architecture, a router can have up to four local connections with neighbor cores. Therefore, neighbors can exchange data through a single router, reducing communication latency. The generic architecture also considers the adjustment of the bandwidth between routers to accommodate the expected traffic at a specific link. Link bandwidth is adjustable by changing the number of wires.

The careful customization of the NoC structure with the most appropriate number and type of routers and the proper number of connections and bandwidth will lead us to a communication structure that uses less area and exhibits lower average communication latency than the typical NoC structure.

3   Router Design

After receiving a data packet, the router reads the packet destination address and forwards it to the correct output port. To attain this, a router has several input and output ports connected to neighbor routers and to local IP cores, a switch that establishes a connection between any pair of input and output ports, a routing policy to determine through which output port a packet should be forward and a set of arbiters to control the simultaneous accesses to output ports. The communication ports include buffers to temporarily store packets (see a router with four ports in figure 3).

The routing policy is implemented in each input port using the route block. Our implementation uses the simple XY routing algorithm. Having determined the destination port, the routing block sends a request to the arbiter associated with the destination output port.

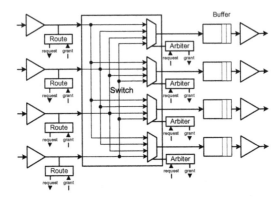

Fig. 3. Router architecture with four input and four output ports

Since the arbiter may receive more than one request from different input ports, it uses an arbitration policy to choose among the requesting input ports. The arbiter of our router uses a round-robin technique. The packet is finally switched from the input port to the output port through the switch, which is nothing more than a set of multiplexers, as represented in figure 3.

The switching policy of our router is a trade-off between wormhole routing and store-and-forwarding routing, which we designate *n-flit wormhole routing*. In this algorithm, the router receives n-flits before forwarding them. For each group of n-flits, only the first one contains the destination address. A router only receives a packet if it has enough buffer space available to store the n-flits. This way, it avoids leaving flits along the path, like in wormhole, and reduces the latency of store-and-forward by reducing the number of stored flits before being forwarded. The only disadvantage is that each group of n-flits must include a flit with the routing information. In our approach, we are using n = 4.

We have described our generic router in VHDL and than implemented it in an XC2V6000 FPGA. From the implementation, we concluded that in the worst case it can operate at a frequency around 100 MHz. Since the switch of the router is fully connected, the router is able to forward n packets at a time, where n is the number of ports. It means that it has a total bandwidth of b x n, where b is the bandwidth of a single port. For example, a router with six ports, a datawidth of 16 bits operating at 100MHz has a total bandwidth of 9,6 Gbps.

The areas occupied by routers are resumed in table 1.

Table 1. Area of router (slices)

Num of Ports	8 bits	16 bits
5	232	284
6	380	459

Table 1 contains the number of slices used to implement routers with different number of ports and bitwidths, and FIFOs with a depth of 16 words. These routers support a SoC with up to 256 cores. The block of the router using more area is the switch. A switch with 6 ports consumes 192 slices for 16 bit words.

4   NoC Area/Performance Evaluation

To get an idea of the total area reduction and the influence over the latency that is attainable if we use different NoC topologies, we have conducted the analysis of two different NoC topologies with 6 x 6 nodes for two different traffic patterns.

One topology is the typical one previously illustrated in figure 1 where a router have 5 ports including a local port (5-router topology). The other NoC topology consists of a mesh of routers with two local ports, where routers have 6 ports, allowing the connection of two cores to a single router (6-router topology) (see figure 4).

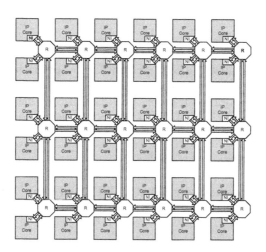

Fig. 4. Second network topology pattern used in the experiments

The traffic patterns used were the complement traffic pattern (type 1) and the local neighbor traffic (type 2).

The 5-router topology uses 7248 slices and the 6-router uses 5702 slices, which is about 31% lower than the former topology. This happens because it has half the routers and a router with six ports is smaller than two routers with five ports. However, the 5-router topology has 252 links and the 6-router topology has just 192. Therefore, the average bandwidth used per link is higher in the second topology, which may potentially create more hot spots of traffic congestion.

We have also analyzed the influence of NoC configurations over the average latency communication (see figure 5).

From the graphics, we conclude that for traffic type 1, the 6-ports router topology has lower average communication latency for injection rates over 40%. One explanation for this fact is that this topology has on average fewer routers

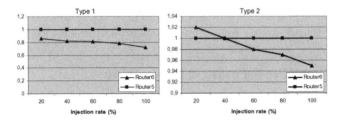

Fig. 5. NoC average latency for traffic type 1 and type 2

in the communication paths. For traffic type 2, the 6-ports router topology has obtained very good results (almost 25% reduction in average latency) because it is tailored to local traffic patterns.

5   Conclusion

The generic architecture proposed in this work allows the improvement of the total area and performance of a NoC structure. Our approach has obtained good results when tested with some topologies and traffic patterns. We are implementing a design space exploration tool for the design of NoC-based systems-on-chip that includes our generic NoC architecture and configurable router.

Acknowledgments

The authors thank the support granted by ISEL and INESC-ID.

References

1. Guerrier, P., Greiner, A.: A generic architecture for on-chip packet-switched interconnections. DATE (2000)
2. Hemani, A., et al.: Network on chip: An arquitectura for billion transistor era. Proceedings of the IEEE NorChip Conference (2000)
3. Dally, W., Towles, B.: Route packets, not wires: on-chip interconnection networks. Proceedings of DAC (2001)
4. Murali, S., Micheli, G.: Bandwidth-constrained mapping of cores onto NoC architetcures. DATE (2004)
5. Lei, T., Kumar, S.: A two-step genetic algorithm for mapping task graphs to a NoC architecture. DSD (2003)
6. Kreutz, M., et al.: Design space exploration comparing homogeneous and heterogeneous network-on-chip architectures. SBCCI (2005)
7. Benini, L., Micheli, G.: Networks on chips: a new SoC paradigm. SBCCI (2005) Computer **35(1)** (2002) 70–78

Implementation of Inner Product Architecture for Increased Flexibility in Bitwidths of Input Array

Kwangsup So, Jinsang Kim[*], Won-Kyung Cho, Young-Soo Kim,
and Doug Young Suh

School of Electronics and Information, Kyung Hee University
#1 Seocheon, Giheung, Yongin, Gyeonggi 449-701 Korea
Tel.: +82-31-201-2942, 2996; Fax: +82-31-203-4968
ssyop79@vlsi.khu.ac.kr, jskim27@khu.ac.kr

Abstract. Most digital signal processing (DSP) algorithms for multimedia and communication applications require multiplication and addition operations. Especially matrix-matrix or matrix-vector multiplication are frequently used in DSP algorithms needs inner product arithmetic which takes most processing time. Also multiplications for the DSP algorithms have different input bitwidths. Therefore, the multiplications for inner product need to be sufficiently flexible in terms of bitwidths to utilize the multiplication resources efficiently. This paper proposes a novel reconfigurable inner product architecture thas is using a pipelined adder array, which features increased flexibility in bitwidths of input arrays. The proposed architecture consists of sixteen 4x4 multipliers and a pipelined adder array and can compute the inner product of input arrays with any combination of multiples of 4 bitwidths such as 4x4, 4x8, 4x12, ...16x16. Experimental results show that the proposed architecture has latency of maximum 9 clock cycles and the throughput of 1 clock cycle for inner product of various bitwidths of input arrays. When TSMC 0.18 um libraries are used, the chip area and power dissipation of the proposed architecture are 332162 (nand gates) and 3.46 mW, respectively. The proposed architecture can be applied to a reconfigurable arithmetic engine for real-time DSP applications.

1 Introduction

Reconfigurable hardware architecture which processes various DSP algorithms in one hardware resource have been increasing studied recently. To achieve real time processing of multimedia and communication signal processing algorithms, the efficient reconfigurable computational elements for addition, multiplication, and inner product operations are needed. Especially matrix-matrix or matrix-vector multiplication frequently used in DSP algorithms needs inner product arithmetic which takes most processing time. Also multiplications for the DSP algorithms have different input bitwidths (e.g. 4x4, 4x8, 4x16, 8x8 ...). Multiplications and inner product operations require complex arithmetic and large hardware resources. Therefore the multiplications for inner product need to be sufficiently flexible in terms of bitwidths to utilize multiplication resources efficiently.

---

[*] Corresponding author.

K. Bertels, J.M.P. Cardoso, and S. Vassiliadis (Eds.): ARC 2006, LNCS 3985, pp. 199 204, 2006.
© Springer-Verlag Berlin Heidelberg 2006

Many researches have been performed to improve the performance of the multiplier and the inner product architecture. Dedicated multipliers for faster multiplication have been studied [1], [2], [3], [4]. These dedicated multipliers lead to high performance. Similar to this, inner product researches have been studied [5], [6], [7], [8]. All the existing multipliers and inner product architectures have tried to improve the processing speed. However, the bitwidths of the input data or input arrays of the existing architectures are fixed or less flexible for dynamic processing various DSP algorithms which usually have different bitwidths of input data to be processed.

This paper proposes a novel reconfigurable inner product architecture using a parallel 4x4 multiplier array and a pipelined adder array, which features increased flexibility in bitwidths of input arrays (any combination of multiples of 4 bitwidths such as 4x4, 4x8, 4x12, ...16x16). The proposed inner product architecture uses 4x4 multipliers to compute the partial products of inner product and then the partial products are fed into a parallel and pipelined adder tree to compute the final inner product result.

2   Proposed Reconfigurable Pipelined Inner Product Architecture

The proposed reconfigurable inner product architecture has two functional blocks, parallel 4x4 multiplier array and pipelined 4-bit adder array. The functional block diagram of the proposed architecture is shown in Fig. 1. Parallel 4x4 multiplier array generates the partial product of 4n x 4m multiplication and the pipelined 4-bit adder array computes additions for inner products. Bitwidths signal controls the input bitwidths of both multiplicand and multiplier.

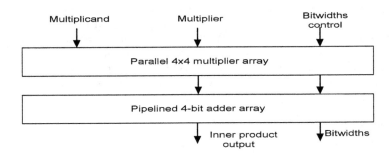

Fig. 1. Functional block diagram of the proposed reconfigurable inner product architecture

2.1   Parallel 4x4 Multiplier Array

Parallel 4x4 multiplier array consists of sixteen 4x4 multipliers, output register which stores the 16 4x4 multiplier's result which is fed into the pipelined adder array. The multiplicand and the multiplier are the input data of the parallel multipliers. The bitwidths of input data are determined by Bitwidths control signal. (e.g. 4x4, 4x8, 4x12 ... 16x16). Fig. 2 shows the architecture of the parallel 4x4 multiplier array.

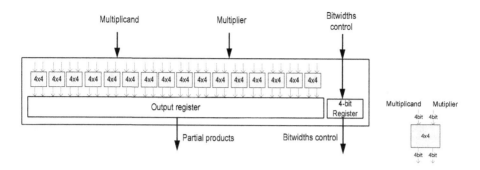

Fig. 2. Parallel 4x4 multiplier array and 4x4 multiplier

2.2 Pipelined Adder Array

Pipelined adder array is used for the summation of partial products to reduce the critical path in the adder tree. We modify Dadda algorithm [6] for additions of the partial products by grouping 4-bit data. Fig. 3 shows the examples of the partial product additions with different bitwidths of input data.

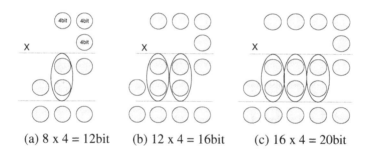

(a) 8 x 4 = 12bit   (b) 12 x 4 = 16bit   (c) 16 x 4 = 20bit

Fig. 3. Examples of the partial product addition with different bitwidths

A configuration example of pipelined adder array is shown in Fig. 4. In multiplier array block, each output of the 4x4 multiplier has the size of 8-bit results. Thus the parallel sixteen 4x4 multipliers lead to 128-bit (=16x8 bits) output. This result is fed into input data of the pipelined adder array. At the first stage, the adder array accumulates the 4 bits of LSB. At the second stage, the adder array accumulates the 4 bits of MSB. The carry-out generated during addition of the 4 LSB bits, is used for carry-in during addition of the 4 MSB bits. The carry-outs generated during addition of the 4 MSB bits, can be computed by two 7:3 counters. In this way, we can reduce the pipeline stage. Therefore, we get maximum 12-bit inner product result: 4 bits (2 counter's result) + 4 bits (addition result of 4 MSB bits) + 4 bits (addition result of 4 LSB bits).

Table 1 shows the analysis results of hardware resource utilization for inner products with various configurations. For 4n x 12 multiplication (n=1, 2, 3, 4), there are unused multipliers. These unused multipliers may consume power dissipation. Thus, the unused multipliers or counters can be turned-off for low-power applications.

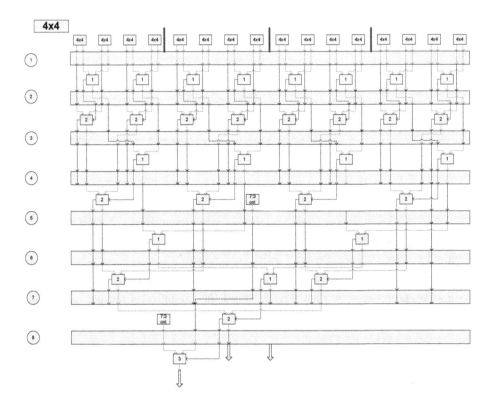

Fig. 4. Configuration example of inner product for sixteen 4x4 elements

Table 1. Utilization of hardware resources

Multipli-cation	Needed # of 4x4 multipliers	Unused 4x4 multipliers	# of partial products	Bitwidths of a partial product	Inner product result
4x4	1	0	16	8 bits	8 bits x 2^4 = 12 bits
4x8	2	0	8	12 bits	12 bits x 2^3 = 15 bits
4x12	3	4	4	16 bits	16 bits x 2^2 = 18 bits
4x16	4	0	4	20 bits	20 bits x 2^2 = 22 bits
8x8	4	0	4	16 bits	16 bits x 2^2 = 18 bits
8x12	6	4	2	20 bits	20 bits x 2^1 = 21 bits
8x16	8	0	2	24 bits	24 bits x 2^1 = 25bits
12x12	9	7	1	24 bits	24 bits x 2^0 = 24 bits
12x16	12	4	1	28 bits	28 bits x 2^0 = 28 bits
16x16	16	0	1	32 bits	32 bits x 2^0 = 32 bits

Compared the proposed architecture to the multiplication and multiplication-accumulation architecture of Chin-Long Wey and Jin-Fu Li [4], the proposed architecture is more flexible in terms of the bitwidths of input data than Chin-Long Wey and Jin-Fu Li's n x n input bitwidths (n is multiples of 8). Also, the Chin-Long Wey and Jin-Fu Li's architecture has an amount of unused hardware resources to produce multiplication and multiplication-accumulation with bitwidths of nonmultiple of 8.

3 Experimental Result

Fig. 5 show the functional simulation result of the proposed multiplier. In the simulation, the multiplicand and multiplier A and B are set all '1'. Therefore the partial product result of parallel 4x4 multiplier array is 11100001(E1 Hex). When the 4x4 inner product scheme is selected, this partial product output E1(Hex) is fed to the input data of pipelined adder array. Therefore the inner product result is the addition of the sixteen E1 (16 x 225 = 3600). The latency and throughput of the proposed reconfigurable inner product architecture are 9 clock cycles and 1 clock cycle, respectively. Also, we can confirm the results are correct when inputs of A and B are changed every clock.

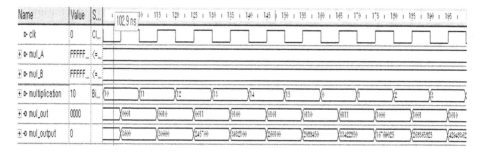

Fig. 5. Functional simulation result

The proposed inner product architecture was synthesized by using Synopsys Design Vision and placed and routed by using Synopsys Astro. TSMC 0.18um CMOS libraries were used in this experiment. Table 2 shows chip area of the proposed multiplier. The chip area of parallel multiply array block and the pipelined adder array block are 160506 (nand gates) and 171655 (nand gates), respectively. Since the proposed architecture performs inner products with various reconfigurable bitwidths, the parallel adder array block requires larger chip area. And the critical path is 0.19ns at adder array block. Table 3 shows the power dissipation measured by using Design vision.

Table 2. Chip area of the proposed multiplier (unit: nand gate)

Parallel multiply array	Pipelined adder array	Total
160506	171655	332162

Table 3. Power dissipation of the proposed multiplier

Cell internal power	Net switching power	Total dynamic power	Cell leakage power
2.748 mW	708.747 uW	3.457 mW	1.970 uW

4 Conclusion

In this paper, we proposed reconfigurable inner product architecture for the multimedia and communication processing applications. The proposed architecture utilizes parallelism and pipelining for reconfigurable high-speed inner product arithmetic with various bitwidths of input array. Experimental results show that the proposed architecture generates the inner product output of various bitwidths of input arrays every clock and can compute the inner product of input arrays with any combination of multiples of 4 bitwidths such as 4x4, 4x8, 4x12,...,16x16. The proposed architecture has advantages over existing architectures in terms of flexibility and the processing speed. Therefore, the proposed architecture can be applied to a reconfigurable arithmetic engine for real-time DSP applications.

Acknowledgement

This work was supported by the Korean Science and Engineering Foundation under grant R01-2003-000-10149-0 and by IDEC (CAD tools).

References

1. K. Hwang, *Computer Arithmetic,*. New York: Wiley, 1979.
2. Rong Lin, "Reconfigurable parallel Inner product processor architectures," IEEE Trans. VLSI Syst. vol. 9 April 2001, pp. 261-272, 2001.
3. Hanho Lee, "A power-aware scalable pipelined Booth multiplier," SOC Conference, 2004. Proc. IEEE International pp. 123-126, Sept. 2004.
4. Chin-Long Wey and Jin-Fu Li, "Design of reconfigurable array multipliers and multiplier-accumulators," in proc. IEEE Asia-pacific conference, vol. 1, pp. 37-40 , Dec. 2004.
5. S. P. Smith and H. C. Torng, "Design of a fast inner product processor," in Proc. IEEE Symp Computer Arithmetic, pp. 38-43, 1985.
6. L. Breveglieri and L. Dadda, "A VLSI inner product macrocell," *IEEE Trans. VLSI Syst.*, vol. 6, no.2, pp. 292-298, June 1998.
7. L. Dadda, "Fast serial input serial output pipelined inner product units," Internal Rep. 87-031, Dep. Elec. Eng. Inform. Sci. Politecnico di Milano, Milano, Italy, 1987
8. E. Swartzlander, "Merged arithmetic," *IEEE Trans. Computers*, vol. C-29, pp. 946–950, 1980.

A Flexible Multi-port Caching Scheme for Reconfigurable Platforms

Su-Shin Ang[1], George Constantinides[1], Peter Cheung[1], and Wayne Luk[2]

[1] Dept. of Electrical and Electronics Engineering, Imperial College, London
[2] Dept. of Computing, Imperial College, London
sa4@imperial.ac.uk

Abstract. Memory accesses contribute sunstantially to aggregate system delays. It is critical for designers to ensure that the memory subsystem is designed efficiently, and much work has been done on the exploitation of data re-use for algorithms that exhibit static memory access patterns in FPGAs. The proposed scheme enables the exploitation of data re-use for both static and non-static parallel memory access patterns through the use of a multi-port cache, where parameters can be determined at compile time and matched to the statistical properties of the application, and where sub-cache contentions are arbitrated with a semaphore-based system. A complete hardware implementation demonstrates that, for a motion vector estimation benchmark, the proposed caching scheme results in a cycle count reduction of 51% and execution time reduction of up to 24%, using a Xilinx XC2V6000 FPGA on a Celoxica RC300 board. Hardware resource usage and clock frequency penalties are analyzed while varying the number of ports and cache size. Consequently, it is demonstrated how the optimum cache size and number of ports may be established for a given datapath.

1 Introduction

FPGAs have become natural platforms for design implementation or prototyping due to their re-programmability and comparatively short design cycle. One of the main advantages that FPGAs have over traditional processors is the massive amount of available parallelism. External memory bandwidth available for reconfigurable logic, however, has not developed at the same rate, limiting the effective amount of achievable parallelism. Hence, it is critical to account for the memory subsystem during the design process.

Much work has been done in the development of scratchpad memories (SPM) [1,2,3] for algorithms with static memory access patterns. However, algorithms such as the Huffman decoder and some motion vector estimation approaches [4] exhibit data dependent memory access patterns, and as a result, the memory accesses cannot be predicted at compile time.

In this work, a flexible multi-port caching scheme is presented. Besides the exploitation of data re-use inherent in an algorithm, this scheme allows accesses for an arbitrarily parallelized data path and so may be transparently used alongside an existing hardware design. Parallel cache-system accesses are detected and

K. Bertels, J.M.P. Cardoso, and S. Vassiliadis (Eds.): ARC 2006, LNCS 3985, pp. 205–216, 2006.

arbitrated if they are contending for the same sub-cache. A significant speed-up of up to 24% in execution time and a cycle count reduction of up to 51% is observed for a cache size that is approximately 3% of image size for a benchmark application involving motion vector estimation. The contributions of this work are as follows:

1. A novel parameterisable cache design, based on a semaphore-style arbitration scheme, is developed to allow user transparency and parallel accesses to multiple sub-caches.
2. A complete implementation of the caching scheme, including the quantification of clock period degradation and area overhead.
3. FPGA-based *in situ* hardware profiling to determine the trade-off between resource usage and performance benchmark algorithm.

This paper is organized as follows: in Section 2, work related to this paper will be discussed and an overview of the multi-port caching system is given in Section 3. The architecture of the caching system will be discussed in Section 4. In Section 5, implementation details and experimental results for a motion vector estimation algorithm are presented and analyzed and finally, the paper is concluded in Section 6.

2 Related Work

Caches are widely used to exploit data re-use within algorithms. A large volume of work has been done on the improvement of cache performance for software applications [5]. These include techniques to optimize data placement and reduce cache misses [6,7], as well as to reduce the number of tag and way accesses [8].

In [9], a dynamic scheme is used for the allocation of variables to scratchpad memory (SPM) which is implemented using block RAMs. Profiling and loop transformation are carried out by the compiler. Based on this profile, the variables are allocated to the SPM for the exploitation of data re-use. However, this approach only considers static memory access patterns. Another compiler that is capable of detecting data re-use is [10]. Smart buffers are inserted at the input and output of the datapath and these in turn interface with external memory. These buffers store windows of data that are re-used within the loop body such that external memory accesses are reduced. Similarly, this technique only accounts for static memory access patterns.

Some papers have been published on multi-port caches: in [11], a multi-port cache is implemented using interleaved cache banks targeting the MIPS 2000 instruction set. This work targets superscalar processors, enabling multiple instructions to be carried out in parallel. The cache bandwidth, however, is limited by the maximum number of instructions that can be issued, restricting the design space that can be explored. In [12], a multi-port cache is implemented by cache duplication. This requires the updating of multiple cache locations in the event of cache misses. The number of ports is restricted to two on the particular platform so the trade off between resources and parallelism is not explored.

This work is targeted at FPGAs. Consequently, cache parameters have to be chosen to match well with the underlying device granularity. The user can determine the number of ports to access cache contents, providing greater leverage over total execution time and resource usage. By taking advantage of the reconfigurability of FPGAs, profiling is carried out *in situ*, on a hardware platform. This allows a wide range of designs to be explored quickly and accurately compared to software modelling. Most importantly, this scheme allows the exploitation of data re-use for non-static memory access patterns.

3   Overview of Multi-port Caching System

Memory accesses can be categorized into different types. During compile time, it might be impossible to determine the exact cycle that main memory is accessed due to data-dependent control. This type of access has *dynamic* timing. Accesses with non-dynamic timing are referred to as *static*. Statically timed memory accesses can have either static or dynamic addresses sequences (dynamic address sequences occur as a result of data dependency). Three major points distinguish this work from others:

1. Previous schemes [9,10] for FPGAs are capable of handling accesses with static timing and address sequence. The proposed caching scheme on the other hand is able to handle dynamic accesses. Therefore, it is potentially more effective for data dependent algorithms.
2. Memory-based optimizations often involve substantial changes to the code [10]. The proposed caching scheme optimizes memory accesses with minimal changes to the high-level code. Further, it does not require the user to sequentialize external memory accesses manually.
3. Multi-ported caches [11] have been explored before. However, our work targets FPGAs where the design space is often larger but permits more rapid and accurate exploration.

In Figure 1(a), the datapath and the proposed caching system are illustrated. Data items are retrieved from external main memory through the cache. N sub-caches are used to provide the parallel accesses required by the datapath, and each of the sub-caches is a variant of a direct-mapped cache.

There are two levels of connectivity in this system. The first level connects the datapath to the cache. M ports allow communication between the caching system and the datapath. Specifically, the datapath can access any of the N sub-caches using any of the given ports. A crossbar switch is therefore necessary to realize this functionality. Given that addresses presented at these ports could contend for the same sub-cache, there is a need for an arbiter to sequentialize accesses should this situation occur. The second level connects the sub-caches to external main memory, which it is assumed has only one port. Since more than one sub-cache might wish to access main memory, the interface to main memory again needs to be able to sequentialize accesses in that situation.

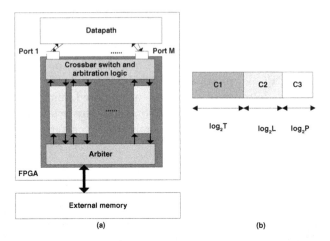

Fig. 1. Proposed multi-port cache: (a) Top-level diagram of caching system. (b) Address mapping scheme.

The address mapping scheme has a transparent address interface; this is shown in Figure 1(b). The address is split into three components: the most significant $\log_2 T$ bits make up the tag of the address, the middle $\log_2 L$ bits are used to determine the correct line within the cache, and the least significant $\log_2 P$ bits are used to determine the sub-cache that is currently targeted. The components are arranged in this order to allow spatial locality of memory accesses to be exploited. Indeed, consecutive sub-caches will store items from consecutive addresses of main memory because the address bits that determine the target sub-cache are the least significant bits.

4   Usage and Arbitration Scheme

This caching scheme is designed in a completely user-transparent way, using a semaphore-based system. An example usage of the cache is shown in Figure 2. Figure 2(a) shows the original source code containing a function stub *func*. The input parameters of the function, *address0* and *address1*, which may not be known at compile time, are used in the retrieval of data items *data0* and *data1* from a common external memory. The result of the computation is then returned to register *O*. To make use of the cache, the external memory access macros are replaced with cache access macros as shown in Figure 2(b). Parallel cache accesses are made possible through the use of the crossbar switch and arbitration logic. It is important to note that in Figure 2(a), assuming only one port of access, the user has to ensure that multiple external memory accesses have to take place in different cycles or the data retrieved will be incorrect, whereas this is transparently ensured by the cache access macros in Figure 2(b).

In Figure 2(b), sub-cache contention may occur. This type of access has static timing but dynamic addressing since the addresses are data-dependent, whereas

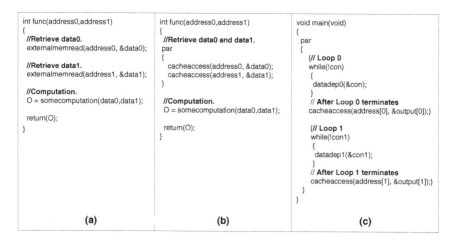

```
int func(address0,address1)
{
  //Retrieve data0.
  externalmemread(address0, &data0);

  //Retrieve data1.
  externalmemread(address1, &data1);

  //Computation.
  O = somecomputation(data0,data1);

  return(O);
}
```

(a)

```
int func(address0,address1)
{
  //Retrieve data0 and data1.
  par
  {
    cacheaccess(address0, &data0);
    cacheaccess(address1, &data1);
  }

  //Computation.
  O = somecomputation(data0,data1);

  return(O);
}
```

(b)

```
void main(void)
{
  par
  {
    {// Loop 0
    while(!con)
    {
      datadep0(&con);
    }
    // After Loop 0 terminates
    cacheaccess(address[0], &output[0]);}

    {// Loop 1
    while(!con1)
    {
      datadep1(&con1);
    }
    // After Loop 1 terminates
    cacheaccess(address[1], &output[1]);}
  }
}
```

(c)

Fig. 2. Cache usage: (a) Original code. (b) Cache substitution. (c) Indeterminate memory access. Note: construct *par* indicates that statements encapsulated within its braces are carried out in parallel.

in the latter example, an example of a memory access with dynamic timing is seen in Figure 2(c). Two concurrent loops are running in parallel and two data dependent functions: *datadep0* and *datadep1* determine when the loops terminate; cache access takes place after loop termination. If *con* and *con1* are asserted in the same cycle, then concurrent cache accesses will take place. If the two accesses are targeting different sub-caches, accesses will take place concurrently. However, under the proposed scheme, these accesses will be sequentialized if the same sub-cache is targeted.

In the proposed scheme, semaphores are used for the architecture of the arbiters at both levels of connectivity to automatically ensure sequential access to the sub-caches as well as external memory when there are multiple requests, facilitating user transparency. The architecture of the arbitration scheme is detailed in the rest of this section.

In [13], algorithms described in a high-level language are translated into hardware by complementing the data path with a token-based control path: a statement is executed when it captures a token; the statement releases this token only upon completion of the task specified by the statement. The token may be duplicated and passed to mutiple statements meant to be carried out in parallel. Upon completion of the task, the token belonging to the statement that consumes the largest number of cycles will be transferred to the next statement in sequence. The proposed arbitration architecture uses such a token-based control scheme. Figure 3(a) shows the block diagram of the semaphore-based system. Token I_x, $1 \leq x \leq N$, is captured by the request block when an assertion is detected. Subsequently, a request for the semaphore guarding the resource is submited using a *trysema* statement; up to N *trysema* statements potentially compete for the semaphore but only one is allowed access to the resource.

Equivalently, only one token, S_x may be granted such that only one statement, x is allowed access to that resource at a time. The semaphore is released when token R_y, $1 \leq y \leq M$, is captured by the Sema state block, which in turn activates the *releasesema* statement, making the semaphore available to other requests. Signal *State* is asserted if the semaphore is captured.

Specifically, the function of individual blocks is described by Boolean equations in Figure 3(b). If I_x is asserted, the corresponding Request block is used to check if the resource is currently occupied. If the resource is free, Q_x is asserted. Otherwise, Q_x is not asserted, but the request is remembered by asserting input of register, P_x^+ for consecutive cycles until the resource is eventually free as shown in line 2 of Figure 3(b). P_x^+ will also be asserted if the semaphore is free but the request is over-ridden by other statements, such that $S_x = 0$. If the semaphore is free, the Priority encoder block is used to determine the statement that is allowed access to this resource. Among the asserted Q_x values, it chooses one with the smallest value of x resulting in lines 3 to 4. If any $S_x = 1$, then *Captured* $= 1$. The state of the semaphore in the next cycle, *State*$^+$, determined by the Sema State block will be asserted if *Captured* $= 1$, or if the resource is currently busy and none of the *releasesema* statements have been asserted as shown in line 5. For this system, the area and delay growth are $O(N^2)$ and $O(\log N + \log M)$ respectively.

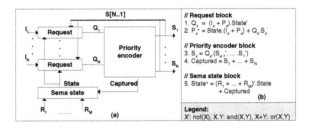

Fig. 3. Architecture of a semaphore-based system: (a) Block diagram. (b) Boolean equations for individual blocks.

5   Implementation and Results

The effectiveness of the caching system is shown in the following sections. The cache is expected to reduce the cycle count. However, degradation in clock speed as well as greater resource utilization will also occur. The experimental setup used to investigate this caching scheme and the performance-resource usage trade-offs in practice will be presented in the following sections.

5.1   Experimental Setup

A memory intensive variant of motion vector estimation [14] is used as a benchmark circuit to test the effectiveness of the caching system. This algorithm and the proposed multi-port cache are implemented using the Handel-C [15] language, which includes semaphores as a built-in construct.

The RC300 board [16] from Celoxica containing a Xilinx Virtex XC2V6000 FPGA is used for this experiment. The FPGA contains 33792 slices and 144 block RAMs [17]. Two external synchronous SRAMs (SSRAM) are used to store image frames. Only one port of access exists for each SSRAM and each access requires two cycles [18]. On-chip block RAMs are used for the implementation of the cache. The access time for block RAM access is one cycle, but logic overheads prolong access time to two cycles for the semaphore-based system which is the same as external memory access time. Therefore, a reduction in overall cycle count comes only by parallelizing accesses to the sub-caches.

Two experiments were conducted. For both experiments, each design is indicated by $S\_X\_Y\_Z$ in Sections 5.2 and 5.3, where X indicates the number of ports, Y indicates the logarithm of the number of cache lines (base 2) within 1 sub-cache, and Z represents the search window size. Two motion vector search window sizes, 7 and 15 pels, are used where a pel indicates a block region in an image frame of size of 16 by 16 pixels. The number of pels represents the distance of the search center from the boundary of a square search area. In Experiment 1, execution time and resource usage are monitored while the number of ports is varied. The number of data items in the cache is held constant at 2^{11} (approximately 3% of frame size). These designs are compared with a reference design where no cache is included. Intuitively, execution time will fall with the increasing parallelism afforded by the increasing memory bandwidth. At the same time, the extent to which spatial locality is exploited increases under the mapping scheme described in Section 3, implying an increased incidence of cache hits. However, degradation in clock speed and resource usage are expected because of logic resources used in the implementation of increasing numbers of semaphores as well as the size of the crossbar switch. In the experiment, the optimum number of ports is established empirically.

In Experiment 2, for each window size, the execution time and resource usage is monitored while the number of cache lines is varied for a constant number of ports, which are found to give the minimum execution time in Experiment 1. With an increase in the number of cache lines, the number of cache hits should increase resulting in execution time reduction. However, more storage and routing resources are needed to accommodate the extra cache lines, leading to degradation in clock speed. Therefore, an optimum trade-off point is again expected.

5.2   Experiment 1

In Table 1, $Baseline\_Z$ indicates the design where no cache is added and external memory accesses are sequentialized by hand; Z represents the search window size. The performance columns are partitioned into two sub-columns. The left column corresponds to values for a search window size of 7 pels and the right column corresponds to 15 pels. A significant reduction of up to 50.6% in cycle count is seen for both $S\_16\_7\_7$ and $S\_16\_7\_15$. However, due to degradation in the clock period, the execution time is reduced by at most 23.6% ($S\_4\_9\_15$) for 15 pels. The maximum reduction in execution time for 7 pels $S\_2\_10\_15$ is 14.7%, for design $S\_2\_10\_7$. Given that the number of cycles required to access data items in the cache is the same as the number of cycles used to access external memory, no significant benefit is observed in a cache with a single port. Indeed, designs $S\_1\_11\_7$ and $S\_1\_11\_15$ have larger cycle counts compared to $Baseline\_7$ and $Baseline\_15$ respectively because each cache miss results in an access time of 3 cycles (the additional cycle consumed over normal external memory access is due to the overhead of tag checking). It can be seen that a reduction in execution time can, however be obtained by parallelizing cache accesses. Also, there is an increase of approximately 52.8% in execution time, comparing the lowest execution time of both 7 and 15 pels, with an increase of search area by 76.5% for each reference block. This increase in resource usage and execution time represents a trade-off between motion vector quality and search window size. The resource usage for both window sizes is the same because they have the same data paths.

Table 1. Table of timing and resource usage for a fixed cache size for window sizes of 7 and 15 pels

Design	Period /ns		Cycle Count /10^8		Execution time /sec per frame		Slice Count	Block RAMs
	Z/pels		Z/pels		Z/pels			
	7	15	7	15	7	15		
Baseline_Z	29.5	29.7	5.78	13.5	17.0	40.2	1166	4
S_1_11_Z	32.8	35.8	5.93	13.9	19.4	49.7	1224	7
S_2_10_Z	34.1	30.4	4.31	10.1	14.7	30.7	1539	8
S_4_9_Z	41.9	43.9	3.47	8.13	14.5	35.7	2363	12
S_8_8_Z	51.4	52.1	3.06	7.15	15.7	37.3	4650	20
S_16_7_Z	62.5	62.9	2.85	6.67	17.8	41.9	10927	36

For the cache design, the number of *trysema* statements, N is equal to the number of *releasesema* statements, M. The slice count increases superlinearly with the number of ports, in line with the $O(N^2)$ prediction of section 4.

A Pareto-optimum trade-off curve between execution time and resource usage is shown in Figure 4. Resource usage is obtained by taking the larger of the proportions of block RAM and slice usage [19] as seen in (1). Note that each point on the graph represents a fully placed and routed design. The leftmost point of the trade-off curve shows the *Baseline* design and the number of ports increase from the left to the right. For 7 pels, beyond a port count of 4, there is an increase in execution time even when more resources are used due to clock period degradation, indicating that the designs are sub-optimal. For 15 pels, $S\_4\_9\_15$ does not lie on the Pareto-optimum curve because of the comparatively smaller clock period of $S\_2\_10\_15$.

$$\text{Resource usage} = \max\left(\frac{B}{T_\text{B}}, \frac{S}{T_\text{S}}\right) \tag{1}$$

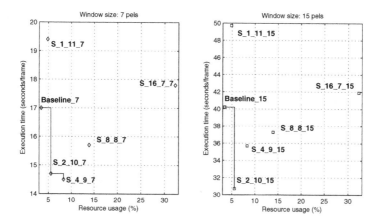

Fig. 4. Graph of execution time versus resource usage for different number of ports on a Xilinx XC2V6000 chip

$$B = \text{Number of block RAMs used in the design}$$
$$T_B = \text{Total number of block RAMs on-chip}$$
$$S = \text{Number of slices used in the design}$$
$$T_S = \text{Total number of slices on-chip}$$

5.3   Experiment 2

In Table 2, the timing and resource usage information with varying number of cache lines are shown for a fixed port count of 4 and 2, for window sizes of 7 and 15 pels respectively. The number of cache lines is not extended beyond 2^{14} because the number of items in the cache exceeds the size of the image beyond that point. An optimum point is seen in the execution time where number of cache lines is 2^{10}. A block RAM is able to hold 2^{11} pixels, so no reduction of block RAM usage is seen below 2^{11} cache lines. However, a reduction of slice count still occurs. The number of data block RAMs for 15 pels is the same for 2^9 and 2^{10} cache lines for the same reason, but two additional block RAMs are required for 2^{11} cache lines to hold the tag and valid bits because of the fixed number of wordlength formats allowed in block RAMs.

The Pareto-optimum curve is shown in Figure 5. The number of cache lines increases with resource usage from the left to the right; For 7 pels, aside from *Baseline_7* and *S_4_11_7*, all other designs are clearly sub-optimal. *S_4_9_7* and *S_4_10_7* are sub-optimal because, by employing design *S_4_11_7*, execution time can be reduced without additional resource usage. This behaviour is attributed to the granularity of the FPGA platform; a block RAM has a storage capacity of 2^{11} pixels so that further reductions in the number of cache lines will still employ one block RAM. Further, designs not lying on the Pareto-optimum curve require more resources but require longer execution times because of clock period

Table 2. Table of timing and resource usage for fixed number of ports (Z refers to the window size in pels and X refers to the number of ports)

Design	Period /ns		Cycle Count /10^8		Execution time /sec per frame		Slice Count		Block RAMs	
	X=4, Z=7	X=2, Z=15	X=4, Z=7	X=2, Z=15	X=4, Z=7	X=2, Z=15	X=4, Z=7	X=2, Z=15	X=4, Z=7	X=2, Z=15
S_X_9_Z	41.9	32.3	3.47	10.2	14.5	33.1	2363	1531	12	8
S_X_10_Z	42.3	30.4	3.31	10.1	14.0	30.7	2374	1539	12	8
S_X_11_Z	40.8	33.2	3.28	9.68	13.4	32.1	2370	1544	12	10
S_X_12_Z	44.6	37.6	3.28	9.64	14.6	36.3	2386	1552	20	14
S_X_13_Z	49.0	37.3	3.28	9.62	16.1	35.9	2399	1556	36	18
S_X_14_Z	47.4	43.5	3.28	9.62	15.5	41.9	2404	1536	48	28

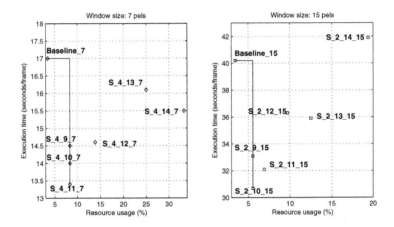

Fig. 5. Graph of execution time versus resource usage for different cache sizes on a Xilinx XC2V6000 chip

degradation. For a window size of 15 pels, the trade-off characteristic is similar. However, *Baseline_15* and *S_2_10_15* are optimal.

6   Conclusion

In this work, a novel multi-port caching scheme for circuits with parallel data-paths has been described. This scheme detects parallel accesses to cache contents dynamically and uses a semaphore-based system to sequentialize these accesses if they are targeted at the same sub-cache. This scheme requires minimal changes to the algorithm description. Significant savings of up to 51% and up to 24% in cycle count and execution time are seen, respectively, for a benchmark application. Further, it was verified in hardware that parallel sub-cache accesses were responsible for the cycle count reduction. However, degradation in clock speed reduces the extent of these gains. Due to the varying degree of clock degradation, the savings are different for different window sizes. A 24% reduction in execution time is seen for a window size of 15 pels compared to 15% for 7 pels. In addition, beyond a specific number of ports and cache size, this degradation negates further reductions in cycle count, leading to an increase in execution time. Finally, the trade-off between resource usage and execution time were shown via hardware profiling. It has been explicitly shown that in the process of selecting Pareto-optimal designs, it is important to account for clock speed degradation. Indeed, considering cycle count reduction and resource usage alone are insufficient in the selection process.

Current and future work includes the investigation of the trade-off between energy consumption and resource usage. Also, trade-offs between dynamic and static memory accesses will be explored in greater detail. Potentially, more work could be done to tune the cache parameters during run-time to exploit trade-offs between resource usage and execution time to cater to statistical properties of the algorithm. However, re-configuration overheads have to be considered in determining the benefit and timing of re-configuration.

References

1. Issenin, I., Dutt, N.: Automatic generation of affine functions for memory optimizations. In: Proceedings of the conference on Design, Automation and Test in Europe. (2005) 808–813
2. Kandemir, M., Choudhary, A.: Compiler-directed scratch-pad memory hierarchy design and management. In: Proceedings of the Design Automation Conference. (2002) 628–633
3. Udayakumaran, A., Barua, R.: Compiler-decided dynamic memory allocation for scratch-pad based embedded systems. In: Proceedings of the International Conference on Compilers, Architecture and Synthesis for Embedded Systems. (2003) 276–279
4. Chalidabhongse, J., Kuo, C.: Fast motion vector estimation using multiresolution-spatio-temporal correlations. IEEE transactions on circuits and systems for video technology 7(3) (1997) 477–488
5. Patterson, D.A., L.Hennessy, J.: Computer Architecture: A Quantitative Approach. Morgan Kaufmann, San Francisco (1996)
6. Kulkarni, C., Catthoor, F., Man, H.: Data and memory optimization techniques for embedded systems. In: Proceedings of the IPDPS Workshops on Parallel and Distributed Processing. (2000) 186–193
7. Panda, P., Catthoor, F., Danckaert, K., Brockmeyer, E., Kulkarni, C., Vandercappelle, A., Kjeldsberg, P.: Data and memory optimization techniques for embedded systems. IEEE Transactions on Very Large Scale Integr. Syst. 6(2) (2001) 149–206
8. Ishihara, T., Fallah, F.: A way memoization technique for reducing power consumption in caches in Application Specific Integrated Procesors. In: Proceedings of the conference on Design, Automation and Test in Europe. (2005) 358–363
9. Nastaran, B., Park, J., Diniz, P.: A compiler analysis and algorithm for exploiting data reuse in configurable architectures with RAM blocks. In: Proceedings of the Field-Programmable Logic and Applications. (2004) 1113–1115
10. Guo, Z., Buyukkurt, B., Najjar, W., Vissers, K.: Optimized generation of datapaths from C codes for FPGAs. In: Proceedings of the conference on Design, Automation and Test in Europe. (2005) 112–118

11. Sohi, G., Franklin, M.: High-bandwidth data memory systems for superscalar processors. In: Proceedings of the Fourth International Conference on Architectural Support for Programming Languages and Operating Systems. (1991) 53–62
12. Edmondson, J., Rubinfield, P., Bannon, P., Benschneider, B., Berstein, D., Castelino, R., Cooper, E., Dever, D., Donchin, D., Fischer, T., Jain, A., Mehta, S., Meyer, J., Preston, R., Rajagopalan, V., Somanathan, C., Taylor, S., Wolrich, G.: Internal organization of the Alpha 21164 a 300MHz 64-bit quad-issue CMOS RISC microprocessor. Digital Technical Journal **7**(1) (1995) 119–135
13. Page, I., Luk, W.: Compiling Occam into FPGAs. In: Proceedings of the Field-Programmable Logic and Applications. (1991) 271–283
14. Intel: (Understanding memory access characteristics of motion estimation algorithms) http://www.intel.com/cd/ids/developer/asmo-na/eng/182345.htm?page=2, accessed 1 October 2005.
15. Celoxica: (DK compiler) http://www.celoxica.com, accessed 1 October 2005.
16. Celoxica: (RC300 board) http://www.celoxica.com/rc300/default.asp, accessed 1 October 2005.
17. Xilinx: (Virtex 2 datasheet) http://www.xilinx.com/bvdocs/publications/ds031.pdf, accessed 1 October 2005.
18. Celoxica: (RC300 manual) http://www.celoxica.com/techlib/CEL-WO4110816VG-316.pdf, accessed 1 October 2005.
19. Bouganis, C.S., Constantinides, G., Cheung, P.Y.K.: A novel 2-D design methodology for heterogeneous devices. In: Proceedings of the IEEE International Symposium on Field Programmable Custom Computing Machines. (2005) 1–10

Enhancing a Reconfigurable Instruction Set Processor with Partial Predication and Virtual Opcode Support*

Nikolaos Vassiliadis, George Theodoridis, and Spiridon Nikolaidis

Section of Electronics and Computers, Department of Physics,
Aristotle University of Thessaloniki, 54124 Thessaloniki, Greece
nivas@skiathos.physics.auth.gr

Abstract. A previously proposed Reconfigurable Instruction Set Processor (RISP) architecture, which tightly couples a coarse-grain Reconfigurable Functional Unit (RFU) to a RISC processor, is considered. Two architectural enhancements, namely partial predicated execution and virtual opcode are presented. An automated development framework for the introduced architecture is proposed. In order to evaluate both the architecture and the development framework a complete MPEG-2 encoder application is used. The efficiency of the predicated execution is proved and impressive speedup of the application is produced. Also, the use of virtual opcode to alleviate the opcode space explosion is demonstrated.

1 Introduction

Modern applications, implemented in embedded systems, are characterized by diversity of algorithms, rapid evolution of standards, and high-performance demands. To amortize cost over high production volumes, embedded systems must exhibit high levels of flexibility and adaptation to achieve fast time-to-market and increased reusability. An appealing option -broadly referred to as reconfigurable computing- is to couple a standard processor with reconfigurable hardware combining this way the advantages of both resources [1]. The processor can serve as the bulk of the flexibility that can be used to implement any algorithm. On the other hand, the incorporation of the Reconfigurable Hardware (RH) features potentially infinite dynamic instruction set extensions offering the adaptation of the system to the targeted application.

In this paper, we target at a dynamic RISP architecture [2], which consists of a RISC processor extended by a coarse-grain RFU. We present two enhancements performed to the architecture to increase its efficiency. The first, which aims to increase performance, supports partial predicated execution [3]. It is used to remove control dependencies and expose larger clusters of operations as candidates for execution in the RFU. The second enhancement, namely "virtual opcode", attempts to alleviate the opcode space explosion. This is achieved by assigning the same opcode to different operations across the application space.

---

* This work was supported by PENED 2003 programme of the General Secretariat for Research and Technology of Greece and the European Union.

K. Bertels, J.M.P. Cardoso, and S. Vassiliadis (Eds.): ARC 2006, LNCS 3985, pp. 217–229, 2006.

Specifically, a natural opcode accompanied with information regarding the region of the application where it is used forms a virtual opcode. Thus, a virtually almost arbitrary number of reconfigurable instruction set extensions can be supported.

Furthermore, in order to program and evaluate the introduced architecture a development framework is presented. The framework is fully automated in the sense that it hides all RH related issues requiring no interaction with the user other than that of a traditional compiler flow. Using this framework a complete MPEG-2 encoder application is implemented and evaluated. Results indicate that an x2.9 speedup is obtained. Finally, we demonstrate how performance can be traded-off with opcode space and configuration memory size, using the proposed virtual opcode technique.

2   Related Work

Based on the coupling type between the processor and the reconfigurable hardware, the overwhelming majority of the proposed reconfigurable systems fall into two main categories which are: 1) the reconfigurable hardware is a co-processor communicating with the main processor and 2) the reconfigurable hardware is a functional unit of the processor pipeline (we will state this category as RFU from now on).

The first category includes, Garp, NAPA, Molen, REMARC, and PipeRench [4,5,6,7,8]. In this case, the coupling between the processor and the RH is loosely; communication is performed implicitly using special instructions to move data and control directives to and from the RH. To hide the overhead introduced by this type of communication, the number of clock cycles for each use of the RH must be high. Furthermore, the RH usually has direct connection to memory and features state registers, while can operate in parallel with the processor. In this way, the allowed performance improvements are significant. However, only parts of the code weakly interacting with the rest of the code can be mapped to the RH to exploit this performance gain. These parts of the code must be identified and replaced with the appropriate special instructions. Garp and Molen features automation of this process but only for loop bodies and complete functions, respectively. For NAPA and PipeRench this process is performed manually.

Examples of the second category are systems such as PRISC, Chimaera, and XiRisc [9,10,11]. Here, the coupling is tightly and communication is performed explicitly. Data is read and written directly to and from the processor's register file, while the RH is treated as another functional unit of the processor. This makes control logic simple, while the communication overhead is eliminated. However, the explicit communication can cause an opcode space explosion, a drawback of this approach. In this case, parts of the code implemented in the RH are smaller and can be seen as dynamic extensions of the processor's instruction set. Fully automated compilers are not reported in the literature neither for this category. For example, in XiRisc the identification of the extracted computational kernel is performed manually, while PRISC and Chimaera feature no selection process for the identified instructions.

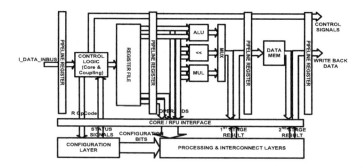

Fig. 1. Target RISP Architecture

Our approach falls in the second category, since it tightly couples an RFU to the processor core. The implicit communication offers the possibility to consider for acceleration the whole application and not just kernels, which is usually the case for the co-processor approach. Even though smaller speedups are achieved for the kernels compared to the co-processor approach, they are achieved in all application's space. Thus, the average speedup is preserved as it is proven in the following.

3 Target Architecture

The target architecture, which is shown in Figure 1, is a RISP processor described in [2]. The processor is based on standard 32-bit, single-issue, five-stage pipeline RISC architecture that has been extended to support the following features:

- Extended ISA to support three types of operations performed by the RFU, namely: 1) complex computations, 2) complex addressing modes, and 3) complex control transfer operations.
  An interface supporting the tightly couple of an RFU to the processor pipeline.
  An RFU array of Processing Elements (PEs).

On each execution cycle an instruction is fetched from the Instruction Memory. If the instruction is identified as reconfigurable its opcode and four operands from the register file are forwarded to the RFU. In addition, the opcode is decoded and produces the necessary control signals to drive the interface and pipeline. At the same time the RFU is appropriately configured by downloading the necessary configuration bits from a local configuration memory.

The processing of the reconfigurable instruction is initiated in the execution pipeline stage. If the instruction has been identified as addressing mode or control transfer then its result is delivered back to the execution pipeline stage to access the data memory or the branch unit, respectively. Otherwise, the next pipeline is also used in order to execute longer chains of operations and to improve performance. Since instructions are issued and completed in-order, while

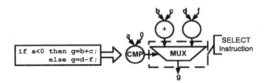

Fig. 2. If-then-else statement implementation using partial predicated execution

all hazards are resolved in hardware, the architecture is totally synchronized and does not require any special attention by the compiler.

The RFU consists of a 1-Dimension array of PEs. The array features an interconnection network that allows connection of all PEs to each other (fully connected). The granularity of PEs is 32-bit allowing the execution of the same word-level operations with the processor's datapath. Furthermore, each PE can be configured to provide its unregistered or registered result. In the first case, spatial computation is exploited (in addition to parallel execution) by executing chains of operations in the same clock cycle. When the delay of a chain exceeds the clock cycle, the registered output is used to exploit temporal computation by providing the value to the next pipeline stage for further computation.

In the following, a description of partial predicated execution and virtual opcode architectural enhancements, performed to the RISP architecture are presented.

3.1   Support for Partial Predicated Execution

Predicated execution [3] provides an effective mean to eliminate branches from an instruction stream. It is referred to the conditional execution of an instruction based on the value of a Boolean source operand, called the predicate. Typically, it is utilized by the compiler and/or hardware to remove control dependences and expose Instruction Level Parallelism (ILP) in superscalar and VLIW processors.

In our approach, partial predicate execution is supported to eliminate the branch in an if-then-else statement. Figure 2 presents an implementation example of such a statement. The two alternative paths of the statement are executed unconditionally and the final result is selected using a special three source operand SELECT operation. The SELECT operation can be implemented with a multiplexer as shown in Figure 2. Furthermore, the two alternative paths including the comparison path can include a large number of operations forming a complex reconfigurable instruction. This type of instructions, implemented in the RFU, offer the possibility for high performance improvement.

Figure 3 illustrates the modifications (marked with gray) performed in the RFU to support predicated execution. As detailed presented in [2], the RFU features an output network responsible to select the appropriate PE result. The selection is performed based on the corresponding configuration bits. Two multiplexers controlled by two new configuration bits are added to control each stage result. In this way, the configuration that will drive the output network is selected between the standard configuration bits and hardwired comparison

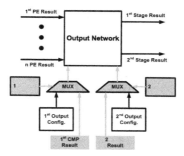

Fig. 3. Hardware extensions to support partial predicated execution

results, for predicated execution. The comparison results are provided by the PEs that already support comparison operations.

3.2   Virtual Opcode Support

As previously mentioned, the explicit communication between the processor and the RFU involves the direct encoding of reconfigurable instructions to the opcode of the instruction word. This fact limits the number of reconfigurable instructions that can be supported, leaving unutilized available performance improvements. On the other hand, the decision to increase the opcode space requires hardware and software modifications. Such modifications can be in general unacceptable. This is also the case for our approach since our intention is to extend a conventional RISC processor with reconfigurable instruction set extensions with small architectural and design modifications. Virtual opcode assists to increase the available opcodes without increasing the size of the opcode bits or modify the instruction's word format.

Each virtual opcode consists of two parts. The fist is the natural opcode contained in the instruction word that has been fetched for execution in the RFU. The second is a value indicating the region of the application in which this instruction word has been fetched. Thus, different operations can be assigned to the same natural opcode across different regions of the application featuring a virtually "unlimited" number of reconfigurable instructions.

Figure 4 presents the new organization of the local configuration memory in order to support virtual opcodes. The original organization has been presented in [2] and is capable to provide at each cycle the appropriate configuration bits to the RFU based on the reconfigurable instruction opcode. The extended configuration memory is characterized by two levels. The first one, with size of K instructions, stores the configuration bits assigned to each one of the natural opcodes. The second, with size of L contexts, indicates the different copies of the natural opcodes each one assigned in a different region of the application. Therefore the size of the local configuration memory equals to KxLxN (where N is the number of configuration bits required for each reconfigurable instruction). Each time only one of the L contexts can be active and the configuration bits

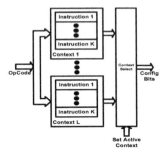

Fig. 4. Local configuration memory organization to support virtual opcodes

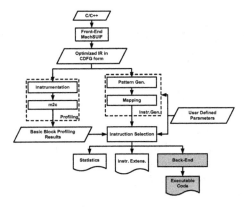

Fig. 5. Automated Development Framework organization

assigned to a natural opcode of this specific context are driven to the output. A special instruction is used to set active the appropriate context. This instruction is issued by the processor when the control flow of the application is entering a specific region. The compiler is responsible to identify these regions, create the virtual opcodes, and issue the activation of the correct context.

4   Development Framework

Our approach of compiling for the target architecture involves primarily the transparent to the user incorporation of compiler extensions to support the re-configurable instruction set extensions. Under this demand, we developed an automated development framework for the target RISP architecture, whose organization is depicted in Figure 5. The complete flow is divided in five distinct stages, namely: 1) Front-End, 2) Profiling, 3) Instruction Generation, 4) Instruction Selection and 5) Back-End. Each stage of the flow is presented below.

Front-End: The framework supports C/C++ codes that are firstly fed to the front-end. MachSUIF [12] is used to generate the Control and Data Flow Graph (CDFG) of the application using the SUIFvm Intermediate Representation (IR).

A MachSUIF pass that performs if-conversion [15] is used to support partial predicated execution. The pass eliminates branch instructions by introducing conditional SELECT instructions, which can be implemented in the RFU as previously described. The output of this stage is an optimized IR in the form of a CDFG.

Profiling: A MachSUIF pass which instruments the CDFG with profiling annotations marking the entrances and exits of basic blocks (we will state DFGs as basic blocks from now on), has been developed. A modified m2c pass (the original is supplied with the MachSUIF) translates the CDFG to equivalent C code, while the annotations regarding the basic blocks are converted to program counters. Compiling and executing the generated code, profiling information for the execution frequency of the basic blocks is collected.

Instruction Generation: The instruction generation stage is divided in two steps. The goal of the first step (pattern generation) is the identification of complex patterns of primitive operations (e.g. SUIFvm operations) that can be merged into one reconfigurable instruction. Pattern generation is performed using an in-house framework for automated extension of embedded processors described in [13]. The patterns generation engine is based on the MaxMISO (maximal multiple-input single-output) algorithm [14].

In the second step, the mapping of the previously identified patterns in the RFU is performed and the actual candidate reconfigurable instruction set extensions are generated. A mapper for the target RFU has been developed for this reason. The steps performed by the mapper are:

1. Calculate the latency of each operation in the pattern. This latency includes the accumulated latencies of the operation's presidencies in the pattern's chains. The latency is calculated using user parameters defining the delay of the modules of the RFU (PEs, interconnection etc.).
2. Place each operation in a PE and appropriately configure its functionality.
3. Put the PE for execution in the appropriate pipeline stage based on the calculated latency and the type of the pattern (e.g. computation, addressing, and control). This is performed by selecting the registered or the unregistered output of the PE (see [2] for more details).
4. Configure the multiplexers of the 1-D array for appropriate interconnection of the PEs.
5. Report the reconfigurable instruction set semantics (e.g. latency, type, resources etc.).

Instruction Selection: In this stage, the final instruction set extensions are selected. Firstly, the static speed-up of each instruction is calculated. This is accomplished by considering the software versus the hardware (RFU) execution cycles of the instruction. The software execution cycles are equal to the number of operations of which the instruction consists, while the hardware cycles have been reported by the mapper in the previously stage. The static speed-ups are multiplied by the execution frequency of the basic block (derived at profiling stage) and the dynamic speed-ups are calculated. Finally, we perform pair-wise graph isomorphism on the set of instructions. A set of isomorphic instructions defines a group for which the offered speed-up is calculated by summing the dynamic speed-ups of the group members.

The instructions/groups are then ranked based on the dynamic speed-ups that they can produce. This ranking can be performed in two different modes regarding the support of virtual opcodes. When such support is not consider, the instructions are ranked unified across all the application's space. The best K instructions (where K is the maximum number of available opcode space) are selected to be included as reconfigurable instruction set extensions.

In the case where virtual opcode technique is used, the application is partitioned in regions. Currently, the framework is capable to consider only function bodies as different regions. This time, the ranking of the candidate instructions is performed partial for each function. Furthermore, the possible overhead introduced by the requirement to set each time active the specific region context is considered. This information is provided by the profiling stage. The regions are then ranked based on their available speed-up. The first L regions, (where L is the number of the available contexts) are considered and the first K instructions of each region are selected.

Back-End: The back-end of the framework flow is the only stage that has not yet been fully implemented. However, since reconfigurable instructions do not require any special manipulation for the communication and synchronization between processor and RFU, the back-end is much like any traditional processor back-end performing tasks like scheduling, register allocation etc.

5   Experimental Results

To evaluate the architecture and the development framework, we used an MPEG-2 encoding application. The source code of the application was taken by the MediaBench suite [16]. As input data a video sequence consisting of 12 frames with resolution of 144x176 pixels was considered. Since no Operating System (OS) support is currently available for our architecture, all OS calls (like printf, fopen etc.) was omitted. Therefore, it was considered that all data were initially available in the data memory and results of the application were delivered back to the same memory. Speedups have been calculated by comparing the instruction count of the base RISC processor of the architecture with and without support of the RFU unit.

The following experimental results are divided in two sections. In the first, we consider the architecture without virtual opcodes support and present the achieved speedups for the MPEG-2 encoder application. We analyze the speedup over the whole application space and quantify the benefits by the incorporation of the partial predicated execution support. In the second section, we demonstrate the usage of virtual opcodes to achieve speedups with limited opcode space.

5.1 MPEG-2 Encoder Application Speedup Analysis

Table 1 presents instruction counts for the most timing consuming functions of the MPEG-2 encoder application. Results are presented for both execution on the core processor alone (No RFU) and with RFU support. The experiments were performed considering the initial version of the target architecture [2], where 64 different reconfigurable instructions are supported. All instructions were consider available in the local configuration memory requiring no cycle penalty to use them. The third column contains speedups achieved for the specific part of the application. Fourth column holds incremental speedups achieved when the specific function including those before it are considered for acceleration. The SAD operation is actually contained in the dist1 function and results are presented to help in the following discuss.

Table 1. Instruction Counts for the most timing consuming functions, without (No RFU) and with RFU support (RFU)

	Instr. Counts (NoRFU) (10^6)	Instr. Counts (RFU) (10^6)	SpeedUp	SpeedUp (Incremental)
SAD	589.0	89.0	6.6	1.5
dist1	1206.0	375.0	3.4	2.3
fullsearch	73.5	35.0	2.0	2.5
bdist1	18.0	9.0	2.0	2.5
putbits	16.3	7.0	2.3	2.6
fdct	15.6	6.8	2.3	2.6
quant_non_intra	13.1	5.1	2.6	2.7
idctcol	11.4	4.8	2.4	2.7
dct_type_estimation	10.4	4.5	2.3	2.7
pred_comp	10.1	5.4	1.9	2.7
iquant_non_intra	9.9	5.6	1.8	2.8
add_pred	8.0	4.1	2.0	2.8
bdist2	7.3	4.1	1.8	2.8
idctrow	7.0	3.2	2.2	2.8
putnonintrablk	6.9	4.0	1.8	2.8
sub_pred	6.6	3.7	1.8	2.9
Overall	**1448.7**	**499.6**	**2.9**	**2.9**

Regarding the profiling of the application it is observed that the most timing consuming part is the dist1 function. As Table 1 shows, this part of the code accounts for the 83% of the total execution time and it is speeded-up by 3.4. If only this part were considered for acceleration, x2.3 speedup for the whole application is produced. Moreover, this is the part of the code where the well known computation intensive Sum-of-Absolute-Difference (SAD) is located. The SAD function consumes 41% of the total application execution time. Table 1 actually demonstrates what was expected based on the well-known Amdahl's

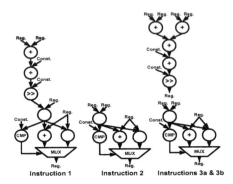

Fig. 6. Implementation of the SAD operation as reconfigurable instructions in the RFU using partial predicated execution

law. That is, attempting to accelerate only the hot-spots of the application by a factor S, produces an overall application speedup that is only a fraction of S. As Table 1 indicates, our approach attempts to accelerate all the spectrum of the application achieving an overall speedup x2.9 for the entire MPEG-2 encoder application.

Finally, in order to evaluate the limitation of the opcode space, we perform again the same experiments assuming an infinite number of available opcodes. The speedup in this case is x3.1. Thus, in our case we are able to utilize the 94% of the available performance improvements.

Evaluation of partial predicated execution support: Although the Mach-SUIF pass that performs if-conversion was available in [15], partial predicated execution is not yet fully integrated in our framework. Therefore, we had to manually identify and exploit this type of operations. To reduce complexity we target only the most time consuming part of the code which is function dist1 as already mention. Specifically, we target the computation intensive SAD operation which is part of the dist1 function. Three instructions were selected for implementation in the RFU, which are presented in Figure 6. The third one was partitioned in two distinct instructions to resolve inputs and delay constraints.

These instructions are capable to deliver significant performance improvements. Specifically, when partial predicated execution is not used the achieved speedup for the dist1 function drops from x6.6 to x1.7, resulting in a reduction in the overall speedup from x2.9 to x1.7. Clearly, there are significant benefits by the incorporation of partial predicated execution technique that we expect to be increased by fully incorporation of the technique in our framework.

5.2   Experimental Results with Virtual Opcode Support

As previously stated, opcode explosion is a limitation of the explicit communication between the core processor and the RFU. To provide opcode space for the

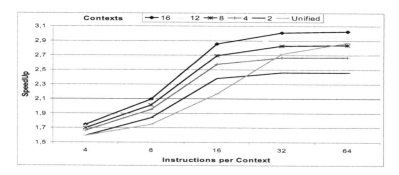

Fig. 7. Achieved speedups with virtual opcode support for varied number of contexts and instructions per context

encoding of the reconfigurable operations, modifications to the base processor are required. Such modifications include redesign of the instruction format and the instruction decoder of the base processor. In fact, this is the case for our architecture in order to support 64 different reconfigurable instructions [2]. In the following we demonstrate the use of virtual opcode to exploit any available opcodes without modifying the design of the base processor.

Experiments were re-performed with the virtual opcode support in the instruction selection stage of the development framework enabled. The experiments were performed for different number of contexts and instructions per context. The overhead to set each time active the appropriate context was taken into account. Figure 7 presents the speedups achieved for a number of contexts varied from 2 to 16. For comparisons purposes the speedups without virtual opcode support (Unified) are included. The number of instructions per context varied from 4 to 64.

As it is observed virtual opcode can be employed when targeting a base processor with limited opcode space, to increase achievable speedups. Thus, in the case when 4 or 8 instructions per contexts are available, speedups of x1.7 and x2.0, respectively, can be achieved by utilizing 8 contexts. This way the 55% and 65%, respectively, of the maximum speedup (that is x3.1) is utilized. Although this is a moderate fraction of the available speedup, it is clearly well above the one with no virtual opcode support (Unified). The configuration memory requirements in this case are 0.5KB and 1.1KB for 4 and 8 instructions, respectively. Memory requirements are calculated by the expression KxLxN as described in 3.2 section (N=136 configuration bits per instruction).

In the case where more opcodes are becoming available, virtual opcode becomes more efficient. Thus, with 16 instructions x2.8 speedup is possible with 12 contexts. The memory requirement in this case is 3.2KB. Furthermore, when 32 instructions are becoming available, results indicate that actually all performance is utilized without the need for more opcode space. The maximum memory requirement in this case is 8.7KB and they can produce x3 speedup for the complete MPEG-2 encoder application. In general, the overhead in memory requirements can be characterized as reasonable.

6 Conclusions

In this paper, a previously proposed RISP architecture was considered and was enhanced with partial predicated execution to improve performance and virtual opcode to relax opcode space pressure. Using an automated development framework a complete MPEG-2 encoder application was implemented. Experimental results present an impressive x2.9 speedup for the application. Speedup is achieved by accelerating the whole space of the application with efficient reconfigurable instruction set extensions. This fact is in contrast with the co-processor approach were usually only the heavily executed kernels of the application are considered.

References

1. DeHon, A. and Wawrzynek, J.: Reconfigurable Computing: What, Why, and Implications for Design Automation. In DAC'99. (1999) 610-615.
2. Vassiliadis, N., Kavvadias, N., Theodoridis, G., and Nikolaidis S.: A RISC Architecture Extended by an Efficient Tightly Coupled Reconfigurable Unit. In ARC'05. (2005) 41-49.
3. Mahlke, S., Hank, R., McCormick, J., August, D., and Hwu, D.: A comparison of full and partial predicated execution support for ILP processors. In ISCA'95. (1995) 138-150.
4. Callahan, T. J., Hauser, J. R., and Wawrzynek, J.: The Garp Architecture and C Compiler. In IEEE Computer, vol. 33, no. 4. (2000) 62-69.
5. Gokhale, M. B. and Stone J. M.: NAPA C: Compiling for a Hybrid RISC/FPGA Architecture. In FCCM'98. (1998) 126.
6. Vassiliadis, S., Wong, S., Gaydadjiev, G., Bertels, K., Kuzmanov, G., and Moscu Panainte, E.: The MOLEN Polymorphic Processor. In IEEE Trans. on Computers, vol. 53, no. 11. (2004) 1363-1375.
7. Miyamori, T. and Olukotun, K.: REMARC: Reconfigurable Multimedia Array Co-Processor. In IEICE Trans. Information Systems, vol. E82-D, no. 2. (1999) 389-397.
8. Goldstein, S. C., Schmit, H., Moe, M., Budiu, M., Cadambi, S., Taylor, R., and Laufer, R.: Piperench: A Coprocessor for Streaming Multimedia Acceleration. In ISCA'99. (1999) 28-39.
9. Razdan, R. and Smith, M. D.: A High-Performance Microarchitecture with Hardware-Programmable Functional Units. In MICRO 27. (1994) 172-180.
10. Ye, Z. A., Shenoy, N., and Baneijee, P.: A C compiler for a Processor with a Reconfigurable Functional Unit. In FPGA'00. (2000) 95-100.
11. La Rosa, A., Lavagno, L., and Passerone, C.: Software Development for High-Performance, Reconfigurable, Embedded Multimedia Systems. In IEEE Design and Test of Computers, vol. 22, no. 1. (2005) 28-38.
12. Machine-SUIF research compiler. See website: http://www.eecs.harvard.edu/hube /research/machsuif.html.

13. Kavvadias, N. and Nikolaidis S.: Automated Instruction-Set Extension of Embedded Processors with Application to MPEG-4 Video Encoding. In ASAP'05. (2005) 140-145.
14. Alippi, C., Fornaciari, W., Pozzi, L., and Sami, M.: A DAG Based Design Approach for Reconfigurable VLIW Processors. In DATE'99. (1999) 778-779.
15. Optimization Passes for Machine Suif. See website: http://lapwww.epfl.ch/dev /machsuif/opt_passes/.
16. Lee, C., Potkonjak, M., and Mangione-Smith, W. H.: MediaBench: A Tool for Evaluating and Synthesizing Multimedia and Communications Systems. In MICRO. (1997) 330-335.

A Reconfigurable Data Cache
for Adaptive Processors[*]

D. Benitez[1], J.C. Moure[2], D.I. Rexachs[2], and E. Luque[2]

[1] IUSIANI and DIS Department, University of Las Palmas G.C.,
35017 Las Palmas, Spain
dbenitez@dis.ulpgc.es

[2] Computer Architecture and Operating System Department,
Universitat Autonoma Barcelona, 08193 Barcelona, Spain
{JuanCarlos.Moure, Dolores.Rexachs, Emilio.Luque}@uab.es

Abstract. Adaptive processors can exploit the different characteristics exhibited by program phases better than a fixed hardware. However, they may significantly degrade performance and/or energy consumption. In this paper, we describe a reconfigurable cache memory, which is efficiently applied to the L1 data cache of an embedded general-purpose processor. A realistic hardware/software methodology of run-time tuning and reconfiguration of the cache is also proposed, which is based on a pattern-matching algorithm. It is used to identify the cache configuration and processor frequency when the programs data working-set changes. Considering a design scenario driven by the best product execution time×energy consumption, we show that power dissipation and energy consumption of a two-level cache hierarchy and the product time×energy can be reduced on average by 39%, 38% and 37% respectively, when compared with a non-adaptive embedded microarchitecture.

1 Introduction

Programs and their execution phases exhibit different efficiencies when fixed processor hardware is adopted [12]. Adaptive processors can exploit this phenomenon to provide higher efficiency than fixed hardware systems [14]. These processors activate the reconfiguration of its microarchitecture under architectural criteria: highest performance, lowest energy consumption, etc. Hardware reconfigurability is a more general concept related to physical resources needed to modify the hardware organization after chip fabrication. Some reconfigurable cache memories have been proposed to improve the performance or power dissipation of general-purpose processors ([1], [7], [9]). However, improvements are limited by the level of reconfigurability, which has been forced to not degrade the operating frequency of processor. We have observed that if the clock speed of the reconfigurable system is allowed to be slightly slower, higher performance

---

[*] This work was supported by the MCyT-Spain under contract TIN 2004-03388, the Gobierno de Canarias, the Generalitat de Catalunya, and the HiPEAC Network.

K. Bertels, J.M.P. Cardoso, and S. Vassiliadis (Eds.): ARC 2006, LNCS 3985, pp. 230–242, 2006.

and reduced power dissipation can be achieved at the same time compared with non-reconfigurable hardware systems.

In this paper, we propose the microarchitecture of the Field-Programmable Cache Array (FPCA). FPCA is a specialized reconfigurable circuit for the cache memory of a general-purpose processor. In comparison with a conventional cache, the clock speed is only slightly slower. The temporal and power overheads are low because programs exhibit large execution phases and reconfigurations are only sporadically activated. The additional hardware is also small because the circuit is specialized in memory caches. Our field-programmable cache memory is similar to others reconfigurable caches in that they try to obtain the highest performance or the lowest energy consumption by selecting the best configuration at critical runtime points ([1], [7], [9]). However, their range of configurations is fixed at design-time and is not scalable to different chip area budgets. In these cases, we have observed that it can be possible that a single cache configuration is selected for the majority of applications. The FPCA cache can be used in scalable designs with different initial budgets for the processor development, each of them can adopt a distinct FPCA.

Some control algorithms for adaptive caches spend long times in the tuning process because they explore all the configurations for picking the best cache configuration ([1], [4]). Then, the temporal and energy overheads are higher as the number of tuneable cache configurations increases. The large number of cache configurations that can be implemented with a FPCA cache would damage the potential of FPCA for achieving improvements. We also propose an on-line control algorithm called Cache Matching Algorithm for instantaneously tuning a FPCA-based L1 data cache with accuracy, minimal hardware cost, and an overhead that is independent of the number of tuneable configurations.

Section 2 contains discussion of related work. Section 3 presents the internal organization of the reconfigurable FPCA circuit, and the parameters required for architectural simulations. Section 4 describes the control algorithm to reconfigure a FPCA in adaptive processors and its hardware implementation. In Section 5, we describe the simulation methodology employed to evaluate our proposals. Section 6 evaluates our control methodology for real processors with a FPCA-based L1 data cache. Section 7 contains concluding remarks and future work.

2 Related Work

Two aspects of the reconfigurable systems that are integrated into a general-purpose processor are needed to be determined in the design process: the hardware organization, and its control methodology. Both aspects are reviewed next.

Some sections of a general-purpose processor have been proposed to be reconfigurable: the ALU functional unit ([5], [14]), the clock generator and power supply [10], the cache memory ([1], [7], [9], [15]). Our proposal of reconfigurable cache memory differentiates from these systems in the following ways. (1) The number of possible cache configurations can be two orders of magnitude higher than other adaptive caches, with approximately a 10% increase in chip area.

Depending on each application, some configurations are used to provide the highest performance and other configurations are used to provide the lowest power dissipation. (2) The operating frequency of the processor/cache system and cache hit latency can be independently varied. A wide range of frequencies and chip areas can be used in different scenarios, from low-cost processors to high-performance processors. (3) The configuration bitstream is sufficiently small to not significantly impact performance and energy consumption.

The control algorithm is used to determine the hardware configuration that best suits the characteristics of a given program or execution phase. Depending on the dynamic or static system behaviour, two groups of control methodologies can be identified: on-line and off-line control. Methodologies for on-line control take clues from the processor hardware to infer characteristics of programs. Different hardware events have been used: branch frequency [1], cache misses [7], cache hits [7], utilization of the issue queues [10], and the invocation of subroutines [6]. Work on this subject has explored three basic properties of algorithms ([1], [4]): (a) efficiency on detecting a phase boundary, (b) the tuning overhead, and (c) the reconfiguration overhead. Additionally, we have observed that the set of tuneable configurations is required to be analyzed. Our on-line control algorithm differentiates from other methods in the following ways: (1) We do not use the same tuneable cache configurations for all programs; (2) We propose a methodology based on basic block vectors to know the most efficient configurations for each program; (3) The tuning and reconfiguration overheads are relatively low and independent of the number of tuneable configurations, as we do not prove all the possible cache configurations each time a program phase change is detected; (4) Most of the adaptive techniques that have been proposed for energy saving in cache memory reduce the energy or the time×energy product but also reduce performance [1]. On the other hand, prior adaptive systems proposed for performance improvement increase energy consumption ([1], [10]). For the programs in which the effect of L1 misses dominates, our proposal can improve performance and reduce energy consumption at the same time.

Off-line compiling, profiling and instrumentation of the application can be used to alternatively implement the adaptation control ([6], [15]). Our FPCA cache can be exclusively managed by a software procedure. We have observed that a high percentage of the performance improvement and energy saving demonstrated by on-line adaptation is achieved. This approach decreases the chip area by avoiding the use of a hardware coprocessor [2].

3   The Field-Programmable Cache Array

In this section, we describe a specialized reconfigurable circuit for cache memories called Field-Programmable Cache Array (FPCA), which is based on Field-Program-mable Gate Array technology. The FPCA circuit can be integrated into conventional processors, from high-performance to low-cost processors. The FPCA circuit is organized into an array of reconfigurable cells called

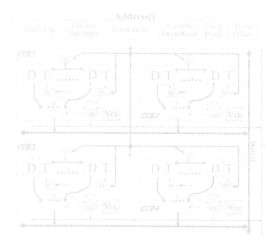

Fig. 1. Block diagram of the Field-Programmable Cache Array (FPCA)

Configurable Cache Blocks (CCB), which are selectively connected by a power-on configuration bit (called Vcc). Fig. 1 shows a block diagram of the FPCA where four CCBs can be identified.

A CCB is based on the classical organization of CMOS memories, and its design was guided by results of the architectural study of the cache adaptation shown in Section 6. Each CCB consists of eight complete cache memories called T-D, each of them consists of 128 sets with 20 bits for tags and 8 bytes for data (T and D respectively in Fig. 1). Some tag bits can be selectively activated, depending on the cache configuration. The overall capacity of each CCB is 8 Kbytes, and the reconfigurability of CCBs allows up to three degrees of set-associativity: 2-way, 4-way and 8-way, and up to four line sizes: 8, 16, 32, 64 bytes. A FPCA includes 10 additional configuration bits which are shared by all CCBs. When a different cache organization is required, the FPCA can implement it by changing the configuration area.

Reconfigurability requires additional hardware resources: SL, OE, and RC. SL represents the selection logic that selects the index bits which are the same for all CCBs. This module uses four configuration bits to select the appropriate bits from the variable sections of the address called Tag/Index and Index/Block (see Fig. 1). OE represents the hardware module that selects the output data, which uses other four configuration bits and the block bits of the address (fixed block and variable index/block in Fig. 1). RC represents the reconfigurable comparator where the information read from the tag array T is compared to the tag bits of the address (fixed tag and variable index/tag in Fig. 1).

The range of configurations that can be implemented with FPCA has the following constrains: the number of sets has to be higher than or equal to 128, 8-way set-associativity is the highest allowed associativity, the cache lines can store data from 8 to 64 bytes, and the biggest size depends on the number of CCBs, which is related with the chip area devoted to FPCA. Therefore, FPCA allows different cache configurations to be implemented, in which capacity, associativity and line size can be varied independently. The hit latency (in cycles) can also be variable and depends on the operating frequency. Supposing that the critical path of the processor is determined by the L1 data cache, we have observed that better performance can be achieved when the operating frequency is reduced slightly in order to maintain a minimal hit latency in cycles of FPCA accesses. This is the reason why we do not fix the operating frequency, which is supposed to be limited by the maximum frequency allowed by the L1 data cache of a non-reconfigurable processor which is taken as reference system.

3.1   Architectural Model

An architectural model of the FPCA circuit is required for detailed cycle-by-cycle simulations of complete processors. We modified the analytical model used by CACTI tool [13], which predicts the access time, power dissipation and chip area of conventional CMOS cache memories. Our modification was guided by PSPICE simulations of the FPCA circuit and provided the following average results: (a) The conventional paths that are affected by the specialized reconfigurable architecture are the address decoder, comparator, multiplexer driver, and wire lines of the input address and output data (see dotted line in Fig. 1). The access time and cycle time of a FPCA cache configuration on average was 20% longer than provided by original CACTI for the same CMOS technology; (b) Each FPCA has more transistors than the equivalent non-reconfigurable cache memory. So, the power consumption of a memory access is on average 10% higher; (c) The reconfiguration time is a temporal overhead which is proportional to the number of configuration bits. For the FPCA shown in Fig. 1, its four CCBs has 14 configuration bits, which are loaded when a change of cache organization is activated. Supposing that these bits are serially loaded with a 100 MHz configuration clock signal, the reconfiguration time of FPCA is 0.14 ms. During this reconfiguration phase, we suppose that FPCA can not be accessed, and the previous content of the cache is discarded; (d) The FPCA was 10% larger in chip area than the equivalent non-reconfigurable memory cache.

4   Run-Time Adaptation

In this section, we show how Basic Block Vectors (BBV) obtained from dynamic program traces can be used to determine changes in some characteristics of the data working-set accessed by an instruction interval. Then, we explain how a hardware algorithm called Cache Matching Algorithm collects BBV vectors during program run-time for reconfiguring a L1 data cache implemented with a FPCA circuit in order to adapt to changes in the data working-set.

4.1   Predictor of the Data Working-Set

The size of a Basic Block (BB) is determined from the instruction count between branches. A BBV vector is gathered for each instruction interval during the program execution. Each component of a BBV collects the frequency of basic blocks with a determined size. Up until now, BBV-based techniques have been used for accelerating simulation time of general-purpose processors [11].

A program phase is characterized by a large number of consecutive instruction intervals with similar data working-sets. We propose a method for adapting a reconfigurable data cache, which consists in using a unique BBV vector to recognize instruction intervals with recurring data working-sets. Working-set representations have the advantage that they can be used to estimate the working-set size directly [4]. They are useful in cases where performance and/or power consumption of a hardware unit is directly related to the working-set characteristics. In our reconfigurable system, the detection of one of these BBVs can predict the volume and characteristics of accessed data. So, a cache configuration accommodated to the data working-set can be activated when a BBV vector is recognized during program execution.

4.2   Reconfiguration Algorithm

We use a pattern-matching algorithm called Cache Matching Algorithm (CMA) to associate each unique BBV with a distinct cache configuration. It dynamically detects changes of data working-set to reconfigure an FPCA-based L1 data cache. Three stages are required: Learning, Recognition, and Actuation.

Learning Stage. The Learning Stage is used to identify patterns/phases of recurring data working-sets, and associates each pattern with a configuration of the reconfigurable FPCA cache. This task is performed by software and is divided into three major steps. In the first learning step, a BBV vector is read from some hardware registers. Every BBV vector may have thousands of components. A feature extraction method called Decision Boundary Feature Extraction was used to calculate the optimal transformation to a three dimensional space [8]. Thus, for each instruction interval, three BB sensors (counters) in the processor core hold the components of a three-dimensional BBV vector (called 3-D BBV). The BB sensors collect the number of all executed basic blocks whose sizes are in three ranges, which were identified during this research for each program. BBV vectors that are close together represent instruction intervals with similar data working-sets, i.e. a recurring program pattern/phase.

In the second learning step, the K-means clustering algorithm [11] runs iteratively on 3-D BBV vectors collected from the execution of a relatively large number of 100,000 instruction intervals. So, the 3-D BBV vectors are grouped into a set of K clusters called "SimPoint (SP) Classes", where each SP class represents a different program pattern/phase. Finally, the 3-D representation space is partitioned into hypercubes; each of them encloses the 3-D BBV vectors assigned to an SP class.

In the last learning stage, associating each SP class with an optimal cache configuration involves executing several instructions intervals for every tuneable configuration, and monitoring the respective SP classes and products "execution time $\times$ energy consumption ($t \times E$)". After picking all configurations, each SP class is assigned to the cache configuration which exhibits the highest t×E in most of the instruction intervals assigned to that SP class. Since we are assuming that the best cache configuration is the same for all the intervals belonging to the same SP class, a single program execution will suffice. In fact, learning time can be reduced by testing configurations on-the-fly, as the program is run for the first time. Since an SP class should be composed of many intervals, the learning time is negligible in comparison with the total execution time.

A Representation Space Table is used to store the SP class assigned to each 3-D BBV. Another Pattern Table contains the association between an SP class and the cache configuration ID with the highest t×E (see Fig. 2). Both tables are implemented in hardware for a fast look-up, and are set-up by software after the last learning step.

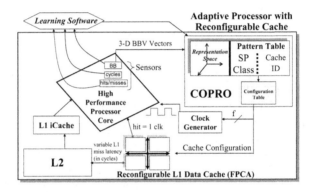

Fig. 2. Microarchitecture of the adaptive processor with Field-Programmable Data Cache (FPCA) and hardware support (COPRO) for the Cache Matching Algorithm

Recognition and Actuation Stages. The Recognition stage tunes the cache configuration for optimum performance and energy consumption. It detects if the current cache configuration does not provide the highest t×E for the running program pattern/phase, and determines what different cache configuration should be used instead. A hardware coprocessor performs this task by firstly reading the 3-D BBV vector from the BB sensors after each execution interval (see Fig. 2). Next, the vector position in the Representation Space Table allows the SP class of the interval to be recognized. If the activated cache configuration does not match with the configuration associated with this SP class, which is stored in the Pattern Table, it means that the instruction interval was not efficiently executed. The tuning task can be executed in parallel with the instruction flow and does not modify the critical path of instruction execution.

The Actuation stage is activated by the coprocessor when the SP classes of three consecutive instruction intervals are assigned in the Pattern Table to the same cache configuration (identified by a Cache ID) and this is different from the currently activated configuration. When the actuation stage starts, the instruction flow is stalled and a Configuration Table is read to obtain the bitstream required for the reconfiguration process, including the operating frequency (see Fig. 2). After reconfiguring the hardware, the cache content is lost and the instruction flow and recognition process are restarted. Before running a different program, the Representation Space Table, Pattern Table and Configuration Table are loaded with the information derived from the respective Learning Stage.

In summary, the association of a cache configuration with a program phase is learned once, stored, and used each time the program phase is recognized. Therefore, the runtime overhead is independent of the number of configurations.

4.3   Reconfiguration Controller

Supposing intervals of 10^5 instructions, three 17-bit counters measure the number of executed instructions in BBs with three different ranges of sizes. The three more significant bits from each counter builds one of the components of the 3-D BBV vectors. Six 12-bit registers load the upper and lower limits of the three ranges of BB sizes before running the program. Another 17-bit counter registers the clock cycles for each instruction interval, and a pair of 16-bit counters measures hits and misses in the cache.

The hardware coprocessor required for the Recognition and Actuation stages contains three small tables (see Fig. 2). The Representation Space Table provides for each 3-D BBV the respective SimPoint Class. Since each BBV component has three bits and 16 is an appropriate number of SP classes, its size is $2^9 \times 4$ bits. The Pattern Table contains the association between SP Class and cache configuration (identified by a Cache ID). Supposing that the maximum number of different configurations is 256, its size is $2^4 \times 8$ bits. The Configuration Table stores for each Cache ID the configuration bits needed for reconfiguring the FPCA data cache (14 bits), including the operating frequency and the hit and miss latencies. Its size is 50 bytes.

A FIFO memory is used to store the Cache ID of the last three instruction intervals, and a single register stores the current FPCA configuration ID. Another hardware module provides the activation signal of the Actuation stage when the four IDs are the same. Additionally, a small circuit is needed to read the Configuration Table and configure the FPCA in the Actuation stage. Supposing eight instructions/cycle, 100,000 instructions are executed in 12,500 clock cycles. It is enough for reading the Representation Space and Pattern tables, and for the glue logic to activate the Actuation Stage.

5   Experimental Methodology

We have used the Simplescalar tool set [3] to generate the dynamic trace of the first 2 billion instructions for 20 SPEC programs (Alpha ISA, cc DEC 5.9, O4): applu, gcc, apsi, gzip, art, ijpeg, bzip, mcf, eon, mesa, equake, parser, facerec, perlmbk, fma3d, sixtrack, galgel, vpr, gap, wupwise. They were chosen to demonstrate how our proposed hardware/software methodology can outperform both highly efficient non-adaptive approaches on SPEC benchmarks, and additionally, because they represent different program domains (Integer, FP, Multimedia).

Accurate cycle-by-cycle simulation was performed using a superscalar CPU simulator based on Simplescalar [3], to subsequently calculate for each tuneable L1 data cache configuration the execution time, energy consumption, power dissipation, and product "execution time × energy consumption". The parameters used for the simulated out-of-order microarchitecture are: up to 8 instructions renamed, dispatched, issued and retired per cycle; Fetch Queue of 16 instructions; a perfect Branch Predictor; Issue Queue of 48 instructions; Reorder Buffer of 256 instructions; Operation latencies like Pentium 4; Load/Store Queues of 64/32 instructions; perfect I-Cache with 2-cycle load-use latency; a perfect L2-Cache with 4.6 ns access time; and a 16GB/s L1-L2 interface. The simulated configurations for the Reconfigurable L1 Data Cache were: Size: 1KB, ..., 32KB; Set-Associativity: 2-way, 4-way, 8-way; Line Size: 8, ..., 64 Bytes; Load-use Latency: 1 clock cycle; 2 read/write ports. All simulations considered in this paper included the following penalizations for the reconfigurable cache with respect to the same cache configuration built with fixed hardware: CPU stall time during cache reconfiguration (1 μs), energy consumption during cache reconfiguration (5 μJ), cache content is lost after reconfiguration.

Benchmarks were simulated using intervals of 10^5 instructions per 1 billion instructions executed, after a warming-up of 1 billion instructions. The whole analysis interval was divided into two equal intervals of 0.5 billion instructions. The first one was used for learning, and the second one for recognition/actuation.

The standard SimPoint Toolkit [11] was used to extract basic block vectors (BBV) from the dynamic execution of benchmarks during the analysis interval. As previously described in Section 4.2, each instruction interval provides a 3-D BBV vector. The BBVs of the learning interval were classified into SP classes, which determined the content of the Representation Space Table. Our CPU simulator takes 3-D BBV vectors obtained from the recognition interval and associates each of them with the FPCA configuration of the respective SP class, which was assigned in the Learning Stage.

We used a modified version of CACTI 3.2 [13] to estimate the access time, energy consumed in each memory access, and chip area of each FPCA configuration, for a CMOS technology with $\lambda = 100$ nm. Our experiments used the original CACTI tool to characterize the reference configuration: 32 Kbytes, 8-way set-associative, and line size of 32 bytes. This reference cache is very popular among current embedded processors [15]. We supposed that the operating frequency of the reference processor (f_{base}) and the maximum operating frequency of the adaptive processor (f_{limit}) are determined by the L1 data cache of the reference processor, with a hit latency of 1 cycle. This means that $f_{base}=f_{limit}=$ 1.0 GHz. Additionally, the chip area of the reconfigurable cache is limited by the chip area of the reference L1 data cache: $A_{limit}=$ 1.5 mm^2.

This paper reports results for three architectural metrics: execution time, static and dynamic energy consumption and power dissipation of the L1 data cache and unified L2 cache, and execution time × energy product. As CACTI only provides estimates of dynamic energy, we calculate static energy as described in [15], with k_static = 50%, i.e. static energy is 50% of the total energy. In the

experiments, we have supposed that in each reconfiguration of the FPCA cache
the instruction flow is stalled during 1 ms and the contents of the L1 data cache
is discarded. The energy consumed by sensors was not considered since they
are very small. In each cache reconfiguration, the additional energy consumed
by FPCA and coprocessor is 5 μJ. When reconfiguration is not activated, the
energy consumed by coprocessor is negligible because the activated hardware is
also small: Representation Space Table, Pattern Table and glue logic.

6   Results

This section evaluates the potential of our reconfigurable FPCA cache memory
for embedded processors. We simulate the Learning Stage as described in Section 4.2 by taking into account intervals of 100,000 instructions and prioritizing
the product time $\times$ energy. Once the Learning Stage has provided the contents
of the coprocessors tables, the Recognition and Actuation Stages of the adaptive L1 data cache can be simulated. After each instruction interval, the BBV
vector provided by the hardware sensors and the contents of the representation
table are used to find the corresponding SP class. A reconfiguration is activated
only when three consecutive instruction intervals are assigned to the same SP
class, and this SP class is assigned in the pattern table to a cache configuration that is different from the currently activated. We assume that each cache
reconfiguration additionally introduces an overhead delay of 1 μs and consumes
5 μJ, which includes the overheads of the Actuation Stage and the update of
L2 memory. The number of reconfigurations performed during the experiments
(f_{limit}= 1.0 GHz, A_{limit}= 1.5 mm^2, 5,000 instruction intervals) oscillated from 0
(eon) to 423 (gzip) with an average of 139 reconfigurations per interval, i.e. less
than 3%. These results indicate that the program phases exhibit high temporal
locality, which reduces the performance and energy overheads due to hardware
reconfiguration.

Results of the evaluation of the adaptive processor with reconfigurable FPCA
data cache are shown in Fig. 3. As can be seen, FPCA adaptation achieves a

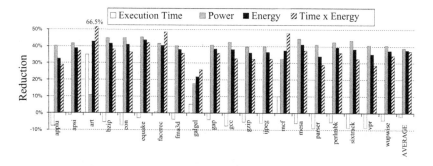

Fig. 3. Reduction of execution time, power dissipation, energy consumption and
time×energy for the adaptive processor with respect to the reference system

39% mean reduction of power dissipation of the cache hierarchy, a 38% mean reduction of energy consumption of the cache hierarchy, and a 37% mean reduction of time×energy. Performance is only degraded on average by 2%. These results are presented relative to the same reference machine mentioned earlier.

This phenomenon is mainly due to the frequent selection of FPCA configurations with lower energy cost per memory access than the reference configuration, while the operating frequency of the adaptive processor is close to the maximum frequency (f_{limit}). We have observed that it is better to reduce the operating frequency of the adaptive processor in order to maintain the same hit latency as the reference configuration than increasing the frequency to the maximum and adding one clock cycle to the hit latency of the adaptive L1 data cache. This would increase the average CPI (cycles per retired instruction), which is not compensated by the increase in operating frequency.

The maximum improvement of energy, time×energy, and performance was achieved by art (43%, 67%, and 35% respectively). This and other three programs (facerec, galgel, mcf) show no degradation in all four architectural metrics. This is due to the high miss rate for the L1 data cache. For these programs, the miss rates of the reference cache configuration range from 20% for facerec to 49% for art. Then, the L1 miss latency provides a significant delay. The non-adaptive L2 cache requires a different miss penalty for each FPCA cache configuration, since the operating frequency depends on the FPCA access time. A tunable L1 cache configuration with lower frequency and lower energy per memory access allows the L1 miss latency and energy consumption to be reduced. Therefore, in programs with high L1 miss rate, the saving in L1 miss penalty can compensate the reduction in operating frequency, while achieving higher performance and power saving at the same time.

The maximum saving of power dissipation was 45% for equake. In this case, the L1 miss rate is very low (0.03% with the reference configuration). The picked FPCA cache configurations can double this L1 miss rate, which is also very low. However, the respective energy per access can be halved. At the same time, the operating frequency is only slightly lower than reference system, and so, the execution time is also slightly lower than reference system. Therefore, power dissipation (energy / execution time) can be significantly reduced by using the reconfigurable FPCA cache. Note that, after finalizing the learning phase, the selection during run-time of a cache configuration does not require previous tuning of all available configurations before the selection of the preferred cache, as proposed in [1] and [10]. Therefore, our adaptation control method requires lower overhead for the determination of the stable state of the L1 data cache configuration than previously reported methods.

7 Conclusions and Future Work

We have proposed and evaluated the performance, power dissipation, and energy consumption of a reconfigurable L1 data cache, which is based on field-programmable technology and managed by a hardware/software algorithm. With this proposal, a high efficiency of use of the data cache of an embedded processor can be achieved by using a specialized reconfigurable circuit. The main contributions of the paper are the following. The reconfigurable data cache (1) provides a change mechanism with low reconfiguration overhead, (2) is characterized by access times only slightly larger than similar non-adaptive circuits, (3) uses a learning mechanism applied to reduce tuning overhead, (4) improves energy consumption and power dissipation of the cache hierarchy and the product time × energy at the same time. We additionally (5) proposed a predictor mechanism of the data working-set of a program, and discovered that (6) energy and power saving can be achieved with minimal performance degradation when for each program, the set of preferred cache configurations is accurately determined, which justifies the existence of a reconfigurable cache. The efficiency provided by the reconfigurable FPCA cache that is presented in this paper can be exploited in other cache levels. This is one of our research goals in the near future.

References

1. R. Balasubramonian, D. Albonesi, A. Buyuktosunoglu, S. Dwarkadas: A Dynamically Tunable Memory Hierarchy. IEEE Tran. Computers, 52(10):1243-1257, 2003
2. D. Benitez, J.C. Moure, D.I. Rexachs, E. Luque: Performance and Power Evaluation of an Intelligently Adaptive Data Cache. Springer LNCS, Vol. 3769
3. D. Burger, T.M. Austin: The SimpleScalar Toolset, Ver. 2.0. Computer Architecture News, 25(3):13-25, 1997
4. A.S. Dhodapkar, J.E. Smith: Managing Multi-Configuration Hardware via Dynamic Working Set Analysis. Proc. 29th Intl. Symp. Computer Architecture, IEEE Computer Society (2002) 233–244
5. M. Epalza, P. Ienne, D. Mlynek: Adding limited reconfigurability to superscalar processors. Proc. 13th Intl. Conf. on PACT, pp.53-62, 2004
6. M. C. Huang, J. Renau, J. Torrellas: Positional Adaptation of Processors: Application to Energy Reduction. Proc. 30th Intl. Symp. Computer Architecture, IEEE Computer Society (2003) 157–168
7. C. Kim, D. Burger, S.W. Keckler: An Adaptive, Non-Uniform Cache Structure for Wire-Delay Dominated On-Chip Caches. Proc. 10th Intl. Conf. Architectural Support for Program. Languages and Operating Syst., ACM Press (2002) 211–222
8. C. Lee, D.A. Landgrebe: Feature Extraction Based On Decision Boundaries. IEEE Tran. Pattern Analysis and Machine Intelligence, 15(4)388-400, 1993
9. P. Ranganathan, S. Adve, N.P. Jouppi: Reconfigurable Caches and their Application to Media Processing. Proc. 27th Intl. Symp. Computer Architecture, ACM Press (2000) 214–224
10. G.Semeraro et al: Energy-Efficient Processor Design Using Multiple Clock Domains with Dynamic Voltage and Frequency Scaling. Proc. 8th Symp. High Performance Computer Architecture, IEEE Computer Society (2002) 29–40
11. T. Sherwood, E. Perelman, G. Hamerly, B. Calder: Automatically Characterizing Large Scale Programs. Proc. Intl. Conf. on ASPLOS, ACM Press (2002)45-57
12. T. Sherwood, S. Sair, B. Calder: Phase Tracking and Prediction. Proc. 30th Intl. Symp. Computer Architecture. ACM Press (2003) 336–349

13. P.Shivakumar, N.P. Jouppi CACTI 3.0: An Integrated Cache Timing, Power, and Area Model. Compact WRL Technical Report 2001/2, 2001
14. S. Vassiliadis, S. Wong, S. Cotofana: The MOLEN coded processor. Springer-Verlag LNCS, Vol. 2147 (2001) 275–285
15. C. Zhang, F. Vahid, W. Najjar: A Highly Configurable Cache Architecture for Embedded Systems. Proc. Int. Symp. Computer Architecture, pp.136-146, 2003

The Emergence of Non-von Neumann Processors

Daniel S. Poznanovic

SRC Computers, Inc.
Colorado Springs, CO
poz@srccomp.com

Abstract. The von Neumann processor has been the foundation of computing from the start. Today's instruction processors are powerful and scale to thousands to yield large compute power, but a small fraction of the peak. The ASIC chip technology that implementations the fixed design microprocessor is placing significant constraints on the design of processors. At the same time reconfigurable Processors based upon FPGA chip technology are growing in capability and performance using a nontraditional processor architecture without instructions (the non-von Neumann architecture). Both processor types are trending to a common design point. This paper explores these trends and explains the technology of the emerging non-von Neumann processor and presents an example implementation.

1   Introduction

The von Neumann instruction processor has been with us since ENIAC at the University of Pennsylvania's Moore School [1] and has led to the creation of powerful computers that scale from single processor to thousands of interconnected processors. Applications are consuming as much compute power as can be delivered. At the same time processor designers in their search for even greater performance levels are reaching limits in complexity, power and cooling in the chips from which new processors are created. Costs and time to market are increasing while the delivered performance of processor chips is failing to keep up with the Moore's law growth in transistor count per chip. The traditional instruction processor is going through dramatic changes, all dealing with reducing complexity and power consumption, while increasing delivered performance.

The Moore's law gains in transistor count have also benefited other chip type besides the traditional processor chip. Field Programmable Gate Array (FPGA) chips, which can be configured with logic, have dramatically increased in capacity and clock rate. FPGAs are now practical to be used in creating application specific processors that best the traditional processor in performance with reduced power consumption. The evolving changes in current processor design are really just the early indications of the need for non-von Neumann reconfigurable processors. A logical transition is underway. That transition and a projection of the path the technology will support is presented. The trend toward simpler processors and greater parallelism logically extends to the emergence of non-von Neumann processors implemented as reconfigurable computers using FPGA chip technology.

K. Bertels, J.M.P. Cardoso, and S. Vassiliadis (Eds.): ARC 2006, LNCS 3985, pp. 243–254, 2006.

2   The Evolving von Neumann Processor

The tradition processor for today's systems is based on instruction processor architecture, the von Neumann architecture. This processor type has been very successful and has allowed the creation of large high performance systems. However, in recent years the requirement for ever increasing performance has clashed with the need for reasonable development times, and cost of ownership. Ever greater complexity and greater power consumption has caused a reassessment of the basic design of the microprocessor. Addressing these problems has started a move to simpler and more power aware designs. Clock rates have hit a limit or are being reduced, simpler processors are being designed and multiple processors per chip emerging. Several prominent processor designs will be reviewed and the trend analyzed.

2.1   IBM Cell Processor

The Cell processor, joint development by IBM, Sony and Toshiba [2][3][4], is being developed with the objective of orders of magnitude performance gain over the Playstation2, Real time responsiveness, wide applicability and rapid design and introduction. To accomplish these objectives the architecture of this new processor is built upon the Power Architecture while enhanced it with co-operative offload processors called synergistic processor elements (SPEs). The Cell processor combines a Power Processing Element with eight SPEs, an on-chip memory controller, and a configurable I/O interface. Both the PPE and associated SPEs include SIMD instructions.

The SPE is the interesting new component in this architecture. Its goal is to offload processing from the PPE. It has a simple structure with multiple parallel execution units, and with simple sequential instruction issue. Data movement is through multiple explicit DMAs, and there is no cache. Multiple PPEs can chain their computation results to one another with the objective of creating long pipelines of computation and thus achieving significant parallelism.

Through simplification of the processor and elimination of cache, both performance increase is seen as well as reduced power requirements. The cache and its management overhead is eliminated by introducing explicit data management through program controlled DMAs. This form of data access permits overlap of compute with data movement, another addition to parallelism in the processor. The PPE and SPEs are all resident on a single chip and thus reducing synchronization overhead.

Programming the Cell processor requires awareness of the local memory and use of the SIMD functional units. Performance is gained only when the SPEs are fully used. The architecture supports a number of programming models: function offload, computational accelerator, streaming, share memory, and asymmetric thread models [2]. The referenced paper contains details on all of these. The significant characteristic of these models is that the programmer has much mode explicit control that in the traditional microprocessor.

2.2   IBM Blue Gene/L

The Blue Gene/L system from IBM [5][6][7][8] was designed with the goal of exceptional cost/performance while approaching the performance of application specific processors. The system is designed around high level integration of a moderate frequency in system on a chip (SOC) technology. Performance/watt is the measure of performance for this system. The simplicity of the building block of BG/L is desired; since the system is intended to be built up to 65,536 nodes through an efficient interconnect.

Through use of a lower performing processor and SOC technology the system is able to provide all of the functionality of a node on a single chip, and to allow aggregation of a large numbers of high performance/watt nodes. The result is a high aggregate performance system.

2.3   Intel Multi-core Processors

Intel has realigned its focus from pure high GHz clock rate processors to the multi-core architecture [9][10]. This means focusing on greater parallelism and more work done per clock cycle. This change of focus arises from the recognition that Moore's Law advances are no longer delivering the performance to the application at the same rate that the transistor count is growing. A lower clock frequency brings with it lower power consumption, as well as a simpler processor to design. Multi-core architecture simply means more processors on a chip, and simpler inter-processor coordination. Intel has not however followed the Cell processor direction of vastly simplified processors. The multiprocessor on a chip provides more support for threaded applications and therefore more parallel work. The parallelism is however, at a high granularity. Within each processor there is also support for SIMD instructions and the pipelines that they supports. This style of streaming processing also provides functional units parallelism.

2.4   Imagine-Stream Processor

Streams processors [11][12][13] are signal and image processors that provide ASIC performance and programmability. A stream program can be represented as a data flow graph with data flow between computational nodes. A stream processor exploits parallelism at the functional unit level and producer-consumer data locality eliminating the memory load/store overhead. Explicit data management is accomplished through the use of a large Stream Register File (SRF). The stream processor is both an instruction processor and a data flow processor. It is programmable, however it is not reconfigurable. The processor is composed of a fixed number and type of functional unit, but has through the SRF a flexible interconnect between functional units.

The Imagine stream processor is a prototype that contains eight arithmetic clusters each with six 32 bit pipelined floating point arithmetic units. Each functional unit has its own register file. Each cluster is controlled through a wide VLIW instruction.

2.5 The von Neumann Processor Trend

Though there continues to be microprocessors with severe complexity (Itanium), the trend in microprocessor designs is toward:

- simplicity
- reduced power consumption
- greater parallelism
- slower clocks
- application specific functionality
- more on chip parallelism with less complexity
- explicit control

These trends are driven by the reality of cost and time to market. They also are tending to bring the instruction processor architecture closer to that of the non-instruction reconfigurable processor. The following sections will explore these ideas.

3   The Emerging Non-von Neumann Processor

The previous section explored the trends of some prominent microprocessors whose implementation is based on fixed function dense logic devices (ASICs). Processors based upon reconfigurable chip technology have also been evolving. In particular FPGA chip technology is evolving to allow ever greater amounts of logic and higher clock rates. The FPGA-based Reconfigurable Processor is coming of age. Technology trends have enabled the creation of a high performance processor that is not based upon the traditional von Neumann architecture. These trends have enabled the creation of a competitive processor today and will continue to drive this new processor to the computing forefront. FPGA technology, its future and the Reconfigurable Processor architecture that is enabled is discussed next. The trends seen in microprocessor and the reconfigurable processors are leading to a common point which is giving greater importance to the FPGA based non-von Neumann architectures.

3.1   Field Programmable Gate Array Chips

Field Programmable Gate Arrays (FPGA) are commodity chips composed of SRAM memory cells used to define a configuration for the chip. FPGAs contain logic gates, flip-flops, RAMs, arithmetic cores, clocks, and configurable wires to provide interconnection. FPGAs can be configured to implement any arbitrary logic function, and can therefore be used to create custom processors that can be optimized to an application. The chip has a simple and regular structure. Circuits can be built up from the logic gates of the chip. Specific functionality can then be built up from the lower level circuits. Data paths connecting the logic can be configured using routing and switch resources. In this way FPGAs can be configured to implement any arbitrary logic function, and can therefore be used to create chips with any desired functionality.

FPGAs can be configured to create arbitrary circuits. So an FPGA could be configured as a simple interface chip or a complex microprocessor. So, a collection of FPGAs could be configured to be a MIPS, or SPARC, PowerPC, or Xeon processor, as well as a processor of one's own design. Integrating the FPGA with memory and chips providing I/O could then yield an instruction processor capable of being programmed with instructions.

3.2   Direct Execution Logic Processor

Other processor types could be implemented with FPGAs. In fact a processor need not even be an instruction processor. It could be a Direct Execution Logic (DEL) processor which contains only computational logic requiring no instructions to define the algorithm. Specific functional units, such as adders, multipliers, dividers, and logic functions can be instantiated in an FPGA with data paths configured to connect the functional units in such a way as to compute an expression. What is important to application developers is that today's reconfigurable chips have a clock rate and capacity that make it practical to do large scale computing with RC hardware.

DEL processors hold great potential for high performance. A DEL processor can be created with exactly the resources required to perform a specific algorithm. Traditional instruction processors have fixed resources, adders, multipliers, registers, cache memory, and require significant chip real estate and processing power to implement overhead operations such as instruction decode and sequencing, and cache management.

Why should one care that a DEL processor can be created dynamically for an application, and that it uses its chips more effectively than a microprocessor? The answer is simple: PERFORMANCE and POWER EFFICIENCY. A DEL RC processor can be created with all of the parallelism that exists within an algorithm without the overhead present in a microprocessor. For the remainder of this article RC processors will be assumed implemented using FPGAs in order to be more specific in the discussion.

3.3   Performance in DEL Processors

Performance in RC processors comes from parallel execution of logic. RC processor are completely parallel. In fact the task of constructing the logic for a given algorithm is to coordinate the parallel execution such that intermediate results are created, communicated and retained at the proper instants in time.

A DEL processor is constructed as a network of functional units connected with data paths and control signals. Each computational element in the network becomes active with each clock pulse. Even though a microprocessor can operate at a clock frequency of 3 GHz and the FPGA chips operate in the 100 to 300 MHz frequency range the parallelism and internal bandwidth on a DEL processor can out perform the microprocessor by orders of magnitude better delivered performance. Parallel execution of exactly the required number of functional units, high internal bandwidth, elimination of instruction processing overhead, and load/store elimination all contribute to overcoming the 30X difference in clock frequency between the DEL processor and the Intel microprocessor.

3.4   FPGA Technology - The Future

Figures 1 and 2 present a summary of the performance expected in FPGAs over the next few years [14]. Performance gains can be seen on two fronts: parallelism and clock rate, with the resulting gain to application performance being multiplicative. Additional logic capacity of the chips results in additional parallelism. FPGA chip geometry and growing density results in increased clock rates. The basic chip technology that has lead to microprocessor performance advances also produces higher performing FPGAs. However, the performance gains seen in FPGA based processors is more readily delivered to the application, because of

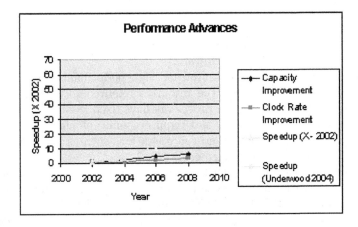

Fig. 1. Performance Advances in FPGAs

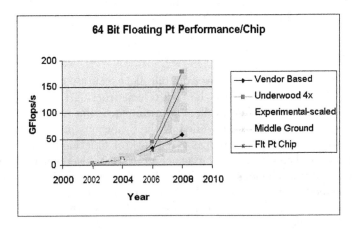

Fig. 2. Floating Point Performance Advances in FPGAs

the application specific processing that takes place. The overhead in the FPGA can be kept to an absolute minimum when compared to a typical microprocessor. So the bottom line is that the Moore's Law gains in transistor count is turned into application level performance at a greater rate than microprocessors.

Raw FPGA clock rate and gate density is not likely to exceed the ASIC implementation of microprocessor chips. Since FPGAs are reconfigurable and implement functionality through configurable lookup tables and route signals through configurable levels of switches, a hardware level of indirection is introduced. However, in the long run, the high degree of available parallelism and reduced overhead available through Direct Execution Logic and the resulting application specific processors overcomes any deficit in clock rate.

A new generation of FPGAs is partially eliminating the indirect routing slowdown by introducing hard cores into the FPGA fabric. These hard cores are essentially ASIC implementations of processors or functional units. They range from integer multipliers, to double precision IEEE floating point units, to DSP processors. The introduction of hard core functional units that provide dense real estate and low latency compute while retaining the flexible routing of signals in and out of the unit is a big performance step forward. It is also a step toward the traditional microprocessor ASIC implementation. The combination of soft core and hard core functional units on a flexible routing fabric provides high performance while maintaining the flexibility of routing that gives a Direct Execution Logic processor its efficiency.

4 A New High Performance Architecture

Previous sections of this paper discuss Reconfigurable Processors in general. This section presents a specific implementation of a systems based on both von Neumann and non-von Neumann processors. SRC Computers, Inc. [15] has created systems that are composed of DEL processors and microprocessors. SRC systems runs Linux as the OS, provide a programming environment called Carte™ for creating applications composed of both microprocessor instructions and DEL, and support microprocessor and DEL processor hardware in a single system. SRC's hardware and software implementation is next presented to illustrate an current implementation of the previously discussed Reconfigurable Computing technology.

4.1 The DEL Processor - MAP®

The MAP processor is SRC's high performance DEL processor. MAP uses reconfigurable components to accomplish control and user-defined compute, data prefetch, and data access functions. This compute capability is teamed with very high on and off-board interconnect bandwidth. MAP's multiple banks of On-Board Memory provides 24 GBs/sec of local memory bandwidth. MAP is equipped with separate input and output ports with each port sustaining a data payload bandwidth of 3.6 GB/sec or 14.4 GB/s total bandwidth. Each MAP

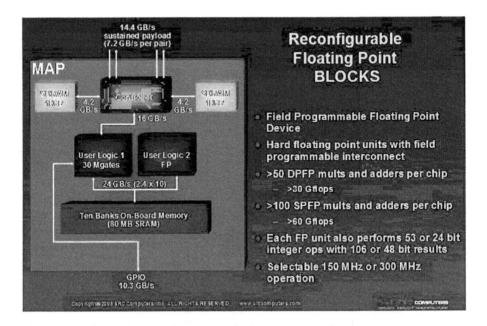

Fig. 3. SRC MAP

also has two general purpose I/O (GPIO) ports sustaining an additional data payload 10.3 GB/sec for direct MAP-to-MAP connections or data source input. Figure 3 presents the block diagram of the MAP processor.

4.2 Microprocessor with SNAP™

The Dense Logic Devices (DLDs) used in these products is the dual processor Intel IA-32 line of microprocessors. These third party commodity boards are then equipped with the SRC developed SNAP interface. SNAP allows commodity microprocessor boards to connect to, and share memory with, MAPs and Common Memory nodes that make up the rest of the SRC system.

The SNAP interface is designed to plug directly into the microprocessors' memory subsystem, instead of its I/O subsystem, allowing SRC systems to sustain significantly higher interconnect bandwidths. SNAP uses separate input and output ports with each port currently sustaining a data payload bandwidth of 3.6 GB/sec.

The intelligent DMA controller on SNAP is capable of performing complex DMA prefetch and data access functions such as data packing, strided access and scatter/gather, to maximize the efficient use of the system interconnect bandwidth. Interconnect efficiencies more than 10 times greater than a cache-based microprocessor using the same interconnect are common for these operations.

SNAP can either connect directly to a single MAP or to SRC's Hi-Bar® switch for system-wide access to multiple MAPs, microprocessors or Common Memory.

4.3   SRC System Level Architectural Implementation

System level configurations implement either a cluster of MAPstations™, or a crossbar switch-based topology. Cluster-based systems utilize the microprocessor and DEL processor previously discussed in a direct connected configuration. While this topology does have a microprocessor-DEL processor affinity, it also has the benefit of using standards-based clustering technology to create very large systems.

When more flexibility is desired, Hi-Bar switch-based systems can be employed. Hi-Bar is SRC's proprietary scalable, high-bandwidth, low-latency switch. Each Hi-Bar supports 64-bit addressing and has 16 input and 16 output ports to connect to 16 nodes. Microprocessors, MAPs and Common Memory nodes can all be connected to Hi-Bar in any configuration as shown in Figure 4. Each input or output port sustains a yielded data payload of 3.6 GB/sec for an aggregate yielded bisection data bandwidth of 9.2 TB/sec per 16 ports. Port-to-port latency is 180 ns with Single Error Correction and Double Error Detection (SECDED) implemented on each port. Hi-Bar switches can also be interconnected in multi-tier configurations, allowing two tiers to support 256 nodes. Each Hi-Bar switch is housed in a 2U-high, 19-inch wide rack mountable chassis, along with its power supplies and cooling solution, for easy inclusion into rack-based servers.

SRC servers that use the Hi-Bar crossbar switch interconnect can incorporate Common Memory nodes in addition to microprocessors and MAPs. Each of these Common Memory nodes contains an intelligent DMA controller and up to 8 GBs of DDR SDRAM. The SRC-7 MAPs, SNAPs, and Common Memory node (CM) support 64 bit virtual addressing of all memory in the system, allowing a single flat address space to be used within applications. Each node sustains memory reads and writes with 3.6 GB/sec of yielded data payload bandwidth.

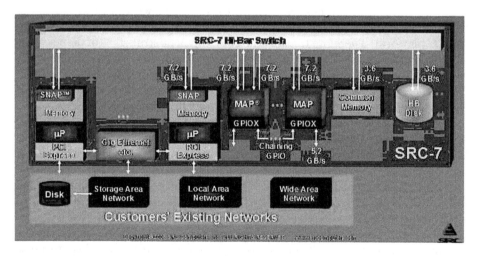

Fig. 4. SRC-7 Hi-Bar System

The CM's intelligent DMA controller is capable of performing complex DMA functions such as data packing, strided access, and scatter/gather to maximize the efficient use of the system interconnect bandwidth. Interconnect efficiencies more than 10 times greater than a cache-based microprocessor using the same interconnect are common for these operations.

In addition, the SRC system have dedicated semaphore circuitry that is also accessible by all MAP processors and microprocessors for synchronization.

5   Programming Model for Reconfigurable Computing

Traditionally the programming model for RC has been one of hardware design. Given that the tools required for the underlying FPGA technology of RC are all logic design tools from the Electronic Design Automation industry, there really has not been a programming environment recognizable to a software developer. The tools have supported Hardware Definition Languages (HDL) such as Verilog, VHDL, and Schematic Capture.

With the introduction of system on a chip (SOC) technology and the complexity associated with hardware definition of such complexity, high level languages have begun to be available. Java and C-like languages are becoming more common for use in programming RC chips. This is a significant step forward, but continues to require quite a leap by application programmers.

The SRC programming model is the traditional software development model where C and Fortran are used to program the MAP processor, and any language capable of linking with the run time libraries (written in C) can be compiled and run on the microprocessor portion of the system.

5.1   Carte Programming Environment

The SRC Carte programming environment was created with the design assumption that application programmers would be writing and porting applications to the RC platform. Therefore the standard development strategies, of design, code in high level languages (HLLs), compile, debug via standard debugger, edit code, re-compile, and so on, until correct, are used to develop for the SRC-7 system. Only when the application runs correctly in a microprocessor environment, is the application recompiled and targeted for the DEL processor, MAP.

Compiling to hardware in a RC system requires two compilation steps that are quite foreign to programming for an instruction processor. The output of the HLL compiler must be a hardware definition language. In Carte the output is either Verilog or Electronic Design Interchange Format (EDIF). EDIF files are the hardware definition object files that define the circuits that will be implemented in the RC chips. If Verilog is generated, then that HDL must be synthesized to EDIF using a Verilog compiler such as Synplify from Synplicity.

A final step, place and route, takes the collection of EDIF files and creates the physical layout of the circuits on the RC chip. The output files for this process is a configuration bitstream which can be loaded into an FPGA to create the hardware representation of the algorithm being programming into the RC processor.

The Carte programming environment performs the compilation from C or FORTRAN to bitstream for the FPGA without programmer involvement. It further compiles the codes targeted to microprocessors into objects modules. The final step for Carte is the creation of a Unified Executable which incorporates the microprocessor object modules, the MAP bitstreams, and all of the required run time libraries into a single Linux executable file.

6   Conclusions

This paper has discussed the trends in recent microprocessor, and in the FPGA based reconfigurable processors. These widely dissimilar architectures are actually on a path of convergence driven by the approaching limits of technology for the microprocessor and by the advances in the FPGA technology seen by the RC processors. Microprocessors are achieving higher performance via parallelism of simpler multi-cores with slower clock rates and efficiency through explicit control. Simplicity of designs and power efficiency are now important processor deign goals. The FPGA based non-von Neumann processor are achieving performance through harnessing parallelism of data-flow processing, utilizing multi-core fixed logic techology, increasing chip capacity and higher clock rates, and delivering power efficient performance. Both the instruction based processors and the data-flow procesors can now be programmed using high level programming languages.

Both processor types have a place in computing. However, if the technology trends continue, the nontraditional (non-von Neumann) processor has a good chance of becoming the dominant processor, while the traditional fixed design microprocessor (von Neumann) processor moves to be the support processor of a computing system.

References

1. Weik, M. H.: The ENIAC Story, ORDINANCE, January-February 1961. http://ftp.arl.army.mil/ mike/comphist/
2. IBM: IBM Cell: http://www.research.ibm.com/cell/cell_chip.html
3. IBM: IBM Cell: http://www.research.ibm.com/cell/cell_systems.html
4. IBM: IBM Cell: http://www.research.ibm.com/cell/cell_programming
5. Gara, A., Blumrich, M. A., Chen, D., Chiu, G. L., Coteus, P., Giampapa, M. E., Haring, R. A., Heidelberger, P., Hoenicke, D., Kopcsay, G. V., Liebsch, T. A., Ohmacht, M., Steinmacher-Burow, B. D., Takken, T. and P. Vranas: Blue Gene/L system architecture. IBM J. Res. & Dev., Vol. **49** No. 2/3 (2005) 195-212.
6. Bright, A. A, Haring, R. A., Dombrowa, M. B., Ohmacht, M., Hoenicke, D., Singh, S., Marcella, J. A., Lembach, R. F., Douskey, S. M., Ellavsky, M. R., Zoellin, C. G., and A. Gara: Blue Gene/L Compute chip: Synthesis, timing and physical design, IBM J. Res. & Dev., Vol. **49** No. 2/3 (2005) 277-288.
7. Ohmacht, M., Bergamaschi, R. A., Bhattacharya, S., Gara, A., Giampapa, M. E., Gopalsamy, B., Haring, R. A., Hoenicke, D., Krolak, D. J., Marcella, J. A., Nathanson, B. J., Salapura, V., and M. E. Wazlowski: Blue Gene/L Compute chip: Memory and Ethernet subsystem. IBM J. Res. & Dev., Vol. **49** No. 2/3 (2005) 255-264.

8. Moreira, J. E., Almsi, G., Archer, C., Bellofatto, R., Bergner, P., Brunheroto, J. R., Brutman, M., Castaos, J. G., Crumley, P. G., Gupta, M., Inglett, T., Lieber, D., Limpert, D., McCarthy, P., Megerian, M, Mendell, M., Mundy, M., Reed, D., Sahoo, R. K., Sanomiya, A., Shok, R., Smith, B., and G. G. Stewart: Blue Gene/L programming and operating environment. IBM J. Res. & Dev. Vol. **49** No. 2/3.(2005) 367-376.
9. Intel: Intel Multi-Core Processor Architecture Development Backgrounder: `http://www.intel.com/multi-core/`
10. Intel: A New Era of Architectural Innovation Arrives with Intel Dual-Core Processors: `http://www.intel.com/multi-core/`
11. Ahn, J. H., Dally, W. J., Khailany, B., Kapasi, U. J., and A. Das: Evaluating the Imagine Stream Architecture. Proceedings of the 31st Annual International Symposium on Computer Architecture, Munich, Germany, June 2004.
12. Dally, W. J., Kapasi, U. J., Khailany, B., Ahn, J. H., and A. Das.: Stream Processors: Programmability with Efficiency. ACM Queue. Vol. **2** No. 1. (2004) 52-62.
13. Kapasi , U. J., Rixner, S., Dally, W. J, Khailany, B., Ahn, J. H., Mattson, P., and J. D. Owens.: Programmable Stream Processors. IEEE Computer. August (2003) 54-62.
14. Underwood, K.: FPGAs vs. CPUs: Trends in Peak Floating-Point Performance. FPGA04, Feb.22-24, 2004.
15. SRC Computers, Inc.: `http://www.srccomp.com`.

Scheduling Reconfiguration Activities of Run-Time Reconfigurable RTOS Using an Aperiodic Task Server*

Marcelo Götz and Florian Dittmann

Heinz Nixdorf Institute, University of Paderborn, Germany
{mgoetz, roichen}@upb.de

Abstract. Reconfigurable computing based on hybrid architectures, comprising general purpose processor (CPU) and Field Programmable Gate Array (FPGA), is very attractive because it can provide high computational performance as well as flexibility to support today's embedded systems requirements. However, the relative high reconfiguration costs often represent an obstacle when using such architectures for run-time reconfigurable systems. In order to overcome this barrier the used real-time operating system must explicitly respect the reconfiguration time. In such systems, the reconfiguration activities need to be carried out during run-time without causing the application tasks to miss their deadlines. In this paper, we show how we model these activities as aperiodic jobs. Therefore, we apply the server-based method from the real-time schedule theory to the scheduling of aperiodic activities.

1 Introduction

In currently available Field Programmable Gate Arrays (FPGAs), the availability of a general purpose processor (GPP) surrounded by a large field of reconfigurable hardware offers the possibility for a sophisticated System-on-Chip (SoC) concept. Moreover, the capability of such devices to be on-the-fly partially reprogrammed allows to dynamically adapt the software and hardware to the current system requirements, performing a Reconfigurable SoC (RSoC). The resulting system is one which can provide higher performance by implementing custom hardware functions in FPGA, and still be flexible by reprogramming the FPGA and/or using a microprocessor (hybrid architecture).

In the scope of our ongoing research we are developing a runtime reconfigurable Real-Time Operating System (RTOS). In the proposed framework, the RTOS is able to adapt itself to the current application requirements, tailoring its components for this purpose. Therefore, the system continuously analysis the application requirements deciding on-the-fly which RTOS components are

* This work was developed in the course of the Special Research Initiative 614 - Self-optimizing Concepts and Structures in Mechanical Engineering - University of Paderborn, and was published on its behalf and funded by the Deutsche Forschungsgemeinschaft. It was also partially supported by DFG SPP 1148.

K. Bertels, J.M.P. Cardoso, and S. Vassiliadis (Eds.): ARC 2006, LNCS 3985, pp. 255–261, 2006.

needed and also to which execution environment (CPU or FPGA) they will be assigned. Thus, techniques for a deterministic system reconfiguration need to be used in order to avoid that a running application will miss its deadlines.

In this paper, we will focus on the mechanisms used to handle the reconfiguration activities in a deterministic way, applying, therefore, techniques from real-time schedule theory. More precisely, our proposal consists of modeling these activities as aperiodic jobs, which will be scheduled together with the running tasks in order to keep the time correctness of the system.

The remainder of the paper is organizes as follows. After summarizing related work, we specify the problem and its model. We then show that reconfiguration activities can be considered as aperiodic jobs (Section 4) and explain how the server is applied (Section 5). The schedulability analysis in Section 6 sums up and proves the applicability of our server. Finally, we conclude and give an outlook.

2   Related Work

The hardware/software allocation of applications tasks to dynamically reconfigurable embedded systems (by means of task migration) allows the customization of their resources during run-time to meet the demands of executing applications, as can be seen in [1]. Another example is the Operating System (OS) for a heterogeneous RSoC [2], which reallocates on-the-fly the tasks over a hybrid architecture, depending on the Quality of Service expected from the application. Nevertheless, the RTOS itself is still static and reconfiguration and migration costs are not a big issue in the design.

The works presented in [3], [4] and [5] are some examples of RTOS services to support the (re)location, scheduling and placement of application tasks on an architecture composed by FPGA with or without a CPU.

In our work we expand and adapt the existing concepts to the RTOS level. Therefore, technics to take the reconfiguration costs into consideration in order to achieve a deterministic execution environment is here proposed.

3   Problem Statement and Modeling

The target architecture is composed of one CPU, FPGA, memory and a bus connecting the components. Most of these elements are provided on a single die, such as the Virtex II Pro, from Xilinx company. The RTOS services that are able to be reconfigured are stored on an external SDRAM chip in two different implementations: as software object and as FPGA configuration bitstream.

Abstractly, the system concept is based on the microkernel approach of DReaMs RTOS [6]. Only absolutely essential core OS functions are provided by the kernel (which is fixed and can not be reconfigured). The other functionalities (services) are provided by components dynamically attached to the kernel.

The RTOS is composed of a set of services that may run either on the CPU or on the FPGA. In our system, only application critical tasks use FPGA resources. The allocation of the currently required RTOS services is decided by an algorithm presented in [7]. This algorithm decides where to place each RTOS service taking into consideration its current cost and available resources (limited FPGA area: A_{max} and limited CPU processor utilization: U_{max}).

Due to the application dynamism, the allocation decision needs to be checked continuously. Whenever the specified constraints are no longer fulfilled, a system reconfiguration takes place. This implies that a set of RTOS components need to be relocated (reconfigurated) by means of migration. However, this activity must not compromise the correctness of the running application, which under real-time system means also the respecting of time-constraints.

In typical embedded real-time systems the application may be modeled as a set of periodic activities. Even sporadic tasks can be modeled as periodic ones through the assumptions that their minimum interarrival time being the period. Therefore, we consider the application and the RTOS services as a set of periodic tasks. However, without dependencies among tasks. From the point of view of the microkernel level, the application as well as RTOS activities are tasks that compete for system resources. Hence, to schedule the reconfiguration activities, it is enough to consider the whole system as a single set of periodic tasks. Let us define a set S of tasks that will suffer a reconfiguration: $S = \{s_1, ..., s_m\}$. Each task $s_i \in S$ is characterized by the parameters shown in the following table:

Parameter	Description
$E_{sw,i}$; $E_{hw,i}$	Execution time of a task i in software and in hardware
P_i; D_i	Period and Relative deadline of a task i
a_i; s_i; f_i	Arrival, Starting and Finishing time of a task i
$RP_{sw,i}$; $RP_{hw,i}$	Time to program a task i in software and in hardware
$RM_{shw,i}$	Time to migrate a task i between software and hardware

Additionally, every task i running in software utilizes some processor, which is defined to be: $U_i = \frac{E_{sw,i}}{P_i}$. Similarly, for every task i running in hardware, some amount of FPGA area is used: A_i.

The notations RP and RM are used to represent the times needed to program a task in its new execution environment and to actually migrate it, respectively. When a task is placed in hardware, RP represents the time needed to partially program the FPGA with its related bitstream. Likewise, RP represents the activity to link the object code of a task in the software CPU.

Once having the FPGA programmed with the task's bitstream, or the CPU software linked with the task's object code, the effective migration of the task can start: RM. This phase represents the activity to read the internal data of the task and to write it to the new execution environment, including also the translation of this data between the two different execution environments. After finishing the RM phase, the next task instance will start in its new execution environment. Based on our current implementation status, we consider the RM time as being the same for a task migrating from software or from hardware.

Although there are some methods that allow the preemption of hardware tasks, (as readback, scan-path methods and etc., e.g. [8]), we do not consider that a task may be preempted in FPGA and resumed at CPU (or vice-versa). In our approach, each hardware periodic task saves its internal data onto a particular set of registers after every finishing of its execution instance. These registers are made available to the CPU in order to perform the data migration.

4 Scheduling Reconfiguration Activities

Due to the application dynamism, the task set S and its arrival time is not known a priory. Thus, this scenario can be seen as a set of aperiodic jobs arriving into a running system. In real-time schedule theory, when real-time periodic tasks and non (or firm) aperiodic jobs need to be scheduled together, a server for aperiodic jobs is generally used. The basic idea of this approach is to include a new periodic task to the system which will be responsible to carry out the aperiodic jobs without causing a periodic task to miss its deadline. A more comprehensive and detailed explanation of this idea is given in [9].

Among different types of server, we focus our analysis on the Total Bandwidth Server (TBS) due to the following reasons:

We are currently using Earliest Deadline First (EDF) as our schedule policy;
- This server presents a high performance/cost ratio [10];
Limiting the complexity, TBS allows the improvement of the response time.

The TBS assigns the deadline d_i for an aperiodic job i arriving to the system at time a_i: $d_i = \max(a_i, d_{i-1}) + \frac{C_i}{U_s}$. Where d_{i-1} represents the deadline of the aperiodic job arrived before task i, U_s is the server capacity and C_i is the execution time requested by the job i. Deadline d_{i-1} is 0 if task i is the first one, or if all pending aperiodic jobs arrived before i has been already finished.

5 Applying TB Server

The activity of the phase RP_i from a task i, either in software or in hardware, does not imply an extra synchronization with the running task i. This activity may even be preempted by task i without causing a data consistency problem. Thus, its execution is carried out during the server activation time and does not impose any extra constraint (the server appliance is straightforward). Differently, the RM_i phase must completely execute between two consecutive instances of a task i. The Figure 1 illustrate the scenario where a RM phase of a periodic task i is schedule between two consecutive instances (k and $k+1$) of this task.

To ensure that RM_i will not start before task $s_{i,k}$, we free the RM_i only when $s_{i,k}$ has finished: $a_{RM,i} \geq f_{i,k}$. In order to give more time to the server to execute the RM_i job, one may think that the optimal arrival time ($a^*_{RM,i}$) is in the specific instance k^* where the lateness of task i is minimal: $a^*_{RM,i} = f_{i,k^*} | (d_{i,k^*} - f_{i,k^*}) = \min_k(d_{i,k} - f_{i,k})$ (see Figure 1(a). However, to find the instance that provides the minimum lateness when periodic task set is scheduled under EDF is not easy. This would increase the complexity of our algorithms. Moreover, a non wanted

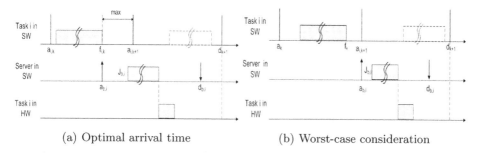

(a) Optimal arrival time   (b) Worst-case consideration

Fig. 1. Scenario where a task migrates from software to hardware

delay in the complete reconfiguration time may be included due to shifting of $a_{RM,i}$ from $f_{i,k}$ to $f_{i,k*}$ (depending on the hyperperiod).

The Figure 1(b) shows a pessimistic scenario where the arrival of the job RM_i occurs at the arrival time of the next instance $a_{i,k+1}$. This scenario covers also the worst-case where a task i finishes exactly in its deadline (when relative deadline is equal to period). Under EDF schedule, the running task is always the one which has the smallest absolute deadline among the ready tasks. Thus, we can ensure that RM_i will not be preempted by $s_{i,k+1}$, making $d_{RM,i} \leq d_{i,k+1}$.

As we free the RM phase only after RP has been finished, the deadline assigned to RM_i ($d_{RM,i}$), using TBS and respecting the conditions explained above is shown in Equation 1. Noting that $d_{i,k+1} = a_{i,k+1} + P_i$ and $a_{i,k+1} = a_{RM,i}$ and knowing that $U_i = \frac{E_{sw,i}}{P_i}$, the Equation 1 can be rewritten in terms of the processor utilization factor (Equation 2).

$$d_{RM,i} = a_{RM,i} + \frac{RM_{shw,i}}{U_s} \leq d_{i,k+1} \quad (1) \qquad U_s \geq \frac{RM_{shw,i}}{E_{sw,i}} U_i \quad (2)$$

The Equation 2 shows that the required server capacity, to migrate a task from software to hardware, can even be smaller than the task processor utilization of the correspondent task if the RM phase takes less time than the execution time of the task in software. In addition, if under all tasks that will migrate from software to hardware the condition expressed in Equation 2 is fulfilled, we can guarantee that the precedence conditions defined in this section will be satisfied when EDF and TBS are used. Another condition implicity assumed during this analysis, is that the execution time of a task in hardware is smaller (at maximum equal) than its execution in software (which is true in most of the cases).

Similar analysis can be applied on the scenario where tasks are migrating from hardware to software. Due to the true parallelism capability offered by the hardware execution environment, the finishing time of a task can be calculated more precisely. Thus, the deadline assigned to RM by TBS is given by Equation 3. Noting that $a_{i,k+1} = a_{i,k} + P_i$ and knowing that $U_i = \frac{E_{sw,i}}{P_i}$, we derive the minimum server capacity required (Equation 4).

$$d_{RM,i} = a_{i,k} + E_{hw,i} + \frac{RM_{shw,i}}{U_s} \leq d_{i,k+1} \quad (3) \qquad U_s \geq \frac{RM_{shw,i}}{2P_i - E_{hw,i}} \quad (4)$$

The Equation 4 give us the minimal server capacity that is necessary to migrate a task from hardware to software under the precedence constraints explained in the beginning of the Section 5.

6 Schedulability Analysis

All analysis made in the sections before were based on the proper assignment of arrival time of aperiodic reconfiguration activities and the establishment of conditions for the definition of the server capacity. These analysis were made in order to proper represent the precedence constraints imposed in our scenario to achieve a consistent data transfer during task migration. Thus, a schedulability analysis is necessary. As we are restricting ourself to a scenario were periodic tasks do not have dependency, a simple schedulability analysis can be made. As long as the sum of the processor utilization from all periodic tasks (even those ones that do not suffer a migration) together with the server capacity does not exceed a maximum (U_{max}) the feasibility of the schedule is guaranteed. Therefore, after every task migration, the processor utilization cannot be greater than U_{max}. Furthermore, after every task migration to FPGA, the remaining area needs to be enough to receive a new possible task.

7 Conclusion and Future Work

In this work, we have introduced the use of a server to carry out the reconfiguration activities of a reconfigurable RTOS in a deterministic way. The concept proposed explicitly respects the reconfiguration time and migration costs and derives, by analytical analysis, the minimal server capacity knowing the execution times and reconfiguration costs of every task.

In the future, we will investigate the scenario where tasks are scheduled under fixed priority schedule. Additionally, we want to derive an analysis that will be able to determine the amount of time necessary to migrate/reconfigure the complete set S of tasks, using also less pessimistic assumptions.

References

1. Harkin, J., McGinnity, T.M., Maguire, L.P.: Modeling and optimizing run-time reconfiguration using evolutionary computation. Trans. on Emb. Comp. Sys. (2004)
2. Nollet, V., Coene, P., Verkest, D., Vernalde, S., Lauwereins, R.: Designing an Operating System for a Heterogeneous Reconfigurable SoC. In: IPDPS. (2003)
3. Baskaran, K., Jigang, W., S., T.: Hardware Partitioning Algorithm for Reconfigurable Operating System in Embedded Systems. In: 6th RTLinux W. (2004)
4. Wigley, G., Kearney, D.: The Development of an Operating System for Reconfigurable Computing. In: FCCM. (2001)
5. Mignolet, J.Y., et al: Infrastructure for Design and Management of Relocatable Tasks in a Heterogeneous Reconfigurable System-on-Chip. In: DATE. (2003)

6. Ditze, C.: Towards Operating System Synthesis. Dissertation, Universität Paderborn, Heinz Nixdorf Institut, Entwurf Paralleler Systeme (2000)
7. Götz, M., Rettberg, A., Pereira, C.E.: Towards Run-time Partitioning of a Real Time Operating System for Reconfigurable Systems on Chip. In: IESS. (2005)
8. Ahmadinia, A., Bobda, C., Koch, D., Majer, M., Teich, J.: Task scheduling for heterogeneous reconfigurable computers. In: SBCCI. (2004)
9. Buttazzo, G.C.: Hard Real-time Computing Systems: Predictable Scheduling Algorithms And Applications (Real-Time Systems Series). Kluwer (1997)
10. Buttazzo, G.C.: Rate Monotonic vs. EDF: Judgment Day. RT Systems (2005)

A New Approach to Assess Defragmentation Strategies in Dynamically Reconfigurable FPGAs[*]

Manuel G. Gericota[1], Gustavo R. Alves[1], Luís F. Lemos[1],
and José M. Ferreira[2]

[1] Department of Electrical Engineering - ISEP,
Rua Dr. António Bernardino de Almeida, 4200-072 Porto, Portugal
{mgg, gca, lfl}@isep.ipp.pt
[2] Department of Electrical and Computer Engineering - FEUP,
Rua Dr. Roberto Frias, 4200-465 Porto, Portugal
jmf@fe.up.pt

Abstract. Fragmentation on dynamically reconfigurable FPGAs is a major obstacle to the efficient management of the logic space in reconfigurable systems. When resource allocation decisions have to be made at run-time a rearrangement may be necessary to release enough contiguous resources to implement incoming functions. The feasibility of run-time relocation depends on the processing time required to set up rearrangements. Moreover, the performance of the relocated functions should not be affected by this process or otherwise the whole system performance, and even its operation, may be at risk.

Relocation should take into account not only specific functional issues, but also the FPGA architecture, since these two aspects are normally intertwined. A simple and fast method to assess performance degradation of a function during relocation and to speed up the defragmentation process, based on previous function labelling and on the application of the Euclidian distance concept, is proposed in this paper.

1 Introduction

Field Programmable Gate Arrays (FPGAs) experienced a considerable evolution in the last two decades. Shorter reconfiguration times and the new features introduced recently, such as run-time partial reconfiguration and self-reconfiguration, made possible the implementation of the concept of virtual hardware defined in the early 1990s: the hardware resources are supposed to be unlimited and implementations that oversize the reconfigurable logic space available are resolved by temporal partitioning [1].

Generally, an application comprises a set of functions that are predominantly executed in sequence, or with a low degree of parallelism, in which case their

---

[*] This work is supported by an FCT program under contract POSC/EEA-ESE/55680/2004.

K. Bertels, J.M.P. Cardoso, and S. Vassiliadis (Eds.): ARC 2006, LNCS 3985, pp. 262–267, 2006.

simultaneous availability is not required. Functions may be swapped in real time, becoming operational only when needed and being substituted if their availability is no longer required. However, when the logic space of an FPGA is shared among several functions belonging to a number of different applications, each with its own requirements in spatial and temporal terms, fragmentation of the logic space may occur [2]. The solution to this problem is to consolidate unused areas within the FPGA without halting the operation of currently running functions. If a new function cannot be allocated immediately due to lack of contiguous free resources, a suitable rearrangement of a subset of the executing functions must be implemented to overcome the problem.

In general, there is a tendency to model the FPGA as a regular array structure and to regard defragmentation as a strictly packing problem [3, 4, 5]. While in the first generations of FPGAs this assertion was true regarding the CLBs position inside the array, it was inaccurate when other resources were considered. The presence of dedicated routing resources available to enhance specific applications (like counters and adders), which have a tremendous impact on function performance, were mainly responsible for this inaccuracy. The problem was aggravated in more recent generations by the introduction of memory blocks and of dedicated Digital Signal Processing (DSP) blocks distributed among the FPGA array.

In an FPGA, the access to the reconfiguration mechanism is independent from the operation of the running functions. Therefore, defragmentation may be implemented as a background process, running concurrently with the operation of currently implemented functions, without disturbing or impairing them, instead of just when a new incoming function is claiming area to be implemented. As a result, waiting times will be reduced and the overall system performance improved. A metric to determine when to perform defragmentation is proposed in [6].

2 Labelling Functions

To enhance the performance of specific types of functions, FPGA architectures present some special features, like dedicated carry lines to increase speed of arithmetic functions (e.g. counters or adders). In the architecture of Virtex FPGAs from Xilinx, which were used during the experimental phase of this research work, these lines span the FPGA vertically, enabling only the interconnection of vertically adjacent CLBs. The use of dedicated carry lines, with very low propagation delays (in the order of a few picoseconds), enabled us to achieve an operating frequency of circa 145 MHz for a 24-bit binary counter implemented on an XCV200, and 450 MHz in the case of an XC4VFX12.

However, the maximum frequency of operation decreased dramatically if one or more of these dedicated carry lines were substituted by generic interconnection resources. Figure 1 shows how the maximum frequency of operation of the 24-bit counter decreases, in percentage terms, for both FPGAs, as a function of the number of dedicated carry lines that are broken. Notice that despite belonging to different FPGA generations, the counter exhibited a similar behavior in both cases. From this simple example it becomes obvious that it is mandatory for any defragmentation procedure to take into account both architectural and functional aspects, before making any function relocation decisions.

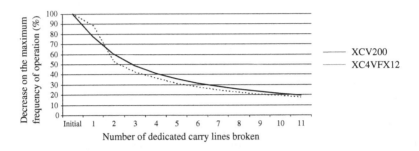

Fig. 1. Performance degradation

If this function is active, i. e. if the function is currently being used by an application, dynamic relocation techniques, as those described in [2], must be applied during the defragmentation procedure, otherwise the function operation will be temporarily halted, which may consequently disrupt the operation of the whole system. Moreover, relocation must be performed keeping as much as possible the vertical orientation of the function placement. Besides, no more than one of the dedicated carry lines linking vertically adjacent CLBs should be broken. This means that only one adjacent CLB may be relocated at a time and that vertical adjacency must not be lost.

These two pieces of information, verticality and adjacency, are essential to enable an efficient defragmentation and should be attached as a label to the function configuration file.

To evaluate the influence of changes in shape and in relative position of CLBs in different functions, the same type of experiments were performed over a subset of the ITC'99 benchmark circuits [7]. The objective was to determine which parameters are involved in the performance degradation of particular functions so as to be able to formulate a simple set of rules to support logic space management. The experiments consisted of displacing vertically and horizontally each one of the functions and changing its relative shape, from a square-like shape to a rectangular one and rotating it 90°. These stressing conditions helped to bring into evidence which parameters are mostly responsible for performance degradation, when functions are moved around. The results of the experiments are summarised in table 1. It is evident that circuits B04, B05, B07, B11, B13 and B14 experienced considerable performance degradation when the relocation of the whole function was carried out horizontally, since all these functions use dedicated carry lines on their implementation. This conclusion confirmed the extremely high importance of keeping intact dedicated carry lines.

Some functions, like B11, comprise hundreds of gates but have a reduced number of carry lines. In this case, it is necessary to have a simple method to quickly

Table 1. Evaluation of function performance degradation due to reshaping

Circuit reference	Number of occupied CLBs	Variation in the maximum frequency of operation (%)	
		Vertical relocation	Horizontal relocation
B01	6	−5.5	0.0
B02	1	0.0	0.0
B03	11	−1.9	−4.9
B04	54	−6.1	−29.3
B05	103	−17.3	−36.9
B06	5	−2.7	0.0
B07	31	−23.6	−37.8
B08	17	−5.8	−5.8
B09	12	−1.8	−4.9
B10	20	−7.5	−7.6
B11	39	−10.5	−36.0
B12	119	0.0	−1.2
B13	37	−4.3	−42.8
B14	333	−13.5	−47.8

identify the columns that contain these lines. Otherwise, the ability to reshape the function during defragmentation will be heavily constrained. The label attached to the function configuration file must indicate the relative position inside the function of the column that must be left as it is.

3 Proximity Vectors

The first circuit on the list, B01, exhibits a different behaviour when compared to those previously observed. Horizontal relocations do not degrade its performance, most probably because it uses no carry lines. However, vertical relocations decrease its maximum frequency of operation.

The most noticeable aspect of its implementation was the great number of high fanout signals that leave the CLBs located in the central column. To reduce propagation delays these CLBs were strategically positioned by the design tools in the centre of the function floorplan. If the circuit is shifted horizontally, the relative position of the central CLBs is not affected. However, if the central location of these two CLBs is changed, propagation delays will increase and the maximum frequency of operation of this function will decrease. This hypothesis was confirmed by rotating the function 90° and relocating it in only one CLB column.

The CLBs with output signals that drive a large number of inputs, despite keeping their central location, are now, on average, far from their destination inputs than they were before. This means an increase on the propagation delay not only due to an increase in the length of interconnection lines, whose impact is minor, but mainly because each line has to cross a greater number of

Programmable Interconnect Points (PIPs). The small distance that signals have to cross means that small segments linking adjacent routing arrays are used to route them. Therefore, if a new segment has to be added, a new PIP has also to be used, which leads to a noticeable increase in the propagation delay. The other benchmark circuits exhibited a similar behaviour.

A systematic analysis of this problem led to the development of a new method to assess the impact of relocating CLBs whose output signals drive a large number of inputs: the application of the concept of *proximity vectors*, a vector associated to each interconnection and linking the CLB source to the CLB destination.

The length of each vector, called *proximity factor*, is expressed in CLB units and calculated as the modulus of the distance between the CLB source and the CLB destination:

$$|f_{px}| = \sqrt{r^2 + c^2} \qquad (1)$$

where:

r=CLB destination row - CLB source row
r=CLB destination column - CLB source column

If the sum of all proximity vectors of one CLB output is minimised (eq. 2), the proximity factor associated to that output will also be minimised. This corresponds, in terms of the propagation delay of a given output, to the best position of that CLB inside the function.

$$|f_{pox}| = \min_{d} \quad (f_{p1}, f_{p2}, ..., f_{pd}) \qquad (2)$$

When relocating the CLB, if the proximity factor F_{pox} increases, then performance degradation of the function will occur. Generically, we can say that minimising each output proximity factor of a function results in the minimisation of its global proximity factor, which corresponds to the best performance (maximum frequency of operation). The application of this concept to the remaining circuits showed a consistent reproduction of results, confirming the initial hypothesis.

The concept of proximity vectors is based on the application of the Euclidian distance measurement to each net. Since routing is constrained to horizontal and vertical wires, it seems, at first, that the use of the Manhattan distance measurement would be more reasonable. However, a series of experiments performed to compare the use of the two distance measurement methodologies showed a greater correlation between maximum frequency of operation and the Euclidian distance measurement.

The main advantages of this approach are as follows:

1. It can be easily automated and integrated in existing design tools;
2. The computation time of the proximity vectors is extremely low when compared to previous proposed approaches, since only the nets that will be affected by relocation need to have their proximity factor (before and after the relocation) calculated;

3. There is no need to perform a complete analysis of the function performance after each CLB relocation, since, if the minimisation of the global proximity factor of the CLB was assured, the minimisation of the global proximity factor of the overall function is assured, and therefore, no performance degradation occurs.

All these factors enable this method to be used at run time to quickly and reliably assess the strategy used to manage the defragmentation procedure.

4   Conclusions

This paper presents a new approach to assess the performance degradation introduced by the relocation of functions during defragmentation procedures applied to dynamically reconfigurable FPGAs. The proposed approach is able to guide the defragmentation procedure in a reliable and fast way enabling the run-time relocation of running functions, timely releasing enough contiguous space for new incoming ones while avoiding performance degradation.

Current work is aimed at evaluating the influence of other array heterogeneities (that are present in more recent generations of FPGAs), namely memory blocks and dedicated DSP blocks. The influence of hardware embedded processors and the rule they may play in the implementation of defragmentation strategies on run time reconfigurable systems will also be addressed in the future.

References

[1] Ling, X.-P., Amano, H.: WASMII: a Data Driven Computer on a Virtual Hardware, Proc. 1st IEEE Workshop on FPGAs for Custom Computing Machines (1993), 33–42

[2] Gericota, M. G., Alves, G. R., Silva, M. L., Ferreira, J. M.: Run-Time Defragmentation for Dynamically Reconfigurable Hardware, in: New Algorithms, Architectures and Applications for Reconfigurable Computing. Springer (2005) 117–129

[3] Teich, J., Fekete, S., Schepers, J.: Compile-time optimization of dynamic hardware reconfigurations, Proc. Intl. Conf. on Parallel and Distributed Processing Techniques and Applications (1999) 1097–1103

[4] Handa, M., Vemuri, R.: An efficient algorithm for finding empty space for online FPGA placement, Proc. Design, Automation Conf. (2004) 960–965

[5] Vinh, P. C., Bowen, J. P.: Continuity Aspects of Embedded Reconfigurable Computing, Innovations in Systems and Software Engineering: A NASA Journal, Springer-Verlag, Vol. 1, No. 1, (2005) 41–53

[6] Ejnioui, A., DeMara, R. F.: Area Reclamation Strategies and Metrics for SRAM-Based Reconfigurable Devices, Proc. Intl. Conf. on Engineering of Reconfigurable Systems and Algorithms (2005)

[7] Politcnico di Torino ITC'99 benchmarks. Available at: http://www.cad.polito.it/tools/itc99.html

A 1,632 Gate-Count Zero-Overhead Dynamic Optically Reconfigurable Gate Array VLSI

Minoru Watanabe and Fuminori Kobayashi

Department of Systems Innovation and Informatics,
Kyushu Institute of Technology
680-4 Kawazu, Iizuka, Fukuoka, 820-8502, Japan
Tel.: +81-948-29-7749; Fax: +81-948-29-7749
{watanabe, koba}@ces.kyutech.ac.jp

Abstract. A Zero-Overhead Dynamic Optically Reconfigurable Gate Array (ZO-DORGA), based on a concept using junction capacitance of photodiodes and load capacitance of gates constructing a gate array as configuration memory, has been proposed to realize a single instruction set computer that requires zero-overhead fast reconfiguration. To date, although the concept and architecture have been proposed and some simulation results of designs have been presented, a ZO-ORGA VLSI chip has never been fabricated. In this paper, the first 1,632 gate-count zero-overhead VLSI chip fabricated using 0.35 um CMOS process technology is presented. The 1,632 ZO-DORGA-VLSI is not only the first prototype VLSI chip; it is also the largest gate-count ORGA. Such a large gate count ORGA had never been fabricated until this study. The performance of ZO-DORGA-VLSI is clarified and discussed using experimental results.

1 Introduction

In recent years, high-speed reconfigurable processors have been developed: DAP/ DNA chips [1][2][3] and DRP chips [4][5]. However, the reconfiguration contexts of currently available multi-context devices, for example, those of DAP/DNA and DRP chips, are limited quantitatively to 4-16 as a result of die-size limitations that depend on cost. Therefore, rapid reconfiguration capability is achievable, but achievement of continuous reconfiguration is difficult. On the other hand, a field programmable gate array (FPGA) [6,7] architecture in which context memory and gate arrays are situated separately onto different chips renders it difficult to realize rapid reconfiguration. Therefore, conventional electrical techniques are insufficient to realize a high-speed reconfigurable device with many reconfiguration contexts.

In recent years, optically programmable gate arrays (OPGAs) [8][9][10] have been proposed, in which an optical holographic memory is introduced and connected directly to the gate array part of a VLSI circuit. These devices can provide rapid reconfiguration and numerous reconfiguration contexts. Currently, OPGAs have achieved over a hundred reconfiguration contexts and a 16–20 us reconfiguration period. However, the OPGAs have a problem: the gate density of the VLSI part is very low. As one example, a previously fabricated OPGA-VLSI had only 80 gates because an optical receiver array and memory array, which are necessary to temporarily store one context

K. Bertels, J.M.P. Cardoso, and S. Vassiliadis (Eds.): ARC 2006, LNCS 3985, pp. 268–273, 2006.
© Springer-Verlag Berlin Heidelberg 2006

of a gate array, occupy two-thirds of the implementation area of the gate array VLSI.V Furthermore, a second problem exists: the 16–20 us reconfiguration speed cannot support clock-by-clock reconfiguration. Moreover, the reconfiguration period can engender large overhead in any dynamically reconfigurable applications because the gate array cannot function during reconfiguration in the OPGAs.

For those reasons, a Zero-Overhead Dynamic Optically Reconfigurable Gate Array (ZO-DORGA) has been proposed, which has removed static memory function to temporarily store one context of a gate array and has decreased the reconfiguration overhead by using load capacitance of gates constructing a gate array as configuration memory. The ZO-DORGA presents two advantages: the ZO-DORGA can achieve a large gate count and the reconfiguration speed can reach nanoseconds without any overhead.

In this paper, the first 1,632 gate-count zero-overhead VLSI chip fabricated using 0.35 um CMOS process technology is presented. The 1,632 ZO-DORGA-VLSI is not only the first prototype VLSI chip. It is also the largest gate-count ORGA. Such a large gate count ORGA was fabricated for the first time in this study. The performance of ZO-DORGA-VLSI is clarified and discussed using experimental results.

2   Zero-Overhead Dynamic Optical Reconfiguration Circuit

A conventional ORGA necessitates the same architecture as FPGAs and has many programming elements, similar to FPGAs. Therefore, reducing the size of each optical reconfiguration circuit corresponding to the configuration memory of FPGAs is very important. A single-bit optical reconfiguration circuit in conventional ORGAs comprises: a photodiode; a static memory function such as a latch, a flip-flop or a bit of memory; and some transistors. However, the static memory function requires a large implementation area, which strictly prohibits the realization of high gate-count ORGAs. To date, the gate counts of fabricated ORGAs with static memory functions have remained limited to 68-476 gates.

Furthermore, the VLSI component of previously proposed OPGAs has remained incapable of keeping pace with clock-by-clock high-frequency reconfiguration. The 16-20 us slow reconfiguration capability of OPGAs is attributable to its architecture, which uses serial transfer between optical receiver arrays and gate arrays. For example, in a five-input look-up table (LUT) of an OPGA, a serial transfer between a 32 bit-optical receiver array with a 32-bit latch and a five-input LUT with a 32-bit SRAM requires 16-20 μs. However, for clock-by-clock reconfiguration of a gate array, the 16–20 μs reconfiguration period is too long and the reconfiguration operation consumes 99% of the entire operation time when implementation circuits with a 10 ns operation period are reconfigured at every clock cycle. Therefore, because the optical reconfiguration procedure of the VLSI part can occupy large overhead for the circuit execution, improvement is also important.

Therefore, to improve those two issues, a ZO-DORGA has been developed. The optical reconfiguration circuits of a ZO-DORGA are based on a concept using junction capacitance of photodiodes and load capacitance for constructing a gate array as configuration memory. The state of the gate array is maintained using load capacitance of the

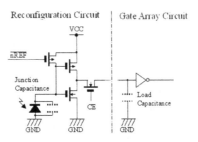

Fig. 1. A schematic diagram of a zero-overhead dynamic optical reconfiguration circuit

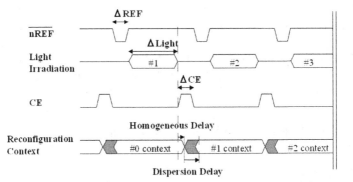

Fig. 2. Timing diagram of the zero-overhead dynamic optical reconfiguration circuit

gates that comprise the gate array during reconfiguration. Therefore, the zero-overhead dynamic optical reconfiguration circuit allows parallel execution of the reconfiguration operation and circuit operation implemented on the gate array.

The zero-overhead dynamic optical reconfiguration circuit consists of a refresh transistor, an inverter, a photodiode, and a pass transistor, as shown in Fig. 1. This zero-overhead dynamic optical reconfiguration circuit uses a pass transistor to exploit the load of gates comprising the gate array as a memory function. Each load of inverter gates, transmission gates, and so on composing the gate array is sufficient to maintain the gate array state during the gate-array reconfiguration. The additional pass transistor realizes a function to block off the connection between the gate array and dynamic optical reconfiguration circuit during reconfiguration. Because they are blocked, the load of gates that compose the gate array can retain their states during the next reconfiguration.

Figure 2 shows a timing diagram. One reconfiguration procedure is initiated by activating a refresh signal (nREF) with a certain pulse width ΔREF to charge the junction capacitance of photodiodes. Then, the context light is illuminated using an optical memory with a laser light that has a certain pulse width $\Delta Light$. Finally, the gate-array state can be changed by activation of the Configuration Enable signal (CE) with a certain pulse width ΔCE. Therefore, the reconfiguration period $\Delta RPeriod$ of ZO-DORGA can be calculated through summation of ΔREF, $\Delta Light$, and ΔCE as

$$\Delta RPeriod = \Delta REF + \Delta LIGHT + \Delta CE. \tag{1}$$

3   VLSI Design

A new 1,632-gate-count DORGA-VLSI chip was designed and fabricated using a 0.35 μm standard CMOS process technology. Voltages of core and I/O cells were designed identically using 3.3 V. The acceptance surface size of the photodiode and photodiode-cell size, including an optical reconfiguration circuit, are, respectively, 9.5 μm × 8.8 μm and 25.5 μm × 16.5 μm. The photodiodes were constructed between N+ diffusion and the P-substrate. Photodiode cells are arranged at 34.5 μm horizontal intervals and at 33.0 μm vertical intervals. This design incorporates 6,213 photodiodes. The average aperture ratio of the overall VLSI is 4.24%. In this design, considering the resolution of optical components and simplified justification of the positioning between a VLSI part and an optical part, photodiodes and their spacing were designed to be large. The top metal layer was used for guarding transistors from light irradiation; the other two layers were used for wiring.

The gate array of the DORGA-VLSI uses an island style. In all, 48 optically reconfigurable logic blocks (ORLBs) including two 4 input - 1 output LUTs, 63 optically reconfigurable switching matrices (ORSMs), and 24 optically reconfigurable I/O bits (ORIOBs) were implemented in the gate array. The ORLBs, ORSMs, and ORIOBs are programmable block-by-block respectively through 59, 49, 49 optical connections.

4   Experimental Results and Discussion

This section presents some experimental results using a fabricated ZO-DORGA-VLSI chip. The merits and demerits of the ZO-DORGA architecture are discussed using experimental results. Figure 3 shows a photograph of a fabricated ZO-DORGA-VLSI chip. The optical experimental system with a liquid crystal television panel and a 633 nm, 20 mW He-Ne laser was constructed to measure the optical reconfiguration performance of the ZO-DORGA-VLSI chip. Firstly, the reconfiguration speed of the

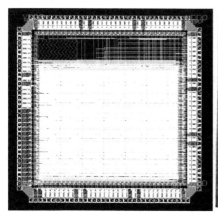

Fig. 3. CAD layout and chip photograph of a fabricated DORGA chip using 0.35 μm standard CMOS process

ZO-DORGA-VLSI chip was measured using the experimental system. Experimental results showed that the photodiode response time is less than 10.0 ns. In this experimental board, because all timing signals are generated using a 48 MHz clock, the pulse-wide of a refresh signal to charge the junction capacitance of photodiodes and CE pulse-wide are all equal: 20.8 ns. Therefore, 62.4 ns optical reconfiguration was confirmed experimentally. However, we have also confirmed that the minimum pulse width extracted from HSPICE simulation results is less than 1 ns. Therefore, if a DORGA-VLSI chip has a short pulse generator in the own chip, the reconfiguration cycle is estimated as less than 12 ns. In addition, the retention time of the load capacitance of gate array in ZO-DORGA has been measured as longer than 100 us.

In the case of previously proposed DORGA-VLSI, because the reconfiguration contexts are stored only in junction capacitances, the retention time depends on the contrast and background light noise of a holographic memory and lasers. Therefore, partial reconfiguration is extremely difficult because the diffraction light of the other partial reconfiguration reduces the electrical charge of the junction capacitance, which must be retained. However, this ZO-DORGA architecture allows partial reconfiguration because the reconfiguration light never affects the gate-array load capacitances. Fast reconfiguration, partial reconfiguration, and numerous reconfiguration context capabilities are the salient advantages of ZO-DORGA-VLSI.

5   Conclusion

In this paper, the first prototype chip of ZO-DORGA-VLSI was presented. The ZO-DORGA architecture described herein was capable of achieving a high gate-count and rapid reconfiguration without any overhead. Now, the 1,632 gate count is the largest gate count ORGA. The ZO-DORGA performance was measured using the fabricated chip and an experimental optical system. Its 62.4 ns optical reconfiguration performance was confirmed experimentally. Furthermore, this paper showed that the reconfiguration cycle can be reduced to less than 12 ns using a short pulse generator inside the chip. In addition, the retention time for partial reconfiguration was confirmed 100 us. We conclude that ZO-DORGA architecture with a holographic memory enables clock-by-clock reconfiguration without overhead, overall reconfiguration, and partial reconfiguration. The ZO-DORGA architecture is suitable for the next generation of clock-by-clock reconfigurable single instruction set computers.

Finally, using 14.2 mm by 14.2 mm 0.35 um CMOS process chip and the ORLB, ORSM and ORIOB designs, we have confirmed that a 29,172 gate count VLSI can be achieved. The virtual gate count will reach 29,172,000 if a holographic memory can store a thousand reconfiguration contexts. That huge virtual gate count emphasizes the great advantages of the ORGA architecture.

Acknowledgment

This research was partially supported by the project of development of high-density optically and partially reconfigurable gate arrays under Japan Science and Technology

Agency. Also, this research was partially supported by the Ministry of Education, Science, Sports and Culture, Grant-in-Aid for Young Scientists (B), 16760275, 2004. The VLSI chip in this study was fabricated in the chip fabrication program of VLSI Design and Education Center (VDEC), the University of Tokyo in collaboration with Rohm Co. Ltd. and Toppan Printing Co. Ltd.

References

1. http://www.ipflex.co.jp
2. Yu Yunquing, K. Murakami, "Reconfigurable neural network using DAP/DNA," International Conference on High Performance Computing and Grid in Asia Pacific Region, pp. 432–433, 2004.
3. M. Yoshida, T. Soga, N. Yoshimatsu, K. Murakami, "SysteMorph prototyping on DAP/DNA," IEEE Asia-Pacific Conference on Advanced System Integrated Circuits, pp. 420 – 423, 2004.
4. H. Nakano, T. Shindo, T. Kazami, M. Motomura, "Development of dynamically reconfigurable processor LSI," NEC Tech. J. (Japan), vol. 56, no. 4, pp. 99–102, 2003.
5. M. Suzuki, Y. Hasegawa, Y. Yamada, N. Kaneko, K. Deguchi, H. Amano, K. Anjo, M. Motomura, K. Wakabayashi, T. Toi, T. Awashima, "Stream applications on the dynamically reconfigurable processor," IEEE International Conference on Field-Programmable Technology, pp. 137 – 144, 2004.
6. Altera Corporation, "Altera Devices," http:/www.altera.com/products/devices/dev–index.html
7. Xilinx Inc., "Xilinx Product Data Sheets," http://www.xilinx.com/ partinfo/databook.html
8. J. Mumbru, G. Panotopoulos, D. Psaltis, X. An, F. Mok, S. Ay, S. Barna, E. Fossum, "Optically Programmable Gate Array," SPIE of Optics in Computing 2000, Vol. 4089, pp. 763–771, 2000.
9. J. Mumbru, G. Zhou, X. An, W. Liu, G. Panotopoulos, F. Mok, and D. Psaltis, "Optical memory for computing and information processing," SPIE on Algorithms, Devices, and Systems for Optical Information Processing III, Vol. 3804, pp. 14–24, 1999.
10. J. Mumbru, G. Zhou, S. Ay, X. An, G. Panotopoulos, F. Mok, and D. Psaltis, "Optically Reconfigurable Processors," SPIE Critical Review 1999 Euro-American Workshop on Optoelectronic Information Processing, Vol. 74, pp. 265-288, 1999.

PISC: Polymorphic Instruction Set Computers

Stamatis Vassiliadis, Georgi Kuzmanov, Stephan Wong,
Elena Moscu-Panainte, Georgi Gaydadjiev, Koen Bertels, and Dmitry Cheresiz

Computer Engineering, EEMCS,
Delft University of Technology,
Mekelweg 4, 2628 CD Delft, The Netherlands
S.Vassiliadis@ewi.tudelft.nl
http://ce.et.tudelft.nl/

Abstract. We introduce a new paradigm in the computer architecture referred to as Polymorphic Instruction Set Computers (PISC). This new paradigm, in difference to RISC/CISC, introduces hardware extended functionality on demand without the need of ISA extensions. We motivate the necessity of PISCs through an example, which arises several research problems unsolvable by traditional architectures and fixed hardware designs. More specifically, we address a new framework for tools, supporting reconfigurability; new architectural and microarchitectural concepts; new programming paradigm allowing hardware and software to coexist in a program; and new spacial compilation techniques. The paper illustrates the theoretical performance boundaries and efficiency of the proposed paradigm utilizing established evaluation metrics such as potential zero execution (PZE) and the Amdahl's law. Overall, the PISC paradigm allows designers to ride the Amdahl's curve easily by considering the specific features of the reconfigurable technology and the general purpose processors in the context of application specific execution scenarios.

1 Introduction

Overall performance measurements in terms of Millions Instructions Per Cycle (MIPS) or cycles per instruction (CPI) depend greatly on the CPU implementation. Potential performance improvements due to the parallel/concurrent execution of instructions, independent of technology or implementations, can be measured by the number of instructions which may be executed in zero time, denoted by PZE (potential zero-cycle execution) [1]. The rationale behind this measurement, as described in [1] for compound instruction sets is:

"If one instruction in a compound instruction pair executes in n cycles and the other instruction executes in $m \leq n$ cycles, the instruction taking m cycles to execute appears to execute in zero time. Because factors such as cache size and branch prediction accuracy vary from one implementation to the next, PZE measures the potential, not the actual, rate of zero-cycle execution. Additionally, note that zero-cycle instruction execution does not translate directly to cycles per instruction (CPI) because all instructions do not require the same number

K. Bertels, J.M.P. Cardoso, and S. Vassiliadis (Eds.): ARC 2006, LNCS 3985, pp. 274–286, 2006.

of cycles for their execution. The PZE measure simply indicates the number of instructions that potentially have been removed from the instruction stream during the execution of a program."

Consequently, PZE is a measurement that indicates maximum speedup attainable when parallelism/concurrency mechanisms are applied. The main advantage of PZE is that given a base machine design the benefits of proposed mechanisms can be measured and compared. We can thus evaluate the efficiency of a real design expressed as a percentage of the potentially maximum attainable speedup indicated by PZE. An example is illustrated in Figure 1. Four instructions, executing in a pipelined machine are considered. The instructions from the example are parallelized applying different techniques, such as instruction level parallelism (ILP), pipelining, technological advances, etc., as depicted in Figure 1. Timewise, the result is that the execution of 4 instructions is equivalent to the execution of 2 instructions, which corresponds to a seeming code reduction by 50%, i.e., *2 out of 4 instructions potentially have been removed from the instruction stream during the program execution*. It means that the maximum theoretically attainable speedup (i.e., again potentially) in such a scenario is a factor of 2. In the particular example from Figure 1, the execution cycles count for 4 instructions is reduced from 8 to 6 cycles, allowing 1.33 times speedup, which compared to the maximum speedup of 2, suggests efficiency of 65%. The above example suggests that PZE allows to measure the efficiency of a real machine implementation by comparing to a theoretical base machine, i.e., PZE gives an indication of how close a practical implementation performs to the theoretically attainable best performance boundaries. These theoretical boundaries are described by Amdahl's law [2].

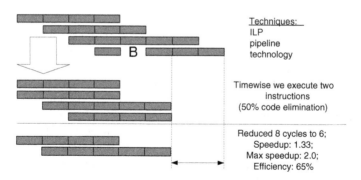

Fig. 1. PZE example

Amdahl's law and the new polymorphic paradigm. The maximum theoretically attainable (i.e., the potentially maximum) speedup, considered for the PZE, with respect to the parallelizable portion of the program code, is determined by Amdahl's law. Amdahl's curve, graphically illustrated in Figure 2, suggests that if, say half of an application program is parallelized and that its entire parallel fraction is assumingly executed in zero time, the speedup would potentially be 2.

Moreover, the Amdahl's curve suggests that to achieve an order of magnitude speedup, a designer should parallelize over 90% of the application execution. In such cases, when over 90% of the application workload is considered for parallelization, it is practical to create an ASIC, rather than utilizing programmable GPP. The design cycle of an ASIC, however, is extremely inflexible and very expensive. Therefore, ASICs may not appear to be an efficient solution when we consider smaller portions (i.e., less than 90%) of an algorithm for hardware acceleration. Obviously, there exist potentials for new hardware proposals that perform better than GPPs and are more flexible alternative to design and operate than ASICs.

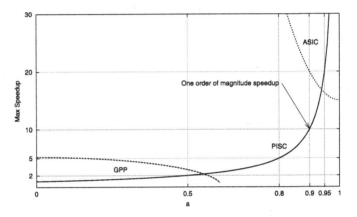

Fig. 2. The Amdahl's curve and PISC

In this paper, we introduce a new architectural paradigm targeting the existing gap between GPPs and ASICs in terms of flexibility and performance. This new paradigm exploits specific features of the reconfigurable hardware technologies. In consistence with the classical RISC and CISC paradigms [3,4], we refer to the new architectural paradigm as to a Polymorphic Instruction Set Computer (PISC). The practically significant scope of PISC covers between 50% and 90% application parallelization illustrated with the Amdahl's curve in Figure 2. This interval provides a designer with potentials to benefit from the best of two worlds, i.e., with a synergism between purely programmable solutions on GPPs and reconfigurable hardware. That is, the infinite flexibility of the programmable GPPs combined with reconfigurable accelerators results into a PISC - a programmable system that substantially outperforms GPP. Therefore, we believe that the gap between GPP and ASIC, illustrated in Figure 2, belongs to PISC. More specifically, we address the following research areas related to the PISC paradigm:

New HW/SW co-design tools
Processor architecture and microarchitecture
Programming paradigm
– Compilation for the new programming paradigm

The remainder of this paper is organized as follows. In Section 2, we present a motivating example and derive key research questions. Section 3 describes the general approach to solve these research questions. The polymorphic architectural extension is presented in Section 4. Section 5 introduces some compiler considerations targeting the new architectural paradigm. Finally, the paper is concluded in Section 6.

2 Motivating Example and Research Questions

To illustrate the necessity of the PISC computing paradigm, we present a motivating example based on the Portable Network Graphics (PNG) standard [5]. PNG is a popular standard for image compression and decompression, it is a native standard for the graphics implemented in *Microsoft Office* as well as in a number of other applications. We consider the piece of C-code presented in Figure 3, which is extracted from an implementation of the PNG standard. This code fragment implements an important stage of the PNG coding process. It computes the Paeth prediction for each pixel d of the current row, starting from the second pixel. The Paeth prediction scheme, illustrated in Figure 4, selects from the 3 neighboring pixels a, b, and c, that surround d, the pixel that differs the least from the value $p = a + b - c$ (which is called the initial prediction). The selected pixel is called the *Paeth prediction* for d. If the pixel rows contained *length + 1* elements, *length* prediction values are produced. This prediction

```
void Paeth_predict_row(char *prev_row, char *curr_row, char *predict_row, int length)
{char *bptr, *dptr, *predptr;
char a, b, c, d;
short p, pa, pb, pc;

bptr = prev_row+1;
dptr = curr_row+1;
predptr= predict_row+1;

for(i=1; i<length; i++)
{c = *(bptr-1); b = *bptr;
a = *(dptr-1); d = *dptr;
p = a + b - c; /* this is the initial prediction */
pa = abs( p - a ); /* distance of each member */
pb = abs( p - b ); /* to the */
pc = abs( p - c ); /* initial estimate */
if ((pa≤pb)&&(pa≤pc)) *predptr = a;
else if (pb≤pc) *predptr = b;
else *predptr = c;

bptr++; dptr++; predptr++; } }
```

Fig. 3. The Paeth prediction routine according to PNG specification [5]

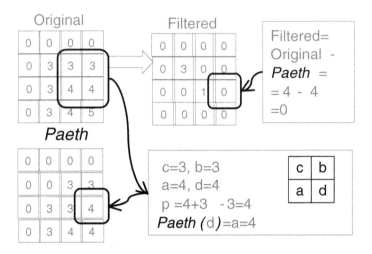

Fig. 4. The Paeth prediction scheme

scheme is used during the image filtering stage of the image coding and decoding. Figure 5 presents an implementation of the code fragment in pseudocode derived from the AltiVec assembly. In this figure, the general-purpose register GPRi of the underlying ISA is denoted by `ri`, `vri` denotes the i-th vector register of AltiVec.

Analysis of the motivating example presented above suggests the following. If the Paeth predictor must be computed for a row of 1024 pixels, the complete AltiVec code presented in Figure 5 will result in a dynamic instruction count of $8(prologue) + 64 \cdot [3(load) + 6(unpack) + 76(compute) + 1(pack) + 1(store) + 2(miscellaneous) + 3(pointerupdate) + 3(loopcontrol)] = 8 + 6464 \cdot 95 = 6088$ *instructions*. This high instruction count, which limits the performance, is caused by the following features of the short-vector media extensions. First, if the main operation to be performed is relatively complex, it requires multiple instructions. Second, the overhead tasks associated with stream sectioning, loading, storing, packing, unpacking, and data rearrangement require separate instructions.

Considering Figure 5, we can substitute all loop iterations in the Paeth code with a single instruction and add only a few instructions to interface with the remainder of the program code. In such a case, we can expect considerable decrease of the instructions count and execution time improvements. The Paeth loop is transformed now in a single instruction [6] that takes 5 cycles to complete[1] and requires 20 setup instructions. The improvement attained is nearly two orders of magnitude reduction of the instructions count and two orders of magnitude reduction of the execution time. Obviously, the scale of these improvements depends on the implementability of the Paeth coding into hardware as a single instruction. An efficient Paeth hardware implementation comprises 24 32-bit adders allowing a throughput of 16 pixels/cycle (i.e., 6 8-bit adders per pixel).

---

[1] One cycle is the duration of a single ALU operation.

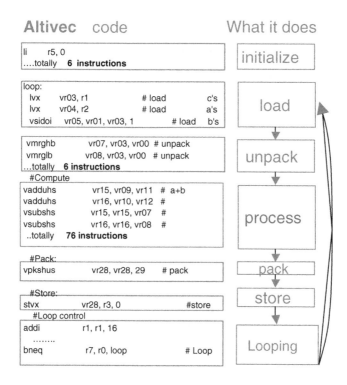

Fig. 5. AltiVec code for the *Paeth predict* kernel

Research Questions. The Paeth encoding is just one computationally demanding kernel identified in a particular program. To implement an entire application efficiently, however, it is very likely that a number of such kernels should be identified within a single program execution context and each of them should be implemented in hardware. Therefore, traditional approaches, which introduce a new instruction for each portion of the application considered for hardware implementation, are restricted by the unused opcode space of the core processor architecture. Moreover, due to the large number of candidate kernels for hardware implementation, it may appear that their fixed hardware realization is impossible within limited silicon resources. The latter problem can be overcome, if the hardware can change its functionality at the designer's wish, i.e., using reconfigurable hardware. For many traditional reconfigurable approaches, however, the above problems become even more dramatic if an arbitrary number of new operations should be considered for hardware implementation [7,8]. In such scenarios,the traditional design methods can not be employed. The above observations arise the following research questions:

1. How to identify the code for hardware implementation?
2. How to implement "arbitrary" code?
3. How to avoid adding new instructions per kernel?

4. How to substitute the hardwired code with SW/HW descriptions say at source level?
5. How to generate the "transformed" program automatically?

With respect to the above questions, in this paper we address the following research topics:

1. New kind of tools.
2. Microarchitecture design.
3. Processor architecture (behavior and logical structure).
4. New programming paradigm allowing HW and SW to coexist in a program.
5. New compilation techniques.

3   General Approach

To solve the research questions stated in the previous section, we propose a synergism between a general-purpose processor (GPP) and a reconfigurable processor (RP) referred to as the Molen $\rho\mu$-coded processor. In the discussion to follow, we present the general concept of transforming an existing program to one that can be executed on the reconfigurable computing platform we propose and hints to the new mechanisms, intended to improve existing approaches.

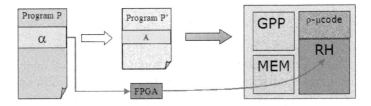

Fig. 6. Program transformation example

The conceptual view of how program P (intended to execute only on the general-purpose processor (GPP) core) is transformed into program P' (executing on both the GPP core and the reconfigurable hardware) is depicted in Figure 6. The purpose is to obtain a functionally equivalent program P' from program P which (using specialized instructions) can initiate both the configuration and execution processes on the reconfigurable hardware. The steps involved in this transformation are the following:

1. identify code "α" in program P to be mapped in reconfigurable hardware.
2. show that "α" can be implemented in hardware in an existing technology, e.g., FPGA, and map "α" onto reconfigurable hardware (RH).
3. eliminate the identified code "α" and add "equivalent" code (A) assuming that A "calls" the hardware with functionality "α". The code A comprises the following:

Repair code inserted to communicate parameters and results to/from the reconfigurable hardware from/to the general-purpose processor core. "HDL"-like hardware code and emulation code inserted to configure the reconfigurable hardware and to perform the functionality that is initialized by the "execute code".

4. compile and execute program P' with original code plus code having functionality A (equivalent to functionality "α") on the GPP/reconfigurable processor.

The mentioned steps illustrate the need for a new programming paradigm in which both software and hardware descriptions are present in the same program. It should also be noted that the only constraint on "α" is implementability, which possibly implies complex hardware. Consequently, the microarchitecture may have to support emulation [9] via microcode. We have termed this reconfigurable microcode ($\rho\mu$-code) as it is different from the traditional microcode. The difference is that such microcode does not execute on fixed hardware facilities. It operates on facilities that the $\rho\mu$-code itself "designs" to operate upon. We refer to such facilities as to configurable computing units (CCU). A processor supporting $\rho\mu$-code is referred to as a $\rho\mu$-coded processor and we also call it a Molen processor. More details on the Molen machine organization are presented in [11,12].

The methodology of the transformation described previously for the reconfigurable computing platform is depicted in Figure 7. First, the code to be executed on the reconfigurable hardware must be determined. This is achieved by high-level to high-level instrumentation and benchmarking. This results in several

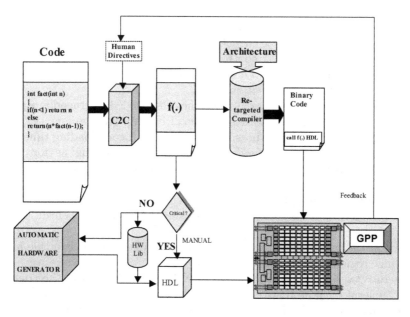

Fig. 7. Program transformation methodology for reconfigurable computing

candidate pieces of code. Second, we must determine which piece of code is suitable for implementation on the reconfigurable hardware. The suitability is solely determined by whether the piece of code is implementable (i.e., "fits in hardware"). Those parts can then be mapped into hardware via a hardware description language (HDL). In case the HDL corresponds to "critical" hardware in terms of, for instance, area, performance, memory and power consumption, the translation will be done manually. Otherwise, the translation can be done automatically or extracted from a library [13].

4   The Polymorphic ISA

In order to target the $\rho\mu$-code processor, we propose a sequential consistency programming paradigm [10]. The paradigm allows for parallel and concurrent hardware execution and requires only a one-time architectural extension of few instructions to provide a large user reconfigurable operation space. The complete list of the eight required instructions, denoted as polymorphic ($\pi o\lambda v\mu o\rho\phi\iota\kappa\acuteo$) Instruction Set Architecture (πISA), is as follows:

Six instructions are required for controlling the reconfigurable hardware, namely:

- Two **set** instructions: these instructions initiate the configurations of the CCU. Two instructions are added for partial reconfiguration:
  * the partial set (p **set** <*address*>) instruction performs those configurations that cover common parts of multiple functions and/or frequently used functions.
  * the complete set (c **set** <*address*>) instruction performs the configurations of the remaining blocks of the CCU (not covered by the p **set**) to *complete* the CCU functionality.
- **execute** <*address*>: controls the execution of the operations implemented on the CCU. These implementations are configured onto the CCU by the **set** instructions.
- **set prefetch** <*address*>: prefetches the needed microcode responsible for CCU reconfigurations into a local on-chip storage facility (the $\rho\mu$ code unit) in order to possibly diminish microcode loading times.
- **execute prefetch** <*address*>: the same reasoning as for the **set prefetch** instruction holds, but now relating to microcode responsible for CCU executions.
- **break**: facilitates the parallel execution of both the reconfigurable processor and the core processor. It is utilized as a synchronization mechanism to complete the parallel execution.

Two *move* instructions for passing values between the register file and exchange registers (XREGs):

- **movtx** XREG$_a$ ← R$_b$: (move to XREG) used to move the content of general-purpose register R$_b$ to XREG$_a$.
- **movfx** R$_a$ ← XREG$_b$: (move from XREG) used to move the content of exchange register XREG$_b$ to general-purpose register R$_a$.

The <*address*> field in the instructions introduced above denotes the location of the reconfigurable microcode responsible for the configuration and execution processes. The parameters are passed via the exchange registers (XREGs). In order to maintain correct program semantics, the code is annotated. It is not imperative to include all instructions when implementing the Molen organization. The programmer/implementor can opt for different ISA extensions depending on the performance that needs to be achieved and the available technology. There are basically three distinctive πISA possibilities with respect to the Molen instructions introduced earlier - the *minimal*, the *preferred* and the *complete* πISA extension:

- **The minimal πISA:** This is essentially the smallest set of Molen instructions needed to provide a working scenario. The four basic instructions needed are **set** (more specifically: c **set**), **execute**, **movtx** and **movfx**.
- **The preferred πISA:** In order to address reconfiguration latencies both p **set** and c **set** instructions are utilized. The two **prefetch** instructions (**set prefetch** and **execute prefetch**) provide a way to diminish the microcode loading times by scheduling them well ahead of the moment that the microcode is needed.
- **The complete πISA:** This scenario involves all πISA instructions including the **break** instruction. The **break** instruction provides a mechanism to synchronize the parallel execution of instructions by halting the execution of instructions following the **break** instruction.

Parallel execution. Parallel execution, for all πISA modifications is initiated by a **set**/**execute** instruction. For both minimal and preferred πISA, a parallel execution is ended by a general-purpose instruction as described in Figure 8(a). When a complete πISA is implemented and a sequence of instructions is performed in parallel, the end of the parallel execution is marked by the **break** instruction. It indicates where the parallel execution stops (see Figure 8 (b)).

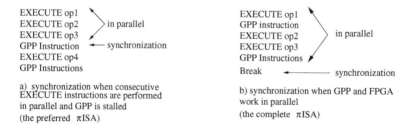

Fig. 8. Parallel execution and models of synchronization

Microarchitecture and its implementation. An example of a PISC is the Molen $\rho\mu$-coded processor introduced in [11]. More details on the Molen microarchitecture have been published in [12]. We have implemented a prototype design of a Molen processor using the Xilinx Virtex II Pro technology [14], which demonstrates many advantages of the PISCs and can be utilized for real-life application implementations. The core processor of the Molen prototype from [14] is the PowerPC hardcore embedded in the Xilinx virtex II Pro FPGAs.

5   Compiler

The specific PISC compiling techniques will be illustrated with examples from the Molen compiler [15]. Currently, the Molen compiler relies on the Stanford SUIF2 [16] (Stanford University Intermediate Format) Compiler Infrastructure for the front-end and for the back-end on the Harvard Machine SUIF [17] framework. The following essential features for a compiler targeting custom computing machines (CCM) have currently been implemented:

> Code identification: for the identification of the code mapped on the reconfigurable hardware, we added a special pass in the SUIF front-end. This identification is based on code annotation with special pragma directives (similar to [18]). In this pass, all the calls of the recognized functions are marked for further modification.
>
> Instruction set extension: the compiler takes into account the instruction set extension and inserts the appropriate **set/ execute** instructions both at the medium intermediate representation level and at low intermediate representation (LIR) level.
>
> Register file extension: the register file set has been extended with the exchange registers. The register allocation algorithm allocates the XREGs in a distinct pass applied before the register allocation; it is introduced in Machine SUIF, at LIR level. The conventions introduced for the XREGs are implemented in this pass.
>
> Code generation: code generation for the reconfigurable hardware (as previously presented) is performed when translating SUIF to Machine SUIF intermediate representation, and affects the function calls marked in the front-end. The code generation schedules the **set** instructions to hide the reconfiguration latency and to guarantee that the functions can be mapped on the available area [19].

An example of the code generated by the extended compiler for the Molen programming paradigm is presented in Figure 9. On the left, the C code is depicted. The function implemented in reconfigurable hardware is annotated with a pragma directive named *call_fpga*. It has incorporated the operation name, *op1* as specified in the hardware description file. In the middle, the code generated by the original compiler for the C code is depicted. The pragma annotation is ignored and a normal function call is included. On the right, the code generated by the compiler extended for the Molen programming paradigm is depicted; the function call is replaced with the appropriate instructions for sending parameters to the reconfigurable hardware in XREGs, hardware reconfiguration, preparing the fixed XREG for the microcode of the **execute** instruction, execution of the operation and the transfer of the result back to the general-purpose register file.

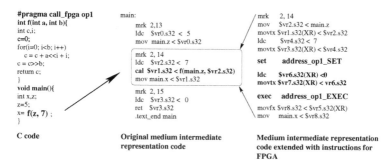

Fig. 9. Medium intermediate representation code

The presented code is at medium intermediate representation level in which the register allocation pass has not been applied yet.

The compiler extracts from a hardware description file the information about the target architecture such as the microcode address of the **set** and **execute** instructions for each operation implemented in the reconfigurable hardware, the number of XREGs, the fixed XREG associated with each operation, etc. The compiler may also decide not to use a reconfigurable hardware function and to include a pure software based execution.

6   Conclusions

We presented a new paradigm in computer architecture referred to as Polymorphic Instruction Set Computer (PISC). This new computing paradigm allows general purpose programming code and reconfigurable hardware descriptions to coexist within the same application program. We showed that a one-time instruction set extension of minimum 4 and maximum 8 polymorphic instructions is sufficient to implement an arbitrary number of application specific functionalities. Additional architectural features such as exchange registers and shared memory allow performance efficient communications, parameter and data exchange. We also presented the programming paradigm, supporting the polymorphic architectural extension and sketched some compiling considerations. Overall, we conclude that the PISC paradigm allows the designers to ride easily the Amdahl's curve towards the invention of more flexible and performance efficient computing machines.

References

1. S. Vassiliadis, B. Blaner, and R. J. Eickemeyer, *SCISM: A scalable compound instruction set machine.* IBM J. Res. Develop. Vol. 38, No. 2, Jan 1994, pp. 59–78.
2. G. M. Amdahl, Validity of the single processor approach to achieving large scale computing capabilities, in *Proc. AFIPS 1967 Spring Joint Computer Conference*, 1967, pp. 483–485.

3. D. A. Patterson and D. R. Ditzel, *The case for the reduced instruction set computer*, SIGARCH Comput. Archit. News, Vol. 8, No. 6, Oct 1980, pp. 25–33.

4. D. Bhandarkar and D. W. Clark. *Performance from Architecture: Comparing a RISC and a CISC with Similar Hardware Organization*. Communications of the ACM, Sep 1991, pp. 310–319.

5. G. Roelofs. *PNG: The Definitive Guide*. O'Reilly and Associates, 1999.

6. E. A. Hakkennes and S. Vassiliadis, Hardwired Paeth codec for portable network graphics (PNG), in *Proc. Euromicro 99*, Sep 1999, pp. 318–325.

7. S. Hauck, T. Fry, M. Hosler, and J. Kao, The Chimaera Reconfigurable Functional Unit, in *Proc. IEEE Symp. on Field-Programmable Custom Computing Machines*, 1997, pp. 87–96.

8. A. L. Rosa, L. Lavagno, and C. Passerone, Hardware/Software Design Space Exploration for a Reconfigurable Processor, in *Proc. Design, Automation and Test in Europe 2003 (DATE 2003)*, 2003, pp. 570–575.

9. S. Vassiliadis, S. Wong, and S. Cotofana, *Microcode Processing: Positioning and Directions*, IEEE Micro, vol. 23, no. 4, Jul 2003, pp. 21–30.

10. S. Vassiliadis, G. Gaydadjiev, K. Bertels, and E. Moscu Panainte, The Molen Programming Paradigm, in *Proc. Third International Workshop on Systems, Architectures, Modeling, and Simulation (SAMOS'03)*, Jul 2003, pp. 1–7.

11. S. Vassiliadis, S. Wong, and S. Cotofana, The MOLEN $\rho\mu$-Coded Processor, in *Proc. 11th Int. Conf. on Field Programmable Logic and Applications (FPL 2001)*, Aug 2001, pp. 275–285.

12. S. Vassiliadis, S. Wong, G. N. Gaydadjiev, K. Bertels, G. Kuzmanov, and E. M. Panainte, *The Molen Polymorphic Processor*, IEEE Transactions on Computers, vol. 53, Nov 2004, pp. 1363–1375.

13. J. M. P. Cardoso and H. C. Neto, *Compilation for FPGA-Based Reconfigurable Hardware*, IEEE Design & Test of Computers, vol. 20, no. 2, Apr 2003, pp. 65–75.

14. G. Kuzmanov, G. N. Gaydadjiev, and S. Vassiliadis, The MOLEN Processor Prototype, in *Proc. IEEE Symposium on Field-Programmable Custom Computing Machines (FCCM'04)*, Apr 2004, pp. 296–299.

15. E. Moscu Panainte, K. Bertels, and S. Vassiliadis, Compiling for the Molen Programming Paradigm, in *Proc. 13th Int. Conf. on Field Programmable Logic and Applications (FPL)*, Sep 2003, pp. 900–910.

16. http://suif.stanford.edu/suif/suif2.

17. http://www.eecs.hardvard.edu/hube/research/machsuif.html.

18. M. Gokhale and J. Stone, Napa C: Compiling for a Hybrid RISC/FPGA Architecture, in *Proc. IEEE Symp. on Field-Programmable Custom Computing Machines*, Apr 1998, pp. 126–135.

19. E. Moscu Panainte, K. Bertels, and S. Vassiliadis, Compiler-driven FPGA-area Allocation for Reconfigurable Computing, in *Proc. Design, Automation and Test in Europe 2006 (DATE 06)*, Mar 2006, pp. 369–374.

Generic Network Interfaces for Plug and Play NoC Based Architecture

Sanjay Pratap Singh, Shilpa Bhoj, Dheera Balasubramanian, Tanvi Nagda, Dinesh Bhatia, and Poras Balsara

Center for Integrated Circuits and Systems,
University of Texas, Dallas, TX 75080, USA
{sps042000, sxb043000, dxb039000, tmn041000, dinesh, poras}@utdallas.edu

Abstract. The emergence of the Network on chip (NoC) as a communication backbone for System on chip (SoC) based designs requires standardized interfaces for integrating IP (Intellectual Property) cores with diverse communication requirements. These interfaces have to be simple and generic for rapid plug and play implementation with minimal overhead. In this paper we describe the design and implementation of a programmable fabric based Network interface architecture. We have mapped the JPEG compression application on our architecture to demonstrate the feasibility of our design. The network interfaces seamlessly connect existing IP modules (Processor core, JPEG core, Memory core and UART core) to the NoC. The network, IP cores and the network interfaces are implemented on an FPGA device.

1 Introduction and Prior Work

Recent advances in VLSI and fabrication technology have given designers the ability to create System on a Chip (SoC) based architecture using several IP blocks and embedded memories. The SoC concept facilitates the reuse of IP cores in a plug and play manner.This reduces the time involved in design of the new system. The IP cores are connected by on-chip interconnects like a system bus, ad-hoc global wiring structures and more recently Networks on Chip. The concept of a Network on a chip (NoC) has gained popularity due to the fact that as technology scales, device sizes reduce, chip density increases and problems associated with interconnects arise [1] . The key ingredient in a plug and play architecture is the decoupling of computation from communication. This requires that the interfaces that connect the IP cores to the communication network are well defined and hide the implementation details of the interconnect [2]. Although much work has been carried out in designing the routing architecture and protocols for NoCs [3,4,5], little research has been done on the architectural design and implementation of interfaces required to connect standard IP cores to an NoC.

The definition of standard interfaces also facilitates the deployment of reusable system components without the need for different controllers for each component. However, the variety of cores necessitates the need for a certain amount of

K. Bertels, J.M.P. Cardoso, and S. Vassiliadis (Eds.): ARC 2006, LNCS 3985, pp. 287–298, 2006.

customization in the interfaces. Prior work in designing network interfaces primarily involves interfacing standard buses to NoCs [6,7]. In [7] a design of an interface to the On-chip Peripheral Bus (OPB) has been prototyped. However, in this architecture the bulk of the interface functionality (packetization and depacketization) lies with the core specific part of the interface. This increases the amount of redesign required to attach a new core. In [8] a design for a dual layered network interface along with a router has been synthesised. We propose a novel architecture in which most of the interfacing functionality is incorporated in the generic part of the interface to which different cores can be attached with minimum redesign of the specific interfaces. The generic network interface is universal and can incorporate mixed signal and mixed technology cores. The focus of our work is the implementation of generic network interfaces that allow any core to be attached to the NoC using core specific wrappers. To demonstrate the feasibility of the interface architecture we have implemented JPEG compression using a variety of IP cores (Processor, JPEG, Memory and UART) . Apart from the generic network interfaces, application specific core specific wrappers have been developed to allow cores to be interfaced without making any modifications to the cores and the Network Interfaces. This preserves the generic nature of the Network Interface.

The rest of the paper is organized as follows. Section 2 provides the architectural description of the generic network interface. This is followed by a section which outlines the data flow through the interface. The next section describes the architecture of the communication network used in the design. Section 5 gives a brief overview of the experimental framework in which we have proved the feasibility of our architecture. Section 6 discusses the results of our implementation. We conclude with a summary of the work presented in this paper and a brief description of future work.

2   Network Interface Architecture

The Network Interface translates packet-based communication of the network into a form that is required by the IP cores. In general, the tasks performed by network interface are:

Abstraction of the network communication protocol from the core so that the latter can be developed independently of the communication infrastructure. This allows any core to be connected to the Network interface.

Allowing the core specific wrapper to interface with any NoC protocol or topology. Since the size of all the fields in the protocol are parameterized, the network interface is generic with respect to the Network. The network interface provides a field to hold the routing information bits to route the data packets and this can be interpreted by the router as required by the network topology.

Data packetization and depacketization for relaying and receiving signals over the NoC.

We split the design of the Network Interface into the following parts: the Generic Core Interface, the Packet Maker and Disassembler along with their respective memories and the Asynchronous FIFOs as shown in the Figure 1.

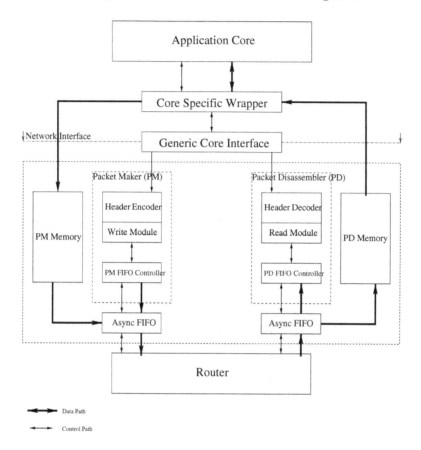

Fig. 1. The Network Interface Architecture

2.1   Generic Core Interface (GCI) Architecture

The GCI lies between the network and the Core Specific Wrapper. This unit forms the foundation of the generic nature of the architecture as it prevents the wrapper from directly interacting with the rest of the Network interface. The GCI abstracts the packet information from the core specific wrapper, and provides it with the actual data/control information only.

Any core specific wrapper can interface with the GCI with simple predefined handshaking signals. When a core needs to communicate with another core on the network, the trigger signals (*start_read* ,*start_write*) to initiate packetization, the number of words to be read/written and the destination address are passed between the specific wrapper and GCI. When the core is reading from/writing to the Network Interface memory, *perform_read/perform_write, read_complete/write_complete* signals are exchanged between GCI and core specific wrapper. In our design, various core specific wrappers share similar handshaking signals with the GCI. For a few cores some signals are not required, however the GCI includes support for these signals to preserve its generic nature. E.g, Processor and JPEG engine have *processing_start* and *processing_done* signals, which are really not needed for memory core. If a new core is added to the system, only the core specific wrapper has to be designed without modifying the GCI or network interface. Hence, the Core Specific Wrapper views the network interface as a black box.

2.2 Packet Maker (PM)

This unit functions at the source core (core from which packets originate in the network) and performs the following critical tasks that maintain data integrity:

1. Creates the Packet Header with correct routing and control information required by the routers and the destination core.
2. Ensures that the entire block of data is broken down into packets with the correct payload size (size of the actual data to be processed).
3. Writes the packet into the packet maker (PM) memory to provide for in-order packet routing by the network.
4. Converts the data stored in the PM memory (Figure 1) into flits (the smallest data transfer unit) before queuing them in the asynchronous FIFO.

The Packet Maker is divided into three main units, the Header Encoder, the Write Module and the FIFO controller. The Header Encoder unit forms the packet header based on the information provided by the GCI. It includes the address of the destination core and control information which depends on the type of operation the core is requesting for, and the core it is communicating with. The encoder breaks down the entire data according to the maximum payload size and keeps count of the number of packets to be sent. The Header Encoder also contains a parameterized lookup table which provides the destination address. The Write Module exercises control over the address and read/write line of the PM memory. It decides whether the Header Encoder (when the header is written into the memory) or the Specific Core Wrapper (when the payload is written into memory) has access to the PM memory. Once the entire packet is written, the Write Module transfers control to the FIFO Controller. The function of Packet Maker FIFO Controller(PMFC) is to convert the data written into the PM shared memory into flits and dispatch them to the network through the asynchronous FIFO. It may sometimes be necessary to break a packet into many flits.The PMFC sets the end of packet (EOP) field in the flit to 1 when it transmits the last flit to the FIFO.

2.3 Packet Disassembler (PD) Architecture

This unit functions at the destination core. It performs the tasks of reading data from the incoming asynchronous FIFO, decoding the Packet Header, extracting the control information required by the core and obtaining the total message size if the message is split into many packets. The Packet Disassembler includes the Packet Disassembler FIFO controller, the Read Module and the Header Decoder. The Packet Disassembler FIFO controller (PDFC) reads flits from the Async FIFO and writes them into the Packet Disassembler (PD) Memory. After writing a complete packet it triggers the Read Module to initiate further transfer. The Read Module controls the address bus and control line to the PD memory. The read module gives control of the PD memory data bus to the Header Decoder to obtain the header bytes. It then transfers the control to the Core Wrapper, to read the payload. The Header Decoder extracts information from the packet header and passes it to the GCI. Each field of the header set by the encoder of the source core is decoded to obtain information for the destination core such as the operation to be performed, the total number of words to be written into the destination core, the number of words to be read from the destination core and the address of the source core in case packets are to be sent back to the source. The next section explains the flow of data for read and write operations.

3   Data Flow

The core specific wrapper performs read and write operations. As the initiating core specific wrapper, it can perform the following:

1. Initiate a write operation: The source core sends data over the network to the destination core. In this case the Packet Maker sends data packets with a header and payload.
2. Initiate a Read operation: This operation initiates a read from the destination core. The packet maker sends a single control packet (header only).

In response to the above operations the reciprocating core performs the following:

1. Reads data sent over the network: The reciprocating core reads the data from its PD memory and processes it.
2. Reciprocating core sends data over the network: In response to the source core's read request, the reciprocating core sends data through its PM memory and the network back to the source.

4   Communication Architecture

Communication among the IP cores is handled by a parameterized NoC. Since the focus of this research is on developing generic interfaces to support a plug and play architecture, a simple mesh based NoC architecture has been used for this project. As shown in Figure 2 the NoC consists of a grid of routers that are connected to the network interfaces through asynchronous FIFOs. The buffer sizes in the routers and asynchronous FIFOs as well as the data line width in the communication network are parameterized according to the requirements of the application. The network of routers has been designed to allow simultaneous

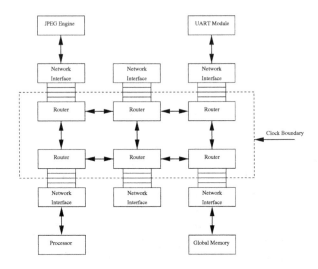

Fig. 2. JPEG Mapped on NoC

communication among cores. Each router has four input and four output ports with one pair connected to the network interface that it serves. In addition it also has a switch controller to coordinate the transfer of flits among the routers. An internal buffer is used to store flits inside the router in case of any congestion.

4.1 Packet Header Structure

Information between routers is sent through packets. There are two types of packets, a control packet containing only the header, and a data packet containing both the header and payload. In this architecture, the parameterized packet header is 48 bits. The packet header structure is depicted in figure 3. The field sizes are chosen to ensure scalability. The Source address field represents the address of each core. The read/write bit specifies the type of the data transfer operation. If memory is one of the IP cores then the Base address field indicates the address of the memory for read/write operations. The 8 bits are interpreted as the higher order bits of the address, hence the number of addresses

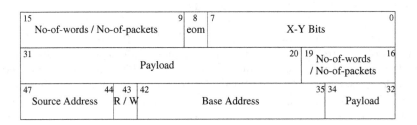

Fig. 3. Packet header Structure

are not restricted to 256. The total payload size field gives the size of the data transmitted in each packet with a maximum value of 32767 bits. This size ensures that a significant amount of data can be packed into one packet. For instance, one pixel is 3 bytes and to pack an image of 16x16 just one packet is needed. The field *No-of-packets/No-of-words* indicates the number of packets for a write operation or the number of words for a read operation. An asserted EOM (end of message) bit indicates the end of the message. The XY bits denote the routing information. Each packet is transmitted as more than one flit. A flit is the smallest unit of data transfer. The size of a flit is parameterized and we have chosen a size of 16-bits in our implementation.

4.2 Communication Protocol

Data packets are routed through the network using a wormhole routing scheme. This has low latency and requires less routing resources. A simple X-Y routing [9] scheme has been adopted to eliminate the need for lookups at the router level. In our protocol, the first flit that is transmitted is the header flit that contains the routing information in the first 8 bits. To transmit a data packet across the router, the payload and the encapsulating header are divided into flits. The sequence of flits is brought from the PM memory into the asynchronous FIFO connected to the router. The router transmits the flits according the to the XY routing information specified in the header flit. At the destination router, the flits are reassembled by the Packet Disassembler and delivered to the core. The latency of the header flit depends on the number of hops through the network. For the flits that follow, the latency is independent of the number of hops as the entire operation is pipelined. This is also verified by the experimental results in section 7.

5 Experimental Framework

In order to demonstrate the feasibility of our proposed Network Interface architecture we have mapped a JPEG compression application using four cores. These cores are placed around the network and exchange data using packet based communication. The uncompressed image is initially stored in the global memory of the system. The processor sends a read request packet for the image to the global memory. On receiving the packet, global memory sends the uncompressed RGB image to the processor via the network. Once the image is converted to the YUV format, it is sent to the JPEG engine for compression. JPEG engine compresses the BMP image to JPG format and sends it to the UART core to be transmitted to the terminal. Below is a description of each core and the specific application wrapper attached to it.

5.1 Processor

YACC, the processor used in this implementation, is an open source 32 bit, 5 stage pipelined RISC processor based on the MIPS I intruction set. The processor is a soft core in which the Instruction and the Data Memory are configurable according to the application requirement (image size). The processor follows the Von-Neumann architecture which limits the number of ports available to the external hardware for Direct Memory Access (DMA) of data memory. Therefore we have added a local memory to the processor as an additional hardware unit. This is mapped to the processor's address space. This local memory is accessed by the processor using memory mapped General Purpose Input Output (GPIO). In our experimental setup, YACC converts gamma corrected RGB image to YUV (Y Cb Cr) format for compression.

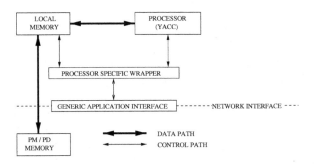

Fig. 4. Processor with Specific Wrapper

Processor Specific Wrapper. The Processor Specific Wrapper provides the interface between the processor core and Network Interface through the Generic Core Interface. Figure 4 shows the flow of control signals and data. The wrapper sends a request for image to be processed along with information such as the address of the destination core and the amount of data needed (image size) to the Generic Core Interface. Once the image arrives in the Shared Memory, the wrapper dumps the RGB image into the Local Memory of the processor. The processor converts the image into YUV format and simultaneously writes it into the Local Memory. The wrapper moves the processed image from the Local Memory to the Shared Memory to route it to the next core for further processing.

5.2   JPEG Engine

The JPEG ENGINE is a standard Baseline DCT compressor (JFIF header) with 2:1:1 sub sampling [10]. It takes a YUV image as input and outputs a compressed JPEG image.

At the input to the JPEG encoder, source image samples are grouped into 8x8 blocks and are fed into the Forward DCT (FDCT) block. After output from the FDCT, each of the 64 DCT coefficients is uniformly quantized in conjunction with a 64-element quantization table, which is specified as an input to the encoder. After quantization, the DC coefficient is treated separately from the 63 AC coefficients and is encoded as the difference from the DC term of the previous block in the encoding order. The final DCT-based encoder processing step is entropy coding. Here we achieve additional compression in a lossless manner by encoding the quantized DCT coefficients more compactly through Huffman coding.

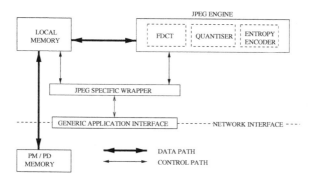

Fig. 5. JPEG Engine with Specific Wrapper

JPEG Specific Wrapper. Similar to the Processor Specific Wrapper, the JPEG Specific Wrapper provides the interface between the JPEG core and Network Interface through Generic Core Interface. Figure 5 shows the flow of control signals and data in the JPEG engine and wrapper. The JPEG core sends a request for YUV Image to be compressed along with the information such as address of destination core (Processor) and the amount of data needed (Image size) to the Generic Core Interface. Once the image arrives in the Shared Memory of the Network Interface, the wrapper dumps the YUV image in Local Memory of the core. The JPEG engine compresses the image and places it back into the Local Memory. The wrapper transfers the com-pressed image from the Local Memory to the Shared Memory, from where the image is routed via the network to UART core to display on the terminal.

5.3   Universal Aysnchronous Receiver Transmitter(UART)

The UART core comprises of 3 modules: a finite state machine, a buffer and a transmit module. The finite state machine generates the handshaking signals between the modules. The buffer stores the data received from the other cores through the network. The transmit module receives a byte of data at a time, serializes it, attaches the start and the stop bits and transmits it to the RS 232 port at proper time intervals. The transmit module is parameterized with respect to the transmission speeds that it can handle. The UART specific wrapper that interfaces the UART core with the Generic Core Interface coordinates the transfer of data packets from the shared memory in Network Interface to the buffer in the UART transmitter core. The wrapper also converts the data into 8 bit words to make it compatible with the UART transmitter core.

5.4   Global Memory

The Global Memory core is a dual port RAM of a parameterized size. The wrapper is a finite state machine that includes the functionality of a memory controller while interacting with the network interface. The wrapper handles variations in word size between the memory and the network interface and contention in memory access.

6   Application Mapping and Testing

The interfaces, communication network and the cores were implemented on the Xilinx FPGA (XC2VP30). Post place and route simulation was used to find out how the architecture responds to real time data communication between independ-ently developed cores which are connected using the on-chip network.

For the purpose of analysis, we evaluate the case where the processor retrieves the image from the shared memory, processes it and sends it to the JPEG engine for compression. Table 1 gives the latency in terms of clock cycles between modules for different image sizes.

As can be seen from the table, the Processor has a larger computational latency compared to the JPEG engine. Therefore, the percentage overhead in latency incurred due to the network interface is much lower. Hence, it can be inferred that the network interfaces do not significantly degrade the performance of computationally intensive cores.

Table 1. Latency (in clock cycles) from Processor to JPEG engine

Source Module	Destination Module	16x16 img	32x32 img	64x64 img	128x128 img
NI Shared memory1	Proc Local memory	2651	10600	42378	169546
Processor latency	Processor latency	85926	309043	1111509	3890283
Proc Local memory	NI Shared memory2	2651	10600	42378	169546
NI Shared memory2	NI Shared memory1	8318	32475	129105	515264
NI Shared memory1	JPEG Engine	1536	6141	24564	98256
JPEG latency	JPEG latency	3882	16054	65098	259412
JPEG Engine	NI Shared memory2	1656	6258	25032	100128

Table 2. Latency(in clock cycles) of Network Interface and Router Network

Source Module	Destination Module	16x16 img	32x32 img	64x64 img	128x128 img
NI Shared memory1	NI Shared memory2	8318	32475	129405	515624
NI Shared memory1	NI Router1	8073	31677	126095	511567
Router1	Router2	8219	32202	128142	511896
Router2	NI shared memory1	8283	32475	129105	515264

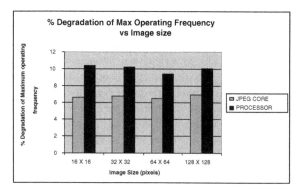

Fig. 6. Plot of percentage overhead in operating frequency with image size

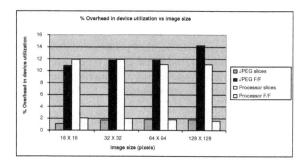

Fig. 7. Plot of percentage degradation in device utilisation with image size

Table 2 shows the latencies incurred during the transfer of data packets between the two network interfaces across the routing network. We observe that the latencies of packet transfer remain approximately the same at every stage of communication. This behavior can be attributed to the pipelined architecture of the interface and the routing network.

Figure 6 shows the degradation of the maximum operating frequency of the different cores. It can be seen that the degradation is reasonably low and uniform with increasing image size. Thus it can be stated that the degradation effect of the application specific wrapper is not substantial even with large data sizes.

The effect of the core specific wrappers on the device utilization is shown in figure 7. The percentage overhead is uniformally low. Therefore attaching a wrapper to a core does not significantly increase resource requirements.

7   Conclusions

In this paper we proposed a comprehensive interface architecture that can seamlessly integrate different IP cores to a communication fabric. We tested the functionality and robustness of our design by mapping a JPEG compression algorithm on our architecture. We used a variety of IP cores to evaluate the performance of the interfaces under a variety of traffic conditions. After extensive testing we found that for computationally intensive cores, the overhead of the interfaces is not substantial. The generic characteristic of the interface facilitates IP core reuse as only the core specific wrapper needs minor modification. It is the authors' belief that an NoC approach driven by generic interfaces will change the way SoCs are designed in the years to come. Our future exploration in this area would be in the direction of designing better communication architectures and refining the layered structure of the network interface. Our ultimate goal would be to develop an Application Specific Integrated Circuit of the communication network and the generic interfaces for performance driven applications.

References

1. G. D. Micheli and L. Benini, "Networks on chips: A new soc paradigm," *IEEE Computer*, vol. 35, no. 1, 2002.
2. B. P. M. R., "Interfacing cores with on-chip packet-switched networks," *VLSI Design, 2003. Proceedings. 16th International Conference*, pp. 382 – 387, Jan. 2003.
3. A. Adriahantenaina, H.Charlery, A.Greiner, L.Mortiez, and C. Zeferino, "Spin: a scalable, packet switched, on-chip micronetwork," in *Proc. IEEE Design Automation and Test*, 2003.
4. C. Zeferino and A. Susin, "Socin: a parametric and scalable network-on-chip," in *Proc. 16th Symposium on Integrated Circuits and Systems Design*, Sept. 2003.
5. Z. C. K. M. S. A.A, "Rasoc: a router soft-core for networks-on-chip," in *Proc. Design, Automation and Test in Europe Conference and Exhibition*, Feb. 2001, pp. 198–203 Vol.3.
6. P. Gurrier and A. Greiner, "A generic architecture for on-chip packet switched interconnections," in *Proc. IEEE Design Automation and Test*, Mar. 2000.
7. R.Holsmark, A.Johansson, and S. Kumar, "On connecting cores to packet switched on-chip networks: A case study with microblaze processor cores," in *IEEE Workshop on Design and Diagnostics of Electronic Circuits and Systems*, Apr. 2004.
8. J. Dielissen, A. Radulescu, K. Goossens, and E. Rijpkema, "Concepts and implementation of the philips network-on-chip," in *IP-SOC Workshop*, Nov. 2003.
9. L. M. Ni and P. K. McKinley, "A survey of wormhole routing techniques in direct networks," *IEEE Transaction on Computers*, pp. 62–76, Feb. 1993.
10. G.K.Wallace, "The jpeg still picture compression standard," *IEEE Transactions on Comsumer Electronics*, vol. 38, no. 1, pp. xviii–xxxiv, 1992.

Providing QoS Guarantees in a NoC by Virtual Channel Reservation

Nikolay Kavaldjiev, Gerard J.M. Smit, Pascal T. Wolkotte,
and Pierre G. Jansen

Faculty of Electrical Engineering, Mathematics and Computer Science
University of Twente, the Netherlands
{n.k.kavaldjiev, g.j.m.smit, p.t.wolkotte, p.g.jansen}@utwente.nl

Abstract. Virtual channel reservation is a simple approach for providing guaranteed throughput services in a virtual channel network-on-chip. However, its performance is limited by the number of virtual channels per physical channels. In this paper we explore the limits of the approach and investigate how these limits depend on the routing algorithm, the traffic locality, the network topology and the network size. The results show the the approach can be applied in a network of size 10-by-10 nodes with four virtual channels per physical channel. The traffic locality has strong influence on the performance limits of the approach and can also help in reducing the communication energy cost by 50% to 70%. The type of the routing algorithm does not practically influence the performance limits.

1 Introduction

Multiprocessor System-on-Chip (MPSoC) is an emerging platform for the future mobile devices, e.g. PDAs, media players, mobile phones etc. To meet the functional requirements of these devices, such a platform should provide flexibility together with high performance and low power consumption. A promising approach for satisfying these contradicting requirements is though reconfigurable domain-specific computing. The work presented in this paper is performed as a part of the Gecko project which addresses architectural and design issues in low-power dynamically reconfigurable multimedia systems. The platform we envision for these devices is a MPSoC consisting of a large array of coarse grain reconfigurable processing elements (PEs) and distributed memories. The PEs are heterogeneous and domain specific, performing efficient high performance computation for specific application domains. One of the major issues in such a system is the communication between the PEs. The traditional system bus is not a solution because it is not scalable and cannot sustain the increasing bandwidth demands. The bus easy becomes a bottleneck and hence in the future MPSoC it is replaced by a light weighted communication network built on-chip, also known as Network-on-Chip (NoC) [1]. In this paper we discuss the NoC we propose for our MPSoC.

The network we consider is constructed in the following way. The PEs in our system are arranger in a two-dimensional array. Each PE is equipped with a

K. Bertels, J.M.P. Cardoso, and S. Vassiliadis (Eds.): ARC 2006, LNCS 3985, pp. 299–310, 2006.

network router it uses for inter processor communication. The network routers are connected in a grid by full-duplex channels build by two unidirectional channels - one in each direction. The unidirectional channels are referred to as *physical channels*. In our system we use a virtual channel network [2]. In a virtual channel network, on each physical channel there are several *virtual channels* (VCs). Data in the network is transported over the VCs.

The system we envision is dynamic and reconfigurable at run-time. The applications that will run in the system are not known in advance, but are decided at run-time. A central system authority starts and terminates applications at run-time. When an application is started, the central authority allocates and configures PEs for the application and reserves communication channels in the NoC to carry the data streams between the PEs. When the application is terminated the resources it uses are freed.

Since many of the applications in mobile multimedia devices are real-time, predictable system communications are important. Predictable communications in our network are provided by means of guaranteed throughput (GT) services. The network can provide connections with a guaranteed minimal throughput bound. To guarantee the bound we use a *virtual channel reservation* - the VCs traversed by a connection are reserved and not used by other communications. Such approach is simple, but its potential is limited by the number of VCs in the network. Since there are finite number of VCs on each physical channel, the number of connections that can traverse a physical channel is limited and thus is limited the number of connections that can be opened simultaneously in the network. The number of VCs cannot be increased arbitrary, because it has a strong impact on the router area.

In this paper we explore the limits of the virtual channel reservation approach in a network of size 10-by-10 PEs with four VCs per physical channel. Considering the available chip area and the size of the processing elements this network size is feasible for the today and near future systems. The number of VCs is chosen such that the routers have reasonable size. We also investigate how the limits of the virtual channel reservation approach depend on the network routing algorithm, the network traffic locality and the network topology.

The paper is organized as follows. Section 2 discusses related work. The network is presented in Section 3. Section 4 discusses how the GT traffic is routed in the network and what algorithms are used for that. In Section 5 a model of the GT traffic in the network is constructed. Section 6 describes the performed experiments and Section 7 discussed the simulation results.

2   Related Work

In this section we briefly review the QoS solutions in NoCs. In the Ethereal network-on-chip [3] guaranteed services are based on time-division multiplexing (TDM). The communications on the physical channels are globally scheduled in time slots. A TDM approach is used also in the Nostrum network [4]. Although simple from implementation point of view, the TDM approach is static and not flexible enough for a dynamic system. Small changes in the network configuration may require complete recomputation of the schedule. The distribution of the new schedule requires reconfiguration of all the routers along the changed paths. Furthermore, the global schedule requires a global notion of time in the system which may become a disadvantage in the near future when systems are expected to be Globally Asynchronous Locally Synchronous (GALS) [5].

A circuit switching NoC is another solution for providing guaranteed services. It benefits from small size and low energy consumption but is restrictive in the number of circuits that can be established. Wolkotte et al [6] overcome the problem by providing more than one physical channel between the neighbour routers. However, an additional network is needed for handling the best effort traffic in the system and for network configuration. The time for establishing a circuit cannot be neglected because all the switches along the circuit have to be reconfigured.

Another approach for providing guaranteed services in a network-on-chip is by introducing priorities. Such an approach is used by Felicijan et al [7] to provide guarantees in a virtual channel network. The VCs over a physical channel have statically assigned priorities. The high priority VCs are used for guaranteed traffic and the low priority VCs are used for best effort traffic. While this approach can guarantee better services for the traffic using higher priority VCs it cannot give exact bound on the provided services.

3   Network Operation

Here we briefly present the on-chip network we propose for interconnecting the PEs in the system. It is a packet switching virtual channel network that provides GT as well as Best Effort (BE) services [8]. The network consists of a grid of routers interconnected by physical channels. Each router is connected to a PE which serves as a source and sink of data. On each physical channel there are 4 VCs , this number being motivated by the trade-off between performance and area of a virtual channel router studied by Dally [2]. The VCs time-share the physical channel but are separately buffered at the router input. The physical channel is shared on a cycle-by-cycle basis in a round-robin fashion, but cycles are only used by the VCs that transmit data; the idle VCs do not use cycles. Since sharing is done in a round-robin fashion, the VCs equally share the physical channel bandwidth. If on a physical channel of bandwidth b there are v VCs currently transmitting data, then each of these v VCs is guaranteed a throughput of

$$TH_{min} = \frac{b}{v} \qquad (1)$$

This is the worst case throughput the traffic on the v VCs can experience. Whatever traffic load is applied to the v VCs their throughput will never go below TH_{min}. Therefore, guarantees on the throughput bound of a VC can be given by restricting the number of VCs used on the same physical channel.

If a minimal throughput bound TH_R is requested for a VC, then according to Eq. (1) the number v of VCs used on the same physical channel should be

$$v \leq \left\lfloor \frac{b}{TH_{min}} \right\rfloor \qquad (2)$$

With four VCs per physical channel in our network we can guarantee throughput of b, b/2, b/3 or b/4.

In traditional virtual channel networks VCs are allocated to packets dynamically by the routers [2]. In such a network the number of currently occupied VCs depends on the current traffic and cannot be determined. Therefore no throughput guarantees can be given for a VC. In contrast, in our network VCs are statically allocated. We use a source routing, which is a technique where the packet destination address describes the exact route in terms of VCs that the packet takes to the destination. The addresses are generated by the central authority and given to the PEs during their configuration. Knowing the routes already in use, the central authority can determine which VCs are used. Therefor, it can predict their throughput and give guarantees.

In our network GT services are provides on a connection basis. A route is found between the source and the destination node and the VCs the route traverses are reserved and not used for other communications. Such a route is called *connection*. The throughput of the connection is determined by the VC with minimal throughput among the traversed. If Eq. (2) holds for all VCs the connection traverses then it guarantees minimal throughput bound of TH_R.

Routes for connections are provided by the central authority using a routing function. The routing function searches for a route traversing only VCs that can satisfy the connection throughput request TH_R according to Eq. (2). Thus, the routing function is in charge of providing GT connections for the application.

4   Routing Function

The task of the routing function is to find routes for the GT connections in the network. The function has the form $R(S,D,TH_R)$. It takes as input a of a connection description and returns as a result a description of network route. The connection description consists of a source node S, a destination node D and a requested throughput TH_R. The route description is an ordered sequence $<vc_1, vc_2, , vc_n>$ of the virtual channels vc_i traversed by the route. The requested throughput can be a real number but according to Eq. (2) the guaranteed throughput bound is always discrete and takes values b, b/2, b/3 and b/4.

To guarantee the specified throughput the routing function looks for a route traversing only VCs for which Eq. (2) holds. To find such a route, the routing function needs to know the current state of all VCs in the network. The state of a VC is represented by one integer set to 0 when the VC is not used or indicating the throughput that is guaranteed when the VC is used. The states of all VCs form the network state. When searching for a route, the routing function checks the network state and uses only free VCs that satisfy the following two *GT routing criteria*: i) the VC can guarantee the requested throughput according Eq. (2), ii) the use of the VC will not violate the throughput guarantees already given (if any) by the other VCs on the same physical channel (Eq. (2) will still hold for them). After the route has been constructed, the routing function updates the state of the used VCs. When the route is not needed anymore, e.g. the application using it has terminated, the VCs constructing the route are freed and their state is updated.

Finding a route in a network is equivalent to finding a path between two nodes in a graph - the network topology is represented as a graph and a path searching algorithm is run on it. Among all possible paths the shortest is preferable, because shorter network routes result in less network traffic and less energy for communication. Therefore, the routing function is based on an algorithm for the shortest path search in graphs. However, our routing function runs on a subgraph I=(N,C) of the full network graph, derived by deleting all channels that do not satisfy the two GT routing criteria. Here N represent the set of network nodes and C represent the set on channels.

The routing function is used at run-time and therefore has to be as fast and simple as possible. But a simple algorithm may lead to poor network utilization generating congestions at some parts of the network while other parts stay unutilized. To examine the influence of the routing algorithm, we experiment with two shortest path search algorithms [9]: *Breadth-first search* and *Dijkstra's algorithm*.

Breadth-first search (BFS) is the simplest possible shortest path search algorithm. It works on non-weighted graphs and finds a shortest path in terms of the number of edges. It routes without taking into account the network condition - weakly and heavy loaded physical channels are equally preferred. The computational complexity of the algorithm is $O(N)$. The memory complexity of the algorithm is also linear in the number of network nodes.

Dijkstra's algorithm (DA) is more complex and allows the routing decision to adapt according the current network conditions. The algorithm works on weighted, directed graphs, where all edge weights are nonnegative. It finds shortest paths in terms of the minimal weighted sum. In our network, the weight assigned to an edge is proportional to the load of the corresponding physical channel. The weight equals the number of occupied VCs on the corresponding physical channel plus one, as one stands for a unit physical distance. Thus, if no virtual channel is occupied the weight is one and if all four VCs are occupied the weight is 5. One is added to avoid zero weight and thus to provide that the algorithm always prefers shorter paths. Every time a connection is routed the state of the reserved VCs is changed which increases the weights of the physical channels traversed by the connection. When the connection is deleted, the VCs are released and the weights are reduced. Hence, the weights reflect the current network state and the routing algorithm adapt its decision according to this state. The computational complexity of Dijkstra's algorithm is $O(N^2)$. The memory complexity of the algorithm is linear in the number of vertices.

BFS and DA have the same memory complexity but DA has a higher computational complexity than BFS. We examine how the routing algorithm influences the performance of the routing function and whether it is profitable to use DA instead of the simpler BFS.

5   Traffic Model

In this section we construct a model of the GT traffic in the network. The model is later used for evaluation of the routing function. We model only the spatial aspects of the traffic, like communication pattern and communication distances, and not the timing aspects. The timing aspects, like data generation rate or data inter arrival time are entirely hidden behind the requested throughput TH_R. The traffic spatial characteristics are determined by two factors - topology of the application graphs and strategy for mapping of the application graphs on the multiprocessor architecture. The application is represented as a graph $G_A = (V_A, E_A)$. The graph vertices V_A represent processes to run on the PEs and the graph edges E_A represent the communication between the processes. To run an application, the vertices of the application graph are mapped on PEs in the system. After the mapping the edges between the processes define the communications between the PEs to be handled by the network.

GT traffic in the system is generated by streaming applications which typically have application graphs with simple pipeline structure [10][11]. At a certain moment in time a number of streaming applications are running simultaneously in the system, hence there are number of pipeline graphs scattered over the PEs. To model such traffic conditions we use a large graph of ring topology which nodes are scatter over the PEs. A large ring graph can be seen as a serial connection of many short pipeline graphs. The number of nodes in the ring graph is equal to the number of PEs in the system and every node is mapped on a separate PE. Thus, we model a system where every PE generates and consumes a data stream.

The mapping decides the actual PEs where the application processes will run and therefore it has a strong influence on the communication locality. To model the effect of traffic locality we use three different strategies for mapping the ring topology graph. The three strategies produce mappings that approximate respectively the best, the average and the worst case of traffic locality. The three mapping strategies use the same algorithm for choosing the PEs, but differ in a parameter given to the algorithm. The algorithm operates on the ring graph as follows. The graph nodes are mapped sequentially in the order they appear in the graph. For every next node a PE is chosen randomly among those which are at distance less than or equal d hops from the PE where the previous graph node was mapped. Here d is a parameter of the algorithm that sets a diameter for the preferred network distance. If there is no free PE within that distance, then a PE is chosen randomly among all free PEs. The three mappings strategies differ only in the value they set the parameter d to. The first strategy tries to maximize the traffic locality; it sets the parameter d to 1 and approximates *best* case locality.

The second strategy sets d to 4 and approximates some *average* case locality. The third strategy approximates *worst* case locality. It sets the parameter d to the diameter of the network (the longest network distance). Hence, the mapping algorithm uniformly scatters the vertices of the ring graph over the PEs and no locality should be expected.

6 Simulation Experiments

To explore the performance limits of the routing function and hence of the virtual channel reservation approach, we perform a number of simulation experiments using the traffic model from Section 5. In an simulation experiment a ring graph of 100 nodes is mapped on a network of size 10-by-10 nodes. The mapping is randomized but generated with specific locality characteristics (worst, average, best case locality). After the mapping, a routing function provides GT connections for the communication channels defined by the edges of the ring graph, all with the same requested throughput TH_R. Thus, 100 GT connections following a ring communication pattern are routed. The routing is considered to be *successful* when all the 100 GT connections are routed. When routes cannot be found for all connections, the routing is considered to fail. If a routing is successful, information is collected about the network distances of the routed GT connections and the utilization of the VCs in the network. Experiments are performed for the three traffic locality conditions (worst, average, best case locality), with two network topologies (mesh and torus), with two routing functions based respectively on the BFS and DA algorithms and with four values for the requested throughput TH_R (b, b/2, b/3 and b/4). All 24 combinations of these factors are explored. To asses the average performance of the routing function, for each of the 24 combinations we perform 1000 experiments, each experiment setting a *sample* in the space of the possible traffic patterns. The number 1000 was chosen empirically such that to provide enough samples for representative average results in acceptable simulation time. Thus in total 24x1000 samples are collected.

7 Simulation Results

In this section we present and discuss the results of the conducted experiments. We compare how the different factors influence the performance of the virtual channel reservation approach in order to decide which of them are of importance and can be used to improve the performance of the approach and which can be neglected.

7.1 Number of Successful Samples

Figure 1 shows how many of the 1000 samples taken in each of the 24 combination of factors are successful . The three graphs correspond to the three cases of traffic locality, each graph presenting the results for mesh and torus topology. Of interest for us are the cases for which all 1000 samples are successful. We assume that in these cases the requested GT connections can always be provided; therefore, the virtual channel reservation approach can be safely applied. In the cases when not all samples are successful the routing function cannot always provide all the requested GT connections and the virtual channel reservation approach performs insufficiently for these requirements.

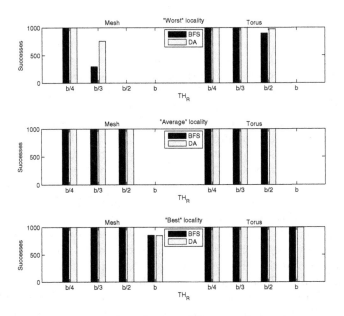

Fig. 1. Number of successfully routed mappings

Figure 1 we see that for worst case traffic locality the virtual channel reservation approach can be safely applied if the requested throughput TH_R is restricted to $b/4$ for mesh topology and up to $b/3$ for torus topology. The torus topology helps improving the performance in such traffic conditions by increasing the throughput limit from $b/4$ to $b/3$. When locality is introduced the performance is improved by increasing the limits on the TH_R to b/2 and b. But for local traffic the improvement achieved by replacing mesh with torus topology is not significant. The routing algorithms do not change the performance of the approach for any traffic conditions. Among the three factors - locality, topology and routing function - the traffic locality has the strongest influence on the performance limits of the virtual channel reservation approach while the routing algorithm does not influence it significantly. The results show also that four VCs per physical channel provide enough network resource for applying the virtual channel reservation in a 10-by-10 network; in all the cases, if TH_R is restricted, the approach can be applied . Restriction on TH_R restricts the maximal throughput guaranteed to a connection to some fraction of the capacity b of the physical channel. Thus, at network design time an appropriate b has to be chosen (e.g. by choosing the operation frequency of the network and the width of the physical channel).

7.2   Detour Cost

The routing function tries to route the requested connections using minimal distance routes, but this is not always possible because some VCs along the minimal distance routes might be occupied. In such a case the routing function takes a detour - a route which is not minimal. *Detour cost* is defined as the difference between the real route distance and the minimal distance. The real distances are the result of the routing, while the minimal distances are idealistic, assuming there is no other traffic in the network. The better routing algorithms manage to route the traffic using shorter paths and therefore with less detour cost.

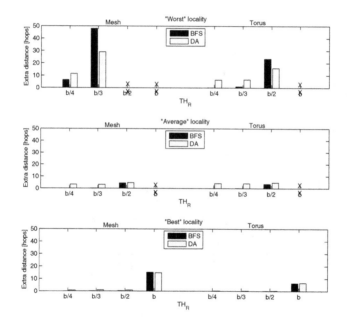

Fig. 2. Average detour cost (sum over 100 connections)

The detour cost is shown in Figure 2. The presented figures give the sum of the detour cost of all 100 connections in the ring graph. In most of the cases the sum detour cost is less than ten hops, which is negligible compared to the sum distances of the 100 connection (at least 100 hops). The detour cost exceeds 10 hops only when the requested GT connection cannot always be provided, therefore the approach cannot be used.

7.3 Communication Energy Cost

Wolkotte et al [12] performs power analysis of our virtual channel router and derives a energy model of the network. An energy model of a circuit switching network is also derived. We use the two energy models to estimate and compare the average communication energy cost in the proposed virtual channel network and in the circuit switching network proposed by Wolkotte. The energy models estimate the energy cost in [pJ/bit] for transporting a bit in the network

$$E_{ps} = E_R(N_{hop} + 1) + (0.39 + 0.12l_{wire})N_{hop} \qquad (3)$$

Here l_{wire} is the length of a physical channel in mm. N_{hop} is the network distance in number of hops. E_R stands for the energy cost for traversing a router; for the packet-switching and the circuit-switching network E_R takes values $E_{R\_PS} = 0.98$ and $E_{R\_CS} = 0.37$. The second term in the energy model estimates the energy for traversing the wires between two routers (a physical channel). The model captures only the dynamic energy cost for transporting a bit.

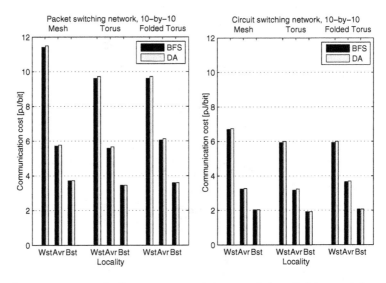

Fig. 3. Average communication energy cost in a packet switching and in a circuit switching network

The energy cost is estimated for three topologies - mesh, torus, and folded torus. A folded torus has the same graph structure as torus, but its nodes are reshuffled in the plane such that the torus wraparound channels are avoided in expense of regular channels with doubled length [13]. We assume that the size of a PE is 1.5x1.5 mm or 2.25 mm^2 [14]. Thus, the length of the physical channels and therefore of l_{wire} in mesh is 1.5 mm. In the torus topology the wraparound channels cross the entire array of 10-by-10 PEs and hence are 15 mm long. In the folded torus the channels in the middle of the network cross two PEs and are 3 mm long. The network distance N_{hop} in Eq. (3) is substituted with the mean communication distances calculated from the simulation results. To take into account that the wraparound channels in torus has different length, Eq. (3) is modified to contain two terms that capture the wires energy contribution - one term for the regular channels and one for the wraparound channels. During the experiments information is collected about the utilization of the single hop channels and the wraparound channels. This information is used to weight the number of hops N_{hop} in the two terms.

Figure 3 presents the results for the communication energy cost in our virtual channel network (packet switching) and in the circuit switching network proposed by Wolkotte. The results show that by exploiting the communication locality the average communication energy cost can be reduced by 50% to 70% for the different topologies. For worst case locality traffic, the torus topology reduces the communication energy cost compared to mesh because of its smaller network diameter. But since the traffic locality reduces the communication distances, for local traffic the smaller diameter of the torus is not advantageous. The routing algorithm can influence the communication energy cost by the detour cost - higher detour cost entails more energy for communication. But as we saw, the detour cost is negligibly small, which explains the insignificant influence of the routing algorithm on the communication energy.

The energy cost results for the circuit switching network is reduced compared to the results for the packet switching network. This is due to the smaller energy cost for traversing a router in the circuit-switching network - a clear advantage of this approach. Unfortunately, the circuit switching solution is less flexible - it requires external configuration, cannot handle best effort traffic.

8   Conclusion

In this paper we explored the possibility to provide guaranteed throughput services in a virtual channel network by virtual channel reservation. We test the limits of the virtual channel reservation approach for variety of traffic conditions. The results show that the approach is feasible and can be used for providing throughput guarantees in a 10-by-10 network in worst case traffic conditions. For this network size a mesh topology and four virtual channels per physical channel provide enough connectivity for predictable system operation. Amongst the considered factors that influence the performance limits of the approach, the communication locality has the strongest influence. By exploiting communication locality the network performance is improved and, at a certain extend, made independent of the network size. Furthermore, exploiting the locality the communication energy cost can be reduced by 50% to 70%. The routing algorithms, based respectively on the simple Breath-first search algorithm and the more complex Dijkstra's algorithm, do not show noticeable performance difference. Therefore the Breath-first search is preferred because of its lower computational complexity.

References

1. Dally, W., Towles, B.: Route packets, not wires: on-chip interconnection networks. In: Proceedings of the 38th Conference on Design Automation (DAC'01), ACM Press (2001) 684 – 689
2. Dally, W.: Virtual-channel flow control. IEEE Transactions on Parallel and Distributed Systems, **3** (1992) 194–205
3. Goossens, K., van Meerbergen, J., Peeters, A., Wielage, R.: Networks on silicon: combining best-effort and guaranteed services. In: Proceedings of the Design, Automation and Test in Europe Conference (DATE'02). (2002) 423 – 425
4. Millberg, M., Nilsson, E., Thid, R., Jantsch, A.: Guaranteed bandwidth using looped containers in temporally disjoint networks within the nostrum network on chip. In: Proceedings of the Design, Automation and Test in Europe Conference (DATE'04). Volume 2., IEEE Computer Society (2004) 890 – 895
5. Muttersbach, J., Villiger, T., Kaeslin, H., Felber, N., Fichtner, W.: Globally-asynchronous locally-synchronous architectures to simplify the design of on-chip systems. In: Proceedings of the 12-th Annual IEEE International ASIC/SOC Conference. (1999) 317–321
6. Wolkotte, P., Smit, G., Rauwerda, G.: An energy-efficient reconfigurable circuit switched network-on-chip. In: Proceedings of the 19th IEEE International Parallel and Distributed Processing Symposium (IPDPS'05). (2005) 155–161
7. Felicijan, T., Furber, S.: An asynchronous on-chip network router with quality-of-service (qos) support. In: Proceedings of the IEEE International System-on-Chip Conference (SOCC'04), IEEE Computer Society (2004) 274–277
8. Kavaldjiev, N., Smit, G., Jansen, P.: A virtual channel router for on-chip networks. In: Proceedings of the IEEE International System-on-Chip Conference (SOCC'04), IEEE Computer Society (2004) 289–293
9. Cormen, T., Leiserson, C., Rivest, R., Stein, C.: Introduction to algorithms. 2 edn. MIT Press, Cambridge, Massachusetts (2001)
10. Rauwerda, G., Heysters, P., Smit, G.: Mapping wireless communication algorithms onto a reconfigurable architecture. Journal of Supercomputing **30** (2004) 263–282
11. Wolkotte, P., Smit, G., Smit, L.: Partitioning of a drm receiver. In: Proceedings of the 9th International OFDM-Workshop. (2004) 299–304
12. Wolkotte, P., Smit, G., Kavaldjiev, N., Becker, J., Becker, J.: Energy model of networks-on-chip and a bus. In: Proceedings of the International Symposium on System-on-Chip (SoC'05). (2005) 82–85
13. Dally, W., Towles, B.: Principles and Practices of Interconnection Networks. The Morgan Kaufmann Series in Computer Architecture and Design. Morgan Kaufmann, San Francisco, CA (2003)
14. Heysters, P., Smit, G., Molenkamp, E.: A flexible and energy-efficient coarse-grained reconfigurable architecture for mobile systems. Journal of Supercomputing **26** (2003) 283–308

Efficient Floating-Point Implementation of High-Order (N)LMS Adaptive Filters in FPGA*

Milan Tichy[1], Jan Schier[2], and David Gregg[1]

[1] University of Dublin, Trinity College,
Dept. of Computer Science, Dublin 2, Ireland
{Milan.Tichy, David.Gregg}@cs.tcs.ie
[2] Institute of Information Theory and Automation,
Academy of Sciences of the Czech Republic,
Dept. of Signal Processing, Prague 8, Czech Republic
schier@utia.cas.cz

Abstract. Adaptive filters are used in many applications of digital signal processing. Digital communications and digital video broadcasting are just two examples. This paper deals with floating-point-like implementation of LMS and NLMS algorithms using FPGA hardware. We present an optimized cores for both algorithms, built using logarithmic arithmetic which provides very low cost multiplication and division. The designs are crafted to make efficient use of the pipelined logarithmic addition/subtraction units. The resulting cores can be clocked at more than 80 MHz on the one million gate Xilinx XC2V1000-4 FPGA performing 295 MFLOPS. They can be used to implement adaptive filters of orders 20 to 1022 with a sampling rate exceeding 70 kHz.

1 Motivation

Adaptive filters are widely used in digital signal processing (DSP) for countless applications in telecommunications, digital broadcasting, etc. Adaptive filtering algorithms are often suitable for FPGA implementation, because they involve very regular computations with very fine-grain parallelism capabilities.

A wide variety of adaptive filtering algorithms have been proposed with various trade-offs in the filtering properties (convergence, etc.) and computational requirements. Perhaps the simplest is the *least means squares (LMS)* [1] algorithm, which has very low computational requirements and is thus widely used in resource-constrained embedded systems. The LMS performs large numbers of addition and multiplication operations and requires no other functional units.

---

* This work was supported and funded by the European Commission under the Sixth Framework Programme within the Marie Curie Intra-European Fellowship scheme, Project No. MEIF-CT-2003-502085, and by the Czech Ministry of Education within the Centre of Applied Cybernetics scheme, Project No. 1M0567. The paper reflects only the authors' view and the European Commission and the Czech Ministry of Education are not liable for any use that may be made of the information contained herein.

K. Bertels, J.M.P. Cardoso, and S. Vassiliadis (Eds.): ARC 2006, LNCS 3985, pp. 311–316, 2006.
© Springer-Verlag Berlin Heidelberg 2006

More sophisticated algorithm with better convergence properties is the *normalized LMS (NLMS)* [1] but it requires divison.

The LMS algorithm can be described as

$$\mathbf{w}_k = \mathbf{w}_{k-1} + \mu \mathbf{u}_k \left(d_k - \mathbf{u}_k^{\mathrm{T}} \mathbf{w}_{k-1} \right)$$

where $\mathbf{w}_k$ is the *coefficient vector* of length L (which is referred to as the *filter order*), $\mathbf{u}_k$ is the *excitation signal vector* consisting of the delayed sequence of L input samples, d_k denotes *desired signal* sample, and the index k denotes discrete time. The symbol μ is *step-size* parameter. The NLMS differs from LMS by using (time-variable) power normalized step-size $\bar{\mu} = \frac{\mu}{\delta + \mathbf{u}_k^{\mathrm{T}} \mathbf{u}_k}$ where parameter δ prevents overflow. The time complexity of both algorithms is $\mathcal{O}\left(2N\right)$ multiply-accumulate (MACC) operations.

2   Logarithmic Arithmetic

In order to maintain accuracy of the algorithms in the FPGA implementation, we decided to implement the computations using a floating-point-like logarithmic arithmetic. The parameters of the library are briefly presented in this section.

The *logarithmic number system (LNS)* was chosen in order to reduce resource requirements and to achieve short latency as compared to other floating-point solutions. Logarithmic multiplication and division require only very simple logic. Although addition and subtraction are more complex in LNS, recent advances have made them feasible in small FPGA devices. We use the High Speed Logarithmic Arithmetic (HSLA) cores, described in [2].

Table 1 shows the parameters of our LNS units in comparison to Underwood's [3] highly-optimized IEEE single-precision floating-point (FLP) units. The major disadvantage of LNS arithmetic is the number of Block RAMs used by the ADD/SUB unit for storing the look-up tables. These units are always instantiated in pairs. While the resource requirements for a pair of LNS ADD/SUB pipes is significantly higher than for a pair of the FLP cores, LNS multiplier units need a small fraction of the size of the FLP multipliers. The most common operations in many matrix algorithms are multiplication and addition. When we sum the resources required by two multiply-add pipes, we see that the LNS units require fewer resources (except for Block RAMs). Since many DSP algorithms require division and/or square root the advantage of LNS is evident.

Table 1. Comparison of single-precision floating-point and 32-bit LNS units

	ADD		2-pipe ADD		MUL		DIV		SQRT	
	FLP	LNS	FLP	LNS	FLP	LNS	FLP	LNS	FLP	LNS
Slice Flip Flops	696	—	1,392	1,702	821	35	2,476	35	—	35
4 input LUTs	611	—	1,222	2,135	722	139	2,220	145	—	42
Occupied Slices	496	—	992	1,648	598	83	1,929	82	—	28
Block RAMs	0	—	0	28	0	0	0	0	—	0
MULT18X18s	0	—	0	8	4	0	0	0	—	0

Another important issue is the clock speed and latencies. Underwood's adder can be clocked at up to 165 MHz on the XC2V6000-5 FPGA, with a latency of up to 13 cycles, the multiplier at 125 MHz with a latency of 16 cycles, whereas the divider at 105 MHz, but with a latency of 37 cycles. In contrast, the latencies of the LNS adder, multiplier and divider are 8, 1, and 1 cycles respectively, at clock rates over 80 MHz (add/sub) and 200 MHz (mul, div, and sqrt) on the XC2V6000-4 FPGA. From this we can conclude that if latency is important, the LNS cores can give considerable advantage.

3   Architecture

In this section we briefly present architecture of our cores. The mapping of the (N)LMS algorithm onto the LNS arithmetic units as well as of data structures to Block RAMs is described. The algorithmic description of the NLMS algorithm is given in Fig. 1(a). The top-level architecture of the NLMS core is depicted in Fig. 1(b). The blocks in the diagram correspond to individual steps in the algorithm. The LMS algorithm employs one LNS addition/subtraction (ADD/SUB **A** and **B**—two separate, parallel pipelines) unit and two LNS multipliers (MUL **A**, **B**). The NLMS algorithm uses one LNS divider (DIV **A**). Non-scalar data structures are stored in Virtex-2 Block RAMs.

The $L+1$ most recent input signal samples is stored in the Block RAM referred to as **UX** (vector). To avoid shifting each time a new input signal is sampled, the **UX** vector storage is implemented as a circular buffer. The filter coefficient vector **w** is split into two parts which are stored in separate Block RAMs **WW0** and **WW1**.

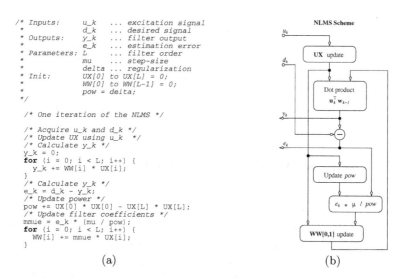

(a)   (b)

Fig. 1. Algorithmic description of the NLMS algorithm (a) and block diagram and data dependencies of top-level architecture of the NLMS core (b)

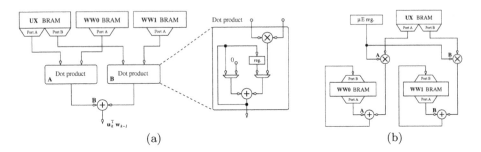

Fig. 2. Architecture schematics of the calculation of the filter output $\mathbf{u}_k^T \mathbf{w}_{k-1}$ (a) and of the update of the coefficient vector $\mathbf{w}$ stored in the Block RAMs $\mathbf{WW[0,1]}$ (b)

First, the filter output $y_k = \mathbf{u}_k^T \mathbf{w}_{k-1}$ is calculated. We use two parallel multiply-accumulate (MACC) pipelines, each operating on one half of the vectors $\mathbf{u}$ and $\mathbf{w}$. The hardware structure of this step is schematically depicted in Fig. 2(a). The "Dot product" module denoted as $\mathbf{A}$ uses the ADD/SUB $\mathbf{A}$ and the MUL $\mathbf{A}$ units; the same is for the module $\mathbf{B}$. The operation is fully pipelined except for the stage of the final summation.

The next step of the algorithms is to compute the estimation error e_k, which requires a single subtraction also performed on the ADD/SUB $\mathbf{B}$ unit. Subsequently, μe_k is calculated using MUL $\mathbf{B}$ unit. This is the only step which is different for the LMS and NLMS algorithms. In the NLMS algorithm, μ is divided by the signal power which is calculated recursively as $p_k = p_{k-1} + u_k u_k - u_{k-L} u_{k-L}$, where $p_0 = \delta$ and values u_k and u_{k-L} are retrieved from the Block RAM $\mathbf{UX}$, rather than calculating $p_k = \delta + \mathbf{u}_k^T \mathbf{u}_k$. The ADD/SUB $\mathbf{A}$, MUL $\mathbf{A}$, and DIV $\mathbf{A}$ units are employed to normalize the step size μ.

Finally, the vector $\mathbf{w}$ is updated. The hardware structure of this stage is shown in Fig. 2(b). The data bandwidth to $\mathbf{w}$ is limited by the number of ports on the Block RAM, so we split the vector $\mathbf{w}$ into two vectors as mentioned above. This allows us to use two independent pipelines to update both halves of $\mathbf{w}$ in parallel as depicted in the figure. This stage utilizes both pipelines of the ADD/SUB unit and the MUL $\mathbf{A}$ and $\mathbf{B}$ units. At the end of this step one (N)LMS iteration is complete and the core is ready to acquire new data samples.

4   Experimental Results and Discussion

We created separate cores for LNS 32- and 19-bit precision. The parameters of all cores are fully configurable. It is possible to vary filter order L for values $20 \leq L \leq 1022$, and filter parameters μ and δ. For the experiments in this section, we fixed the length of the filter as $L = 1000$ to demonstrate performance. In this configuration, a full iteration of the LMS algorithm takes 1083 cycles and performs 4003 logarithmic operations (3.69 ops/cycle). With the corresponding filter parameters, the NLMS algorithm can perform a full iteration in 1088 clock cycles, and performs 4008 logarithmic operations (3.68 ops/cycle).

Table 2. Resource utilization of the 32-bit and 19-bit LNS LMS cores

	LNS 32-bit		LNS 19-bit	
	XC2V1000-4	XC2V6000-4	XC2V1000-4	XC2V6000-4
Slice Flip Flops	4,261 41%	3,922 5%	2,931 28%	2,751 4%
4 input LUTs	4,674 45%	4,683 6%	3,197 31%	3,246 4%
Occupied Slices	4,302 84%	4,006 11%	2,857 55%	2,703 7%
Tbufs	1,280 50%	1,280 7%	192 7%	192 1%
Block RAMs	32 80%	32 22%	10 25%	10 6%
MULT18X18s	8 20%	8 5%	8 20%	8 5%
Clock rate	80.013 MHz	80.090 MHz	80.887 MHz	80.038 MHz
Total Power	731 mW	822 mW	509 mW	618 mW

Table 3. Resource utilization of the 32-bit and 19-bit LNS NLMS cores

	LNS 32-bit		LNS 19-bit	
	XC2V1000-4	XC2V6000-4	XC2V1000-4	XC2V6000-4
Slice Flip Flops	4,408 43%	4,069 6%	3,026 29%	2,846 4%
4 input LUTs	4,834 47%	4,831 7%	3,301 32%	3,369 4%
Occupied Slices	4,473 87%	4,160 12%	2,973 58%	2,820 8%
Tbufs	1,280 50%	1,280 7%	192 7%	192 1%
Block RAMs	32 80%	32 22%	10 25%	10 6%
MULT18X18s	8 20%	8 5%	8 20%	8 5%
Clock rate	80.051 MHz	80.058 MHz	80.652 MHz	80.483 MHz
Total Power	732 mW	839 mW	512 mW	594 mW

Our cores were developed on a Xilinx XC2V6000-4 (6-million gate, speed grade 4) FPGA and on a much smaller Xilinx XC2V1000-4 (1-million gate, speed grade 4) device. Tables 2 and 3 show parameters of developed cores. All designs can be clocked at a little over 80 MHz. This is very close to the maximum clock rate of the LNS cores, indicating that our architecture is not the limiting factor on clock speed. At this clock speed the designs are performing around 295 million logarithmic operations per second which is equivalent to 295 MFLOPS and can operate on signals at a sampling rate of around 73 kHz.

Both LMS and NLMS 32-bit LNS cores occupy only a small fraction (11% and 12%) of the 6-million gate XC2V6000-4 device. On the 1-million gate XC2V1000-4, it uses quite large percentage of available resources—in particular, LMS occupies 84% and NLMS 87% of slices; both employ 80% of Block RAMs. For 19-bit LNS implementations, the figures show that the cores occupy a little bit over a half of available slices and 25% of Block RAMs. It can clearly be seen that for all cores there is a potential for implementing other logic on the same chip using the free resources.

As presented in Section 3, both LMS and NLMS modules use one 2-pipe LNS addition/subtraction unit and two LNS multiplication units to reduce overall latency of the cores. In order to perform normalization, the NLMS module needs a divider. When using the 32-bit LNS divider the NLMS core is only about 4% bigger than the LMS core. Considering the size of two multiply-add pipelines which is 1814 slices for LNS and 2188 for floating-point units, one can argue that there is little difference in slice counts between using either LNS or floating-point. Floating-point might be more convenient because it does not require Block RAMs, and there is no need to convert values to LNS. Nevertheless, the advantages are minor because Block RAMs are not usually a limiting resource for LNS in current FPGAs and the conversions [4] to/from LNS can be done easily.

However, when implementing NLMS, the need for a divider tips the balance decidedly in the favour of log arithmetic, because the LNS divider is both tiny and extremely fast. Summing the resources required by two multiply-add pipes and a divider we find that the floating-point units alone would occupy around 80% (4117 of 5120 slices) of the XC2V1000 device whereas the LNS units use only 37% (1896 of 5120 slices) of the same chip. These facts clearly demonstrate the advantages of using logarithmic arithmetic instead of standard floating-point arithmetic, particularly in applications where division or square root operations are required, and even for such simple algorithms as (N)LMS.

5   Conclusions and Future Work

This paper describes work-in-progress on using the unique features of LNS arithmetic to create highly-optimized implementations of adaptive filtering algorithms in FPGAs. We show that although LNS addition is resource expensive, the low resource requirements of LNS multiplication offsets this cost. We describe implementations of two algorithms: LMS and NLMS. NLMS has significantly better adaptive properties, but may be expensive to implement because it requires a divider. We present IP cores for both algorithms that achieve clock speeds of over 80 MHz on an XC2V1000-4 (1-million gate, speed grade 4) device, and perform around 295 MFLOPS. Our log implementation of NLMS requires only slightly more (84% versus 80%) occupied slices than our LMS implementation, due to the low cost of LNS division unit. The cores can be used to implement adaptive filters of orders 20 to 1022 with a sampling rate exceeding 70 kHz.

Our future work will concentrate on two areas: implementation of more sophisticated algorithms with greater complexity and resource requirements; and better comparisons with other number representations, such as floating-point.

References

1. Haykin, S.: Adaptive Filter Theory. 4th edn. Prentice Hall (2002)
2. Matousek, R., Tichy, M., Pohl, Z., Kadlec, J., Softley, C., Coleman, N.: Logarithmic number system and floating-point arithmetics on FPGA. In: 12th Int. Conference on FPL and Applications. Volume 2438., Springer-Verlag (2002) 627–636
3. Underwood, K.: FPGAs vs. CPUs: Trends in peak floating-point performance. In: ACM SIGDA 12th Int. Symp. on FPGA. (2004) 171–179
4. Pohl, Z., Matousek, R., Kadlec, J., Tichy, M., Licko, M.: Lattice adaptive filter implementation for FPGA. In: ACM SIGDA 11th Int. Symp. on FPGA. (2003) 246

A Reconfigurable Architecture for MIMO Square Root Decoder

Hongzhi Wang, Pierre Leray, and Jacques Palicot

IETR/Supelec
Campus de Rennes
Av. de la Boulais, BP 81127
35511 Cesson-sevigne, France
{hongzhi.wang, pierre.leray, jacques.palicot}@supelec.fr

Abstract. An implementation of reconfigurable architecture for MIMO V-BLAST (Vertical Bell Laboratories Layered Space-Time) detection based on the square root algorithm is proposed in this paper. This reconfigurable square root decoder supports MIMO system with various number of antennas, different throughputs and different signal constellations. The decoder architecture is based on various number of operators CORDIC (COordinate Rotation DIgital Computer). The system prototype of the decoder reaches 600Mbit/s data rate on an Xilinx Virtex-II FPGA for a 2 antennas system with a QPSK signal constellation.

1 Introduction

Multiple-Input Multiple-Output (MIMO) is an attractive technology for future wireless systems because of their huge bandwidth capacity. It is well known that an extraordinary spectral efficiency can be achieved in MIMO system [1]. The MIMO technology is a promising technology to increase performance in future wireless system. For example, it will be adopted in the next phase of the 3GPP (3rd Generation Partnership Project) standards in order to further increase the HSDPA (High-Speed Downlink Packet Access) system capacity and enhance the quality of Internet and multimedia services. The MIMO system is also the candidate to answer the high performance expected in 4G broadband wireless for future mobile services [2]. In order to be used in these wireless standards, future MIMO systems will need to support multiple air-interfaces and modulation formats. These are the reasons for the recent interest in reconfigurable architectures to MIMO system.

In various MIMO detection algorithms, the complexity of the optimal ML (maximum likelihood) detector is too huge to be implemented for a system with a large number of antennas and a large signal constellation size. The sphere detector has more complexity than the V-BLAST square root detector [5]. The linear detector like MMSE (Minimum Mean Squared Error) and ZF (Zero-Forcing) is poor in BER (bit error rate) performance. Hence the square root detector is an attractive solution to obtain a high performance with reasonable complexity.

K. Bertels, J.M.P. Cardoso, and S. Vassiliadis (Eds.): ARC 2006, LNCS 3985, pp. 317–322, 2006.

DSP (Digital Signal Processing) processors and ASIC (Application-Specific Integrated Circuit) are the traditional architecture solutions for MIMO wireless system. But DSP processors cannot achieve high performance on throughput in highly parallel 3G/4G applications. ASIC implementations are the most computationally efficient system, but its implementations are not flexible enough to the wide diversity of the future systems. FPGAs are widely used in signal processing because of their reconfigurability and support of parallelism. An implementation of square root algorithm is realized by Z.Guo in [5], which is not adaptable to different requirements of the future system. We will propose here a FPGA implementation of the square root algorithm for V-BLAST detection which is based on various number of operators CORDIC. We will show that this square root detector is reconfigurable to be adapted to a various number of antennas, different signal constellations and throughputs.

In this paper we will first overview the MIMO detection techniques in Section 2. The square root algorithm is briefly described in section 3. The reconfigurable architecture for square root decoder is detailed in section 4. The experimental results and performance analysis are provided in Section 5. The conclusions will be stated in section 6.

2   Overview of MIMO Detection

The multiple antennas system with M transmits antennas and $N \geq M$ receive antennas is modeled in baseband by following relation:

$$r = Hs + v \, . \tag{1}$$

In the relation(1), $s = [s_1, s_2, \ldots, s_M]^T$ is the transmitted symbol vector, in which each component s_i is independently drawn from a complex constellation. The total transmit power is normalized to unity. The vector $r = [r_1, r_2, \ldots, r_N]^T$ is the received symbol vector and $v = [v_1, v_2, \ldots, v_N]^T$ is an independently identically distributed (i.i.d) complex zero-mean Gaussian noise vector with variance σ^2 per dimension. The channel matrix H is considered in a block-fading and rich-scattering channel model[1]. The elements h_{ij} represent complex channel gain between the j-th transmit antenna and the i-th receive antenna. Each channel gain is assumed to be i.i.d complex zero-mean Gaussian with unit variance. The channel matrix is assumed to be perfectly known to the receiver in this paper.

3   Decoding Algorithm

The V-BLAST square root algorithm is proposed in [4], which successfully avoids the repeated pseudo-inverse and matrix inverse computations by using unitary transformations. The computational cost is reduced effectively from $O(M^4)$ to $O(M^3)$ without degradation in BER performance, where M is the number of transmit antennas. The whole algorithm is described in the following steps:

A) Compute $P^{1/2}$ and Q_a : for $i= 1, 2,\ldots,N$:

$$
\begin{bmatrix} 1 & H_i^{1\times M} P_{i-1}^{1/2M\times M} \\ 0^{M\times 1} & P_{i-1}^{1/2M\times M} \\ -e_i^{N\times 1} & Q_{i-1}^{N\times M} \end{bmatrix} \Theta_i = \begin{bmatrix} \times & 0^{1\times M} \\ \times & P_i^{1/2M\times M} \\ \times & Q_i^{N\times M} \end{bmatrix} \tag{2}
$$

In this relation, $P_0^{1/2} = \beta\, I$, $Q_0 = 0^{N\times M}$, e_i is the i-th unit vector of dimension N, Θ_i is any unitary transformation that block lower triangularizes the pre-array and $\times$ is the result ignored. After N steps, we obtain: $P^{1/2} = P_N^{1/2}$ and $Q_\alpha = Q_N$.

B) Determine the optimal ordering and nulling vectors: for $i=M, M\text{-}1,\ldots,1$:

B_1)Find the minimum length row of $P^{1/2}$ and permute it to be the last (Mth) row. Permute s accordingly.

B_2) Find a unitary Σ to block upper triangularize $P^{1/2}$:

$$
P_i^{1/2}\Sigma_i = \begin{bmatrix} P_{i-1}^{1/2} & \times^{i-1\times 1} \\ 0 & p_i \end{bmatrix} \tag{3}
$$

B_3)Update Q_a to $Q_a\Sigma_i$, the nulling vector for the i-th signal is given by

$$
w_i = p_i q_{\alpha,i}^* \tag{4}
$$

where $q_{\alpha,i}^*$ is the i-th column of $Q_a{}^*$.

B_4)Compute $y_i = w_i r$, and then the i-th transmitted signal in s is detected as the closest point in the signal constellation.

B_5) Cancel the interferences of the detected signal in the remaining received signal s:

$$
r = r - s_i(H)_i \tag{5}
$$

B_6) Go back to the step B_1, but now with $P_{i-1}^{1/2}$ and $Q_{\alpha,i-1}$ (the first i-1 columns of Q_a).

4   Architecture

The architecture of the MIMO square root decoder is illustrated in figure 1. It consists of 6 processing modules. The values of matrix channel H and messages r are assumed to have been pre-calculated. The three first modules(M_1,M_2,M_3) use unitary transformations to compute $P^{1/2}$(Step A), Q_a(Step A), p_i(Step B_2) and $q_{a,i}^*$(Step B_3) by employing various numbers of CORDIC. The following module(M_4) calculates the optimal ordering and nulling vectors w_i. Module M_5 compute the transmitted symbol vector.The last module(M_6) performs interferences cancellation.

The three unitary transformation modules have the similar architecture, as shown in figure 2. In these modules, unitary transformations are used instead of the conventional QR triangular array which employs too high number of processors [6]. Unitary transformations are performed by a sequence of numerically

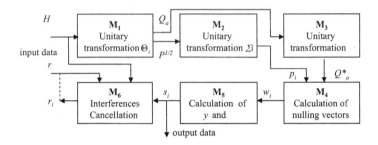

Fig. 1. Block diagram of square root decoder architecture

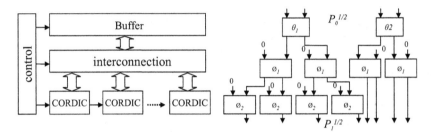

Fig. 2. Block diagram of unitary transformation module and calculation of $P_1^{1/2}$(first iteration) in the module M_1

stable complex Givens rotations which is suitable for implementation because the hardware elementary is based on CORDIC in which only shifters and adder are involved [3]. It reduces the computational complexity significantly. In the module M_1, the elements of equation (2) are passed by column to operator CORDIC which performes Givens rotations. Then the products are stocked in the buffer waiting to be passed to operator CORDIC again. This complets an iteration. After N iterations, the module output becomes $P^{1/2}$ and Q_a.

We propose a structure in which the number of CORDIC is adaptable depending on the throughput required and the number of antennas. A total parallel structure may lead to a waste of computational capabilities, since the channel data changes slower than the received symbol data. Therefore several operators CORDIC are used iteratively to optimize the resources. We take an example, the calculation of $P^{1/2}$(first iteration), to show how to use different number of operators CORDIC. Ten CORDIC operations required are illusted in figure 2. The angles(θ_1, θ_2, ϕ_1, ϕ_2) for the CORDIC are given by the elements of equation(2).

We compare here two architecture A_1(2 parallel CORDIC) and A_2(4 parallel CORDIC). The organization of calculations is showed in the figure 3. Five cycles are required to complete the computation by A_1. But the same computation can be performed in three cycles by A_2. The throughput is increased 1.6 times. In contrary, A_2 takes more surface of FPGA architecture than A_1. The detecting throughput can be improved further by increasing the number of CORDIC. On the other hand, if the throughput requirement is not crucial, the number of CORDIC can be decreased by a single CORDIC. Because there is no place to explain the internal details of CORDIC, the reader can see the reference [3].

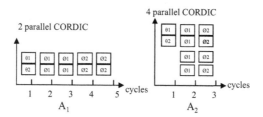

Fig. 3. Different number of parallel CORDIC for different throughput

The throughput of square root decoder for a MIMO system with M transmit and N receive antennas is determined as:

$$Throughput = (Freq \times N \times b) \times (\frac{NC_{used}}{NC_{required}}) \tag{6}$$

In the equation(6), *Freq* represents the clock frequency, b is the bit per symbol, NC_{used} is the number of parallel CORDIC used, $NC_{required}=f(M,N)$ is the number of CORDIC required which depends on the number of transmit and receive antennas.

The last three modules(M_4,M_5,M_6) are based on PE(Processor Elementary). Every PE unit consists of a multiplier-accumulation unit, a adder-subtractor and a buffer. The module can improve the throughput by paralleling several modules.

5   Experimental Results

The decoder for 2 antennas system with QPSK signal constellation is designed in VHDL, simulated with Modelsim. The decoder is implemented and tested on a Virtex-II from Xilinx. Table 1 shows synthesis results of different architectures with various number of CORDIC. It can operate at 148.6 MHz when prototyped on Virtex-II from Xilinx.

Table 1. Synthesis results of MIMO square root decoder

Target FPGA Xilinx Virtex	Number of slices	Max.Freq (MHz)	Throughput (Mbits/s)
50 CORDIC	29036	148.6	600
16 CORDIC	14380	148.6	600
8 CORDIC	9936	148.6	300

The first architecture have a total parallel structure which wastes some operators to compute the same channel matrix. The optimal number of CORDIC for this application is 16. When the number of CORDIC is reduced to 8, the throughput is reduced 2 times smaller than the second one. But the number of slices in FPGA architecture is not reduced proportionally to number of CORDIC, because the size of controller becomes important, when the number of parallel operators CORDIC is decreased. The throughput obtained is widely superior to the requirements of current standards. For instant, the emerging IEEE 802.11n standard requires a data rate of 150 Mbits/s. In that case the number of operator CORDIC can be still reduced.

6   Conclusion and Future Work

A reconfigurable MIMO square root decoder has been designed and implemented. It is attractive for the future wireless applications, supporting different antenna sizes, different modulation and throughputs. Comparing with the architecture of GUO, this decoder has less performance on throughput, but it is more adaptable for the different requirements by using different number of operators CORDIC. The operator CORDIC can be also used like a common operator for the SDR applications [7]. The architectures of all modules are defined synthesized individually by Xilinx software tool [8]. Future works will carry on managing dynamic reconfiguration of this decoder.

References

1. G. J. Foshini: Layered space-time architecture for wireless communication in a fading environment when using multi-element antennas. Bell Labs Technical Journal, pages 41-57, Autumn 1996.
2. J. Hu, W.Lu: Open wireless architecture - the core to 4G mobile communications, Communication Technology Proceedings. ICCT 2003, Volume: 2 , 9-11 April 2003 pp:1337 - 1342 vol.2
3. R.Andraka: A Survey of CORDIC Algorithms for FPGAs, FPGA '98. Proceedings of the 1998 ACM/SIGDA sixth international symposium on Field programmable gate arrays, Feb. 22-24, 1998, Monterey, CA. pp191-2000.
4. B. Hassibi: An efficient square-root algorithm for BLAST, http://mars.bell-labs.com/.
5. Z. Guo and P. Nilsson: A VLSI implementation of MIMO detection for future wireless communications,in Proc. IEEE PIMRC'03, vol. 3, 2003, pp. 2852-2856.
6. C. M. Rader: VLSI Systolic Arrays for daptive Nulling, IEEE Sig. Proc. Mag,Vol. 13, No. 4, pp. 29-49, 1996.
7. J. Palicot, C. Roland: FFT : A basic function for a reconfigurable receiver, in ICT february 2003, Papeete, Tahiti.
8. http://www.xilinx.com/support/mysupport.htm.

Time-Memory Trade-Off Attack on FPGA Platforms: UNIX Password Cracking

Nele Mentens, Lejla Batina, Bart Preneel, and Ingrid Verbauwhede[*]

Katholieke Universiteit Leuven, ESAT/SCD-COSIC
Kasteelpark Arenberg 10
B-3001 Leuven-Heverlee, Belgium
{Nele.Mentens, Lejla.Batina, Bart.Preneel,
Ingrid.Verbauwhede}@esat.kuleuven.ac.be

Abstract. This paper presents a hardware architecture for UNIX password cracking using Hellman's time-memory trade-off; it is the first hardware design for a key search machine based on the rainbow variant proposed by Oechslin. The implementation target is the Berkeley BEE2 FPGA platform which can run at 400 million password calculations/second. Our design targets passwords of length 48 bits (out of 56). This means that with one BEE2 module the precomputation for one salt takes about 8 days, resulting in a storage of 56 Gigabyte. For the precomputation of all salts in one year we would need 92 BEE2 modules. Recovering an individual password requires a few minutes on a Virtex-4 FPGA.

Keywords: cryptanalysis, hash-functions, time-memory trade-off, exhaustive key search, rainbow table, FPGA implementation.

1 Introduction

Symmetric-key cryptography deals with algorithms that use a secret key to provide confidentiality, identification and data authentication. A basic problem in symmetric-key cryptology is the computation of preimages or inversion of one-way functions. For example, a brute-force attack on a block cipher in a known plaintext attack considers the mapping of the key to the ciphertext, which should be a one-way function. If no shortcut method is known, and the function has an n-bit result, there are two straightforward methods: first one can perform an exhaustive search over an average of 2^{n-1} values until the target is reached. A second solution is to precompute and store 2^n input and output pairs in a table (for a random function this will not result in different values – if the input space is large enough, the coupon collector's formula tells us that a space of about $n \cdot 2^n$ elements needs to be searched). If one then needs to invert a particular value, one just looks up the preimage in the table, so inverting requires only a single table lookup.

---

[*] Nele Mentens, Lejla Batina, Bart Preneel and Ingrid Verbauwhede are funded by FWO projects (G.0450.04, G.0141.03). This work is also supported by EU IST FP6 projects SCARD and ECRYPT and GOA Ambiorix 2005/11.

K. Bertels, J.M.P. Cardoso, and S. Vassiliadis (Eds.): ARC 2006, LNCS 3985, pp. 323–334, 2006.

The time-memory trade-off attack invented by Hellman in 1980 [7] proposes a solution that lies in between the two solutions. The precomputation time is still on the order of 2^n, but the memory complexity is $2^{2n/3}$ and the inversion of a single value requires only $2^{2n/3}$ function evaluations. In [6] Fiat and Naor propose a more general and rigorous variant at the cost of extra workload and/or memory. Kusuda and Matsumoto generalize the Hellman method in [8]; they derive stricter bounds on the success probability and give relationships between the memory complexity, processing complexity and success probability. Note that for cryptanalyzing stream ciphers more complex time/memory/data trade-offs are known – see for example Biryukov and Shamir [4].

Hellman's basic idea was improved in 1982 by Rivest who suggested to use distinguished points in order to reduce the number of memory accesses. This idea was elaborated independently by Borst *et al.* [5] and Stern [13]. The first FPGA design of this method was proposed by Quisquater *et al.* [12] for a 40-bit DES variant; they also presented cost estimations for the cryptanalysis of a full DES (with 56 bits). A detailed analysis for this platform was given in [15]. A more generic full cost analysis of the time-memory trade-off with and without distinguished points has been provided by Wiener in [16].

At Crypto 2003, Oechslin [10] suggested to use so-called rainbow tables for precomputations; this method combines the advantage of the distinguished point approach (reduced number of memory accesses) with the higher success probability and easier analysis of Hellman's original method. He has developed further details in [11].

In this paper we propose an FPGA platform for cryptanalysis of the UNIX password hashing scheme [9] using the rainbow table approach. The implementation target is an existing FPGA platform called BEE2 (Berkeley Emulation Engine 2) [1]. The paper is organized as follows. Section 2 provides the theoretical background and some definitions as well as specifics related to our case. In Sect. 3 the details of the proposed FPGA implementation are described together with future improvements. More future work is depicted in Sect. 4 and Sect. 5 concludes the paper.

2   Theoretical Background

In this section we give some definitions that are used in the remainder of the paper.

2.1   Time-Memory Trade-Off

Let $E : \{0,1\}^n \times \{0,1\}^k \longrightarrow \{0,1\}^n$ be a block cipher with block length n and key length k. We will consider DES with $n = 64$ and $k = 56$, or rather a variant of DES. The encryption is denoted as: $C = E_K(P)$ where C, K and P are respectively ciphertext, key and plaintext. For a fixed and known plaintext P, the mapping $E_K(P)$ is a one-way function from the key to the ciphertext. For a time-memory trade-off two functions are usually defined. The first one is $g : \{0,1\}^{64} \longrightarrow \{0,1\}^{56}$ that maps a ciphertext to a k-bit string, hence we can write:

$$g(C) = g(C_1, C_2, \ldots, C_{64}) = (X_1, X_2, \ldots, X_{56}) \,. \tag{1}$$

This function is usually called a mask function or a reduction function. There are many possibilities to define this function; one often proposes to drop 8 bits and to permute the other 56 ones, which results in more than 2^{280} choices. Other options that are more suitable for hardware implementations include bit swaps, xor functions, etc. We discuss these options in more detail in Sect. 3.1. Second, we define a function $f : \{0,1\}^{56} \longrightarrow \{0,1\}^{56}$ that maps the key space to itself:

$$f(K) = g(E_K(P)) = g(C_1, C_2, \ldots, C_{64}) = g(C), \forall K \in \{0,1\}^{56} \,. \tag{2}$$

This construction originates from Hellman [7]; it was generalized by Kusuda and Matsumoto in [8]. By succession of ciphertexts with keys a chain can be constructed:

$$K_i \xrightarrow{E_{K_i}(P)} C_i \xrightarrow{g(C_i)} K_{i+1} \,,$$

which can be written as a chain of keys

$$K_i \xrightarrow{f} K_{i+1} \xrightarrow{f} K_{i+2} \,.$$

In the original algorithm of Hellman m chains of length t are created; one stores only the first and the last element of each chain in a table. Given a ciphertext C (with a known plaintext) one can try to find a key that was used to generate C in the following way. Chains (up to some fixed length t) are searched until a key that matches the last key of some chain is found. Using the first key, the chain can be reconstructed and the right key is the one just before C. The typical parameter sizes for a k-bit key are $t = m = 2^{k/3}$. If one uses $r = 2^{k/3}$ tables, the total precomputation time is 2^k evaluations of f and one needs to store $2^{2k/3}$ values of $2k$ bits. Recovering a single key requires $2^{2k/3}$ evaluations of f. The success probability of this method depends on the number of repeated elements in the chains; repetitions occur due to merging chains and due to chains that enter a loop. For the typical parameter sizes $t = m = r = 2^{k/3}$, with a precomputation complexity of 2^k, the success probability is around 0.55 [7].

The approach of distinguished points avoids a table lookup after every function computation, since an efficient implementation of a lookup in a large table would be too expensive. A distinguished point is a key that has a property that is easy to identify (for example the 20 most significant bits are zero); this means that one only needs to check after each iteration whether or not a value is a distinguished point. One creates chains starting and ending with a distinguished point: this also allows to reduce the storage per chain and to check for some merged chains (but throwing away such chains implies that one needs to increase the precomputation time). However, in the distinguished point variant, chains are of unequal length and will have a larger probability to merge (reducing the success probability of the attack).

The rainbow tables approach proposed by Oechslin [10] uses a different function g in every iteration. More precisely, rainbow chains have a fixed length t and use t different mask functions inside one chain: $g_1, \ldots, g_t$. In order to recover a key one first starts in the one but last column (1 application of g_t); next one starts in the second but last column and one applies g_{t-1} and g_t. In the final iteration one applies g_1 through g_t; the total number of iterations is $\frac{t(t-1)}{2}$. This also allows to reduce the memory accesses, but at the same time it reduces the probability of merging chains; indeed, two chains will only merge if the two merging points are at the same position in a chain. Because of the reduced merge probability, rainbow tables can be much larger; typically only a few tables are needed [11]. The method has been implemented in software (a.o. for Windows passwords), but we are not aware of any hardware implementations. This article explores some options for hardware implementations of rainbow chains applied to the UNIX password system.

2.2   UNIX Password Hashing

Here we consider the application of the time-memory trade-off to the UNIX password system. In this case, 25 DES operations are performed where the ciphertext of one DES is used as the plaintext of the next DES. The plaintext of the first DES consists of all zeros and the key to all DES functions is the user password consisting of 8 ASCII characters. The ciphertext of the last DES block is the hash-value of the password. To increase the security of the UNIX password system, these 25 DES functions are modified based on a 12-bit salt; this salt defines an extra permutation in the expansion function in each round. The salt is a public value that is allocated to the user when she registers to the system; it is stored together with the hash value. The salt is often derived from the system clock. The black-box representation of this scheme is shown in Fig. 1. Assuming password characters consisting of capitals, small letters, numbers and two special characters " \ " and "." every character contains only 6 bits of information which results in a key space of 48 bits. The password salting results in 2^{12} extra variations, hence the time-memory trade-off precomputation needs to be repeated for all salts: both the storage and the precomputation time increase with a factor 4096, but a single password can still be recovered with $2^{48 \cdot 2/3} = 2^{32}$ function evaluations. Of course one can also choose to mount the attack for a subset of salts.

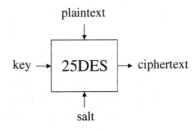

Fig. 1. Black-box of one UNIX password hashing

2.3   Bounds and Parameters

We now introduce some notation. Let t be the length of the chains, let m denote the number of chains in each table and r the number of tables. These parameters can be varied in order to tune the success rate as the time-memory trade-off is a probabilistic method. The schematics of one chain and the total structure are shown in Fig. 2 and Fig. 3. The bounds on the memory M (used to store the precomputation tables) and the time T (required to find the password starting from the hash) are as follows:

$$M = m \cdot r \cdot m_0$$
$$T = t \cdot r \cdot t_0$$

Here, m_0 is the amount of memory required to store each chain *i.e.* its start and end point. In our case m_0 is 14 bytes. Likewise, t_0 is the time in which one password hash is generated.

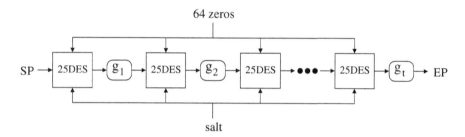

Fig. 2. Schematics of one rainbow chain. The inputs and outputs of one hash function are depicted in Fig. 1. SP = start point, EP = end point.

The success rate of a single rainbow table can be estimated as follows [10]:

$$P = 1 - \prod_{i=1}^{t} (1 - \frac{m_i}{N}),$$

where

$$m_1 = m, \quad m_{n+1} = N(1 - e^{-\frac{m_n}{N}}).$$

In Fig. 4 the success rate is shown as a function of the length of the chains t. It is obvious that the probability grows fast at the beginning with the length of the chains. After a length of around $102\,400$ ($\approx 2^{16.64}$) the probability is almost stagnating.

By taking the direct approach from the original paper of Hellman we derived the following lower bound. By approximating $mt^2 \approx N$ the lower bound can be estimated to be 0.75, which is similar to the result of Standaert *et al.* [15]:

$$P \geq \frac{mt}{N}\left[1 - \frac{mt^2}{4N} + \frac{(mt^2)^2}{18N} - \frac{(mt^2)^3}{96N} + \frac{(mt^2)^4}{600N} - \cdots\right] \qquad (3)$$

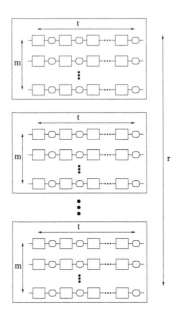

Fig. 3. Schematics and parameters of the complete structure

The success rate for multiple tables can be calculated from

$$P \geq 1 - (1 - P_{one\,table})^r.\qquad(4)$$

Here we consider only one rainbow table, which can be justified by the result of Oechslin. In his work the best cryptanalysis results were achieved using only five tables.

3   Hardware Implementation Options and Results

We now elaborate on the implementation of the precomputation in hardware. We describe the FPGA design and give performance estimates.

3.1   Our FPGA Solution

The first crucial choice is related to the mask functions. The mask function is actually a reduction function that maps a ciphertext to a key. There exist various options among which we mention:

    permutations *i.e.* S-boxes
 − xor functions
    bit swaps

As we are interested in hardware implementations, it is important to choose mask functions with a low hardware complexity. From this point of view, all

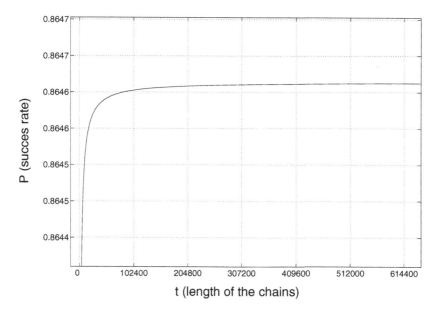

Fig. 4. Success rate as a function of the length of the chains

three suggested options are suitable. However, for rainbow tables a chain contains many different mask functions which implies that the overhead in control logic should also be minimized. With respect to this, xor-ing with a register containing a variable value is the best solution. Moreover, in our case permutations may not even offer enough choices for different masks. Since the complexity of our key space is 2^{48} we chose to throw away the last 16 bits and to xor with a 48-bit counter. In this way, we can use just one generic mask function which is varied by different states of the counter resulting in a total of 2^{48} different mask functions. Finally, the 48-bit output of the xor function passes through some logic gates to obtain a 56-bit result which is a valid 56-bit key (containing only capitals, small letters, numbers and the characters " \" and ".").

Fig. 5 depicts the architecture of our design. To construct a chain, an alternating sequence of block cipher computations and mask functions is applied. This is done using a feedback loop.

The generation of start points is implemented in hardware in order to contribute to a more efficient precomputation. More precisely, loading start points of chains from outside of the FPGA would create an overhead in communication time. Namely, because of pipelining, the design has to deal with many start points at the same time. For this reason, we implemented a counter to generate the start points. The value of the counter in the mask functions, padded with 8 zeros, can be re-used for this purpose.

Next a buffer design needs to be developed to take into account the variable output rate of the rainbow algorithm. The start point-end point pairs are stored in a hash table with the end point as the index. After sorting the table entries,

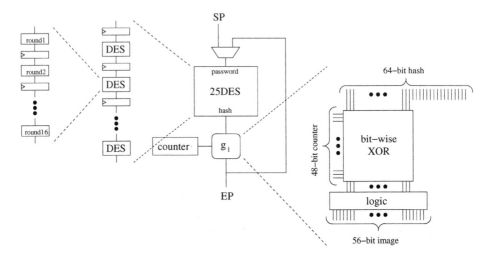

Fig. 5. Pipelined architecture for performing the rainbow chains

the on-line part has to be performed. It looks up the values output by the FPGA until the targeted key is found. Recovering an individual password in a rainbow chain takes $\frac{t(t-1)}{2}$ function evaluations. This part can be done in software or, to make it faster, on an FPGA. Using a XC4VLX200 Virtex-4, a non-pipelined version of the Unix password system can find the key in less than an hour. A pipelined key search on this FPGA can be done in a few minutes.

There are two cases when finding an end point does not lead to the correct key; these are usually referred to as false alarms. First, the key may be a part of a chain with the same end point but which is not in the table. The second false alarm situation occurs when a key is in a chain which merges with another chain in the table. For rainbow chains, the merging will occur only if the collision happens at the same position in two chains. For chains of length t, the probability that a collision is a merge is only $\frac{1}{t}$. As noted in [10], it is possible to generate tables without any merging. However, this solves only some false alarm situations and it remains a problem to create tables that cover the key space as much as possible.

3.2   Hardware Precomputation Platform and Results

We chose an existing platform to perform the precomputation part: the Berkeley Emulation Engine 2 (BEE2) [1]. One BEE2 module consists of 5 Xilinx Virtex-2Pro70 FPGAs of which 4 can be used to implement digital circuits and one to take care of global routing and control logic. The floorplan of one module is depicted in Fig. 6. The Virtex-2Pro70 is a high performance FPGA which comes at a cost of approximately US$ 1500. The BEE2 platform is designed for high-speed applications with a communication bandwidth up to 360 Gbit/s. Every module contains a 20 GB DDR-RAM and a 10 Gbit/s ethernet connector.

However, our application only requires a 14-byte value to be written in the RAM after every 2^{16} hash operations, which comes down to a write speed of 85 449 bytes/s for one BEE2 module. This is achievable by a hard disk supplemented with 500 MB or 1 GB of RAM. Furthermore, for recovering one key, we need approximately 2^{32} 7-byte table lookups in a 56 GB memory. Assuming it takes 2 minutes to perform the on-line computations, this comes down to 36 million read operations per second at a bandwidth to the memory of 250 MB/s. This means that for the on-line part it is also not required to have a bandwidth of 360 Gbit/s nor a 20 GB RAM. Hence, a dedicated design with a slower memory access rate could reduce the full cost.

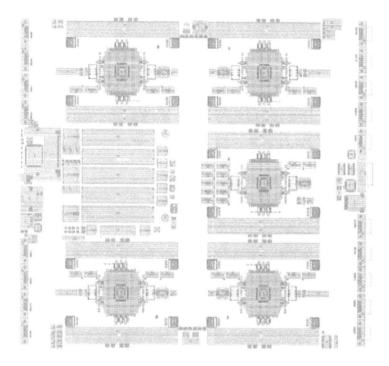

Fig. 6. Floorplan of one BEE2 module

Synthesis results show that one precomputation unit uses almost 200% of the slices of a Virtex-2Pro70 (33 088 slices). That is why we use one BEE2 module to implement two precomputation units. Each pipelined architecture in Fig. 5 can compute 200 million password hashes per second at a frequency of 200 MHz. Targeting 48-bit passwords using one BEE2 module, this would mean a precomputation time of 8 days. The upper bound on the storage for one salt is $2^{32} \times$ 14 Bytes, resulting in 56 GB of memory. To make the precomputation for all salts in one year, we need 92 BEE2 modules. Figures 7 and 8 depict the precomputation time as a function of the number of BEE2 modules used in parallel.

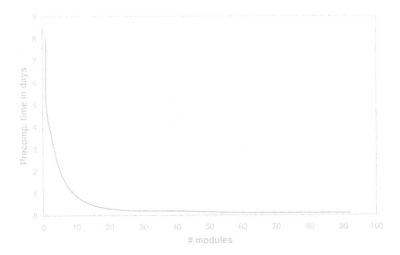

Fig. 7. Precomputation time for one salt as a function of the number of BEE2 modules

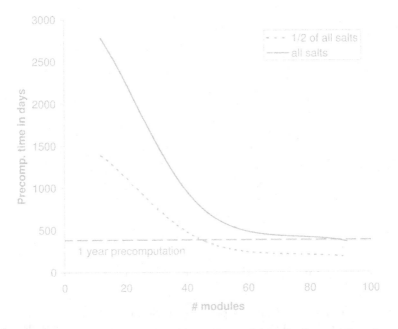

Fig. 8. Precomputation time for half of the salts and for all salts as a function of the number of BEE2 modules

Table 1 compares our results with other hardware as well as software solutions. The only known hardware solution is [12] which attacked one 40-bit DES while our target was 25 56-bit DES blocks. The other are software options dedicated to cracking 56-bit DES.

Table 1. Comparison of implementation results for symmetric key cryptanalysis

	platform	algorithm	speed (enc/s)
[2]	64-bit Alpha computer	56-bit DES	2 M
[12]	Virtex1000	40-bit DES	66 M
[10]	P4, 1.5 GHz, 500 MB RAM	56-bit DES	0.7 M
this work	BEE2	25 x 56-bit modified DES	400 M

4   Future Work

The results described in this paper can be further optimized by considering the work of Biryukov *et al.* [3], in which time-memory-data trade-off attacks show an improvement of a factor 2 to 3.

Another standard for computing UNIX password hashes is based on the MD5 algorithm [14]. The feasibility of attacking these kinds of UNIX password systems should be investigated.

5   Conclusions

In this paper we presented an FPGA architecture for cracking UNIX passwords using the rainbow tables approach from Oechslin. The attack targets passwords consisting of capitals, small letters, numbers and a few special characters, *i.e.* 48-bit passwords. The implementation platform consists of BEE2 modules developed at UC Berkeley. We give the implementation results for one BEE2 module precomputing the rainbow tables for one salt. Furthermore, we estimate the number of modules needed for the precomputation of all salts in one year.

References

1. University of California Berkeley Wireless Research Center. Bee home page. http://bwrc.eecs.berkeley.edu/Research/BEE/.
2. E. Biham. A fast new DES implementation in software. In E. Biham, editor, *Proceedings of 4th International Workshop on Fast Software Encryption Workshop (FSE)*, number 1267 in Lecture Notes in Computer Science. Springer-Verlag, 1997.
3. A. Biryukov, S. Mukhopadhyay, and P. Sarkar. Improved time-memory trade-offs with multiple data. In B. Preneel and S. Tavares, editors, *Proceedings of the 12th Annual Workshop on Selected Areas in Cryptography*, Lecture Notes in Computer Science, page 19 pages. Springer, 2005.
4. A. Biryukov and A. Shamir. Cryptanalytic time/memory/data tradeoffs for stream ciphers. In Tatsuaki Okamoto, editor, *Advances in Cryptology: Proceedings of ASIACRYPT*, volume 1976 of *Lecture Notes in Computer Science*, pages 1–13. Springer, 2000.
5. J. Borst, B. Preneel, and J. Vandewalle. On the memory trade-off between exhaustive key-search and table precomputation. In *Proceedings of the 19th Symposium on Information Theory in the Benelux*, pages 111–118. Werkgemeenschap voor Informatie- en Communicatietheorie, Enschede, The Netherlands, 1998.

6. A. Fiat and M. Naor. Rigorous time/space tradeoffs for inverting functions. In *Proceedings of the 23rd Annual ACM Symposium on Theory of Computing*, pages 534–541, 1991.

7. M. Hellman. A cryptanalytic time-memory trade-off. *IEEE Transactions on Information Theory*, 26:401–406, 1980.

8. K. Kusuda and T. Matsumoto. Optimization of time-memory trade-off cryptanalysis and its application to DES, FEAL-32 and Skipjack. *IEICE Transcations on Fundamentals of Electronics, Communications and Computer Science*, E-79A:35–48, 1996.

9. A. J. Menezes, P. C. van Oorschot, and S. A. Vanstone. *Handbook of Applied Cryptography*. CRC Press, 1997.

10. P. Oechslin. Making a faster cryptanalytic time-memory trade-off. In D. Boneh, editor, *Advances in Cryptology: Proceedings of CRYPTO*, number 2729 in Lecture Notes in Computer Science, pages 617–630. Springer-Verlag, 2003.

11. P. Oechslin. Les compromis temps-mémoire et leur utilisation pour casser les mots de passe Windows. In *Symposium sur la Sécurité des Technologies de l'Information et de la Communication SSTIC, Rennes*, June 2004.

12. J.-J. Quisquater, F.-X. Standaert, G. Rouvroy, and J.D. Legat. A cryptanalytic time-memory trade-off: First FPGA implementation. In *Proceedings of the 8th International Workshop on Field-Programmable Logic and Applications (FPL)*, volume 2438 of *Lecture Notes in Computer Science*, pages 780–789. Springer-Verlag, 2002.

13. J.-J. Quisquater and J. Stern. Time-memory tradeoff revisited. *Unpublished*, 1998.

14. R. Rivest. The MD5 Message-Digest Algorithm. `http://www.ietf.org/rfc/rfc1321.txt` , 1992.

15. F.-X. Standaert, G. Rouvoy, J.-J Quisquater, and J.-D. Legat. A time-memory trade-off using distinguished points: New analysis and FPGA results. In B. S. Kaliski Jr., Ç. K. Koç, and C. Paar, editors, *Proceedings of 4th International Workshop on Cryptographic Hardware and Embedded Systems (CHES)*, number 2535 in Lecture Notes in Computer Science, page 593609. Springer-Verlag, 2002.

16. M. J. Wiener. The full cost of cryptanalytic attacks. *Journal of Cryptology*, 17(2):105–124, 2004.

Updates on the Security of FPGAs Against Power Analysis Attacks

F.-X. Standaert[*], F. Mace, E. Peeters, and J.-J. Quisquater

UCL Crypto Group, Place du Levant 3, B-1348 Louvain-la-Neuve, Belgium
{fstandae, mace, peeters, quisquater}@dice.ucl.ac.be

Abstract. This paper reports on the security of cryptographic algorithms implemented on FPGAs against power analysis attacks. We first
present some improved experiments against these reconfigurable devices,
due to an improved measurement process. Although it is usually believed
that FPGAs are noisy targets for such attacks, it is shown that simple
power consumption models can nearly perfectly correlate with actual
measurements. Then, we evaluate how these correlation values depend
on the resources used in the FPGAs. Finally, we investigate the possibility to counteract these attacks by using random pre-charges in the devices and determine how this technique allows a designer to increase the
security of an implementation. These results confirm that side-channel
attacks present a serious threat for most microelectronic devices, including FPGAs. To conclude, we discuss the security *vs.* efficiency tradeoffs.

1 Introduction

Hardware designs are usually evaluated within an area-time implementation
space. However, in the context of cryptographic implementations, the efficiency
is not the only metric by which one can measure an implementation's quality.
In particular, the physical security of microelectronic circuits has recently attracted a lot of attention. While originally applied to small devices like smart
cards, certain attacks have recently been shown quite efficient to defeat FPGA
implementations as well (*e.g.* [10,14]). As an illustration, in this paper, we consider the resistance of FPGA implementations against power analysis attacks
and update certain assumptions on their actual security.

In these attacks, an adversary uses a hypothetical model of a target device
in order to predict its power consumption. The predictions are then compared
to the real, measured power consumption in order to recover secret information.
Therefore, the better a power consumption model can correlate with actual measurements, the more efficient the resulting attack is. In this context, previously
published results against FPGA devices suggested that these are challenging
components to target with power analysis. Assumed reasons for this notably
were (1) the difficulty of obtaining good power consumption measurements for
FPGAs, (2) the possibility to perform parallel computing within these devices.

[*] François-Xavier Standaert is a post doctoral researcher funded by the FNRS (Funds
for National Scientific Research, Belgium).

K. Bertels, J.M.P. Cardoso, and S. Vassiliadis (Eds.): ARC 2006, LNCS 3985, pp. 335–346, 2006.
© Springer-Verlag Berlin Heidelberg 2006

In this paper, we first suggest that, as far as the quality of the measurements is concerned, FPGAs do not significantly differ from small devices like smart cards. In particular, even very simple power consumption models based on the prediction of the number of bit transitions within a device can nearly perfectly correlate with actual measurements, if some simple signal processing is applied. In practice, we perform and evaluate some improved experimental correlation attacks against FPGA implementations of cryptographic algorithms. We also discuss how these attacks depend on the resources used in the devices.

In a second part of the paper, we investigate the possibility to counteract these attacks by using random pre-charges in the FPGAs and evaluate how this technique allows to increase the security of an implementation. In particular, as already observed in the context of smart cards, such a proposal makes it impossible to predict bit transitions. This is because one every two consecutive values in a device is then random and unknown. As a consequence, targeting such designs requires the use of more complex power consumption models (e.g. based on distinguishing $0 \rightarrow 1$ from $1 \rightarrow 0$ bit transitions), for which the correlations obtained are lower. We evaluate these correlation values in the paper.

The rest of the paper is structured as follows. Section 2 describes the principles of power analysis attacks. Section 3 evaluates the correlation obtained between a simple power consumption model based on the switching activity within an FPGA and actual measurements. Section 4 illustrates how these correlations depend on the resources used by a target design. Section 5 performs the same experiments if random prcharges are used within the FPGA. Section 6 discusses the resulting security vs. efficiency tradeoff and our conclusions are in Section 7.

2   Correlation Power Analysis Attacks

Power analysis attacks [6] generally require a hypothetical model of the device under attack to predict its power consumption. For example, FPGAs are usually made of CMOS gates, for which it is reasonable to assume that the main component of the power consumption is due to the switching activity. For a single CMOS gate, we can express it as follows [12]:

$$P_S = C_L V_{DD}^2 P_{0 \rightarrow 1} f \tag{1}$$

where C_L is the gate load capacitance, V_{DD} the supply voltage, $P_{0 \rightarrow 1}$ the probability of a $0 \rightarrow 1$ output transition and f the clock frequency. Equation (1) specifies that the power consumption of CMOS circuits is data-dependent. An attacker may consequently estimate a device power consumption at time t by the number of bit transitions inside the device at this time. Based on this simple observation, power analysis attacks have been applied to numerous algorithms and devices, including smart cards, ASICs and FPGAs. In practice, the use of secret key information in cryptographic designs only allows us to predict a part of the bit transitions, but it is sufficient to correlate with actual measurements of the power consumption.

We illustrate the attack principle (*e.g.* see [2]) with the simple encryption network of Figure 1, which contains the same basic elements as most present block ciphers *e.g.* the DES [7] and AES Rijndael [8]. That is, the plaintext is XORed with a secret key, then goes through a layer of relatively small substitution boxes and is finally sent to a larger permutation (*e.g.* a linear diffusion layer for the AES Rijndael). The same operations are iterated a number of times. For the purposes of this paper, it is not necessary to know more details on these algorithms. The attack proceeds as follows.

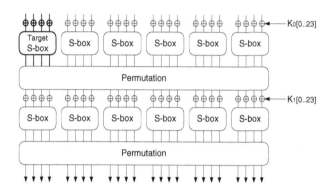

Fig. 1. A simple encryption network

Let the adversary target the 4 key bits entering the left S-box of Figure 1, denoted as $K_0[0..3]$. Then, for N different plaintexts, he first predicts the number of transitions at the S-box output, for every possible value of $K_0[0..3]$. The result of this prediction is a $N \times 2^4$ selected prediction matrix $\mathbf{P}$, containing numbers between 0 and 4. For simulation purposes, it is also interesting to produce the global prediction matrix $\mathbf{G}$ that contains the number of bit transitions inside the whole design. This can of course not be computed by an actual adversary, but can be done if the secret key is known (*i.e.* when evaluating the attacks).

In the second part of the attack, the adversary let the circuit encrypt the same N plaintexts with a fixed key (the same as during the predictions if $\mathbf{G}$ was computed, a secret one in case of real attacks) and he measures the power consumption of the device while the chip is operating the targeted operation. This results in a $N \times 1$ measurement vector $\mathbf{M}$.

Finally, the attacker computes the correlation between the measurement vector and all the columns of the selected prediction matrix (corresponding to all the possible key guesses). If the attack is successful, it is expected that only one value, corresponding to the correct key bits, leads to a high correlation. An efficient way to compute the correlation is to use the Pearson coefficient that can be expressed as follows:

$$C(\mathbf{M}, \mathbf{P}) = \frac{\mu(\mathbf{M}.\mathbf{P}) - \mu(\mathbf{M}).\mu(\mathbf{P})}{\sqrt{\sigma^2(\mathbf{M}).\sigma^2(\mathbf{P})}} \tag{2}$$

In this expression, $\mu(\mathbf{M})$ denotes the mean of the set of measurements $\mathbf{M}$ and $\sigma^2(\mathbf{M})$ its variance. For a more detailed explanation of the power analysis attack principles, we refer to previous publications, *e.g.* [2,14]. We note that different statistical tools could be considered to mount power analysis attacks and the use of the correlation coefficient is not optimal with this respect. For example, maximum likelihood techniques [4] may yield better results. However, with the simple power consumption models considered here, correlation attacks provide good results and are extremely easy to manipulate (*e.g.* they do not require any estimation of the noise in the target devices).

Finally, let us recall two simple formulas, proven in [15]. Firstly, the correlation coefficient we are interested in during an attack is the one between the selected predictions and the measurements. It can be rewritten as:

$$C(\mathbf{P}, \mathbf{M}) = C(\mathbf{P}, \mathbf{G}) \times C(\mathbf{G}, \mathbf{M}) \tag{3}$$

In this equation, the coefficient $C(\mathbf{G}, \mathbf{M})$ only relates to the quality of the measurement and for example, is independent of the FPGA design considered. On the contrary, the coefficient $C(\mathbf{P}, \mathbf{G})$ is specifically related to the implementation under attack and depends on the number of bit transitions that can actually be predicted. In our previous example, we did only predict the transitions of one target S-box, out of the 12 S-boxes in Figure 1. Secondly, the number of generated plaintexts N required to have a successful correlation attack is worth:

$$N = c \times \frac{1}{C(\mathbf{P}, \mathbf{M})^2}, \tag{4}$$

where c is a small constant value. In the following sections, we would like to answer the question: "How precisely can we correlate our simple power consumption models with actual measurements of the power consumption?"

3   Correlations Measurements and Consequences

Target Designs: For all our experiments, we used the four target designs represented in Figure 2. They are again made of XOR operations, substitution boxes and diffusion layers. The three first designs loop on one iteration while the fourth one loops on two iterations. These designs also differ by their various number of pipeline stages. For simplicity purposes, we forced all the operations to be performed by one single layer of look up tables (LUTs) in the FPGA (*e.g.* we used the 4-bit substitution boxes of the Khazad block cipher [1] that perfectly fit to these constraints). Also, the potential leaking points, corresponding to the points in the design for which the transitions consume power, are denoted as a, b, c and d (and further letters for the fourth design). All the architectures are 128-bit wide. When the values $a, b, c, d, ...$ are stored in registers, and according to the terminology introduced in [14], the dark gray registers are *full* (meaning that their bit transitions are strongly correlated to the key values) while the light gray ones are *empty* (meaning the opposite). Also, the small black boxes suggest that a part of the register can actually be predicted by an adversary, because it does only depend on a limited number of key bits. On the opposite, registers without black boxes cannot be predicted. This is typically the case of the registers after the diffusion layer.

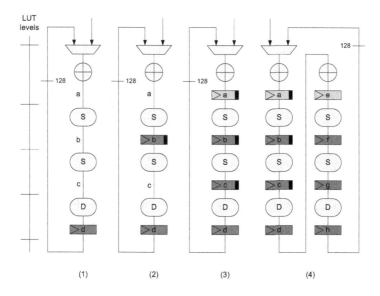

Fig. 2. Target designs

Our measurements were performed on a Xilinx Spartan-2 device. Although the building of a good measurement setup is an important step in side-channel attacks, the technical description of such a setup is out of the scope of this work. We simply note that our approach was to use a dedicated board in order to isolate the FPGA from any other component, representing potential noise sources in the observations. It is important to have in mind that the following results highly depend on our measurement capabilities and the context considered. For example, targeting an FPGA on a prototyping board including various processors, memories, ... would be more challenging. On the other hand, the measurement process itself could still be improved and is under progress. Again, the objective of this paper is to suggest that basic methods can already yield good results.

Our initial strategy to evaluate the correlation coefficient $C(\mathbf{G},\mathbf{M})$ was the following. We considered the third design of Figure 2, with four pipeline stages. Then, we assumed that the leaking points a,b,c,d (all of them being stored in registers) contributed for a similar part of the power consumption and predicted the bit transitions in these registers. On a power trace like the one in the left part of Figure 3, we finally observed the peaks occurring at the rising edges of the clock signal and evaluated how the values of these peaks were correlated with the total number of bit transitions predicted.

Two simple signal processing steps were applied. First, the spectrum of the power traces was observed (partially represented in Figure 3) and we identified

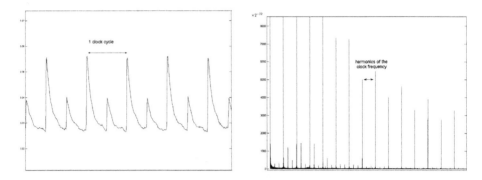

Fig. 3. A single power trace: time and frequency domains

a number of parasitic signals that were filtered with their harmonics. Second, we performed a small averaging on the filtered traces.

The correlations between our predictions and a single FPGA power trace, filtered or not, are represented in the left part of Figure 4, for different numbers of generated plaintexts. The correlations after averaging are in the right part of the figure. Roughly, we observe that a single trace allows to reach a correlation of up to 75% while a small averaging increases this value behind 90%. As a comparison, previously published results, *e.g.* [14] suggested correlation values of around 45%, roughly corresponding to our single non-filtered trace experiment. Therefore, referring to Equation 4, the number of required plaintexts to perform a successful attack would be divided by 4.

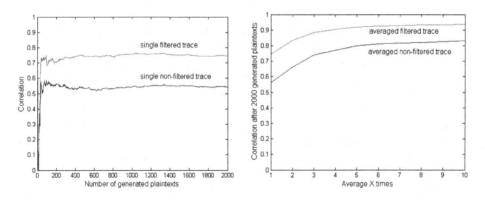

Fig. 4. Correlation between our predictions and actual power consumption measurements for the design (3), without random pre-charges: single trace and averaged traces

4   Resources Dependencies

In the previous experiment, we correlated the total number of bit transitions in the device registers with actual power consumption measurements. As already mentioned, this involves the important assumption that all the leaking points contribute identically to the power consumption. Obviously, this may not be formally correct and the aim of this section is to evaluate how relevant is this assumption for practical applications. In particular, we would like to answer two questions: (1) do the use of registers in a design influence its power consumption? (2) how do the various FPGA resources contribute to the power consumption?

In order to answer the first question, we implemented the designs (1),(2) and (3) of Figure 2. Since they only differ in their number of pipeline stages, they actually require (roughly) the same number of LUTs and slices. The only difference is in their number of flip flops. Then, we measured the power consumption of these three architectures when fed with the same inputs. We could not distinguish any significant difference between the power consumption patterns. The assumed reason for this observation is that the overall power consumed by an FPGA mainly depends on the amount of resources (*e.g.* the slices) used by a design, that is roughly the same in the three experiments.

To answer the second question, we used again the designs (1), (2) and (3) and evaluated separately the correlations between their power consumption measurements and the bit transitions for the leaking points a, b, c, d. It is illustrated for the design (1) in the left part of Figure 5 where we can clearly observe that the leaking points do not correlate the same way and therefore do not contribute for equal parts to the global power consumption. Then, to obtain better results, we used a weighted sum of the predictions of the different leaking points. It is represented in the right part of the figure where it is compared with a non-weighted sum (as we used in the previous section).

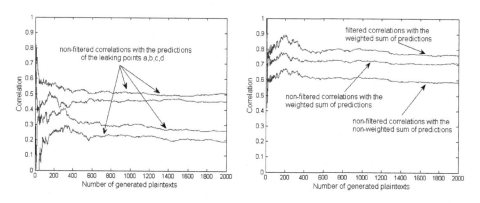

Fig. 5. Resource dependent correlations without random pre-charges

These results confirm the experiments performed in [13] where it is shown that the dynamic power consumption in FPGAs actually depends on the effective capacitances of the resources used. For example, it is shown that the effective capacitances of signals within a slice are much lower than the ones of long connection wires. This could explain that the correlations with certain bit transitions appear to be much higher than others. It is also interesting to observe that filtering the trace can again yield an even better correlation. This could be easily understood since filtering reduces the noise due to parasitic frequencies within the signal while the use of weighted predictions increases the quality of our leakage model. That is, both techniques relate to different noise sources.

From a practical point of view, it is important to have in mind that the use of weighted predictions involves a different attack context, usually denoted as template attacks [4]. Indeed, in the most general setting, an actual adversary will not be able to determine precisely which transitions in a design contribute the most to the power consumption. Therefore, the naive strategy (without attributing weights to the bit transitions) is the only one applicable. On the opposite, if the adversary can use a programmable device to build a better power consumption model (*i.e.* in the template attack context), improved strategies as the one presented in this section are applicable. Note that, in our example, we only used four different weights (*i.e.* for the a,b,c,d leaking points), although it would be possible to further improve the process by considering more different weights.

To further analyze these observations, we use the following lemma, also applied in [15]: *the correlation coefficient between the sum of n arbitrary independent identically distributed random variables and the sum of the first $m < n$ of these equals $\sqrt{m/n}$.* If we assume that various bit transitions in a design contribute additively to the global power consumption, it means that the four correlations in the left part of Figure 5 respectively correspond to $0.2^2 \simeq 4\%$, $0.25^2 \simeq 6\%$, $0.45^2 \simeq 20\%$ and $0.5^2 \simeq 25\%$ of the total power consumption. That is a sum of 55%. Such a prediction should allow a correlation of $\sqrt{0.55} \simeq 74\%$ which is close to the one observed in the right part of the figure, for the (non-filtered) weighted sum experiment. This re-confirms that a significant part of the power consumption is not predicted, which may be caused by various noise sources and/or parasitic signals. Those could be removed by filtering (as the right part of Figure 5 suggests) or averaging as the previous section underlined.

To conclude this section, we note that although the knowledge of a design's details may allow to improve correlation analysis attacks, a basic side-channel adversary will probably be limited to simple strategies, *e.g.* assuming all the bit transitions to contribute equally to the power consumption. It must be observed that, if the leaking points targeted by an adversary are connected to low effective capacitances within a FPGA, the actual attack may become more challenging. Another remark is that, due to their high diffusion properties, encryption algorithms usually require the use of long connection wires, which probably increases their power consumption compared to other designs. Finally, we reproduced the attack against an FPGA implementation of the AES Rijndael performed in [14] with the improved measurement process corresponding to the right part of Figure 4. It is represented in the left part of Figure 6 where we observe that the attack is successful after 300 generated plaintexts. Compared with the results in [14], it confirms our expectations that this number is roughly divided by 4.

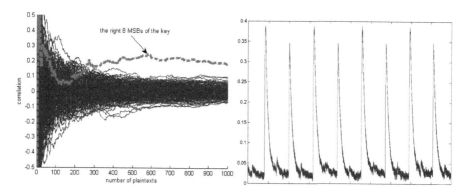

Fig. 6. An attack against the AES Rijndael, $0 \rightarrow 1$ and $1 \rightarrow 0$ bit transition differences

5   Random Pre-charges and Consequences

A common countermeasure used in the smart card industry to counteract side-channel analysis is to pre-charge the buses with random values. Such a solution can be straightforwardly transposed in the context of FPGA implementations at the cost of a reduction of the throughput. Indeed, if one every two inputs of the encryption design is a random number generated within the FPGA[1], an adversary will not be able to predict the transitions within the implementation anymore (of course, the resulting ciphertext should not be outputted from the device). As suggested in [11], the only solution is then to distinguish $0 \rightarrow 1$ from $1 \rightarrow 0$ bit transitions through the leakages. In the latter case, one can predict the number of 0's and 1's in the device at some time, rather than predicting the number of bit transitions at this time. That is, we use a model based on the Hamming weight of the data manipulated rather than on its Hamming distance. To confirm that such a model is applicable, we performed a preliminary experiment, pictured on the right part of Figure 6. We observed the power traces of large bit-vectors switching between "all zeroes" or "all ones" patterns. Typically, this experiment suggested power consumption differences of about 10%.

The correlations between Hamming weight-based predictions and a single FPGA power trace (using the design (3) of Figure 2, as in Section 3), filtered or not, are represented in the left part of Figure 7, for different numbers of generated plaintexts. The correlations after averaging are in the right part of the figure. Roughly, we observe that a single trace allows to reach a correlation of up to 15% while a small averaging increases this value behind 20%. One can conclude that, although the correlations obtained are significantly lower (due to a much higher model matching noise), they are still sufficient to perform the attacks. This is specially true when considering that the measurement process is still likely to be improved and that other side-channel information could be used to increase these correlations, *e.g.* the electromagnetic radiation. On the other hand, if com-

---

[1] *E.g.* [5] could be used to produce the initial seeds of a pseudo-random number generator which will consequently generate the pre-charges.

bined with other countermeasures, such random pre-charges may increase the difficulty of performing the attacks at a relatively low implementation cost.

Let us finally remark that the differences between $0 \to 1$ and $1 \to 0$ bit transitions could also be used to slightly improve our power consumption model of the previous sections, again using different weights for these different transitions.

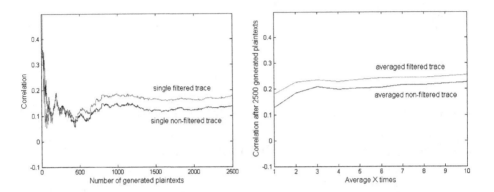

Fig. 7. Correlation between our predictions and actual power consumption measurements, with random pre-charges: single trace and averaged traces

6   Security vs. Efficiency Tradeoffs

The previous considerations can be summarized in order to easily determine the number of plaintexts required to have a successful attack [15]:

$$N = c \times \frac{1}{C(\mathbf{P}, \mathbf{G})^2 \times C(\mathbf{G}, \mathbf{M})^2} \tag{5}$$

In this expression:

1. $C(\mathbf{G}, \mathbf{M})$ is the expected correlation obtained between the power consumption model and the actual measurements (investigated in this paper). Our results suggest that reasonable values for this parameter are:
   $0.50 < C(\mathbf{G}, \mathbf{M}) < 0.95$ if no random pre-charges are used (we observed values in this range). The better the correlation is, the more efficient the resulting attack is.
   $0.10 < C(\mathbf{G}, \mathbf{M}) < 0.50$ if random pre-charges are used. Our results suggest no more than 0.25 but could possibly be improved. Therefore, a small security margin is reasonable.
2. $C(\mathbf{P}, \mathbf{G})$ relates to the number of bits for which the power consumption can be predicted in the attack. If n_{pred} is this number of predictable bits and n_{tot} is the total number of bits in the design, we roughly[2] have $C(\mathbf{P}, \mathbf{G}) = \sqrt{\frac{n_{pred}}{n_{tot}}}$.

---

[2] More precisely, if n_{pf} is the number of predictable and full bits, n_{pe} the number of predictable and empty bits and n_u the number of unpredictable bits, with $n_{tot} = n_{pf} + n_{pe} + n_u$, the correlation we are interested in is $\sqrt{\frac{n_{pf}}{n_{tot} - n_{pe}}} = \sqrt{\frac{n_{pf}}{npf + n_u}}$.

3. c is a small constant value depending on the number of key bits targeted during the attack. For example, it could be estimated once for 8-bit substitution boxes (like the ones of the AES Rijndael) as follows. Knowing that:

the attack of Figure 6 is using $C(\mathbf{G},\mathbf{M}) \simeq 0.9$,

the ratio of predictable registers (from [14]) is worth $\sqrt{\frac{48}{1536}} \simeq 0.18$,

the attack of Figure 6 is successful after 300 plaintexts,

we find that a reasonable value (including a small security margin) is $c \simeq 10$.

From Equation 5, it is now extremely simple to evaluate the security of our different implementations in Figure 2. For example, let us consider a correlation attack against implementation (3), without random pre-charges. First, we assume a reasonable value for $C(\mathbf{G},\mathbf{M}) \simeq 0.8$. Then, we know that we have a total of $4 \times 128 = 512$ bits in the design, among which $3 \times 8 = 24$ are predictable. This yields $C(\mathbf{P},\mathbf{G}) = \sqrt{\frac{24}{512}}$. Finally, we find: $N \simeq 333$. Now, let us consider the fourth design for which the total number of bits is $8 \times 128 = 1024$ and we still have $n_{pred} = 32$. It yields $N \simeq 666$. If we additionally consider random pre-charges in the same fourth design, we could have $C(\mathbf{G},\mathbf{M}) \simeq 0.25$ (at the cost of a throughput reduction) and therefore $N \simeq 6882$. That is, any possible similar hardware architecture could be analyzed. As already frequently discussed, we observe that the attacks efficiencies depend on the implementation size and therefore involve a security *vs.* efficiency tradeoff. Note that in addition to the use of random pre-charges, various combinations of repetition codes (*e.g.* sending one true plaintexts for x random ones, in variable orders to the encryption device) could be considered. Also, as suggested in [9], such countermeasures could be particularly interesting in the context of feedback implementations, where pipelining cannot be used for increasing the performances, but possibly for fault detection or improved side-channel resistance.

We finally mention that in all our experiments, we only considered the peak values of the power traces occurring at the rising edges of the clock. It is reasonable (and verified in our experiments) to assume that these values give a good image of the power consumption because of the inherently synchronous behavior of RAM-based FPGAs. However, this could not be the case for other devices.

7   Conclusion

The correlation between the power consumption measurements of an isolated FPGA implementation of a cryptographic algorithm and a simple prediction based on the number of bit transitions within the devices can be up to 90%. Using random pre-charges in the FPGA allows to decrease these correlation values (our experiments suggest 25%) but is not sufficient to counteract the attacks. We provide simple techniques for estimating the number of measurements required to defeat one particular implementation. The latter estimations suggest that most FPGA implementations of symmetric-key block ciphers can be defeated in a low (*e.g.* a few hundred) number of power traces.

References

1. P. Barreto, V. Rijmen, *The KHAZAD Legacy-Level Block Cipher*, Submission to NESSIE project, available from http://www.cosic.esat.kuleuven.ac.be/nessie/
2. E. Brier, C. Clavier, F. Olivier, *Correlation Power Analysis with a Leakage Model*, in the proceedings of CHES 2004, Lecture Notes in Computer Science, vol 3156, pp 16-29, Boston, USA, August 2004.
3. P. Buysschaert, E. De Mulder, S. B. Örs, P. Delmotte, B. Preneel, G. Vandenbosch, I. Verbauwhede, *Electromagnetic Analysis Attack on an FPGA Implementation of an Elliptic Curve Cryptosystem*, in the proceedings of EUROCON 2005 - The International Conference on Computer as a Tool, IEEE, 4 pages, 2005.
4. S. Chari, J. Rao, P. Rohatgi, *Template Attacks*, in the proceedings of CHES 2002, Lecture Notes in Computer Science, vol 2523, pp 13-28, Redwood City, CA, USA, August 2002.
5. V. Fischer, M. Drutarovsky, *True Random Number Generator Embedded in Reconfigurable Hardware*, in the proceedings of CHES 2002, Lecture Notes in Computer Science, vol 2523, pp 415-430, Redwood Shores, California, USA, August 2002.
6. P. Kocher, J. Jaffe, B. Jun, *Differential Power Analysis*, in the proceedings of Cypto 1999, Lecture Notes in Computer Science, vol 1666, pp 398-412, Santa-Barbara, USA, August 1999, Springer-Verlag.
7. National Bureau of Standards, *FIPS PUB 46, The Data Encryption Standard*, Federal Information Processing Standard, NIST, U.S. Dept. of Commerce, Jan 1977.
8. National Bureau of Standards, *FIPS 197, Advanced Encryption Standard*, Federal Information Processing Standard, NIST, U.S. Dept. of Commerce, November 2001.
9. T.G. Malkin, F.-X. Standaert, M. Yung, *A Comparative Cost/Security Analysis of Fault Attack Countermeasures*, in the proceedings of FDTC 2005, Edinburgh, Scotland, September 2005.
10. S.B. Ors, E. Oswald, B. Preneel, *Power-Analysis Attacks on an FPGA – First Experimental Results*, in the proceedings of CHES 2003, Lecture Notes in Computer Science, vol 2279, pp 35-50, Cologn, Germany, September 2003, Springer-Verlag.
11. E. Peeters, F.-X. Standaert, J.-J. Quisquater, *Power and Electromagnetic Analysis: Improved Model, Consequences and Comparisons*, to appear in Integration, the VLSI Journal, Spring 2006, Elsevier.
12. J.M. Rabaey, *Digital Integrated Circuits*, Prentice Hall International, 1996.
13. L. Shang, A. Kaviani, K. Bathala, *Dynamic Power Consumption in Virtex-2 FPGA Family*, in the proceedings of FPGA 2002, pp 157-164, Monterey, California, USA, February 2002.
14. F.-X. Standaert, S.B. Ors, B. Preneel, *Power Analysis of an FPGA Implementation of Rijndael : Is Pipelining a DPA Countermeasure?*, in the proceedings of CHES 2004, Lecture Notes in Computer Science, vol 3156, pp 30-44, Cambridge, MA, USA, August 2004.
15. F.-X. Standart, E. Peeters, G. Rouvroy, J.-J. Quisquater, *Power Analysis Attacks and Countermeasures of Field Programmable Gate Arrays: Recent Results*, to appear in the Proceedings of the IEEE, special issue on Cryptographic Hardware and Embedded Systems, Spring 2006.
16. K. Tiri, I. Verbauwhede, *Synthesis of Secure FPGA Implementations*, in the proceedings of the International Workshop on Logic and Synthesis (IWLS 2004), pp 224-231, June 2004.

Reconfigurable Modular Arithmetic Logic Unit for High-Performance Public-Key Cryptosystems*

K. Sakiyama, N. Mentens, L. Batina, B. Preneel, and I. Verbauwhede

Katholieke Universiteit Leuven, ESAT/COSIC, Kasteelpark Arenberg 10,
B-3001 Leuven-Heverlee, Belgium
{Kazuo.Sakiyama, Nele.Mentens, Lejla.Batina,
Bart.Preneel, Ingrid.Verbauwhede}@esat.kuleuven.be

Abstract. This paper presents a reconfigurable hardware architecture for Public-key cryptosystems. By changing the connections of coarse grain Carry-Save Adders (CSAs), the datapath provides a high performance for both RSA and Elliptic Curve Cryptography (ECC). In addition, we introduce another reconfigurability for the flip-flops in order to make the best of hardware resources. The results of FPGA implementation show that better performance is obtained for ECC on the same hardware platform.

Keywords: Public-Key Cryptography (PKC), RSA, Elliptic Curve Cryptography (ECC), FPGA implementation, Reconfigurable architecture.

1 Introduction

Diffie and Hellman introduced the idea of public-key cryptography [4] in the mid 70's. They showed that one can eliminate the need for prior agreement of a key in order to exchange some confidential data. Public-key cryptosystems also enable digital signatures. The best-known and most commonly used public-key cryptosystems are RSA and Elliptic Curve Cryptography (ECC). The RSA public-key cryptosystem is named after its inventors Rivest, Shamir and Adelman [11]. ECC, which was proposed in the mid 80's by Miller [9] and Koblitz [5], is based on a different algebraic structure. In the case of ECC, the group used is the group of points on an elliptic curve. It is important to point out that ECC offer equivalent security as RSA for much smaller key sizes. Other benefits include higher speed, lower power consumption and smaller certificates which is especially useful in constrained environments (smart cards, mobile phones, PDAs, *etc.*).

The security of the RSA cryptosystem is based on the difficulty of the RSA problem. It is still the most popular cryptosystem, especially for high-end devices that are typically used in e-commerce and Virtual Private Network (VPN)

---

* Kazuo Sakiyama, Nele Mentens and Lejla Batina are funded by FWO projects (G.0450.04, G.0141.03). This research has been also partially supported by the EU IST FP6 projects SCARD and ECRYPT.

K. Bertels, J.M.P. Cardoso, and S. Vassiliadis (Eds.): ARC 2006, LNCS 3985, pp. 347–357, 2006.
© Springer-Verlag Berlin Heidelberg 2006

servers. RSA, still the most popular public key cryptosystem, has at its root the modular exponentiation operation. Modular exponentiation consists of repeated modular multiplications, which is also the basic operation for ECC.

Our contribution deals with an FPGA implementation of RSA and ECC over a field of a prime characteristic. We used a reconfigurable datapath to achieve arbitrary precision in bits, hence easily bridging the gap between the bit-lengths for ECC from 160 bits to 2,048 bit long moduli for RSA. We use modular exponentiation based on Montgomery's method without any modular reduction which is also beneficial for side-channel attacks.

The results show that the proposed reconfigurable datapath is indeed a suitable solution for high-performance public-key cryptosystems such as RSA and ECC. Comparing the two with the same hardware resources and with corresponding bit-lengths that provide the similar security, we found that ECC-256p allows a better performance than RSA-2048. This research is of interest because due to a constant progress in cryptography and security applications an alternative solution for public-key services such as signatures, key-distribution *etc.* is needed.

This paper is organized as follows. Sect. 2 lists some relevant previous work. In Sect. 3 the details of our architecture are given. The main contribution of our work *i.e.* the reconfigurable datapath is explained in Sect. 4. The details of two cryptosystems that are implemented and the results are given in Sect. 5. Sect. 6 concludes the paper.

2   Related Work

This section reviews some of the most relevant previous work in hardware implementations for RSA and ECC. To consider both RSA and ECC on the same platform has only recently became more popular, since ECC have proven to be a mature technology. Some of the work is done on FPGAs and only very few implementations are presenting an ASIC implementation of ECC in the field of prime characteristic.

More recent work on hardware implementation of RSA includes the work by McIvor *et al.* [7]. They use Carry Save Adders (CSAs) to perform the large word length additions required for MMM. The obtained performance for one 1024 bit RSA decryption on the Xilinx Virtex2 board was 2.63 *msec*. The work of Crowe *et al.* [3] also proposed a unique architecture for RSA and ECC. A hardware optimized version of MMM is used for modular multiplication. The so-called dual processor could operate in parallel for ECC or in a pipelined series for RSA.

The contribution presented in [1] is combining a systolic array architecture with a Montgomery based RSA implementation, achieving the notion of scalability as introduced originally in the work by Tenca and Koç [12]. The optimal bound for Montgomery's parameter R is achieved which, with some savings in hardware, omits completely all reduction steps that are presumed to be vulnerable to side-channel attacks. By using the optimal scheduling for the architecture the authors have obtained a substantial speed-up for ECC when compared with RSA implementation on the same platform.

3   Modular Arithmetic Logic Unit

3.1   Datapath of the MALU

The proposed architecture is a Montgomery modular multiplier with digit-serial multiplications (Algorithm 1). Four-to-two (4-2) CSAs (Fig.1-a) are used in the hardware implementation because they are considered as one of the most optimal solutions for a multi-operand addition including Algorithm 1.

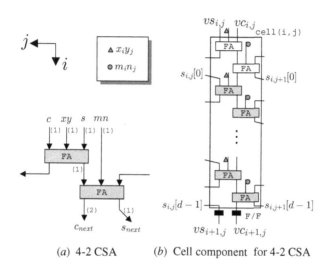

(a) 4-2 CSA   (b) Cell component for 4-2 CSA

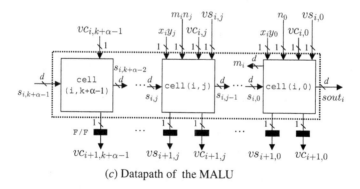

(c) Datapath of the MALU

Fig. 1. Configuration of the MALU with 4-2 CSAs

The cell, a column of the datapath of the MALU uses d sets of 4-2 CSAs (Fig.1-b), *i.e.*, the inputs and outputs of the cell are presented in 2-bit CS-form during the operation. Therefore, the cell needs $2d$ sets of FAs. The critical path of the datapath is estimated with the critical path delay of the cell as follows.

$$T_{4-2CSAs} = 2dT_{FA}. \tag{1}$$

Here, we assumed that the delay for the sum and carry calculations are the same. The propagation of $s_{i,j}$ goes through d sets of the cell and uses two FAs in every cell. The right-most cell, cell(i,0) provides m_i vector for the rest of cells. As expressed in Eq.(2), the path for generating a bit of m_i only consists of 3-input XOR in the right-most cell.

$$m_i[0] = vs_{i,0} \oplus vc_{i,0} \oplus x_i[0]y_0$$
$$m_i[1] = s_{i,0}[1] \oplus c0_{next}[0] \oplus x_i[1]y_0$$
$$\vdots$$
$$m_i[d-1] = s_{i,0}[d-1] \oplus c0_{next}[d-1] \oplus x_i[d-1]y_0 .$$

$$(2)$$

In the worst combination of the paths through the logic generating m_i, it takes:

$$dT_{m_i} + dT_{FA} .$$

$$(3)$$

This path delay is assumed to be equivalent to or shorter than $T_{4-2CSAs}$.

As can been seen from the hardware configuration and the delay calculations, the datapath of the MALU has an area and delay that can be adapted with the size of d. In this way the propagation can be tuned to the speed of the system. The proposed array is flexible regarding the size of d: it can be decided by exploring the best combination of performance and cost.

3.2   Functionality of the MALU

Before explaining the general case, the main functionality of the MALU is explained with the case that $d = 1$. In this configuration, each cell is composed of one 4-2 CSA (Fig1-a). The 4-2 CSA sums up the four-bit inputs xy, mn, s and c and outputs two bits in the redundant CS-form whose value is $2(c_{next}) + s_{next}$ where s and c are the virtual sum and carries. The bit multiplications xy and mn are main inputs for computing the bit level of Montgomery multiplication in Algorithm 1, i.e. $(T + xy + mn)/2$.

Simply thinking, a multiplication can be computed with $(k + \alpha)^2$ times 4-2 CSA operations if the multiplicand and multiplier have $(k + \alpha)$ bit. However, considering that there are no carry propagations in the j-direction shown on Fig.1, it is natural to allocate $(k + \alpha)$ sets of cells in the j-direction to take the speed merit. This CSA array is defined as the minimal configuration of our proposed MALU. The connection of the CSA arrays in the i-direction are determined by the bit weights of the CSA's outputs (numbers in parenthesis in Fig.1-a,b) and the division of the bit-level Montgomery algorithm (1-bit right-shift). The connection is latched with $(2k + 2\alpha - 1)$ sets of F/Fs for virtual carries.

The explanation of the MALU for a general d is given as follows. As illustrated in Fig.1-c, the introduced MALU with 4-2 CSAs has four types of input vectors, $X = (x_g \cdots x_1 x_0)_{2^d}$, $Y = (y_{k+1} \cdots y_1 y_0)_2$, $N = (n_{k-1} \cdots n_1 n_0)_2$, and $S = (s_{h,k+\alpha-1} \cdots s_{1,k+\alpha-1} s_{0,k+\alpha-1})_{2^d}$ where $g = \lceil (k+1)/d \rceil$ and $h = \lceil k/d \rceil$. Here, X is the multiplier, Y is the multiplicands, and N is the modulus. The

---

Algorithm 1. Algorithm for d-digit serial Montgomery Modular Multiplication over GF(p) without final subtraction

---

Require: $N = (n_{k-1} \cdots n_1 n_0)_2$, $X = (x_k \cdots x_1 x_0)_2$, $Y = (y_k \cdots y_1 y_0)_2$
   with $x, y \in [0, 2N - 1]$, $R = 2^{k+2}$, $gcd(N, 2) = 1$
Ensure: $T = XYR^{-1} \bmod 2N$
   1. $T \leftarrow 0$
   2. **for** i from 0 to $k + 1$ **do**
   3. $m_i \leftarrow t_0 \oplus x_i y_0$
   4. $T \leftarrow (T + x_i y + m_i N)/2$ // addition stage
   5. $m_{i+1} \leftarrow t_0 \oplus x_{i+1} y_0$
   6. $T \leftarrow (T + x_{i+1} y + m_{i+1} N)/2$ // addition stage
         $\vdots$
   1+2d. $m_{i+d-1} \leftarrow t_0 \oplus x_{i+d-1} y_0$
   2+2d. $T \leftarrow (T + x_{i+d-1} y + m_{i+d-1} N)/2$ // addition stage
   3+2d. **end for**
   4+2d. Return T

---

augend vector S is provided to the MALU by d bits in every cycle and eventually added to the result of the modular multiplication of X and Y (modulo N). The intermediate results are stored in $VS = (vs_{i,k+\alpha-1} \cdots vs_{i,1} vs_{i,0})_2$ and $VC = (vc_{i,k+\alpha-1} \cdots vc_{i,1} vc_{i,0})_2$. They are reset to zero when a modular multiplication starts to execute ($i = 0$). After finishing a Montgomery multiplication, the result is output from the right-most cell by d bits in every cycle as $Sout = (sout_g \cdots sout_1 sout_0)_{2^d}$.

The MALU has two independent stages for GF(p) operation. One is the Carry-Save(CS)-stage that implements the Montgomery algorithm in a CS-form. Another converts the CS-form integer into a normal integer by propagating carries, namely the Carry-Propagate(CP)-stage. Moreover the CP-stage is capable of adding/subtracting S to/from the result of the CS-stage. When subtracting S from XY, we use the 2's complement of S. More precisely, each bit of S is inverted in setting a register for S and $2N + 1$ is provided from inputs of mn at the first cycle of the CP stage. For reducing the hardware cost and the critical path delay, the CP calculations are executed in the same datapath of the MALU as the CS-calculations. The operation of the MALU is explained in Eq.(4).

$$\text{MALU}_N(XR, YR, SR) = (XY \pm S)R \bmod N. \tag{4}$$

Here R is selected as $R = 2^{k+\alpha}$ where k is the bit-length of the secret key and α is a value determined so that the final reductions can be avoided. In our case, we chose $\alpha = 4$. The details are explained by the following Lemma [2].

Lemma 1. *If the Montgomery parameter R satisfies the following inequality $R > 16N$, then for inputs $X, Y < 4N$ and $S < 2N$ the result T will satisfy: $T < 4N$ (as required).*

Proof: The Montgomery multiplication as implemented in the MALU calculates the following:

$$T = \text{MALU}_N(X, Y, S) = \frac{XY + MN}{R} + S$$
$$< \frac{4N \cdot 4N}{16N} + N + 2N \leq 4N. \tag{5}$$

While the reduction step was needed in the original notation of Montgomery's algorithm, we use a method which does not require the reduction. For convenience of repeating usage of Eq.(4), the so-called Montgomery form is applied because the output is in the Montgomery form as well. The latency to calculate a MALU_N needs $2 \cdot \lceil (k + \alpha)/d \rceil$ cycles in total.

4   Reconfigurable Datapath

In order to obtain high-performance modular operations, we should allocate $k + \alpha - 1$ cells for the datapath of the MALU. For instance, the case of ECC-256p and RSA-2048 need 260 and 2,052 cells, respectively. Since we target a platform which supports both ECC-256p and RSA-2048, we introduce a coarse grain datapath of the $\text{MALU}_{260 \times 1}$ ($k = 256$ and $d = 1$) and allocate its clones. For the general case ($K \times D$ sets of $\text{MALU}_{k \times d}$) the block diagram of the reconfigurable datapath is illustrated in Fig.2.

The datapath can be configured by changing the interconnection of the $\text{MALU}_{d \times k}$ that is determined by the three multiplexors (Fig.3) and two- or three-bit registers for selecting them. The *sel1* and *sel2* are used for configuring the datapath, and the *sel3* is used for configuring the flip-flops. Those multiplexors and flip-flops for the configuration are considered as the area overhead (denoted as AO) introduced by the reconfigurable feature. It is approximately estimated as follows:

$$AO_{base} = DK(A_{MUX(sel1)} + A_{MUX(sel2)} + A_{MUX(sel3)} + A_{FF(config)})$$
$$= \{(6d + k)DK - 2dK\} \cdot A_{2-1MUX} + \{3DK - K\} \cdot A_{FF}. \tag{6}$$

Here, we ignored the area increase caused by the complexity of the wiring. In addition to the AO_{base}, some more flip-flops are not used depending on the configuration. As an example, we consider the case of using eight clones of $\text{MALU}_{260 \times 1}$ ($K = 2$ and $D = 4$). When supporting RSA-2048, the datapath is configured as $\text{MALU}_{2080 \times 1}$. In this configuration, the horizontal connections of the MALUs are not re-timed by flip-flops for S and R (REG_S and REG_R). Therefore, the total area overhead becomes as follows:

$$AO_{RSA-2048} = AO_{base} + 14A_{FF}$$
$$= 11,448A_{2-1MUX} + 36A_{FF}. \tag{7}$$

Likewise, for RSA-2048 with CRT (Chinese Remainder Theorem) [10], the datapath is configured to have two sets of $\text{MALU}_{1040 \times 1}$. Therefore, the area overhead for RSA-2048 with CRT is estimated as follows:

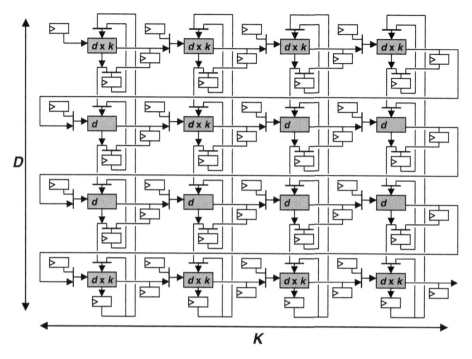

Fig. 2. Reconfigurable Datapath using $D \times K$ sets of MALU$_{d \times k}$

$$AO_{RSA-2048(CRT)} = AO_{base} + 12A_{FF}$$
$$= 11,448A_{2-1MUX} + 34A_{FF}. \tag{8}$$

For ECC-256p, we configure the datapath so that two sets of MALU$_{260 \times 4}$ can be used in parallel. This configuration uses vertical series of MALU$_{260 \times 1}$. The intermediate values, the virtual carry and sum, are stored in the flip-flops for VS and VC only at the bottom of Fig.2. In this configuration, only one-fourth of of REG$_X$, REG$_Y$ and REG$_N$ are used in each MALU$_{260 \times 1}$. Therefore, the total area of the overhead becomes as follows:

$$AO_{ECC-256p} = AO_{base} + (260 \times 12 + 260 \times 24 \times 3/4)A_{FF}$$
$$= 11,448A_{2-1MUX} + 7,822A_{FF}. \tag{9}$$

In the case of the RSA configuration, we can utilize the flip-flops with almost no waste, while the configuration of ECC can not use them effectively. In order to exploit the unused flip-flops, we introduce another reconfigurability. Different from RSA, ECC needs to store the intermediate variables during point operations. For the purpose, two sets of 14 words of 260-bit RAM (28×260-bit RAM) can be configured with the unused flip-flops. In this case, the area overhead becomes as follows:

$$AO_{ECC-256p} = 11,448A_{2-1MUX} + 542A_{FF}. \tag{10}$$

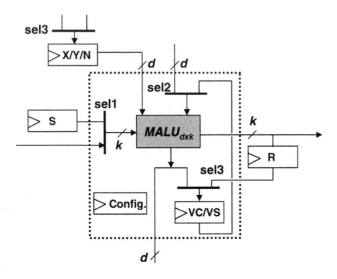

Fig. 3. Flip-Flops and and Multiplexors of MALU$_{d \times k}$

Thus, we can make the best use of the hardware resources also for the ECC configuration. For the critical path delay for each configuration, we have different delays as follows:

$$
\begin{aligned}
T_{RSA-2048} = T_{RSA-2048(CRT)} &= 2T_{FA} + 2T_{2-1MUX} + T_{FF} + T_{wiring} \\
T_{ECC-256p} &= 8T_{FA} + 4T_{2-1MUX} + T_{FF} + 4T_{wiring}.
\end{aligned}
\tag{11}
$$

We assumed that the wiring delay in the critical path of ECC is four times longer than that of RSA. As seen from the Eq.(11), the critical path delay of ECC is about four times longer than RSA. Therefore, we need to assume a circumstance where we can use two different clock frequency, *e.g.*, providing a divided clock in the ECC configuration, in order to facilitate a high performance for both configurations.

5   Performance Comparison

5.1   RSA

The main operation in the RSA algorithm is a modular exponentiation [11]. The two most straightforward algorithms to implement this are given in Algorithm 2, where G is a finite abelian group and e is a positive integer. The basic operations in both algorithms are multiplications and squarings. To be able to use the same datapath for both operations and also for side-channel issues [6] the squarings are not performed on a dedicated squarer, but on the multiplier. Taking into account an expected value of $\frac{n}{2}$ ones in e, the total number of multiplications in both algorithms is $\frac{3n}{2}$. In the left-to-right algorithm the multiplications have to be performed consecutively requiring one memory location for intermediate values.

Algorithm 2. Algorithms for left-to-right and right-to-left binary exponentiation

Require: $g \in G$, $e = (e_{n-1}e_{n-2}\cdots e_1 e_0)_2$	**Require:** $g \in G$, $e = (1\ e_{n-2}\cdots e_1 e_0)_2$
Ensure: g^e	**Ensure:** g^e
1: $A \leftarrow 1$	$A \leftarrow 1$, $S \leftarrow g$
2: **for** i from $n-1$ downto 0 **do**	**for** i from 0 to $n-1$ **do**
3: $\quad A \leftarrow A \cdot A$	$\quad$ **if** $e_i = 1$ **then**
4: $\quad$ **if** $e_i = 1$ **then**	$\quad\quad A \leftarrow A \cdot S$
5: $\quad\quad A \leftarrow A \cdot g$	$\quad$ **end if**
6: $\quad$ **end if**	$\quad S \leftarrow S \cdot S$
7: **end for**	**end for**
8: Return A	Return A

In the right-to-left algorithm the multiplications can be parallelized, which doubles the speed. However, the right-to-left algorithm uses two memory locations for intermediate values.

5.2 ECC

In ECC, the equivalent operation of the modular exponentiation in RSA is a point multiplication, which multiplies a point on the elliptic curve with a scalar, resulting in another point on the curve. Similar to the left-to-right and right-to-left binary algorithms for modular exponentiation, a point multiplication can be performed using Algorithm 3 [8], where P is a point on the elliptic curve and k is a positive integer. The point at infinity $\mathcal{O}$ is the identity element for elliptic curve operations. Similar to modular the modular exponentiation algorithms, the left-to-right algorithm will be used when the storage of intermediate values is the bottleneck, while the right-to-left algorithm will be used for higher speed when the datapath allows parallelism.

The point operations in Algorithm 3 are point additions and point doublings. In our case a point addition and a point doubling respectively consist of 14 and 21 multiply/add operations by the MALU in the underlying finite field. Therefore the total number of multiplications for point multiplication is estimated as $\frac{49l}{2}$.

Algorithm 3. Algorithm for left-to-right and right-to-left binary point multiplication

Require: $P = (x, y)$, $k = (k_{l-1}k_{l-2}\cdots k_0)_2$	**Require:** $P = (x, y)$, $k = (1\ k_{l-2}\cdots k_0)_2$
Ensure: $Q = (x', y') = kP$	**Ensure:** $Q = (x', y') = kP$
1: $Q \leftarrow \mathcal{O}$	$Q \leftarrow \mathcal{O}, S \leftarrow P$
2: **for** i from $l-1$ downto 0 **do**	**for** i from 0 to $l-1$ **do**
3: $\quad Q \leftarrow 2Q$	$\quad$ **if** $k_i = 1$ **then**
4: $\quad$ **if** $k_i = 1$ **then**	$\quad\quad Q \leftarrow Q + S$
5: $\quad\quad Q \leftarrow Q + P$	$\quad$ **end if**
6: $\quad$ **end if**	$\quad S \leftarrow 2S$
7: **end for**	**end for**
8: Return Q	Return Q

However, as we allocate two MALUs for the ECC case, the number becomes $21l$ by processing point additions and doublings in parallel.

5.3   Performance Estimation for RSA and ECC from FPGA Implementation

We implemented the proposed datapath on a Xilinx FPGA (Spartan 3). The place-and-route result is shown in Table 1. The design is set as the ECC configuration and the critical path delay for the RSA configuration is estimated by the result of STA (Static Timing Analysis).

Table 1. Implementation result of the proposed datapath

Target Platform	Number of Slices	Critical Path [$nsec$] RSA config.	ECC config.
xc3s5000	27,597	10.6	25.3

Based on the required number of multiplications for RSA and ECC, we estimate the performance and compare them with each other. The result is summarized in Table 2. For the ECC case, the latency of point multiplication is used for the performance, and the latency of modular exponentiation is estimated for the RSA case. As seen from the result, the performance of modular exponentiation for RSA-2048 is slower than ECC by a factor of 7 approximately. Even when applying CRT for RSA-2048, the performance is almost half of that of ECC-256p. Moreover, ECC-256p offers stronger security than RSA-2048.

Table 2. Performance comparison of RSA-2048, RSA-2048 with CRT, and ECC-256p

Type of PKC	MALU Config.	Max. Clock Freq. [MHz]	Performance [$msec$]
RSA-2048	MALU$_{2048 \times 1}$	95	133.1
RSA-2048(CRT)	2× MALU$_{1024 \times 1}$	95	33.3
ECC-256p	2× MALU$_{260 \times 4}$	40	17.7

6   Conclusions

We presented a new reconfigurable datapath that enables modular operations for different bit-widths. In addition, the flip-flops are also reconfigured depending on the configuration in order to use hardware resources effectively. The estimated performance based on an FPGA implementation is shown as a case study of RSA-2048 (with and without CRT) and ECC-256p. The results prove that our proposed datapath is suitable for a high-performance cryptosystem supporting both RSA and ECC over GF(p). Especially in our case, ECC-256p shows a better performance than RSA-2048 on the same amount of hardware resources.

References

1. L. Batina, G. Bruin-Muurling, and S.B. Örs. Flexible hardware design for RSA and elliptic curve cryptosystems. In T. Okamoto, editor, *In Topics in Cryptology - CT-RSA - The Cryptographers' Track at the RSA Conference*, volume 2964 of *Lecture Notes in Computer Science*, pages 250–263. Springer-Verlag, 2004.
2. L. Batina and G. Muurling. Montgomery in Practice: How to Do It More Efficiently in Hardware. In B. Preneel, editor, *In Topics in Cryptology - CT-RSA - The Cryptographers' Track at the RSA Conference*, number 2271 in Lecture Notes in Computer Science, pages 40–52, San Jose, USA, February 18-22 2002. Springer-Verlag.
3. F. Crowe, A. Daly, and W. Marnane. A Scalable Dual Mode Arithmetic Unit for Public Key Cryptosystems. In *Proc. IEEE International Conference Conference on Information Technology - ITCC'05*, pages 568–573, Las Vegas, 2005.
4. W. Diffie and M.E. Hellman. New directions in cryptography. *IEEE Transactions on Information Theory*, 22:644–654, 1976.
5. N. Koblitz. Elliptic curve cryptosystem. *Math. Comp.*, 48:203–209, 1987.
6. P. Kocher, J. Jaffe, and B. Jun. Introduction to differential power analysis and related attacks. http://www.cryptography.com/dpa/technical, 1998.
7. C. McIvor, M. McLoone, J. McCanny, A. Daly, and W. Marnane. Fast Montgomery Modular Multiplication and RSA Cryptographic Processor Architectures. In *Proceedings of 37th Annual Asilomar Conference on Signals, Systems and Computers*, pages 379–384, November 2003.
8. A.J. Menezes. *Elliptic Curve Public Key Cryptosystems*. Kluwer Academic Publishers, 1993.
9. V. Miller. Uses of elliptic curves in cryptography. In H. C. Williams, editor, *Advances in Cryptology: Proceedings of CRYPTO'85*, number 218 in Lecture Notes in Computer Science, pages 417–426. Springer-Verlag, 1985.
10. J.-J. Quisquater and C. Couvreur. Fast decipherment algorithm for RSA public-key cryptosystem. *Electronics Letters*, 18:905–907, October 1982.
11. R.L. Rivest, A. Shamir, and L. Adleman. A method for obtaining digital signatures and public-key cryptosystems. *Communications of the ACM*, 21(2):120–126, 1978.
12. A.F. Tenca and Ç.K. Koç. A scalable architecture for Montgomery multiplication. In Ç.K. Koç and C. Paar, editors, *Proceedings of 1st International Workshop on Cryptographic Hardware and Embedded Systems (CHES)*, number 1717 in Lecture Notes in Computer Science, pages 94–108, Worcester, Massachusetts, USA, August 12-13 1999. Springer-Verlag.

FPGA Implementation of a $GF(2^m)$ Tate Pairing Architecture

Maurice Keller*, Tim Kerins, Francis Crowe, and William Marnane

Dept. of Electrical and Electronic Engineering,
University College Cork, Cork City, Ireland.
{mauricek, timk, francisc, liam}@rennes.ucc.ie

Abstract. This paper presents a hardware implementation of a dual mode Tate pairing/elliptic curve processor over fields of characteristic 2. The architecture can be reconfigured for different underlying field sizes and hence can support different security levels. The processor also performs elliptic curve point scalar multiplication. The performance of the architecture implemented on an FPGA is evaluated for various security levels.

1 Introduction

Pairing based cryptography has recently generated a significant amount of research interest due to its potential for the construction of many new and interesting cryptosystems [1]. An example of a pairing based system is Identity Based Encryption [2], which has many applications from securing emails to ad-hoc networks. Pairings also find a use in securing Internet protocols [3].

Pairing based cryptography is based on mathematical operations known as bilinear pairings. In practice, a bilinear pairing is a map which takes as inputs two points on an elliptic curve defined over a finite field $GF(p^m)$ and outputs an element of the extension field $GF(p^{km})$. The Tate pairing is used in practice as it can be efficiently computed using Miller's Algorithm and its variants [4,5,6,7]. For elliptic curves over fields of characteristic $p = 2$ the security multiplier k takes a maximum value of $k = 4$ [4,5].

For security comparable to 1024-bit RSA it is desirable to have $km > 1000$, i.e. $k \leq 4$ when $p = 2$ [4,5] so $m > 250$, and m prime. The underlying arithmetic over such field sizes is computationally intensive and can require significant computation time on a general purpose serial processor. Varying the underlying field size m allows the security of the system to be changed, resulting in a trade-off between security level and speed.

Dedicated hardware can potentially provide much faster Tate pairing computation times. It is noted that many pairing based cryptosystems require elliptic

---

* This research was funded by the Embark Initiative Postgraduate Research Scholarship Scheme from the Irish Research Council for Science, Engineering and Technology (IRCSET).

K. Bertels, J.M.P. Cardoso, and S. Vassiliadis (Eds.). ARC 2006, LNCS 3985, pp. 358–369, 2006.

curve point scalar multiplication [1]. Therefore it is desirable that this operation also be accelerated in hardware.

This work details a dual mode Tate pairing accelerator architecture, which is also capable of performing elliptic curve point scalar multiplication. The architecture can be reconfigured to support different security levels by changing the underlying field size m. The architecture was prototyped on a Xilinx Virtex II FPGA and fully implemented in hardware on an $RC2000$ development board from Celoxica [8].

2   Related Work

Two efficient methods for calculating the Tate pairing based on the elliptic curve group law and line function evaluation have appeared in the literature [4,5]. These are the BKLS and GHS methods respectively. More recently a number of newer algorithms $Duursma - Lee$, η and η_T have appeared, which decouple the Tate pairing calculation from elliptic curve point scalar multiplication [6,7]. An advantage of the BKLS/GHS approach from a hardware perspective is that the same hardware can be used for point scalar multiplication and Tate pairing evaluation

Although the algorithms for computing pairings are well studied in the literature, their hardware implementation is less so. A hardware implementation of the BKLS/GHS algorithm for fields of characteristic 3 was reported in [9]. A hardware implementation of the η pairing over fields of characteristic 2 has been reported in [10] but this is based on hyperelliptic curves. To the best of the authors knowledge this is the first hardware implementation of a pairing on elliptic curves over fields of characteristic 2.

3   Elliptic Curves and the Tate Pairing

A supersingular elliptic curve over the field $GF(2^m)$ is defined by the equation:

$$E(GF(2^m)) : y^2 + y = x^3 + x + b, b \in \{0, 1\} \tag{1}$$

The set of points on $E(GF(2^m))$ is defined as the set of all $(x, y) \in GF(2^m)$ which satisfy Eq.(1) and a special point φ, known as the point at infinity. Addition and doubling of elliptic curve points is defined by Eq.(2) and Eq.(3), where $P_i = (x_i, y_i)$. The underlying operations are Galois Field addition, multiplication, squaring and division. The equation of the line function $d(x, y)$, where d is the line between P_0 and P_1, is defined in Eq.(4).

$$
\begin{aligned}
P_2 &= P_0 + P_1 \\
\lambda &= \frac{y_0 + y_1}{x_0 + x_1} \\
x_2 &= \lambda^2 + x_1 + x_0 \\
y_2 &= \lambda(x_0 + x_2) + y_0 + 1
\end{aligned}
\tag{2}
$$

$$
\begin{aligned}
P_2 &= [2]P_0 = P_0 + P_0 \\
\lambda &= x_o^2 + 1 \\
x_2 &= \lambda^2 \\
y_2 &= x_0^4 + y_0^4
\end{aligned}
\tag{3}
$$

$$d(x, y) = y + y_0 + \lambda(x + x_0) \tag{4}$$

Algorithm 1. BKLS/GHS Algorithm

Input:	$P \in E(GF(2^m)), \ Q \in E(GF(2^{4m})), l = \sum_{i=0}^{t-1} l_i 2^i$	
Output:	$t_l(P, Q)$	
Initialise: 1.	$f = 1; \ V = P$	
Run: 2.	for $i = t - 1$ downto 0 do	
3.	$V = 2V$	/* Point Double */
4.	$f = f^2.d(Q)$	/* $GF(2^{4m})$ Multiplication */
5.	if($l_i = 1$) then	
6.	$V = V + P$	/* Point Addition */
7.	$f = f.d(Q)$	/* $GF(2^{4m})$ Multiplication */
8.	end if	
9.	end for	
Return: 10.	$t_l = f^{\epsilon_l}$	/* $GF(2^{4m})$ Exponentiation */

The order of the curve is the total number of points on $E(GF(2^m))$ and it dictates the computational complexity of the Tate pairing. It is denoted $\#E(GF(2^m))$ and is given by Eq.(5) for the curve defined in Eq.(1). The curve order can be broken into two factors $n = h.l$, where l is a large prime and the cofactor h is small compared to l. In some cases the curve order itself may be prime in which case $h = 1$. For good security it is necessary to ensure that l is approximately 160 bits [5]. For this work Eq.(1) with $b = 1$ was used as the underlying curve.

$$\#E(GF(2^m)) = n = \begin{cases} 2^m + 1 + (-1)^b 2^{(m+1)/2}, \ m \equiv 1, 7 \mod 8 \\ 2^m + 1 - (-1)^b 2^{(m+1)/2}, \ m \equiv 3, 5 \mod 8 \end{cases} \quad (5)$$

Point scalar multiplication of an elliptic curve point, R by a scalar k is computed using repeated point additions i.e. $T = [k]R = R + R + \ldots + R$. An elliptic curve point P is said to have order l if l is the smallest number such that $[l]P = \varphi$. The set of all points of order l on the curve $E(GF(2^m))$ is denoted by $E(GF(2^m))[l]$.

Let E be the curve given in Eq.(1). The lth-order Tate pairing maps two points, $P \in E(GF(2^m))[l]$ and $Q \in E(GF(2^{4m}))[l]$, to an element of the multiplicative group $GF(2^{4m})^*$. It is defined as:

$$t_l(P, Q) = f_P(Q)^{\epsilon_l} \quad (6)$$

The Tate pairing is raised to the power $\epsilon_l = \frac{2^{4m}-1}{l}$ to obtain a unique value for cryptographic applications. The BKLS/GHS algorithm presented in Algorithm 1 is an optimised version of Miller's algorithm for computing the Tate pairing where $Q = \phi(R), \ R \in E(GF(2^m)), \ Q \in E(GF(2^{4m}))$ for some suitable distortion map $\phi(x, y)$ as described in [4]. The final exponentiation stage of the algorithm can be performed using the binary square and multiply method as described in [11].

The Tate pairing can also be computed in terms of the curve order n. This is the nth-order Tate pairing and is denoted $t_n(P, Q)$ where $P \in E(GF(2^m))[l]$ and $Q \in E(GF(2^{4m}))[l]$. The final exponentiation in this case is to the power

Table 1. Example Secure Field Sizes for Pairing Based Cryptography

m	km	$hw(n)$	Bits in l	$hw(l)$
251	1004	3	154	76
283	1132	3	284	3

Algorithm 1a. Point Scalar Multiplication

Input:	$P \in E(GF(2^m)), k = \sum_{i=0}^{t-1} k_i 2^i$
Output:	$[k]P$
Initialise:	1. $V = P$
Run:	2. for $i = t - 1$ downto 0 do
	3. $V = 2V$ /* Point Double */
	4. if($k_i = 1$) then
	5. $V = V + P$ /* Point Addition */
	6. end if
	7. end for
Return:	8. $V = [k]P$

$\epsilon_n = \frac{2^{4m}-1}{n}$. Algorithm 1 can be used to compute the nth-order Tate pairing by replacing the binary expansion of l with the binary expansion of n and performing the final exponentiation to ϵ_n. From [7] it is known that $t_n(P, Q) = t_l(P, Q)$.

It can be seen that the run time of Algorithm 1 will depend heavily on the Hamming weight of l or n depending on which order Tate pairing is computed. The Hamming weight of n is given by Eq.(7) (see Appendix A for proof). Choosing the field size m such that $m \equiv 3, 5 \mod 8$ and computing the nth-order Tate pairing will result in a fast computation time due to the low Hamming weight of n.

$$hw(n) = \begin{cases} \frac{m+1}{2}, & m \equiv 1, 7 \mod 8 \\ 3, & m \equiv 3, 5 \mod 8 \end{cases} \tag{7}$$

In choosing the field size however it is necessary to also consider the prime order l of the group of points on the curve . Two field sizes suitable for use in pairing based cryptosystems and their associated parameters are presented in Table 1. For $m = 251$ it can be seen that $hw(n) << hw(l)$ therefore the nth-order Tate pairing is more efficiently computable using Algorithm 1. For $m = 283$ a special case is seen where the cofactor is 1 and both n and l have the same Hamming weight. Therefore either order Tate pairing is optimal.

It is noted that the BKLS/GHS algorithm is a modified version of the binary algorithm for elliptic curve point scalar multiplication. Therefore if steps $4, 7$ and 10 are omitted from the algorithm it can be used to perform point scalar multiplication i.e. computing $[k]P$. This is given in Algorithm 1a. This is advantageous from a hardware implementation point of view as it means that the same architecture can perform both operations.

4   Hardware Architecture

4.1 $GF(2^m)$ Components

The underlying arithmetic in Algorithm 1 is performed over $GF(2^m)$. Addition is simply bitwise XOR of the two elements to be added with the result available after one XOR gate delay. Therefore it is considered virtually free from both a time and area perspective in hardware, in comparison to the other operations. Multiplication is implemented using a Digit-Serial multiplier architecture as described in [12]. This computes the result in $n = \lceil \frac{m}{D} \rceil$ clock cycles, where D is the digit size of the multiplier. Varying D allows an area/speed trade-off to be explored. Squaring is a special case of multiplication which can be implemented in hardware using a Bit-Parallel architecture which computes the result in one clock cycle. Division is provided by the architecture described by Shantz in [13]. It computes the result in $2m$ clock cycles.

4.2 $GF(2^{4m})$ Multiplier

A multiplier architecture based on the Karatsuba-Ofman algorithm [14] was used for the extension field multiplication. The architecture, shown in Figure 1, computes $c(x) = a(x)b(x) \mod f(x)$, $a(x), b(x), c(x) \in GF(2^{4m})$. A full description of the architecture is given in [15]. The architecture features nine parallel $GF(2^m)$ Digit-Serial multipliers and performs the extension field multiplication in the time taken for one $GF(2^m)$ multiplication i.e. $n = \lceil \frac{m}{D} \rceil$ clock cycles. This architecture also allows an area/speed trade-off to be explored by varying D.

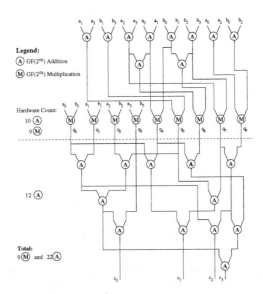

Fig. 1. $GF(2^{4m})$ Karatsuba Multiplication Architecture

4.3 $GF(2^{4m})$ Squarer

It is desired to compute $c(x) = a^2(x) \mod f(x)$, $a(x), c(x) \in GF(2^{4m})$. The square is given simply by $a^2(x) = a_3^2 x^6 + a_2^2 x^4 + a_1^2 x^2 + a_0^2$ and the polynomial modular reduction is performed using matrix multiplication as described in [15]. This leads to the closed equations for $c(x)$ given in Eq.(8). These can be implemented in hardware using four $GF(2^m)$ squarers and two $GF(2^m)$ adders. The $GF(2^{4m})$ squaring is performed in three clock cycles.

$$
\begin{aligned}
c_3 &= a_3^2 \\
c_2 &= a_1^2 + a_3^2 \\
c_1 &= a_2^2 \\
c_0 &= a_0^2 + a_2^2
\end{aligned}
\tag{8}
$$

4.4 Line Function Evaluator

This block must compute $d(Q) = d(x_Q, y_Q) \in GF(2^{4m})$ as per Eq.(4) where $x_0, y_0, \lambda \in GF(2^m)$ and $x_Q, y_Q \in GF(2^{4m})$. On each iteration of the algorithm the values (x_0, y_0) correspond to the coordinates of V before it is updated. Using $x_Q(x) = x_{Q_3} x^3 + x_{Q_2} x^2 + x_{Q_1} x + x_{Q_0}$, $y_Q(x) = y_{Q_3} x^3 + y_{Q_2} x^2 + y_{Q_1} x + y_{Q_0}$ and $(x_0, y_0) = (x_V, y_V)$ the following expressions for $d(Q)$ can be obtained:

$$
\begin{aligned}
d_i &= y_{Q_i} + \lambda x_{Q_i}, \ i = 1, 2, 3 \\
d_0 &= y_{Q_0} + y_V + \lambda(x_{Q_0} + x_V)
\end{aligned}
\tag{9}
$$

where λ is computed using either Eq.(2) or Eq.(3). For maximum speed, four $GF(2^m)$ multipliers are used in parallel along with six $GF(2^m)$ adders. The computation time of the block is equal to the time taken for one $GF(2^m)$ multiplication i.e. $N_{line} = n$ clock cycles.

4.5 Elliptic Curve Processor

This block implements elliptic curve point additions and doublings as per Eq.(2) and Eq.(3). The processor takes four m-bit inputs $(x_0, y_0), (x_1, y_1)$ and outputs $(x_2, y_2) = (x_0, y_0) + (x_1, y_1)$ or $(x_2, y_2) = 2(x_0, y_0)$ depending on whether the double/add input is 0 or 1.

Elliptic curve point addition is performed using Eq.(2). For implementation the equation for y_2 is rearranged to $y_2 = \lambda(\lambda^2 + x_1) + y_0 + 1$, which saves one addition in the critical path. It is implemented in hardware using six adders, a squarer, a divider and a multiplier as shown in Figure 2. The critical path through the design is $3A + D + S + M$. Therefore the number of clock cycles required to perform a point addition is $N_{add} = n + 2m$, neglecting the additions and the squaring. It is noted however that λ is available once the division is complete i.e. after $2m$ clock cycles. A doubling block implements Eq.(3). It computes λ in 2 clock cycles and (x_2, y_2) in 3 clock cycles.

The elliptic curve processor consists of an adder block and a doubling block as shown in Figure 3. The processor has two done pins, one to indicated that

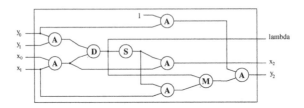

Fig. 2. Point Addition Block Structure

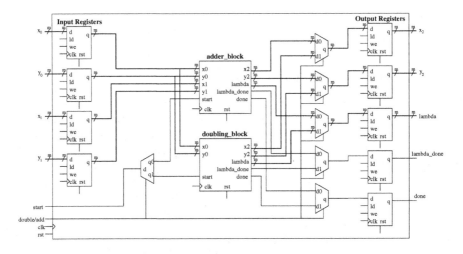

Fig. 3. Elliptic Curve Processor (without bus interface)

λ is ready and one to indicate that (x_2, y_2) is ready. This means that in the evaluation of Algorithm 1 the line function block can begin computing $d(Q)$ once λ is available.

4.6   Bus Interface

The overall architecture utilises an m-bit data bus. Each component to be used in the Tate pairing architecture has multiple m-bit inputs and outputs, and therefore requires an interface to this bus. The bus interface consists of an m-bit data bus, an address bus, a read/write pin and a load pin. Each m-bit input and output has its own register, which is assigned an address. To write m-bits of data read/write is set to low, the appropriate address is selected (enabling the appropriate register) and then load is asserted. To read the outputs read/write is asserted, which allows the component to drive the data bus. The individual output registers are then read by setting the appropriate address. Each component also has a done pin, used to indicate to the control circuitry that it has completed a calculation.

4.7   Dual Mode Tate Pairing Processor

The Tate pairing processor architecture is illustrated in Figure 4. The mode input selects between the two modes of operation. With mode low the architecture takes four input values: $P = (x_p, y_p), Q = (x_q, y_q), j, \epsilon_j$. It then computes $t_j(P, Q)$ using Algorithm 1 ($j = n$ or l depending on which order Tate pairing is to be computed). With mode high the architecture takes as input $P = (x_p, y_p), k$ and computes $[k]P$ using Algorithm 1a.

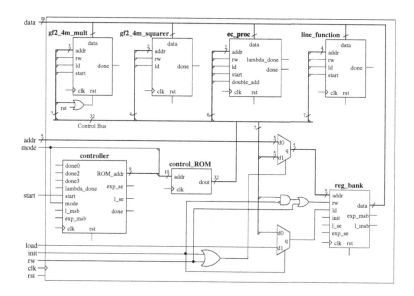

Fig. 4. Dual Mode Tate Pairing Processor Architecture

The controller is based on a 32-bit wide ROM which stores a set of instructions for controlling the bus interfaces of the individual components in the design. In Tate pairing mode a state machine addresses the ROM in the appropriate sequence to perform Algorithm 1. A second state machine is used to perform Algorithm 1a when mode is high. Tri-state buffers enabled by the mode input are used to control which state machine is in control and addressing the ROM.

The register bank contains the memory necessary to store the inputs and f, t_j which are the outputs of Algorithm 1. Shift registers within the register bank are used to store j and ϵ_j with their shift enable (se) and msb's being direct inputs and outputs of the register bank. The other variables require 18 m-bit registers. The FPGA block RAM resources are used for this purpose.

Figure 5 illustrates the schedule of operations (excluding data transfers) for the point addition stage of Algorithm 1 i.e. lines 6 and 7. From this graph it is seen that the point addition stage requires $N_{add} = 2m + 2n + 81$ clock cycles including those for data transfer. It is noted that $d(Q)$ does not need to be evaluated on the last iteration of Algorithm 1, leading to a special point addition stage with a reduced cost $N_{add2} = n + 41$. Similarly $N_{double} = 2n + 95$.

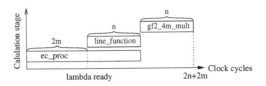

Fig. 5. Point Addition Stage Operation Scheduling

The exponentiation operation also has two stages, namely squaring and multiplying. Their cost is given by $N_{square} = 3 + 31$ and $N_{mult} = n + 36$. At the start of Algorithm 1 and before the exponentiation there are $N_{setup} = 57$ clock cycles in total required to setup the architecture for the calculation. The exponent is stored in four cascaded m-bit shift registers, however it will generally be less than $4m$ bits. Therefore it will be shifted s times at the start of the exponentiation stage to ensure that the msb output is 1. The total cost of the Tate pairing calculation including all data transfer clock cycle overheads is given by Eq.(10).

$$N_{tate} = N_{setup} + mN_{double} + (hw(l) - 1)N_{add} + N_{add2} \\ + s + (4m - s)N_{square} + hw(\epsilon)N_{mult} \tag{10}$$

This cost can be further split into control clock cycles ($N_{control}$) and calculation clock cycles (N_{calc}) as given by Eq.(11) and Eq.(12). The control clock cycles include the cycles required for the setup stages and all the data transfers across the data bus of the architecture. The number of calculation clock cycles is a measure of the latency of the components performing calculations.

$$N_{control} = 17 + 219m + 81hw(l) - 30s + 36hw(\epsilon) \tag{11}$$

$$N_{calc} = (2m + hw(\epsilon) + 1)n + (hw(l) - 1)(2m + 2n) + (4m - s)3 \tag{12}$$

When in point multiplication mode the clock cycles required for each stage of Algorithm 1a are $N_{Psetup} = 9$, $N_{Pdouble} = 22$ and $N_{Padd} = n + 2m + 19$. The number of clock cycles required to perform a point scalar multiplication $[k]P$ depends on the Hamming weight of the scalar k and is given by Eq.(13).

$$N_{Pmult} = N_{Psetup} + mN_{Pdouble} + hw(k)N_{Padd} \tag{13}$$

5   Results

The processor architecture of Figure 4 was prototyped on a Xilinx Virtex 2 $xc2v6000 - 4$ device using Xilinx ISE. The design was implemented on an $RC2000$ development board from Celoxica [8] and the maximum clock frequency determined.

Tables 2 and 3 give the implementation results of the architecture for 1004 and 1132 bit finite fields respectively. The post synthesis (PS) and actual implementation (RC2000) clock frequencies are reported along with the area requirement

Table 2. Dual Mode Processor Results, $m = 251$, $km = 1004$

D	CLK freq. (MHz)		area	T_{tate}	T_{mult}	$\frac{N_{control}}{N_{calc}}$
	PS	RC2000	(slices)	(ms)	(ms)	
1	72.4	50.0	16621 (49%)	6.44	2.06	0.26
6	72.4	43.0	21955 (64%)	2.58	1.78	1.44
10	72.4	40.0	27725 (82%)	2.37	1.86	2.22

Table 3. Dual Mode Processor Results, $m = 283$, $km = 1132$

D	CLK freq. (MHz)		area	T_{tate}	T_{mult}	$\frac{N_{control}}{N_{calc}}$
	PS	RC2000	(slices)	(ms)	(ms)	
1	71.2	50.0	18599 (55%)	7.98	2.59	0.23
4	71.2	49.0	22636 (66%)	3.23	2.03	0.87
6	71.2	47.0	24655 (72%)	2.81	2.05	1.23

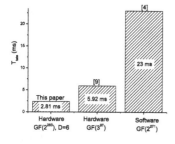

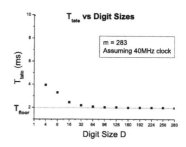

Fig. 6. Performance of the architecture presented in this paper compared with other implementations

Fig. 7. Illustration of T_{floor} for $m = 283$

for various different digit sizes D of the underlying $GF(2^m)$ multipliers. Tate pairing and average point multiplication times are given based on the actual $RC2000$ implementation clock frequency and Eq.(10) and Eq.(13) (an average Hamming weight of $(m + 1)/2$ was assumed for k).

These results provide significant acceleration over the software result of $23ms$ reported in [4] for a Tate pairing calculation over $GF(2^{271})$ on a $1GHz$ Pentium III processor. This architecture is smaller and faster than the $GF(3^m)$ BKLS/GHS architecture reported in [9]. This reports a fastest BKLS/GHS Tate pairing computation time of $5.92ms$ over $GF(3^{97})$ with an area of 50286 slices. As can be seen from Table 3 the architecture detailed in this paper gives a faster Tate pairing computation time with a 50% reduction in area for $D = 6$. The area time product of this architecture for $m = 283$, $D = 6$ is 70 $slice.secs$ which is a significant improvement over the area time product of 298 $slice.secs$ for the $GF(3^{97})$ design reported in [9]. It is noted that $GF(2^{283})$ provides a comparable level of security to $GF(3^{97})$. A comparison of the various results is given in Figure 6.

The final column of Tables 2 and 3 gives the ratio of control clock cycles to calculation clock cycles. For a small digit size the ratio is quiet low. This means that most of the Tate pairing calculation time comes from waiting for the underlying components to perform a calculation. However, as the digit size increases the ratio becomes larger and the Tate pairing calculation time is dominated by the control i.e. data transfers between the components in the architecture and the setup time for each. Figure 7 illustrates this effect for $m = 283$. Neglecting the area requirements and assuming a constant clock frequency of $40MHz$ it can be seen that the Tate pairing computation time approaches a "floor" of $2ms$ as the digit size is increased to its maximum value of 283.

6   Conclusions

A dual mode architecture to perform the Tate pairing or elliptic curve point scalar multiplication over $GF(2^m)$ is presented in this paper. The architecture was implemented on an FPGA for two different security levels and various digit sizes of the underlying multiplier. The Tate pairing computation time of the architecture provides significant speed-ups compared to recent software implementations of the same algorithm. It also outperformed an implementation of the same algorithm over $GF(3^m)$ reported in the literature.

The advantage of this hardware architecture is that it can be reconfigured to suit different security levels by varying the underlying field size m. The digit size of the underlying multiplier can also be varied to obtain an area/speed trade-off to suit the particular application. It is also advantageous from an area perspective that the same architecture can be used to accelerate elliptic curve point scalar multiplication.

References

1. R. Dutta, R. Barua and P. Sarkar: Pairing-Based Cryptographic Protocols: A Survey. Cryptology ePrint Archive, Report 064/2004, (2004)
2. D. Boneh and M. Franklin: Identity Based Encryption from the Weil Pairing. *SIAM J. of Computing*, Vol. 32, No. 3, (2003) 586–615
3. M. Zhao, S. W. Smith and D. M. Nicol: Aggregated Path Authentication for Efficient BGP Security. *Proc. 12th ACM Conference on Computer and Communications Security*, (November 2005) 128–138
4. P. S. L. M. Barreto, H. Y. Kim, B. Lynn and M. Scott: Efficient Algorithms for Pairing-Based Cryptosystems. *Proc. CRYPTO '02*, (2002) 354–368
5. S. D. Galbraith, K. Harrison and D. Soldera: Implementing the Tate Pairing. *Proc. Fifth Algorithmic Number Theory Symp. (ANTS-V)*, (2002) 324–337
6. I. Duursma and H.-S. Lee: Tate Pairing Implementation for Hyperelliptic Curves $y^2 = x^p - x + d$. *Proc. ASIACRYPT '03*, (2003) 111–123
7. P. S. L. M. Barreto, S. Galbraith, C. O'hEigeartaigh and M. Scott: Efficient Pairing Computation on Supersingular Abelian Varieties. Cryptology ePrint Archive, Report 375/2004, (2004)
8. Celoxica RC2000, http://www.celoxica.com/products/rc2000/default.asp

9. T. Kerins, W. P. Marnane, E. M. Popovici and P. S. L. M. Barreto: Hardware Accelerators for Pairing Based Cryptosystems. *IEE Proceedings on Information Security*, Vol 152, No. 1, (October 2005) 47–56

10. R. Ronan, C. O'hEigeartaigh, C. Murphy, M. Scott, T. Kerins and W. P. Marnane: A Dedicated Processor for the eta Pairing. Cryptology ePrint Archive, Report 330/2005, (2005)

11. D. Knuth: The Art of Computer Programming: Seminumerical Algorithms. Vol 2, Second Edition, Addison-Wesley, (1981)

12. L. Song and K. Parhi: Low Energy Digit-Serial/Parallel Finite Field Multipliers. *Kulwer Journal of VLSI Signal Processing Systems*, Vol 19, No. 2, (1998) 149–166

13. S. C. Shantz: From Euclid's GCD to Montgomery Multiplication to the Great Divide. TR-2001-95, Technical Report, Sun Microsystems, (2001)

14. A. Karatsuba and Y. Ofman: Multiplication on Many-Digital Numbers by Automatic Computers. *Translation in Physics-Doklady*, Vol 7, (1963) 595–596

15. M. Keller, T. Kerins and W. Marnane: FPGA Implementation of a $GF(2^{4m})$ Multiplier for use in Pairing Based Cryptosystems. *Proc. International Conference on Field Programmable Logic and Applications 2005*, (August 2005) 594–597

A   Determining the Hamming Weight of n

In deciding which order Tate pairing to compute for minimum computation time it is desirable to know the Hamming weight of the curve order n as given in Eq.(5). Assuming $b = 1$ Eq.(5) simplifies to

$$\#E(GF(2^m)) = n = \begin{cases} 2^m + 1 - 2^{(m+1)/2}, \, m \equiv 1, 7 \mod 8 \\ 2^m + 1 + 2^{(m+1)/2}, \, m \equiv 3, 5 \mod 8 \end{cases} \tag{14}$$

When $m \equiv 3, 5 \mod 8$ the Hamming weight is trivially $hw(n) = 3$.

When $m \equiv 1, 7 \mod 8$ a closed equation for the Hamming weight of $2^m + 1 - 2^{(m+1)/2}$ represented using $(m + 1)$ bits can be deduced as follows.

Consider some number 2^j. It is known that $hw(2^j) = 1$. Now consider the $(m + 1)$-bit binary representation of $2^j = 000...010...000$, where the 1 is in bit position j. Two's complement representation can be used to represent -2^j in binary. To convert 2^j to -2^j all the bits are inverted and 1 is added. This gives $-2^j = 111...110...000$. This has 1's in all the bit positions between the jth bit and the mth bit. Therefore $hw(-2^j) = m - j + 1$.

Next consider the number $2^m - 2^j + 1$. Firstly $2^m - 2^j = 011...110...000$ i.e. only the msb changes. Adding 2^m to 2^j reduces its hamming weight by 1. Secondly $2^m - 2^j + 1 = 011...110...001$ i.e. only the lsb changes. Adding 1 to $2^m - 2^j$ increases its hamming weight by 1. Therefore the addition of 2^m and 1 to -2^j have no effect on the hamming weight of the number as they cancel each other out. Therefore $hw(2^m - 2^j + 1) = m - j + 1$.

With $j = \frac{(m+1)}{2}$ this yields $hw(n) = \frac{m+1}{2}$ for $m \equiv 1, 7 \mod 8$.

Iterative Modular Division over $\mathrm{GF}(2^m)$: Novel Algorithm and Implementations on FPGA

Guerric Meurice de Dormale* and Jean-Jacques Quisquater

Université Catholique de Louvain, UCL Crypto Group, DICE
Place du Levant 3, B-1348 Louvain-La-Neuve, Belgium
{gmeurice, quisquater}@dice.ucl.ac.be

Abstract. Public key cryptography is a concept used by many useful functionalities such as digital signature, encryption, key agreements, ... For those needs, elliptic curve cryptography is an attractive solution.

Cryptosystems based on elliptic curve need a costly modular division. Depending on the choice of coordinates, this operation is requested at each step of algorithms, during a precomputation phase or at the end of the whole computation. As a result, efficient modular division implementations are useful for both area constrained designs working in affine coordinates and high-speed processors.

For that purpose, this work highlights the most efficient iterative modular division algorithm and explores different time and area tradeoffs on FPGA. First, thanks to a novel algorithm, the computational time is divided by two with an area increase of one half. Second, using the *Single-Instruction Multiple-Data* feature of the selected algorithm, the area is divided by two with a doubling of the computational time.

To the best of our knowledge, it is the first report about an iterative digit-serial modular division algorithm, the first area and time tradeoff analysis of an iterative algorithm and the best result among the very few implementations on FPGA.

1 Introduction

With the advent of public key cryptography, many useful functionalities appeared such as digital signature, public key encryption, key agreements, ... For those needs, elliptic curve cryptography (ECC) is an attractive solution. Co-invented by V. Miller [16] and N. Koblitz [15] in 1985, it provides one of the highest security per bit of known public key scheme. This means highly wanted properties like less processing power, storage, bandwidth and power consumption. For a thorough description of the topic, the reader is referred to [4] for mathematical background and to [12] for implementation issues.

As the underlying operations of public key cryptosystems are computer-intensive, hardware processor or co-processor are often needed to speed up the computation. As a result, efficient algorithms and specific implementations of the critical arithmetic operations are needed.

---

* Supported by the Belgian fund for industrial and agricultural research (FRIA).

K. Bertels, J.M.P. Cardoso, and S. Vassiliadis (Eds.): ARC 2006, LNCS 3985, pp. 370–382, 2006.

The main operation of ECC is the scalar point multiplication. The underlying modular arithmetic operations are addition, squaring, multiplication and the costly division. Depending on the choice of coordinates, a modular division is needed for each point addition and point doubling or only at the end of the scalar multiplication. With precomputation strategy, it could also be used to precompute points in affine coordinates in order to enable mixed coordinates addition [18]. As a result, a cost-effective modular division is useful for area constrained designs based on affine coordinates (e.g. [1]). High-speed processors using projective coordinates require also efficient modular division to handle the conversion of the final result back to affine representation (e.g. [10]). Indeed, this operation must not constrain the area and working frequency of the processor.

One of the aims of this paper is to emphasize the most efficient iterative modular division algorithm over GF(2^m). On this basis, different time and area tradeoffs are analyzed on Xilinx Virtex FPGAs.

First, a novel algorithm processing simultaneously two bits is presented. Compared to the serial design, the computational time is divided by two and the optimized implementation needs only an area increase of one half. To the best of our knowledge, it is the first proposal of an iterative digit-serial algorithm. This method could be further exploited to carry out algorithms processing more than two bits (with an exponential complexity), but it is not the topic of this paper.

Second, using the *Single-Instruction Multiple-Data* (SIMD) feature of the selected algorithm, the division is processed in two different phases with the same hardware. As a result, the area is halved at the expense of the doubling of the computational time.

The joint utilization of the novel algorithm and the SIMD feature leads to another tradeoff: the throughput of the serial algorithm is reduced by one third while improving the area by one seventh. This is unexpected since the serial implementation seemed to be area-optimal.

This paper is structured as follows: Sect. 2 introduces the previous works on modular division over GF(2^m) and emphasizes the most efficient one. Sect. 3 displays the selected algorithm and presents the novel digit-serial modular division. The optimized designs for the selected platform stands in Sect. 4. Then, those implementations modified with the SIMD feature are reported in Sect. 5. The results are discussed in Sect. 6 and finally, conclusions are in Sect. 7.

2   Previous Works

There are three main methods to perform the modular division X/Y over GF(2^m):

Little Fermat's theorem, computed as $X \cdot Y^{2^m-2} \bmod p(x)$ [14].
Solution of a system of m linear equations over GF(2) using Gaussian elimination [13].
Iterative transformations of the *gcd* (greatest common divisor) function based on Euclid or Stein [19] algorithms.

The latter exhibits the best area-time complexity [20]. Therefore, this paper focusses on *gcd* based algorithms and especially on the binary versions of Stein.

In the literature, this kind of algorithms are usually considered as very slow (e.g. [8]). One reason is that modular divisions using the basic Euclid and Stein algorithms are not favorable to efficient implementations. They need degree comparisons at each step, increasing the area-time complexity and thwarting digit-serial techniques. A method replacing this comparison by a much more simple counter has been described as early as in the mid 80's by Brent and Kung [3].

Exploiting this counter idea, Brunner et al. [2] presented an efficient binary shift-left algorithm. Recently, Wu et al. [20][1] and Kim et al. [7] presented two very similar serial binary shift-right algorithms. The authors show that this modification leads to an even better area-time complexity.

The next step was to adapt this algorithm to a digit-serial version, favorable to an iterative design. For an m-degree irreducible polynomial $p(x)$, the aim of the digit-serial technique is to divide the $2m - 1$ steps required by the algorithm by the digit size d. The complexity of the circuit increase with d, but small d can already achieve an interesting improvement on the latency.

It should be emphasized here that the proposed method is different from a "multi bit-shift" technique. As shown by Gutub [11], it saves at most 15% of the $2m - 1$ step instead of 50% with a digit size of 2 for example.

A systolic digit-serial algorithm has already been presented in [9], but the atomic piece of circuits needs more than one cycle to process the data. As a result, it is not suitable for an iterative implementation. Moreover, they do not provide an explicit algorithm: the digit-serial feature is obtained by domain partition of a systolic dependence graph. Therefore, they do not benefit from algorithmic optimization.

3   Modular Division Algorithms

Let $p(x) \in GF(2)[x]$ be an irreducible polynomial of degree m generating the field $GF(2^m)$. Let X and Y be two polynomials with coefficient in $GF(2)$ represented by $X = (x_{m-1}, \ldots, x_1, x_0)$ and $Y = (y_{m-1}, \ldots, y_1, y_0)$. Only the polynomial basis is considered.

Algorithm 1 is equivalent to the binary shift-right algorithm of Wu et al. and Kim et al. It is used to process the division $X/Y \bmod p(x)$ and it needs $2m - 1$ iterations to compute the result.

The following notations are used: p stands for the irreducible polynomial $p(x)$. The addition, a bitwise *xor* operation, is written $\oplus$. The bit *IsPos* is used to store the sign of the unsigned counter D. It is equal to 1 when the counter represents a positive value. Finally, the operations between brackets are performed in parallel.

One adjustment has also been made to ease the implementations covered by the Section 4 and 5: for D, a simple unsigned arithmetic counter is used instead of a one-hot counter. It has been chosen in order to reduce the chip area while keeping good working frequency.

---

[1] Notice that, because their r and s variables converge towards zero, they should reduce the size of their systolic array design in a triangular shape.

Algorithm 1. Serial modular division over GF(2^m), $X/Y \bmod p$

$U \leftarrow Y$, $V \leftarrow p$, $R \leftarrow X$, $S \leftarrow 0, k \leftarrow 2m - 2$, $D \leftarrow 1$, $IsPos \leftarrow 0$
while $k \geq 0$ **do**
  if $u_0 = 0$ **then** $U \leftarrow U/x$, $R \leftarrow R/x \pmod p$
    if $IsPos = 0$ **then** $D \leftarrow D + 1$
    else if $D = 0$ **then** $D \leftarrow D + 1$, $IsPos \leftarrow 0$ **else** $D \leftarrow D - 1$
  else if $IsPos = 1$ **then** $U \leftarrow U/x \oplus V/x$, $R \leftarrow R/x \oplus S/x \pmod p$
    if $D = 0$ **then** $D \leftarrow D + 1$, $IsPos \leftarrow 0$ **else** $D \leftarrow D - 1$
  else $D \leftarrow D - 1$, $IsPos \leftarrow 1$
    $\{U \leftarrow U/x \oplus V/x$, $V \leftarrow U\}$, $\{R \leftarrow R/x \oplus S/x \pmod p$, $S \leftarrow R\}$
  $k \leftarrow k - 1$
return S

Algorithm 2. 2-bit Digit-serial modular division over GF(2^m), $X/Y \bmod p$

$U \leftarrow 2Y$, $V \leftarrow p$, $R \leftarrow 2X$, $S \leftarrow 0$, $k \leftarrow m - 1$, $D \leftarrow 1$, $IsPos \leftarrow 0$
while $k \geq 0$ **do**
  if $u_1 = 0$ **then**
    if $u_2 = 0$ **then** $U \leftarrow U/x^2$, $R \leftarrow R/x^2 \pmod p$
      if $IsPos = 0$ **then** $D \leftarrow D + 1$
      else if $D = 1$ **then** $IsPos \leftarrow 0$ **else** $D \leftarrow D - 1$
    else if $IsPos = 1$ **then** $U \leftarrow U/x^2 \oplus V$, $R \leftarrow R/x^2 \oplus S \pmod p$
      if $D = 1$ **then** $IsPos \leftarrow 0$ **else** $D \leftarrow D - 1$
    else $IsPos \leftarrow 1$, $\{U \leftarrow U/x^2 \oplus V$, $V \leftarrow U/x^2\}$,
      $\{R \leftarrow R/x^2 \oplus S \pmod p$, $S \leftarrow R/x^2 \pmod p\}$
  else if $IsPos = 1$ **then**
    if $u_2 \oplus v_1 = 0$ **then**
      $U \leftarrow U/x^2 \oplus V/x$, $R \leftarrow R/x^2 \oplus S/x \pmod p$
    else $U \leftarrow U/x^2 \oplus V/x \oplus V$, $R \leftarrow R/x^2 \oplus S/x \oplus S \pmod p$
    if $D = 1$ **then** $IsPos \leftarrow 0$ **else** $D \leftarrow D - 1$
  else
    if $u_2 \oplus v_1 = 0$ **then** $\{U \leftarrow U/x^2 \oplus V/x$, $V \leftarrow U/x\}$,
      $\{R \leftarrow R/x^2 \oplus S/x \pmod p$, $S \leftarrow R/x \pmod p\}$
    else $\{U \leftarrow U/x^2 \oplus V/x \oplus U/x$, $V \leftarrow U/x\}$,
      $\{R \leftarrow R/x^2 \oplus S/x \oplus R/x \pmod p$, $S \leftarrow R/x \pmod p\}$
    if $D = 1$ **then** $D \leftarrow D - 1$, $IsPos \leftarrow 1$
  $k \leftarrow k - 1$
return S

For the division by the polynomial root (a right shift), $U/x \equiv (0, u_{m-1}, \ldots, u_1)$, the degree of the polynomials decreases by one. If the division must be performed modulo the irreducible polynomial, the degree zero of the divided polynomial must be used: $R/x \pmod p \equiv (r_0, r_{m-1} \oplus r_0 p_{m-1}, \ldots, r_1 \oplus r_0 p_1)$ (using the fact that coefficients of the degree m and zero of $p(x)$ always equal one).

The Algorithm 2 is the proposed digit-serial division with a digit size of 2. To improve readability, this algorithm is renamed as "2-bit digit". It needs m iterations to compute the result. The notations used for the Algorithm 1 are kept and the same choice for the counter is applied. Furthermore, the variables

U and R are loaded with a left shift of the operands Y and X. The bits u_1 and u_2 must therefore be used for the control instead of u_0 and u_1.

In the building process of the 2-bit digit algorithm, two successive steps of the serial algorithm are concatenated. As the body of the serial algorithm is split in three different cases, with the set of three operations {shift, shift-add, shift-add & swap}, the 2-bit digit could be expected to need nine cases. Fortunately, the two operations (shift-add – shift-add & swap) and (shift-add & swap – shift-add & swap) never happen and the complexity is reduced.

As two steps are processed at each iteration, the D' counter would never be incremented or decremented by 1 but only by 2. So, it has been modified to $D = D'/2$ to only handle increment and decrement of 1. Moreover, the counter D' is initialized with an odd value, so D never reaches zero. It is important to take care of the counter to ensure an optimal implementation: it is an essential element of the control logic and its performances have a non negligible impact on the working frequency.

4   Hardware Implementations

This Section presents the hardware implementations of the two algorithms from Section 3. In order to exhibit the best performances, the designs have been optimized for the selected hardware platform: the Virtex family of Xilinx FPGA. Their basic building block will therefore be reminded.

The three extension degrees covered are: 163, 193 and 233. For each degree, two different kinds of irreducible polynomials are handled. First, the polynomials recommended by the NIST [17] and the SECG [5] are used: $p(x) = x^{163} + x^7 + x^6 + x^3 + 1$, $p(x) = x^{193} + x^{15} + 1$ and $p(x) = x^{233} + x^{74} + 1$. They are hardwired in the circuit. Secondly, arbitrary polynomials are considered. Nevertheless, it has been decided that only 10% of their monomials, located in the lowest degrees, may have a variable coefficient. The other monomials are hardwired to zero. For applications, another choice for the kind of irreducible polynomial is very unlikely because random irreducible polynomials thwart many improvements (as illustrated in [10]).

For the operative circuits of the two implementations, the register-to-register combinational logic needs few serially connected look-up tables. As a result, the control circuits will dominate the critical path. More precisely, the D counter and its different operations are the most time consuming elements of the control part. To guarantee a high working frequency for each design, the D counter has been optimized with precomputation of the different test flags and commands.

4.1   Targeted Platform

As the implementations have been optimized in order to map the resources of Xilinx Virtex FPGAs in the best possible way, it is important to remind their basic building block. For that purpose, Fig. 1 illustrates the half of a Virtex slice.

This logic cell includes a 4-input look-up table (LUT), carry logic and a storage element. Only those basic features are used in the implementations. Among other functionalities, this logic cell can also provide a 16-bit shift register.

4.2 Serial Modular Division

The implementation of Alg. 1 is illustrated in Fig. 2. In order to consume as few resources as possible, the design takes into account the basic structure of the FPGA. Therefore, when it is possible, each register storing the bits of U,V,R and S variables is driven by a 4-input combinational circuit.

The main optimization is the splitting into two phases of the loading step. To save one input in the logic driving the U and R registers, the operands $2Y$ and $2X$ are loaded in the registers V and S. Then, using the available wires of the circuit, the content of V and S is moved to the appropriate U and R registers (with a shift right operation).

For hardwired irreducible polynomials, each bit of the U,V,R and S variables is dynamically specified by four inputs. With m-degree polynomials, this circuit will consume only $2m$ slices. For arbitrary polynomials, 10% of m additional slices are required to handle the low-degree monomials of $p(x)$.

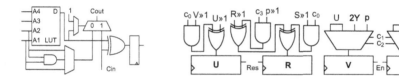

Fig. 1. Basic half of a Virtex slice   **Fig. 2.** Serial modular divider

As this algorithm needs four registers, an area of $4m$ half slices seems optimal. Nevertheless, this can be improved as explained in Section 5.

4.3 Digit-Serial Modular Division

The implementation presented in Fig. 3 is based on the proposed digit-serial algorithm (Alg. 2). The same design principles as the serial algorithm are followed and another feature of the FPGA is exploited: the *xor* gate of the dedicated carry chain is used in order to extend the number of available inputs. As a result, the slices are equivalent to a combinational function with $2 * 4 + 1$ inputs, and 2 outputs. Indeed, if the carry input is embezzled[2], it is shared for the whole slice. The design is then constrained to use the two *xor* gates and to use them with the same input (otherwise half of the slice is wasted).

For hardwired irreducible polynomials, this circuit will consume only $3m$ slices plus a few additional slices for the gates driven by c_8 and c_9 (due to the sparse

---

[2] To achieve this optimization, constraints have to be added for the mapping tool.

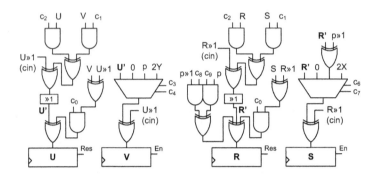

Fig. 3. Digit-serial modular divider with a digit size of 2

$p(x)$). For arbitrary polynomials, 10% of m additional slices are required for the logic driving the V and S registers. Another 10% of m additional slices are needed for the R register.

5   Exploiting the SIMD Feature

With the use of the digit-serial algorithm, computational time has been saved at the cost of extra area. In this section, the serial and digit-serial implementations are modified in order to save area at the cost of more computational time [6].

In the selected algorithm, the set of three different operations (Sect. 3) are executed on two groups of variables: $(U\quad V)$ and $(R\quad S)$. This SIMD feature can therefore be used to process both groups of variables at a different time. Since almost the same hardware is required for both groups, area saving is expected.

Two different techniques are analyzed. The first interleaves the processing of both groups of variables. This approach is easier because the command signals are computed and directly used during two cycles. Nevertheless, during the processing of the first group of variables, registers are needed to store the second group. The second technique processes both groups of variables entirely at a different time. The extra registers are no longer required but the sequence of operations must be recorded for the processing of the second group. Fortunately, this recording will consume only a little area since the Virtex slices can be used as 32-bit shift registers.

5.1   Interleaved Processing

Serial Modular Divider. The design of the interleaved serial modular divider is presented in Fig. 4. From the implementation of Fig. 2, the operative part of the R and S registers are used. Two registers are also added to store the temporary variables. Nevertheless, some modifications are made compared with the serial implementation. In order to exploit the LUTs before the UR registers, the regular loading operation is used instead of the two phases. The reset signal is therefore no longer needed. The LUTs before the VS registers must also be used for the loading operation since a multiplexor has been added before the SV registers. In the previous implementation, this multiplexor was not required thanks to the *hold* capability of the V and S registers. The enable signal of the VS registers is used to hold the final result.

Unfortunately, the required amount of resources is the same as the serial implementation. This design is therefore useless.

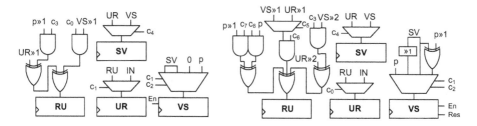

Fig. 4. Interleaved serial divider   **Fig. 5.** Interleaved 2-bit digit divider

Digit-Serial Modular Divider. The design of the interleaved 2-bit digit modular divider is presented in Fig. 5. It is quite different from the implementation of Fig. 3. The regular loading operation is used and a reset signal for the VS registers is added to perform the loading of the S variable. Unfortunately, the carry chain is not usable anymore. This is also a consequence of the loss of the *hold* capability of the V and S registers. The enable signal of the VS registers is also used to hold the final result.

This design requires roughly $2.5m$ slices. Compared to the $3m$ slices needed by the 2-bit digit design, the improvement begins to be interesting.

5.2   Non-interleaved Processing

Serial Modular Divider. For the recording of the sequence of operations, only one bit is required for each cycle. Indeed, with the use of the D counter while replaying the sequence, the successive u_0 bits are enough to perform the processing on the R and S variables. Thanks to the specific shift registers of the FPGA, a complete sequence holds in around ten slices only.

The design of the non-interleaved serial modular divider, presented in Fig. 6, is derived from the operative part of the R and S registers of Fig. 2. The only difference is the loading capability of both 0 and p in the VS registers. This design requires roughly the half of the slices needed by the serial modular divider. It is therefore useful for applications demanding a small throughput.

Digit-Serial Modular Divider. For the recording of the sequence of operations, only two bits are required for each cycle. Indeed, with the use of the D counter, the successive u_1 bits are needed. Then if the bit u_1 equals zero, the u_2 bit is stored; otherwise, the $u_2 \oplus v_1$ bit is stored. This information is enough to perform the processing on the R and S variables. A complete sequence holds also in around ten slices only.

The design of the non-interleaved 2-bit digit modular divider, shown in Fig. 7, is also derived from the operative part of the R and S registers of Fig. 3. The loading capability of p in the VS registers is extended through the added reset signal.

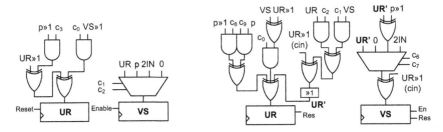

Fig. 6. Non-interleaved serial modular divider   **Fig. 7.** Non-interleaved 2-bit digit modular divider

This design requires also roughly half of the slices needed by the 2-bit digit modular divider. It is therefore interesting for applications demanding a regular throughput. Compared with the serial modular divider, the required amount of resources decreases by about a seventh whit a computational time increase of one third. The seeming area-optimality of the serial divider is therefore improved.

6   Results

The designs of the serial modular divider and the 2-bit digit modular divider, with and without the non-interleaved modification, have been implemented on a last generation Xilinx Virtex4 XC4VLX15-12sf363 and a small and low-cost Xilinx Spartan3[3] XC3S200-4ft256. The performances of the designs based on the interleaved modification are not reported since the improvements are much smaller than the non-interleaved modification. The VHDL synthesis and place & route have been achieved on Xilinx ISE 7.1.03i with the best speed effort. In order to evaluate the chip area and the working frequency of the four modular divider cores, shift registers have been added for the inputs and the outputs. These resources are not considered for the area count.

The performances of the two dividers together with the two kinds of irreducible polynomials $p(x)$ are reported in table 1. The results of the non-interleaved implementations are shown in table 2. The throughput of the serial, the 2-bit digit and their non-interleaved versions are respectively computed with a latency of $2m$, $m+1$, $4m+2$ and $2m+2$ cycles (considering the 2 cycles needed by the load operation).

---

[3] Spartan3 devices have a Virtex structure.

For the throughput enhancement in table 1, the serial and the 2-bit digit implementations are compared for each extension field degree and $p(x)$. For the area saving (LUTs) in table 2, the left value is the comparison between both algorithms, with and without the non-interleaved modification. The right value evaluates the area sparing between the non-interleaved 2-bit digit modular divider and the serial divider. The same analysis is done for the throughput decrease in the next column. The 4-input LUTs count is reported and used for comparisons because the mapping tool of ISE gives priority to combining the related logic. As a result, when the constraint on the working frequency is strong, many slices of the digit-serial design are half empty (but are still available for other purposes).

Table 1. Implementation results on Virtex4 and Spartan3

Designs	Frequency [Mhz]	Area [Slices]	Area [LUTs]	Throughput [Mbit/s]	Throughput enhancemement
163 NIST					
Serial	**480** 210	504 552	716 712	240 105	
2-bit digit	325 177	699 648	1124 1093	323 146	35% 39%
163 arbit.					
Serial	451 193	543 562	747 742	225 96	
2-bit digit	326 137	695 675	1154 1144	324 136	44% 42%
193 SECG					
Serial	457 178	641 622	837 832	228 89	
2-bit digit	324 141	858 751	1298 1277	322 140	41% 57%
193 arbit.					
Serial	446 167	675 629	873 869	223 83	
2-bit digit	324 133	910 798	1359 1337	322 133	44% 60%
233 NIST					
Serial	446 173	753 789	999 998	223 86	
2-bit digit	324 140	982 877	1526 1520	322 139	44% 61%
233 arbit.					
Serial	436 167	798 791	1043 1043	218 83	
2-bit digit	322 133	1055 950	1648 1597	321 132	38% 59%

As expected, the working frequency of the digit-serial divider decreases compared with the serial divider. Nevertheless, the throughput enhancement shows that the improved latency overtakes this diminution. For each design, the reported area count follows the estimation of Section 4. Due to the best speed effort constraint, the area is slightly augmented by the logic replication of the control circuit. An important point is that the 2-bit digit designs appear to have a reasonable increase of complexity: only 55 % of additional LUTs are required. This is far from the 100 % increase expected with the simple concatenation of two serial circuits.

For the non-interleaved implementations, the working frequency decreases due to a stronger complexity of the finite state machine. As a result, the throughput decrease slightly exceeds 50 %. Nevertheless, the area improvement is close to 50 % as expected. Comparing the serial divider and the joint use of the 2-bit digit algorithm and the SIMD feature, the resultant throughput is decreased by 35 % due to a higher complexity. However, the required amount of resources is reduced by 15 %.

Comparing the performances between implementations based on the recommended irreducible polynomials (NIST, SECG) and the chosen arbitrary polynomials, the differences are non significative. This follows also the predictions.

The performances of the modular divider are usually not reported in the different implementations of elliptic curve cryptosystems. The only found FPGA implementation of an equivalent serial modular divider is presented in [10]. While their performances are much less interesting, the comparison is not really fair: they use completely arbitrary polynomials and they do not try to exceed a working frequency of 66 Mhz. The frequency result of [7] are not really comparable since they used the very small field $GF(2^8)$.

Table 2. Non-interleaved results on Virtex4 and Spartan3

Designs	Frequency [Mhz]	Area [LUTs]	Area saving	Throughput decrease
163 NIST				
Serial	**418** 195	**403** 408	**44%** 43%	**57%** 53%
2-bit digit	**278** 131	**628** 618	**44% 12%** 43% 13%	**57% 42%** 55% 38%
163 arbit				
Serial	**394** 185	**434** 439	**42%** 41%	**56%** 52%
2-bit digit	**272** 127	**657** 675	**43% 12%** 41% 9%	**58% 40%** 54% 35%
193 SECG				
Serial	**425** 195	**463** 468	**45%** 44%	**54%** 45%
2-bit digit	**275** 132	**717** 707	**45% 14%** 45% 15%	**57% 40%** 53% 26%
193 arbit.				
Serial	**395** 187	**501** 505	**43%** 42%	**56%** 44%
2-bit digit	**272** 126	**798** 780	**41% 9%** 42% 10%	**58% 39%** 53% 25%
233 NIST				
Serial	**418** 195	**543** 548	**46%** 45%	**53%** 46%
2-bit digit	**277** 128	**849** 834	**44% 15%** 45% 17%	**57% 38%** 54% 26%
233 SECG				
Serial	**394** 187	**588** 564	**44%** 46%	**55%** 44%
2-bit digit	**272** 126	**936** 925	**43% 10%** 42% 11%	**58% 38%** 52% 25%

7   Conclusion

A full set of time and area tradeoffs for the modular division over $GF(2^m)$ has been proposed. First, an iterative digit-serial algorithm has been introduced to decrease the computational time at the expense of more area. The presented 2-bit digit algorithm reduces the latency by a factor two and is well suited for hardware implementations. Second, using the SIMD feature of the selected algorithm, non-interleaved implementations of both modular dividers have been carried out to decrease the required resources at the cost of more computational time. These two techniques have then been jointly used to provide another interesting tradeoff. Among other fields of applications, the novel algorithm and the different implementations are particularly interesting for elliptic curve cryptography and more precisely for area constrained designs working in affine coordinates and high-speed processors.

The different techniques have been implemented on FPGA of the Xilinx Virtex family, with different kinds of irreducible polynomials and extension field degrees. The designs have been optimized for this platform and resulting performances exhibit a high working frequency and small area requirements.

The 2-bit digit implementation appears to have a throughput improvement between 35 % and 60 % compared with the serial implementation while only 55 % of additional area is required. It can therefore be used when a higher throughput is requested, with a better area efficiency. The non-interleaved implementations exhibit an area improvement of 45 % with a latency increase of 55 %. They can therefore be used to save area when a smaller throughput is needed. For applications demanding an intermediate throughput, both techniques can be jointly used to even further optimize the resource requirements.

References

1. H. Aigner, H. Bock, M. Hütter, J. Wolkerstorfer, *A Low-Cost ECC Coprocessor for Smartcards*, CHES'04, LNCS 3156, pp. 107-118, 2004.
2. H. Brunner, A. Curiger, M. Hofstetter, *On Computing Multiplicative Inverses in GF(2^m)*, IEEE Trans. on computers, vol. 42(8), pp. 1010–1015, 1993.
3. R.P. Brent and H.T. Kung, *Systolic VLSI Arrays for Polynomial GCD Computation*, IEEE Trans. on Computers, vol. 33(8), pp. 731–736, 1984.
4. I.F. Blake, G. Seroussi, N.P Smart, *Elliptic Curves in Cryptography*, London Mathematical Society, Lecture Notes Series 265, Cambridge University Press, 1999.
5. Certicom Research, *SEC 2: Recommended Elliptic Curve Domain Parameters*, v1.0, 2000.
6. A.K. Daneshbeh et al., *A Class of Unidirectional Bit Serial Systolic Architectures for Multiplicative Inversion and Division over GF(2^m)*, Tr. on Comp., vol. 54(3), pp. 370–380, 2005.
7. C.H. Kim, S. Kwon, J.J. Kim, C.P. Hong, *A Compact and Fast Division Architecture for a Finite Field GF(2^m)*, ICCSA'03, LNCS 2667, pp. 855–864, 2003.
8. K. Fong, D. Hankerson, J. López, A. Menezes, *Field Inversion and Point Halving Revisited*, IEEE Trans. on Computers, vol. 53(8), pp. 1047–1059, 2004.
9. J.-H. Guo and C.-L. Wang, *Novel digit-serial systolic array implementation of Euclid's algorithm for division in GF(2^m)*, ISCAS'98, pp. 478–481, 1998.
10. N. Gura, S. C. Shantz, H. Eberle, S. Gupta, V. Gupta, D. Finchelstein et al., *An End-to-End Systems Approach to Elliptic Curve Cryptography*, CHES'02, LNCS 2523, pp. 349-365, 2002.
11. A. A.-A. Gutub, *New Hardware Algorithms and Designs for Montgomery Modular Inverse Computation in Galois Fields GF(p) and GF(2^n)*, Ph.D. Thesis, 2002.

12. D. Hankerson, A. Menezes, S. Vanstone, *Guide to Elliptic Curve Cryptography*, Springer Professional computing, Springer, 2004.
13. M.A. Hasan and V.K. Bhargava, *Bit-Serial Systolic Divider and Multiplier for Finite Fields GF(2^m)*, IEEE Trans. on Computers, vol. 41(8), pp. 972–980, 1992.
14. T. Itoh and S. Tsujii, *A Fast Algorithm for Computing Multiplicative Inverses in GF(2^m) Using Normal Bases*, Information and Comp., vol. 78, pp. 171–177, 1988.
15. N. Koblitz, *Elliptic curve cryptosystems*, Math. of Comp., vol. 48, pp. 203–209, 1987.
16. V. Miller, *Uses of elliptic curves in cryptography*, CRYPTO'85, LNCS 218, pp. 417–426, 1986.
17. U.S. Department of Commerce/National Institute of Standards and Technology (NIST), *Digital Signature Standard (DSS)*, FIPS PUB 182-2change1, 2000.
18. K. Okeya, K. Sakurai, *Fast Multi-scalar Multiplication Methods on Elliptic Curves with Precomputation Strategy Using Montgomery Trick*, CHES'02, LNCS 2523, pp. 564–578, 2002.
19. J. Stein, *Computational problems associated with Racah algebra*, J. Computational Physics, vol. 1, pp. 397–405, 1967.
20. C.-H. Wu et al., *High-Speed, Low-Complexity Systolic Designs of Novel Iterative Division Algorithms in GF(2^m)*, IEEE Trans. on Computers, vol. 53(3), pp. 375–380, 2004.

Mobile Fingerprint Identification Using a Hardware Accelerated Biometric Service Provider

David Rodríguez, Juan M. Sánchez, and Arturo Duran

Área de Arquitectura y Tecnología de los Computadores
Esuela Politécnica, Universidad de Extremadura
Campus Universitario S/N 10071 Cáceres
{drlozano, sanperez, aduran}@unex.es

Abstract. This paper describes a BioAPI compatible Architecture for mobile biometric fingerprint identification and verification, based on a XML Web Service and a Field Programmable Gate Array (FPGA). We present a client-server system that uses a Personal Digital Assistant (PDA) with a built-in fingerprint sensor and wireless LAN (WLAN) connectivity as a mobile client, and a Biometric Service Provider (BSP) running as a BioAPI compatible XML Web Service on the server side. BioAPI high level functions *enrolment*, *identification* and *verification* are implemented using BSP primitives, *capture, process, createtemplate, verifymatch*, and *identifymatch* that are partially hardware implemented using Handel-C and the Celoxica RC1000-PP platform.

1 Introduction

Biometric authentication is the verification of a user's identity by means of a physical trait or behavioural characteristic that can't easily be changed. Examples of physical characteristics include fingerprints, eye retinas and irises and patterns, while examples of behavioural characteristics include signature, gait and typing patterns. Fingerprint-based identification is the oldest method which has been successfully used in numerous applications.

New handheld computers and smart phones can be provided with biometric fingerprint sensors. These devices can be used with wireless LAN and mobile technologies for the development of biometric applications that allow easy and quick identification of an individual in public or open spaces, like airports, schools, parks, etc.

These devices have computational and storage limitations, so we need a client-server architecture to achieve fast and reliable authentication on one individual fingerprint among a large population, 1:N identification.

On other hand, XML Web Services provides a simple and flexible model based on neutral Web technologies for publishing software services. Web Services are shown to be the natural evolution of distributed application architectures on Internet [1]. Web Services allow mobile clients the use, on-demand, of a FPGA implementing the primitives of a BSP, reducing the cost of dedicated reconfigurable hardware.

Finally, FPGA-based systems have been used with success in pattern matching algorithms, digital image processing and different security and biometric applications, all with high computational complexity [5].

K. Bertels, J.M.P. Cardoso, and S. Vassiliadis (Eds.): ARC 2006, LNCS 3985, pp. 383 388, 2006.
© Springer-Verlag Berlin Heidelberg 2006

According to these considerations, we present the design and implementation of a BioAPI compatible architecture, which allows wireless and mobile identification/verification of biometric fingerprints, using a hardware-accelerated BSP. The key ideas for this work are:

To present the basis of fingerprint biometry and the BioAPI standard, section 2.
To identify the different elements of the proposed architecture, section 3.
To define the functions and components of mobile client software, section 4.
Finally, to implement the XML Web Service and the hardware accelerated BSP primitives, section 5.

2 Biometric Identification Based on Fingerprints. BioAPI

A fingerprint is made of a series of ridges and valleys on the surface of the finger. The uniqueness of a fingerprint can be determined by the pattern of ridges and valleys called minutiae. Minutiae points are local characteristics that occur at either a ridge bifurcation or a ridge ending [2].

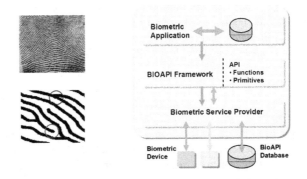

Fig. 1. Scanned fingerprint (left-up) and example of ridge bifurcation and ridge ending (left-down). BioAPI layered architecture (right).

The BioAPI Specification provides a high-level generic biometric authentication model. BioAPI has been defined to allow the biometric developer the maximum freedom in the placement of the processing involved, and allows the processing to be shared between the client and a server. BioAPI specification also defines the Biometric Service Provider (BSP) Interface. Theoretically, BSPs supplied by vendors conforming to this interface specification could then be used within any application developed to this BioAPI. There are three principal high-level abstraction functions in the API, *Enroll*, *Verify* and *Identify* [3].

3 System Architecture

The design of the system is based on the tier architecture showed in the figure 2. We use a client-server scheme over an IP network, to support the access using wireless networks (WiFi and Internet/Intranet). We use standard web technology to connect the client application with the server. The main components are:

The Client application, it's based on a web browser and its extensions. This is the interface of the biometric application.

The Application server and the BSP, it's a XML Web Service with the software and hardware extensions needed to implement the primitive functions proposed in the BioAPI specification. The designed BSP implements a subset of its functions using reconfigurable hardware. The reconfigurable logic device used is a Xillinx Virtex FPGA with a Celoxica platform RC1000.

The Database, it's compliant with the ISO CBEFF (NISTIR 6529) standard.

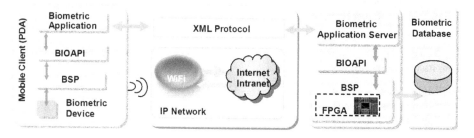

Fig. 2. Main components of the proposed architecture

Using a client-server architecture and standard Internet technologies, has two main advantages, the design of the client hardware and software is independent of the access medium (WiFi, Ethernet, Bluetooth or GPRS/UMTS), and the client application maintenance and distribution can be automated using Web technologies.

4   Client Application

To develop the client application we study two choices:

A Java Applet running in a *Java Virtual Machine* (JVM) enabled Web browser. With this choice, we take advantage of the interoperability between Operative Systems (OS) and platforms. On the other hand, the execution of this choice is slower than native code and there's less support and drivers to access to biometric hardware.

An ActiveX Control running in Internet Explorer. In this case, the native execution mode is faster and there are several developing tools. On the contrary, the interoperability between operative systems is limited to Windows or a compatible plug-in is required.

4.1   Prototype of Client Application

For the client device we choose the Hewlett-Packard Ipaq H5550 PDA, with an Intel PXA225 400MHz microprocessor, wireless Bluetooth/WLAN 802.11b, and a biometric sensor. The PDA software version is Pocket PC 2003 and Windows CE 4.20.

Fig. 3. Ipaq H5550 requesting the user authenticate to begin the session (left). Client application running in Internet Explorer.

The IPaq H5550 biometric sensor (AT77C101B) is developed by Atmel Corporation, its main features are:

CMOS thermal sensor.
Scanning resolution 0,4 mm x 14 mm.
Image array 8 x 280 = 2240 pixels
Pixel size 50 μm x 50 μm = 500 dpi

Finally, we implement the client application using an ActiveX control. This control is hosted by the Internet Explorer for Pocket PC Web browser. We have to install the following libraries into the PDA to support the biometric application.

HP Ipaq Biometric Toolkit.
BioAPI Consortium Framework.
Microsoft .Net Compact Framework

5 XML Web Service for Biometric Identification

The RC1000_BIOAPI Web Service implements and supports remote clients connectivity, allowing the access to high level BioAPI functions *enrolment*, *identification* and *verification*.

When a remote client invokes a high level API function, this is translated into a sequence of primitives implemented by the BSPs in the client side (*capture*) or server side (*process, match and create_template*). The server side BSP partially implements these primitives using a VIRTEX FPGA and Handel-C.

Web Services can be used by mobile clients in two different modes, as shown in Fig. 4:

1) Using an Application Server, that acts as a Proxy between the remote clients and the BSP. In this scenario the XML Web Service methods are invoked using dynamic Web pages with .aspx extension. The Application Server must control the access to BSP and may perform pay-per-use billing functions. The used protocols are HTTP for the interchange between the Web Client and Application Server and XML-SOAP between the Proxy class and the Web Service.

2) Using ASP.NET asmx pages, this option allows to remote clients direct access to XML Web Services. The Web Service can be implemented using a C#, Visual Basic .Net or C++ class. Namespace, classes, properties, and methods of the Web Service are defined in this class, which is referenced in the asmx page. Remote clients can use different protocols and applications to access the XML Web Services.

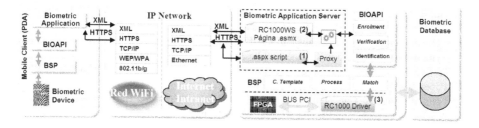

Fig. 4. Architecture, protocols and devices used in the prototype

5.1 Hardware Accelerated BSP

We have tested the proposed architecture, by programming the BSP *process* primitive using Handel-C. The *process* function provides the image preprocessing and minutiae extraction. This function takes as input a scanned fingerprint image acquired by the biometric client sensor.

The implementation of *process* primitive involves programming digital image processing algorithms as convolution filters, threshold, skeleton and morphological operators. Previous works have successfully implemented these algorithms using Handel-C and RC1000 platform [4]. Pattern matching algorithms [6] are usually used for the implementation of *verifymatch* and *identifymatch* functions. These algorithms are easily parallelizable and can be implemented using Handel-C parallel sentences [7].

The access to the hardware application is carried out using the RC1000PP platform libraries (pp1000.lib) and the PCI board drivers as shown in Fig. 4.

6 Conclusions and Acknowledgements

We have described a BioAPI compatible architecture based on XML Web Services and reconfigurable hardware. The main goal of this work is present standard Web technologies and commercial hardware-software platforms for the design, programming and execution of the proposed Architecture. These decisions make very easy the implementation of this Architecture in a real scenario.

The present and future work includes programming the Java version of the client, and the full implementation of the BSP primitives using the Celoxica RC2000 platform.

This work has been partially supported by the project OPLINK TIN2005-08818-C04-03.

References

1. Newcomer E.: Understanding Web Services: XML, WSDL, SOAP, and UDDI. Addison-Wesley (2002).
2. R.M. Bolle, A.W. Senior, N. K. Ratha and S. Pankanti, "Fingerprint Minutiae: A Constructuive Definition". Lecture Notes in Computer Science.
3. The BioAPI Consortium, BioAPI Specification Version 1.1 March 16, 2001
4. Rodríguez, D., Sánchez J.M., Gómez J.A.: Reconfigurable Hybrid Architecture for web Applications. Proceedings Field-Programmable Logic and Applications, 13th International Conference, FPL'03 (2003) pág. 1091-1094.
5. V.K. Prasanna and A. Dandalis, "FPGA-based Cryptography for Internet Security". Online Symposium for Electronic Engineers. (2000).
6. O. Svedin, M. Öbrink, J. Bergenek, "Precise BioMatch™ FingerPrint Technology". White Paper April 2004.
7. Fons M., Fons F., Canyellas N., Lopez M., Cantó E., "Codiseño Hardware-software de un Algoritmo de Matching Biométrico", JCRA 2003, pag. 399-406.

UNITE: Uniform Hardware-Based Network Intrusion deTection Engine

S. Yusuf, W. Luk, M.K.N. Szeto, and W. Osborne

Department of Computing, Imperial College London,
180 Queen's Gate, London SW7 2BZ
{sherif.yusuf, w.luk, man.szeto, william.osborne}@imperial.ac.uk

Abstract. Current software implementations of network intrusion detection reach a maximum network connection speed of about 1Gbps (Gigabits per second). This paper analyses the Snort software network intrusion detection system to highlight the bottlenecks of such systems. It proposes a novel packet processing engine called UNITE that deploys a uniform hardware architecture to perform both header classification and payload signature extraction utilising a Content Addressable Memory (CAM) which is optimised by techniques based on Binary Decision Diagrams (BDDs). The proposed design has been implemented on an XC2VP30 FPGA, and we achieve an operating frequency of 350MHz and a processing speed in excess of 2.8Gbps. The area resource usage for UNITE is also shown to be efficient, with a Look Up Tables (LUTs) per character ratio of 0.82 for a rule set of approximately 20,000 characters.

1 Introduction

Many mechanisms have been developed which aim to address and enhance network security, of which firewalls and NIDS are the two most common examples. Many of these mechanisms have initially been developed through software implementation, but there is increasing interest in transforming these mechanisms into hardware-based implementations to obtain improved speed performance. One hardware platform for such implementations is Field Programmable Gate Arrays (FPGAs).

Network speed and flexibility are the two major concerns for network managers; networks must be adaptable enough to accommodate the enhancement of invasive technology, without allowing the financial and performance costs of network security to spiral out of control. Contemporary networks enable extremely high data rates, and any security measures used in such networks must be capable of equal or higher data rates if they are not to degrade overall network performance. In a 'Denial of Service' (DoS) attack, network security countermeasures must process packets faster than the attacker can deliver them, but current software-based security systems cannot operate at the data rates of the networks they protect.

Attackers on network security are notorious for their ability to adapt, evolve and innovate. This requires network security to be equally, or even more, adaptable in order to effectively deal with the attacks that are thrown at it. In the

K. Bertels, J.M.P. Cardoso, and S. Vassiliadis (Eds.): ARC 2006, LNCS 3985, pp. 389–400, 2006.

case of new attacks, existing systems must be able to use emerging information about the new attack to update the system to cope with the current and future such attacks. This means a system capable of almost limitless adaptability is vital, but this should not be obtained at the cost of network performance. The software implementation of network security measures provides a high level of flexibility, but cannot offer performance even approaching the speed required by networks. An alternative hardware implementation using Application Specific Integrated Circuits (ASICs), is capable of providing much faster processing speeds, but ASICs are generally inflexible and not cost effective. The aim of this project is to develop an NIDS for deployment on an FPGA platform, with the following contributions:

> The study and profiling of Snort NIDS, demonstrating that the decoding and detection phase of Snort are the best candidates for further optimisation.
> A pipelined packet processing engine called UNITE (for Uniform hardware-based Network Intrusion deTection Engine) that employs a uniform architecture to perform both header classification and payload signature extraction utilising a Content Addressable Memory (CAM) which is optimised a Binary Decision Diagram (BDD) technique.
> – The implementation of UNITE is shown to be capable of achieving a high processing speed. The results show that it is capable of handling in excess of 3Gbps traffic.

2   Network Intrusion Detection Systems

Existing research into NIDS techniques explores two different directions: header classification and payload matching. The header classification of a packet has been researched for the longest period and is well-established in theory and practise, with a focus on efficient software implementation. The payload matching of the packet is more recent, and here research concentrates more on hardware implementation. This has lead to a split between the development of these two fundamental parts of NIDS solutions: although individual research for each part may yield promising results, the final result may not be as promising when attempting to integrate different parts to develop a "complete" NIDS. This is because some techniques applied to header classification may not be directly applicable to payload matching and vice versa. There is currently limited research into the area of complete hardware NIDS, that is, those that can integrate both header and packet filtering [10,11]. In this paper, therefore, we aim to develop a complete NIDS using a uniform technique which will strengthen and improve integration.

2.1   Profiling of Network Intrusion Detection Systems

Earlier security measures were mainly concentrated on the packet header classification, but as technology has developed, such security measures, if employed on their own, are not enough to guard against evolved attacks.

Current security systems have now extended to allow the examination of packet payload content as an extra precaution, and this allows recognised patterns or attack signatures, of intrusions to be easily detected. The attack signatures are represented as strings, and are used to match against the packet payload content by the NIDS.

In this section, a study is carried out for two NIDS: one for software and one for hardware. The motivation behind this study is to strengthen the understanding of NIDS and to aid its development. Further, this study should prove that it is necessary to develop NIDS in hardware, rather than software, for performance considerations.

Software NIDS. Snort is one of the most popular software-based NIDS systems, deployed as a security measure on many real-world networks [1]. It is Open-Source Software (OSS) so its source code is freely available, allowing any interested party to study, modify and improve its methods. Snort is supplied with a database of the attack signatures of many known attacks, and matches the payload of incoming packets against this database: packets with payloads that match those of malicious packets will be rejected.

Hardware NIDS. Although the performance of a hardware implementation will, in general, exceed that of software, there are still many constraints that must be taken into account when designing an NIDS. The main constraint within hardware (FPGA) is its area resource.

Hardware NIDS has been implemented through several stages [9], starting with the Snort signature list, and culminating in a compact representation of the signatures. The implementation runs at a rate of approximately 2.5 Gbps. The entire SNORT rule set was implemented on the FPGA platform with around 12% of the area on a Xilinx XC2V8000 FPGA. Although the design in runs at high speed, it does not perform header classification.

It has been shown how FPGA based multiprocessors can be used to increase the performance of network applications [10]. The system was demonstrated performing rule processing in reconfigurable hardware. They achieved a processing rate of 2.5 Gbps, with a suggestion that 10 Gbps is also possible with the most recent FPGA chips, such as the Virtex4.

Another design [11] combines and optimises the TCAM and Bit Vector algorithms for packet header classification in NIDS. The throughput of the design is also approximately 2.5 Gbps, with a combination of Block RAMs (BRAMs) and FPGA logic used for the implementation.

2.2 Snort

Snort is profiled using a Linux-based profiling tool called GProf[3]. Snort was compiled and linked with optimisations, and profiling enabled, in order to profile it with GProf. Then the execution of Snort is carried out as a normal execution, and GProf collects the data and outputs it at the end of execution. The result of most interest to us is the call graph, which provides the number of times a function in the program is called. Snort 2.4.0 was executed in NID mode with several different tcpdump data sets; some of these data sets were obtained from [14] and contained packets of a malicious nature.

The Snort system can be divided into five parts which carry out the main functions. Here we focus mainly on the *Packet Decode* and *Detection Engine*; interested readers can consult [1] for more details.

Packet Decoder. The Packet Decoder decodes the captured packets and identifies set pointers to all the different parts of information needed for the detection phase. The packet decoder decodes the packet through the protocol stack, from the Data Link layer up through to the Application layer. The decoding routine is to decode the Data Link frame (the medium that the packet came from, i.e. ethernet), then it decodes the IP protocol, and it also decodes the TCP/UDP packet left at the end.

Detection Engine. The detection engine takes the packet data from the packet decoder and preprocessor, and performs the detection process. The match of signature to packet is done on the transport and application layers. The matching on the transport layer is generally for checking the source and destination IP addresses and ports, or even the flags if it is TCP protocol. The application layer is for matching the payload in the packet to the attack signatures; this matching process employs the Boyer-Moore Search Algorithm [6].

Results. Table 1 shows the results of Snort analysis of several different tcpdump data sets. These data sets contain packets with activity ranging from a distributed denial of service attack run by a novice attacker (LLDOS 1.0) and a second more stealthy DDOS attack (LLDOS 2.0.2), inside sniffing (2000 Inside) and outside sniffing (2000 Outside)[14]. There is also a data set with no malicious packets (Pack100000 & Pack1000000), were captured on a student machine connected to the ethernet network in the Department of Computing at Imperial College.

Table 1. Processing Speed of Snort

Dataset	Processing Speed (Mbps)
1998 DARPA	105
2000 Inside	60
2000 Outside	57
LLS(DDoS) 1.0 DMZ	38
LLS(DDoS) 1.0 Inside	21
LLS(DDoS) 2.0.2 DMZ	45
LLS(DDoS) 2.0.2 Inside	44
Pack100000	22
Pack1000000	44

There is a small variation in the processing speed of Snort, as with the different data sets, there are different characteristics, and so the behaviour of Snort in each execution is quite different. The processing speed of snort is generally below

Table 2. Result for profiling of Snort

Operation	Percentage of Execution Time
Alert/logging	8
Decode Frame, Packet	25
Payload matching	51
Miscellaneous	4
Preparation for rules and pattern	4
Preprocessing of packet	8

100Mbps, regardless of whether or not the data set contains malicious packets. The average processing speed of Snort reported is approximately 48Mbps.

Table 2 shows the percentage of the total execution time for each phase in Snort. The phase that uses up most of the execution time is the payload matching phase. The decoding phase uses the second most execution time, but only half the time of the payload matching process. The preprocessing phase and alert/logging phase both took approximately 8% of the execution time, and preparation for rules/patterns and miscellaneous items took approximately 4%.

The high execution time for decoding is a result of decoding every packet received, unlike other phases. The payload matching is not necessarily performed on all packets, but rather depends on the result of the decoding phase. The result of this profiling shows that the decoding and payload matching phases of Snort are ideal for optimisation, as the execution times are longer than other phases. In a hardware implementation, the decoding phase would be eliminated and its function would be integrated into the detection or payload matching phase.

3   A Uniform Hardware NIDS

This section presents the UNITE architecture. It adopts a uniform way of computing both header classification and payload signature detection utilising a Content Addressable Memory (CAM), which is optimised by techniques based on Binary Decision Diagrams (BDDs).

3.1   Design

In NIDS, some rules are often specified in terms of both header and payload. In the header section, it defines which IP source/destination address and port, and protocol to match against the packet's header. In the payload section, it defines the pattern that this rule is looking for in the packet's payload.

In the case of the header, the required fields will be located at the beginning of the IP packet and will be the same in every packet that arrives, with the fields of a fixed length. However, the signature being searched for in the payload will not always be in the same position, nor will it be of a fixed sized. Due to these differences, most research focuses on either header classification or payload matching.

Figure 1 shows a block diagram of the construction of the UNITE structure. The process, consisting of 5 stages, performs both header classification and

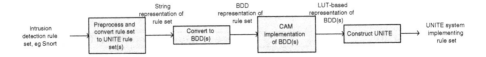

Fig. 1. An overview of our UNITE device

payload signature extraction utilising a Content Addressable Memory (CAM) which is optimised by techniques based on Binary Decision Diagrams (BDDs).

Stage 1. This stage, takes the intrusion detection (in this case Snort) signature list and parses the header and payload security requirements into a simple list of strings for the matching engine. The wildcard (or don't cares) option in the header section of the rules is a characteristic that can result in large BDDs. To combat this explosion in the BDD, we perform a preprocessing step on the rules. This preprocessing step groups the rules into smaller groups that exhibit the wildcards in the same field of the rules. In this way, the resulting BDDs with the wildcard options are shared between as many rules as possible, minimizing their impact on the overall hardware size.

Stage 2. This stage, corresponding to the second block in Figure 1, converts the strings into a boolean expression, from which a reduced ordered binary decision diagram is generated. The string is converted to boolean expression by taking the ASCII value of each character as a parameter, then constructing an BDD representation. After all string has been converted to BDDs, the common and non-common bits of all the BDD are extracted, which are then used to build smaller BDD structures, consequently achieving a more compact hardware implementation.

Stage 3. This stage (third block in Figure 1) uses look up tables to implement an CAM. The circuits that are to be implemented are based on the common and non-common tree structures extracted from the second stage above.

Stage 4. This stage uses additional BDD manipulations on the non-common BDDs obtained in Stage 2 to further reduce the logic required in the hardware implementation. This is achieved by manipulating the two branches separately and further finding common and non-common bits within each branch to further reduce the size of the BDD structure of each branch. This stage and stage 5, both correspond to fourth block in Figure 1.

Stage 5. This final stage logically connects all sub circuits built in previous stages in order to generate an BDD-based CAM structure, which then is implemented in hardware in a highly condensed form, resulting in a much smaller area resource consumption.

Figure 2 shows the BDD representation of the non-common bits of a simple rule set (Figure 2(a)) and the corresponding LUT-based architecture (Figure 2(b)). This design results from applying stages 1 to 3 and stage 5 to the original BDD representation of the rule set. Figure 3 illustrates a typical end result of applying all five stages to the simple rule set. The labels *High Branch* and *Low Branch* relate to the optimisation phase in stage 2. In Figure 2(a), each node in the BDD leads to another node or two different nodes, and in the case where a node, x (node 3 in Figure 2) leads to two different nodes, y and z (the two node 6 in Figure 2), a logic '0' (the Low Branch) from node x leads to node y, and a logic '1' (High Branch) from node y leads to node z. Therefore, the two branches stem from the further optimisation of the *non-common* BDD stated in stage 4. Note that since we adopt a uniform way in optimising header classification and payload matching, we obtain better results than using different methods in optimising them.

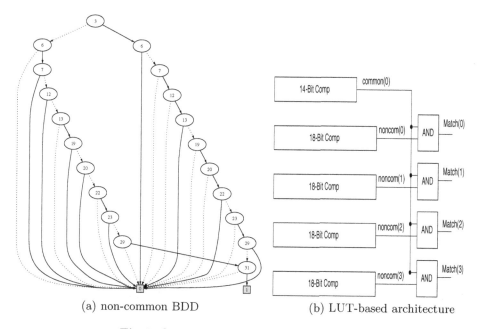

(a) non-common BDD   (b) LUT-based architecture

Fig. 2. Optimisation of BDD representation

For the technique to work, we only need to shift the payload section of the rules, but keep the header fields fixed. To achieve this, we developed an interface (shown in Figure 4) to the UNITE device which we use to keep the header section fixed, while still shifting the payload.

3.2   Implementation

We develop a system capable of both header classification and payload matching, using a combination of software and hardware.

The board used is the Xilinx University Program (XUP) board[15] with a XC2VP30 [2] FPGA chip, and it consists of multiple cores which are used in this project. The cores of most interest are: PowerPC (PPC) processor [2],

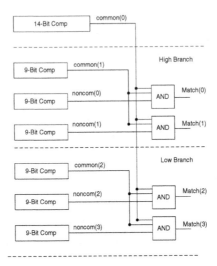

Fig. 3. A complete LUT-based architecture of a simple rule set

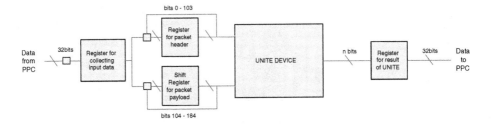

Fig. 4. The interface for the UNITE device

Ethernet controller [13], and the FPGA chip. Figure 5 illustrates the communication between the different components of the system.

The main use of the PPC processor is to run programs, written in C, to access and utilise both the FPGA logic and the ethernet controller. The PPC processor is used to receive ethernet frames from the ethernet port through the use of the EMAC core, and then to disassemble the ethernet frame and extract different fields from the frames (source/destination address and port, and protocol). These fields are of particular importance because they will be used as input to the UNITE device. The payload is then identified and extracted, and also used as input to the UNITE device.

The Xilinx library functions provide a set of functions which allow the user to manipulate the EMAC core. These functions include the ability to:

start and stop the device,
set the MAC address of the device,
collect statistics of the device,
set the receiving mode of the device(e.g broadcast, unicast).

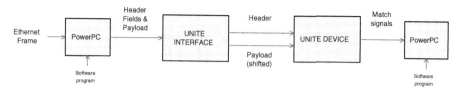

Fig. 5. Communication between component of System

4   Performance Evaluation

In this section, we present the results for both area resource and timing of the UNITE device.

Testing Methods. The testing framework provides methods for the user to run various tests on the device. For testing, a user may wish to use "real" packet data to test the NIDS rather than reading in made up data in memory as input.

The testing framework uses a Linux program called Packit[12] to create the input data for testing. Packit is an ethernet frame construction and injection tool, and is capable of creating an ethernet frame and inject/send it down the physical ethernet interface. Packit can construct the packet from the data link layer through the network layer to the transport layer. The network layer and the transport layer are of most interest to us because network layer contains the IP addresses and the transport layer contains the source and destination ports. Users can specifies the IP addresses and ports to be the value they required as long as the value for the IP addresses and ports are of valid value within the protocol. The user can also specify the payload content for the packet to send.

One drawback of Packit is that it does not provide a function to create random payload. To overcome this drawback, a script was written to generate random or user-defined payload content for the packets and then pass the payload generated to Packit. The script can also be used for stress testing, and this is done by using loops to repeatedly generate random or user-defined packets and then send them to the NIDS using Packit. The user can specify how often the script sends user-defined packets to the UNITE device in between randomly generated packets. The user can also specify the interval between sending each packet to the UNITE device and also the total number of packets sent to the UNITE device.

Area. The UNITE implementation was compiled for a number of rule sets provided by Snort. The result for area resource usage is on average 0.82 Lut/Byte. This is in contrast to the 0.6 Lut/Byte ratio achieved in [9], an increase of 0.22. This is acceptable, since [9] does not perform header classification. The area resource usage in [10,11] is not comparable to UNITE as their implementation uses a combination multiple FPGA and BRAMs in order to perform the complete NIDS detection, but our UNITE only makes use of one FPGA platform.

Speed. In order to process the entire payload, it is shifted and passed to the device to perform matching again. The shifting and matching phase is repeated until the end of payload, or when the payload has an exact match to the rule

Table 3. Area result for UNITE implementation

Snort rule set	Number of Rules	Total Number of Byte	Number of LUTs	Luts/Byte
Finger	13	203	132	0.65
ICMP	11	488	507	1.03
Oracle	22	547	498	0.91
Porn	26	595	521	0.88
X11	2	54	34	0.63

Table 4. Result for profiling of UNITE device

Operation	Average Number of Clock Cycles	Percentage of Execution Time
Frame Capture	3311	66
Frame Decoding	1147	23
Data Transfer through Bus	336	7
Packet Matching	182	4

Table 5. Comparison between different designs of NIDS

	Header & Payload	Area (Logic/Byte)	Throughput (Gbps)
UNITE	Both	0.82	2.85
BCAM[9]	Payload only	0.6	2.5
WashU Rule Processor[10]	Both	3.16	2.5
TCAM & BV[11]	Both	2.16	2.5
Snort[1]	Both		<1

set. The implementation of the UNITE device is pipelined, so this shifting and matching process will only increase the execution time by 1 clock cycle per 1 byte shifted.

An example UNITE device was implemented for the rule set of ICMP. The size of the header information is 12 bytes and the shortest payload pattern to match is 8 bytes of payload, hence needing 1455 shift operations if the 8 bytes pattern is at the very end of the maximum payload size, resulting in a total execution time of 1455 clock cycles. The clock rate for the implementation is 356MHz, and the processing speed of the device is 2.848Gbps.

Table 4 shows the results of profiling UNITE. However, only the packet capture and detection phase has been implemented in hardware, with software being used as an aid to provide the extraction of the header fields and the payload to the UNITE device.

The packet matching phase only used up 4% of the total execution time; this is a very good result because it shows that the hardware element of the system uses much less time than other software phases. This provides a major motivation in migrating the design for other software parts into hardware implementation. The migration of software parts to hardware implementation will not only improve the speed of execution, but will also eliminate some of the communication phase, e.g. data transfer through bus, between hardware and software if all software elements are eliminated. In Table 5, we show the merits between different designs of NIDS.

5   Conclusion

This paper describes UNITE, a novel network intrusion detection engine which adopts a uniform hardware architecture to perform both header classification and payload and payload signature extraction. Both CAM and BDD techniques are used in optimising the sharing of resources in this architecture.

UNITE achieves higher processing speeds than Snort, and also shows comparable performance to the designs in [10,11], which also support header classification and payload matching. However, UNITE is developed on a single FPGA, whereas the designs in[10,11] uses multiple FPGAs and BRAMs for their implmentation.

We have shown that the UNITE architecture, with its simplicity and scalability, has significant potential. Its performance can be further enhanced by two means: first, arranging for multiple engines to process packets in parallel, since currently each engine only takes around 10% on an advanced FPGA; second, to migrate functions currently implemented on the processor to the FPGA, so that both the software processing speed and the hardware/software interface will no longer have an impact on performance for the UNITE approach.

References

1. Sourcefire, "Snort - The Open Source Network Intrusion Detection System", http://www.snort.org, 2005.
2. Xilinx Inc, "Virtex II Pro Platform FPGA", http://www.xilinx.com/products/silicon_solutions/fpgas/virtex, 2005.
3. J. Fenlason and R. Stallman, "The GNU Profiler", http://www.gnu.org/software/binutils/manual/gprof-2.9.1/html_mono, 2005.
4. W. R. Cheswick and S. M. Bellovin, "Firewalls and Internet Security", *Addison-Wesley Professional*, 1994.
5. E. D. Zwicky, S. Cooper and B. D. Chapman, "Building Internet Firewalls (2nd Edition)", *O'Reilly*, 2000.
6. S. R. Boyer and S. J. Moore, "A Fast String Searching Algorithm", *ACM Press*, pp. 762–772, 1977.
7. D. Knuth, J. Morris and V. Pratt, "Fast Pattern Matching in Strings", *SIAM Journal on Compting*, pp. 323–350, 1977.
8. G. A. Stephen, "String Searching Algorithms", *World Scientific Publishing Co., Inc.*, 1974.
9. S. Yusuf and W. Luk, "Bitwise Optimised CAM for Network Intrusion Detection Systems", *Field Programmable Logic Conference Proceedings*, pp. 444–449, 2005.

10. M. E. Attig and J. Lockwood, "A Framework for Rule Processing in Reconfigurable Network Systems", *Proc. IEEE Symp. on Field Programmable Custom Computing Machines*, 2005.
11. H. Song and J. Lockwood, "Efficient Packet Classification for Network Intrusion Detection using FPGA", *Proc. IEEE Symp. on Field Programmable Custom Computing Machines*, 2005.
12. D. Bounds, "Packit - Network Injection and Capture", http://packit.sourceforge.net/, 2005.
13. Xilinx Inc, "OPB EMAC", http://www.xilinx.com, 2005.
14. Massachusetts Institute of Technology Lincoln Laboratory, "DARPA Intrusion Detection Evaluations", http://www.ll.mit.edu/IST/ideval/data/data_index.html.
15. Xilinx Inc, "Xilinx University Program", http://www.xilinx.com/univ/, 2005.

Impact of Loop Unrolling on Area, Throughput and Clock Frequency in ROCCC: C to VHDL Compiler for FPGAs

Betul Buyukkurt, Zhi Guo, and Walid A. Najjar

Department of Computer Science and Engineering
University of California - Riverside
Riverside CA 92507, USA

Abstract. Loop unrolling is the main compiler technique that allows reconfigurable architectures achieve large degrees of parallelism. However, loop unrolling increases the area and can potentially have a negative impact on clock cycle time. In most embedded applications, the critical parameter is the throughput. Loop unrolling can therefore have contradictory effects on the throughput. As a consequence there exists, in general, a degree of unrolling that maximizes the throughput per unit area.

This paper studies the effect of loop unrolling on the area, clock speed and throughput within the ROCCC, C to VHDL compilation framework. Our results indicate that due to the unique design of the ROCCC compilation framework, FPGA area either *shrinks* or *increases at a very low rate* for the first few times the loops are unrolled. This reduced area causes the clock cycle time to decrease and thus a great gain in throughput. Our results also show that there are different optimal unrolling factors for different programs.

1 Introduction

Loop unrolling is the main compiler technique that allows reconfigurable architectures achieve large degrees of parallelism. Loops that do not carry dependencies from earlier iterations can theoretically be fully unrolled to achieve maximum parallelism. However due to the adverse impact of loop unrolling on clock cycle time, there exists, in general, a degree of unrolling that maximizes the throughput per unit area. Since in most embedded systems, the critical parameter is the throughput, this implies that there should be different optimal unrolling factors for different programs.

This paper studies the effect of loop unrolling on the FPGA area, clock speed and throughput within the ROCCC C to VHDL compiler framework. Our results indicate that the consumed FPGA area either shrinks or grows at a very low rate for the first few times the loops are unrolled. In most cases, decrease in area leads to a decrease in the clock cycle time thus a great gain in throughput. Such results indicate that a design space exploration in the loop-unrolling factor vs.

K. Bertels, J.M.P. Cardoso, and S. Vassiliadis (Eds.): ARC 2006, LNCS 3985, pp. 401–412, 2006.

performance would indicate an optimal number of times to unroll for maximum throughput.

The impact of loop unrolling on FPGA area has been reported in [1] and [2]. Crowe et. al. [1] implements a AES symmetric key cryptosystem, SHA-512 secure hashing algorithm and a public key cryptography algorithm on a single FPGA. The area increases from no unrolling to an unrolling factor of 2 by 15% and to an unrolling factor of 4 by 75%. Park et. al. [2] implements binary image correlation on an FPGA which is used in template matching computations in image processing systems. Binary image correlation operates a window over a 2D array. This study reports FPGA areas for unrolling factors of 2x16, 4x16, 8x16 and 16x16. The overall area increases less than 50% and the area of the datapath shrinks, when the design is moved from no unrolling to an unrolling factor of 2. For unrolling factor 4x16, the area increases by little over 50% compared to no unrolling and their datapath area increases around 25%.

Both of the above studies did not report generating their VHDL from high-level languages, whereas in our work the VHDL is generated using our ROCCC, C to VHDL compiler system. Both [1][2] included the areas of the entire datapath, the controller logic and the memory interface area in their results. Our work reasons about the advantages of our ROCCC system that lead to the shrinkage of area on the FPGA. We give a breakdown of the area as the loops are unrolled and how the FPGA real estate is allocated between two main components of our design: 1) the datapath & the controller and 2) the smart buffer, which helps maximize data reuse across iterations.

This paper is organized as follows. Next section describes the ROCCC system. Section 3 talks about the experimental setup and results. Section 4 talks about other existing HLL to HDL compilers. Finally, Section 5 concludes the paper.

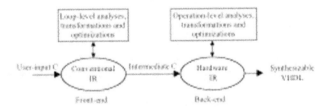

Fig. 1. ROCCC system overview

2   The ROCCC System

ROCCC is a compiler system built on top of the SUIF2 [3] and MACHSUIF [4][7] compiler infrastructures. The ROCCC system, shown in a diagram in Figure 1, is composed of two main components: a front-end that applies the high-level transformations and a back-end that handles the low-end optimizations as well as the VHDL code generation. The objectives of the ROCCC optimizations are threefold:

1. **Parallelism.** Maximize the throughput by exploiting the largest amount of loop and instruction level parallelism within the resource constraints of the FPGA.
2. **Storage.** Optimize the use of on-chip storage by effecting smart re-use of data and minimizing the accesses to memory.
3. **Pipelining.** Generate an efficient, pipelined datapath within the resource constraints in order to minimize clock cycle time.

Among the main strengths of the ROCCC system is the number of loop-level transformations it implements. The ROCCC system currently performs the following loop transformations: Invariant code motion, partial and full loop unrolling, loop peeling, loop un-switching, loop tiling, strip-mining and loop fusion. At the procedure level ROCCC performs the following optimizations: Constant propagation of scalars and constant array masks, constant folding, elimination of algebraic identities, copy propagation, dead and unreachable code elimination, code hoisting, code sinking, scalar renaming and division by constant approximation using shifts and additions. ROCCC also generates reduction on scalars that accumulate values through associative and commutative operations on themselves. Although some of the above analysis/passes exists inside the SUIF2 framework, we wrote our own passes to be able to easily gather and annotate the IR with all the ROCCC specific information. Our analysis and optimization passes use the high-level IR in SUIF2, where all the control structures and arithmetic expressions are preserved as close to their format in the original source code as possible.

Once the above passes are executed, the optimizer output is then analyzed and prepared to generate the data-path and controller information. There are few passes that ROCCC runs on the optimizer output to extract and format the datapath of the loop bodies. These passes are as follows:

- **Scalar I/O detection:** This pass marks all scalar variables that are computed or updated with in the loop body and referenced by the rest of the code once the loop completes execution.
- **Scalar replacement:** This pass decouples array accesses from computation. Figure-2(b) shows the moving filter code after the scalar replacement pass. The middle code block is isolated from memory accesses and is used to form the datapath. The top array read and bottom array write chunks are analyzed to form the smart buffer [18], address generation and the controller circuits.
- **Feedback variable detection:** This pass annotates the scalar variables, which are dependent upon their values from the loop's previous iteration.

The extracted datapath code is then transferred to Machine-SUIF IR, where most of the instruction level parallelism is brought up and pipelines are formed. We modified Machine-SUIF's virtual machine (SUIFvm) IR to build our data flow. All arithmetic opcodes in SUIFvm have corresponding functionality in IEEE 1076.3 VHDL with the exception of division. Machine-SUIF's existing passes, like the Control Flow Graph (CFG) library [8], Data Flow Analysis library [9] and Static Single Assignment library [10] provide useful optimization

```
void main(){
    int sum_of_9, i;
    int A[256], X[256];
    for(i = 0; i < 247; i=i+1) {
        sum_of_9 = A[i] + A[i+1] + A[i+2] + A[i+3] + A[i+4] +
A[i+5] + A[i+6] + A[i+7] + A[i+8];
        X[i] = sum_of_9 / 9;
    }
}
```

(a) 9-tab Moving filter

```
for(i = 0; i < 246; i = 2+i) {
    A0 = A[i]; A1 = A[1+i]; A2 = A[2+i]; A3= A[3+i]; A4 = A[4+i];
    A5 = A[5+i]; A6 = A[6+i]; A7 = A[7+i]; A8 = A[8+i]; A9 = A[9+i];

    sum_of_9 = A0+A1+A2+A3+A4+A5+A6+A7+A8;
    T0 = (sum_of_9>> 12)+(sum_of_9>> 11) +(sum_of_9>> 10)+
(sum_of_9>> 6)+(sum_of_9>> 5) +(sum_of_9>>4);
    sum_of_9 = A1+A2+A3+A4+A5+A6+A7+A8+A9;
    T1 = (sum_of_9>> 12)+(sum_of_9>> 11) +(sum_of_9>> 10)+
(sum_of_9>> 6)+(sum_of_9>> 5)+(sum_of_9>> 4);

    X[i] = T0;
    X[1+i] = T1;
}
```

(b) Moving filter loop after being unrolled twice, and applied the
constant folding, division by constant elimination and scalar
replacement transformations

Fig. 2. Moving filter code before and after ROCCC transformations

and analysis tools for our compilation system. Our compiler at this level automatically places latches in the data flow graph to pipeline the datapath.

ROCCC analyzes the array accesses at the SUIF2 level and generates the
smart buffer, which is a storage mechanism that helps minimize the accesses to
off-chip memory bandwidth for programs that operates on windows sliding over
arrays such as signal/image processing applications. The smart buffer stores the
input data for future iterations and removes old data to save room for new input
data.

The controllers generated by ROCCC include address generators, which ex-
port a series of memory addresses according to the memory access pattern of the
loop, and a higher-level controller, which controls the address generators. They
are all implemented as pre-existing parameterized FSMs (finite state machine)
in a VHDL library.

3   Experimental Evaluation

3.1   Experimental Set-Up

We used Xilinx ISE 6.2.03i to synthesize and place-and-route the generated VHDL code. Our target was the Xilinx Virtex-II xc2v8000-5 FPGA. We used five benchmarks to collect our data. fir5 and fir15 are 5-tap and 15-tap constant-coefficient finite-impulse-response filters and mf9 is a 9-tap moving average filter. fir5, fir15 and mf9 all operate on one-dimensional arrays. dwt (Discrete Wavelet Transform) is part of the JPEG 2000 compression standard. It is a doubly nested loop operating on a 5x3 block of pixels. mvc computes the first step of the three step Moravec corner detection algorithm, which computes the variance of the center pixel within a 3x3 window of 9 pixels. Being image-processing kernels, both dwt and mvc operate on 2D arrays.

fir5, fir15, mf9, dwt and mvc are all kernel loops. The source codes are directly read into the SUIF2 intermediate format and the ROCCC optimizations described in the previous section are applied. Further, we assumed that the I/O bandwidth between the datapath and the on-chip memory is sufficient, when performing unrolling, since the required data bus width increases with unrolling. The 1-D benchmarks are unrolled for 2, 4, 8 and 16 times. mvc is unrolled for 2x2 and 4x4 times. Finally, the dwt code is unrolled at different unrolling factor combinations ranging from 1 to 8 in powers of 2 in either dimension. un1, un2, un4 and un8, un16 labels on the figures indicate the unrolling factors of none, 2, 4, 8 and 16 for benchmarks operating on one dimensional arrays and unxXy labels indicate an unrolling factor of x applied to the outer loop and an unrolling factor of y to the inner loop respectively. We collected data for 8-bit data size. The reported area and clock frequency results are place-and-route results.

3.2   Area

Figure three displays our area results for our benchmarks that execute on one-dimensional arrays. The area results on these figures show the combined areas of the datapath, the controller and smart buffers. As the results indicate, the overall area shrinks from the original version to un2, even un4 for some cases such as that of mf9. In figure three (b) and (c) the not unrolled cases are not the minimal area points. This fact shows that there exist optimal times to unroll.

Figure four (a) shows the results of unrolling a dwt code. Note that an unrolling of 8x8 means that the 5x3 block is replicated eight times in each direction. In other words 64 windows of 5x3 are operated simultaneously. From no unrolling to 64 concurrent loops the area grows by 12 while the throughput grows by 16 in spite of the clock cycle time being about twice as long. Here also it seems that the 1x2, 2x2, 2x4, 4x4 and 4x8 unrolling factors achieve a better throughput per area. Note that the 8x8 unrolling achieves a throughput of 240 MegaPixels/sec, which is more than twice the rate necessary for high-definition TV.

Moravec's pixel variance computation kernel results indicate an almost linear increase in area. However, for this example the operator has a doubly nested

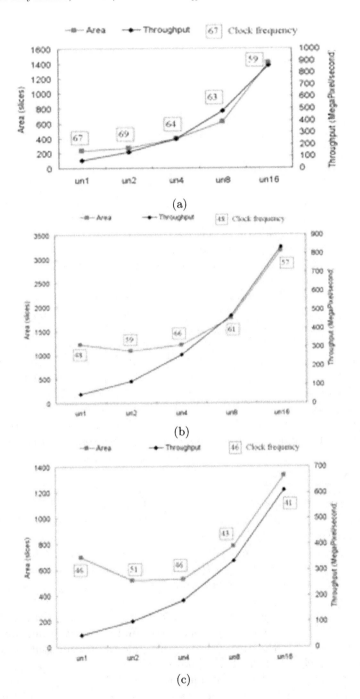

Fig. 3. Area, clock frequency and throughput for (a)fir5, (b)fir15 and (c)mf9

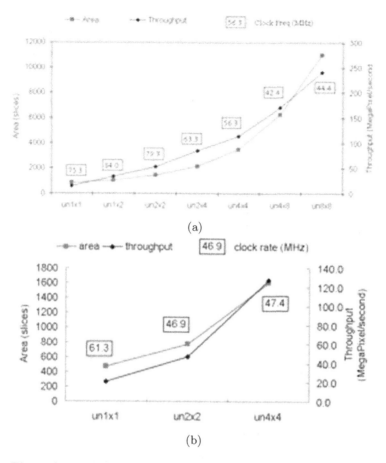

Fig. 4. Area, clock frequency and throughput for (a)dwt and (b)mvc

loop, as does the DWT code. Thus, the unrolled version operates not just on one more set of input data as it would be over a 1-D array, but three more sets of input data since it is twice unrolled towards both directions over a 2-D array.

3.3   Breakdown of the FPGA Area

Table-1 shows the slice and percentage breakdown of the FPGA area into datapath, smart buffer and controllers. To produce the table, we first mapped the entire circuit on to the FPGA, which gave us the results in figures three and four. Since place and route merges the circuits to use the FPGA area as efficiently as possible, it is not possible to distinguish which slices on the FPGA belonged to which component of the design. Thus to be able to obtain an estimate of the area breakdown, we separately mapped the datapath and the smart buffer circuits on to the FPGA, through which we obtained areas of the datapath and smart buffers. Then, to obtain the controller area we summed up the datapath and the smart buffer results and subtracted it from the total area shown in the figures. Obviously, this procedure would not give a correct area estimate of the area occupied by the control logic - the subtraction operation resulted in negative computed area values in some cases as in the case of fir15 -, however it adequately shows where the reduction in area came from. We did not see it necessary to map the controllers separately, since the areas of the controllers stay around the same due to the fact that the controllers are all implemented as pre-existing parameterized FSMs in a VHDL library, whose size does not depend on the unrolling factor.

Table 1. The Area Breakdown (8-bit)

		Datapath		Smart Buffer		Control Logic		Total
		slices	%	slices	%	slices	%	slices
	un1	42	17.8	172	72.9	22	9.3	236
	un2	80	29.5	164	60.5	27	10.0	271
Fir5	un4	159	40.2	201	50.8	36	9.1	396
	un8	317	51.2	250	40.4	52	8.4	619
	un16	769	54.6	483	34.3	157	11.1	1409
	un1	168	13.7	1086	88.9	-32	-2.6	1222
	un2	310	28.6	721	66.5	54	5.0	1085
Fir15	un4	604	49.9	528	43.6	79	6.5	1211
	un8	1186	66.9	490	27.7	96	5.4	1772
	un16	2358	74.2	566	17.8	254	8.0	3178
	un1	45	6.5	620	89.5	28	4.0	693
	un2	83	16.1	406	78.5	28	5.4	517
Mf9	un4	166	31.6	324	61.6	36	6.8	526
	un8	332	42.5	399	51.0	51	6.5	782
	un16	662	49.7	513	38.5	156	11.7	1331
	un1x1	33	7.0	181	38.3	258	54.7	472
Moravec	un2x2	133	17.1	368	47.4	275	35.4	776
	un4x4	532	33.3	714	44.7	352	22.0	1598
	un1x1	205	23.7	425	49.1	235	27.2	865
	un2x1	351	31.1	496	43.9	283	25.0	1130
	un1x2	338	31.9	515	48.5	208	19.6	1061
DWT 5x3	un2x2	590	40.4	618	42.3	252	17.3	1460
	un2x4	1068	49.3	750	34.6	347	16.0	2165
	un4x4	2003	57.5	996	28.6	487	14.0	3486
	un8x4	3875	63.1	1498	24.4	767	12.5	6140

We could not collect the smart buffer's place and route data, for the case of DWT unrolled 8x8 times, due to the fact that the smart buffer's ports exceeded the chip I/O capacity. When the smart buffers are mapped together with the datapath and the controllers, smart buffers' I/O ports become just on-chip wires connected to the datapath and the controllers.

According to the figures in Table-1, the circuit area of the datapath increased almost at a linear rate, although it is known that loop unrolling introduces more opportunities for optimizations especially on the datapath. The reason for the

```
for (i=0; i<N; i=i+1) {
    C[i] = 3*A[i] + 5*A[i+1] + 7*A[i+2]
    9*A[i+3] - A[i+4] ;
}
```

Fig. 5. 5-tap-FIR in C

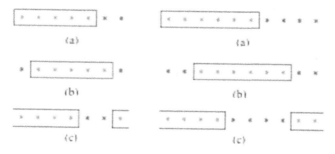

Fig. 6. Windows No.0, No.1 and No.6 in the smart buffer for the not unrolled 5-tap-FIR (left) and the windows No.0, No.1 and No.4 in the smart buffer for the twice-unrolled 5-tap-FIR (right)

linear increase is that all the data path codes are mapped after being decoupled from all memory accesses, all address computation code, and being applied an extensive set of procedure level optimizations.

The gain in area on the FPGA comes mainly from the shrinkage of the circuit size of the smart buffers due to its unique design. Smart buffer organizes the data that is received from the memory in windows. Each window has its own control logic enabling when and which sets of windows are to be exported to the datapath. For the un1 case, the number of windows in the smart buffer is large, although anytime only one of the windows is active. When we unroll the loop, the buffer size increases to hold more loops of input data, however the control logic cost decreases since the number of windows decreases due to the increase in the window size. Window size represents the amount of data that has to be dispatched to the datapath per clock cycle. Since the control logic size diminishes, the overall area for the smart buffer decreases.

To illustrate, if the not unrolled 5-tap-FIR in Figure-5 has a smart buffer whose size is seven words (Figure 6), then every five words constitutes a window, since the loop stride is one. Thus, this seven-word smart buffer contains seven windows. In Figure 6-left (a), (b) and (c) shows the No. zero, No. one and No. six windows. However, at any clock cycle at most one window's data is valid. The inactive words in the smart buffer could be receiving new data while the active window is sending its data to the datapath. To illustrate better, Figure 6-right shows smart buffer for the twice unrolled 5-tap-FIR. If we say the smart buffer size is two-word larger than the not-unrolled one, then, since and the loop stride is two, the size of each window is now six-word. Therefore inside the buffer in Figure 6-right, there are only five windows in total. Although the buffer size increased a bit, the number of windows decreases and so does the control logic. As a result, the overall area shrinks due to the control logic shrinkage.

3.4 Clock Cycle and Throughput

A circuit's clock rate is affected by many factors. The smaller a design is, the easier it is for the synthesis tool chain to generate a faster circuit for it. The data points on the figures where clock frequency increases are the points where the design area shrinks. However, the overall decrease in clock speed for higher unroll factors should not be taken as that the overall throughput is decreasing. The number of parallel iterations generated by high unroll factors imply that the number of outputs generated per clock cycle on a pipelined datapath increases. Thus, the effect of the clock rate decrease with increased unrolling is overcome with the increased parallelism in the unrolled codes.

4 Related Work

Many projects have worked on translating high-level languages into hardware using various approaches. SystemC [12] is designed to provide roughly the same expressive functionality of VHDL or Verilog and is suitable to designing software-hardware synchronized systems. Handel-C [13], a low level hardware/software construction language with C syntax, supports behavioral descriptions and uses a CSP-style (Communicating Sequential Processes) communication model.

SA-C [14] is a single-assignment, high-level, synthesizable language. Because of special constructs specific to SA-C (such as window constructs) and its functional nature, its compiler can easily exploit data reuse for window operations. SA-C does not support while-loops. ROCCC compiler transforms the IR into single-assignment form at back-end. Users are not required to write algorithms in a single-assignment fashion.

Streams-C [15] relies on the CSP model for communication between processes, both hardware and software. Streams-C can meet relatively high-density control requirements. The compiler generates both the pipelined datapath and the corresponding state machine to sequence the basic and pipeline blocks of the datapath. ROCCC supports two-dimensional array access and performs input data reuse analysis on array accesses to reduce the memory bandwidth requirement. Streams-C does not handle 2D arrays.

The DEFACTO [16] system takes C as input and generates VHDL code. It allows arbitrary memory accesses within the datapath. The memory channel architecture has its FIFO queue and a memory-scheduling controller. ROCCC has abundant loop transformations to increase parallelism and performs data reuse using the smart buffer.

GARP's [17] compiler is designed for the GARP reconfigurable architecture. The compiler generates a GARP configuration file instead of standard VHDL. GARP's memory interface consists of three configurable queues. The starting and ending addresses of the queues are configurable. The queues' reading actions can be stalled. The GARP-C compiler is specific to the GARP reconfigurable architecture while ROCCC targets commercial available configurable devices and generates synthesizable VHDL. GARP does not handle 2D arrays.

SPARK [11] is another C to VHDL compiler. Its optimizations include code motion, variable renaming and loop unrolling. The transformations implemented in SPARK reduce the number of states in the controller FSM and the cycles on the longest path. SPARK does not perform optimizations on input data reuse. Thus, ROCCC explores more parallelism than SPARK. ROCCC performs loop pipelining if there are no loop carried dependencies. SPARK handles 2D arrays by converting them into a one-dimensional array and computes memory addresses on the datapath, however ROCCC decouples computation from address calculation using scalar replacement.

CASH [19] is a C to Verilog compiler that generates a hardware dataflow machine that directly executes the input program. It targets asynchronous ASIC implementations. Catapult C [20] is a C++ to RTL compiler that generates hardware for ASICs/FPGAs. The compiler performs loop unrolling, loop pipelining and bit-width resizing. ROCCC harnesses its smart buffer architecture to increase the throughput by reusing input data.

Compared to previous efforts in translating C to HDLs, ROCCC's distinguishing features are its emphasis on maximizing parallelism via loop transformations, maximizing clock speed via pipelining and minimizing area and memory accesses, a feature unique to ROCCC. ROCCC handles 2D arrays and can optimize memory accesses for window operations. On an image processing code operating over an image using a 3x3 window, unrolling and reusing of already fetched data from the smart buffers reduces the memory re-fetches from 800% (without any optimizations) down to 6.25% (when the unrolling factor is 32x32).

5 Conclusions

Compilers for reconfigurable architectures achieve parallelism through unrolling and optimizing the kernel loops inside source codes. This paper studied the effect of loop unrolling on the FPGA area within the ROCCC compiler system. Our results indicate that the relation between the unrolling factor and the overall area growth on the FPGA is non-linear for the ROCCC, C to HDL compiler. This indicates that for systems where area is a constraint, using ROCCC's technology designers can gain more throughout with less area applying loop unrolling. We observed that overall FPGA area either shrinks or increases at a very low rate for the first few times the loops are unrolled. This shows that there are different optimal times to unroll for different programs.

References

1. Crowe. F., Daly A., Kerins T. and Marnane W.: Single-Chip FPGA Implementation of a Cryptographic Co-Processor. International Conference on Field Programmable Technology, Brisbane, December 2004
2. Park J., Diniz P.C., Shayee K.R.S.: Performance and Area Modeling of Complete FPGA Designs in the Presence of Loop Transformations. IEEE Transactions on Computers, Nov. 2004, pgs. 1420-1435, Vol 53, Issue 11, ISSN: 0018-9340

3. SUIF Compiler System. http://suif.stanford.edu, 2004
4. Machine-SUIF. http://www.eecs.harvard.edu/hube/research/machsuif.html, 2004
5. Z. Guo, W. Najjar, F. Vahid and K. Vissers. A Quantitative Analysis of the Speedup Factors of FPGAs over Processors, In. Symp. on Field-Programmable gate Arrays (FPGA), Monterrey, CA, February 2004
6. M. D. Smith and G. Holloway. An introduction to Machine SUIF and its portable libraries for analysis and optimization. Division of Engineering and Applied Sciences, Harvard University.
7. G. Holloway and M. D. Smith. Machine-SUIF SUIFvm Library. Division of Engineering and Applied Sciences, Harvard University 2002.
8. G. Holloway and M. D. Smith. Machine SUIF Control Flow Graph Library. Division of Engineering and Applied Sciences, Harvard University 2002.
9. G. Holloway and A. Dimock. The Machine SUIF Bit-Vector Data-Flow-Analysis Library. Division of Engineering and Applied Sciences, Harvard University 2002.
10. G. Holloway. The Machine-SUIF Static Single Assignment Library. Division of Engineering and Applied Sciences, Harvard University 2002.
11. SPARK project. http://mesl.ucsd.edu/spark/, 2005.
12. SystemC Consortium. http://www.systemc.org, 2005.
13. Handel-C Language Overview. Celoxica, Inc. http://www.celoxica.com. 2004.
14. W. Najjar, W. Bohm, B. Draper, J. Hammes, R. Rinker, R. Beveridge, M. Chawathe and C. Ross. From Algorithms to Hardware - A High-Level Language Abstraction for Reconfigurable Computing. IEEE Computer, August 2003.
15. M. B. Gokhale, J. M. Stone, J. Arnold, and M. Lalinowski. Stream-oriented FPGA computing in the Streams-C high level language. In IEEE Symp. on FPGAs for Custom Computing Machines (FCCM), 2000.
16. P. Diniz, M. Hall Park, J. Park, B. So and H. Ziegler. Bridging the Gap between Compilation and Synthesis in the DEFACTO System. Proceedings of the 14th Workshop on Languages and Compilers for Parallel Computing Synthesis (LCPC'01), Oct. 2001.
17. T. J. Callahan, J. R. Hauser, J. Wawrzynek. The Garp Architecture and C Compiler. IEEE Computer, April 2000.
18. Z. Guo, A. B. Buyukkurt and W. Najjar. Input Data Reuse In Compiling Window Operations Onto Reconfigurable Hardware. Proc. ACM Symp. On Languages, Compilers and Tools for Embedded Systems (LCTES 2004), Washington DC, June 2004.
19. M. Budiu, G. Venkataramani, T. Chelcea and S. C. Goldstein. Spatial Comput-ing. ASPLOS 2004.
20. http://www.mentor.com/products/c-based_design/

Automatic Compilation Framework for Bloom Filter Based Intrusion Detection

Dinesh C. Suresh, Zhi Guo*, Betul Buyukkurt, and Walid A. Najjar

Department of Computer Science and Engineering
*Department of Electrical Engineering
University of California, Riverside, CA 92521
{dinesh, zguo, najjar, betul}@cs.ucr.edu

Abstract. Virus detection at the router level is rapidly gaining in importance. Hardware-based implementations have the advantage of speed and hence can support a large throughput. In this paper we describe an FPGA-based implementation of the Bloom filter virus detection code that is compiled from the native C to VHDL and mapped onto a Virtex XC2V8000 FPGA. Our results show that a single engine tailored for handling virus signatures of length eight bytes can achieve a throughput of 18.6 Gbps while occupying only 8% of the FPGA area.

1 Introduction

Studies on economic impact of computer viruses have shown that global businesses incurred an estimated $55 billion in damages during the year of 2003 [12]. The report also estimates that the monetary losses due to viruses could further increase in the forthcoming years. Therefore, containing new virus outbreaks is one of the greatest challenges facing networks and organizations. One way to control virus outbreaks is to scan for viruses at the router/interconnection points. Packets generated from infected files contain *signatures*, which are strings that uniquely identify the presence of malicious code in an incoming packet. Signatures could be distributed anywhere within a packet or across packets. By accurately identifying signatures in incoming packets, malicious packets could be blocked at the router level, thereby making the networks more secure.

Speed is the greatest concern while handling packets at the routers and hence, any router-level signature detection mechanism should be capable of identifying signatures accurately at high throughputs. This could be accomplished by a dedicated hardware (ASIC or FPGA) that inspects packets in parallel to detect signatures. Advances in high density FPGAs have provided designers with a viable commercial alternative to ASICs. Unlike ASICs, FPGAs do not require a prohibitively high cost of mask production.

In this paper, we present ROCC, a C to native VHDL compiler framework. We demonstrate this tool by using it to generate hardware for Bloom-filter based virus detection. Our compiler framework can be easily adapted to accommodate new algorithms for virus detection and our generated hardware achieves multi-gigabit throughputs. Our contributions in this paper can be summarized as follows. This

K. Bertels, J.M.P. Cardoso, and S. Vassiliadis (Eds.): ARC 2006, LNCS 3985, pp. 413–418, 2006.

paper presents the first work in which a Bloom-filter based virus detection system is automatically generated from C code. We illustrate that automatic code generation is a feasible option in terms of the performance and area utilization of the FPGA. Our 8-byte Bloom filter code delivers a throughput of 18.6 Gbps while occupying a modest chip area of 8%.

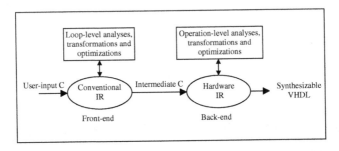

Fig. 1. ROCC compiler framework

2   Overview of the ROCC C to VHDL Compiler

ROCC [15] is built on the SUIF2 [13] and Machine-SUIF [14] platforms.Figure 1 shows ROCC's system overview. It compiles code written in C/C++ or Fortran to VHDL code for mapping onto the FPGA fabric of a CSoC device. In the execution model underlying ROCC, sequential computations are carried out on the microprocessor in the CSoC, while the compute intensive code segments are mapped onto the FPGA. These typically consist of loop nests, most often parallel loops, operating on large arrays or streams of data. Therefore, most loop level analysis and optimizations are done at this level. Most of the information needed to design high-level components, such as controllers and address generators, is extracted from this level's IRs.

The front-end of ROCC performs a very extensive set of loop analysis and transformations aiming at maximizing parallelism and minimizing the area. The transformations include loop unrolling and strip-mining, loop fusion and common sub-expression elimination across multiple loop iterations. . The work reported in [7] shows that in less than one millisecond and within 5% accuracy compile time area estimation can be achieved. Information to generate high-level units, such as controllers and buffers, is also extracted from SUIF IRs. The restrictions on the C code that can be accepted by the ROCC compiler, for mapping on an FPGA fabric, include no recursion, no usage of pointers that cannot be statically unaliased. Function calls will either be inlined or whenever feasible made into a lookup table. In the following section, we explain the operation of a Bloom filter for virus detection.

3   Bloom Filters

A Bloom filter [3] s a space-efficient data structure used to test the set membership of an element. An empty Bloom filter is described by an array of m bits, initially all set to 0. A Bloom filter uses K independent hash functions $h_1....h_k$ with range *{0... m-1}*. Each of these hash functions map an incoming item to a number in the range of *{0 ...m-1}*.During insertion, hash functions $h_1....h_k$ are applied to the input item. Each return value from the hash function is used as an index to the Bloom filter (array of m bits) and the appropriate bit position is set to 1. A location can be set to 1 multiple times, but only the first change has an effect.

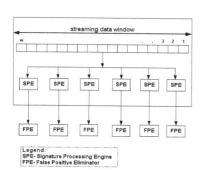

```
for (k=0;k<224;k++)
{
    for (j =0; j < 32; j ++)
    {
        for(i=0;i<8;i++)
        {
            temp = value & 0xff;
            result_location1 = temp ^ hash_function1[i];
            result_location2 = temp ^ hash_function2[i];
            result_location3 = temp ^ hash_function3[i];
            result_location4 = temp ^ hash_function4[i];

            value = value >> 8;

            found = bit_array[result_location1] & bit_array[result_location2]
            bit_array[result_location3] & bit_array[result_location4];
            return (found);
        }
    }
}
```

Fig. 2. The Bloom filter detects malicious packets at the network layer. The output of the Signature Processing Engine (SPE) is fed to the False Positive Eliminator (FPE).

Fig. 3. Bloom filter code for identifying signatures of width 8 bytes each in a stream of size 256 bytes. The packet size is assumed to be 64 bytes. The data structure bit array is a Bloom filter of size 256 entries.

During a search operation, the locations returned by the hash functions are checked to see if they are already set to '1'. If bit values in all the return locations are set, then the Bloom filter is said to contain the pattern else it is a miss. An item x belongs to the set S with some probability if all $h_i(x)$ are set to 1 for 1<i<k. .If not, then x is not a member of S. A Bloom filter may yield a *false positive* when it suggests that an element x belongs to S even though it does not. The probability of a false positive is given by

$$\left(1-\left(1-\frac{1}{m}\right)^{kn}\right)^{k} \approx \left(1-e^{-kn/m}\right)^{k}$$

Where, k,m and n denote the number of hash functions, number of bits in the bloom filter array and the number of elements currently inserted into the bloom filter, respectively. In the event of a match in the Bloom filter, a detailed string matching is performed using a RAM to ensure that the hit was not a false positive.

A functional prototype of the Bloom-filter based intrusion detection system has been implemented. We used a Bloom filter of length 256 bytes to detect patterns of length 8 bytes. Figure 2 shows the block diagram for a bloom-filter based virus detection system. Figure 3 shows a Bloom filter code that uses four hash functions on a 256 entry Bloom filter array. The hash functions are implemented as a simple XOR operation. The result of each hash operation sets a location in the Bloom filter. The compiler unrolls the inner most loop to compare the 8-byte patterns in parallel. We used the rule sets contained in bleeding snort database [11]. Each rule consists of two parts: a header and a rule option. The header is mainly used for packet classification and contains information like the protocol, source IP, source port, destination IP and the destination port. The rule option contains the signatures to be used in intrusion detection.

Figure 5 shows the frequency of the signature width of all rules in the bleeding snort database. As evident from the figure, most of the rules present in the bleeding snort database have a signature width of less than 30 bytes. In the following section, we present the generation of datapath and throughput evaluation for the Bloom filter code.

4 Datapath Generation and Throughput Analysis

Figure 4 shows the three-stage pipeline for the generated Bloom filter circuit. The XOR operation shown in the figure represents each byte of the input being XOR ed with one byte of the hashing function. The location returned by the hashing function is looked up and if all four hashing function lookups return a value of '1', then the circuit reports the current input pattern as malicious.

The compiler groups the instructions in each node into different execution levels to exploit instruction (operation) level parallelism. Instructions at the same level are executed simultaneously. Every level of the dataflow graph corresponds to the instantiation of one loop iteration. ROCC automatically places latches in the data-path for pipelining. Every latched level corresponds to one pipeline stage, and has a delay of one cycle.

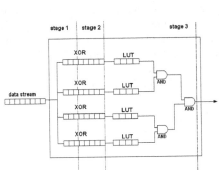

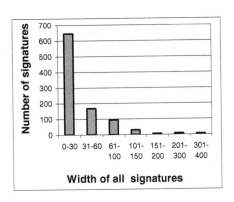

Fig. 4. Three-stage pipeline for the Bloom filter signature code. Each box in the XOR filed represents a byte of the input being XOR ed with one byte of the hashing function.

Fig. 5. Histogram of signature width for all rules in the snort database. The most frequently occurring signatures have a width of around 32 bytes.

Our Bloom filter code does not have loop-carried-dependency and the compiler fully pipelines the data-path. Therefore, the generated data-path can be fed with new set of input every clock cycle and the throughput is one iteration per cycle. We process 8 bytes during each iteration. When we do loop unrolling, we assume that the memory-bus width also scales up with unrolling.

The clock frequency of the FPGA was found to be 73 MHz. The system uses a total of 4692 slices, which accounts for 8% of the total FPGA area. The BRAM on our target FPGA (XC2V8000) can process 256 bits (32 bytes) per cycle. Hence, the BRAM can support eight such hardware instances during each cycle. The total throughput of our hardware is given by

$$Throughput = bits\ per\ cycle * clock\ frequency$$
$$T = 8 * 32 * 73 * 10^{6}\ bits/\ sec. = 18.6\ Gbps.$$

The throughput shown above is for a system that detects multiple signatures of a single width. When multiple instances for each signature width are instantiated, the overall circuit area would also increase proportionately. Synthesis tools tend to produce slower circuits when the design size increases. However, with increase in area, the compiler produces more parallel iterations and hence, the performance loss due to decrease in clock speed is overcome by the increase in parallelism. In order to provide a better insight into our estimated throughput values, we examine the throughput achieved by previously published works.

5   Related Work

Hashmem [9] combines memory and hashing effectively to achieve exact matching of intrusion signatures at throughputs of up to 3.7Gbps while using nearly 0.15 logic cells per character. Baker and Prasanna [2] use automatic compilation to synthesize FPGA architectures that perform deep packet inspection at 10Gbps. Clark et al.[5] use NFAs with predecoded inputs to achieve excellent area and throughput performance. Lockwood et. al.[8] used the Field Programmable Port extender (FPX) platform for expression matching. Their synthesized circuit achieved clock speeds of 37MHz on a virtex XCV2000E FPGA.

Gokhale et.al [6] used CAM to implement snort rules on a virtex XCV1000E FPGA. Their hardware delivered a throughput of 2.2Gbps. Cho et. al [4] generated structural VHDL for deep packet filtering on an FPGA. Their design runs at 90MHz on an Altera EP20K device and achieves a throughput of 2.88Gbps. Attig et. al..[1] have implemented a Bloom filter circuit on a Virtex E2000 FPGA. Their circuit operates at 62.8MHz and provides a throughput of 502Mbps. This paper presents the first reported work that *automatically generates native VHDL for Bloom filter based intrusion detection code written in C.*

6   Conclusion

In this paper, we have described using ROCC, a C to VHDL compiler, to generate Bloom-filter based virus detection system on FPGAs. Ours is the first work that automatically generates VHDL for Bloom filter code written in C. We evaluate the performance and area of the synthesized hardware and prove that automatic compilation to hardware is a feasible design option. Our synthesized hardware runs at 73 MHz and delivers a throughput of 18.6 Gbps while occupying a modest FPGA real estate of 8%.

References

[1] M. Attig, S. Dharmapurikar, J. Lockwood. "Implementation Results of Bloom Filters for String Matching,", In proceedings of the *12th Annual IEEE Symposium on Field-Programmable Custom Computing Machines (FCCM'04)*, pages. 322-323, 2004

[2] Z. Baker and V.K. Prasanna, "High Throughput Linked-Pattern Matching for Intrusion Detection Systems, In Proceedings of *Symposium on Architectures for Networking and Communication Systems* (ANCS' 05) , Princeton, New Jersey, October 2005.

[3] B.H. Bloom. "Space/time tradeoffs in hash coding with allowable errors", *Communications of the ACM,* 13(7): pages 422-426, July 1976.

[4] Y. H. Cho, W. M. Smith, "Specialized Hardware for deep packet filtering", In *Proceedings of the 12th International Conference on Field Programmable Logic and Applications* (2002), France.

[5] C. R. Clark and D. E. Schimmel, "Scalable Parallel Pattern-Matching on High-Speed Networks," in IEEE Symposium on Field-Programmable Custom Computing Machines, Napa, California, April 2004.

[6] M. Gokhale, D. Dubois, A. Dubois, M. Boorman, S. Poole, and V. Hogsett. "Granidt: Towards gigabit rate network intrusion detection technology", . In *Proceedings of International Conference on Field Programmable Logic and Applications*, pages 404–413, 2002.

[7] D. Kulkarni, W. Najjar, R. Rinker, and F. Kurdahi, Fast Area Estimation to Support Compiler Optimizations in FPGAbased Reconfigurable Systems, IEEE Symp. on Field-Programmable Custom Computing Machines (FCCM), Napa, CA, April 2002.

[8] J. Moscola, J. Lockwood, R. P. Loui, and M. Pachos, "Implementation of a content-scanning module for an internet firewall",. In *Proceedings of the IEEE Symposium on Field-Programmable Custom Computing Machines*, 2003.

[9] G. Papadopoulos and D. Pnevmatikatos, "Hashing + Memory = Low Cost, Exact Pattern Matching," in Proceedings of 15th International Conference on Field Programmable Logic and Applications, Tampere, Finlad, August 2005

[10] I. Sourdis and D. Pnevmatikatos, "Fast, large-scale string match for a 10Gbps FPGA-based network intrustion detection system",. In *Proceedings of International Conference on Field Programmable Logic and Applications*, 2003.

[11] http://www.bleedingsnort.com

[12] http://news.designtechnica.com/article2401.html.

[13] SUIF Compiler System. http://suif.stanford.edu.

[14] Machine-SUIF. http://www.eecs.harvard.edu/hube/research/machsuif.html .

[15] Z. Guo, B. Buyukkurt, W. Najjar and K. Vissers. "Optimized Generation of Data-Path from C Codes". In ACM/IEEE Design Automation and Test Europe (DATE), Munich, Germany, March 2005.

A Basic Data Routing Model for a Coarse-Grain Reconfigurable Hardware

Jie Guo[1], Gleb Belov[2], and Gerhard P. Fettweis[1]

[1] Vodafone Chair Mobile Communication Systems, T.U. Dresden, Germany
{guojie, fettweis}@ifn.et.tu-dresden.de
[2] Fak. Mathematics and natural sciences, T.U. Dresden, Germany
bg@math.tu-dresden.de

Abstract. Synchronous Transfer Architecture (STA) is a coarse-grain reconfigurable hardware. It is modelled by using a common machine description that is suitable for both compiler and core generator. STA is a Very Long Instruction Word (VLIW) architecture and in addition it uses a non-orthogonal Instruction Set Architecture (ISA). Generating efficient code for such ISA needs highly optimizing techniques. This paper presents a basic data routing Integer Linear Programming (ILP) model for STA code generation. We will also show in this paper, the execution time of the assembly code can be dramatically reduced. The code generation can be accomplished in acceptable time and it can even be real time by reducing the degree of optimality.

1 Introduction

Integer Linear Programming (ILP) has a long tradition as a method for investigating scheduling problem. Daniel Kästner et al. [1] [2] built two well-structured ILP formulations for global phase-coupled code optimization of irregular architectures. Kent Wilken et al. developed instruction scheduling [3] and precise register allocation for irregular architectures [4]. Besides using some of their ideas, our ILP model is specially designed for the architectural features of STA. Our model requires that operations can be explicitly assigned to functional units. The amount of STA modules, instruction latency and data type can be reconfigured in our model according to the machine description.

This paper is organized as follows: Sec. 2 gives an overview of the STA features and explains why a new model is developed for STA code generation. Sec. 3 shows the basic ILP model about data routing. Sec. 4 gives the experimental results, followed by a conclusion and discussion on future work in sec. 5.

2 Synchronous Transfer Architecture (STA)

Figure 1 gives an overview over the STA concept. STA [5] processors are built up from modules, each with a set of input and output ports. The output ports are buffered. The buffer at the output holds the result of the last operation, until

K. Bertels, J.M.P. Cardoso, and S. Vassiliadis (Eds.): ARC 2006, LNCS 3985, pp. 419–424, 2006.

the next operation of the belonging module is executed. The data at an input port is selected from a set of connected output ports by a multiplexer. Thus, data can be obtained directly from an output register of connected Functional Unit (FU), which lowers the requirement for additional register strongly. This kind of data routing will be called *direct data routing* (DDR) in the rest of this paper. Direct data routing can dramatically reduce the number of required registers in a register file.

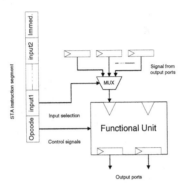

Fig. 1. STA modules

If results of calculations will be kept in output registers of used FUs (direct data routing), a fewer amount of FUs will be available in the following cycles. This will lead to a decrease of instruction level parallelism. Writing the data always back to register files (register access) would increase the time to read the data and hence is not optimal for this architecture. Finding an optimal tradeoff bases on the question "When will the result be used again?". At the scheduling time of the instructions the answer to this question is still unknown because the scheduling of the following instructions is not finished.

3   Basic Idea of Integer Linear Programming (ILP) Model

The developed ILP model is restricted to basic blocks [6]. First we did global data flow analysis [6] to find the original IN and OUT data for each basic block. Here, IN is the set of definitions that come from other basic blocks or from the last iteration of this block and reach the beginning of each basic block. OUT is the set of definitions that reach the end of basic block and is passed to other basic blocks or to the next iteration of this block.

After the IN and OUT are found according to our definition, all the registers are divided into two groups: group I is used for IN and OUT data, group II is used for the temporary results which appear only in one basic block. We did experiments with our ILP model, we found *data direct routing* is often used in optimal scheduling and the amount of registers used for saving temporary results is very small.

We assigned 80% registers to group I and the remaining 20% to group II. If the amount of registers in group I is not enough, memory spill code will be generated in our Medium-Level Intermediate Representation (MIR). Otherwise, the remaining registers in addition to the registers of group II will be used for determining an optimal tradeoff between *direct data routing* and register access in each basic block. In the following paper, we will only show how to find this optimal tradeoff in our model.

3.1 Definitions

Before we explain how to model the *direct data routing* and register access, we need to do the following definitions:

C: Maximal number of the clock cycles for one basic block
J: Set of all the clock cycles $1..C$.
- **set** I: All the MIR instructions in the basic block
- **set** $\mathbb{DDR\_U}$: Instruction i_u and i_v are in the same basic block of MIR, and i_v uses the result of i_u (possible to be used for data direct routing of STA)
N_{FUi}: The amount of ith different type of Functional Units
N_{write}: The amount of register write ports
N_{read}: The amount of register read ports

3.2 Data Routing (Direct Data Routing or Register Access)

We assume there are always a pair of virtual register read $r(u, v, j)$ and write $w(u, v, j)$ between each pair of instructions $(i_u, i_v) \in \mathbb{DDR\_U}$ and the execution time of all the instructions is one clock cycle, there are two cases which may take place in our model:

1. the write instruction $w_{u,v}$ appears before the read instruction $r_{u,v}$
2. the read instruction $r_{u,v}$ appears before the write instruction $w_{u,v}$

The first one is considered as *real*, which means register write and read operations are really used between a *DDR pair* (i_u, i_v). The second case is defined as *unreal*, where the related register operations are physically infeasible and the result of i_u is transferred to i_v with *direct data routing*. In our model, it is explicitly modelled that the corresponding read and write instructions cannot appear in the same cycle.

3.3 Modelling Constraints

We define a series of binary variables $x(u, j), j \in J$. The value of $x(u, j)$ is 1 when i_u begins to be scheduled in cycle j, otherwise 0. Equation (1) guarantees that each instruction i_u must be started and can be only started once. In the same way, we define the corresponding binary variables $x(v, j), j \in J$ and $r(u, v, j)$, $w(u, v, j), (i_u, i_v) \in \mathbb{DDR\_U}, j \in J$.

$$\sum_{j=1}^{C} x(u, j) = 1, \forall i_u \in \mathbb{I} \tag{1}$$

Observing a *DDR pair* $(i_u, i_v), (i_u, i_v) \in \mathbb{DDR\_U}$ as shown in Figure 2.

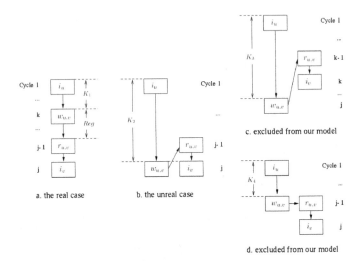

Fig. 2. The sequence of the virtual read and write instructions

Firstly, the write instruction $w_{u,v}$ must appear after instruction i_u. The equation (2) describes this constraint.

$$\sum_{j=1}^{C} x(u,j) * j + 1 \leq \sum_{j=1}^{C} w(u,v,j) * j, \qquad (i_u, i_v) \in \text{DDR\_U} \qquad (2)$$

Secondly, the read instruction $r_{u,v}$ should be placed exactly one cycle before instruction i_v. If a true register write instruction exists, a new read instruction is generated directly before each instruction which uses i_u's result in our compiler. Read instructions can be only executed on the read port. If the data is stored in the register's read port until last use, this read port cannot perform other read instructions for many clocks. If the data is always read before it will be used, this read port is free for some time slots. The free time slots can be available to the other read instructions, they may improve the instruction level parallelism without increasing the cost of read port. Equation (3) is used to describe this constraint.

$$\sum_{j=1}^{C} r(u,v,j) * j + 1 = \sum_{j=1}^{C} x(v,j) * j, \qquad (i_u, i_v) \in \text{DDR\_U} \qquad (3)$$

Thirdly, in a *DDR pair* (i_u, i_v), if $w_{u,v}$ is scheduled before $r_{u,v}$, then the case is considered as *real* (Fig. 2.a) and register is used to transfer the result of i_u to i_v. Otherwise, if $w_{u,v}$ is scheduled after $r_{u,v}$, it is considered as *unreal* (Fig. 2.b) and *direct data routing* is used. We further define that the read instruction can appear at most one cycle before the corresponding write instruction. Equation (4) is used to represent this constraint. An additional equation (5) is the constraint that the read and write operation cannot take place in the same cycle. Thus, the virtual instructions in fig. 2.c and fig. 2.d are excluded in our model.

$$\sum_{j=1}^{C} w(u,v,j) * j - 1 \leq \sum_{j=1}^{C} r(u,v,j) * j, \qquad (i_u, i_v) \in \mathbb{DDR\_U} \qquad (4)$$

$$w(u,v,j) + r(u,v,j) \leq 1, \qquad (i_u, i_v) \in \mathbb{DDR\_U}, \forall j \in \mathbb{J} \qquad (5)$$

Under these two constraints, the *unreal* case is reduced to just one situation: $r_{u,v}$ appears one cycle before $w_{u,v}$. Remember that $r_{u,v}$ appears also one cycle before i_v, so $w_{u,v}$ and i_v must be in the same cycle as shown in Fig. 2.b. In our model, this case represents the *direct data routing* for data transferring. The FU used by the instruction i_u must be kept (i.e. not to be used by the other instructions so that the data in the output register of the FU is not changed), until the cycle in which i_v is scheduled. Then, it is equivalent to count from the cycle of i_u to the cycle of $w_{u,v}$. This period is illustrated by K_2 in Fig. 2.b.

In the *real* case, the FU should also be kept from the cycle of i_u to that of $w_{u,v}$ as shown by K_1 in Fig. 2.a. Thus, the occupation of FU can be uniformly expressed for both cases by very concise ILP equations. The *Reg* in Fig. 2.a indicates that a data unit should take a register space during the period.

4   Experimental Results

We tested the completed model with one user licence of ILOG CPLEX (9.1 version) on one CPU. Table 1 shows the execution time (cycles) of the assembly code for same input data. Column 2 is cycles of the assembly code generated by traditional compiler. The instruction scheduling of this compiler uses some heuristic algorithm for STA [8].

Column 3, 6 and 9 show the cycles of the code generated by our ILP based compiler. P10, P15, P20 mean that each basic block includes maximal 10, 15 and

Table 1. Performance comparison between ILP and traditional code generator

1	2	3	4	5	6	7	8	9	10	11
benchmark	trad.	P10	D	T(s)	P15	D	T(s)	P20	D	T(s)
firparallel	175	114	65.1%	1.44	90	51.4%	2.9	82	46.9%	87.8
iirparallel	196	133	67.9%	1.73	105	53.6%	2.4	89	45.4%	19
firserial	117	75	64.1%	0.94	60	51.3%	2.5	55	47%	3.7
iirserial	113	62	54.9%	0.66	49	43.4%	5.1	43	38.1%	5.9
lmsparallel	1204	1079	89.6%	19.7	904	75.1%	63.5	779	64.7%	842.1
lmsserial	295	149	50.5%	2.1	129	43.7%	7.9	103	34.9%	45
fft648	1269	922	72.7%	29.7	723	56.9%	330.5	681	53.7%	1558.8
fft1288	1439	1125	78.2%	35.1	890	61.8%	481.8	828	57.5%	1890.6
fft2568	1781	1292	72.5%	44.3	1022	57.4%	555.8	951	53.4%	2092.1

20 instructions. Column 4, 7, 10 are the results of (ILP_cycles/trad_cycles*100%). Column 5, 8 and 11 show the solving and proving time of CPLEX (in seconds).

The assembly code generated by our code generator uses much less memory than the former code. ILP-based code generator uses the output buffers of FUs very efficiently, that leads to less necessary registers and much less memory spill code.

5   Conclusion and Future Work

The limitation of such ILP-based code generator is that it can optimize the code in a small area. The advantage of this work is that it can reduce the execution time of the assembly code with block partition in acceptable time. Our code generator can not only be used for the real time application, but also as a reference to the heuristic algorithms. As the future work, we will make better block partition for our code generator, then some heuristic algorithms will also be implemented.

References

1. Daniel Kästner. "Retargetable Postpass Optimisation by Integer Linear Programming", PHD Thesis, Oktober 2000.
2. L.Zhang, SILP. Scheduling and allocation with Integer Linear Programming. PHD Thesis, Saarland University, 1996.
3. Kent Wilken, Jack Liu, and Mark Heffernan. "Optimal Instruction Scheduling Using Integer Programming." Proceedings of the ACM SIGPLAN 2000 conference on Programming language design and implementation, p121-133.
4. Timothy Kong and Kent Wilken. "Precise Register Allocation for Irregular Architectures." Proceedings of the 31st annual ACM/IEEE international symposium on Microarchitecture.
5. Gordon Cichon, P. Robelly, H. Seidel, E. Matus, M. Bronzel and Gerhard Fettweis. "Synchronous Transfer Architecture (STA)." SAMOS-04, p126-130, Juni, 2004.
6. Steven S. Muchnick. "Advanced Compiler Design Implementation." Morgan Kaufmann Publishers, 1997.
7. A.V.Aho, R.Sethi, and J.D.Ullman. "Compilers, Principles, Techniques and Tools." Addison-Wesley, Redding, MA, 1985.
8. Gordon Cichon, P. Robelly, H. Seidel,M. Bronzel and Gerhard Fettweis. "Compiler Scheduling for STA-Processors." PARELEC'04, Dresden, Germany, 07. - 10. September 2004

Hardware and a Tool Chain for ADRES

Bjorn De Sutter[1], Bingfeng Mei[1], Andrei Bartic[1], Tom Vander Aa[1],
Mladen Berekovic[1], Jean-Yves Mignolet[1], Kris Croes[1], Paul Coene[1],
Miro Cupac[1], Aïssa Couvreur[1], Andy Folens[1], Steven Dupont[1],
Bert Van Thielen[1], Andreas Kanstein[2] Hong-Seok Kim[3], and Suk Jin Kim[3]

[1] IMEC vzw, Belgium
desutter@imec.be
[2] Freescale Semiconducteurs France SAS, France
a.kanstein@freescale.com
[3] Samsung Advanced Institute of Technology
hong-seok.kim@samsung.com

Abstract. Until recently, only a compiler and a high-level simulator of
the reconfigurable architecture ADRES existed. This paper focuses on
the problems that needed to be solved when moving from a software-only
view on the architecture to a real hardware implementation, as well as
on the verification process of all involved tools.

1 Introduction

A new class of programmable processor architectures for embedded applications
is emerging: coarse-grained reconfigurable architectures (CGRAs) [3]. Due to
difficult programming models and a vast overuse of resources compared to DSP
processors, none of them have yet been widely adopted. ADRES (Architecture
for Dynamically Reconfigurable Embedded Systems) and DRESC (Dynamically
Reconfigurable Embedded System Compiler) try to overcome these issues [6,5].

An ADRES instance consists of an array of basic components, including
FUs, register files (RFs) and routing resources (wires, muxes and busses), of
which the top row can operate in a VLIW processor mode. This mode shares
the central RF with the second mode, the array mode, in which all entities of
the architecture operate in parallel. By providing two functional views on the
same physical resources, ADRES tightly couples a VLIW processor, which offers an (on other published CGRAs absent) easy path for mapping complex
code, and a coarse-grained array that offers unprecedented loop acceleration.
The shared central RF minimizes communication and mode-switching costs and
enables the compiler to seamlessly generate code for both modes, including data
transfers.

In array mode, a loop is executed that consists of the instructions between
two configuration memory addresses. To remove control flow from loops, the
FUs support predicated execution. The result of each FU can be written to local
RFs, which are smaller and have less ports than the shared RF, or routed directly
to the inputs of other FUs. The multiplexers in the array are used for routing

K. Bertels, J.M.P. Cardoso, and S. Vassiliadis (Eds.): ARC 2006, LNCS 3985, pp. 425–430, 2006.

data from different sources. The configuration memory stores the configuration contexts, from which a single context is loaded onto the FUs and muxes on a cycle-by-cycle basis, thus in effect reconfiguring them every single cycle.

ADRES is programmed in ANSI C. Our tool chain until recently consisted of three tools. First, the IMPACT C compiler front-end parses C code, optimizes it and generates assembly code in the Lcode instruction format. Next, our DRESC compiler takes an ADRES instance description and maps the loop kernels onto the array [5]. The generated schedules are then simulated with the simulator.

ADRES was designed from a compiler perspective to achieve high-performance, low-power computing with automated C compilation. Until recently, however, ADRES was a virtual architecture for which only the compiler and the high-level simulator existed. Here, we take an important step as we now have a full tool chain that compiles C code and generates binary configuration files that can be executed on a hardware implementation in VHDL. *In concreto*, we have compiled an MPEG2 decoder written in C and we have executed it on an FPGA-based demonstrator, thus proving the concept of ADRES. This short paper focuses on the efforts needed to move from a software-only perspective to a hardware implementation and a full tool chain. Performance results are discussed in other work [5,6]. For a discussion of related work, we refer to Bingfeng Mei's thesis [4].

2   Hardware-Software Interface Issues

Instruction Set. To execute an MPEG decoder on an FPGA implementation of ADRES, without writing a full compiler, the instruction set architecture (ISA) needs to meet three requirements. (1) The VLIW ISA needs to be dense enough to store the program on the limited amount of FPGA memory. (2) For proving to be a potential low-power solution, the decoding of the instructions needs to be simple. (3) The ISA should be close enough to that of the intermediate code representation generated by Lcode representation of the IMPACT compiler. Unfortunately, however, Lcode is much too expressive to be dense. First, Lcode supports a wide range of predicate generating instructions, as available on Intel's EPIC architecture. Most of them are rarely used, so supporting all of them implies a large code size overhead. Secondly, Lcode allows all operands of instructions to be 32-bit immediates. Clearly, this is not feasible in any real ISA.

As a temporary solution, we decided to support only the most common type of *unconditional predicates* [1]. Our tool detects when other types are present in the Lcode, and informs the programmer that he must rewrite his code to avoid the use of that predicate. For rather simple applications, such as an MPEG2 decoder, this solution proved to be satisfactory. To support more complex code, however, such as the H.264 codec, adapting the compiler to generate only the supported predicates is the only feasible solution. Furthermore, ADRES VLIW instructions can have only one immediate operand. When Lcode instructions have more of them, our assembler inserts instructions that first put them in free registers. Because the insertion of additional instructions happens after the code is scheduled, the final schedules are sometimes far from optimal. In a production tool chain, this workaround solution will need to be replaced by a better instruction selector and post-pass scheduler. Furthermore, our assembler cannot insert instructions in array schedules, because these are too complex to change in a post-pass tool. Instead, we again notify the programmer to change his source code in such a way that constants occurring in CGA-mode loops are first put in temporary variables, and hence in registers instead of in immediate operands. This required only modest source code transformations. Future versions of our tool chain will perform this rather trivial transformation automatically.

Compiler Perspective. We encountered several unexpected problems during the combined development of both the VHDL specification and the binary code format of our architecture. Most often, these problems surfaced because the compiler developers that developed the compiler-supported architecture, approached it from the software perspective, and not from a hardware perspective. In the former, undefined behavior is non-existent in the sense that only specified computations are performed. For example, a nop instruction executed on some FU is supposed not to change the processor state, and is hence given little consideration. In hardware, by contrast, all signals that can influence the program state need to be specified correctly. This impedance mismatch between the two perspectives became apparent when different simulators were developed. Until recently, the only available simulator was a compiled simulator that basically is an RTL-level implementation of the program in C. This C code is then compiled with a standard C compiler, and executed to simulate the program's execution on ADRES. One of the main differences between real hardware, and the compiled simulator, is that the simulator operates on virtual registers that are modeled through variables. Rotating registers are implemented with simple copy operations on the live variables. Consider the following loop on the left hand side:

```
                                i_2 = 0;
                                while (cont = (i_2<10) || epilogue_is_running) {
for (i=0;i<10;i++) {               if (cont) i_1 = i_2 + 1 ;
   ... // loop body                ... // software-pipelined loop body
}                                  i_2 = i_1; // register rotation
                                }
```

As the loop index is a loop-carried variable, it is allocated to (virtual) rotating registers, as depicted on the right hand side above. The variable `cont` models the loop continuation predicate, which becomes `false` during the final iteration of the loop, thus informing the processor that the array mode needs to be exited. Because loops are software pipelined, it might still be necessary to continue the loop execution for some cycles, however, in order to finish the execution of the ongoing iterations in the loop epilogue. Until recently, we assumed that the continuation predicate could be set during any stage of the loop: the value of `cont` in the above fragment only depends on the initial value in `i_2`.

During the verification of the hardware, we noted that the above assumption on the `cont` predicate was in fact invalid. In real hardware, not only the live registers rotate, but the other ones do so as well, as shown in the following fragment, that contains two copy statements to mimic register rotation.

```
i_2 = 0; cont = true;
while ((cont && cont = i_2<10) || epilogue_still_running) {
  if (cont) i_1 = i_2 + 1 ;    // loop body
  ...
  i_2 = i_1; i_1 = i_0;         // register rotation
}
```

During the normal operation of the loop, the undefined value of i_0 that is rotated into i_1 is overwritten by the guarded increment operation. During the epilogue, however, this is no longer the case, and hence the undefined value in i_0 is not only copied into i_1, but one iteration later also into i_2. As a result, cont becomes true again, and the loop keeps executing.

When we discovered that our assumption was wrong, we were too close to our deadline to start changing the compiler and to not rely on the incorrect assumption. Instead, we opted for slightly adapting the way we used the loop continuation predicate. In the adapted C-code, the continuation predicate is only evaluated as long as it has been true, as can be seen from the while statement in the above fragment. In later versions of our tool chain we will of course adapt the compiler to generate the continuation predicate only at correct schedule times.

While the loop continuation problem is only one issue that arose during this design project, it is very typical for our approach from a compiler perspective. While this approach guaranteed from the start that a full-fledged C-compiler will exist for ADRES, it also resulted in a number of unanticipated problems, like the above one. Consequently, the specification of the architecture needed several updates during its implementation in hardware, because of which a significant amount of time was lost. The lesson we learned is that the hardware and software people involved should learn to speak the same language upfront, and that they should understand the issues involved on both sides of the system.

3   Verification

Several components of our now complete tool chain and hardware implementation needed verification. While the compiler and the compiled simulator had been used and tested for a long period, these tools were largely developed by one PhD. student. [4]. It was expected that there would be hidden assumptions about the compiler in the simulator and vice versa that might need to be reevaluated. Furthermore, the assembler and the linker, that map the assembly-like program representation generated by DRESC onto binary object code, needed to be validated. Finally, the VHDL implementation needed verification. To support these verification needs, a number of tracing tools were developed or extended.

Symbolic Tracing. First, the compiled simulator was extended with tracing capabilities to dump traces containing in and outputs of FUs, RFs and memory accesses. It should be understood that this compiled simulator is just a simple implementation in C of the RTL-like ADRES operations that where generated by the DRESC compiler. In this implementation, local variables of the original program have been replaced by variables that model virtual registers at the RTL level. Data structures that reside in memory in the original program still reside in memory in the compiled simulator. In fact, the data structure declarations are simply copied from the original program to the compiled simulator. As such, the memory accesses on the compiled program all happen in the address space of the compiled simulator on the host system, and not in the memory space of the binary ADRES program as it would be assembled and linked. In practice, this means that all addresses occurring the RF and FU traces not only depend on the actual program being traces, but also on how the simulator was compiled. After every change to the simulator, the addresses change.

Cycle-Accurate Tracing. Secondly, we developed a cycle-accurate μ-arch simulator by means of Esterel [2]. This simulator simulates binary ADRES executables at the RTL-level at a lower level of abstraction than the compiled simulator. This cycle-accurate simulator thus offers the same tracing capabilities as the compiled simulator, but it's traces are closer to the actual hardware.

The main goal of the cycle-accurate tracing is the verification of the compiler back-end and of the correct operation of the whole ADRES concept. For that purpose, its traces could be compared to those produced with the trusted compiled simulator, thus inheriting the thrust from it. Unlike the compiled simulator, however, the μ-arch simulator runs the program in the ADRES address space. Hence addresses occurring in the traces of both simulators are different, which complicates the comparison of their traces.

A first workaround involves eliminating addresses from the traces. This can be done by only tracing instructions that do not usually operate on absolute addresses, such as multiplications, shifting, or the loading/storing of bytes and words. An alternative is to use two versions of the compiled simulator that executes on different addresses. Then we can first compare the traces of those versions, and detect (and later neglect) the values that are in fact addresses, as these are exactly those values that are different in the two versions. A final alternative is the replacement of addresses in traces by symbol names. This can only be done for data whose symbol information is available in the compiled code, however, and hence it is only applicable for statically-allocated data, of which the Linux tool objdump gives us the symbol mapping.

VHDL Tracing. Instead of having the VHDL simulation dump traces, and then verifying the correctness of them, we decided to let the VHDL code verify itself. To that extent, the VHDL implementation reads the FU traces from the cycle-accurate simulation, and then raises assertions when the values observed during the VHDL simulation differ from them. After having validated the cycle-accurate simulator, this on-the-fly trace comparison would allow us to debug, and eventually validate, the VHDL code. Unfortunately, the trace comparison is not without problems. Because these two simulators operate at different abstraction levels, defined behavior in one simulator can correspond to undefined behavior in another, in which cases false-positive assertions are raised.

As a workaround, the cycle-accurate simulator tags the values in a trace with tags that indicate whether a value is defined or not. The addition of the correct tags was a time-consuming process, largely guided by trial and error. We feel this cannot be avoided however, as the goal of having an RTL-level cycle-accurate μ-arch simulator is precisely to enable the verification at a more abstract level.

Furthermore, when loops are mapped onto the array mode, many instructions are executed speculatively to shorten the critical code paths. This again implies that some operations are executed on undefined operands. To detect those during the verification of the tool chain, all possible operands are initialized to easily detectable values in the compiled and in the cycle-accurate μ-arch simulator. For example, the value 0xdeadcafe is well suited because the human eye spots it easily in traces. In hardware, these values do not occur of course, and hence they were replaced by zeroes to generate traces for automated trace comparisons.

4   Conclusion

The ADRES CGRA was developed from a compiler perspective to ensure that C-code could be mapped onto it automatically. This paper presented some of the issues that were dealt with during the development of a hardware implementation and a concrete instruction set, and the verification of all (new) back-end tools and code. All issues were resolved in relatively simple ways, without imposing impractical or unrealistic constraints on either the source code or on the ISA.

Acknowledgement. This research has been carried out in the context of IMEC's multimode multimedia program which is partly sponsored by Samsung and Freescale Semiconductor.

References

1. AUGUST, D. I., SIAS, J. W., PUIATTI, J.-M., MAHLKE, S. A., CONNORS, D. A., CROZIER, K. M., AND MEI W. HWU, W. The program decision logic approach to predicated execution. In *Proc. ISCA '99* (1999), pp. 208–219.
2. BERRY, G. The foundations of esterel. *Proof, language, and interaction: essays in honour of Robin Milner* (2000), 425–454.
3. HARTENSTEIN, R. A decade of reconfigurable computing: a visionary retrospective. In *Proc. of Design, Automation and Test in Europe (DATE)* (2001), pp. 642–649.
4. MEI, B. *A coarse-grained reconfigurable architecture template and its compilation techniques.* PhD thesis, Katholieke Unvirsiteit Leuven, 2005.
5. MEI, B., VERNALDE, S., VERKEST, D., MAN, H. D., AND LAUWEREINS, R. DRESC: A retargetable compiler for coarse-grained reconfigurable architectures. In *International Conference on Field Programmable Technology* (2002), pp. 166–173.
6. MEI, B., VERNALDE, S., VERKEST, D., MAN, H. D., AND LAUWEREINS, R. ADRES: An architecture with tightly coupled VLIW processor and coarse-grained reconfigurable matrix. In *Field-Programmable Logic and Applications* (2003).

Integrating Custom Instruction Specifications into C Development Processes

Jack Whitham and Neil Audsley

Department of Computer Science, University of York, York, YO10 5DD, UK
{jack, neil}@cs.york.ac.uk

Abstract. We describe a new approach for creating hardware description language (HDL) specifications for custom instructions, to form part of the instruction-set architecture (ISA) of an application specific instruction set processor (ASIP). Our approach integrates fully into the traditional C development process, binding tightly with software source code and simplifying the ASIP optimisation process. Our tool is also free software, facilitating its use in future research.

1   Introduction

Increasing system efficiency by extending processors with application specific instructions has been considered widely, with many commercial products available [10,5,3]. However, existing commercial and research solutions separate the description of custom instructions from the actual software using these instructions. This paper proposes an integrated approach, allowing the user to specify custom instructions within the software source code itself.

This approach simplifies build processes by integrating into industry-standard compilation tools, permits easy testing of custom hardware, and makes full use of existing compiler optimisations. C programmers will need little specialist hardware design knowledge to make use of our approach. No new language needs to be learnt, the tool flow is the same as that used in most Unix `make` files, and separate compilation is fully supported.

Application-specific instruction set processor (ASIP) tools [10,5] generate ASIP cores. [15] gives a good overview of ASIP design methodologies. Today, ASIPs are usually soft processor cores, intended for use as part of an FPGA design. Typical ASIP tools permit rapid optimisation of a hardware platform to a particular application. The processor can be tuned to developer requirements, such as reducing power consumption or increasing speed.

But the tools either do not attempt to integrate software and hardware development [8], or do so only within a graphical integrated development environment (IDE) [4,2,23], which constrains development options to those foreseen by the tool vendor. Additionally, the tools are closed, inextensible software, generally operating on secret ASIP cores. This reduces their utility to researchers, who are unable to adapt the tools for experimental purposes. Some adaptations of ASIP technology, such as the introduction of reconfigurable functional units

K. Bertels, J.M.P. Cardoso, and S. Vassiliadis (Eds.): ARC 2006, LNCS 3985, pp. 431–442, 2006.

(RFUs) [26,25], are currently impossible without either a manual implementation or a new tool.

In this paper, Sect. 2 examines the state of the art in ASIP tools and research. Section 3 discusses our approach and the implementation of our tool. Section 4 deals with our evaluation process and Sect. 5 concludes.

2   Existing ASIP Tools

2.1   General Overview

ASIP tools allow an existing "base" processor core to be customised to an application, by providing instruction set customisation (add or remove instructions), architectural customisation (add or remove execution, control or storage elements), and interface customisation (alteration of bus size and type).

Figure 1 illustrates a typical use of instruction set customisation. Software code is replaced by a custom instruction. Instruction fetches and clock cycles are saved. Overall, this approach may permit a smaller processor to be used, or slower, cheaper hardware may become usable. The cost, size and/or power consumption of the entire system may be reduced. Correct choice of code is essential [22,7], but outside the scope of this paper. The typical approach involves profiling the application to find the most frequently executed code [4].

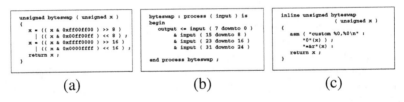

$$(a) \qquad\qquad (b) \qquad\qquad (c)$$

Fig. 1. Acceleration of C function (a) through dedicated hardware (b), accessed by a special opcode (c)

2.2   Commercial Tools

Tensilica Corporation [23] sells ASIP cores and tools under the trade name "Xtensa"[10]. The "Xplorer" IDE is used to modify the Xtensa cores. Custom instructions are described using the Tensilica Instruction Extension (TIE) [24,7], a proprietary Verilog-like HDL. Architectural and interface customisation are also available: for example, multiplier execution units can be added if the application requires them. ARC Corporation [3] makes a similar set of tools for their own ASIP cores, including the "ARCitect" and "Metaware" IDEs, for building ASIP cores and software to execute on them.

ASIP Meister [5] provides an IDE for defining ASIP core features, but lacks features for software development. ASIP Meister permits a higher level of customisation than ARCitect and Xplorer - it is possible to change instruction encoding and processor microcode, even to the extent of implementing other processors [18].

Coware sells the LISATek tool [8], a general purpose processor definition tool based on the Language for Instruction Set Architectures (LISA). Coware's tools generate a compiler, simulator and VHDL processor model from a LISA description.

2.3   Development Using an ASIP Tool

Tensilica tools make use of the TIE [24] language for instruction specification. ASIP Meister allows custom instructions to be specified in a GUI. Other tools follow one of these two models: hardware is specified separately from software, and then used from the software in some way (e.g. compiler macros, in the case of Tensilica). This has the advantage that changes to the software are independent of the custom instructions. Changes to software alone will not force the ASIP to be rebuilt.

However, it has the disadvantage that the two descriptions are kept separate. This forces poor programming practice - functionally related items are in separate files, making the program harder to understand, debug, change and test. Programmers should aim to keep interfaces between modules to a minimum, but the TIE and ASIP Meister methodologies force an inter-module link for every custom instruction.

2.4   ASIP Research

ASIP technology predates the use of FPGAs. The term was first introduced to describe any processor designed for a particular application, not just a soft core to which instructions could be added.

ASIPs in today's form are a development of research into classic co-design, a methodology discussed in [13,19]. Co-design tools are enhanced compilers that produce both a hardware description and a software binary for a particular application, with the intention of producing a faster implementation than software alone. This is done by migrating code fragments between hardware and software implementations: *partitioning* the program.

ASIP researchers initially attempted to derive the best ASIP instruction set for a program in its entirety [1], echoing the work of co-design researchers. Later work took a different direction, starting with a base instruction set and adding new instructions where necessary. This was more effective, as common instructions are always needed. Some ASIP tools try to automatically derive the partition [6,22,7,11], but this is by no means essential. The automatic ASIP design problem has the same limitation as classic co-design: an exponential number of possible partitions.

All ASIP tools allow the developer to define the partition by hand, making use of the developer's understanding of the problem as a guide to partitioning. The developer may also directly define the hardware for each custom instruction. This avoids the suboptimal nature of automatic software hardware to translation [12].

2.5   ASIPs as a Basis for Research

Generally, existing ASIP tools are a good basis for research provided that they can be used as intended. Tensilica's Xtensa tools have formed the basis for some academic work, for example [22,7]. [22] cites the flexibility of Xtensa as the reason for its choice. The work required both a processor with an extensible instruction set, and tools that provided easy access to the extensions. Xtensa provides both of these. Similarly, [21] chose LISATek over ASIP Meister as it provides direct access to the underlying processor definition language.

However, existing ASIP tools were not useful during the development of Chimaera [26], in which hard-wired custom instruction units are replaced by a run-time reconfigurable unit. No existing tools have support for such designs, and since existing tools are not open technology, they are not sufficiently extensible to act as a basis for fundamentally new designs. Thus, the Chimaera researchers were forced to start from scratch.

2.6   A Free ASIP: OpenRISC

The OpenRISC processor [16] is a freely available soft processor core, with a MIPS-like architecture and a five-stage single issue pipeline. OpenRISC already has ASIP features, but lacks ASIP tools.

Space is available within the instruction set for extensions to be added, and stubs exist within the Verilog source to allow custom execution units to be implemented. Additionally, some OpenRISC features can be "switched on" using definitions in a configuration file, allowing architectural customisation. OpenRISC also has a complete GCC tool chain, and similar performance to other 32-bit RISC soft cores.

3   Our Approach

3.1   Design Choices

Section 2.1 described the common features of ASIP tools. Of these, we consider instruction set customisation to be the most important, as it has a high potential for improvements that are easily quantifiable [22,11]. It is this feature that our tool provides.

We have based our approach and tool on the C language and the free GNU C Compiler [9]. Despite its many shortcomings, C remains a widely-used language for embedded system development, and it is thus a good starting point. We chose not to define a new hardware description language, as Tensilica did with TIE, instead making extensions to C and allowing hardware descriptions to be specified using a C subset. The subset is restricted: for example, at present, only single clock cycle operations are supported (see Sect. 3.4).

Noting that custom instructions are often only a small part of an application's software, and that functionally-related lines of code should be close together, our approach requires the programmer to specify hardware within software. Figures 2 and 3 illustrate our tool flow.

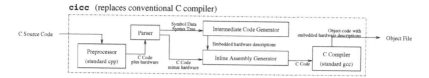

Fig. 2. Tool flow (a): The Custom Instruction C Compiler (`cicc`) is used in place of the regular C compiler. Note that both the hardware and software for each C module are placed in the same object file.

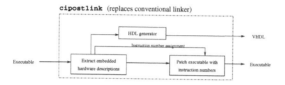

Fig. 3. Tool flow (b): After object files are linked in the usual way, the Custom Instruction Post-linker (`cipostlink`) extracts hardware descriptions from the executable, and then patches the executable to assign custom instruction numbers

The traditional Unix **make** development process is used in place of an IDE. However, a generic IDE may be used. Our approach is fully modular, never requiring a compiler rebuild, and only forcing a processor rebuild if a custom instruction definition changes.

3.2   Data Paths

In a typical RISC architecture, only two input and one output bus are linked to an execution unit. The OpenRISC custom instruction unit is subject to this limitation, which is adequate for all RISC instructions, but not necessarily for custom instructions.

For example, an encryption operation will typically require both plain text and key inputs. Access to more than two registers is required. One solution to this problem is to provide access to all CPU registers. However, this requires register assignments to be fixed at the time of custom instruction generation, making the register file non-orthogonal, as it now includes special purpose registers. In this environment, optimisations are less effective.

Local registers within the custom unit are a better solution. These are single-purpose registers, programmed with appropriate data as required. This approach does not break GCC optimisations, but it does force the programmer to consider thread safety, as the local registers cannot be saved during context switches. Despite this, it is a simple and effective solution.

3.3   Describing Custom Instructions

Suppose that we wish to write a custom instruction that replaces C code:

```
x = ( a + b + 4 ) & b ;
```

This would be written in Tensilica's TIE [24] language as:

```
operation Op ( out int x , in int a , in int b ) {
    assign x = ( a + b + 4 ) & b ;
}
```

The TIE code will be in a separate file, called from the main program using a generated Op macro: `x = Op ( a , b )`. The Op macro will expand to an appropriate instruction within the C file, in the form of inline assembly code. Meanwhile, the TIE code will be compiled separately into Verilog or VHDL, for inclusion in the basic ASIP core provided by Tensilica.

In our approach, the custom instruction would be described in the C source itself. The meaning of the operation is no longer hidden in a separate file. Here is the same example:

```
hardware {
    x = ( a + b + 4 ) & b ;
}
```

hardware marks the statement following it as a custom instruction. hardware statements are extracted automatically by our pre-compiler cicc (Fig. 2), which carries out the work of TIE. cicc is used in place of the regular C compiler (GCC): it is intended to be used as a drop-in replacement.

Pre-compilation is the process of extracting hardware statements and generating hardware descriptions and inline assembly for each. cicc does this by analysing the source file, building a complete symbol table, and then converting each hardware statement into a syntax tree, which is then converted into an intermediate hardware description language.

The pre-compilation step ends with the generation of inline assembly code, to call the generated hardware, and a new .hardware section within the generated object files, to contain the hardware description. This description may be compiled for simulation, or synthesised as hardware. Links are maintained between inline assembly and the associated hardware description using relocatable symbols. The post-linker, cipostlink, is run on the final executable to extract intermediate code and emit a description of the custom unit as VHDL (Fig. 3).

3.4   Custom Instruction Language

hardware blocks may contain a subset of C. The subset includes most expressions, but no loops. Loops cannot be permitted as all operations within a single hardware block must complete within a single clock cycle. Memory accesses are not permitted at present, as a modification to the OpenRISC processor would be required to support them.

The permitted statements are all arithmetic and logical expressions, except division and modulo, conditionals (if/else and x?y:z), assignments, and variable declarations and type casts. Accepted variable types are also restricted to char (8 bit), short (16 bit), int (32 bit) and long long (64 bit).

Variables may cross the interface between a hardware block and the surrounding C code, but at most two different external variables can be read from with the block, and at most one external variable can be written (see Data

Paths, Sect. 3.2). This restriction is offset by local registers, declared using the `localregister` keyword, and temporary variables (declared in the local scope). These variables may be accessed without limitation.

4   Test and Evaluation Process

Evaluation of our free ASIP tool was carried out in two distinct areas: a test for correct operation, and a cost/benefit evaluation against other approaches.

4.1   Test Platform

To test correctness and efficiency, a variety of benchmark programs were set up to run on our target platform, a Xilinx Spartan-2E FPGA with 512Kb of 32-bit SRAM and a serial port attached. The platform is clocked at 12.5MHz. The FPGA holds an OpenRISC processor with a hardware multiplier, in addition to a boot ROM, drivers for the serial port and memory, timer, and hardware profiler. A Linux PC is able to download bitfiles to the FPGA via a parallel interface, then download software and obtain results via the serial port.

On the test platform, the OpenRISC version of the RTEMS [20] operating system is used as the host for the various benchmark programs. Although RTEMS adds a significant memory overhead (160Kb of code), it does not reduce execution speed when used in single-task mode. The Unix-like API of RTEMS makes it easy to compile the benchmark programs.

On the Linux PC, our `cicc` and `cipostlink` tools are installed in addition to the OpenRISC cross-compiler (GCC 3.2.3) and the Xilinx FPGA build tools (Xilinx ISE 7.1). Scripts were written to control the build process: each benchmark program can be built in "normal" mode, in which only standard Open-RISC instructions are used, or in "custom" mode, in which custom instructions are generated, built into the OpenRISC core, and then used.

The "normal" mode program is code from either the MiBench [14] or Medi-aBench [17] suite. We chose applications from these benchmark suites as representatives of the real applications that ASIPs are used in. Each benchmark was minimally modified to run on RTEMS/OpenRISC, with no change in the test data used, and support for our hardware profiler and timer was added. These features allowed the time taken by the benchmark to be examined and improvements to be evaluated.

The "custom" mode program is almost the same as the "normal" mode program, but preprocessor directives (`#ifdef`, etc.) are used to substitute custom instructions for normal code in appropriate places. All other source is unchanged, and the same optimisation settings are used.

Our scripts are able to run an automated test cycle, in which benchmarks are built, downloaded onto the FPGA and tested. Table 1 lists the benchmarks used.

Having run each benchmark in "normal" mode, we examined the profile data from the built-in profiler to find the correct places to add custom instructions. The profiler identified a clear candidate in every case, such as:

The quan() function in g721,
the core of the CRC routine in crc32,
64-bit multiplier code in fft and basicmath, and
fixed-point multiplier code in mad.

Each of these candidates was replaced by a small number of custom instructions, resulting in speed-ups at the cost of extra hardware, as shown in Table 1.

Table 1. The benchmarks that were used, and the relative efficiencies of their "normal" and "custom" implementations

Benchmark name	Clock cycles, normal mode	Clock cycles, custom mode	Total hw (LUTs)	Extra hw (LUTs)	Max clock freq (MHz)	Speedup factor
basicmath	1456m	1449m	5958	1312	28.4	1.01
crc32	13m	11m	4840	194	30.9	1.23
dijkstra	772m	636m	4785	139	30.9	1.21
fft	192m	191m	5958	1312	28.4	1.01
g721	886m	446m	4672	26	30.9	1.99
jpeg	25m	19m	6069	1423	21.8	1.31
mad	129m	123m	5329	683	28.8	1.05

4.2   Operational Testing

Built-In Testing. A simple extension to cicc provides testing support. As the syntax of each custom instruction is a subset of C, it is possible to automatically add a test harness during the pre-compilation step. The step compares the result of the operation carried out in hardware with the result from software. In the event of a mismatch, a failure function is called with information about the location of the error. This test approach was used for every example, which ensures that the generated hardware matches the original specification.

Checksum Testing. All of the benchmarks produce some output. Checksums were used to ensure that the output of each benchmark did not change between the unmodified benchmark code, the "normal" mode benchmark, and the "custom" mode benchmark.

Functional Verification. It is important that each feature that can be placed within a hardware block works correctly. Fortunately, due to the support for built-in testing, this is easily arranged. Across all the benchmarks, all the available features of the hardware block were used, and therefore tested.

4.3   Cost/Benefit Evaluation

Efficiency. Table 1 indicates the improvement gained in each benchmark, plus the additional hardware cost in look-up tables (LUTs) and the change in maximum clock frequency. On our hardware, OpenRISC and associated hardware drivers run at up to 31.0 MHz, and take up 4646 LUTs. Each custom instruction will require some additional LUTs. The maximum clock frequency may also be affected by some custom instructions, if a new critical path is added. Our jpeg benchmark includes a custom instruction with a new critical path: its presence reduces the maximum clock frequency.

It is clear from this data that the tool can provide speed-ups for the various benchmarks. However, its efficiency in comparison to other ASIP tools is not obvious, and cannot be evaluated without access to those tools, which is not available for cost reasons. As comparisons with vendor-supplied benchmarks are only useful if all variables can be standardised, we decided to evaluate efficiency by comparison to the best possible case - direct manual implementation on hardware.

Manual implementation is far more laborious than any ASIP approach. There is no tool assistance: the developer must modify the processor directly. However, the developer may optimise the hardware directly to match the application requirements. There is no intermediate layer, as with our C subset, or Tensilica's TIE language. Greater efficiency is possible at the cost of developer time.

Table 2 illustrates the difference between a manual implementation and a tool-driven implementation for some of our test cases. The same interface into the processor was used for all implementations. As can be seen, the two implementations are very similar in each case, although manual implementations generally require less hardware.

Table 2. Comparison of manually implemented custom units and automatically generated ones

Benchmark name	Extra hw using tool (LUTs)	Extra hw, by hand (LUTs)	Max clock freq using tool (MHz)	Max clock freq, by hand (MHz)
crc32	194	169	30.9	30.9
dijkstra	139	105	30.9	31.0
g721	26	23	30.9	31.0
jpeg	1423	1265	21.8	23.8
mad	683	644	28.8	31.5

Expressiveness of Our Language. As our language is a subset of C, it is easily used by any C programmer. The concepts required to use it are simple enough that C programmers will become custom instruction designers with very little effort. In this respect, it improves upon Tensilica's TIE language, which is really a language for hardware engineers, being based upon the Verilog language.

However, TIE is more expressive than our language. Firstly, TIE allows for direct bit manipulation: every variable is an array of bits, as in Verilog. Our language only permits bit manipulation indirectly through the standard C bit operators. It is our intention that the use of these operators will be optimised out and replaced with direct bit manipulation during synthesis, but we cannot guarantee that this will always happen.

Secondly, TIE allows instructions to take several clock cycles. This feature is not available in our language at present.

Improvements on Other ASIP Tools. Our approach permits ASIP programs to be built in several stages. This is useful if ASIP instructions are required within the C library, operating system, or other supporting libraries. Conventional software engineering processes do not compile these parts together - rather, the operating system and libraries are built into a software development kit first, and the applications are added later. But other ASIP tools force them to be compiled together if customisations are made.

Our approach also permits recompilation of single code modules. Even modules that use ASIP features can be changed: a rebuild of the ASIP itself is only required if the ASIP features change. The approach tightly binds hardware descriptions with the code that uses them, making code more maintainable and well structured. Despite this, the separation between hardware and software is explicit and controlled by the programmer. Nothing is inferred or guessed "intelligently" by our system, so nothing can be guessed wrongly.

Although our approach only works for the OpenRISC processor at present, the interfaces could be adapted for most soft core processors for which HDL is available.

Our approach may appear to permit each custom instruction to be used once. However, this is not the case. Identical custom instructions are merged by the `cipostlink` program, permitting custom instructions to be replicated explicitly (by macros and inline functions) and implicitly (by GCC optimisations).

Disadvantages of Our Tool. We do not consider the additional pre-compilation and post-linking steps to be a disadvantage, as they integrate into traditional **make** files and take very little time.

However, a serious disadvantage of our tool is the single clock cycle limitation. Loops must involve several instructions, and complex operations cannot be pipelined within a single instruction. The Tensilica ASIP tools are not subject to this limitation, so more complex custom instructions can be written in the TIE language without adverse effects on the clock frequency.

The tool also limits the data types that are usable from a custom instruction. Floating point is not available, and nor is integer division.

The tool does not yet try to merge hardware within the custom unit, when it can be shared between two or more instructions. This results in some instructions requiring far more hardware than strictly necessary. We rely on the synthesis tool to optimise the custom unit, but that tool does not have access to all of the available information about the function of each instruction. Thus, the tool could do a better job of optimisation with an instruction merging extension.

5   Conclusion

We have described a new approach for the generation of ASIPs, in which hardware descriptions for ASIP custom units are specified within the software code that makes use of them. Our approach is intended to integrate well into traditional development tool flows, permitting separate compilation and acting as a plug-in replacement for GCC. This allows ASIP features to be used within large projects.

We have also demonstrated our approach using a prototype tool, and showed its effectiveness using a series of benchmarks. Topics for future work will include the implementation of an optimiser for the custom unit inside `cipostlink`, the possible addition of code to permit multi-cycle instructions, and support for RFUs.

References

1. A. Alomary, T. Nakata, Y. Honma, M. Imai, and N. Hikichi. An ASIP instruction set optimization algorithm with functional module sharing constraint. In *Proc. ICCAD*, pages 526–532, Los Alamitos, CA, USA, 1993. IEEE Computer Society Press.
2. Anonymous. Nios II Custom Instruction User Guide. Manual UG-N2CSTNST-1.2, Altera Corporation, 2004.
3. ARC International. Home page (accessed 16 Jan 06). http://www.arc.com/.
4. ARC International. Integrated profiler (accessed 16 Jan 06). http://www.arc.com/software/developmenttools/codeprofiling/integratedprofiler.html.
5. ASIP Meister. Home page (accessed 16 Jan 06). http://www.eda-meister.org/asip-meister/.
6. N. N. Binh, M. Imai, A. Shiomi, and N. Hikichi. A hardware/software partitioning algorithm for designing pipelined ASIPs with least gate counts. In *Proc. DAC*, pages 527–532, New York, NY, USA, 1996. ACM Press.
7. N. Cheung, J. Henkel, and S. Parameswaran. Rapid configuration and instruction selection for an ASIP: a case study. In *Proc. DATE*, page 10802, Washington, DC, USA, 2003. IEEE Computer Society.
8. Coware Corporation. LisaTEK Datasheet (accessed 16 jan 06). http://www.coware.com/PDF/products/LISATek.pdf.
9. Free Software Foundation. GNU Compiler Collection (accessed 16 Jan 06). http://gcc.gnu.org/.
10. R. E. Gonzalez. Xtensa — A configurable and extensible processor. *IEEE Micro*, 20(2):60–70, 2000.
11. D. Goodwin and D. Petkov. Automatic generation of application specific processors. In *Proc. CASES*, pages 137–147, New York, NY, USA, 2003. ACM Press.
12. B. Grattan, G. Stitt, and F. Vahid. Codesign-extended applications. In *Proc. 10th Int. Symp. Hardware/Software Codesign*, pages 1–6, 2002.
13. R. K. Gupta and G. D. Micheli. Hardware-software cosynthesis for digital systems. *IEEE Des. Test*, 10(3):29–41, 1993.
14. M. R. Guthaus, J. S. Ringenberg, D. Ernst, T. M. Austin, T. Mudge, and R. B. Brown. Mibench: A free, commercially representative embedded benchmark suite. In *Proc. 4th IEEE Workshop on Workload Characterization*, 2001.

15. M. K. Jain, M. Balakrishnan, and A. Kumar. ASIP Design Methodologies: Survey and issues. In *Proc. VLSID*, page 76, Washington, DC, USA, 2001. IEEE Computer Society.
16. D. Lampret. OpenRISC 1200 (accessed 16 Jan 06). http://www.opencores.org/.
17. C. Lee, M. Potkonjak, and W. H. Mangione-Smith. Mediabench: A tool for evaluating and synthesizing multimedia and communicatons systems. In *Int. Symp. Microarchitecture*, pages 330–335, 1997.
18. Masaharu Imai. ASIP Meister-DAC participation information (accessed 16 jan 06). http://www.sigda.org/programs/UniversityBooth/Ubooth2002/p/infodetail.html.
19. G. D. Micheli, W. Wolf, and R. Ernst. *Readings in Hardware/Software Co-Design.* Morgan Kaufmann Publishers Inc., 2001.
20. OAR Corporation. RTEMS (accessed 16 Jan 06). http://www.rtems.com/.
21. Scharwaechter, H. and Kammler, D. and Wieferink, A. and Hohenauer, M. and Zeng, J. and Karuri, K. and Leupers, R. and Ascheid, G. and Meyr. H. ASIP Architecture Exploration for Efficient IPSec Encryption: A Case Study. In *Proc. SCOPES*, Amsterdam (Netherlands), Sept 2004.
22. F. Sun, S. Ravi, A. Raghunathan, and N. K. Jha. Synthesis of custom processors based on extensible platforms. In *Proc. ICCAD*, pages 641–648, 2002.
23. Tensilica Corporation. Home page. http://www.tensilica.com/.
24. Tensilica Corporation. TIE: Product brief (accessed 16 Jan 06). http://www.tensilica.com/pdf/TIE_T1050.qxd.pdf.
25. D. Vassiliadis, N. Kavvadias, G. Theodoridis, and S. Nikolaidis. A RISC architecture extended by an efficient tightly coupled reconfigurable unit. In *Proc. ARC*, 2005.
26. Z. A. Ye, A. Moshovos, S. Hauck, and P. Banerjee. Chimaera: a high-performance architecture with a tightly-coupled reconfigurable functional unit. In *Proc. 27th Int. Symp. Computer Architecture*, pages 225–235, 2000.

A Compiler-Oriented Architecture Description for Reconfigurable Systems

Jens Braunes and Rainer G. Spallek

Institute of Computer Engineering
Technische Universität Dresden
D-01062 Dresden, Germany
{braunes, rgs}@ite.inf.tu-dresden.de

Abstract. In this paper an architecture description for reconfigurable architectures is introduced which is not limited on a special architecture or a parameterisable template. The main objective is to adapt a compiler from it to cover different reconfigurable architectures. By means of two examples we will illustrate the applicability of our concept.

1 Introduction

Prospectively coarse-grained, dynamically reconfigurable architectures will be provided in terms of IP cores for SoC and multicore systems. But important for the success at this marked is the availability of development tools, especially compilers, targeting them. According to different derivatives and families of the reconfigurable IP cores an adaptation of the compilers is indispensable. One possibility is to use a formal description of the architecture in terms of a architecture description language (ADL) to extract the instruction set and retarget the compiler as used for SoCs in some cases [1].

Basically compiling an application for reconfigurable systems[1] is a Place & Route problem. The structure of an algorithm – the data and control flow – has to be mapped to the processing elements (PEs) and the routing resources. The possibility to change the behaviour of the hardware at run-time adds another dimension to this problem. Hence instruction set descriptions typically provided by compiler-oriented ADLs are not suitable. Rather there is a need for a mix of behavioural and structural descriptions.

In this paper we propose an architecture description for reconfigurable systems. In contrast to other work we are not limited to a special architecture or a parameterisable template but cover a whole class of architectures which is defined by dedicated computational resources (processing elements), routing resources as well as configuration contexts specified at compile-time (but interchangeable at run-time). The work is still in progress so no final results are presented here.

---

[1] In this paper we are only focusing on coarse-grain reconfigurable architectures, even if we do not state this explicitly.

K. Bertels, J.M.P. Cardoso, and S. Vassiliadis (Eds.): ARC 2006, LNCS 3985, pp. 443–448, 2006.
© Springer-Verlag Berlin Heidelberg 2006

2   Reconfigurable Architecture Description

The fundamental idea behind our modelling concept for reconfigurable architectures is derived from the concept of virtualised hardware. Thus the architecture description is not a representation of the real hardware, rather the
virtual resources provided by reconfiguration are modelled. Transfered to virtual memory, our model represents the addressable memory, not the physical
cells. From the compilers point of view and for the considered class of architectures the real hardware realisation of the virtual resources plays a tangential
role.

The architecture description is built up hierarchically. More complex components can be composed of less complex components or basic elements. A reuse of
already defined components is supported by instantiation. The basis description
elements, we are using in our prototypic implementation based on XML, are
explained in the following.

Operations. The smallest possible items to specify the behaviour of a reconfigurable system are operations. They are predefined and correspond to the nodes
of the CDFGs of the compilers intermediate representation. For each operation
source and destination operands are defined. Typically the set of operations
contains arithmetic and logical functions and data movements (memory access
or register copy). By putting operations together and connecting the according
operands DFGs can be built, which represents a dedicated configuration of a
computational resource. To define different configurations, e.g. of a processing
element, a number of single configurations are put together sharing the source
and destination operands as shown in figure 1. During the mapping, the compiler
selects the corresponding datapaths from the set of alternatives for each source
and destination and forms one continuous DFG.

Components. Two different kinds of components are defined: basic components
and compound components. Both have a real hardware counterpart.

The basic components again are split into three different classes: a *processing
element* class which models the computational resources, a component class
representing the *interconnects* between the PEs as well as a component class
modelling the behaviour of *memory*. From these three classes representations of
the real hardware components can be built.

The processing elements are defined by a set of configurations (see above).
They are connected with the world outside via input and output ports. In contrast to the term port used in HDLs or other ADLs a port in our case does not
transfer signals but connects two or more subgraphs of a DFG.

The data flow between the particular PEs is implemented by interconnect
components. Dedicated ports are defined to connect them with other components
when building compound components. Inside the interconnects only routing of
the data flow is specified. For this purpose two different types of routings are
defined: broadcast and cross connection. Broadcast routing transfers data from
one input port to all specified output ports. The routes between the ports are not

```
                                    <pe name="PE" bitsize="16"        <config name="muladd">
 Selected                             latency="1">                       <baseop name="MUL">
 configuration  Sources               <ports>                              <src name="s1"/>
                                         <port name="s1" type="IN"/>       <src name="s2"/>
                                         <port name="s2" type="IN"/>       <dst name="t"/>
                                         <port name="s3" type="IN"/>    </baseop>
                            Alternative  <port name="d"  type="OUT"/>   <baseop name="ADD">
                            datapaths   </ports>                           <src name="s3"/>
                                      <configs>                            <src name="t"/>
 Configurations                         <config name="add">                <dst name="dst"/>
                                          <baseop name="ADD">           </baseop>
       Destination                          <src name="s1"/>          </config>
          (a)                               <src name="s2"/>              ...
                                            <dst name="d"/>
                                          </baseop>
                                        </config>
```

(b)

Fig. 1. Defining a PE using configurations (a) Alternative datapaths through configurations (b) Fragmentary XML based PE description

configurable. For configurable routing full cross connects are used. The routes between the input and output ports are configurable but only one route to a particular output port can be active at the same time.

The behaviour of memory is modelled by data movement operations (load / store). They will be connected to other components by ports too.

Instances of basic components will be composed to more complex compound components e.g. a configurable unit. Compound components define the data paths between the particular basic components as point to point connections of their input and output ports. These connections are not configurable.

Configuration Contexts. Configurations for a single processing element where already introduced. They are part of the configuration contexts.

In our architecture description configuration contexts are described explicitly. They look like a compound component but they do not have a real hardware counterpart. Rather they represent virtual resources. Contexts are derived from a previously defined configurable unit which is not necessarily an one to one relation.

As a result, a context contains all DFGs as well as the alternatives built by configurations of all included basic components. The actual task of the compiler is to find a mapping of the applications CDFG by selecting from the alternatives and build one connected dataflow.

Each context specification is parameterised by a latency, the time needed to switch between two contexts and the number of different configurations between one can be switched. From one configurable unit more than one contexts can be derived. Thus different load latencies, e.g caused by a configuration memory hierarchy, can be modelled.

Contexts may contain special data paths to transfer data between two consecutive contexts. These intercontext connections are realised by connecting every pair of input and output ports of the same or different basic components included in the context. They are implicitly buffered so no data is lost during a context switch.

3   Interpreting the Model

As mentioned above the prototype of the architecture description is realised using XML. An XML parser transforms the file into an internal graph representation. The generated graph is typed and directed and comprises all possible data paths through the configurable units within the defined contexts as well as back edges to model the intercontext connections.

The nodes of the graph represent the operations, the edges the data paths between them. The edges are attributed by the latencies of the source operation. We distinguish between three different types of edges.

Routing edges: Fixed data paths which are not configurable.

Configurable edges: Alternative data paths. From a set of configurable edges either outgoing from or ingoing to one node exactly one edge can be selected contemporaneously to be a routing edge.

Intercontext edges: Virtual but fixed data paths connecting two contexts. They appears as back edges and insert cycles into the graph. A intercontext edge has a latency of at least one.

The implementation of the model based compiler is still work in progress, so the details are not discussed in this paper. However a few remarks on the key concepts should be made.

As mentioned before the intermediate representation of the compiler is based on a CDFG. For mapping parts of an application the CDFG is split into subgraphs which are purely DFGs. The nodes of these DFGs, which are intermediate operations, correspond to the available operation nodes of the model graph. So a mapping function can be defined to map portions of the DFGs to the virtualised reconfigurable hardware. Therefore different strategies are possible, e.g. *simulated annealing*, or *graph matching algorithms*. To cope with the cycles caused by the intercontext connections, subgraphs inside a context are duplicated and joined together in a sequential manner, comparable to unrolling loops. This can be done as often as contexts are available, but identical contexts might be reused.

4   Examples

The concept of modelling virtualised hardware is illustrated by two examples.

Figure 2(a) shows the realisation of a pipeline reconfigurable architecture similar to the PipeRench [2]. The PipeRench is composed of several pipeline stages, called virtual stripes. A virtual stripe is nothing else than a dedicated context for a physical stripe. A physical stripe can be reconfigured within one cycle while the other stripes are in execution. Thus a large pipeline can be built by reconfiguring physical stripes again and again. The old state of the stripe is saved before the replacement takes place. From the compilers point of view, a large number of pipeline stages are available, which can be filled with operations without having to worry about the real number of physical stripes. Thus our architecture model does contain only one stripe which is embedded

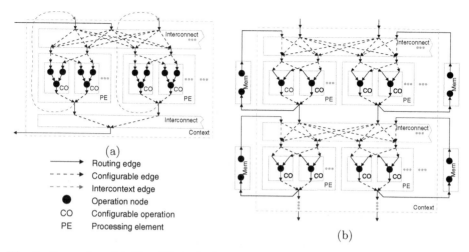

Fig. 2. Examples: (a) Simplified pipeline reconfigurable architecture (derived from PipeRench [2]), (b) Reconfigurable array with registers assigned to the PEs

into a context element. The pipelined reconfiguration can be easily realised by intercontext connections as described above.

With the second example (fig. 2(b)) the realisation of a reconfigurable array is illustrated. Similar to the reconfigurable ALU of the ARRIVE architecture [3] the array consists of processing elements arranged line-by-line. Between the lines a switched routing network transfers the data horizontally. For vertical data movements the processing elements are responsible. The array can be reconfigured cycle-by cycle. Results from the preceding configuration context have to be stored explicitly in a register file before they can be fed into to the succeeding configurations (due to limited space this is not pictured in figure 2(b)). So intercontext connections must not be used in the model. Our example differs from the original ARRIVE by the fact that registers are assigned to each processing element. Some other reconfigurable architectures, e.g. ADRES [4], use these registers to route data between consecutive configuration contexts. Because the data stored in these registers may not be lost, the registers must not be part of the context element.

5   Related Work

Architecture description languages (ADLs) are widely used for SoC or embedded processor design. In the field of reconfigurable architectures they are often used to define the hardware realisation, e.g. structure of the PEs, or interconnect network. However the virtualisation of hardware is not covered by them.

The ADL *EXPRESSION* [5] is used to describe the microarchitecture of PEs of a dynamically reconfigurable ALU array (DRAA) [6]. However EXPRESSION is not designed to meet the special requirements of reconfigurable architectures.

A specialised XML based description is used to define an instance of the ADRES architecture template [4]. The definition comprises the topology of the interconnect network, the operation sets of the configurable functional units, the timing and availability of the particular resources as well as the internal structure of the reconfigurable cells. Due to the fact that the ADRES architecture appears as a VLIW processor from the compilers point of view, explicit modelling of configuration techniques are not necessary.

The ADL presented in [7] is designed with special support for reconfigurable architectures. In contrast to the others the ADL does not target on a specific architecture. To cope with dynamic reconfiguration dynamic instruction sets can be defined.

6   Conclusion and Further Work

In this paper we have presented an architecture description for coarse-grained reconfigurable systems which is aimed to retarget a compiler. In contrast to other work we are not limited to a special architecture or a parameterisable template. By means of two examples we have illustrated the applicability of the description to model different architectures.

The implementation of the compiler is still work in progress. Different techniques will be examined to map portions of algorithms to the reconfigurable hardware. Further it is planed to build a graphical editor on top of the architecture description for a better usability.

References

1. Tomiyama, H., Halambi, A., Grun, P., Dutt, N., Nicolau, A.: Architecture Description Languages for Systems-on-Chip Design. In: Proceedings of 6th Asia Pacific Conference on Chip Design Languages. (1999) 109–116
2. Goldstein, S.C., Schmit, H., Budiu, M., Cadambi, S., Moe, M., Taylor, R.R.: PipeRench: A Reconfigurable Architecture and Compiler. Computer **33** (2000) 70–77
3. Köhler, S., Braunes, J., Preußer, T., Zabel, M., Spallek, R.G.: Increasing ILP of RISC-Microprocessors through Control-Flow based Reconfiguration. In: Proceedings of the 14th International Conference on Field Programmable Logic and Applications (FPL'04). (2004) 781–790
4. Mei, B.: A Coarse-Grained Reconfigurable Architecture Template and its Compilation Techniques. PhD thesis, Katholieke Universiteit Leuven (2005)
5. Halambi, A., Grun, P., Ganesh, V., Khare, A., Dutt, N., Nicolau, A.: EXPRESSION: a Language for Architecture Exploration through Compiler/Simulator Retargetability. In: Proceedings of the Conference on Design, Automation and Test in Europe (DATE'99). (1999) 485–490
6. Lee, J., Choi, K., Dutt, N.D.: Compilation Approach for Coarse-Grained Reconfigurable Architectures. IEEE Design and Test of Computers **20** (2003) 26–33
7. Preußer, T.B., Köhler, S., Spallek, R.G.: Modelling and Simulating Dynamic and Reconfigurable Architectures for Embedded Computing. In: Proceedings of the 5th EUROSIM Congress on Modeling and Simulation. (2004)

Dynamic Instruction Merging and a Reconfigurable Array: Dataflow Execution with Software Compatibility

Antonio Carlos S. Beck, Victor F. Gomes, and Luigi Carro

Instituto de Informática – Universidade Federal do Rio Grande do Sul
Caixa Postal 15064 – 90501-970 – Porto Alegre, RS, Brazil
{caco, vfgomes, carro}@inf.ufrgs.br

Abstract. As Moore's law is loosing steam, one already sees the phenomenon of clock frequency reduction caused by the excessive power dissipation. New technologies that will completely or partially replace silicon are arising, and new architectural alternatives are necessary. Reconfigurable fabric appears to be one of these solutions, and has shown speed ups of critical parts of several data stream programs. However, its wide spread use is still withhold by the need of special tools and compilers, which clearly preclude software portability. Based on all these facts, in this work we propose a coarse-grain dynamic reconfigurable array, tightly coupled to a traditional RISC machine. Besides taking advantage of using combinational logic to speed up the execution, we implement dynamic analysis of the code at run time to reconfigure the array, maintaining full software compatibility. Using the Simplescalar Toolset together with the embedded benchmark suite MIBench, we show performance improvements until 2 times, thanks to the implementation of the proposed approach.

1 Introduction

Moore's law as known will no longer exist in a near future, and one can already see the phenomenon of reduction of clock frequency due to excessive power dissipation. The reason is very simple: physical limits of silicon, since it is not possible to shrink atoms.

Additionally, traditional high performance architectures as the diffused superscalar machine are also achieving their limits, and recent increases in performance occurred mainly thanks to boosts in clock frequency. As an example, the clock frequency of Intel's Pentium 4 processor only increased from 3.06 to 3.2 GHz between 2002 and 2003 [1]. This way, the frequency increase reduction together with the foreseen slow technologies are new architectural challenges to be dealt with.

Reconfigurable fabric appears to be one of these solutions, and has shown speed ups of critical parts of several data stream programs. Using the same idea of instruction reuse, by translating a sequence of operations into a combinational circuit performing the same computation, one could speed up the system and

K. Bertels, J.M.P. Cardoso, and S. Vassiliadis (Eds.): ARC 2006, LNCS 3985, pp. 449–454, 2006.

reduce energy consumption at the obvious price of extra area. Dataflow architectures put this concept to the edge, achieving huge speedups.

Nevertheless, one must be very careful when proposing new possibilities, since there is a clear need to keep software compatibility and traditional programming paradigms. These are key factors to reduce the design cycle allowing one to deploy the product as soon as possible on the market. And that is precisely the major problem precluding the usage of the reconfigurable fabric today: one needs special tools and compilers, which clearly do not sustain software portability.

Keeping all the above restrictions in the mind, one solution already proposed is the dynamic reuse, in someway, of instructions or its dependence analysis [2]. This approach has several advantages. At the same time that it sustains software compatibility and traditional models of computation, it does not require repeated parallelism analysis when executing the same set of instructions. The latter, in turn, is an advantage over superscalar architectures, which repeat exactly the same job again and again on the same set of instructions, discovering every time what they had already discovered.

Concerning the reconfigurable fabric and instruction reuse, recent work has already proposed dynamic analysis of the code to reconfigure an array at run-time [3]. However, this proposal uses a fine-grain array in a FPGA that, besides being dependent on just one technology, results in a huge control overhead that increases the complexity of dynamic detection and the reconfiguration as well, thus requiring a large cache size to store the configurations of the array. As a consequence, just critical parts of the software, like the most executed loops, with some restrictions, are optimized. This way, gains are achieved just in algorithms where the kernel is very distinct from the rest of the software, as filters. Algorithms with more control flow parts or a mixed behavior can not take advantage of such technique.

On the other hand, our work proposes the use of a coarse-grain reconfigurable array composed by simple functional units and multiplexers that, besides being technology independent, is not limited to the complexity of fine-grain configurations. We coupled this coarse-grain array with a technique called Dynamic Instruction Merging, which is used to detect potential sequences of instructions at run time to be executed on the array. Transforming in combinational logic any sequence of instructions, not being limited to critical parts of the software, speedups are obtained even in control-flow algorithms or algorithms that do not present a high level of parallelism. It is exactly the coarse grain nature of the array that makes this possible: the algorithm for the dynamic detection and configuration of the array becomes simpler, and less memory to store these configurations is necessary.

Thus, in this work we show first results of the potential of using such technique. Using the Simplescalar tool [4] and a subset of the MIBench benchmark [5], our approach has a mean acceleration of 2 times, just optimizing instructions inside Basic Blocks.

2   The Reconfigurable Array

The reconfigurable array is tightly coupled to the processor. It is implemented as an ordinary functional unit in the execution stage, using the same approach of Chimaera [7]. This way, no new instructions or external accesses to the array are necessary (which in turn could increase the delay and power consumption).

The unit is a bidimensional array composed by lines and columns. Each instruction is allocated in a column. If two instructions do not have data dependence, they can be executed in parallel, in the same line. The columns are divided in groups, where each group takes a determined number of cycles to be executed. In the example, observed in the Figure 1b, the first group of columns is composed by simple operations, such as arithmetic and logic functions (Figure 1a). Each vertical sequence of three of these columns takes one cycle to be executed. The second group is for the loads execution, which takes one cycle to be executed, and the third group is for the multiplier that takes 3 cycles. The reconfigurable array can not afford floating point or division operations. Note that in the first group supports until four simple instructions to be executed in parallel, while in the second group two loads are allowed and in the third group just one multiply instruction can be executed per time.

A separated unit is responsible for analyzing the instructions at the same time that the main processor fetches them. When this unit realizes that there are a certain number of instructions which are worth to be executed in the array, the configuration for this sequence is saved in a reconfiguration cache.

For each incoming instruction, the first thing done is the verification about RAW (read after write) dependences. The source operands are compared to a bitmap of target registers of each line (Figure 1d). If the current line and all above do not have that target register equal to one of the source operands of the current instruction, this instruction can be allocated in that line, in a column as left as possible, depending on the group, as explained before.

When this is instruction is allocated in that line, the bitmap of target registers is updated. This way, for each instruction just one bitmap per line is necessary to be analyzed. Indirectly, such technique increases the size of the window of instructions, which is one of major limiting factors of ILP, exactly because the number of comparators that is necessary [6].

For each line there is also the information about what registers can be written back or saved to the memory. This way, it is possible to write results back that will not be used anymore in the array in parallel to the execution of other operations (Figure 1c).

After that, these data are saved in the reconfiguration cache, indexed by the PC (Program Counter) register, with the necessary information for future reconfigurations in the array.

As explained before, the array is reconfigured using the data of the cache designed specially for it. While the program executes, when an address of a reconfigurable instruction group is found, the reconfigurable unit detector sends a information to the main processor. Then, its control unit configures the array as the active functional unit, stops the rest of the processor while the array

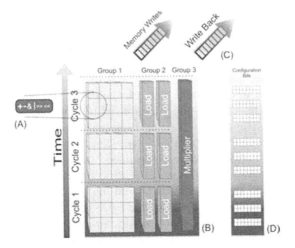

Fig. 1. The structure of the reconfigurable array

is performing it functions, and upgrades the Program Counter with the new address, in order to continue the normal operation after the execution of the array.

As the detection for the address that will be used in the reconfiguration is done in the first stage of the pipeline, and the reconfigurable array is in the fifth stage, there are 4 cycles available between the detection and the use of the array. As one cycle is necessary to find the cache line that has the array configuration, three cycles are available for the reconfiguration, which involves the load of the values of all registers that will be used by that configuration, the load of immediate values, the configuration for the multiplexers and functional units and so on.

During the execution of the operations in the array, one issue is the load instructions. They stay in a special group in the array as showed before, and the number of columns of this group depends on the number of read ports available in the memory (which means the number of loads that can occur simultaneously). Operations that depend on the result of a load have already allocated in the array during the detection phase considering a cache hit as load delay. If a miss occurs, the whole array stops until it is resolved.

Finally, the results that need to be written back either in the memory or in the local registers are allocated in a buffer. The values will be written back just when they are not used anymore for that configuration in the array. For instance, if there are two writes in the same register in a determined configuration, just the last one will be performed, since the first one was already consumed inside the array by other instructions.

It is important to point out that both the reconfigurable array and the additional hardware to detect the sequence of instructions work parallel to the processor, bringing no delay overhead in its pipeline structure.

3   Results

In this section we show the potential of using Dynamic Instruction Merging with the reconfigurable array. Our approach was implemented using the Simplescalar ToolSet [4] running the PISA architecture, executing a subset of the MiBench [5].

We considered a memory where it is possible to make two reads and one write per cycle and a latency of one cycle to fetch values from the cache. This assumption is in somehow very pessimistic. For instance, in [2] was considered for trace reuse the capability to perform 16 reads+writes per cycle, including register and memory values. Developed architectures such as the Alpha 21264 [6] can perform until 14 reads+writes per cycle (8 register reads, 4 register writes and 2 memory references). Therefore, our configuration could be easily implemented in nowadays memory systems.

Figure 2 shows the percentage of performance improvement, where the Y axis is the relative time spent by the algorithm conforming the size of the reconfiguration cache, showed in the X axis (where zero means not using the reconfigurable array).

Analyzing the figure, one could notice that depending on the algorithm a small number of cache positions is enough. As the cache replacement policy implemented for initial analysis was FIFO (First In, First Out), this cache must be large enough to support all the basic blocks that are being executed inside a determined period of time in order to allow their reuse. For instance, consider that an algorithm is composed by a main loop and inside this loop there are five basic blocks. If we have four slots available in the cache, the first time the first basic block will be reused (in the second iteration of the loop), it will not be anymore in the cache and all the detection process should be done again. Therefore, in this case, no optimization would be achieved.

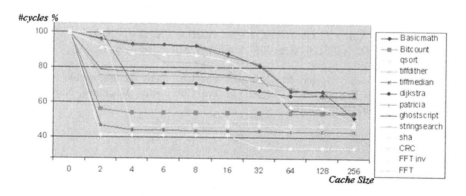

Fig. 2. The structure of the reconfigurable array

Finally, it is important to stand out that we are not exploring beyond basic blocks. However, it is common sense that in order to achieve higher performance improvements this exploration should be done, and that is way the overspread superscalar processors use aggressive speculation to increase even more the instruction level parallelism. Even not taking advantage of such approach, good results are achieved. Depending on the size of the reconfiguration cache, the algorithms can be executed in almost half the original time.

4   Conclusions and Future Work

In this work we presented the potential of replacing the traditional execution flow for combinational logic. Employing similar techniques used by well known data-flow architectures, but maintaining software compatibility, good performance improvements were achieved, even when not exploring beyond basic blocks.

For future work, we intend explore the relation among basic blocks. This way, more parallelism can be achieved and the delay caused by branch instructions avoided. Moreover, other benchmarks such as SPEC will be evaluated, and studies about the area overhead (size of array and number of configurations) and cache replacement policies will be done.

References

1. Flynn, M.J., Hung, P.: Microprocessor design issues: thoughts on the road ahead. IEEE Micro, Vol. 25, Issue 3, May-June (2005) 16 - 31
2. González, A., Tubella, J., Molina, C.: Trace-Level Reuse. Int'l Conf. on Parallel Processing, Sep. (1999)
3. Stitt, G., Lysecky, R., Vahid, F.: Dynamic Hardware/Software Partitioning: A First Approach. Design Automation Conference, (2003)
4. Burger, D., Austin, T. M.: The SimpleScalar Tool Set, Version 2.0. Computer Architecture News, Vol. 25, No. 3, June (1997) 13-25
5. Guthaus, M.R., Ringenberg, J.S., Ernst, D., Austin, T.M., Mudge T., Brown, R.B.: MiBench: A Free, Commercially Representative Embedded Benchmark Suite. 4th Workshop on Workload Characteriza-tion, Austin, TX, Dec. (2001)
6. Gwennap, L.: Digital 21264 Sets New Standard, Microprocessor Report, vol. 10, no. 14, Oct. (1996)
7. Hauck, S., Fry, T., Hosler, M., Kao, J.: The Chimaera reconfigurable functional unit. Proc. IEEE Symp. FPGAs for Custom Computing Machines, Napa Valley, CA, 87-96 (1997)

High-Level Synthesis Using SPARK and Systolic Array

Jae-Jin Lee and Gi-Yong Song

School of Electrical and Computer Engineering, Chungbuk National University,
Cheongju, 361-763, Korea
gysong@chungbuk.ac.kr

Abstract. Recently, SPARK parallelizing high-level synthesis software tool has been developed. It takes a behavioral ANSI-C code as an input, schedules it using speculative code motions and loop transformations, generates a finite state machine for the scheduled design graph, and then finally outputs a synthesizable RTL VHDL code. To handle loop algorithm, SPARK employs various loop transformations such as loop invariant code motion, loop unrolling, loop index variable elimination and loop shifting. In loop synthesis, however, SPARK does not produce circuit description whose quality can compete with manual designs. With the objective of improving the quality of high-level synthesis results for designs with loops, this paper shows an upgrade of SPARK through transforming nested loops into a 2-D systolic array to increase parallelism. The C-to-VHDL loop synthesis in this paper achieves synthesis results that are better than those achieved from a current version of SPARK for matrix-matrix multiplication and FIR filter, and can be incorporated into SPARK parallelizing high-level synthesis framework.

1 Introduction

High-level synthesis [1][2] has received significant attention over the past decade. Early work focused mainly on scheduling heuristics as well as algebra and retiming optimization for data flow design. Current work has presented scheduling heuristics for mixed control data flow designs, many of which apply speculative code motions [3][4]. Several high-level synthesis tools have been released over the past decade [5][6][7], with adoptions being limited.

Recently, SPARK parallelizing high-level synthesis software tool [2][8] has been developed. It is a high-level synthesis methodology that incorporates parallelizing compiler and compiler transformation into a traditional high-level synthesis framework, both during pre-synthesis phase and scheduling phase. To handle loop algorithm, SPARK employs various transformations such as loop invariant code motion, loop unrolling, loop index variable elimination and loop shifting. In practice, however, SPARK does not produce circuit description whose quality can compete with manual designs in term of circuit complexity and execution time. Our work has been motivated by an enhancement of SPARK through synthesizing a loop construct onto a systolic array.

A systolic array [9][10] formed by interconnecting a set of identical data processing cells in a uniform manner is a combination of an algorithm and a

K. Bertels, J.M.P. Cardoso, and S. Vassiliadis (Eds.): ARC 2006, LNCS 3985, pp. 455–460, 2006.

circuit that implements it, and is closely related conceptually to arithmetic pipeline. The underlying principle of systolic array is to achieve massive parallelism with a minimum communication overhead, and generally speaking, a systolic array is easy to implement because of its regularity and easy to reconfigure because of its modularity. Most algorithms of signal processing and other engineering application require the use of a massively parallel computing structure, that is, systolic array structure, to achieve acceptable performance. The transformation of a loop into a systolic array structure is an interesting and challenging problem, which has been extensively studied so far [9][11]. Previous research on the implementation of algorithm with nested loops on 2-D mesh-connected systolic array by Moldovan [11] contributed to and is quoted in this paper, providing a necessary rationale.

This paper shows an upgrade of SPARK by transforming loops into a 2-D systolic array to improve the quality of high-level synthesis results for design with nested loops. The C-to-VHDL synthesis in this paper achieves synthesis results that are better than those achieved from a current version of SPARK for matrix-matrix multiplication and FIR filter from the viewpoint of hardware complexity and execution speed, and can be incorporated into SPARK parallelizing high-level synthesis framework.

2   Mapping Nested Loops onto 2-D Systolic Array

This section is on implementation of behavioral description with nested loop on a mesh-connected systolic array processor. Our work is based on the previous research by Moldovan [11], however, the presented method outperforms the one in [11] when it comes to execution time of algorithm and hardware complexity of implementation without decreasing total running time of the derived systolic array, since it reduces the time required to find valid transformation by simplifying neighbor interconnections, considering sufficient conditions of a systolic array, and utilizing minimum number of cells required by transformation.

We assume that the computational structure consists of a 2-D mesh connected systolic array processor. Each cell in a 2-D systolic array can be indexed 2-tuple in 2 coordinates as shown in Fig. 1. We show only 4 by 4 cells for the purpose of simplicity. In this structure, each cell can only be connected to its neighbor. The structure of Moldovan consists of 9 interconnections between cells, but we use at most 5 communication directions, 4-neighbor bidirectional connections and a connection within the cell. The diagonal links of Moldovan's mesh structure can be deleted without violating the dependence mapping. In addition, it has been shown that most of the circuit area is occupied by local and global interconnections, and the delay of interconnections is responsible for about 40-50% or more of the total delay associated with a circuit. The interconnections between cells are described by the difference vectors between the coordinates of adjacent cells, and can be represented by matrix of interconnection as shown in expression (1).

$$P = \begin{bmatrix} p_1 & p_2 & p_3 & p_4 & p_5 \end{bmatrix} = \begin{matrix} 0 & 0 & 1 & 0 & -1 \\ 0 & 1 & 0 & -1 & 0 \end{matrix} \quad \begin{matrix} j_1 \\ j_2 \end{matrix} \tag{1}$$

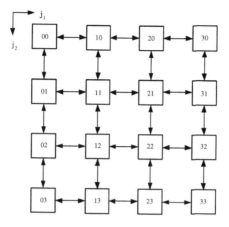

Fig. 1. Structure of 2-D Systolic array

The structural details of the PEs, I/O, execution time, and communication is determined after mapping loops onto systolic array processor. Throughout this paper we are interested in algorithms that are regular in terms of the computational patterns, and we focus on algorithms which have the form of the nested FOR-loop structure with uniform data dependencies. When extracting parallelism from a nested loop, the first step is to trace for relation between variables belonging to different instances of the nested loop. The relation is defined as difference vectors of index points where a variable is used and where that variable is generated [11].

Two steps are involved in mapping a loop algorithm into systolic array [9]. The first step is a scheduling. Once the scheduling is fixed, the second step is process assignment. Scheduling specifies the sequence of operation in all the cells. A schedule function represents a mapping from the N-dimensional index space onto a 1-D schedule (time) space. A linear schedule is based on a set of parallel and uniformly spaced hyperplanes. These hyperplanes are called equitemporial hyperplanes, all the nodes on the same hyperplane must be processed at the same time. Mathematically, the schedule can be represented by a schedule vector S, pointing to the normal direction of the hyperplane. Processor assignment maps each node of DG into a systolic array cell. It is common to use linear projection for processor assignment. Mathematically, linear projection is often represented by projection vector N. The main idea behind Moldovan's method is the transformation of an algorithm $A = (J^n, D)$ to another $A' = (J'^n, D')$ with less total execution time, which is equivalent to A.

To map loops into systolic array mathematically, we search for the transformation matrix defined below.

$$M = \begin{matrix} S \\ R \end{matrix} = \begin{bmatrix} t_{11} & t_{12} & t_{13} \\ t_{21} & t_{22} & t_{23} \\ t_{31} & t_{32} & t_{33} \end{bmatrix} \qquad (2)$$

Where mapping S and R are defined as $S : J^n \to J^1$ and $R : J^n \to J^{n-1}$. M is n by n matrix since we consider only linear transform in this paper. Algorithm dependencies D are transformed into $D' = MD$. The mapping S is selected such that the transformed data dependencies matrix D' has positive entry in the first row. This means that a causality should be enforced in a permissible schedule.

A transformation algorithm of Moldovan considers only minimizing parallel execution time with the exception of hardware complexity, However, our approach calculates the minimum makespan for the time schedule and then we establish minimum number of systolic cells required by specific schedule. The final object also contributes to reduce the time finding mapping R. In the case of Moldovan, the complexity of an algorithm finding R is 9^m, where m is the number of dependence vectors. It may not be applied to find out solutions in real problems due to its complexity. Here our motivation is to reduce the time finding mappings R by simplifying neighbor interconnections from 9 to 5, considering sufficient conditions such as spatial locality [9] of a systolic array and utilizing minimum number of cell required to implement it. If the number of dependence vector of different variables a and b is two, then the 8 mappings shown in Fig. 2 are considered to be valid among 5^2 possible mappings because only thesis mappings satisfy the spatial locality of a systolic array. As a result, our approach finding mappings $R \, (m \geq 2)$ considers the candidate mappings to be valid among 5^m possible mappings if the mapping is belongs to one of 8 in Fig. 2 for at least arbitrary two p_i's.

During finding valid mappings R among 5^m possible mappings by considering sufficient condition of a systolic array, we also try to find mapping R which minimizes the number of cells. If the mapping R satisfies the sufficient condition of a systolic arrays and then we calculate the number of cells required by corresponding mapping R. If the number of cells is the same as makespan we select it as the best mapping to fit our needs and stop the search.

After mapping loop algorithms into systolic array processor, a backend code generation pass outputs RTL VHDL which is synthesizable using Synopsys design compiler. The length of the register is easily identified from algorithm code. The computational elements (multiplier, adder and comparator etc) are selected from a set of computation C and designed using simply component instantiation of Synopsys design ware. Timing and data communication captured by transformed data dependencies give crucial information on generating VHDL code for data path of each cell and intercommunication between cells. The generated VHDL output is structural description, because it determines the exact of the systolic architecture through mapping methodology and leaves no freedom to the CAD tool to reconstruct it.

3   Synthesis Results

To compare the results from transforming loops into a 2-D systolic array mentioned in this paper and those from SPARK, each of the generated VHDL code for matrix-matrix multiplication and FIR filter are synthesized using Synopsys

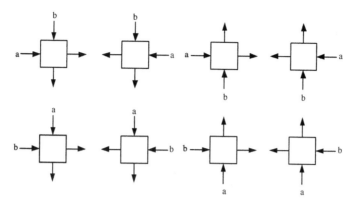

Fig. 2. Acceptable interconnections between cells for $m = 2$

Table 1. Synthesis results of matrix-matrix multiplication

Description	SPARK	The proposed methodology
The size of each matrix	4 by 4	4 by 4
The length of each element(bit)	4	4
Total cell area(2-NAND)	17086	3951
Worst clock cycle(ns)	22.53	13.04
The number of clock cycle	20	10
Total execution time(ns)	450.6	130.4

Table 2. Synthesis results of FIR filter

Description	SPARK	The proposed methodology
The number of taps	4	4
The length of data(bit)	4	4
Total cell area(2-NAND)	6386	957
Worst clock cycle(ns)	20.08	11.19
The number of clock cycle	64	10
Total execution time(ns)	1285.12	111.9

design compiler based on Hynix $0.35\mu m$ cell library. Table 1 and Table 2 list the synthesis results of matrix-matrix multiplication and FIR filter, respectively.

Only 1-D array type is used in the program code for SPARK description, since SPARK does not currently support multi-dimensional array. To fully unroll a loop, loop unrolling and pipelining parameters of SPARK are set to a maximum number of the iteration of loops. The number of hardware resources allocated to schedule the design is set equal to that of resources required by systolic arrays.

As shown in Table 1 and Table 2, the proposed C-to-VHDL loop synthesis achieves results that are better than those achieved from a current version of SPARK. Compared to SPARK, our approach achieves up to 77% reduction in the hardware complexity and up to 70% speed up in the execution time for two designs.

4   Conclusions

This paper shows an upgrade of SPARK through transforming nested loop constructs into a 2-D systolic array with the objective of improving the quality of high-level synthesis results by increasing parallelism. The proposed approach results in about 70% reduction in both area and execution time for two designs, and can be incorporated into SPARK parallelizing high-level synthesis framework.

References

1. G.De Micheli, Synthesis and Optimization of Digital Circuits, McGraw-Hill, 1994.
2. S.Gupta, R.K.Gupta, N.D.Dutt and A.Nicolau, SPARK: A Parallelizing Approach to the High-Level Synthesis of Digital Circuits, Kluwer Academic, 2004.
3. K.Wakabayashi and H.Tanaka, "Global scheduling independent of control dependencies based on condition vectors," DAC, 1992.
4. G.Lakshminarayana et al, "Incoporating speculative execution into scheduling of control flow intensive behavioral description," DAC, 1998.
5. Behavioral compiler, Synopsys
6. Get2Chip Incorporated (now a Cadence subsidiary), G2C architectural compiler, http://www.get2chip.com
7. Forte Design Systems, Behavioral design suit, http://www.forteds.com
8. S.Gupta, User Manual for the SPARK Parallelizing High-Level Synthesis Framework version 1.1, http://mesl.ucsd.edu/spark, 2004.
9. S.Y.Kung, VLSI Array Processors, Prentice Hall, 1988.
10. H.T.Kung, "Why Systolic Architectures?," IEEE Computers, vol.15, no.1, pp.37-46, 1982.
11. Dan I.Moldovan, "ADVIS : A software package for the design of systolic arrays," IEEE Trans. CAD, vol.CAD-6, no.1, 1987.

Super Semi-systolic Array-Based Application-Specific PLD Architecture

Jae-Jin Lee and Gi-Yong Song

School of Electrical and Computer Engineering, Chungbuk National University,
Cheongju, 361-763, Korea
gysong@chungbuk.ac.kr

Abstract. FPGAs have become a critical part of every system design. However, they lag far behind ASICs because of the speed of designs which can be accommodated. Systolic array is an ideal for ASICs because of its massive parallelism with minimum communication overhead, regularity and modularity, but most of commercial FPGAs cannot handle systolic structure with fast sampling rate for their general-purpose architecture nature. Recently, a super-systolic array-based PLD architecture has been proposed. This paper proposes a new PLD architecture targeting a super semi-systolic array — a derivative from a super-systolic array — for application-specific arithmetic operations such as MAC. The proposed super semi-systolic array-based PLD architecture achieves implementation results that are better than those achieved on the super-systolic array-based PLD in terms of hardware complexity and P&R time as well as existing FPGAs in terms of hardware complexity, P&R time and clock speed.

1   Introduction

A systolic array [1][2] formed by interconnecting a set of identical data processing cells in a uniform manner is a combination of an algorithm and a circuit that implements it. In order to raise the cell utility it is needed to reorganize the cell of a systolic array itself as another systolic array, that is, a super-systolic array [3]. In a systolic array, there should be at least one latch sharing the same clock signal between cells. This constraint can be relaxed by modifying the structure of a systolic array to adapt itself to the PLD architecture. The implementation of a systolic array on a PLD with horizontal and vertical channel can be transformed to a semi-systolic design through retiming [1] using PLD channels because global data transfer of semi-systolic design is easily accepted through the horizontal and/or vertical channels around the logic units, eliminating the need for latches.

Most commercial FPGAs [4][5][6] cannot handle designs with very fast sampling rate for their general purpose architecture nature. Recently a super-systolic array-based PLD architecture which combines the performance of a ASIC with the flexibility of a PLD has been proposed in [7].

This paper proposes a new PLD architecture targeting a super semi-systolic design which combines the signal broadcasting capability of horizontal and vertical channel in a PLD and the operation concurrency of the pipelined implementation of a super-systolic array. Compared with existing super-systolic array-based

K. Bertels, J.M.P. Cardoso, and S. Vassiliadis (Eds.): ARC 2006, LNCS 3985, pp. 461–466, 2006.
© Springer-Verlag Berlin Heidelberg 2006

PLD architecture, the proposed super semi-systolic array-based PLD architecture offers improvements in hardware complexity and P&R time without degenerating performance, and improvement in hardware complexity, P&R time and clock speed compared with existing FPGAs.

2   Super Semi-systolic Array

For coefficient sequence of four M-bit integers, $f(n)$, the bit-level super semi-systolic array for FIR filter with semi-systolic multiplier and internal structure of its cell are shown in Fig. 1(a) and Fig. 1(b), respectively.

As shown in Fig. 1, the cell of semi-systolic array for FIR filter contains the bit-serial semi-systolic multiplier, making the FIR filter a super semi-systolic array and the cell of FIR filter a super-cell [3]. Note that the critical path of the proposed a super semi-systolic FIR filter is limited only by one AND gate and one full adder as shown in Fig. 1(c).

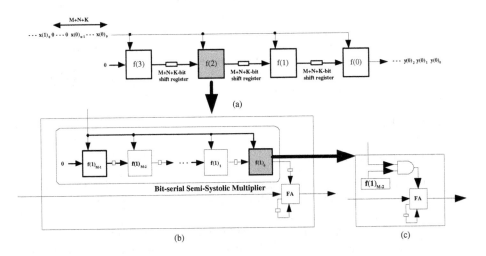

Fig. 1. (a) A super semi-systolic FIR filter (b) Structure of a super-cell (c) Structure of the cell of semi-systolic multiplier

3   Application-Specific PLD Architecture

A proposed PLD architecture targeting a super semi-systolic array for arithmetic operations is similar to that in [7]. The architecture consists of configurable Logic Modules(LMs), configurable I/O Blocks, and programmable interconnections to route signals.

3.1   Logic Module (LM)

Each LM is made up of a Logic Block(LB) which consists of five Logic Units(LUs) and an Array Block(AB) as shown in Fig. 2. There are three kinds of

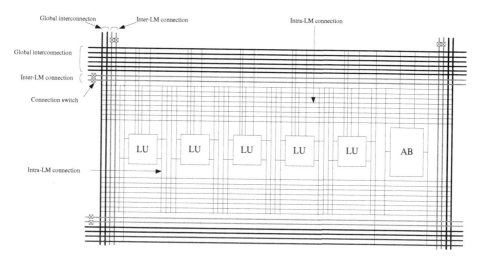

Fig. 2. Structure of a Logic Module

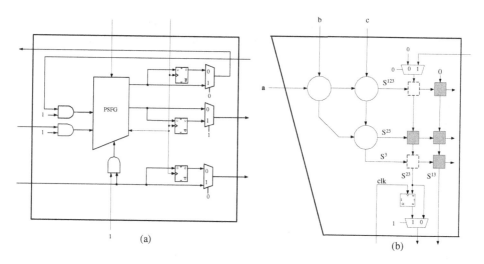

Fig. 3. (a) Structure of a Logic Unit (b) Structure of a PSFG in [7]

programmable interconnections [7]: global interconnection, inter-LM connection and intra-LM connection. The routing channel in Fig. 2 is set up with the aim of implementing arithmetic and signal processing operations such as matrix-matrix multiplication and FIR filter. Each LB which can efficiently implement 4-bit ripple carry adder or 4-bit bit-serial semi-systolic multiplier is based on the super-cell of a super semi-systolic array shown in Fig. 1(b). A ripple carry adder of any length including 8, 16, 32 and 64-bit, and a bit-serial semi-systolic multiplier can efficiently be implemented by cascading the LBs.

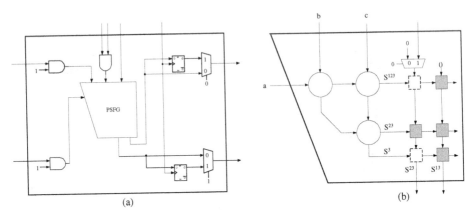

Fig. 4. (a) Structure of a Logic Unit (b) Structure of a PSFG proposed in this paper

3.2 Logic Unit (LU)

The fundamental logic cell, LU, in the proposed PLD is based on PSFG [7] and builds semi-systolic array especially while that of existing FPGAs such as Xilinx is based on multiplier and look-up table without any preference for computational structure. Compared with LU in [7], the proposed LU in this paper is area efficient for its simpler data flows as shown in Fig. 3 and Fig. 4. The LU in Fig. 4(a) is programmed as a systolic multiplier. In Fig. 4(b), one PSFG slice implements both sum and carry of a 1-bit full adder. Symmetric function with more than three inputs can be implemented as a cascade of 3-variable PSFG through EXOR-based Davio expansion [7].

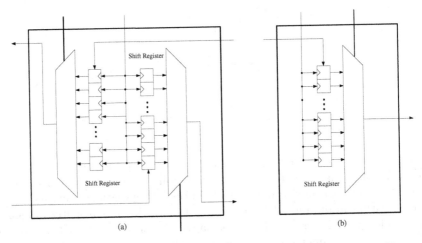

Fig. 5. (a) Structure of an AB in [7] (b) Structure of an AB proposed in this paper

3.3 Array Block (AB)

The AB is introduced to synchronize the bit dataflow between LBs to guarantee the generation and summation of the intermediate results according to recurrence relation of the applications. Fig. 5(a) shows AB proposed in [7], and Fig. 5(b) shows AB proposed in this paper. As shown Fig. 5(a) and Fig. 5(b) the AB proposed in this paper consumes less area than that in [7]. The improvement of hardware complexity is achieved by transforming designs from super-systolic array to super semi-systolic array because global data transfer of semi-systolic design is easily accepted through the horizontal and/or vertical channels around the logic units, eliminating the need for latches.

4 Performance Evaluation

To show the advantage of the PLD architecture proposed in this paper to the existing FPGA architecture and the PLD architecture proposed in [7], super semi-systolic array for matrix-matrix multiplication and super semi-systolic FIR filter are implemented onto a Xilinx FPGA [8]. Table 1 and Table 2 show that our proposed architecture does much better in speed for two designs under test.

Table 1. Implementation results of a super semi-systolic matrix-matrix multiplier

Description	XCV200	The proposed PLD
The size of matrix	3 by 3	3 by 3
The length of each element(bit)	4	4
Hardware complexity	47 SLICEs	45 LUs
P&R time(second)	2	0.5
Worst clock cycle(ns)	5.152	1.25
System clock(MHz)	194.1	800

Table 2. Implementation results of a super semi-systolic FIR filter

Description	XCV200	The proposed PLD
The number of taps	4	4
The length of data(bit)	4	4
Hardware complexity	67 SLICEs	20 LUs / 3 ABs
P&R time(second)	2	0.5
Worst clock cycle(ns)	4.857	1.25
System clock(MHz)	205.89	800

5 Conclusions

This paper proposes a new application-specific PLD architecture targeting a super semi-systolic array for arithmetic operations with recurrence relation. The proposed PLD can achieve implementation results that are better than those achieved on the PLD proposed in [7] in terms of hardware complexity and P&R time as well as existing FPGAs in terms of hardware complexity, P&R time and clock speed, and can easily implement basic arithmetic operations and signal processing algorithms such as ripple carry adder, bit-serial multiplier, matrix-matrix multiplication, FIR filter, IIR filter, 2D convolution, and FFT according to the property that the recurrence relation of such an algorithm is efficiently mapped onto a semi-systolic structure.

References

1. S.Y.Kung, VLSI Array Processors, Prentice Hall, 1988.
2. H.T.Kung, "Why Systolic Architectures?," IEEE Computers, vol.15, no.1, pp.37-46, 1982.
3. J.J.Lee and G.Y.Song, "Implementation of the Super Systolic Array for Convolution," ASP-DAC 2003, pp. 491-494, 2003.
4. Bob Zeidman, Designing with FPGAs and CPLDs, CMP books, 2002.
5. J.S.Rose, R.J.Francis, D.Lewis, and P.Chow, "Architecture of Field-Programmable Gate Arrays: The Effect of Logic Block Functionality on Area Efficiency," IEEE JSSC, vol. 25 no. 5, pp. 1217-1225, 1990.
6. V.Betz and J.Rose, "Automated Generation of FPGA Architectures," in FPGA 2000, ACM Symp. on FPGAs, pp. 175-186, 2000.
7. J.J.Lee and G.Y.Song, "A New Application-Specific PLD Architecture," IEICE Trans. on Fundamentals., vol. E88-A, no. 6, pp. 1425-1433, 2005.
8. Xilinx, Vertex 2.5V Field Programmable Gate Arrays, http://www.xilinx.com

Author Index

Lecture Notes in Computer Science

For information about Vols. 1–3999

please contact your bookseller or Springer

Vol. 4048: L. Goble, J.-J.C.. Meyer (Eds.), Deontic Logic and Artificial Normative Systems. X, 273 pages. 2006. (Sublibrary LNAI).

Vol. 4047: M. Robshaw (Ed.), Fast Software Encryption. XI, 434 pages. 2006.

Vol. 4046: S.M. Astley, M. Brady, C. Rose, R. Zwiggelaar (Eds.), Digital Mammography. XVI, 654 pages. 2006.

Vol. 4045: D. Barker-Plummer, R. Cox, N. Swoboda (Eds.), Diagrammatic Representation and Inference. XII, 301 pages. 2006. (Sublibrary LNAI).

Vol. 4044: P. Abrahamsson, M. Marchesi, G. Succi (Eds.), Extreme Programming and Agile Processes in Software Engineering. XII, 230 pages. 2006.

Vol. 4043: A.S. Atzeni, A. Lioy (Eds.), Public Key Infrastructure. XI, 261 pages. 2006.

Vol. 4042: D. Bell, J. Hong (Eds.), Flexible and Efficient Information Handling. XVI, 296 pages. 2006.

Vol. 4041: S.-W. Cheng, C.K. Poon (Eds.), Algorithmic Aspects in Information and Management. XI, 395 pages. 2006.

Vol. 4040: R. Reulke, U. Eckardt, B. Flach, U. Knauer, K. Polthier (Eds.), Combinatorial Image Analysis. XII, 482 pages. 2006.

Vol. 4039: M. Morisio (Ed.), Reuse of Off-the-Shelf Components. XIII, 444 pages. 2006.

Vol. 4038: P. Ciancarini, H. Wiklicky (Eds.), Coordination Models and Languages. VIII, 299 pages. 2006.

Vol. 4037: R. Gorrieri, H. Wehrheim (Eds.), Formal Methods for Open Object-Based Distributed Systems. XVII, 474 pages. 2006.

Vol. 4036: O. H. Ibarra, Z. Dang (Eds.), Developments in Language Theory. XII, 456 pages. 2006.

Vol. 4035: T. Nishita, Q. Peng, H.-P. Seidel (Eds.), Advances in Computer Graphics. XX, 771 pages. 2006.

Vol. 4034: J. Münch, M. Vierimaa (Eds.), Product-Focused Software Process Improvement. XVII, 474 pages. 2006.

Vol. 4033: B. Stiller, P. Reichl, B. Tuffin (Eds.), Performability Has its Price. X, 103 pages. 2006.

Vol. 4032: O. Etzion, T. Kuflik, A. Motro (Eds.), Next Generation Information Technologies and Systems. XIII, 365 pages. 2006.

Vol. 4031: M. Ali, R. Dapoigny (Eds.), Advances in Applied Artificial Intelligence. XXIII, 1353 pages. 2006. (Sublibrary LNAI).

Vol. 4029: L. Rutkowski, R. Tadeusiewicz, L.A. Zadeh, J. Zurada (Eds.), Artificial Intelligence and Soft Computing – ICAISC 2006. XXI, 1235 pages. 2006. (Sublibrary LNAI).

Vol. 4028: J. Kohlas, B. Meyer, A. Schiper (Eds.), Dependable Systems: Software, Computing, Networks. XII, 296 pages. 2006.

Vol. 4027: H.L. Larsen, G. Pasi, D. Ortiz-Arroyo, T. Andreasen, H. Christiansen (Eds.), Flexible Query Answering Systems. XVIII, 714 pages. 2006. (Sublibrary LNAI).

Vol. 4026: P.B. Gibbons, T. Abdelzaher, J. Aspnes, R. Rao (Eds.), Distributed Computing in Sensor Systems. XIV, 566 pages. 2006.

Vol. 4025: F. Eliassen, A. Montresor (Eds.), Distributed Applications and Interoperable Systems. XI, 355 pages. 2006.

Vol. 4024: S. Donatelli, P. S. Thiagarajan (Eds.), Petri Nets and Other Models of Concurrency - ICATPN 2006. XI, 441 pages. 2006.

Vol. 4021: E. André, L. Dybkjær, W. Minker, H. Neumann, M. Weber (Eds.), Perception and Interactive Technologies. XI, 217 pages. 2006. (Sublibrary LNAI).

Vol. 4020: A. Bredenfeld, A. Jacoff, I. Noda, Y. Takahashi (Eds.), RoboCup 2005: Robot Soccer World Cup IX. XVII, 727 pages. 2006. (Sublibrary LNAI).

Vol. 4019: M. Johnson, V. Vene (Eds.), Algebraic Methodology and Software Technology. XI, 389 pages. 2006.

Vol. 4018: V. Wade, H. Ashman, B. Smyth (Eds.), Adaptive Hypermedia and Adaptive Web-Based Systems. XVI, 474 pages. 2006.

Vol. 4017: S. Vassiliadis, S. Wong, T.D. Hämäläinen (Eds.), Embedded Computer Systems: Architectures, Modeling, and Simulation. XV, 492 pages. 2006.

Vol. 4016: J.X. Yu, M. Kitsuregawa, H.V. Leong (Eds.), Advances in Web-Age Information Management. XVII, 606 pages. 2006.

Vol. 4014: T. Uustalu (Ed.), Mathematics of Program Construction. X, 455 pages. 2006.

Vol. 4013: L. Lamontagne, M. Marchand (Eds.), Advances in Artificial Intelligence. XIII, 564 pages. 2006. (Sublibrary LNAI).

Vol. 4012: T. Washio, A. Sakurai, K. Nakajima, H. Takeda, S. Tojo, M. Yokoo (Eds.), New Frontiers in Artificial Intelligence. XIII, 484 pages. 2006. (Sublibrary LNAI).

Vol. 4011: Y. Sure, J. Domingue (Eds.), The Semantic Web: Research and Applications. XIX, 726 pages. 2006.

Vol. 4010: S. Dunne, B. Stoddart (Eds.), Unifying Theories of Programming. VIII, 257 pages. 2006.

Vol. 4009: M. Lewenstein, G. Valiente (Eds.), Combinatorial Pattern Matching. XII, 414 pages. 2006.

Vol. 4008: J.C. Augusto, C.D. Nugent (Eds.), Designing Smart Homes. XI, 183 pages. 2006. (Sublibrary LNAI).

Vol. 4007: C. Àlvarez, M. Serna (Eds.), Experimental Algorithms. XI, 329 pages. 2006.

Vol. 4006: L.M. Pinho, M. González Harbour (Eds.), Reliable Software Technologies – Ada-Europe 2006. XII, 241 pages. 2006.

Vol. 4005: G. Lugosi, H.U. Simon (Eds.), Learning Theory. XI, 656 pages. 2006. (Sublibrary LNAI).

Vol. 4004: S. Vaudenay (Ed.), Advances in Cryptology - EUROCRYPT 2006. XIV, 613 pages. 2006.

Vol. 4003: Y. Koucheryavy, J. Harju, V.B. Iversen (Eds.), Next Generation Teletraffic and Wired/Wireless Advanced Networking. XVI, 582 pages. 2006.

Vol. 4001: E. Dubois, K. Pohl (Eds.), Advanced Information Systems Engineering. XVI, 560 pages. 2006.